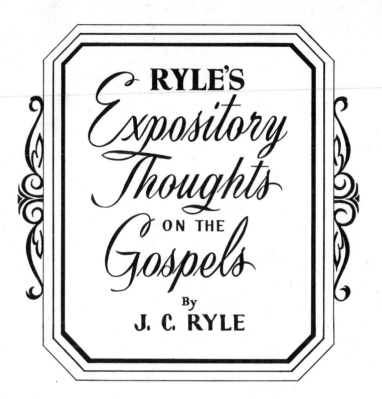

RYLE'S
Expository Thoughts
ON THE
Gospels

By
J. C. RYLE

Anniversary Edition

MATTHEW - MARK

Zondervan Publishing House
GRAND RAPIDS, MICHIGAN

TABLE OF CONTENTS.

EXPOSITORY THOUGHTS

ON THE GOSPELS.

MATTHEW I. 1—17.

1 The book of the generation of Jesus Christ, the son of David, the son of Abraham.

2 Abraham begat Isaac; and Isaac begat Jacob; and Jacob begat Judas and his brethren;

3 And Judas begat Phares and Zara of Thamar; and Phares begat Esrom; and Esrom begat Aram;

4 And Aram begat Aminadab; and Aminadab begat Naasson; and Naasson begat Salmon;

5 And Salmon begat Booz of Rachab; and Booz begat Obed of Ruth; and Obed begat Jesse;

6 And Jesse begat David the king; and David the king begat Solomon of her *that had been the wife* of Urias;

7 And Solomon begat Roboam; and Roboam begat Abia; and Abia begat Asa;

8 And Asa begat Josaphat; and Josaphat begat Joram; and Joram begat Ozias;

9 And Ozias begat Joatham; and Joatham begat Achaz; and Achaz begat Ezekias;

10 And Ezekias begat Manasses; and Manasses begat Amon; and Amon begat Josias;

11 And Josias begat Jechonias and his brethren, about the time they were carried away to Babylon:

12 And after they were brought to Babylon, Jechonias begat Salathiel; and Salathiel begat Zorobabel;

13 And Zorobabel begat Abiud; and Abiud begat Eliakim; and Eliakim begat Azor;

14 And Azor begat Sadoc; and Sadoc begat Achim; and Achim begat Eliud;

15 And Eliud begat Eleazar; and Eleazar begat Matthan; and Matthan begat Jacob;

16 And Jacob begat Joseph the husband of Mary, of whom was born Jesus, who is called Christ.

17 So all the generations, from Abraham to David, *are* fourteen generations; and from David, until the carrying away into Babylon, *are* fourteen generations; and from the carrying away into Babylon unto Christ, *are* fourteen generations.

THESE verses begin the New Testament. Let us always read them with serious and solemn feelings.—The book before us contains not the word of men, but of God. Every verse in it was written by inspiration of the Holy Ghost.

B

Let us thank God daily for giving us the Scriptures. The poorest Englishman who understands his Bible, knows more about religion than the wisest philosophers of Greece and Rome.

Let us remember our deep responsibility. We shall all be judged at the last day according to our light. To whomsoever much is given, of them much will be required.

Let us read our Bibles reverently and diligently, with an honest determination to believe and practise all we find in them. It is no light matter how we use this book. Eternal life or death depends on the spirit in which it is used.

Above all let us humbly pray for the teaching of the Holy Spirit. He alone can apply truth to our hearts, and make us profit by what we read.

The New Testament begins with the life, death, and resurrection of our Lord Jesus Christ. No part of the Bible is so important as this, and no part is so full and complete. Four distinct Gospels tell us the story of Christ's doing and dying. Four times over we read the precious account of His works and words. How thankful we ought to be for this! To know Christ is life eternal. To believe in Christ is to have peace with God. To follow Christ is to be a true Christian. To be with Christ will be heaven itself. We can never hear too much about Jesus Christ.

The Gospel of St. Matthew begins with a long list of names. Sixteen verses are taken up with tracing a pedigree from Abraham to David, and from David to the family in which Jesus was born. Let no one think that these verses are useless. Nothing is useless in creation.

The least mosses, and the smallest insects, serve some good end.—Nothing is useless in the Bible.   Every word of it is inspired.   The chapters and verses which seem at first sight unprofitable, are all given for some good purpose. Look again at these sixteen verses; and you will see in them useful and instructive lessons.

Learn from this list of names, that *God always keeps His word.*   He had promised, that in Abraham's seed all the nations of the earth should be blessed.   He had promised to raise up a Saviour of the family of David. (Gen. xii. 3. Isai. xi. 1.)   These sixteen verses prove, that Jesus was the son of David and the son of Abraham, and that God's promise was fulfilled.—Thoughtless and ungodly people should remember this lesson, and be afraid.   Whatever they may think, God will keep His word.   If they repent not, they will surely perish.—True Christians should remember this lesson, and take comfort. Their Father in heaven will be true to all His engagements.   He has said, that He will save all believers in Christ.   If He has said it, He will certainly do it.   "He is not a man that He should lie."   "He abideth faithful : He cannot deny Himself." (2 Tim. ii. 13.)

Learn next from this list of names *the sinfulness and corruption of human nature.*   Observe how many godly parents in this catalogue had wicked and ungodly sons. The names of Roboam, and Joram, and Amon, and Jechonias, should teach us humbling lessons.   They had all pious fathers.   But they were all wicked men.   Grace does not run in families.   It needs something more than good examples and good advice to make us children of God. They that are born again are not born of blood, nor of the will of the flesh, nor of the will of man, but of God. (John i. 13.) Praying parents should pray night and day, that their children may be born of the Spirit.

Learn lastly from this list of names, *how great is the mercy and compassion of our Lord Jesus Christ.* Think how defiled and unclean our nature is; and then think what a condescension it was in Him to be born of a woman, and "made in the likeness of men." Some of the names we read in this catalogue remind us of shameful and sad histories. Some of the names are those of persons never mentioned elsewhere in the Bible. But at the end of all comes the name of the Lord Jesus Christ. Though He is the eternal God, He humbled Himself to become man, in order to provide salvation for sinners. "Though he was rich, yet for our sakes he became poor."

We should always read this catalogue with thankful feelings. We see here that no one who partakes of human nature can be beyond the reach of Christ's sympathy and compassion. Our sins may have been as black and great as those of any whom St. Matthew names. But they cannot shut us out of heaven, if we repent and believe the gospel. If Jesus was not ashamed to be born of a woman, whose pedigree contained such names as those we have read to-day, we need not think that He will be ashamed to call us brethren, and to give us eternal life.

MATTHEW I. 18—25.

18 Now the birth of Jesus Christ was on this wise . When as his mother Mary was espoused to Joseph, before they came together, she was found with child of the Holy Ghost.

19 Then Joseph her husband, being a just *man*, and not willing to make her a publick example, was minded to put her away privily.

20 But while he thought on these things, behold, the angel of the Lord appeared unto him in a dream, saying, Joseph, thou son of David, fear not to take unto thee Mary thy wife: for that which is conceived in her is of the Holy Ghost.

21 And she shall bring forth a son, and thou shalt call his name JESUS:

for he shall save his people from their sins.

22 Now all this was done, that it might be fulfilled which was spoken of the Lord by the prophet, saying,

23 Behold, a virgin shall be with child, and shall bring forth a son, and they shall call his name Emmanuel, which being interpreted is, God with us.

24 Then Joseph being raised from sleep, did as the angel of the Lord had bidden him, and took unto him his wife:

25 And knew her not till she had brought forth her firstborn son: and he called his name JESUS.

THESE verses begin by telling us two great truths. They tell us how the Lord Jesus Christ took our nature upon Him, and became man. They tell us also that His birth was miraculous. His mother Mary was a virgin.

These are *very mysterious subjects.* They are depths, which we have no line to fathom. They are truths, which we have not mind enough to comprehend. Let us not attempt to explain things which are above our feeble reason. Let us be content to believe with reverence, and not speculate about matters which we cannot understand. Enough for us to know, that with Him who made the world nothing is impossible. Let us rest in the words of the Apostles' Creed: "Jesus Christ was conceived by the Holy Ghost, and born of the Virgin Mary."

Let us observe *the conduct of Joseph* described in these verses. It is a beautiful example of godly wisdom, and tender consideration for others. He saw the "appearance of evil" in her who was his espoused wife. But he did nothing rashly. He waited patiently to have the line of duty made clear. In all probability he laid the matter before God in prayer. "He that believeth shall not make haste." (Isai. xxviii. 16.)

The patience of Joseph was graciously rewarded. He received a direct message from God upon the subject of his anxiety, and was at once relieved from all his fears. How good it is to wait upon God! Who ever cast his cares upon God in hearty prayer, and found Him fail? "In all thy ways acknowledge Him, and He shall direct thy paths." (Prov. iii. 6.)

Let us observe *the two names* given to our Lord in these verses. One is Jesus: the other Emmanuel. One describes His office: the other His nature. Both are deeply interesting.

The name Jesus means "Saviour." It is the same name as Joshua in the Old Testament. It is given to our Lord because "He saves His people from their sins." *This is His special office.* He saves them from the guilt of sin, by washing them in His own atoning blood. He saves them from the dominion of sin, by putting in their hearts the sanctifying Spirit. He saves them from the presence of sin, when He takes them out of this world to rest with Him. He will save them from all the consequences of sin, when He shall give them a glorious body at the last day. Blessed and holy are Christ's people! From sorrow, cross, and conflict they are not saved. But they are saved from sin for evermore. They are cleansed from guilt by Christ's blood. They are made meet for heaven by Christ's Spirit. This is salvation. He who cleaves to sin is not yet saved.

Jesus is a *very encouraging name to heavy-laden sinners.*

He who is King of kings and Lord of lords might lawfully have taken some more high-sounding title. But He does not do so. The rulers of this world have often called themselves Great, Conquerors, Bold, Magnificent, and the like. The Son of God is content to call Himself Saviour. The souls which desire salvation may draw nigh to the Father with boldness, and have access with confidence through Christ. It is His office and His delight to show mercy. "God sent not His Son into the world to condemn the world, but that the world through Him might be saved." (John iii. 17.)

Jesus is a name, *which is peculiarly sweet and precious to believers.* It has often done them good, when the favour of kings and princes would have been heard of with unconcern. It has given them what money cannot buy, even inward peace. It has eased their weary consciences, and given rest to their heavy hearts. The Song of Solomon speaks the experience of many, when it says, "thy name is as ointment poured forth." (Cant. i. 3.) Happy is that person, who trusts not merely in vague notions of God's mercy and goodness, but in "Jesus."

The other name in these verses is scarcely less interesting than that just referred to. It is the name which is given to our Lord from His nature, as "God manifest in the flesh." He is called Emmanuel, "God with us."

Let us take care that we have clear views of our Lord Jesus Christ's *nature and person.* It is a point of the deepest importance. We should settle it firmly in our minds, that our Saviour is perfect man as well as perfect God, and perfect God as well as perfect man. If we once lose sight of this great foundation truth, we may run into

fearful heresies.   The name Emmanuel takes in the whole
mystery.   Jesus is "God with us."   He had a nature
like our own in all things, sin only excepted.   But though
Jesus was "with us" in human flesh and blood, He was
at the same time very God.

We shall often find, as we read the Gospels, that our
Saviour could be weary, and hungry, and thirsty,—could
weep, and groan, and feel pain like one of ourselves.   In
all this we see *"the man"* Christ Jesus.   We see the
nature He took on Him, when He was born of the Virgin
Mary.

But we shall also find in the same Gospels that our
Saviour knew men's hearts and thoughts,—that He had
power over devils,—that He could work the mightiest
of miracles with a word,—that He was ministered to by
angels, that He allowed a disciple to call Him "my God,"
—and that He said, "Before Abraham was I am," and
"I and my Father are one."   In all this we see *"the
eternal God."*   We see Him "who is over all, God
blessed for ever. Amen." (Rom. ix. 5.)

Would you have a strong foundation for your faith
and hope?   Then keep in constant view your Saviour's
divinity.   He in whose blood you are taught to trust is
the Almighty God.   All power is His in heaven and
earth.   None can pluck you out of His hand.   If you
are a true believer in Jesus, let not your heart be troubled
or afraid.

Would you have sweet comfort in suffering and
trial?   Then keep in constant view your Saviour's
humanity.   He is the man Christ Jesus, who lay on the
bosom of the Virgin Mary, as a little infant, and knows

the heart of a man. He can be touched with the feeling of your infirmities. He has Himself experienced Satan's temptations. He has endured hunger. He has shed tears. He has felt pain. Trust Him at all times with all your sorrows. He will not despise you. Pour out all your heart before Him in prayer, and keep nothing back. He can sympathize with His people.

Let these thoughts sink down into our minds. Let us bless God for the encouraging truths which the first chapter of the New Testament contains. It tells us of One who "saves His people from their sins." But this is not all. It tells us that this Saviour is "Emmanuel," God Himself, and yet God with us,—God manifest in human flesh like our own. This is glad tidings. This is indeed good news. Let us feed on these truths in our hearts by faith with thanksgiving.

MATTHEW II. 1—12.

1 Now when Jesus was born in Bethlehem of Judæa in the days of Herod the king, behold, there came wise men from the east to Jerusalem,

2 Saying, Where is he that is born King of the Jews? for we have seen his star in the east, and are come to worship him.

3 When Herod the king had heard *these things*, he was troubled, and all Jerusalem with him.

4 And when he had gathered all the Chief Priests and Scribes of the people together, he demanded of them where Christ should be born.

5 And they said unto him, In Bethlehem of Judæa; for thus it is written by the prophet,

6 And thou Bethlehem, *in* the land of Juda, art not the least among the princes of Juda: for out of thee shall come a Governor, that shall rule my people Israel.

7 Then Herod, when he had privily called the wise men, enquired of them diligently what time the star appeared.

8 And he sent them to Bethlehem, and said, Go and search diligently for the young child; and when ye have found *him*, bring me word again, that I may come and worship him also.

9 When they had heard the king, they departed; and lo, the star, which they saw in the east, went before them, till it came and stood over where the young child was.

10 When they saw the star, they rejoiced with exceeding great joy.

11 And when they were come into the house, they saw the young child with Mary his mother, and fell down, and worshipped him: and when they had opened their treasures, they presented unto him gifts; gold, and frankincense, and myrrh.

12 And being warned of God in a dream that they should not return to Herod, they departed into their own country another way.

IT is not known who these wise men were. Their names and dwelling-place are alike kept back from us. We are only told that they came "from the East." Whether they were Chaldeans or Arabians, we cannot say. Whether they learned to expect Christ from the ten tribes who went into captivity, or from the prophecies of Daniel, we do not know. It matters little who they were. The point which concerns us most is the rich instruction which their history conveys.

These verses show us, *that there may be true servants of God in places where we should not expect to find them.* The Lord Jesus has many "hidden ones" like these wise men. Their history on earth may be as little known as that of Melchizedek, and Jethro, and Job. But their names are in the book of life, and they will be found with Christ in the day of His appearing. It is well to remember this. We must not look round the earth and say hastily, "all is barren." The grace of God is not tied to places and families. The Holy Ghost can lead souls to Christ without the help of many outward means. Men may be born in dark places of the earth, like these wise men, and yet like them be made "wise unto salvation." There are some travelling to heaven at this moment, of whom the church and the world know nothing. They flourish in secret places like the lily among thorns, and "waste their sweetness on the desert air." But Christ loves them, and they love Christ.

These verses teach us, *that it is not always those who have most religious privileges, who give Christ most honour.* We might have thought that the Scribes and Pharisees would have been the first to hasten to Bethlehem, on the slightest rumour that the Saviour was born. But it was not so. A few unknown strangers from a distant land were the first, except the shepherds mentioned by St. Luke, to rejoice at His birth. "He came unto his own, and his own received him not." What a mournful picture this is of human nature! How often the same kind of thing may be seen among ourselves! How often the very persons who live nearest to the means of grace are those who neglect them most! There is only too much truth in the old proverb, "The nearer the church the further from God." Familiarity with sacred things has an awful tendency to make men despise them. There are many, who from residence and convenience ought to be first and foremost in the worship of God, and yet are always last. There are many, who might well be expected to be last, who are always first.

These verses teach us, *that there may be knowledge of Scripture in the head, while there is no grace in the heart.* Mark how king Herod sends to inquire of the priests and elders, "where Christ should be born." Mark what a ready answer they return him, and what an acquaintance with the letter of Scripture they show. But they never went to Bethlehem to seek for the coming Saviour. They would not believe in Him, when He ministered among them. Their heads were better than their hearts.—Let us all beware of resting satisfied with head-knowledge. It is an excellent thing, when rightly used. But a man may have much of it, and yet perish everlastingly. What is the state of our hearts? This is the great question. A little grace is better than many gifts. Gifts alone save no one. But grace leads on to glory.

The conduct of the wise men described in this chapter is *a splendid example of spiritual diligence.* What trouble it must have cost them to travel from their homes to the house where Jesus was born! How many weary miles they must have journeyed! The fatigues of an Eastern traveller are far greater than we in England can at all understand. The time that such a journey would occupy must necessarily have been very great. The dangers to be encountered were neither few nor small. But none of these things moved them. They had set their hearts on seeing Him "that was born King of the Jews;" and they never rested till they saw Him. They prove to us the truth of the old saying, "Where there is a will there is a way."

It would be well for all professing Christians if they were more ready to follow the wise men's example. Where is our self-denial? What pains do we take about our souls? What diligence do we show about following Christ? What does our religion cost us? These are serious questions. They deserve serious consideration.

Last, but not least, the conduct of the wise men is *a striking example of faith.* They believed in Christ when they had never seen Him;—but that was not all. They believed in Him when the Scribes and Pharisees were unbelieving;—but that again was not all. They believed in Him when they saw Him a little infant on Mary's knee, and worshipped Him as a king. This was the crowning point of their faith.—They saw no miracles to convince them. They heard no teaching to persuade them. They beheld no signs of divinity and greatness to overawe them. They saw nothing but a new-born infant, helpless and weak, and needing a mother's care like any one of ourselves. And yet when they saw that infant, they believed that they saw the divine Saviour of the world. "They fell down and worshipped him."

We read of no greater faith than this in the whole volume of the Bible. It is a faith that deserves to be placed side by side with that of the penitent thief. The thief saw one dying the death of a malefactor, and yet prayed to Him, and "called Him Lord." The wise men saw a new-born babe on the lap of a poor woman, and yet worshipped Him, and confessed that He was Christ. Blessed indeed are those that can believe in this fashion!

This is the kind of faith, let us remember, that *God delights to honour*. We see the proof of that at this very day. Wherever the Bible is read the conduct of these wise men is known, and told as a memorial of them. Let us walk in the steps of their faith. Let us not be ashamed to believe in Jesus and confess Him, though all around us remain careless and unbelieving. Have we not a thousand-fold more evidence than the wise men had, to make us believe that Jesus is the Christ? Beyond doubt we have. Yet where is our faith?

MATTHEW II. 13—23.

13 And when they were departed, behold, the angel of the Lord appeareth to Joseph in a dream, saying, Arise, and take the young child and his mother, and flee into Egypt, and be thou there until I bring thee word: for Herod will seek the young child to destroy him.

14 When he arose, he took the young child and his mother by night, and departed into Egypt:

15 And was there until the death of Herod: that it might be fulfilled which was spoken of the Lord by the prophet, saying, Out of Egypt have I called my son.

16 Then Herod, when he saw that he was mocked of the wise men, was exceeding wroth, and sent forth, and slew all the children that were in Bethlehem, and in all the coasts thereof, from two years old and under, according to the time which he had diligently enquired of the wise men.

17 Then was fulfilled that which was spoken by Jeremy the prophet, saying,

18 In Rama was there a voice heard,

lamentation, and weeping, and great mourning, Rachel weeping *for* her children, and would not be comforted, because they are not.

19 But when Herod was dead, behold, an angel of the Lord appeareth in a dream to Joseph in Egypt,

20 Saying, Arise, and take the young child and his mother, and go into the land of Israel: for they are dead which sought the young child's life.

21 And he arose, and took the young child and his mother, and came into the land of Israel.

22 But when he heard that Archelaus did reign in Judæa in the room of his father Herod, he was afraid to go thither: notwithstanding, being warned of God in a dream, he turned aside into the parts of Galilee:

23 And he came and dwelt in a city called Nazareth: that it might be fulfilled which was spoken by the prophets, He shall be called a Nazarene.

OBSERVE in this passage, how true it is that *the rulers of this world are seldom friendly to the cause of God.* The Lord Jesus comes down from heaven to save sinners, and at once we are told that Herod the king "seeks to destroy him."

Greatness and riches are a perilous possession for the soul. They know not what they seek who seek to have them. They lead men into many temptations. They are likely to fill the heart with pride, and to chain the affections down to things below. "Not many mighty, not many noble are called." "How hardly shall a rich man enter the kingdom of God."

Do you envy the rich and great? Does your heart say, "Oh! that I had their place, and rank, and substance?" Beware of giving way to the feeling. The very wealth which you admire may be gradually sinking its possessor down into hell. A little more money might be your ruin. Like Herod, you might run into every excess of wickedness and cruelty. "Take heed, and beware of covetousness." "Be content with such things as you have."

Do you think that Christ's cause depends on the power and patronage of princes? You are mistaken. They have seldom done much for the advancement of true religion. They have far more frequently been the enemies of the truth. "Put not your trust in princes." Those who are like Herod are many. Those who are like Josiah and Edward the Sixth of England are few.

Observe how the *Lord Jesus was "a man of sorrows" even from His infancy.* Trouble awaits Him as soon as He enters into the world. His life is in danger from Herod's hatred. His mother and Joseph are obliged to take Him away by night, and "flee into Egypt." It was only a type and figure of all His experience upon earth. The waves of humiliation began to beat over Him, even when He was a sucking child.

The Lord Jesus is just the Saviour that the suffering and sorrowful need. He knows well what we mean, when we tell Him in prayer of our troubles. He can sympathize with us, when we cry to Him under cruel persecution. Let us keep nothing back from Him. Let us make Him our bosom friend. Let us pour out our hearts before Him. He has had great experience of affliction.

Observe how *death can remove the kings of this world like other men.* The rulers of millions have no power to retain life, when the hour of their departure comes. The murderer of helpless infants must himself die. Joseph and Mary hear the tidings that "Herod is dead;" and at once they return in safety to their own land.

True Christians should never be greatly moved by the persecution of man. Their enemies may be strong, and they may be weak; but still they ought not to be afraid. They should remember that "the triumphing of the wicked

is but short." What has become of the Pharaohs and
Neros and Diocletians, who at one time fiercely persecuted the people of God? Where is the enmity of Charles
the Ninth of France, and bloody Mary of England?
They did their utmost to cast the truth down to the
ground. But the truth rose again from the earth, and
still lives; and they are dead, and mouldering in the
grave. Let not the heart of any believer fail. Death is
a mighty leveller, and can take any mountain out of the
way of Christ's church. "The Lord liveth" for ever. His
enemies are only men. The truth shall always prevail.

Observe, in the last place, *what a lesson of humility is
taught us by the dwelling place of the Son of God*, when
He was on earth. He dwelt with His mother and Joseph
"in a city called Nazareth."

Nazareth was a small town in Galilee. It was an
obscure, retired place, not so much as once mentioned in
the Old Testament. Hebron, and Shiloh, and Gibeon,
and Bethel, were far more important places. But the
Lord Jesus passed by them all, and chose Nazareth.
This was humility.

In Nazareth the Lord Jesus lived thirty years. It was
there He grew up from infancy to childhood, and from
childhood to boyhood, and from boyhood to youth, and
from youth to man's estate. We know little of the
manner in which those thirty years were spent. That
He was "subject to Mary and Joseph," we are expressly
told. That He worked in the carpenter's shop with
Joseph, is highly probable. We only know, that almost
five sixths of the time that the Saviour of the world was
on earth was passed among the poor of this world, and

passed in complete retirement. Truly this was humility.

Let us learn wisdom from our Saviour's example. We are far too ready to " seek great things " in this world. Let us seek them not. To have a place, and a title, and a position in society, is not nearly so important as people think. It is a great sin to be covetous, and worldly, and proud, and carnal-minded. But it is no sin to be poor. It matters not so much where we live, as what we are in the sight of God. Where are we going when we die? Shall we live for ever in heaven? These are the main things to which we should attend.

Above all, let us daily strive to copy our Saviour's humility. Pride is the oldest and commonest of sins. Humility is the rarest and most beautiful of graces. For humility let us labour. For humility let us pray. Our knowledge may be scanty. Our faith may be weak. Our strength may be small. But if we are disciples of Him who "dwelt at Nazareth," let us at any rate be, humble.

MATTHEW III. 1—12.

1 In those days came John the Baptist, preaching in the wilderness of Judæa,

2 And saying, Repent ye: for the kingdom of heaven is at hand.

3 For this is he that was spoken of by the prophet Esaias, saying, The voice of one crying in the wilderness, Prepare ye the way of the Lord, make his paths straight.

4 And the same John had his raiment of camel's hair, and a leathern girdle about his loins; and his meat was locusts and wild honey.

5 Then went out to him Jerusalem, and all Judæa, and all the region round about Jordan,

6 And were baptized of him in Jordan, confessing their sins.

7 But when he saw many of the Pharisees and Sadducees come to his baptism, he said unto them, O generation of vipers, who hath warned you to flee from the wrath to come?

8 Bring forth therefore fruits meet for repentance:

9 And think not to say within yourselves, We have Abraham to *our*

father: for I say unto you, that God is able of these stones to raise up children unto Abraham.

10 And now also the ax is laid unto the root of the trees: therefore every tree which bringeth not forth good fruit is hewn down, and cast into the fire.

11 I indeed baptize you with water unto repentance: but he that cometh after me is mightier than I, whose shoes I am not worthy to bear: he shall baptize you with the Holy Ghost, and *with* fire:

12 Whose fan *is* in his hand, and he will throughly purge his floor, and gather his wheat into the garner; but he will burn up the chaff with unquenchable fire.

THESE verses describe the ministry of John the Baptist, the forerunner of our Lord Jesus Christ. It is a ministry that deserves close attention. Few preachers ever produced such effects. "There went out to him Jerusalem, and all Judæa, and all the region round about Jordan." None ever received such praise from the great Head of the Church. Jesus calls him "a burning and a shining light." The great Bishop of souls Himself declares, that "among them that are born of women there hath not arisen a greater than John the Baptist." Let us then study the leading features of his ministry.

John the Baptist spoke plainly *about sin.* He taught the absolute necessity of "repentance," before any one can be saved. He preached that repentance must be proved by its "fruits." He warned men not to rest on outward privileges, or outward union with the church.

This is just the teaching that we all need. We are naturally dead, and blind, and asleep in spiritual things. We are ready to content ourselves with a mere formal religion, and to flatter ourselves, that if we go to church we shall be saved. We need to be told, that except we "repent and are converted" we shall all perish.

John the Baptist spoke plainly *about our Lord Jesus Christ.* He taught people that one far "mightier than himself" was coming among them. He was nothing more than a servant : the Coming One was the King. He himself could only "baptize with water:" the Coming One could "baptize with the Holy Ghost," take away sins, and would one day judge the world.

This again is the very teaching that human nature requires. We need to be sent direct to Christ. We are all ready to stop short of this. We want to rest in our union with the church, regular use of the sacraments, and diligent attendance on an established ministry. We ought to be told the absolute necessity of union with Christ Himself by faith. He is the appointed fountain of mercy, grace, life, and peace. We must each have personal dealings with Him about our souls. What do we know of the Lord Jesus? What have we got from Him? These are the questions on which our salvation hinges.

John the Baptist spoke plainly *about the Holy Ghost*. He preached that there was such a thing as the baptism of the Holy Ghost. He taught that it was the special office of the Lord Jesus to give it to men.

This again is a teaching which we greatly require. We need to be told that forgiveness of sin is not the only thing necessary to salvation. There is another thing yet; and that is the baptizing of our hearts by the Holy Ghost. There must not only be the work of Christ for us, but the work of the Holy Ghost in us. There must not only be a title to heaven by the blood of Christ, but a preparedness for heaven wrought in us by the Spirit of Christ. Let us never rest till we know something by experience of the baptism of the Spirit. The baptism of water is a great privilege. But let us see to it that we have also the baptism of the Holy Ghost.

John the Baptist spoke plainly *about the awful danger of the impenitent and unbelieving.* He told his hearers that there was a " wrath to come." He preached of an "unquenchable fire," in which the chaff would one day be burned.

This again is a teaching which is deeply important. We need to be straitly warned, that it is no light matter whether we repent or not. We need to be reminded, that there is a hell as well as a heaven, and an everlasting punishment for the wicked, as well as everlasting life for the godly. We are fearfully apt to forget this. We talk of the love and mercy of God, and we do not remember sufficiently His justice and holiness. Let us be very careful on this point. It is no real kindness to keep back the terrors of the Lord. It is good for us all to be. taught, that it is possible to be lost for ever, and that all unconverted people are hanging over the brink of the pit.

In the last place, John the Baptist spoke plainly *about the safety of true believers.* He taught, that there was "a garner" for all who are Christ's wheat, and that they would be gathered together there in the day of His appearing.

This again is a teaching which human nature greatly requires. The best of believers need much encouragement. They are yet in the body. They live in a wicked world. They are often tempted by the devil. They ought to be often reminded, that Jesus will never leave them nor forsake them. He will guide them safely through this life, and at length give them eternal glory.

They shall be hid in the day of wrath. They shall be safe as Noah in the ark.

Let these things sink down deeply into our hearts. We live in a day of much false teaching. Let us never forget the leading features of a faithful ministry. Happy would it have been for the Church of Christ, if all its ministers had been more like John the Baptist!

MATTHEW III. 13—17.

13 Then cometh Jesus from Galilee to Jordan unto John, to be baptized of him.

14 But John forbad him, saying, I have need to be baptized of thee, and comest thou to me?

15 And Jesus answering said unto him, Suffer *it to be so* now: for thus it becometh us to fulfil all righteousness. Then he suffered him.

16 And Jesus, when he was baptized, went up staightway out of the water: and, lo, the heavens were opened unto him, and he saw the Spirit of God descending like a dove, and lighting upon him:

17 And lo, a voice from heaven, saying, This is my beloved Son, in whom I am well pleased

You have here the account of our Lord Jesus Christ's baptism. This was His first step, when He entered on His ministry. When the Jewish priests took up their office at the age of thirty, they were washed with water. When our great High Priest begins the great work He came into the world to accomplish, He is publicly baptized.

Let us learn from these verses *to regard the sacrament of baptism with reverence.* An ordinance of which the Lord Jesus Himself partook, is not to be lightly esteemed. An ordinance to which the great Head of the Church submitted, ought to be ever honourable in the eyes of professing Christians.

There are few subjects in religion on which greater mistakes have arisen than baptism. There are few which require so much fencing and guarding. Let us arm our minds with two general cautions.

Let us beware on the one hand, *that we do not attach a superstitious importance to the water of baptism.* We must not expect that water to act as a charm. We must not suppose that all baptized persons as a matter of course receive the grace of God, in the moment that they are baptized. To say that all who come to baptism obtain like and equal benefit,—and that it matters not a jot whether they come with faith and prayer, or in utter carelessness,—to say such things appears to contradict the plainest lessons of Scripture.

Let us beware on the other hand, *that we do not dishonour the sacrament of baptism.* It is dishonoured when it is thrust out of sight, and never publicly noticed in the congregation. A sacrament ordained by Christ Himself ought not to be treated in this way. The admission of every new member into the ranks of the visible church, whether young or grown up, is an event which ought to excite a lively interest in a Christian assembly. It is an event that ought to call forth the fervent prayers of all praying people. The more deeply we are convinced that baptism and grace are not inseparably tied together, the more we ought to feel bound to join in prayer for a blessing, whenever any one is baptized.

The baptism of our Lord Jesus Christ was attended by circumstances of peculiar solemnity. Such a baptism never will be again, so long as the world stands.

We are told of *the presence of all three persons of the blessed Trinity.* God the Son, manifest in the flesh, is baptized. God the Spirit descends like a dove, and lights upon Him. God the Father speaks from heaven with a voice. In a word we have the manifested presence

of Father, Son, and Holy Ghost. Surely we may regard
this as a public announcement, that the work of Christ
was the result of the eternal counsels of all the Three.
It was the whole Trinity, which at the beginning of creation said, "let us make man." It was the whole Trinity
again, which at the beginning of the Gospel seemed to
say, "let us save man."

We are told of *"a voice from heaven"* at our Lord's
baptism.

This was a circumstance of singular solemnity. We
read of no voice from heaven before this, except at the
giving of the law on Sinai. Both occasions were of
peculiar importance. It therefore seemed good to our
Father in heaven to mark both with peculiar honour.
At the introduction both of the law and Gospel, He
Himself speaks.

How striking and deeply instructive are the Father's
words! "This is my beloved Son, in whom I am well
pleased." He declares, in these words, that Jesus is the
divine Saviour sealed and appointed from all eternity to
carry out the work of redemption. He proclaims, that He
accepts Him as the Mediator between God and man. He
seems to publish to the world, that he is satisfied with
Him as the propitiation, the substitute, the ransom-payer
for the lost family of Adam, and the Head of a redeemed
people. In Him He sees His holy "law magnified and made
honourable." Through Him He can "be just and yet the
justifier of the ungodly." (Rom. iii. 26.)

May we ponder these words well! They are full of
rich food for thought. They are full of peace, joy, comfort and consolation, for all who have fled for refuge to

the Lord Jesus Christ, and committed their souls to Him for salvation. Such may rejoice in the thought, that though in themselves sinful, yet in God's sight they are counted righteous. The Father regards them as members of His beloved Son. He sees in them no spot, and for His Son's sake is "well pleased." (Ephes. i. 6.)

MATTHEW IV. 1—11.

1 Then was Jesus led up of the spirit into the wilderness to be tempted of the devil.

2 And when he had fasted forty days and forty nights, he was afterward an hungred.

3 And when the tempter came to him, he said, If thou be the Son of God, command that these stones be made bread.

4 But he answered and said, It is written, Man shall not live by bread alone, but by every word that proceedeth out of the mouth of God.

5 Then the devil taketh him up into the holy city, and setteth him on a pinnacle of the temple,

6 And saith unto him, If thou be the Son of God, cast thyself down: for it is written, He shall give his angels charge concerning thee: and in *their* hands they shall bear thee up, lest at any time thou dash thy foot against a stone.

7 Jesus said unto him, It is written again, Thou shalt not tempt the Lord thy God.

8 Again, the devil taketh him up into an exceeding high mountain, and sheweth him all the kingdoms of the world, and the glory of them;

9 And saith unto him, All these things will I give thee, if thou wilt fall down and worship me.

10 Then saith Jesus unto him, Get thee hence, Satan: for it is written, Thou shalt worship the Lord thy God, and him only shalt thou serve.

11 Then the devil leaveth him, and, behold, angels came and ministered unto him.

THE first event in our Lord's ministry which St. Matthew records after His baptism, is His temptation. This is a deep and mysterious subject. There is much in the history of it which we cannot explain. But there lie on the face of the history plain practical lessons, to which we shall do well to take heed.

Let us learn, in the first place, *what a real and mighty enemy we have in the devil.* He is not afraid to assault even the Lord Jesus Himself. Three times over he attacks God's own Son. Our Saviour was "tempted of the devil."

It was the devil, who brought sin into the world at the

beginning. This is he, who vexed Job, deceived David, and gave Peter a heavy fall. This is he, whom the Bible calls a "murderer," a "liar," and a "roaring lion." This is he, whose enemity to our souls never slumbers and never sleeps. This is he, who for nearly 6000 years has been working at one work, to ruin men and women, and draw them to hell. This is he, whose cunning and subtlety pass man's understanding, and who often appears "an angel of light."

Let us all watch and pray daily against his devices. There is no enemy worse than an enemy who is never seen and never dies, who is near us wherever we live, and goes with us wherever we go. Not least let us beware of that levity and jesting about the devil, which is so unhappily common. Let us remember every day, that if we would be saved, we must not only crucify the flesh, and overcome the world, but also "resist the devil."

Let us learn in the next place, *that we must not count temptation a strange thing.* "The disciple is not greater than his master, nor the servant than his lord." If Satan came to Christ, he will also come to Christians.

It would be well for all believers, if they would remember this. They are too apt to forget it. They often find evil thoughts arising within their minds, which they can truly say they hate. Doubts, questions, and sinful imaginings are suggested to them, against which their whole inward man revolts. But let not these things destroy their peace, and rob them of their comforts. Let them remember there is a devil, and not be surprised to find him near them. To be tempted is in itself no sin. It is the yielding to the temptation, and giving it a place in our hearts, which we must fear.

Let us learn in the next place, *that the chief weapon we ought to use in resisting Satan is the Bible.* Three times the great enemy offered temptations to our Lord. Three times his offer was refused, with a text of Scripture as the reason, "it is written."

Here is one among many reasons, why we ought to be diligent readers of our Bibles. The Word is the sword of the Spirit. We shall never fight a good fight, if we do not use it as our principal weapon.—The Word is the lamp for our feet. We shall never keep the king's highway to heaven, if we do not journey by its light.—It may well be feared, that there is not enough Bible-reading amongst us. It is not sufficient to have the Book. We must actually read it, and pray over it ourselves. It will do us no good, if it only lies still in our houses. We must be actually familiar with its contents, and have its texts stored in our memories and minds. Knowledge of the Bible [never comes by intuition. It can only be got by hard, regular, daily, attentive, wakeful reading. Do we grudge the time and trouble this will cost us? If we do, we are not yet fit for the kingdom of God.

Let us learn in the last place, *what a sympathizing Saviour the Lord Jesus Christ is.* "In that he himself hath suffered being tempted, he is able to succour them that are tempted." (Heb. ii. 18.)

The sympathy of Jesus is a truth which ought to be peculiarly dear to all believers. They will find in it a mine of strong consolation. They should never forget, that they have a mighty Friend in heaven, who feels for them in all their temptations, and can enter into all their spiritual anxieties. Are they ever tempted by Satan to distrust God's care and goodness? So was Jesus.—Are they ever tempted to presume on God's mercy, and run into danger without warrant? So also was Jesus.—Are they ever tempted to commit some one great private sin for the sake of some great seeming advantage? So also was Jesus.—Are they ever tempted to listen to some misapplication of Scripture, as an excuse for doing wrong? So also was Jesus.—He is just the Saviour that a tempted people require. Let them flee to Him for help, and spread before Him all their troubles. They will find His ear ever ready to hear, and His heart ever ready to feel. He can understand their sorrows.

May we all know the value of a sympathizing Saviour by experience! There is nothing to be compared to it in this cold and deceitful world. Those who seek their happiness in this life only, and despise the religion of the Bible, have no idea what true comfort they are missing.

MATTHEW IV. 12—25.

12 Now when Jesus had heard that John was cast into prison, he departed into Galilee;

13 And leaving Nazareth, he came and dwelt in Capernaum, which is upon the sea coast, in the borders of Zabulon and Nephthalim:

14 That it might be fulfilled which was spoken by Esaias the prophet, saying,

15 The land of Zabulon, and the land of Nepthalim, *by* the way of the sea, beyond Jordan, Galilee of the Gentiles;

16 The people which sat in darkness saw great light; and to them which sat in the region and shadow of death light is sprung up.

17 From that time Jesus began to preach, and to say, Repent: for the kingdom of heaven is at hand.

18 And Jesus, walking by the sea of Galilee, saw two brethren, Simon called Peter, and Andrew his brother, casting a net into the sea: for they were fishers.

19 And he saith unto them, Follow me, and I will make you fishers of men.

20 And they straightway left *their* nets, and followed him.

21 And going on from thence, he saw other two brethren, James *the son* of Zebedee, and John his brother, in a ship with Zebedee their father, mending their nets; and he called them.

22 And they immediately left the ship and their father, and followed him.

23 And Jesus went about all Galilee, teaching in their synagogues, and preaching the Gospel of the kingdom, and healing all manner of sickness

and all manner of disease among the people.

24 And his fame went throughout all Syria: and they brought unto him all sick people that were taken with divers diseases and torments, and those which were possessed with devils, and those which were lunatick, and those that had the palsy; and he healed them.

25 And there followed him great multitudes of people from Galilee, and *from* Decapolis, and *from* Jerusalem, and *from* Judæa, and *from* beyond Jordan.

WE have in these verses the beginning of our Lord's ministry among men. He enters on His labours among a dark and ignorant people. He chooses men to be His companions and disciples. He confirms His ministry by miracles, which rouse the attention of "all Syria," and draw multitudes to hear Him.

Let us notice *the way in which our Lord commenced His mighty work.* "He began to preach."

There is no office so honourable as that of the preacher. There is no work so important to the souls of men. It is an office which the Son of God was not ashamed to take up. It is an office to which He appointed His twelve apostles. It is an office to which St. Paul in his old age specially directs Timothy's attention. He charges him with almost his last breath to "preach the word." It is the means which God has always been pleased to use above any other, for the conversion and edification of souls. The brightest days of the Church have been those when preaching has been honoured. The darkest days of the Church have been those when it has been lightly esteemed. Let us honour the sacraments and public prayers of the Church, and reverently use them. But let us beware that we do not place them above preaching.

Let us notice *the first doctrine which the Lord Jesus proclaimed to the world.* He began to say "repent."

The necessity of repentance is one of the great foundations, which lie at the very bottom of Christianity. It needs to be pressed on all mankind without exception.—High or low, rich or poor, all have sinned and are guilty before God; and all must repent and be converted, if they would be saved. And true repentance is no light matter. It is a thorough change of heart about sin, a change showing itself in godly sorrow and humiliation,—in heartfelt confession before the throne of grace,—in a complete breaking off from sinful habits, and an abiding hatred of all sin. Such repentance is the inseparable companion of saving faith in Christ. Let us prize the doctrine highly. It is of the highest importance. No Christian teaching can be called sound, which does not constantly bring forward "repentance toward God and faith toward our Lord Jesus Christ." (Acts xx. 21.)

Let us notice *the class of men whom the Lord Jesus chose to be His disciples*. They were of the poorest and humblest rank in life. Peter, and Andrew, and James, and John, were all "fishermen."

The religion of our Lord Jesus Christ was not intended for the rich and learned alone. It was intended for all the world,—and the majority of all the world will always be the poor. Poverty and ignorance of books excluded thousands from the notice of the boastful philosophers of the heathen world. They exclude no one from the highest place in the service of Christ. Is a man humble? Does he feel his sins? Is he willing to hear Christ's voice and follow Him? If this be so, he may be the poorest of the poor, but he shall be found as high as any in the kingdom of heaven. Intellect and money are worth nothing without grace.

The religion of Christ must have been from heaven, or it never could have prospered and overspread the earth as it has done. It is vain for infidels to attempt to answer this argument. It cannot be answered. A religion which did not flatter the rich, the great, and the learned,—a religion which offered no license to the carnal inclinations of man's heart,—a religion whose first teachers were poor fishermen, without wealth, rank, or power,—such a religion could never have turned the world upside down, if it had not been of God. Look at the Roman emperors and the heathen priests with their splendid temples on the one side! Look at a few unlearned working men with the Gospel on the other! Were there ever two parties so unequally matched? Yet the weak proved strong, and the strong proved weak. Heathenism fell, and Christianity took its place. Christianity must be of God.

Let us notice in the last place *the general character of the miracles by which our Lord confirmed His mission.* Here we are told of them in the mass. Hereafter we shall read many of them described particularly. And what is their character? They were miracles of mercy and kindness. Our Lord "went about doing good."

These miracles are meant to teach us our Lord's power. He that could heal sick people with a touch, and cast out devils with a word, is "able to save to the uttermost all them that come unto God by Him." He is almighty.

These miracles are meant to be types and emblems of our Lord's skill as a spiritual physician. He before whom no bodily disease proved incurable, is mighty to cure every ailment of our souls. There is no broken heart that He cannot heal. There is no wound of conscience that He cannot cure. Fallen, crushed, bruised, plague-stricken as we all are by sin, Jesus by His blood and Spirit can make us whole. Only let us go to Him.

These miracles not least are intended to show us Christ's heart. He is a most compassionate Saviour. He rejected no one who came to Him. He refused no one, however loathsome and diseased. He had an ear to hear all, and a hand to help all, and a heart to feel for all. There is no kindness like His. His compassions fail not.

May we all remember that Jesus is "the same yesterday, to-day, and for ever!" High in heaven at God's right hand, he is not in the least altered. He is just as able to save, just as willing to receive, just as ready to help, as He was 1800 years ago. Should we have spread out our wants before Him then? Let us do the same now. He can "heal all manner of sickness and all manner of disease."

MATTHEW V. 1—12.

1 And seeing the multitudes, he went up into a mountain: and when he was set, his disciples came unto him.

2 And he opened his mouth, and taught them, saying,

3 Blessed *are* the poor in spirit: for their's is the kingdom of heaven.

4 Blessed *are* they that mourn: for they shall be comforted.

5 Blessed *are* the meek: for they shall inherit the earth.

6 Blessed *are* they which do hunger and thirst after righteousness: for they shall be filled.

7 Blessed *are* the merciful: for they shall obtain mercy.

8 Blessed *are* the pure in heart: for they shall see God.

9 Blessed *are* the peacemakers: for they shall be called the children of God.

10 Blessed *are* they which are persecuted for righteousness' sake: for their's is the kingdom of heaven.

11 Blessed are ye, when *men* shall revile you, and persecute *you*, and shall say all manner of evil against you falsely, for my sake.

12 Rejoice, and be exceeding glad: for great *is* your reward in heaven: for so persecuted they the prophets which were before you.

THE three chapters which begin with these verses deserve the special attention of all readers of the Bible. They contain what is commonly called the "sermon on the mount."

Every word of the Lord Jesus ought to be most precious to professing Christians.   It is the voice of the chief Shepherd.   It is the charge of the great Bishop and Head of the Church.   It is the Master speaking.   It is the word of Him who "spake as never man spake," and by whom we shall all be judged at the last day.

Would we know what kind of people Christians ought to be?   Would we know the character at which Christians ought to aim?   Would we know the outward walk and inward habit of mind which become a follower of Jesus?   Then let us often study the sermon on the mount. Let us often ponder each sentence, and prove ourselves by it.   Not least let us often consider who they are that are called blessed at the beginning of the sermon.   Those whom the great High Priest blesses are blessed indeed.

The Lord Jesus calls those blessed, who are *poor in spirit*.   He means the humble, and lowly-minded, and self-abased.   He means those who are deeply convinced of their own sinfulness in God's sight.   These are they who are not "wise in their own eyes and holy in their own sight." They are not "rich and increased with goods."   They do not fancy they need nothing.   They regard themselves as "wretched, and miserable, and poor, and blind, and naked."   Blessed are all such!   Humility is the very first letter in the alphabet of Christianity.   We must begin low, if we would build high.

The Lord Jesus calls those blessed, who *mourn*.   He means those who sorrow for sin, and grieve daily over their own short-comings.   These are they who trouble themselves more about sin than about any thing on earth. The remembrance of it is grievous to them. The burden of it is intolerable. Blessed are all such! "The sacrifices of God are a broken and contrite spirit." One day they shall weep no more. "They shall be comforted."

The Lord Jesus calls those blessed, who are *meek*. He means those who are of a patient and contented spirit. They are willing to put up with little honour here below. They can bear injuries without resentment. They are not ready to take offence. Like Lazarus in the parable, they are content to wait for their good things. Blessed are all such! They are never losers in the long run. One day they shall "reign on the earth." (Rev. v. 10.)

The Lord Jesus calls those blessed, who *hunger and thirst after righteousness*. He means those who desire above all things to be entirely conformed to the mind of God. They long not so much to be rich, or wealthy, or learned, as to be holy. Blessed are all such! They shall have enough one day. They shall "awake up after God's likeness and be satisfied." (Psal. xvii. 15.)

The Lord Jesus calls those blessed, who are *merciful*. He means those who are full of compassion towards others. They pity all who are suffering either from sin or sorrow, and are tenderly desirous to make their sufferings less. They are full of good works, and endeavours to do good. Blessed are all such! Both in this life and that to come, they shall reap a rich reward.

The Lord Jesus calls those blessed, who are *pure in heart*. He means those who do not aim merely at outward correctness, but at inward holiness. They are not satisfied with a mere external show of religion. They

strive to keep a heart and conscience void of offence, and
to serve God with the spirit and the inner man.   Blessed
are all such!   The heart is the man.   "Man looketh on the
outward appearance, but the Lord looketh on the heart."
(1 Sam. xvi. 7.)   He that is most spiritual-minded will
have most communion with God.

The Lord Jesus calls those blessed, who are *peacemakers*.   He means those who use all their influence to
promote peace and charity on earth, in private and in
public, at home and abroad.   He means those who strive
to make all men love one another, by teaching that
Gospel which says, "love is the fulfilling of the law."
Blessed are all such!   They are doing the very work
which the Son of God began, when He came to earth the
first time, and which He will finish when He returns the
second time.

Lastly, the Lord Jesus calls those blessed, who are *persecuted for righteousness sake*.   He means those who are
laughed at, mocked, despised, and ill-used, because they
endeavour to live as true Christians.   Blessed are all
such!   They drink of the same cup which their Master
drank.   They are now confessing Him before men, and
He will confess them before his Father and the angels at
the last day.   "Great is their reward."

Such are the eight foundation-stones, which the Lord
lays down at the beginning of the sermon on the mount.
Eight great testing truths are placed before us.   May we
mark well each one of them, and learn wisdom!

Let us learn how entirely contrary are the principles of
Christ to the principles of the world.   It is vain to deny
it.   They are almost diametrically opposed.   The very

characters which the Lord Jesus praises, the world despises. The very pride, and thoughtlessness, and high tempers, and worldliness, and selfishness, and formality, and unloving-ness, which abound everywhere, the Lord Jesus condemns.

Let us learn how unhappily different is the teaching of Christ from the practice of many professing Christians. Where shall we find men and women among those who go to churches and chapels, who are striving to live up to the pattern we have read of to-day? Alas! there is much reason to fear, that many baptized persons are utterly ignorant of what the New Testament contains.

Above all let us learn how holy and spiritual-minded all believers should be. They should never aim at any standard lower than that of the sermon on the mount. Christianity is eminently a practical religion. Sound doctrine is its root and foundation, but holy living should always be its fruit. And if we would know what holy living is, let us often bethink ourselves who they are that Jesus calls "blessed."

MATTHEW V. 13—20.

13 Ye are the salt of the earth: but if the salt have lost his savour, wherewith shall it be salted? it is thenceforth good for nothing, but to be cast out, and to be trodden under foot of men.

14 Ye are the light of the world. A city that is set on an hill cannot be hid.

15 Neither do men light a candle, and put it under a bushel, but on a candlestick; and it giveth light unto all that are in the house.

16 Let your light so shine before men, that they may see your good works, and glorify your Father which is in heaven.

17 Think not that I am come to destroy the law, or the prophets: I am not come to destroy, but to fulfil.

18 For verily I say unto you, Till heaven and earth pass, one jot or one tittle shall in no wise pass from the law, till all be fulfilled.

19 Whosoever therefore shall break one of these least commandments, and shall teach men so, he shall be called the least in the kingdom of heaven: but whosoever shall do and teach *them*, the same shall be called great in the kingdom of heaven.

20 For I say unto you, That except your righteousness shall exceed *the righteousness* of the Scribes and Pharisees, ye shall in no case enter into the kingdom of heaven.

IN these verses the Lord Jesus treats of two subjects. One is the character which true Christians must support and maintain in the world. The other is the relation between His doctrines and those of the Old Testament. It is of great importance to have clear views on both these subjects.

True Christians *are to be in the world like salt.* Now salt has a peculiar taste of its own, utterly unlike anything else. When mingled with other substances it preserves them from corruption. It imparts a portion of its taste to everything it is mixed with. It is useful so long as it preserves its savour, but no longer. Are we true Christians? Then behold here our place and its duties!

True Christians *are to be in the world like light.* Now it is the property of light to be utterly distinct from darkness. The least spark in a dark room can be seen at once. Of all things created light is the most useful. It fertilizes. It guides. It cheers. It was the first thing called into being. Without it the world would be a gloomy blank. Are we true Christians? Then behold again our position and its responsibilities!

Surely, if words mean anything, we are meant to learn from these two figures, that there must be something marked, distinct, and peculiar about our character, if we are true Christians. It will never do to idle through life, thinking and living like others, if we mean to be owned by Christ as His people. Have we grace? Then it must be *seen.* Have we the Spirit? Then there must be *fruit.* Have we any saving religion? Then there must be a difference of habits, tastes, and turn of mind, between us and those who think only of the world. It is perfectly clear that true Christianity is something more than being baptized and going to church. "Salt" and "light" evidently imply *peculiarity* both of heart and life, of faith and practice. We must dare to be singular and unlike the world, if we mean to be saved.

The relation between our Lord's teaching and that of the Old Testament, is cleared up by our Lord in one striking sentence. He says, "Think not that I am come to destroy the law, or the prophets: I am not come to destroy, but to fulfil." These are remarkable words. They were deeply important when spoken, as satisfying the natural anxiety of the Jews on the point. They will be deeply important as long as the world stands, as a testimony that the religion of the Old and New Testament is one harmonious whole.

The Lord Jesus came to fulfil the *predictions of the prophets*, who had long foretold that a Saviour would one day appear. He came to fulfil the *ceremonial law*, by becoming the great sacrifice for sin, to which all the Mosaic offerings had ever pointed. He came to fulfil *the moral law*, by yielding to it a perfect obedience, which we could never have yielded,—and by paying the penalty for our breach of it with His atoning blood, which we could never have paid. In all these ways He exalted the law of God, and made its importance more evident even than it had been before. In a word, "He magnified the law and made it honourable." (Isaiah xlii. 21.)

There are deep lessons of wisdom to be learned from these words of our Lord. Let us consider them well, and lay them up in our hearts.

Let us *beware of despising the Old Testament* under

any pretence whatever. Let us never listen to those who bid us throw it aside as an obsolete, antiquated, useless book. The religion of the Old Testament is the germ of Christianity. The Old Testament is the Gospel in the bud. , The New Testament is the Gospel in full flower.— The Old Testament is the Gospel in the blade. The New Testament is the Gospel in full ear.—The saints in the Old Testament saw many things through a glass darkly. But they all looked by faith to the same Saviour, and were led by the same Spirit as ourselves. These are no light matters. Much infidelity begins with an ignorant contempt of the Old Testament.

Let us, for another thing, *beware of despising the law of the Ten Commandments.* Let us not suppose for a moment that it is set aside by the Gospel, or that Christians have nothing to do with it. The coming of Christ did not alter the position of the Ten Commandments one hair's breadth. If anything, it exalted and raised their authority. (Rom. iii. 31.) The law of the Ten Commandments is God's eternal measure of right and, wrong. By it is the knowledge of sin. By it the Spirit shows men their need of Christ, and drives them to Him. To it Christ refers His people as their rule and guide for holy living. In its right place it is just as important as "the glorious Gospel."—It cannot save us. We cannot be justified by it. But never, never let us despise it. It is a symptom of an ignorant and unhealthy state of religion, when the law is lightly esteemed. The true Christian "delights in the law of God." (Rom. vii. 22.)

In the last place, let us *beware of supposing that the Gospel has lowered the standard of personal holiness,* and that the Christian is not intended to be as strict and particular about his daily life as the Jew. This is an immense mistake, but one that is unhappily very common. So far from this being the case, the sanctification of the New Testament saint ought to exceed that of him who has nothing but the Old Testament for his guide. The more light we have, the more we ought to love God. The more clearly we see our own complete and full forgiveness in Christ, the more heartily ought we to work for His glory. We know what it cost to redeem us far better than the Old Testament saints did. We have read what happened in Gethsemane and on Calvary, and they only saw it dimly and indistinctly as a thing yet to come. May we never forget our obligations! The Christian who is content with a low standard of personal holiness has got much to learn.

MATTHEW V. 21—37.

21 Ye have heard that it was said by them of old time, Thou shalt not kill; and whosoever shall kill shall be in danger of the judgment:

22 But I say unto you, That whosoever is angry with his brother without a cause shall be in danger of the judgment: and whosoever shall say to his brother, Raca, shall be in danger of the council: but whosoever shall say, Thou fool, shall be in danger of hell fire.

23 Therefore if thou bring thy gift to the altar, and there rememberest that thy brother hath ought against thee;

24 Leave there thy gift before the altar, and go thy way; first be reconciled to thy brother, and then come and offer thy gift.

25 Agree with thine adversary quickly, whiles thou art in the way with him; lest at any time the adversary deliver thee to the judge, and the judge deliver thee to the officer, and thou be cast into prison.

26 Verily I say unto thee, Thou shalt by no means come out thence, till thou hast paid the uttermost farthing.

27 Ye have heard that it was said by them of old time, Thou shalt not commit adultery:

28 But I say unto you, That whosoever looketh on a woman to lust after her, hath committed adultery with her already in his heart.

29 And if thy right eye offend thee, pluck it out, and cast *it* from thee: for it is profitable for thee that one of thy members should perish, and not *that* thy whole body should be cast into hell.

30 And if thy right hand offend thee, cut it off, and cast *it* from thee: for it is profitable for thee that one of

thy members should perish, and not *that* thy whole body should be cast into hell.

31 It hath been said, Whosoever shall put away his wife, let him give her a writing of divorcement:

32 But I say unto you, That whosoever shall put away his wife, saving for the cause of fornication, causeth her to commit adultery: and whosoever shall marry her that is divorced committeth adultery.

33 Again, ye have heard that it hath been said by them of old time, Thou shalt not forswear thyself, but shalt perform unto the Lord thine oaths:

34 But I say unto you, Swear not at all; neither by heaven; for it is God's throne:

35 Nor by the earth; for it is his footstool: neither by Jerusalem; for it is the city of the great King.

36 Neither shalt thou swear by thy head, because thou canst not make one hair white or black.

37 But let your communication be, Yea, yea; Nay, nay: for whatsoever is more than these cometh of evil.

THESE verses deserve the closest attention of all readers of the Bible. A right understanding of the doctrines they contain lies at the very root of Christianity. The Lord Jesus here explains more fully the meaning of His words, "I came not to destroy the law, but to fulfil." He teaches us that His Gospel magnifies the law, and exalts its authority. He shows us that the law, as expounded by Him, was a far more spiritual and heart-searching rule than most of the Jews supposed. And He proves this by selecting three commandments out of the ten as examples of what He means.

He expounds *the sixth commandment*. Many thought that they kept this part of God's law, so long as they did not commit actual murder. The Lord Jesus shows, that its requirements go much further than this. It condemns all angry and passionate language, and especially when used without a cause. Let us mark this well. We may be perfectly innocent of taking life away, and yet be guilty of breaking the sixth commandment.

He expounds *the seventh commandment*. Many supposed that they kept this part of God's law, if they did not actually commit adultery. The Lord Jesus teaches, that we may break it in our thoughts, hearts, and imaginations, even when our outward conduct is moral and correct. The God with whom we have to do looks far beyond actions. With Him even a glance of the eye may be a sin.

He expounds *the third commandment*. Many fancied that they kept this part of God's law, so long as they did not swear falsely, and performed their oaths. The Lord Jesus forbids all vain and light swearing altogether. All swearing by created things, even when God's name is not brought forward ;—all calling upon God to witness, excepting on the most solemn occasions, is a great sin.

Now all this is very instructive. It ought to raise very serious reflections in our minds. It calls us loudly to use great searching of heart. And what does it teach?

It teaches us *the exceeding holiness of God*. He is a most pure and perfect Being, who sees faults and imperfections, where man's eyes often see none. He reads our inward motives. He notes our words and thoughts, as well as our actions. "He requireth truth in the inward parts." Oh! that men would consider this part of God's character more than they do! There would be no room for pride, and self-righteousness, and carelessness, if they only saw God "as He is."

It teaches us *the exceeding ignorance of man in spiritual things*. There are thousands and ten thousands of professing Christians, it may be feared, who know no more of the requirements of God's law than the most ignorant Jews. They know the letter of the ten commandments well enough. They fancy, like the young ruler, "all these have I kept from my youth up." They never dream that it is possible to break the sixth and seventh commandments, if they do not break them by outward act or deed. And so they live on satisfied with themselves, and quite content with their little bit of religion. Happy indeed are they who really understand God's law!

It teaches us *our exceeding need of the Lord Jesus Christ's atoning blood to save us.* What man or woman upon earth can ever stand before such a God as this, and plead "not guilty?" Who is there that has ever grown to years of discretion, and not broken the commandments thousands of times? "There is none righteous, no! not one." Without a mighty Mediator we should every one be condemned in the judgment. Ignorance of the real meaning of the law is one plain reason why so many do not value the Gospel, and content themselves with a little formal Christianity. They do not see the strictness and holiness of God's Ten commandments. If they did, they would never rest till they were safe in Christ.

In the last place, this passage teaches us *the exceeding importance of avoiding all occasions of sin.* If we really desire to be holy, we must "take heed to our ways, that we offend not in our tongues."—We must be ready to make up quarrels and disagreements, lest they gradually lead on to greater evils. "The beginning of strife is like the letting out of water."—We must labour to crucify our flesh and mortify our members, to make any sacrifice and endure any bodily inconvenience rather than sin.—We must keep our lips as it were with a bridle, and exercise an hourly strictness over our words.—Let men call us precise, if they will, for so doing. Let them say, if they please, that we are "too particular." We need not be moved. We are merely doing as our Lord Jesus Christ bids us, and, if this is the case, we have no cause to be ashamed.

MATTHEW V. 38—48.

38 Ye have heard that it hath been said, An eye for an eye, and a tooth for a tooth:

39 But I say unto you, That ye resist not evil: but whosoever shall smite thee on thy right cheek, turn to him the other also.

40 And if any man will sue thee at the law, and take away thy coat, let him have *thy* cloak also.

41 And whosoever shall compel thee to go a mile, go with him twain.

42 Give to him that asketh thee, and from him that would borrow of thee turn not thou away.

43 Ye have heard that it hath been said, Thou shalt love thy neighbour, and hate thine enemy.

44 But I say unto you, Love your enemies, bless them that curse you, do good to them that hate you, and pray for them which despitefully use you, and persecute you;

45 That ye may be the children of your Father which is in heaven: for he maketh his sun to rise on the evil and on the good, and sendeth rain on the just and on the unjust.

46 For if ye love them which love you, what reward have ye? do not even the publicans the same?

47 And if ye salute your brethren only, what do ye more *than others?* do not even the publicans so?

48 Be ye therefore perfect, even as your Father which is in heaven is perfect.

YOU have here our Lord Jesus Christ's rules for our conduct one towards another. He that would know how He ought to feel and act towards his fellow men, should often study these verses. They deserve to be written in letters of gold. They have extorted praise even from the enemies of Christianity. Let us mark well what they contain.

The Lord Jesus *forbids everything like an unforgiving and revengeful spirit.* A readiness to resent injuries,—a quickness in taking offence,—a quarrelsome and contentious disposition,—a keenness in asserting our rights,— all, all are contrary to the mind of Christ. The world may see no harm in these habits of mind. But they do not become the character of the Christian. Our Master says, "Resist not evil."

The Lord Jesus *enjoins on us a spirit of universal love and charity.* We ought to put away all malice. We ought to return good for evil, and blessing for cursing. We ought to "love even our enemies."—Moreover we are not to love in word only, but in deed. We are to deny ourselves, and take trouble, in order to be kind and courteous. If any man "compel thee to go a mile, go with him twain." We are to put up with much and bear much, rather than hurt another, or give offence. In all things we are to be unselfish. Our thought must never be, "how do others behave to me?" but "what would Christ have me to do?"

A standard of conduct like this may seem, at first sight, extravagantly high. But we must never content ourselves with aiming at one lower. We must observe the two weighty arguments by which our Lord backs up this part of His instruction. They deserve serious attention.

For one thing, if we do not aim at the spirit and temper which are here recommended, *we are not yet children of God.* Our "Father in heaven" is kind to all. He sends rain on good and on evil alike. He causes "His sun" to shine on all without distinction.—A son should be like his father. But where is our likeness to our Father in heaven, if we cannot show mercy and kindness to everybody? Where is the evidence that we are new creatures, if we lack charity? It is altogether wanting. We must yet be "born again." (John iii. 7.)

For another thing, if we do not aim at the spirit and temper here recommended, *we are manifestly yet of the world.* Even those who have no religion can "love those who love them." They can do good and shew kindness, when their affection or interest moves them.   But a Christian ought to be influenced by higher principles than these.—Do we flinch from the test?   Do we find it impossible to do good to our enemies?   If that be the case, we may be sure we have yet to be converted.   As yet we have not "received the Spirit of God." (1 Cor. ii. 12.)

There is much in all this which calls loudly for solemn reflection.   There are few passages of Scripture so calculated to raise in our minds humbling thoughts.   We have here a lovely picture of the Christian as he ought to be. We cannot look at it without painful feelings.   We must all allow that it differs widely from the Christian as he is. Let us carry away from it two general lessons.

In the first place, if the spirit of these ten verses were more continually remembered by true believers, *they would recommend Christianity to the world far more than they do.*   We must not allow ourselves to suppose that the least words in this passage are trifling and of small moment.   They are not so.   It is attention to the spirit of this passage which makes our religion beautiful.   It is the neglect of the things which it contains by which our religion is deformed.   Unfailing courtesy, kindness, tenderness, and consideration for others, are some of the greatest ornaments to the character of a child of God.   The world can understand these things, if it cannot understand doctrine.   There is no religion in rudeness, roughness, bluntness, and incivility.   The perfection of practical Christianity consists in attending to the little duties of holiness as well as to the great.

In the second place, if the spirit of these ten verses had more dominion and power in the world, *how much happier the world would be than it is.* Who does not know that quarrellings, strifes, selfishness, and unkindness, cause half the miseries by which mankind is visited? Who can fail to see that nothing would so much tend to increase happiness as the spread of Christian love, such as is here recommended by our Lord? Let us all remember this. Those who fancy that true religion has any tendency to make men unhappy, are greatly mistaken. It is the absence of it that does this, and not the presence. True religion has the directly contrary effect. It tends to promote peace, and charity, and kindness, and goodwill among men. The more men are brought under the teaching of the Holy Spirit, the more they will love one another, and the more happy they will be.

MATTHEW VI. 1—8.

1 Take heed that ye do not your alms before men, to be seen of them: otherwise ye have no reward of your Father which is in heaven.

2 Therefore when thou doest *thine* alms, do not sound a trumpet before thee, as the hypocrites do in the synagogues and in the streets, that they may have glory of men. Verily I say unto you, They have their reward.

3 But when thou doest alms, let not thy left hand know what thy right hand doeth:

4 That thine alms may be in secret: and thy Father which seeth in secret himself shall reward thee openly.

5 And when thou prayest, thou shalt not be as the hypocrites *are:* for they love to pray standing in the synagogues and in the corners of the streets, that they may be seen of men. Verily I say unto you, They have their reward.

6 But thou, when thou prayest, enter into thy closet, and when thou hast shut thy door, pray to thy Father which is in secret; and thy Father which seeth in secret shall reward thee openly.

7 But when ye pray, use not vain repetitions, as the heathen *do:* for they think that they shall be heard for their much speaking.

8 Be not ye therefore like unto them: for your Father knoweth what things ye have need of, before ye ask him.

In this part of the sermon on the mount the Lord Jesus gives us instruction on two subjects. One is that of giving alms. The other is that of prayer. Both were subjects to which the Jews attached great importance.

Both in themselves deserve the serious attention of all professing Christians.

Observe that our Lord takes it for granted, *that all who call themselves His disciples will give alms.* He assumes as a matter of course, that they will think it a solemn duty to give, according to their means, to relieve the wants of others. The only point He handles is the manner in which the duty should be done. This is a weighty lesson. It condemns the selfish stinginess of many in the matter of giving money. How many are "rich towards themselves," but poor towards God! How many never give a farthing to do good to the bodies and souls of men! And have such persons any right to be called Christians, in their present state of mind? It may well be doubted. A giving Saviour should have giving disciples.

Observe again that our Lord takes it for granted, *that all who call themselves His disciples will pray.* He assumes this also as a matter of course. He only gives directions as to the best way of praying. This is another lesson which deserves to be continually remembered. It teaches plainly that prayerless people are not genuine Christians. It is not enough to join in the prayers of the congregation on Sundays, or attend the prayers of a family on week-days. There must be private prayer also. Without this we may be outward members of Christ's church, but we are not living members of Christ.

But what are the rules laid down for our guidance about almsgiving and praying? They are few and simple. But they contain much matter for thought.

In giving, *everything like ostentation is to be abhorred and avoided.* We are not to give as if we wished everybody to see how liberal and charitable we are, and desired the praise of our fellow men. We are to shun everything like display. We are to give quietly, and make as little noise as possible about our charities. We are to aim at the spirit of the proverbial saying, "Let not thy left hand know what thy right hand doeth."

In praying, *the principal object to be sought is to be alone with God.* We should endeavour to find some place where no mortal eye sees us, and where we can pour out our hearts with the feeling that no one is looking at us but God.—This is a rule which many find it very difficult to follow. The poor man and the servant often find it almost impossible to be really alone. But it is a rule which we must all make great efforts to obey. Necessity, in such cases, is often the mother of invention. When a person has a real will to find some place, where he can be in secret with his God, he will generally find a way.

In all our duties, whether giving or praying, the great thing to be kept in mind is, *that we have to do with a heart-searching and all-knowing God.* Everything like formality, affectation, or mere bodily service, is abominable and worthless in God's sight. He takes no account of the quantity of money we give, or the quantity of words we use. The one thing at which His all-seeing eye looks is the nature of our motives, and the state of our hearts. "Our Father seeth in secret."

May we all remember these things. Here lies a rock, on which many are continually making spiritual shipwreck. They flatter themselves that all must be right with their souls, if they only perform a certain amount of "religious duties." They forget that God does not regard the quantity, but the quality of our service. His favour is not to be bought, as many seem to suppose, by the formal repetition of a number of words, or the self-righteous payment of a sum of money to a charitable institution. Where are our hearts? Are we doing all, whether we give or pray, "as to the Lord, and not to men?" Do we realize the eye of God? Do we simply and solely desire to please Him, who "seeth in secret," and by whom "actions are weighed?" (1 Sam. ii. 3.) Are we sincere? These are the sort of questions, with which we should daily ply our souls.

MATTHEW VI. 9—15.

9 After this manner therefore pray ye: Our Father which art in heaven, Hallowed be thy name.
10 Thy kingdom come. Thy will be done in earth, as *it is* in heaven.
11 Give us this day our daily bread.
12 And forgive us our debts, as we forgive our debtors.
13 And lead us not into temptation, but deliver us from evil: For thine is the kingdom, and the power, and the glory, for ever. Amen.
14 For if ye forgive men their trespasses, your heavenly Father will also forgive you:
15 But if ye forgive not men their trespasses, neither will your Father forgive your trespasses.

THESE verses are few in number, and soon read, but they are of immense importance. They contain that wonderful pattern of prayer, with which the Lord Jesus has supplied His people, commonly called "the Lord's Prayer."

Perhaps no part of Scripture is so well known as this. Its words are familiar, wherever Christianity is found. Thousands, and tens of thousands, who never saw a Bible, or heard the pure Gospel, are acquainted with "Our Father," and "Paternoster." Happy would it be

E

for the world, if this prayer was as well known in the spirit, as it is in the letter!

Perhaps no part of Scripture is so full, and so simple at the same time, as this. It is the first prayer which we learn to offer up, when we are little children. Here is its simplicity.—It contains the germ of everything which the most advanced saint can desire. Here is its fulness.—The more we ponder every word it contains, the more we shall feel, "this prayer is of God."

The Lord's prayer consists of ten parts or sentences. There is one declaration of the Being to whom we pray. —There are three prayers respecting His name, His kingdom, and His will.—There are four prayers respecting our daily wants, our sins, our weakness, and our dangers.—There is one profession of our feeling towards others.—There is one concluding ascription of praise.— In all these parts we are taught to say "we," and "our." We are to remember others, as well as ourselves.—On each of these parts a volume might be written. We must content ourselves at present with taking up sentence by sentence, and marking out the direction in which each sentence points.

The first sentence declares *to whom we are to pray:* "Our Father which art in heaven." We are not to cry to saints and angels, but to the everlasting Father, the Father of spirits, the Lord of heaven and earth. We call Him Father, in the lowest sense, as our Creator; as St. Paul told the Athenians, "in him we live and move, and have our being,—we are also his offspring." (Acts xvii. 28.) We call Him Father in the highest sense, as the Father of our Lord Jesus Christ, reconciling us to Himself, through the death of His Son. (Col. i. 20—22.) We profess that which the Old Testament saints only saw dimly, if at all,—we profess to be His children by faith in Christ, and to have "the Spirit of adoption whereby we cry, Abba, Father." (Rom. viii. 15.) This, we must never forget, is the sonship that we must desire, if we would be saved. Without faith in Christ's blood, and union with Him, it is vain to talk of trusting in the Fatherhood of God.

The second sentence is *a petition respecting God's name:* "Hallowed be thy name." By the "name" of God we mean all those attributes under which He is revealed to us,—His power, wisdom, holiness, justice, mercy, and truth. By asking that they may be "hallowed," we mean that they may be made known and glorified. The glory of God is the first thing that God's children should desire. It is the object of one of our Lord's own prayers: "Father, glorify thy name." (John xii. 28.) It is the purpose for which the world was created. It is the end for which the saints are called and converted. It is the chief thing we should seek, that "God in all things may be glorified." (1 Peter iv. 11.)

The third sentence is *a petition concerning God's kingdom:* "thy kingdom come." By His kingdom we mean first, the kingdom of grace which God sets up and maintains in the hearts of all living members of Christ, by His Spirit and word. But we mean chiefly, the kingdom of glory which shall one day be set up, when Jesus shall come the second time, and "all men shall know Him from the least to the greatest." This is the time when sin, and sorrow, and Satan shall be cast out of the world. It is the time when the Jews shall be converted, and the fulness of the Gentiles shall come in, (Rom. xi. 25.) and a time that is above all things to be desired. It therefore fills a foremost place in the Lord's prayer. We ask that which is expressed in the words of the Burial service, "that it may please thee to hasten thy kingdom."

The fourth sentence is *a petition concerning God's will :* "thy will be done in earth as it is in heaven." We here pray that God's laws may be obeyed by men as perfectly, readily, and unceasingly, as they are by angels in heaven. We ask that those who now obey not His laws, may be taught to obey them, and that those who do obey them, may obey them better. Our truest happiness is perfect submission to God's will, and it is the highest charity to pray that all mankind may know it, obey it, and submit to it.

The fifth sentence is *a petition respecting our own daily wants :* "give us this day our daily bread." We are here taught to acknowledge our entire dependence on God, for the supply of our daily necessities. As Israel required daily manna, so we require daily "bread." We confess that we are poor, weak, wanting creatures, and beseech Him who is our Maker to take care of us. We ask for "bread," as the simplest of our wants, and in that word we include all that our bodies require.

The sixth sentence is *a petition respecting our sins :* "Forgive us our debts." We confess that we are sinners, and need daily grants of pardon and forgiveness. This is a part of the Lord's prayer which deserves especially to be remembered. · It condemns all self-righteousness and self-justifying. We are instructed here to keep up a continual habit of confession at the throne of grace, and a continual habit of seeking mercy and remission. Let this never be forgotten. We need daily to "wash our feet." (John xiii. 10.)

The seventh sentence is *a profession respecting our own feelings towards others :* we ask our Father to "forgive us our debts, as we forgive our debtors." This is the only profession in the whole prayer, and the only part on which our Lord comments and dwells, when He has concluded the prayer. The plain object of it is, to remind us that we must not expect our prayers for forgiveness to be heard, if we pray with malice and spite in our hearts towards others. To pray in such a frame of mind is mere formality and hypocrisy. It is even worse than hypocrisy. It is as much as saying, "Do not forgive me at all." Our prayer is nothing without charity. We must not expect to be forgiven, if we cannot forgive.

The eighth sentence is *a petition respecting our weakness :* "lead us not into temptation." It teaches us that we are liable, at all times, to be led astray, and fall. It instructs us to confess our infirmity, and beseech God to hold us up, and not allow us to run into sin. We ask Him, who orders all things in heaven and earth, to restrain us from going into that which would injure our souls, and never to suffer us to be tempted above that which we are able to bear. (1 Cor. x. 13.)

The ninth sentence is *a petition respecting our dangers :* "deliver us from evil." We are here taught to ask God to deliver us from the evil that is in the world, the evil

that is within our own hearts, and not least from that
evil one, the devil. We confess that, so long as we are in
the body, we are constantly seeing, hearing, and feeling
the presence of evil. It is about us, and within us, and
around us on every side. And we entreat Him, who alone
can preserve us, to be continually delivering us from its
power. (John xvii. 15.)

The last sentence is *an ascription of praise:* "thine is
the kingdom, the power, and the glory." We declare in
these words our belief, that the kingdoms of this world
are the rightful property of our Father,—that to Him
alone belongs all "power,"—and that He alone deserves
to receive all "glory." And we conclude by offering to
Him the profession of our hearts, that we give Him all
honour and praise, and rejoice that He is King of kings,
and Lord of lords.

And now let us all examine ourselves, and see whether
we really desire to have the things which we are taught
to ask for in the Lord's Prayer. Thousands, it may
be feared, repeat these words daily as a form, but never
consider what they are saying. They care nothing for
the "glory," the "kingdom," or the "will" of God. They
have no sense of dependence, sinfulness, weakness, or
danger. They have no love or charity towards their
enemies. And yet they repeat the Lord's Prayer! These
things ought not to be so. May we resolve that, by God's
help, our hearts shall go together with our lips! Happy
is he who can really call God his Father through Jesus
Christ his Saviour, and can therefore say a heartfelt
"Amen" to all that the Lord's Prayer contains.

MATTHEW VI. 16—24.

16 Moreover when ye fast, be not, as the hypocrites, of a sad countenance: for they disfigure their faces, that they may appear unto men to fast. Verily I say unto you, They have their reward.

17 But thou, when thou fastest, anoint thine head, and wash thy face;

18 That thou appear not unto men to fast, but unto thy Father which is in secret: and thy Father, which seeth in secret, shall reward thee openly.

19 Lay not up for yourselves treasures upon earth, where moth and rust doth corrupt, and where thieves break through and steal:

20 But lay up for yourselves treasures in heaven, where neither moth nor rust doth corrupt, and where thieves do not break through nor steal:

21 For where your treasure is, there will your heart be also.

22 The light of the body is the eye: if therefore thine eye be single, thy whole body shall be full of light.

23 But if thine eye be evil, thy whole body shall be full of darkness. If therefore the light that is in thee be darkness, how great is that darkness!

24 No man can serve two masters: for either he will hate the one, and love the other, or else he will hold to the one, and despise the other. Ye cannot serve God and mammon.

THERE are three subjects brought before us in this part of our Lord's sermon on the mount. These three are fasting, worldliness, and singleness of purpose in religion.

Fasting, or occasional abstinence from food, in order to bring the body into subjection to the spirit, is a practice frequently mentioned in the Bible, and generally in connection with prayer. David fasted, when his child was sick. Daniel fasted, when he sought special light from God. Paul and Barnabas fasted, when they appointed elders. Esther fasted, before going in to Ahasuerus.—It is a subject about which we find no direct command in the New Testament. It seems to be left to every one's discretion, whether he will fast or not.—There is great wisdom in this. Many a poor man never has enough to eat, and it would be an insult to tell him to fast. Many a sickly person can hardly be kept well with the closest attention to diet, and could not fast without bringing on illness.—It is a matter in which every one must be persuaded in his own mind, and not be hasty to condemn

others, who do not agree with him.—One thing only must
never be forgotten. Those who fast should do it quietly,
secretly, and without ostentation. Let them not "appear
to men" to fast. Let them not fast to man, but to God.

Worldliness is one of the greatest dangers that beset
man s soul. It is no wonder that we find our Lord
speaking strongly about it. It is an insidious, specious,
plausible enemy. It seems so innocent to pay close
attention to our business! It seems so harmless to seek
our happiness in this world, so long as we keep clear of
open sins! Yet here is a rock on which many make
shipwreck to all eternity. They "lay up treasure on
earth," and forget to "lay up treasure in heaven." May
we all remember this! Where are our hearts? What
do we love best? Are our chiefest affections on things
in earth, or things in heaven? Life or death depends
on the answer we can give to these questions. If our
treasure is earthly, our hearts will be earthly also.
"Where your treasure is, there will your heart be."

Singleness of purpose is one great secret of spiritual
prosperity. If our eyes do not see distinctly, we cannot
walk without stumbling and falling. If we attempt to
work for two different masters, we are sure to give satisfaction to neither. It is just the same with respect to
our souls. We cannot serve Christ and the world at the
same time. It is vain to attempt it. The thing cannot
be done. The ark and Dagon will never stand together.
God must be king over our hearts. His law, His will,
His precepts must receive our first attention. Then,
and not till then, everything in our inward man will
fall into its right place. Unless our hearts are so ordered,

everything will be in confusion. "Thy whole body shall be full of darkness."

Let us learn from our Lord's instruction about fasting, *the great importance of cheerfulness* in our religion. Those words, "anoint thy head, and wash thy face," are full of deep meaning. They should teach us to aim at letting men see, that we find Christianity makes us happy. Never let us forget that there is no religion in looking melancholy and gloomy. Are we dissatisfied with Christ's wages, and Christ's service? Surely not! Then let us not look as if we were.

Let us learn from our Lord's caution about worldliness, what immense need we all have to *watch and pray against an earthly spirit*. What are the vast majority of professing Christians round us doing? They are "laying up treasure on earth." There can be no mistake about it. Their tastes, their ways, their habits tell a fearful tale. They are not "laying up treasure in heaven." Oh! let us all beware that we do not sink into hell by paying excessive attention to lawful things. Open transgression of God's law slays its thousands, but worldliness its tens of thousands.

Let us learn from our Lord's words about the "single eye," *the true secret of the failures*, which so many Christians seem to make in their religion. There are failures in all quarters. There are thousands in our churches uncomfortable, ill at ease, and dissatisfied with themselves, and they hardly know why. The reason is revealed here. They are trying to keep in with both sides. They are endeavouring to please God and please man, to serve Christ and serve the world at the same time. Let us not commit this mistake. Let us be decided, thorough-going, uncompromising followers of Christ. Let our motto be that of Paul, "One thing I do." (Phil. iii. 13.) Then we shall be happy Christians. We shall feel the sun shining on our faces. Heart, head, and conscience will all be full of light. Decision is the secret of happiness in religion. Be decided for Christ, and "thy whole body shall be full of light."

MATTHEW VI. 25—34.

25 Therefore I say unto you, take no thought for your life, what ye shall eat, or what ye shall drink; nor yet for your body, what ye shall put on. Is not the life more than meat, and the body than raiment?

26 Behold the fowls of the air : for they sow not, neither do they reap, nor gather into barns; yet your heavenly Father feedeth them. Are ye not much better than they?

27 Which of you by taking thought can add one cubit unto his stature?

28 And why take ye thought for raiment? Consider the lilies of the field, how they grow; they toil not, neither do they spin:

29 And yet I say unto you, That even Solomon in all his glory was not arrayed like one of these.

30 Wherefore, if God so clothe the grass of the field, which to day is, and to morrow is cast into the oven, *shall he* not much more *clothe* you, O ye of little faith?

31 Therefore take no thought, saying, What shall we eat? or, What shall we drink? or, Wherewithal shall we be clothed?

32 (For after all these things do the Gentiles seek :) for your heavenly Father knoweth that ye have need of all these things.

33 But seek ye first the kingdom of God, and his righteousness; and all these things shall be added unto you.

34 Take therefore no thought for the morrow : for the morrow shall take thought for the things of itself. Sufficient unto the day *is* the evil thereof.

THESE verses are a striking example of the combined wisdom and compassion of our Lord Jesus Christ's teaching. He knows the heart of a man. He knows that we are all ready to turn off warnings against worldliness, by the argument that we cannot help being anxious about the things of this life. "Have we not our families to provide for? Must not our bodily wants be supplied? How can we possibly get through life, if we think first of our souls?" The Lord Jesus foresaw such thoughts, and furnished an answer.

He forbids us *to keep up an anxious spirit* about the things of this world. Four times over He says, "take no thought." About life,—about food,—about clothing, —about the morrow, "take no thought." Be not over-careful. Be not over-anxious. Prudent provision for the future is right. Wearing, corroding, self-tormenting anxiety is wrong.

He reminds us of *the providential care that God continually takes of everything that He has created.* Has he given us "life?" Then He will surely not let us want anything necessary for its maintenance. Has He given us a "body?" Then He will surely not let us die for want of clothing. He that calls us into being, will doubtless find meat to feed us.

He points out *the uselessness of over-anxiety.* Our life is entirely in God's hand. All the care in the world will not make us continue a minute beyond the time which God has appointed. We shall not die till our work is done.

He sends us *to the birds of the air* for instruction. They make no provision for the future. "They sow not, neither do they reap."—They lay up no stores against time yet to come. They do not "gather into barns." They literally live from day to day on what they can pick up, by using the instinct God has put in them. They ought to teach us that no man doing his duty in the station to which God has called him, shall ever be allowed to come to poverty.

He bids us observe *the flowers of the field.* Year after year they are decked with the gayest colours, without the slightest labour or exertion on their part. "They toil not, neither do they spin." God, by His almighty power, clothes them with beauty every season. The same God is the Father of all believers. Why should they doubt that He is able to provide them with raiment, as well as the "lilies of the field?" He who takes thought for perishable flowers, will surely not neglect the bodies, in which dwell immortal souls.

He suggests to us, that over-carefulness about the things of this world is *most unworthy of a Christian.* One great feature of heathenism is living for the present. Let the heathen, if he will, be anxious. He knows nothing of a Father in heaven. But let the Christian, who has clearer light and knowledge, give proof of it by his faith and contentment. When bereaved of those whom we love, we are not to "sorrow as those who have no hope." When tried by anxieties about this life, we are not to be over-careful, as if we had no God, and no Christ.

He offers us *a gracious promise,* as a remedy against an anxious spirit. He assures us that if we "seek first" and foremost to have a place in the kingdom of grace and glory, every thing that we really want in this world shall be given to us. It shall be "added," over and above our heavenly inheritance. "All things shall work together for good to them that love God." "No good thing will He withhold from them that walk uprightly." (Rom. viii. 28. Psalm lxxxiv. 11.)

Last of all, He seals up all His instruction on this subject, by laying down *one of the wisest maxims.* "The morrow shall take thought for the things of itself.

Sufficient to the day is the evil thereof." We are not to carry cares before they come. We are to attend to to-day's business, and leave to-morrow's anxieties till to-morrow dawns. We may die before to-morrow. We know not what may happen on the morrow. This only we may be assured of, that if to-morrow brings a cross, He who sends it, can and will send grace to bear it.

In all this passage there is a treasury of golden lessons. Let us seek to use them in our daily life. Let us not only read them, but turn them to practical account. Let us watch and pray against an anxious and over-careful spirit. It deeply concerns our happiness. Half our miseries are caused by fancying things that we think are coming upon us. Half the things that we expect to come upon us, never come at all. Where is our faith? Where is our confidence in our Saviour's words? We may well take shame to ourselves, when we read these verses, and then look into our hearts. But this we may be sure of, that David's words are true, "I have been young, and now am old, yet never saw I the righteous forsaken, nor his seed begging their bread." (Psalm xxxvii. 25.)

MATTHEW VII. 1—11.

1 Judge not, that ye be not judged.

2 For with what judgment ye judge, ye shall be judged : and with what measure ye mete, it shall be measured to you again.

3 And why beholdest thou the mote that is in thy brother's eye, but considerest not the beam that is in thine own eye?

4 Or how wilt thou say to thy brother, Let me pull out the mote out of thine eye; and, behold, a beam *is* in thine own eye?

5 Thou hypocrite, first cast out the beam out of thine own eye; and then shalt thou see clearly to cast out the mote out of thy brother's eye.

6 Give not that which is holy unto the dogs, neither cast ye your pearls before swine, lest they trample them under their feet, and turn again and rend you.

7 Ask, and it shall be given you; seek, and ye shall find; knock, and it shall be opened unto you :

8 For every one that asketh receiv-eth; and he that seeketh findeth; and to him that knocketh it shall be opened.

9 Or what man is there of you, whom if his son ask bread, will he give him a stone?

10 Or if he ask a fish, will he give him a serpent?

11 If ye then, being evil, know how to give good gifts unto your children, how much more shall your Father which is in heaven give good things to them that ask him?

THE first portion of these verses is one of those passages of Scripture, which we must be careful not to strain beyond its proper meaning. It is frequently abused and misapplied, by the enemies of true religion. It is possible to press the words of the Bible so far that they yield not medicine, but poison.

Our Lord does not mean that it is wrong, under any circumstances, to pass an unfavourable judgment on the conduct and opinions of others. We ought to have decided opinions. We are to "prove all things." We are to "try the spirits."—Nor yet does He mean that it is wrong to reprove the sins and faults of others, until we are perfect and faultless ourselves. Such an interpretation would contradict other parts of Scripture. It would make it impossible to condemn error and false doctrine. It would debar any one from attempting the office of a minister or a judge. The earth would be "given into the hands of the wicked." (John ix. 24.) Heresy would flourish. Wrong-doing would abound.

What our Lord means to condemn is a *censorious and fault-finding spirit*. A readiness to blame others for trifling offences, or matters of indifference,—a habit of passing rash and hasty judgments,—a disposition to magnify the errors and infirmities of our neighbours, and make the worst of them,—this is what our Lord forbids. It was common among the Pharisees. It has always been common from their day down to the present time. We must all watch against it. We should "believe all things," and "hope all things" about others, and be very slow to find fault. This is Christian charity. (1 Cor. xiii. 7.)

The second lesson contained in this passage, is *the importance of exercising discretion as to the persons with whom we speak on the subject of religion.* Everything is beautiful in its place and season. Our zeal is to be tempered by a prudent consideration of times, places, and persons. "Reprove not a scorner," says Solomon, "lest he hate thee." (Prov. ix. 8.) It is not everybody to whom it is wise to open our minds on spiritual matters. There are many, who from violent tempers, or openly profligate habits, are utterly incapable of valuing the things of the Gospel. They will even fly into a passion, and run into greater excesses of sin, if you try to do good to their souls. To name the name of Christ to such people, is truly to "cast pearls before swine." It does them not good, but harm. It rouses all their corruption, and makes them angry. In short, they are like the Jews at Corinth, (Acts xviii. 6.) or like Nabal, of whom it is written, that he was "such a son of Belial, that a man could not speak unto him." (1 Sam. xxv. 17.)

This is a lesson which it is peculiarly difficult to use in the proper way. The right application of it needs great wisdom. We are most of us far more likely to err on the side of over-caution than of over-zeal. We are generally far more disposed to remember the "time to be silent," than the "time to speak." It is a lesson, however, which ought to stir up a spirit of self-inquiry in all our hearts. Do we ourselves never check our friends from giving us good advice, by our moroseness and irritability of temper? Have we never obliged others to hold their peace and say nothing, by our pride and impatient contempt of counsel? Have we never turned against our kind advisers, and silenced them by our violence and passion? Alas! we may well fear that we have erred in this matter.

The last lesson contained in this passage is *the duty of prayer, and the rich encouragements there are to pray.* There is a beautiful connection between this lesson and that which goes before it. Would we know when to be " silent," and when to " speak,"—when to bring forward "holy" things, and produce our " pearls?" We must pray. This is a subject to which the Lord Jesus evidently attaches great importance. The language that He uses is a plain proof of this. He employs three different words to express the idea of prayer. "Ask." " Seek." " Knock." He holds out the broadest, fullest promise to those who pray. "Every one that asketh receiveth." He illustrates God's readiness to hear our prayers, by an argument drawn from the notorious practice of parents on earth. "Evil " and selfish as they are by nature, they do not neglect the wants of their children according to the flesh. Much more will a God of love and mercy attend to the cries of those who are His children by grace.

Let us take special notice of these words of our Lord about prayer. Few of His sayings, perhaps, are so well known and so often repeated as this. The poorest and most unlearned can tell you, that " if we do not seek we shall not find." But what is the good of knowing it, if we do not use it? Knowledge, not improved and well employed, will only increase our condemnation at the last day.

Do we know anything of this asking, seeking, and knocking? Why should we not? There is nothing so simple and plain as praying, if a man really has a will to pray. There is nothing, unhappily, which men are so slow to do. They will use many of the forms of religion, attend many ordinances, do many things that are right, before they will do this. And yet without this no soul can be saved.

Do we ever really pray? If not, we shall at last be without excuse before God, except we repent. We shall not be condemned for not doing what we could not have done, or not knowing what we could not have known. But we shall find that one main reason why we are lost is this, that we never asked that we might be saved.

Do we indeed pray? Then let us pray on, and not faint. It is not lost labour. It is not useless. It will bear fruit after many days. That word never yet failed, "Every one that asketh receiveth."

MATTHEW VII. 12—20.

12 Therefore all things whatsoever ye would that men should do to you, do ye even so to them: for this is the law and the prophets.

13 Enter ye in at the strait gate: for wide *is* the gate, and broad *is* the way that leadeth to destruction, and many there be which go in thereat:

14 Because strait *is* the gate, and narrow *is* the way, which leadeth unto life, and few there be that find it.

15 Beware of false prophets, which come to you in sheep's clothing, but inwardly they are ravening wolves.

16 Ye shall know them by their fruits. Do men gather grapes of thorns, or figs of thistles?

F

17 Even so every good tree bringeth forth good fruit; but a corrupt tree bringeth forth evil fruit.

18 A good tree cannot bring forth evil fruit, neither *can* a corrupt tree bring forth good fruit.

19 Every tree that bringeth not forth good fruit is hewn down, and cast into the fire.

20 Wherefore by their fruits ye shall know them.

IN this part of the sermon on the mount our Lord begins to draw His discourse to a conclusion. The lessons He here enforces on our notice, are broad, general, and full of the deepest wisdom. Let us mark them in succession.

He lays down *a general principle for our guidance* in all doubtful questions between man and man. We are "to do to others as we would have others do to us." We are not to deal with others as others deal with us. This is mere selfishness and heathenism. We are to deal with others as we would like others to deal with us. This is real Christianity.

This is a golden rule indeed! It does not merely forbid all petty malice and revenge, all cheating and over-reaching. It does much more. It settles a hundred difficult points, which in a world like this are continually arising between man and man. It prevents the necessity of laying down endless little rules for our conduct in specific cases. It sweeps the whole debateable ground with one mighty principle. It shows us a balance and measure, by which every one may see at once what is his duty.—Is there a thing we would not like our neighbour to do to us? Then let us always remember, that this is the thing we ought not to do to him. Is there a thing we would like him to do to us? Then this is the very thing we ought to do to him.—How many intricate questions would be decided at once, if this rule were honestly used!

In the second place, our Lord gives us *a general caution against the way of the many in religion.* It is not enough to think as others think, and do as others do. It must not satisfy us to follow the fashion, and swim with the stream of those among whom we live. He tells us that the way that leads to everlasting life is "narrow," and "few" travel in it. He tells us that the way that leads to everlasting destruction is "broad," and full of travellers. "Many there be that go in thereat."

These are fearful truths! They ought to raise great searchings of heart in the minds of all who hear them.—"Which way am I going? By what road am I travelling?"—In one or other of the two ways here described, every one of us may be found. May God give us an honest, self-inquiring spirit, and show us what we are!

We may well tremble and be afraid, if our religion is that of the multitude. If we can say no more than this, that "we go where others go, and worship where others worship, and hope we shall do as well as others at last," we are literally pronouncing our own condemnation. What is this but being in the "broad way?" What is this but being in the road whose end is "destruction?" Our religion at present is not saving religion.

We have no reason to be discouraged and cast down, if the religion we profess is not popular, and few agree with us. We must remember the words of our Lord Jesus Christ in this passage: "The gate is strait." Repentance, and faith in Christ, and holiness of life, have never been fashionable. The true flock of Christ has always been small. It must not move us to find that we are reckoned singular, and peculiar, and bigotted, and narrow-minded. This is "the narrow way." Surely it is better to enter into life eternal with a few, than to go to "destruction" with a great company.

In the last place, the Lord Jesus gives us *a general warning against false teachers in the church.* We are to "beware of false prophets." The connection between this passage and the preceding one is striking. Would we keep clear of this "broad way?" We must beware of false prophets. They will arise. They began in the days of the apostles. Even then the seeds of error were sown. They have appeared continually ever since. We must be prepared for them, and be on our guard.

This is a warning which is much needed. There are thousands who seem ready to believe anything in religion, if they hear it from an ordained minister. They forget that clergymen may err as much as laymen. They are not infallible. Their teaching must be weighed in the balance of Holy Scripture. They are to be followed and believed, so long as their doctrine agrees with the Bible, but not a minute longer.—We are to try them "by their fruits." Sound doctrine and holy living are the marks of true prophets.—Let us remember this. Our minister's mistakes will not excuse our own. "If the blind lead the blind, both will fall into the ditch."

What is the best safe-guard against false teaching? Beyond all doubt the regular study of the word of God, with prayer for the teaching of the Holy Spirit. The Bible was given to be a lamp to our feet and a light to our path. (Psal. cxix. 105.) The man who reads it aright will never be allowed greatly to err. It is neglect of the Bible which makes so many a prey to the first false teacher whom they hear. They would fain have us believe that "they are not learned, and do not pretend to have decided opinions." The plain truth is that they are lazy and idle about reading the Bible, and do not like the trouble of thinking for themselves. Nothing supplies false prophets with followers so much as spiritual sloth under a cloak of humility.

May we all bear in mind our Lord's warning! The world, the devil, and the flesh, are not the only dangers in the way of the Christian. There remains another yet, and that is the "false prophet," the wolf in sheep's clothing. Happy is he who prays over his Bible and knows the difference between truth and error in religion! There is a difference, and we are meant to know it, and use our knowledge.

MATTHEW VII. 21—29.

21 Not every one that saith unto me, Lord, Lord, shall enter into the kingdom of heaven; but he that doeth the will of my Father which is in heaven.

22 Many will say to me in that day, Lord, Lord, have we not prophesied in thy name? and in thy name have we cast out devils? and in thy name done many wonderful works?

23 And then will I profess unto them, I never knew you: depart from me, ye that work iniquity.

24 Therefore whosoever heareth these sayings of mine, and doeth them, I will liken him unto a wise man, which built his house upon a rock:

25 And the rain descended, and the floods came, and the winds blew, and beat upon that house; and it fell not: for it was founded upon a rock.

26 And every one that heareth these sayings of mine, and doeth them not, shall be likened unto a foolish man, which built his house upon the sand:

27 And the rain descended, and the floods came, and the winds blew, and beat upon that house; and it fell: and great was the fall of it.

28 And it came to pass, when Jesus had ended these sayings, the people were astonished at his doctrine:

29 For he taught them as *one* having authority, and not as the Scribes.

THE Lord Jesus winds up the sermon on the mount by a passage of heart-piercing application. He turns from false prophets to false professors, from unsound teachers to unsound hearers. Here is a word for all. May we have grace to apply it to our own hearts!

The first lesson here is *the uselessness of a mere outward profession of Christianity.* Not every one that saith "Lord, Lord," shall enter the kingdom of heaven. Not all that profess and call themselves Christians shall be saved.

Let us take notice of this. It requires far more than most people seem to think necessary, to save a soul. We may be baptized in the name of Christ, and boast confidently of our ecclesiastical privileges. We may possess head-knowledge, and be quite satisfied with our own state. We may even be preachers, and teachers of others, and do "many wonderful works" in connection with our church. But all this time are we practically doing the will of our Father in heaven? Do we truly repent, truly believe on Christ, and live holy and humble lives? If not, in spite of all our privileges and profession, we shall miss heaven at last, and be for ever cast away. We shall hear those awful words, "I never knew you: depart from me."

The day of judgment will reveal strange things. The hopes of many, who were thought great Christians while they lived, will be utterly confounded. The rottenness of their religion will be exposed and put to shame before the whole world. It will then be proved, that to be saved means something more than "making a profession." We must make a "practice" of our Christianity as well as a "profession." Let us often think of that great day. Let us often "judge ourselves, that we be not judged," and condemned by the Lord. Whatever else we are, let us aim at being real, true and sincere.

The second lesson here is a *striking picture of two classes of Christian hearers*. Those who hear and do nothing,—and those who hear and do as well as hear,—are both placed before us, and their histories traced to their respective ends.

The man who hears Christian teaching, and practices what he hears, is like "a wise man who builds his house upon a rock." He does not content himself with listening to exhortations to repent, believe in Christ, and live a holy life. He actually repents. He actually believes. He actually ceases to do evil, learns to do well, abhors that which is sinful, and cleaves to that which is good. He is a doer as well as a hearer. (James i. 22.)

And what is the result? In the time of trial his religion does not fail him. The floods of sickness, sorrow, poverty, disappointments, bereavements beat upon him in vain. His soul stands unmoved. His faith does not give way. His comforts do not utterly forsake him. His religion may have cost him trouble in time past. His foundation may have been obtained with much labour and many tears. To discover his own interest in Christ may have required many a day of earnest seeking, and many an hour of wrestling in prayer. But his labour has not been thrown away. He now reaps a rich reward. The religion that can stand trial is the true religion.

The man who hears Christian teaching, and never gets beyond hearing, is like "a foolish man who builds his house upon the sand." He satisfies himself with listening and approving, but he goes no further. He flatters himself, perhaps, that all is right with his soul, because he has feelings, and convictions, and desires, of a spiritual

kind.   In these he rests.   He never really breaks off from
sin, and casts aside the spirit of the world.   He never
really lays hold on Christ.   He never really takes up the
cross.   He is a hearer of truth, but nothing more.

And what is the end of this man's religion ?   It breaks
down entirely under the first flood of tribulation.   It fails
him completely, like a summer-dried fountain, when his
need is the sorest.   It leaves its possessor high and dry,
like a wreck on a sand bank, a scandal to the church, a
by-word to the infidel, and a misery to himself.   Most
true is it that what costs little is worth little !   A religion
which costs us nothing, and consists in nothing but
hearing sermons, will always prove at last to be a useless
thing.

So ends the sermon on the mount.   Such a sermon
never was preached before.   Such a sermon perhaps has
never been preached since.   Let us see that it has a
lasting influence on our own souls.   It is addressed to
us as well as to those who first heard it.   We are thoy
who shall have to give account of its heart-searching
lessons.   It is no light matter what we think of them.
The word that Jesus has spoken, " the same shall judge
us in the last day." (John xii. 48.)

MATTHEW VIII. 1—15.

1 When he was come down from
the mountain, great multitudes followed him.
2 And, behold, there came a leper
and worshipped him, saying, Lord, if
thou wilt, thou canst make me clean.
3 And Jesus put forth *his* hand, and
touched him, saying, I will ; be thou
clean.   And immediately his leprosy
was cleansed.

4 And Jesus saith unto him, See
thou tell no man ; but go thy way,
shew thyself to the Priest, and offer
the gift that Moses commanded, for a
testimony unto them.
5 And when Jesus was entered into
Capernaum, there came unto him a
centurion, beseeching him,
6 And saying, Lord, my servant

lieth at home sick of the palsy, grievously tormented.

7 And Jesus saith unto him, I will
come and heal him.

8 The centurion answered and said,
Lord, I am not worthy that thou
shouldest come under my roof: but
speak the word only, and my servant
shall be healed.

9 For I am a man under authority,
having soldiers under me : and I say
to this *man*, Go, and he goeth ; and
to another, Come, and he cometh ;
and to my servant, Do this, and he
doeth *it*.

10 When Jesus heard *it*, he marvelled, and said to them that followed,
Verily I say unto you, I have not
found so great faith, no, not in Israel.

11 And I say unto you, That many

shall come from the east and west,
and shall sit down with Abraham, and
Isaac, and Jacob, in the kingdom of
heaven.

12 But the children of the kingdom
shall be cast out into outer darkness :
there shall be weeping and gnashing
of teeth.

13 And Jesus said unto the centurion, Go thy way ; and as thou hast
believed, *so* be it done unto thee.
And his servant was healed in the
selfsame hour.

14 And when Jesus was come into
Peter's house, he saw his wife's mother
laid, and sick of a fever.

15 And he touched her hand, and
the fever left her : and she arose, and
ministered unto them.

THE eighth chapter of St. Matthew's Gospel is full of our
Lord's miracles.   No less than five are specially recorded.
There is a beautiful fitness in this.   It was fitting that
the greatest sermon ever preached should be immediately
followed by mighty proof, that the preacher was the Son
of God.   Those who heard the sermon on the mount
would be obliged to confess, that, as "none spake such
words as this man," so also none did such works.

The verses we have now read contain three great
miracles.   A leper is healed with a touch.   A palsied
person is made well by a word.   A woman sick with a
fever is restored in a moment to health and strength.
On the face of these three miracles, we may read three
striking lessons.   Let us examine them, and lay them to
heart.

Let us learn, for one thing, *how great is the power of our
Lord Jesus Christ*.   Leprosy is the most fearful disease by
which man's body can be afflicted.   He that has it is like
one dead while he lives.   It is a complaint regarded by

physicians as incurable. (2 Kings v. 7.) Yet Jesus says, "be thou clean, and immediately the leprosy was cleansed."—To heal a person of the palsy without even seeing him, by only speaking a word, is to do that which our minds cannot even conceive. Yet Jesus commands, and at once it is done.—To give a woman prostrate with a fever, not merely relief, but strength to do work in an instant, would baffle the skill of all the physicians on earth. Yet Jesus "touched" Peter's wife's mother, and "she arose, and ministered unto them."—These are the doings of one that is Almighty. There is no escape from the conclusion. This was "the finger of God." (Exod. viii. 19.)

Behold here a broad foundation for the faith of a Christian! We are told in the Gospel to come to Jesus, to believe on Jesus, to live the life of faith in Jesus. We are encouraged to lean on Him, to cast all our care on Him, to repose all the weight of our souls on Him. We may do so without fear. He can bear all. He is a strong rock. He is Almighty. It was a fine saying of an old saint, " my faith can sleep sound on no other pillow than Christ's omnipotence." He can give life to the dead. He can give power to the weak. He can "increase strength to them that have no might." Let us trust Him, and not be afraid. The world is full of snares. Our hearts are weak. But with Jesus nothing is impossible.

Let us learn, for another thing, the *mercifulness and compassion of our Lord Jesus Christ.* The circumstances of the three cases we are now considering were all different. He heard the leper's pitiful cry, " Lord, if thou wilt, thou canst make me clean."—He was told of the centurion's servant, but He never saw him.—He saw Peter's wife's mother, "laid and sick of a fever;" and we are not told that she spoke a word.—Yet in each case the heart of the Lord Jesus was one and the same. In each case He was quick to show mercy, and ready to heal. Each poor sufferer was tenderly pitied, and each effectually relieved.

Behold here another strong foundation for our faith! Our great High Priest is very gracious. He can be "touched with the feeling of our infirmities." He is never tired of doing us good. He knows that we are a weak and feeble people, in the midst of a weary and troublous world. He is as ready to bear with us, and help us, as He was 1800 years ago. It is as true of Him now as it was then, "He despiseth not any." (Job. xxxvi. 5.) No heart can feel for us so much as the heart of Christ.

Let us learn, in the last place, *what a precious thing is the grace of faith*. We know little about the centurion described in these verses. His name, his nation, his past history, are all hidden from us. But one thing we know, and that is, that he believed. "Lord," he says, "I am not worthy that thou shouldest come under my roof. Speak the word only, and my servant shall be healed." He believed, let us remember, when Scribes and Pharisees were unbelievers. He believed, though a Gentile born, when Israel was blinded. And our Lord pronounced upon him the commendation, which has been read all over the world from that time to this, "I have not found so great faith, no, not in Israel."

Let us lay firm hold on this lesson. It deserves to be

remembered.   To believe Christ's power and willingness
to help, and to make a practical use of our belief, is a rare
and precious gift.   Let us be ever thankful if we have it.
To be willing to come to Jesus as helpless, lost sinners,
and commit our souls into His hands is a mighty privilege.
Let us ever bless God if this willingness is our's, for it is
His gift.   Such faith is better than all other gifts and
knowledge in the world.   Many a poor converted heathen,
who knows nothing but that he is sick of sin, and trusts
in Jesus, shall sit down in heaven, while many learned
English scholars are rejected for evermore.   Blessed indeed are they that believe!

What do we each know of this faith?   This is the
great question.   Our learning may be small: but do we
believe?   Our opportunities of giving and working for
Christ's cause may be few: but do we believe?   We
may neither be able to preach, nor write, nor argue for
the Gospel: but do we believe?   May we never rest till
we can answer this inquiry!   Faith in Christ appears
a small and simple thing to the children of this world.
They see in it nothing great or grand.   But faith in
Christ is most precious in God's sight, and like most
precious things, is rare.   By it true Christians live.   By
it they stand.   By it they overcome the world.   Without this faith no one can be saved.

MATTHEW VIII. 16—26.

16 When the even was come, they brought unto him many that were possessed with devils: and he cast out the spirits with *his* word, and healed all that were sick:

17 That it might be fulfilled which was spoken by Esaias the prophet, saying, Himself took our infirmities, and bare *our* sicknesses.

18 Now when Jesus saw great

multitudes about him, he gave commandment to depart unto the other side.

19 And a certain Scribe came, and said unto him, Master, I will follow thee whithersoever thou goest.

20 And Jesus saith unto him, The foxes have holes, and the birds of the air *have* nests; but the Son of man hath not where to lay *his* head.

21 And another of his disciples said unto him, Lord, suffer me first to go and bury my father.

22 But Jesus said unto him, Follow me; and let the dead bury their dead.

23 And when he was entered into a ship, his disciples followed him.

24 And, behold, there arose a great tempest in the sea, insomuch that the ship was covered with the waves: but he was asleep.

25 And his disciples came to *him*, and awoke him, saying, Lord, save us: we perish.

26 And he saith unto them, Why are ye fearful, O ye of little faith? Then he arose, and rebuked the winds and the sea; and there was a great calm.

27 But the men marvelled, saying, What manner of man is this, that even the winds and the sea obey him!

In the first part of these verses we see a striking example of *our Lord's wisdom in dealing with those who professed a willingness to be His disciples.* The passage throws so much light on a subject frequently misunderstood in these days, that it deserves more than ordinary attention.

A certain scribe offers to follow our Lord whithersoever He goes. It was a remarkable offer, when we consider the class to which the man belonged, and the time at which it was made. But the offer receives a remarkable answer. It is not directly accepted, nor yet flatly rejected. Our Lord only makes the solemn reply, " the foxes have holes, and the birds of the air have nests; but the Son of man hath not where to lay his head."

Another follower of our Lord next comes forward, and asks to be allowed to " bury his father," before going any further in the path of a disciple. The request seems, at first sight, a natural and lawful one. But it draws from our Lord's lips a reply no less solemn than that already referred to: "Follow me, and let the dead bury their dead."

There is something deeply impressive in both these

sayings. They ought to be well weighed by all professing Christians. They teach us plainly, that people who
shew a desire to come forward and profess themselves
true disciples of Christ, should be warned plainly to
"count the cost," before they begin.—Are they prepared to
endure hardship? Are they ready to carry the cross?
If not, they are not yet fit to begin.—They teach us
plainly that there are times when a Christian must
literally give up all for Christ's sake, and when even such
duties as attending to a parent's funeral must be left to
be performed by others. Such duties some will always
be ready to attend to; and at no time can they be put
in comparison with the greater duty of preaching the
Gospel, and doing Christ's work in the world.

It would be well for the churches of Christ, if these
sayings of our Lord were more remembered than they
are. It may well be feared, that the lesson they contain
is too often overlooked by the ministers of the Gospel,
and that thousands are admitted to full communion,
who are never warned to "count the cost." Nothing,
in fact, has done more harm to Christianity than the
practice of filling the ranks of Christ's army with every
volunteer who is willing to make a little profession,
and talk fluently of his experience. It has been painfully forgotten that numbers alone do not make strength,
and that there may be a great quantity of mere outward religion, while there is very little real grace.
Let us all remember this. Let us keep back nothing
from young professors and inquirers after Christ. Let
us not enlist them on false pretences. Let us tell them
plainly that there is a crown of glory at the end. But

let us tell them no less plainly, that there is a daily cross in the way.

In the latter part of these verses we learn, *that true saving faith is often mingled with much weakness and infirmity*. It is a humbling lesson, but a very wholesome one.

We are told of our Lord and His disciples crossing the sea of Galilee in a boat. A storm arises, and the boat is in danger of being filled with water, by the waves that beat over it. Meanwhile our Lord is asleep. The frightened disciples awake Him, and cry to Him for help. He hears their cry and stills the waters with a word, so that there is "a great calm." At the same time, He gently reproves the anxiety of His disciples. "Why are ye fearful, O ye of little faith?"

What a vivid picture we have here of the hearts of thousands of believers! How many have faith and love enough to forsake all for Christ's sake, and follow Him whithersoever He goes, and yet are full of fears in the hour of trial! How many have grace enough to turn to Jesus in every trouble, crying, "Lord save us," and yet not grace enough to lie still, and believe in the darkest hour that all is well! Truly believers have reason indeed to be "clothed with humility."

Let the prayer, "Lord, increase our faith," always form part of our daily petitions. We never perhaps know the weakness of our faith, until we are placed in the furnace of trial and anxiety. Blessed and happy is that person who finds by experience that his faith can stand the fire, and that he can say with Job, "though he slay me, yet will I trust in him." (Job xiii. 15.)

We have great reason to thank God that Jesus, our great High-priest, is very compassionate and tender-hearted. He knows our frame. He considers our infirmities. He does not cast off His people because of defects. He pities even those whom he reproves. The prayer even of " little faith " is heard, and gets an answer.

MATTHEW VIII. 28—34.

28 And when he was come to the other side into the country of the Gergesenes, there met him two possessed with devils, coming out of the tombs, exceeding fierce, so that no man might pass by that way.

29 And, behold, they cried out, saying, What have we to do with thee, Jesus, thou Son of God? art thou come hither to torment us before the time?

30 And there was a good way off from them an herd of many swine feeding.

31 So the devils besought him, saying, If thou cast us out, suffer us to go away into the herd of swine.

32 And he said unto them, Go. And when they were come out, they went into the herd of swine: and, behold, the whole herd of swine ran violently down a steep place into the sea, and perished in the waters.

33 And they that kept them fled, and went their ways into the city, and told every thing, and what was befallen to the possessed of the devils.

34 And, behold, the whole city came out to meet Jesus: and when they saw him, they besought *him* that he would depart out of their coasts.

THE subject of these seven verses is deep and mysterious. The casting out of a devil is here described with special fulness. It is one of those passages which throw strong light on a dark and difficult point.

Let us settle it firmly in our minds, *that there is such a being as the devil.* It is an awful truth, and one too much overlooked. There is an unseen spirit ever near us, of mighty power, and full of endless malice against our souls. From the beginning of creation he has laboured to injure man. Until the Lord comes the second time and binds him, he will never cease to tempt, and practice mischief. In the days when our Lord was upon earth, it is clear that he had a peculiar power over the bodies of certain men and women, as well as over their souls. Even in our own times there may be more of this bodily possession than some suppose, though confessedly in a far less degree than when Christ came in the flesh. But that the devil is ever near us in spirit, and ever ready to ply our hearts with temptations, ought never to be forgotten.

Let us, in the next place, settle it firmly in our minds, *that the power of the devil is limited.* Mighty as he is, there is one mightier still. Keenly set as his will is on doing harm in the world, he can only work by permission. These very verses show us that the evil spirits know they can only go to and fro, and ravage the earth, until the time allowed them by the Lord of lords. "Art thou come to torment us," they say, "before the time?" Their very petition shows us that they could not even hurt one of the Gergesene swine, unless Jesus the Son of God suffered them. "Suffer us," they say, "to go into the herd of swine."

Let us, in the next place, settle it in our minds, *that our Lord Jesus Christ is man's great deliverer from the power of the devil.* He can redeem us not only "from all iniquity," and "this present evil world," but from the devil. It was prophesied of old that he should bruise the serpent's head. He began to bruise that head, when he was born of the Virgin Mary. He triumphed over that head, when He died upon the cross. He showed His complete dominion over Satan, by "healing all that were oppressed of the devil," when He was upon earth. (Acts x. 38.) Our great remedy, in all the assaults of the devil, is to cry

to the Lord Jesus, and to seek His help. He can break
the chains that Satan casts round us, and set us free. He
can cast out every devil that plagues our hearts, as surely
as in the days of old. It would be miserable indeed to
know that there is a devil ever near us, if we did not
also know that Christ was "able to save to the uttermost,
because he ever liveth to make intercession for us."
(Heb. vii. 25.)

Let us not leave this passage without observing *the
painful worldliness of the Gergesenes,* among whom this
miracle of casting out a devil was wrought. They besought the Lord Jesus to "depart out of their coasts."
They had no heart to feel for anything but the loss of
their swine. They cared not that two fellow-creatures,
with immortal souls, were freed from Satan's bondage.
They cared not that there stood among them a greater
than the devil, Jesus the Son of God. They cared for
nothing but that their swine were drowned, and the "hope
of their gains gone." They ignorantly regarded Jesus as
one who stood between them and their profits, and they
only wished to be rid of Him.

There are only too many like these Gergesenes. There
are thousands who care not one jot for Christ, or Satan,
so long as they can make a little more money, and have
a little more of the good things of this world. From
this spirit may we be delivered! Against this spirit may
we ever watch and pray! It is very common. It is
awfully infectious. Let us recollect every morning that
we have souls to be saved, and that we shall one day
die, and after that be judged. Let us beware of loving
the world more than Christ. Let us beware of hindering

the salvation of others, because we fear the increase of true religion may diminish our gains, or give us trouble.

MATTHEW IX. 1—13.

1 And he entered into a ship, and passed over, and came into his own city.

2 And, behold, they brought to him a man sick of the palsy, lying on a bed : and Jesus seeing their faith said unto the sick of the palsy ; Son, be of good cheer ; thy sins be forgiven thee.

3 And, behold, certain of the Scribes said within themselves, This *man* blasphemeth.

4 And Jesus knowing their thoughts said, Wherefore think ye evil in your hearts ?

5 For whether is easier, to say, *Thy* sins be forgiven thee ; or to say, Arise, and walk ?

6 But that ye may know that the Son of man hath power on earth to forgive sins, (then saith he to the sick of the palsy,) Arise, take up thy bed, and go unto thine house.

7 And he arose, and departed to his house.

8 But when the multitudes saw *it*, they marvelled, and glorified God, which had given such power unto men.

9 And as Jesus passed forth from thence, he saw a man, named Matthew, sitting at the receipt of custom : and he saith unto him, Follow me. And he arose, and followed him.

10 And it came to pass, as Jesus sat at meat in the house, behold, many Publicans and sinners came and sat down with him and his disciples.

11 And when the Pharisees saw *it*, they said unto his disciples, Why eateth your Master with Publicans and sinners ?

12 But when Jesus heard *that*, he said unto them, They that be whole need not a physician, but they that are sick.

13 But go ye and learn what *that* meaneth, I will have mercy, and not sacrifice : for I am not come to call the righteous, but sinners to repentance.

LET us notice in the first part of this passage *our Lord's knowledge of men's thoughts.*

There were certain of the scribes, who found fault with the words which Jesus spoke to a man sick of the palsy. They said secretly among themselves, " this man blasphemeth." They probably supposed that no one knew what was going on in their minds. They had yet to learn that the Son of God could read hearts, and discern spirits. Their malicious thought was publicly exposed. They were put to an open shame.

There is an important lesson for us in this. " All things are naked and opened unto the eyes of Him with whom we have to do." (Heb. iv. 13.) Nothing can be concealed from Christ. What do we think of, in private, when no man sees us? What do we think of, in church, when we seem so grave and serious? What are we thinking of at this moment, while these words pass under our eyes? Jesus knows. Jesus sees. Jesus records. Jesus will one day call us to give account. It is written that "God shall judge the secrets of men by Jesus Christ according to my Gospel." (Rom. ii. 16.) Surely we ought to be very humble when we consider these things. We ought to thank God daily that the blood of Christ can cleanse from all sin. We ought often to cry, " Let the words of my mouth, and the meditation of my heart be acceptable in thy sight." (Psalm xix. 14.)

Let us notice, in the second place, *the wonderful call of the apostle Matthew to be Christ's disciple.*

We find the man, who afterwards was the first to write a Gospel, sitting at the receipt of custom. We see him absorbed in his worldly calling, and possibly thinking of nothing but money and gain. But suddenly the Lord Jesus calls on him to follow Him, and become His disciple. At once Matthew obeys. He "makes haste, and delays not" to keep Christ's commandment. (Psal. cxix. 60.) He arises and follows Him.

Let it be a fixed principle in our religion, that *with Christ nothing is impossible.* He can take a tax-gatherer, and make him an apostle. He can change any heart, and make all things new. Let us never despair of any one's salvation. Let us pray on, and speak on, and work on to do good to souls, even to the souls of the worst. "The voice of the Lord is mighty in operation." (Psal.

xxix. 4.) When He says by the power of the Spirit, "follow me," He can make the hardest and most sinful obey.

Let us observe Matthew's *decision*. He waited for nothing. He did not tarry for "a convenient season." (Acts xxiv. 25.) And he reaped in consequence a great reward. He wrote a book, which is known all over the earth. He became a blessing to others, as well as blessed in his own soul. He left a name behind him, which is better known than the names of princes and kings. The richest man of the world is soon forgotten when he dies. But as long as the world stands, millions will know the name of Matthew the publican.

Let us notice, in the last place, our Lord's *precious declaration about His own mission*.

The Pharisees found fault with Him, because He allowed publicans and sinners to be in His company. In their proud blindness they fancied, that a teacher sent from heaven ought to have no dealings with such people. They were wholly ignorant of the grand design for which the Messiah was to come into the world, to be a Saviour, a Physician, a healer of sin-sick souls. And they drew from our Lord's lips a rebuke, accompanied by the blessed words, "I came not to call the righteous, but sinners to repentance."

Let us make sure that we thoroughly *understand* the doctrine that these words contain. The first thing needful, in order to have an interest in Christ, is to feel deeply our own corruption, and to be willing to come to Him for deliverance. We are not to keep away from Christ, as many ignorantly do, because we feel bad, and wicked, and unworthy. We are to remember that sinners are those He came into the world to save, and that if we feel ourselves such, it is well. Happy is he who really comprehends that one principal qualification for coming to Christ is a deep sense of sin!

Finally, if by the grace of God we really understand the glorious truth that sinners are those whom Christ came to call, let us take heed that we *never forget it.* Let us not dream that true Christians can ever attain such a state of perfection in this world, as not to need the mediation and intercession of Jesus. Sinners we are in the day we first come to Christ. Poor needy sinners we continue to be so long as we live, drawing all the grace we have every hour out of Christ's fulness. Sinners we shall find ourselves in the hour of our death, and shall die as much indebted to Christ's blood, as in the day we first believed.

MATTHEW IX. 14—26.

14 Then came to him the disciples of John, saying, Why do we and the Pharisees fast oft, but thy disciples fast not?

15 And Jesus said unto them, Can the children of the bridechamber mourn, as long as the bridegroom is with them? but the days will come, when the bridegroom shall be taken from them, and then shall they fast.

16 No man putteth a piece of new cloth unto an old garment, for that which is put in to fill it up taketh from the garment, and the rent is made worse.

17 Neither do men put new wine into old bottles: else the bottles break, and the wine runneth out, and the bottles perish: but they put new wine into new bottles, and both are preserved.

18 While he spake these things unto them, behold, there came a certain ruler, and worshipped him, saying, My daughter is even now dead: but come and lay thy hand upon her, and she shall live.

19 And Jesus arose, and followed him, and *so did* his disciples.

20 And, behold, a woman, which was diseased with an issue of blood twelve years, came behind *him,* and touched the hem of his garment:

21 For she said within herself, If I may but touch his garment, I shall be whole.

22 But Jesus turned him about, and when he saw her, he said, Daughter, be of good comfort; thy faith hath made thee whole. And the woman was made whole from that hour.

23 And when Jesus came into the ruler's house, and saw the minstrels and the people making a noise,

24 He said unto them, Give place : for the maid is not dead, but sleepeth. And they laughed him to scorn.

25 But when the people were put forth, he went in, and took her by the hand, and the maid arose.

26 And the fame hereof went abroad into all that land.

LET us mark in this passage, the gracious name by which the Lord Jesus speaks of Himself. He calls Himself "*the bridegroom.*"

What the bridegroom is to the bride, the Lord Jesus is to the souls of all who believe in Him. He loves them with a deep and everlasting love. He takes them into union with Himself. They are "one with Christ and Christ in them." He pays all their debts to God. He supplies all their daily need. He sympathizes with them in all their troubles. He bears with all their infirmities, and does not reject them for a few weaknesses. He regards them as part of Himself. Those that persecute and injure them are persecuting Him. The glory that He has received from His Father they will one day share with Him, and where He is, there shall they be. Such are the privileges of all true Christians. They are the Lamb's wife. (Rev. xix. 7.) Such is the portion to which faith admits us. By it God joins our poor sinful souls to one precious Husband ; and those whom God thus joins together, shall never be put asunder. Blessed indeed are they that believe !

Let us mark, in the next place, *what a wise principle the Lord Jesus lays down for the treatment of young disciples.*

There were some who found fault with our Lord's followers, because they did not fast as John the Baptist's disciples did. Our Lord defends His disciples with an argument full of deep wisdom. He shows that there would be a want of fitness in their fasting, so long as He, their Bridegroom, was with them. But He does not stop there. He goes on to show, by two parables, that young beginners in the school of Christianity must be dealt with gently. They must be taught as they are able to bear. They must not be expected to receive everything at once. To neglect this rule would be as unwise as to "put new wine into old bottles," or to put "a piece of new cloth to an old garment."

There is a mine of deep wisdom in this, which all would do well to remember, in the spiritual teaching of those who are young in experience. We must be careful not to attach an excessive importance to the lesser things of religion. We must not be in a hurry to require a minute conformity to one rigid rule in things indifferent, until the first principles of repentance and faith have been thoroughly learned. To guide us in this matter, we have great need to pray for grace, and Christian common sense. Tact in dealing with young disciples is a rare gift, but a very useful one. To know what to insist upon as absolutely necessary from the first,—and what to reserve, as a lesson to be learned when the learner has come to more perfect knowledge,—is one of the highest attainments of a teacher of souls.

Let us mark, in the next place, *what encouragement our Lord gives to the humblest faith.*

We read in this passage, that a woman sorely afflicted with disease, came behind our Lord in the crowd, and "touched the hem" of His garment, in the hope that by so doing she should be healed. She said not a word to obtain help. She made no public confession of faith.

But she had confidence, that if she could only " touch His garment," she would be made well. And so it was. There lay hid in that act of her's a seed of precious faith, which obtained our Lord's commendation. She was made whole at once, and returned home in peace. To use the words of a good old writer, "She came trembling, and went back triumphing."

Let us store up in our minds this history. It may perhaps help us mightily in some hour of need. Our faith may be feeble. Our courage may be small. Our grasp of the Gospel, and its promises, may be weak and trembling. But, after all, the grand question is, do we really trust only in Christ? Do we look to Jesus, and only to Jesus, for pardon and peace? If this be so, it is well. If we may not touch His garment, we can touch His heart. Such faith saves the soul. Weak faith is less comfortable than strong faith. Weak faith will carry us to heaven with far less joy than full assurance. But weak faith gives an interest in Christ as surely as strong faith. He that only touches the hem of Christ's garment shall never perish.

In the last place, let us mark in this passage *our Lord's almighty power*. He restores to life one that was dead.

How wonderful that sight must have been! Who that has ever seen the dead, can forget the stillness, the silence, the coldness, when the breath has left the body? Who can forget the awful feeling, that a mighty change has taken place, and a mighty gulf been placed between ourselves and the departed? But behold! our Lord goes to the chamber where the dead lies, and calls the spirit back to its earthly tabernacle. The pulse once more beats. The eyes once more see. The breath once more comes and goes. The ruler's daughter is once more alive, and restored to her father and mother. This was omnipotence indeed! None could have done this but He who first created man, and has all power in heaven and earth.

This is the kind of truth we never can know too well. The more clearly we see Christ's power, the more likely we are to realize Gospel peace. Our position may be trying. Our hearts may be weak. The world may be difficult to journey through. Our faith may seem too small to carry us home. But let us take courage, when we think on Jesus, and not be cast down. Greater is He that is for us, than all they that are against us. Our Saviour can raise the dead. Our Saviour is almighty.

MATTHEW IX. 27—37.

27 And when Jesus departed thence, two blind men followed him, crying, and saying, *Thou* Son of David, have mercy on us.

28 And when he was come into the house, the blind men came to him: and Jesus saith unto them, Believe ye that I am able to do this? They said unto him, Yea, Lord.

29 Then touched he their eyes, saying, According to your faith be it unto you.

30 And their eyes were opened; and Jesus straitly charged them, saying, See *that* no man know *it*.

31 But they, when they were departed, spread abroad his fame in all that country.

32 As they went out, behold, they brought to him a dumb man possessed with a devil.

33 And when the devil was cast out, the dumb spake: and the multitudes marvelled, saying, It was never so seen in Israel.

34 But the Pharisees said, He casteth out devils through the prince of the devils.

35 And Jesus went about all the cities and villages, teaching in their synagogues, and preaching the Gospel of the kingdom, and healing every sickness and every disease among the people.

36 But when he saw the multitudes, he was moved with compassion on them, because they fainted, and were scattered abroad, as sheep having no shepherd.

37 Then saith he unto his disciples, The harvest truly *is* plenteous, but the labourers *are* few;

38 Pray ye therefore the Lord of the harvest, that he will send forth labourers into his harvest.

THERE are four lessons in this passage, which deserve close attention. Let us mark them each in succession.

Let us mark, in the first place, that *strong faith in Christ may sometimes be found where it might least have been expected.* Who would have thought that two blind men would have called our Lord the "Son of David?" They could not, of course, have seen the miracles that He did. They could only know Him by common report. But the eyes of their understanding were enlightened, if their bodily eyes were dark. They saw the truth which Scribes and Pharisees could not see. They saw that Jesus of Nazareth was the Messiah. They believed that He was able to heal them.

An example like this shows us, that we must never despair of any one's salvation, merely because he lives in a position unfavourable to his soul. Grace is stronger than circumstances. The life of religion does not depend merely upon outward advantages. The Holy Ghost can give faith, and keep faith in active exercise, without book-learning, without money, and with scanty means of grace. Without the Holy Ghost a man may know all mysteries, and live in the full blaze of the Gospel, and yet be lost. We shall see many strange sights at the last day. Poor cottagers will be found to have believed in the Son of David, while rich men, full of university learning, will prove to have lived and died, like the Pharisees, in hardened unbelief. Many that are last will be first, and the first last. (Matt. xx. 16.)

Let us mark, in the next place, that our Lord Jesus Christ *has had great experience of disease and sickness.* He "went about all the cities and villages" doing good. He was an eye-witness of all the ills that flesh is heir to. He saw ailments of every kind, sort, and description. He was brought in contact with every form of bodily suffering. None were too loathsome for Him to attend to. None were too frightful for Him to cure. He was a healer of "every sickness and every disease."

There is much comfort to be drawn from this fact. We are each dwelling in a poor frail body. We never know what quantity of suffering we may have to watch, as we sit by the bedside of dear relations and friends. We never know what racking complaint we ourselves may have to submit to, before we lie down and die. But let us arm ourselves betimes with the precious thought that Jesus is specially fitted to be the sick man's friend. That great high-priest to whom we must apply for pardon and peace with God, is eminently qualified to sympathize with an aching body, as well as to heal an ailing conscience. The eyes of Him who is King of kings used often to look with pity on the diseased. The world cares little for the sick, and often keeps aloof from them. But the Lord Jesus cares specially for the sick. He is the first to visit them, and say, "I stand at the door and knock." Happy are they who hear His voice, and let Him in!

Let us mark, in the next place, our Lord's *tender concern for neglected souls*. "He saw multitudes" of people when He was on earth, scattered about "like sheep having no shepherd," and He was moved with compassion. He saw them neglected by those who, for the time, ought to have been teachers. He saw them ignorant, hopeless, helpless, dying, and unfit to die. The sight moved Him to deep pity.   That loving heart could not see such things, and not feel.

Now what are our feelings, when we see such a sight? This is the question that should arise in our minds. There are many such to be seen on every side.   There are millions of idolaters and heathen on earth,—millions of deluded Mahometans,—millions of superstitious Roman Catholics.   There are thousands of ignorant Protestants near our own doors.   Do we feel tenderly concerned about their souls?   Do we deeply pity their spiritual destitution?   Do we long to see that destitution relieved? These are serious inquiries, and ought to be answered. It is easy to sneer at missions to the heathen, and those who work for them.   But the man who does not feel for the souls of all unconverted persons, can surely not have "the mind of Christ." (1 Cor. ii. 16.)

Let us mark, in the last place, that *there is a solemn duty incumbent on all Christians*, who would do good to the unconverted part of the world.   They are to pray for more men to be raised up to work for the conversion of souls.   It seems as if it was to be a daily part of our prayers.   "Pray ye the Lord of the harvest that he would send forth labourers into his harvest."

If we know anything of prayer, let us make it a point of conscience never to forget this solemn charge of our Lord's.   Let us settle it in our minds, that it is one of the surest ways of doing good, and stemming evil. Personal working for souls is good.   Giving money is good.   But praying is best of all.   By prayer we reach Him without whom work and money are alike in vain. We obtain the aid of the Holy Ghost.—Money can pay agents. Universities can give learning. Congregations may elect. Bishops may ordain. But the Holy Ghost alone can make ministers of the Gospel, and raise up lay workmen in the spiritual harvest, who need not be ashamed. Never, never may we forget that if we would do good to the world, our first duty is to pray!

MATTHEW X. 1—15.

1 And when he had called unto *him* his twelve disciples, he gave them power *against* unclean spirits, to cast them out, and to heal all manner of sickness and all manner of disease.

2 Now the names of the twelve apostles are these ; The first, Simon, who is called Peter, and Andrew his brother ; James, *the son* of Zebedee, and John his brother ;

3 Philip, and Bartholomew ; Thomas, and Matthew the Publican ; James *the son* of Alphæus, and Lebbæus, whose surname was Thaddæus ;

4 Simon the Canaanite, and Judas Iscariot, who also betrayed him.

5 These twelve Jesus sent forth, and commanded them, saying, Go not into the way of the Gentiles, and into *any* city of the Samaritans enter ye not :

6 But go rather to the lost sheep of the house of Israel.

7 And as ye go, preach, saying, The kingdom of heaven is at hand.

8 Heal the sick, cleanse the lepers,

raise the dead, cast out devils : freely ye have received, freely give.

9 Provide neither gold, nor silver, nor brass in your purses,

10 Nor scrip for *your* journey, neither two coats, neither shoes, nor yet staves : for the workman is worthy of his meat.

11 And into whatsoever city or town ye shall enter, enquire who in it is worthy ; and there abide till ye go thence.

12 And when ye come into an house, salute it.

13 And if the house be worthy, let your peace come upon it : but if it be not worthy, let your peace return to you.

14 And whosoever shall not receive you, nor hear your words, when ye depart out of that house or city, shake off the dust of your feet.

15 Verily I say unto you, It shall be more tolerable for the land of Sodom and Gomorrha in the day of judgment, than for that city.

THIS chapter is one of peculiar solemnity. Here is the record of the first ordination which ever took place in the church of Christ. The Lord Jesus chooses and sends forth the twelve apostles.—Here is an account of the first charge ever delivered to newly ordained Christian ministers. The Lord Jesus Himself delivers it.—Never was there so important an ordination! Never was there so solemn a charge!

There are three lessons which stand out prominently on the face of the first fifteen verses of this chapter. Let us take them in order!

We are taught, in the first place, that *all ministers are not necessarily good men.* We see our Lord choosing a Judas Iscariot to be one of His apostles. We cannot doubt that He who knew all hearts, knew well the characters of the men whom He chose. And He includes in the list of His apostles one who was a traitor!

We shall do well to bear in mind this fact. Orders do not confer the saving grace of the Holy Ghost. Ordained men are not necessarily converted. We are not to regard them as infallible, either in doctrine or in practice. We are not to make popes or idols of them, and insensibly put them in Christ's place. We are to regard them as "men of like passions" with ourselves, liable to the same infirmities, and daily requiring the same grace. We are not to think it impossible for them to do very bad things, or to expect them to be above the reach of harm from flattery, covetousness, and the world. We are to prove their teaching by the word of God, and follow them so far as they follow Christ, but no further. Above all, we ought to pray for them, that they may be successors not of Judas Iscariot, but of James and John. It is an awful thing to be a minister of the Gospel! Ministers need many prayers.

We are taught, in the next place, that *the great work of a minister of Christ is to do good.* He is sent to seek "lost sheep,"—to proclaim glad tidings,—to relieve those who are suffering,—to diminish sorrow,—and to increase joy. His life is meant to be one of "giving," rather than receiving.

This is a high standard, and a very peculiar one. Let it be well weighed, and carefully examined. It is plain, for one thing, that the life of a faithful minister of Christ cannot be one of ease. He must be ready to spend body and mind, time and strength, in the work of His calling. Laziness and frivolity are bad enough in any profession, but worst of all in that of a watchman for souls.—It is plain, for another thing, that the position of the ministers of Christ is not that which ignorant people sometimes ascribe to them, and which they unhappily sometimes claim for themselves. They are not so much ordained to rule as to serve. They are not intended so much to have dominion over the Church, as to supply its wants, and wait upon its members. (2 Cor. i. 24.) Happy would it be for the cause of true religion, if these things were better understood! Half the diseases of Christianity have arisen from mistaken notions about the minister's office.

We are taught, in the last place, that *it is a most dangerous thing to neglect the offers of the Gospel.* It shall prove "more tolerable for the land of Sodom and Gomorrha" in the judgment day, than for those who have heard Christ's truth, and not received it.

This is a doctrine fearfully overlooked, and one that deserves serious consideration. Men are sadly apt to forget, that it does not require great open sins to be sinned, in order to ruin a soul for ever. They have only to go on hearing without believing, listening without repenting, going to Church without going to Christ, and by and bye they will find themselves in hell ! We shall all be judged according to our light. We shall have to give account of our use of religious privileges. To hear of the "great salvation," and yet neglect it, is one of the worst sins man can commit. (John xvi. 9.)

What are we doing ourselves with the Gospel? This is the question which every one who reads this passage should put to his conscience. Let us assume that we are decent and respectable in our lives, correct and moral in all the relations of life, regular in our formal attendance on the means of grace. It is all well, so far as it goes. But is this all that can be said of us? Are we really receiving the love of the truth? Is Christ dwelling in our hearts by faith? If not, we are in fearful danger. We are far more guilty than the men of Sodom, who never heard the Gospel at all. We may awake to find, that in spite of our regularity, and morality, and correct-ness, we have lost our souls for all eternity. It will not save us to have lived in the full sunshine of Christian privileges, and to have heard the Gospel faithfully preached every week. There must be experimental acquaintance with Christ. There must be personal re-ception of His truth. There must be vital union with Him. We must become His servants and disciples. Without this, the preaching of the Gospel only adds to our responsibility, increases our guilt, and will at length sink us more deeply into hell. These are hard sayings. But the words of Scripture, which we have read, are plain and unmistakeable. They are all true.

H

MATTHEW X. 16—23.

16 Behold, I send you forth as sheep in the midst of wolves: be ye therefore wise as serpents, and harmless as doves.

17 But beware of men : for they will deliver you up to the councils, and they will scourge you in their synagogues;

18 And ye shall be brought before governors and kings for my sake, for a testimony against them and the Gentiles.

19 But when they deliver you up, take no thought how or what ye shall speak : for it shall be given you in that same hour what ye shall speak.

20 For it is not ye that speak, but the Spirit of your Father which speaketh in you.

21 And the brother shall deliver up the brother to death, and the father the child : and the children shall rise up against *their* parents, and cause them to be put to death.

22 And ye shall be hated of all *men* for my name's sake : but he that endureth to the end shall be saved.

23 But when they persecute you in this city, flee ye into another : for verily I say unto you, Ye shall not have gone over the cities of Israel, till the Son of man be come.

THE truths contained in these verses should be pondered by all who try to do good in the world. To the selfish man, who cares for nothing but his own ease or comfort, there may seem to be little in them. To the minister of the Gospel, and to every one who seeks to save souls, these verses ought to be full of interest. No doubt there is much in them, which applies specially to the days of the apostles. But there is much also which applies to all times.

We see, for one thing, *that those who would do good to souls, must be moderate in their expectations.* They must not think that universal success will attend their labours. They must reckon on meeting with much opposition. They must make up their minds to "be hated," persecuted, and ill-used, and that too by their nearest relations. They will often find themselves like "sheep in the midst of wolves."

Let us bear this in mind continually. Whether we preach, or teach, or visit from house to house,—whether we write or give counsel, or whatever we do, let it be a

settled principle with us not to expect more than Scripture and experience warrant. Human nature is far
more wicked and corrupt than we think. The power
of evil is far greater than we suppose. It is vain to
imagine that everybody will see what is good for them,
and believe what we tell them. It is expecting what we
shall not find, and will only end in disappointment.
Happy is that labourer for Christ, who knows these
things at his first starting, and has not to learn them by
bitter experience! Here lies the secret cause why many
have turned back, who once seemed full of zeal to do good.
They began with extravagant expectations. They did not
count the cost. They fell into the mistake of the great
German Reformer, who confessed he forgot at one time,
that "old Adam was too strong for young Melancthon."

We see, for another thing, *that those who would do
good have need to pray for wisdom, good sense, and a
sound mind.* Our Lord tells His disciples to be "wise as
serpents, and harmless as doves." He tells them that
when they are persecuted in one place, they may lawfully "flee to another."

There are few of our Lord's instructions which it is
so difficult to use rightly as this. There is a line marked
out for us between two extremes; but one that it requires great judgment to define. To avoid persecution
by holding our tongues, and keeping our religion entirely
to ourselves, is one extreme. We are not to err in that
direction.—To court persecution, and thrust our religion
upon every one we meet, without regard to place, time,
or circumstances, is another extreme. In this direction
also we are warned not to err any more than in the

other.—Truly we may say, "who is sufficient for these things?" We have need to cry to the only wise God for wisdom.

The extreme into which most men are liable to fall in the present day, is that of silence, cowardice, and letting others alone. Our so-called prudence is apt to degenerate into a compromising line of conduct, or downright unfaithfulness. We are only too ready to suppose that it is of no use trying to do good to certain people. We excuse ourselves from efforts to benefit their souls, by saying it would be indiscreet, or inexpedient, or would give needless offence, or would even do positive harm. Let us all watch and be on our guard against this spirit. Laziness and the devil are often the true explanation of it. To give way to it is pleasant to flesh and blood, no doubt, and saves us much trouble. But those who give way to it often throw away great opportunities of usefulness.

On the other hand, it is impossible to deny that there is such a thing as a righteous and holy zeal, which is "not according to knowledge." It is quite possible to create much needless offence, commit great blunders, and stir up much opposition, which might have been avoided by a little prudence, wise management, and exercise of judgment. Let us all take heed that we are not guilty in this respect. We may be sure there is such a thing as Christian wisdom, which is quite distinct from Jesuitical subtlety, or carnal policy. This wisdom let us seek. Our Lord Jesus does not require us to throw aside our common sense, when we undertake to work for Him. There will be offence enough connected with our religion, do what we will; but let us not increase it without cause.

Let us strive to "walk circumspectly, not as fools but as wise." (Ephes. v. 15.)

It is to be feared, that believers in the Lord Jesus do not sufficiently pray for the spirit of knowledge, judgment, and a sound mind. They are apt to fancy that if they have grace, they have all they need. They forget that a gracious heart should pray that it may be full of wisdom, as well as of the Holy Ghost. (Acts vi. 3.) Let us all remember this. Great grace and common sense are perhaps one of the rarest combinations. That they may go together, the life of David, and the ministry of the apostle Paul are striking proofs. In this however, as in every other respect, our Lord Jesus Christ Himself is our most perfect example. None were ever so faithful as He. But none were ever so truly wise. Let us make Him our pattern, and walk in His steps.

MATTHEW X. 24—33.

24 The disciple is not above *his* master, nor the servant above his lord.

25 It is enough for the disciple that he be as his master, and the servant as his lord. If they have called the master of the house Beelzebub, how much more *shall they call* them of his household?

26 Fear them not therefore: for there is nothing covered, that shall not be revealed; and hid, that shall not be known.

27 What I tell you in darkness *that* speak ye in light: and what ye hear in the ear, *that* preach ye upon the housetops.

28 And fear not them which kill the body, but are not able to kill the soul: but rather fear him which is able to destroy both soul and body in hell.

29 Are not two sparrows sold for a farthing? and one of them shall not fall on the ground without your Father.

30 But the very hairs of your head are all numbered.

31 Fear ye not therefore, ye are of more value than many sparrows.

32 Whosoever therefore shall confess me before men, him will I confess also before my Father which is in heaven.

33 But whosoever shall deny me before men, him will I also deny before my Father which is in heaven.

To do good to souls in this world is very hard. All who try it find out this by experience. It needs a large stock of courage, faith, patience, and perseverance. Satan will fight vigorously to maintain his kingdom. Human nature is desperately wicked. To do harm is easy. To do good is hard.

The Lord Jesus knew this well, when He sent forth His disciples to preach the Gospel for the first time. He knew what was before them, if they did not. He took care to supply them with a list of encouragements, in order to cheer them when they felt cast down. Weary missionaries abroad, or fainting ministers at home,—disheartened teachers of schools, and desponding visitors of districts, would do well to study often the nine verses we have just read. Let us mark what they contain.

Those who try to do good to souls *must not expect to fare better than their great Master.* "The disciple is not above his Master, nor the servant above his Lord." The Lord Jesus was slandered and rejected by those whom he came to benefit. There was no error in His teaching. There was no defect in His method of imparting instruction. Yet many hated Him, and "called Him Beelzebub." Few believed Him, and cared for what He said. Surely we have no right to be surprised if we, whose best efforts are mingled with much imperfection, are treated in the same way as Christ. If we let the world alone, it will probably let us alone. But if we try to do it spiritual good, it will hate us as it did our Master.

Those who try to do good *must look forward with patience to the day of judgment.* "There is nothing covered that shall not be revealed, and hid that shall not be known." They must be content in this present world to be misunderstood, misrepresented, vilified, slandered, and abused. They must not cease to work because their

motives are mistaken, and their characters fiercely
assailed. They must remember continually that all will
be set right at the last day. The secrets of all hearts
shall then be revealed. "He shall bring forth thy righteousness as the light, and thy judgment as the noon-
day." (Psal. xxxvii. 6.) The purity of their intentions,
the wisdom of their labours, and the rightfulness of their
cause, shall at length be made manifest to all the world.
Let us work on steadily and quietly. Men may not
understand us, and may vehemently oppose us. But the
day of judgment draws high. We shall be righted at
last. The Lord, when He comes again, "will bring to
light the hidden things of darkness, and will make manifest the counsels of the hearts, and then shall every man
have praise of God." (1 Cor. iv. 5.)

Those who try to do good *must fear God more than
man*. Man can hurt the body, but there his enmity must
stop. He can go no further. God "is able to destroy
both soul and body in hell." We may be threatened
with the loss of character, property, and all that makes
life enjoyable, if we go on in the path of religious duty.
We must not heed such threats, when our course is plain.
Like Daniel and the three children, we must submit to
anything rather than displease God, and wound our
consciences. The anger of man may be hard to bear,
but the anger of God is much harder. The fear of man
does indeed bring a snare, but we must make it give way
to the expulsive power of a stronger principle, even the
fear of God. It was a fine saying of good Colonel
Gardiner's, "I fear God, and therefore there is none else
that I need fear."

Those who try to do good *must keep before their minds the providential care of God over them.* Nothing can happen in this world without His permission. There is no such thing in reality as chance, accident, or luck. "The very hairs of their heads are all numbered." The path of duty may sometimes lead them into great danger. Health and life may seem to be perilled, if they go forward. Let them take comfort in the thought that all around them is in God's hand. Their bodies, their souls, their characters are all in His safe keeping. No disease can seize them,—no hand can hurt them, unless He allows. They may say boldly to every fearful thing they meet with, "Thou couldest have no power at all against me, except it were given thee from above."

In the last place, those who try to do good *should continually remember the day when they will meet their Lord to receive their final portion.* If they would have Him own them, and confess them before His Father's throne, they must not be ashamed to own and "confess Him" before the men of this world. To do it may cost us much. It may bring on us laughter, mockery, persecution, and scorn. But let us not be laughed out of heaven. Let us recollect the great and dreadful day of account, and not be afraid to show men that we love Christ, and want them to know and love Him also.

Let these encouragements be treasured up in the hearts of all who labour in Christ's cause, whatever their position may be. The Lord knows their trials, and has spoken these things for their comfort. He cares for all His believing people, but for none so much as those who work for His cause, and try to do good. May we seek to be of that number. Every believer may do something if he tries. There is always something for every one to do. May we each have an eye to see it, and a will to do it.

MATTHEW X. 34—42.

34 Think not that I am come to send peace on earth: I came not to send peace, but a sword.

35 For I am come to set a man at variance against his father, and the daughter against her mother, and the daughter in law against her mother in law.

36 And a man's foes *shall be* they of his own household.

37 He that loveth father or mother more than me is not worthy of me: and he that loveth son or daughter more than me is not worthy of me.

38 And he that taketh not his cross, and followeth after me, is not worthy of me.

39 He that findeth his life shall lose it: and he that loseth his life for my sake shall find it.

40 He that receiveth you receiveth me, and he that receiveth me receiveth him that sent me.

41 He that receiveth a prophet in the name of a prophet shall receive a prophet's reward; and he that receiveth a righteous man in the name of a righteous man shall receive a righteous man's reward.

42 And whosoever shall give to drink unto one of these little ones a cup of cold *water* only in the name of a disciple, verily I say unto you, he shall in no wise lose his reward.

IN these verses the great Head of the Church winds up His first charge to those whom He sends forth to make known His Gospel. He declares three great truths, which form a fitting conclusion to the whole discourse.

In the first place, He bids us remember *that His Gospel will not cause peace and agreement wherever it comes.* "I came not to send peace, but a sword." The object of His first coming on earth was not to set up a millennial kingdom in which all would be of one mind, but to bring in the Gospel, which would lead to strifes and divisions. We have no right to be surprised, if we see this continually fulfilled. We are not to think it strange, if the Gospel rends asunder families, and causes estrangement between the nearest relations. It is sure to do so in many cases, because of the deep corruption of man's heart. So long as one man believes, and another remains unbelieving,—so long as one is resolved to keep his sins, and another desirous to give them up, the result of the preaching of the Gospel must needs be division. For this the Gospel is not to blame, but the heart of man.

There is deep truth in all this, which is constantly forgotten and overlooked. Many talk vaguely about unity, and harmony, and peace in the Church of Christ, as if they were things that we ought always to expect, and for the sake of which everything ought to be sacrificed. Such persons would do well to remember the words of our Lord. No doubt unity and peace are mighty blessings. We ought to seek them, pray for them, and give up everything in order to obtain them, excepting truth and a good conscience. But it is an idle dream to suppose that the churches of Christ will enjoy much of unity and peace before the millennium comes.

In the second place, our Lord tells us *that true Christians must make up their minds to trouble in this world.* Whether we are ministers or hearers, whether we teach or are taught, it makes little difference. We must carry "a cross." We must be content to lose even life itself for Christ's sake. We must submit to the loss of man's favour, we must endure hardships, we must deny ourselves in many things, or we shall never reach heaven at last. So long as the world, the devil, and our own hearts, are what they are, these things must be so.

We shall find it most useful to remember this lesson ourselves, and to impress it upon others. Few things do so much harm in religion as exaggerated expectations. People look for a degree of worldly comfort in Christ's

service, which they have no right to expect, and not finding what they looked for, are tempted to give up religion
in disgust. Happy is he who thoroughly understands,
that though Christianity holds out a crown in the end, it
brings also a cross in the way.

In the last place, our Lord cheers us by saying *that
the least service done to those who work in His cause is
observed and rewarded of God.* He that gives a believer
so little as "a cup of cold water only in the name of a
disciple shall in no wise lose his reward."

There is something very beautiful in this promise. It
teaches us that the eyes of the great Master are ever
upon those who labour for him, and try to do good.
They seem perhaps to work on unnoticed and unregarded.
The proceedings of preachers, and missionaries, and
teachers, and visitors of the poor, may appear very
trifling and insignificant, compared to the movements of
kings and parliaments, of armies and of statesmen. But
they are not insignificant in the eyes of God. He takes
notice who opposes his servants, and who helps them.
He observes who is kind to them, as Lydia was to Paul,—
and who throws difficulties in their way, as Diotrephes did
to John. All their daily experience is recorded, as they
labour on in His harvest. All is written down in the
great book of His remembrance, and will be brought to
light at the last day. The chief butler forgat Joseph,
when he was restored to his place. But the Lord Jesus
never forgets any of His people. He will say to many
who little expect it, in the resurrection morning, "I was
an hungered, and ye gave me meat: I was thirsty, and
ye gave me drink." (Matt. xxv. 35.)

Let us ask ourselves, as we close the chapter, in what light we regard Christ's work and Christ's cause in the world? Are we helpers of it, or hinderers? Do we in any wise aid the Lord's "prophets," and "righteous men?" Do we assist His "little ones?" Do we impede His labourers, or do we cheer them on?—These are serious questions. They do well and wisely who give the "cup of cold water," whenever they have opportunity. They do better still who work actively in the Lord's vineyard. May we all strive to leave the world a better world than it was when we were born! This is to have the mind of Christ. This is to find out the value of the lessons this wonderful chapter contains.

MATTHEW XI. 1—15.

1 And it came to pass, when Jesus had made an end of commanding his twelve disciples, he departed thence to teach and to preach in their cities.

2 Now when John had heard in the prison the works of Christ, he sent two of his disciples,

3 And said unto him, Art thou he that should come, or do we look for another?

4 Jesus answered and said unto them, Go and shew John again those things which ye do hear and see:

5 The blind receive their sight, and the lame walk, the lepers are cleansed, and the deaf hear, the dead are raised up, and the poor have the Gospel preached to them.

6 And blessed is *he*, whosoever shall not be offended in me.

7 And as they departed, Jesus began to say unto the multitudes concerning John, What went ye out into the wilderness to see? A reed shaken with the wind?

8 But what went ye out for to see? A man clothed in soft raiment? behold, they that wear soft *clothing* are in kings' houses.

9 But what went ye out for to see? A prophet? yea, I say unto you, and more than a prophet.

10 For this is *he*, of whom it is written, Behold, I send my messenger before thy face, which shall prepare thy way before thee.

11 Verily I say unto you, Among them that are born of women there hath not risen a greater than John the Baptist: notwithstanding he that is least in the kingdom of heaven is greater than he.

12 And from the days of John the Baptist until now the kingdom of heaven suffereth violence, and the violent take it by force.

13 For all the Prophets and the Law prophesied until John.

14 And if ye will receive *it*, this is Elias, which was for to come.

15 He that hath ears to hear, let him hear.

THE first thing that demands our attention in this passage, is *the message which John the Baptist sends to our Lord Jesus Christ.* He "sent two of his disciples, and said unto him, Art thou he that should come, or do we look for another?"

This question did not arise from doubt or unbelief on the part of John. We do that holy man injustice, if we interpret it in such a way. It was put for the benefit of his disciples. It was meant to give them an opportunity of hearing from Christ's own lips, the evidence of His divine mission. No doubt John the Baptist felt that his own ministry was ended. Something within him told him that he would never come forth from Herod's prison-house, but would surely die. He remembered the ignorant jealousies that had already been shown by his disciples towards the disciples of Christ. He took the most likely course to dispel those jealousies for ever. He sent his followers to "hear and see" for themselves.

The conduct of John the Baptist in this matter affords a striking example to ministers, teachers, and parents, when they draw near the end of their course. Their chief concern should be about the souls of those they are going to leave behind them. Their great desire should be to persuade them to cleave to Christ. The death of those who have guided and instructed us on earth ought always to have this effect. It should make us lay hold more firmly on Him who dieth no more, "continueth ever," and "hath an unchangeable priesthood." (Heb. vii. 24.)

The second thing that demands our notice in this passage, is *the high testimony which our Lord bears to the character of John the Baptist.* No mortal man ever received such commendation as Jesus here bestows on His imprisoned friend. "Among them that are born of women, there hath not risen a greater than John the Baptist." In time past John had boldly confessed Jesus before men, as the Lamb of God. Now Jesus openly declares John to be more than a prophet.

There were some, no doubt, who were disposed to think lightly of John Baptist, partly from ignorance of the nature of his ministry, partly from misunderstanding the question he had sent to ask. Our Lord Jesus silences such cavillers by the declaration He here makes. He tells them not to suppose that John was a timid, vacillating, unstable man, "a reed shaken by the wind." If they thought so, they were utterly mistaken. He was a bold, unflinching witness to the truth.—He tells them not to suppose that John was at heart a worldly man, fond of king's courts, and delicate living. If they thought so, they greatly erred. He was a self-denying preacher of repentance, who would risk the anger of a king, rather than not reprove his sins.—In short, He would have them know that John was "more than a prophet." He was one to whom God had given more honour than to all the Old Testament prophets. They indeed prophecied of Christ, but died without seeing Him. John not only prophecied of Him, but saw Him face to face. —They foretold that the days of the Son of man would certainly come, and the Messiah appear. John was an actual eye-witness of those days, and an honoured instrument in preparing men for them.—To them it was given to predict that Messiah would be "led as a lamb to the slaughter," and "cut off." To John it was given to point to Him, and say, "Behold the Lamb of God which taketh away the sin of the world."

There is something very beautiful and comforting to true Christians in this testimony which our Lord bears to John. It shows us the tender interest which our great Head feels in the lives and characters of all His members. It shows us what honour He is ready to put on all the work and labour that they go through in His cause. It is a sweet foretaste of the confession which He will make of them before the assembled world, when He presents them faultless at the last day before His Father's throne.

Do we know what it is to work for Christ? Have we ever felt cast down and dispirited, as if we were doing no good, and no one cared for us? Are we ever tempted to feel, when laid aside by sickness, or withdrawn by providence, "I have laboured in vain, and spent my strength for nought?" Let us meet such thoughts by the recollection of this passage. Let us remember, there is One who daily records all we do for Him, and sees more beauty in His servants' work than His servants do themselves. The same tongue which bore testimony to John in prison, will bear testimony to all His people at the last day. He will say, "Come ye blessed of my Father, receive the kingdom prepared for you from the foundation of the world." And then shall His faithful witnesses discover, to their wonder and surprise, that there never was a word spoken on their Master's behalf, which does not receive a reward.

MATTHEW XI. 16—24.

16 But whereunto shall I liken this generation? It is like unto children sitting in the markets, and calling unto their fellows,

17 And saying, We have piped unto you, and ye have not danced; we have mourned unto you, and ye have not lamented.

18 For John came neither eating nor drinking, and they say, He hath a devil.

19 The Son of man came eating and drinking, and they say, Behold, a man gluttonous, and a winebibber, a friend of Publicans and sinners. But wisdom is justified of her children.

20 Then began he to upbraid the cities wherein most of his mighty works were done, because they repented not:

21 Woe unto thee, Chorazin! woe unto thee, Bethsaida! for if the mighty works, which were done in you, had been done in Tyre and Sidon, they would have repented long ago in sackcloth and ashes.

22 But I say unto you, it shall be more tolerable for Tyre and Sidon at the day of judgment, than for you.

23 And thou, Capernaum, which art exalted unto heaven, shalt be brought down to hell: for if the mighty works, which have been done in thee, had been done in Sodom, it would have remained until this day.

24 But I say unto you, That it shall be more tolerable for the land of Sodom in the day of judgment, than for thee.

THESE sayings of the Lord Jesus were called forth by the state of the Jewish nation, when He was upon earth. But they speak loudly to us also, as well as to the Jews. They throw great light on some parts of the natural man's character. They teach us the perilous state of many immortal souls in the present day.

The first part of these verses shows us *the unreasonableness of many unconverted men in the things of religion.* The Jews, in our Lord's time, found fault with every teacher whom God sent among them. First came John the Baptist preaching repentance,—an austere man, a man who withdrew himself from society, and lived an ascetic life. Did this satisfy the Jews? No! They found fault and said, "He hath a devil."—Then came Jesus the Son of God, preaching the Gospel, living as other men lived, and practising none of John the Baptist's peculiar austerities. And did this satisfy the Jews? No! They found fault again, and said, "Behold a man gluttonous and a wine-bibber, a friend of publicans and sinners." In short, they were as perverse and hard to please as wayward children.

It is a mournful fact, that there are always thousands of professing Christians just as unreasonable as these Jews. They are equally perverse, and equally hard to please. Whatever we teach and preach, they find fault. Whatever be our manner of life, they are dissatisfied. Do we tell them of salvation by grace, and justification by faith? At once they cry out against our doctrine as licentious and antinomian.—Do we tell them of the holiness which the Gospel requires? At once they exclaim, that we are too strict, and precise, and righteous overmuch.—Are we cheerful? They accuse us of levity. —Are we grave? They call us gloomy and sour.—Do we keep aloof from balls, and races, and plays? They denounce us as puritanical, exclusive and narrow-minded. —Do we eat, and drink, and dress like other people, and attend to our worldly callings and go into society? They sneeringly insinuate that they see no difference between us and those who make no religious profession at all, and that we are not better than other men.—What is all this but the conduct of the Jews over again? "We have piped unto you, and ye have not danced: we have mourned unto you, and ye have not lamented." He who spake these words knew the hearts of men.

The plain truth is, that true believers must not expect unconverted men to be satisfied, either with their faith or their practice. If they do, they expect what they will not find. They must make up their minds to hear objections, cavils, and excuses, however holy their own lives

I

may be.   Well says Quesnel, " Whatever measures good
men take, they will never escape the censures of the
world.   The best way is not to be concerned at them."
After all, what saith the Scripture ?   " The carnal mind
is enmity against God."   " The natural man receiveth
not the things of the Spirit of God." (Rom. viii. 7.   1
Cor. ii. 14.)   This is the explanation of the whole matter.

The second part of these verses shows us *the exceeding
wickedness of wilful impenitence.*   Our Lord declares that
it shall be "more tolerable for Tyre, Sidon, and Sodom,
in the day of judgment," than for those towns where
people had heard His sermons, and seen His miracles,
but not repented.

There is something very solemn in this saying.   Let
us look at it well.   Let us think for a moment what
dark, idolatrous, immoral, profligate places Tyre and
Sidon must have been.   Let us call to mind the unspeakable wickedness of Sodom.   Let us remember that the
cities named by our Lord, Chorazin, Bethsaida, and
Capernaum, were probably no worse than other Jewish
towns, and, at all events, were far better than Tyre,
Sidon, and Sodom.   And then let us observe, that the
people of Chorazin, Bethsaida, and Capernaum, are to
be in the lowest hell, because they heard the Gospel, and
yet did not repent,—because they had great religious
advantages, and did not use them.   How awful this
sounds !

Surely these words ought to make the ears of every one
tingle, who hears the Gospel regularly, and yet remains
unconverted.   How great is the guilt of such a man
before God !   How great the danger in which he daily

stands! Moral, and decent, and respectable as his life may be, he is actually more guilty than an idolatrous Tyrian or Sidonian, or a miserable inhabitant of Sodom. They had no spiritual light: he has, and neglects it.— They heard no Gospel: he hears, but does not obey it.—Their hearts might have been softened, if they had enjoyed his privileges. Tyre and Sidon "would have repented." Sodom "would have remained until this day." His heart under the full blaze of the Gospel remains hard and unmoved.—There is but one painful conclusion to be drawn. His guilt will be found greater than their's at the last day. Most true is the remark of an English bishop, "Among all the aggravations of our sins, there is none more heinous than the frequent hearing of our duty."

May we all think often about Chorazin, Bethsaida, and Capernaum! Let us settle it in our minds that it will never do to be content with merely hearing and liking the Gospel. We must go further than this. We must actually "repent and be converted." We must actually lay hold on Christ, and become one with Him. Till then we are in awful danger. It will prove more tolerable to have lived in Tyre, Sidon, and Sodom, than to have heard the Gospel in England, and at last died unconverted.

MATTHEW XI. 25—30.

25 At that time Jesus answered and said, I thank thee, O Father, Lord of heaven and earth, because thou hast hid these things from the wise and prudent, and hast revealed them unto babes.

26 Even so, Father: for so it seemed good in thy sight.

27 All things are delivered unto me of my Father: and no man knoweth the Son, but the Father; neither knoweth any man the Father, save

the Son, and *he* to whomsoever the Son will reveal *him*.

28 Come unto me, all *ye* that labour and are heavy laden, and I will give you rest.

29 Take my yoke upon you, and learn of me; for I am meek and lowly in heart: and ye shall find rest unto your souls.

30 For my yoke *is* easy, and my burden is light.

THERE are few passages in the four Gospels more important than this. There are few which contain, in so short a compass, so many precious truths. May God give us an eye to see, and a heart to feel their value!

Let us learn, in the first place, *the excellence of a childlike and teachable frame of mind.* Our Lord says to His Father, "Thou hast hid these things from the wise and prudent, and revealed them unto babes."

It is not for us to attempt to explain why some receive and believe the Gospel, while others do not. The sovereignty of God in this matter is a deep mystery: we cannot fathom it. But one thing, at all events, stands out in Scripture, as a great practical truth to be had in everlasting remembrance. Those from whom the Gospel is hidden are generally "the wise in their own eyes, and prudent in their own sight." Those to whom the Gospel is revealed are generally humble, simple-minded, and willing to learn. The words of the Virgin Mary are continually being fulfilled, "He hath filled the hungry with good things, and the rich he hath sent empty away." (Luke i. 53.)

Let us watch against pride in every shape,—pride of intellect, pride of wealth, pride in our own goodness, pride in our own deserts. Nothing is so likely to keep a man out of heaven, and prevent him seeing Christ, as pride. So long as we think we are something we shall never be saved. Let us pray for and cultivate humility.

Let us seek to know ourselves aright, and to find out our place in the sight of a holy God. The beginning of the way to heaven, is to feel that we are in the way to hell, and to be willing to be taught of the Spirit. One of the first steps in saving Christianity is to be able to say with Saul, "Lord, what wilt thou have me to do?" (Acts ix. 6.) There is hardly a sentence of our Lord's so frequently repeated as this, "He that humbleth himself shall be exalted." (Luke xviii. 14.)

Let us learn, in the second place, from these verses, *the greatness and majesty of our Lord Jesus Christ.*

The language of our Lord on this subject is deep and wonderful. He says, "All things are delivered unto me of my Father: and no man knoweth the Son save the Father, neither knoweth any man the Father save the Son, and he to whom the Son shall reveal him." We may truly say, as we read these words, "Such knowledge is too wonderful for me; it is high, I cannot attain to it." We see something of the perfect union which exists between the first and second Persons of the Trinity. We see something of the immeasurable superiority of the Lord Jesus to all who are nothing more than men. But still, when we have said all this, we must confess that there are heights and depths in this verse, which are beyond our feeble comprehension. We can only admire them in the spirit of little children. But the half of them, we must feel, remains untold.

Let us, however, draw from these words the great practical truth, that all power and authority, in everything that concerns our soul's interests, is placed in our Lord Jesus Christ's hands. "All things are delivered unto him." He bears the keys: to Him we must go for admission into heaven. He is the door: through Him we must enter. He is the Shepherd: we must hear His voice, and follow Him, if we would not perish in the wilderness. He is the Physician: we must apply to Him, if we would be healed of the plague of sin. He is the bread of life: we must feed on Him, if we would have our souls satisfied. He is the light: we must walk after Him, if we would not wander in darkness. He is the fountain: we must wash in His blood, if we would be cleansed, and made ready for the great day of account. Blessed and glorious are these truths! If we have Christ, we have all things. (1 Cor. iii. 22.)

Let us learn, in the last place, from this passage, *the breadth and fulness of the invitations of Christ's Gospel.*

The three last verses of the chapter, which contain this lesson, are indeed precious. They meet the trembling sinner who asks, "Will Christ reveal His Father's love to such an one as me?" with the most gracious encouragement. They are verses which deserve to be read with special attention. For eighteen hundred years they have been a blessing to the world, and have done good to myriads of souls. There is not a sentence in them which does not contain a mine of thought.

Mark who they are that Jesus invites. He does not address those who feel themselves righteous and worthy. He addresses "all that labour and are heavy laden."—It is a wide description. It comprises multitudes in this weary world. All who feel a load on their heart, of which they would fain get free, a load of sin or a load of sorrow, a load of anxiety or a load of remorse,—all, whosoever they may be, and whatsoever their past lives,—all such are invited to come to Christ.

Mark what a gracious offer Jesus makes. "I will give you rest.—Ye shall find rest to your souls." How cheering and comfortable are these words! Unrest is one great characteristic of the world. Hurry, vexation, failure, disappointment, stare us in the face on every side. But here is hope. There is an ark of refuge for the weary, as truly as there was for Noah's dove. There is rest in Christ, rest of conscience and rest of heart, rest built on pardon of all sin, rest flowing from peace with God.

Mark what a simple request Jesus makes to the labouring and heavy-laden ones. "Come unto me :—Take my yoke upon you, learn of me." He interposes no hard conditions. He speaks nothing of works to be done first, and deservingness of His gifts to be established. He only asks us to come to Him just as we are, with all our sins, and to submit ourselves like little children to His teaching. "Go not," He seems to say, "to man for relief. Wait not for help to arise from any other quarter. Just as you are, this very day, come to me."

Mark what an encouraging account Jesus gives of Himself. He says, "I am meek and lowly of heart." How true that is, the experience of all the saints of God has often proved. Mary and Martha at Bethany, Peter after his fall, the disciples after the resurrection, Thomas after his cold unbelief, all tasted the "meekness and gentleness of Christ." It is the only place in Scripture where the "heart" of Christ is actually named. It is a saying never to be forgotten.

Mark, lastly, the encouraging account that Jesus gives of His service. He says, "My yoke is easy, and my burden is light." No doubt there is a cross to be carried, if we follow Christ. No doubt there are trials to be endured, and battles to be fought. But the comforts of the Gospel far outweigh the cross. Compared to the service of the world and sin, compared to the yoke of Jewish ceremonies, and the bondage of human superstition, Christ's service is in the highest sense easy and light. His yoke is no more a burden than the feathers are to a bird. His commandments are not grievous. His ways are ways of pleasantness, and all His paths are peace. (1 John v. 3. Prov. iii. 17.)

And now comes the solemn inquiry, Have we accepted this invitation for ourselves? Have we no sins to be forgiven, no griefs to be removed, no wounds of conscience to be healed? If we have, let us hear Christ's voice. He speaks to us as well as to the Jews. He says, "Come unto me."—Here is the key to true happiness. Here is the secret of having a light heart. All turns and hinges on an acceptance of this offer of Christ.

May we never be satisfied till we know and feel that we have come to Christ by faith for rest, and do still come to Him for fresh supplies of grace every day! If we have come to Him already, let us learn to cleave to Him more closely. If we have never come to Him yet, let us begin to come to-day. His word shall never be broken: "Him that cometh unto me, I will in nowise cast out." (John vi. 37.)

MATTHEW XII. 1—13.

1 At that time Jesus went on the sabbath day through the corn; and his disciples were an hungered, and began to pluck the ears of corn, and to eat.

2 But when the Pharisees saw *it*, they said unto him, Behold, thy disciples do that which is not lawful to do upon the sabbath day.

3 But he said unto them, Have ye not read what David did, when he was an hungered, and they that were with him;

4 How he entered into the house of God, and did eat the shewbread, which was not lawful for him to eat, neither for them which were with him, but only for the Priests?

5 Or have ye not read in the law, how that on the sabbath days the Priests in the temple profane the sabbath, and are blameless?

6 But I say unto you, That in this place is *one* greater than the temple.

7 But if ye had known what *this* meaneth, I will have mercy, and not sacrifice, ye would not have condemned the guiltless.

8 For the Son of man is Lord even of the sabbath day.

9 And when he was departed thence, he went into their synagogue:

10 And, behold, there was a man which had *his* hand withered. And they asked him, saying, Is it lawful to heal on the sabbath days? that they might accuse him.

11 And he said unto them, What man shall there be among you, that shall have one sheep, and if it fall into a pit on the sabbath day, will he not lay hold on it, and lift *it* out?

12 How much then is a man better than a sheep? Wherefore it is lawful to do well on the sabbath days.

13 Then saith he to the man, Stretch forth thine hand. And he stretched *it* forth; and it was restored whole, like as the other.

THE one great subject which stands out prominently in this passage of Scripture, is the Sabbath day. It is a subject on which strange opinions prevailed among the Jews in our Lord's time. The Pharisees had added to the teaching of Scripture about it, and overlaid the true character of the day with the traditions of men.—It is a subject on which divers opinions have often been held in the Churches of Christ, and wide differences exist among men at the present time. Let us see what we may learn about it from our Lord's teaching in these verses.

Let us, in the first place, settle it in our minds as an established principle, that *our Lord Jesus Christ does not do away with the observance of a weekly Sabbath day.* He neither does so here, nor elsewhere in the four Gospels. We often find His opinion expressed about the Jewish errors on the subject of the Sabbath. But we do not find a word to teach us that His disciples were not to keep a Sabbath at all.

It is of much importance to observe this. The mistakes that have arisen from a superficial consideration of our Lord's sayings on the Sabbath question, are neither few nor small. Thousands have rushed to the hasty conclusion, that Christians have nothing to do with the fourth commandment, and that it is no more binding on us than the Mosaic law about sacrifices. There is nothing in the New Testament to justify any such conclusion.

The plain truth is, that our Lord did not abolish the law of the weekly Sabbath. He only freed it from incorrect interpretations, and purified it from man-made additions. He did not tear out of the decalogue the fourth commandment. He only stripped off the miserable traditions with which the Pharisees had incrusted the day, and by which they had made it, not a blessing, but a burden. He left the fourth commandment where he found it, a part of the eternal law of God, of which no jot or tittle was ever to pass away. May we never forget this!

Let us, in the second place, settle it in our minds, that *our Lord Jesus Christ allows all works of real necessity and mercy to be done on the Sabbath day.*

This is a principle which is abundantly established in the passage of Scripture we are now considering. We find our Lord justifying His disciples for plucking the ears of corn on a Sabbath. It was an act permitted in Scripture. (Deut. xxiii. 25.) They "were an hungered," and in need of food. Therefore they were not to blame.— We find Him maintaining the lawfulness of healing a sick man on the Sabbath day. The man was suffering from disease and pain. In such a case it was no breach of God's commandment to afford relief. We ought never to rest from doing good.

The arguments by which our Lord supports the lawfulness of any work of necessity and mercy on the Sabbath, are striking and unanswerable. He reminds the Pharisees, who charged Him and His disciples with breaking the law, how David and his men, for want of other food, had eaten the holy shew-bread out of the tabernacle.—He reminds them how the priests in the temple are obliged to do work on the Sabbath, by slaying animals and offering sacrifices.—He reminds them how even a sheep would be helped out of a pit on the Sabbath, rather than allowed to suffer and die, by any one of themselves.—Above all, He lays down the great principle, that no ordinance of God is to be pressed so far as to make us neglect the plain duties of charity. "I will have mercy and not sacrifice." The first table of the law is not to be so interpreted as to make us break the second. The fourth commandment is not to be so explained, as to make us unkind and unmerciful to our neighbour. There is deep wisdom in all this. We are reminded of the saying, "Never man spake like this man."

In leaving the subject, let us beware that we are never tempted to take low views of the sanctity of the Christian Sabbath. Let us take care that we do not make our gracious Lord's teaching an excuse for Sabbath profanation. Let us not abuse the liberty which He has so clearly marked out for us, and pretend that we do things on the Sabbath from "necessity and mercy," which in reality we do for our own selfish gratification.

There is great reason for warning people on this point. The mistakes of the Pharisee about the Sabbath were in one direction. The mistakes of the Christian are in another. The Pharisee pretended to add to the holiness of the day. The Christian is too often disposed to take away from that holiness, and to keep the day in an idle, profane, irreverent manner. May we all watch our own conduct on this subject. Saving Christianity is closely bound up with Sabbath observance. May we never forget that our great aim should be to "keep the Sabbath holy." Works of necessity may be done. "It is lawful to do well," and show mercy. But to give the Sabbath to idleness, pleasure-seeking, or the world, is utterly unlawful. It is contrary to the example of Christ, and a sin against a plain commandment of God.

MATTHEW XII. 14—21.

14 Then the Pharisees went out, and held a council against him, how they might destroy him.

15 But when Jesus knew *it*, he withdrew himself from thence : and great multitudes followed him, and he healed them all ;

16 And charged them that they should not make him known :

17 That it might be fulfilled which was spoken by Esaias the prophet, saying,

18 Behold my servant, whom I have chosen : my beloved, in whom my soul is well pleased : I will put my spirit upon him, and he shall shew judgment to the Gentiles.

19 He shall not strive, nor cry ; neither shall any man hear his voice in the streets.

20 A bruised reed shall he not break, and smoking flax shall he not quench, till he send forth judgment unto victory.

21 And in his name shall the Gentiles trust.

THE first thing which demands our notice in this passage, is *the desperate wickedness of the human heart*, which it exemplifies. Silenced and defeated by our Lord's arguments, the Pharisees plunged deeper and deeper into sin. They "went out and held a council against him how they might destroy him."

What evil had our Lord done, that He should be so treated? None, none at all. No charge could be brought against His life : He was holy, harmless, undefiled, and separate from sinners,—His days were spent in doing good. No charge could be brought against His teaching : He had proved it to be agreeable to Scripture and reason, and no reply had been made to His proofs. But it mattered little how perfectly He lived or taught. He was hated.

This is human nature appearing in its true colours. The unconverted heart hates God, and will show its hatred whenever it dares, and has a favourable opportunity. It will persecute God's witnesses. It will dislike all who have anything of God's mind, and are renewed after His image. Why were so many of the prophets killed ? Why were the names of the apostles cast out as evil by the Jews ? Why were the early martyrs slain ? Why were John Huss, and Jerome of Prague, and Ridley, and Latimer burned at the stake ? Not for any sins that they had sinned, — not for any wickedness they had committed. They all suffered because they were godly men. And human nature, unconverted, hates godly men, because it hates God.

It must never surprise true Christians if they meet with the same treatment that the Lord Jesus met with. "Marvel not if the world hate you." (1 John iii. 13.) It is not the utmost consistency, or the closest walk with God, that will exempt them from the enmity of the natural man. They need not torture their consciences by fancying that if they were only more faultless and consistent, everybody would surely love them. It is all a mistake.

They should remember, that there was never but one perfect man on earth, and that He was not loved, but hated. It is not the infirmities of a believer that the world dislikes, but his godliness. It is not the remains of the old nature that call forth the world's enmity, but the exhibition of the new. Let us remember these things, and be patient. The world hated Christ, and the world will hate Christians.

The second thing which demands our notice in this passage, is *the encouraging description of our Lord Jesus Christ's character*, which St. Matthew draws from the prophet Isaiah. "A bruised reed shall he not break, and smoking flax shall he not quench."

What are we to understand by the bruised reed, and smoking flax? The language of the prophet no doubt is figurative. What is it that these two expressions mean? The simplest explanation seems to be, that the Holy Ghost is here describing persons whose grace is at present weak, whose repentance is feeble, and whose faith is small. Towards such persons the Lord Jesus Christ will be very tender and compassionate. Weak as the broken reed is, it shall not be broken. Small as the spark of fire may be within the smoking flax, it shall not be quenched. It is a standing truth in the kingdom of grace, that weak grace, weak faith, and weak repentance, are all precious in our Lord's sight. Mighty as He is, "He despiseth not any." (Job xxxvi. 5.)

The doctrine here laid down is full of comfort and consolation. There are thousands in every church of Christ to whom it ought to speak peace and hope. There are some in every congregation, that hears the Gospel,

who are ready to despair of their own salvation, because
their strength seems so small.   They are full of fears and
despondency, because their knowledge, and faith, and
hope, and love, appear so dwarfish and diminutive.   Let
them drink comfort out of this text.   Let them know
that weak faith gives a man as real and true an interest
in Christ as strong faith, though it may not give him the
same joy.   There is life in an infant as truly as in a
grown up man.   There is fire in a spark as truly as in a
burning flame.   The least degree of grace is an everlasting possession.   It comes down from heaven.   It is
precious in our Lord's eyes.   It shall never be overthrown.

Does Satan make light of the beginnings of repentance
towards God, and faith towards our Lord Jesus Christ?
No! indeed! he does not.   He has great wrath, because
he sees his time is short.—Do the angels of God think
lightly of the first signs of penitence and feeling after
God in Christ?   No! indeed! "there is joy" among them,
when they behold the sight.—Does the Lord Jesus regard
no faith and repentance with interest, unless they are
strong and mighty?   No! indeed!   As soon as that
bruised reed, Saul of Tarsus, begins to cry to Him,
He sends Ananias to him, saying, "Behold he prayeth."
(Acts ix. 11.) We err greatly if we do not encourage the
very first movements of a soul towards Christ.   Let the
ignorant world scoff and mock, if it will.   We may be
sure that "bruised reeds" and "smoking flax" are very
precious in our Lord's eyes.

May we all lay these things to heart, and use them in
time of need, both for ourselves and others.   It should

be a standing maxim in our religion, that a spark is better than utter darkness, and little faith better than no faith at all. "Who hath despised the day of small things?" (Zechar. iv. 10.) It is not despised by Christ. It ought not to be despised by Christians.

MATTHEW XII. 22—37.

22 Then was brought unto him one possessed with a devil, blind, and dumb: and he healed him, insomuch that the blind and dumb both spake and saw.

23 And all the people were amazed, and said, Is not this the Son of David?

24 But when the Pharisees heard *it*, they said, This *fellow* doth not cast out devils, but by Beelzebub the prince of the devils.

25 And Jesus knew their thoughts, and said unto them, Every kingdom divided against itself is brought to desolation; and every city or house divided against itself shall not stand:

26 And if Satan cast out Satan, he is divided against himself; how shall then his kingdom stand?

27 And if I by Beelzebub cast out devils, by whom do your children cast *them* out? therefore they shall be your judges.

28 But if I cast out devils by the Spirit of God, then the kingdom of God is come unto you.

29 Or else how can one enter into a strong man's house, and spoil his goods, except he first bind the strong man? and then he will spoil his house.

30 He that is not with me is against me; and he that gathereth not with me scattereth abroad.

31 Wherefore I say unto you, All manner of sin and blasphemy shall be forgiven unto men: but the blasphemy *against* the *Holy* Ghost shall not be forgiven unto men.

32 And whosoever speaketh a word against the Son of man, it shall be forgiven him: but whosoever speaketh against the Holy Ghost, it shall not be forgiven him, neither in this world, neither in the *world* to come.

33 Either make the tree good, and his fruit good; or else make the tree corrupt, and his fruit corrupt: for the tree is known by *his* fruit.

34 O generation of vipers, how can ye, being evil, speak good things? for out of the abundance of the heart the mouth speaketh.

35 A good man out of the good treasure of the heart bringeth forth good things: and an evil man out of the evil treasure bringeth forth evil things.

36 But I say unto you, That every idle word that men shall speak, they shall give account thereof in the day of judgment.

37 For by thy words thou shalt be justified, and by thy words thou shalt be condemned.

THIS passage of Scripture contains "things hard to be understood." The sin against the Holy Ghost in particular has never been fully explained by the most learned divines. It is not difficult to show from Scripture what the sin is not. It is difficult to show clearly what it is. We must not be surprised. The Bible would not be the book of God, if it had not deep places here and there, which man has no line to fathom. Let us rather thank God that there are lessons of wisdom to be gathered, even out of these verses, which the unlearned may easily understand.

Let us gather from them, in the first place, that there is *nothing too blasphemous for hardened and prejudiced men to say against religion.* Our Lord casts out a devil ; and at once the Pharisees declare that He does it "by the prince of the devils."

This was an absurd charge. Our Lord shows that it was unreasonable to suppose that the devil would help to pull down his own kingdom, and "Satan cast out Satan." But there is nothing too absurd and unreasonable for men to say, when they are thoroughly set against religion. The Pharisees are not the only people who have lost sight of logic, good sense, and temper, when they have attacked the Gospel of Christ.

Strange as this charge may sound, it is one that has often been made against the servants of God. Their enemies have been obliged to confess that they are doing a work, and producing an effect on the world. The results of Christian labour stare them in the face. They cannot deny them. What then shall they say? They say the very thing that the Pharisees said of our Lord, "It is the devil." The early heretics used language of this kind about Athanasius. The Roman Catholics spread reports of this sort about Martin Luther. Such things will be said as long as the world stands.

K

We must never be surprised to hear of dreadful charges being made against the best of men, without cause. "If they called the Master of the house Beelzebub, how much more shall they call them of his household?"—It is an old device. When the Christian's arguments cannot be answered, and the Christian's works cannot be denied, the last resource of the wicked is to try to blacken the Christian's character. If this be our lot, let us bear it patiently. Having Christ and a good conscience, we may be content. False charges will not keep us out of heaven. Our character will be cleared at the last day.

In the second place, let us gather out of these verses *the impossibility of neutrality in religion.* "He that is not with Christ is against him, and he that gathereth not with him scattereth abroad."

There are many persons in every age of the Church, who need to have this lesson pressed upon them. They endeavour to steer a middle course in religion. They are not so bad as many sinners, but still they are not saints. They feel the truth of Christ's Gospel, when it is brought before them, but are afraid to confess what they feel. Because they have these feelings, they flatter themselves they are not so bad as others. And yet they shrink from the standard of faith and practice which the Lord Jesus sets up. They are not boldly on Christ's side, and yet they are not openly against Him. Our Lord warns all such that they are in a dangerous position. There are only two parties in religious matters. There are only two camps. There are only two sides. Are we with Christ, and working in His cause? If not, we are against

Him. Are we doing good in the world? If not, we are doing harm.

The principle here laid down is one which it concerns us all to remember. Let us settle it in our minds, that we shall never have peace, and do good to others, unless we are thorough-going and decided in our Christianity. The way of Gamaliel and Erasmus never yet brought happiness and usefulness to any one, and never will.

In the third place, let us gather from these verses *the exceeding sinfulness of sins against knowledge.*

This is a practical conclusion which appears to flow naturally from our Lord's words about the blasphemy against the Holy Ghost. Difficult as these words undoubtedly are, they seem fairly to prove that there are degrees in sin. Offences arising from ignorance of the true mission of the Son of Man, will not be punished so heavily as offences committed against the noontide light of the dispensation of the Holy Ghost. The brighter the light, the greater the guilt of him who rejects it. The clearer a man's knowledge of the nature of the Gospel, the greater his sin, if he wilfully refuses to repent and believe.

The doctrine here taught is one that does not stand alone in Scripture. St. Paul says to the Hebrews, "It is impossible for those who were once enlightened,—if they shall fall away, to renew them again unto repentance." "If we sin wilfully, after that we have received the knowledge of the truth, there remaineth no more sacrifice for sins, but a fearful looking for of judgment." (Heb. vi. 4—6, and x. 26, 27.) It is a doctrine of which we find mournful proofs in every quarter. The unconverted children of godly parents, the unconverted servants of godly families, and the unconverted members of evangelical congregations are the hardest people on earth to impress. They seem past feeling. The same fire which melts the wax, hardens the clay.—It is a doctrine, moreover, which receives awful confirmation from the histories of some of those whose last ends were eminently hopeless. Pharaoh, and Saul, and Ahab, and Judas Iscariot, and Julian, and Francis Spira, are fearful illustrations of our Lord's meaning. In each of these cases there was a combination of clear knowledge and deliberate rejection of Christ. In each there was light in the head, but hatred of truth in the heart. And the end of each seems to have been blackness of darkness for ever.

May God give us a will to use our knowledge, whether it be little or great! May we beware of neglecting our opportunities, and leaving our privileges unimproved! Have we light? Then let us live fully up to our light. Do we know the truth? Then let us walk in the truth. This is the best safeguard against the unpardonable sin.

In the last place, let us gather from these verses *the immense importance of carefulness about our daily words.* Our Lord tells us, that "for every idle word that men shall speak, they shall give account in the day of judgment." And He adds, " By thy words thou shalt be justified, and by thy words thou shalt be condemned."

There are few of our Lord's sayings which are so heart-searching as this. There is nothing, perhaps, to which most men pay less attention than their words. They go through their daily work, speaking and talking without thought or reflection, and seem to fancy that if they do what is right, it matters but little what they say.

But is it so ? Are our words so utterly trifling and unimportant ? We dare not say so, with such a passage of Scripture as this before our eyes. Our words are the evidence of the state of our hearts, as surely as the taste of the water is an evidence of the state of the spring. "Out of the abundance of the heart the mouth speaketh." The lips only utter what the mind conceives. Our words will form one subject of inquiry at the day of judgment. We shall have to give account of our sayings, as well as our doings. Truly these are very solemn considerations. If there were no other text in the Bible, this passage ought to convince us, that we are all " guilty before God," and need a righteousness better .than our own, even the righteousness of Christ. (Phil. iii. 9.)

Let us be humble as we read this passage, in the recollection of time past. How many idle, foolish, vain, light, frivolous, sinful, and unprofitable things we have all said ! How many words we have used which, like thistle-down, have flown far and wide, and sown mischief in the hearts of others that will never die ! How often when we have met our friends, "our conversation," to use an old saint's expression, "has only made work for repentance." There is deep truth in the remark of Burkitt, "A profane scoff or atheistical jest may stick in the minds of those that hear it, after the tongue that spake it is dead. A word spoken is physically transient, but morally permanent." " Death and life," says Solomon, "are in the power of the tongue." (Prov. xviii. 21.)

Let us be watchful as we read this passage about words,

134 EXPOSITORY THOUGHTS.

when we look forward to our days yet to come. Let us resolve, by God's grace, to be more careful over our tongues, and more particular about our use of them. Let us pray daily that our "Speech may be always with grace." (Coloss. iv. 6.) Let us say every morning with holy David, "I will take heed to my ways, that I offend not in my tongue." Let us cry with him to the Strong for strength, and say, "Set a watch over my mouth, and keep the door of my lips." Well indeed might St. James say, "if any man offend not in word, the same is a perfect man." (Psal. xxxix. 1. cxli. 3. James iii. 2.)

MATTHEW XII. 38—50.

38 Then certain of the Scribes and of the Pharisees answered, saying, Master, we would see a sign from thee.

39 But he answered and said unto them, An evil and adulterous generation seeketh after a sign; and there shall no sign be given to it, but the sign of the prophet Jonas:

40 For as Jonas was three days and three nights in the whale's belly: so shall the Son of man be three days and three nights in the heart of the earth.

41 The men of Nineveh shall rise in judgment with this generation, and shall condemn it: because they repented at the preaching of Jonas; and, behold, a greater than Jonas is here.

42 The queen of the south shall rise up in the judgment with this generation, and shall condemn it: for she came from the uttermost parts of the earth to hear the wisdom of Solomon: and, behold, a greater than Solomon is here.

43 When the unclean spirit is gone out of a man, he walketh through dry places, seeking rest, and findeth none.

44 Then he saith, I will return into my house from whence I came out; and when he is come, he findeth *it* empty, swept, and garnished.

45 Then goeth he, and taketh with himself seven other spirits more wicked than himself, and they enter in and dwell there: and the last *state* of that man is worse than the first. Even so shall it be also unto this wicked generation.

46 While he yet talked to the people, behold, *his* mother and his brethren stood without, desiring to speak with him.

47 Then one said unto him, Behold, thy mother and thy brethren stand without, desiring to speak with thee.

48 But he answered and said unto him that told him, Who is my mother? and who are my brethren?

49 And he stretched forth his hand toward his disciples, and said, Behold my mother and my brethren!

50 For whosoever shall do the will of my Father which is in heaven, the same is my brother, and sister, and mother.

THE beginning of this passage is one of those places

which strikingly illustrate the truth of Old Testament History. Our Lord speaks of the queen of the South, as a real, true person, who had lived and died. He refers to the story of Jonah, and his miraculous preservation in the whale's belly, as undeniable matters of fact. Let us remember this, if we hear men professing to believe the writers of the New Testament, and yet sneering at the things recorded in the Old Testament, as if they were fables. Such men forget, that in so doing they pour contempt upon Christ Himself. The authority of the Old and New Testament stands or falls together. The same Spirit inspired men to write of Solomon and Jonah who inspired the Evangelists to write of Christ. These are not unimportant points in this day. Let them be well fixed in our minds.

The first practical lesson which demands our attention in these verses, is *the amazing power of unbelief.*

Mark how the Scribes and Pharisees call upon our Lord to show them more miracles. "Master, we would see a sign from thee." They pretended that they only wanted more evidence, in order to be convinced, and become disciples. They shut their eyes to the many wonderful works which Jesus had already done. It was not enough for them that He had healed the sick, and cleansed the lepers, raised the dead, and cast out devils. They were not yet persuaded. They yet demanded more proof. They would not see what our Lord plainly pointed at in His reply, that they had no real will to believe. There was evidence enough to convince them, but they had no wish to be convinced.

There are many in the Church of Christ, who are

exactly in the state of these Scribes and Pharisees. They flatter themselves that they only require a little more proof to become decided Christians. They fancy that if their reason and intellect could only be met with some additional arguments, they would at once give up all for Christ's sake, take up the cross, and follow Him. But in the mean time, they wait. Alas! for their blindness. They will not see that there is abundance of evidence on every side of them. The truth is, that they do not want to be convinced.

May we all be on our guard against the spirit of unbelief! It is a growing evil in these latter days. Want of simple, childlike faith is an increasing feature of the times, in every rank of society. The true explanation of a hundred strange things that startle us in the conduct of leading men in churches and states, is downright want of faith. Men who do not believe all that God says in the Bible, must necessarily take a vacillating and undecided line on moral and religious questions. "If ye will not believe, surely ye shall not be established." (Isaiah vii. 9.)

The second practical lesson which meets us in these verses is *the immense danger of a partial and imperfect religious reformation.*

Mark what an awful picture our Lord draws of the man to whom the unclean spirit returns, after having once left him. How fearful are those words, "I will return into my house from whence I came out!" How vivid that description, "He findeth it empty, swept, and garnished!" How tremendous the conclusion, "he taketh with him seven other spirits more wicked than himself,—

and the last state of that man is worse than the first!" It is a picture most painfully full of meaning. Let us scan it closely, and learn wisdom.

It is certain that we have in this picture *the history of the Jewish church and nation*, at the time of our Lord's coming. Called as they were at first out of Egypt to be God's peculiar people, they never seem to have wholly lost the tendency to worship idols. Redeemed as they afterwards were from the captivity of Babylon, they never seem to have rendered to God a due return for His goodness. Aroused as they had been by John the Baptist's preaching, their repentance appears to have been only skin-deep. At the time when our Lord spoke they had become, as a nation, harder and more perverse than ever. The grossness of idol-worship had given place to the deadness of mere formality. Seven other spirits worse than the first had taken possession of them. Their last state was rapidly becoming worse than the first. Yet forty years, and their iniquity came to the full. They madly plunged into a war with Rome. Judæa became a very Babel of confusion. Jerusalem was taken. The temple was destroyed. The Jews were scattered over the face of the earth.

Again, it is highly probable that we have in this picture *the history of the whole body of Christian churches*. Delivered as they were from heathen darkness by the preaching of the Gospel, they have never really lived up to their light. Revived as many of them were at the time of the Protestant Reformation, they have none of them made a right use of their privileges, or "gone on to perfection." They have all more or less

stopped short and settled on their lees. They have all
been too ready to be satisfied with mere external amend-
ments. And now there are painful symptoms in many
quarters that the evil spirit has returned to his house,
and is preparing an outbreak of infidelity, and false
doctrine, such as the churches have never yet seen.
Between unbelief in some quarters, and formal superstition in others, everything seems ripe for some fearful
manifestation of anti-christ. It may well be feared that
the last state of the professing Christian churches will
prove worse than the first.

Saddest and worst of all, we have in this picture *the
history of many an individual's soul.* There are men
who seemed at one time of their lives to be under the
influence of strong religious feelings. They reformed
their ways. They laid aside many things that are bad.
They took up many things that are good. But they
stopped there, and went no further, and by and bye gave
up religion altogether. The evil spirit returned to their
hearts, and found them empty, swept, and garnished.
They are now worse than they ever were before. Their
consciences seem seared. Their sense of religious things
appears entirely destroyed. They are like men given
over to a reprobate mind. One would say it was "impossible to renew them to repentance." None prove so
hopelessly wicked as those, who after experiencing strong
religious convictions have gone back again to sin and the
world.

If we love life, let us pray that these lessons may be
deeply impressed on our minds. Let us never be content
with a partial reformation of life, without thorough con-

version to God, and mortification of the whole body of sin. It is a good thing to strive to cast sin out of our hearts. But let us take care that we also receive the grace of God in its place. Let us make sure that we not only get rid of the old tenant, the devil, but have also got dwelling in us the Holy Ghost.

The last practical lesson which meets us in these verses is *the tender affection with which the Lord Jesus regards His true disciples.*

Mark how He speaks of every one who does the will of His Father in heaven. He says, " the same is my brother, and sister, and mother." What gracious words these are ! Who can conceive the depth of our dear Lord's love towards His relations according to the flesh ? It was a pure, unselfish love. It must have been a mighty love, a love that passes man's understanding. Yet here we see that all His believing people are counted as His relations. He loves them, feels for them, cares for them, as members of His family, bone of His bone, and flesh of His flesh.

There is a solemn warning here to all who mock and persecute true Christians on account of their religion. They consider not what they are doing. They are per-secuting the near relations of the King of kings. They will find at the last day that they have mocked those whom the Judge of all regards as " His brother, and sister, and mother."

There is rich encouragement here for all believers. They are far more precious in their Lord's eyes than they are in their own. Their faith may be feeble, their repentance weak, their strength small. They may be poor and needy in this world. But there is a glorious "whosoever" in the last verse of this chapter which ought to cheer them. "Whosoever" believes is a near relation of Christ. The elder Brother will provide for him in time and eternity, and never let him be cast away. There is not one "little sister" in the family of the redeemed, whom Jesus does not remember. (Cant. viii. 8.) Joseph provided richly for all his relations, and Jesus will provide for His.

MATTHEW XIII. 1—23.

1 The same day went Jesus out of the house, and sat by the sea side.

2 And great multitudes were gathered together unto him, so that he went into a ship, and sat; and the whole multitude stood on the shore.

3 And he spake many things unto them in parables, saying, Behold, a sower went forth to sow;

4 And when he sowed, some *seeds* fell by the way side, and the fowls came and devoured them up:

5 Some fell upon stony places, where they had not much earth: and forthwith they sprung up, because they had no deepness of earth:

6 And when the sun was up, they were scorched; and because they had no root, they withered away.

7 And some fell among thorns; and the thorns sprung up, and choked them:

8 But other fell into good ground, and brought forth fruit, some an hundredfold, some sixtyfold, some thirtyfold.

9 Who hath ears to hear let him hear.

10 And the disciples came, and said unto him, Why speakest thou unto them in parables?

11 He answered and said unto them, Because it is given unto you to know the mysteries of the kingdom of heaven, but to them it is not given.

12 For whosoever hath, to him shall be given, and he shall have more abundance: but whosoever hath not, from him shall be taken away even that he hath.

13 Therefore speak I to them in parables: because they seeing see not; and hearing they hear not, neither do they understand.

14 And in them is fulfilled the prophecy of Esaias, which saith, By hearing ye shall hear, and shall not understand; and seeing ye shall see, and shall not perceive:

15 For this people's heart is waxed gross, and *their* ears are dull of hearing, and their eyes they have closed; lest at any time they should see with *their* eyes, and hear with *their* ears, and should understand with *their* heart, and should be converted, and I should heal them.

16 But blessed *are* your eyes, for they see: and your ears, for they hear.

17 For verily I say unto you, That many prophets and righteous *men* have desired to see *those things* which ye see, and have not seen *them;* and to hear *those things* which ye hear, and have not heard *them.*

18 Hear ye therefore the parable of the sower.

19 When any one heareth the word of the kingdom, and understandeth *it* not, then cometh the wicked *one*, and

catcheth away that which was sown in his heart. This is he which received seed by the way side.

20 But he that received the seed into stony places, the same is he that heareth the word, and anon with joy receiveth it ;

21 Yet hath he not root in himself, but dureth for a while ; for when tribulation or persecution ariseth because of the word, by and by he is offended.

22 He also that received seed among the thorns is he that heareth the word ; and the care of this world, and the deceitfulness of riches, choke the word, and he becometh unfruitful.

23 But he that received seed into the good ground is he that heareth the word, and understandeth *it;* which also beareth fruit, and bringeth forth, some an hundredfold, some sixty, some thirty.

THE chapter which these verses begin is remarkable for the number of parables which it contains. Seven striking illustrations of spiritual truth are here drawn by the great Head of the Church from the book of nature. By so doing He shows us that religious teaching may draw helps from everything in creation. Those that would "find out acceptable words," should not forget this. (Eccles. xii. 10.)

The parable of the sower, which begins this chapter, is one of those parables which admit of a very wide application. It is being continually verified under our own eyes. Wherever the word of God is preached or expounded, and .people are assembled to hear it, the sayings of our Lord in this parable are found to be true. It describes what goes on, as a general rule, in all congregations.

Let us learn, in the first place, from this parable, that *the work of the preacher resembles that of the sower.*

Like the sower, the preacher must sow good seed, if he wants to see fruit. He must sow the pure word of God, and not the traditions of the church, or the doctrines of men. Without this his labour will be vain. He may go to and fro, and seem to say much, and to work much in his weekly round of ministerial duty. But there will be no harvest of souls for heaven, no living results, and no conversions.

Like the sower, the preacher must be diligent. He must spare no pains. He must use every possible means to make his work prosper. He must patiently "sow beside all waters," and "sow in hope." He must be "instant in season and out of season." He must not be deterred by difficulties and discouragements. "He that observeth the wind shall not sow." No doubt his success does not entirely depend upon his labour and diligence. But without labour and diligence success will seldom be obtained. (Isai. xxxii. 20. 2 Tim. iv. 2. Eccles. xi. 4.)

Like the sower, the preacher cannot give life. He can scatter the seed commited to his charge, but cannot command it to grow. He may offer the word of truth to a people, but he cannot make them receive it and bear fruit. To give life is God's sovereign prerogative. "It is the Spirit that quickeneth." God alone can "give the increase." (John vi. 63. 1 Cor. iii. 7.)

Let these things sink down into our hearts. It is no light thing to be a real minister of God's Word. To be an idle, formal workman in the Church is an easy business. To be a faithful sower is very hard. Preachers ought to be specially remembered in our prayers.

In the next place, let us learn from this passage, that *there are various ways of hearing the word of God without benefit.*

We may listen to a sermon with a heart like the hard "way side," careless, thoughtless, and unconcerned. Christ crucified may be affectionately set before us, and we may hear of His sufferings with utter indifference, as a subject in which we have no interest. Fast as the words fall on our ears, the devil may pluck them away, and we may

go home as if we had not heard a sermon at all.   Alas!
there are many such hearers!   It is as true of them as
of the idols of old, "eyes have they, but they see not;
they have ears, but they hear not." (Psal. cxxxv. 16, 17.)
Truth seems to have no more effect on their hearts than
water on a stone.

We may listen to a sermon with pleasure, while the
impression produced on us is only temporary and short-
lived.   Our hearts, like the "stony ground," may yield a
plentiful crop of warm feelings and good resolutions.
But all this time there may be no deeply-rooted work in
our souls, and the first cold blast of opposition or temptation may cause our seeming religion to wither away.
Alas! there are many such hearers!   The mere love of
sermons is no sign of grace.   Thousands of baptized
people are like the Jews of Ezekiel's day: "Thou art
unto them as a very lovely song of one that hath a
pleasant voice, and can play well on an instrument: for
they hear thy words, but they do them not." (Ezek.
xxxiii. 32.)

We may listen to a sermon, and approve of every
word it contains, and yet get no good from it, in consequence of the absorbing influence of this world.   Our
hearts, like the "thorny ground," may be choked with a
rank crop of cares, pleasures, and worldly plans.   We
may really like the Gospel, and wish to obey it, and yet
insensibly give it no chance of bearing fruit, by allowing
other things to fill a place in our affections, and insensibly to fill our whole hearts.   Alas! there are many
such hearers!   They know the truth well.   They hope
one day to be decided Christians.   But they never come

to the point of giving up all for Christ's sake. They never make up their minds to "seek first the kingdom of God,"—and so die in their sins.

These are points that we ought to weigh well. We should never forget that there are more ways than one of hearing the word without profit. It is not enough that we come to hear. We may come, and be careless.—It is not enough that we are not careless hearers. Our impressions may be only temporary, and ready to perish. —It is not enough that our impressions are not merely temporary. But they may be continually yielding no result, in consequence of our obstinate cleaving to the world.—Truly "the heart is deceitful above all things, and desperately wicked : who can know it ? " (Jerem. xvii. 9.)

In the last place, let us learn from this parable, that *there is only one evidence of hearing the word rightly.* That evidence is to bear fruit.

The fruit here spoken of is the fruit of the Spirit. Repentance towards God, faith towards the Lord Jesus Christ, holiness of life and character, prayerfulness, humility, charity, spiritual-mindedness,—these are the only satisfactory proofs that the seed of God's word is doing its proper work in our souls. Without such proofs our religion is vain, however high our profession. It is no better than sounding brass and a tinkling cymbal. Christ has said, "I have chosen you, and ordained you, that ye should go and bring forth fruit." (John xv. 16.)

There is no part of the whole parable more important than this. We must never be content with a barren orthodoxy, and a cold maintenance of correct theological views. We must not be satisfied with clear knowledge, warm feelings, and a decent profession. We must see to it that the Gospel we profess to love, produces positive "fruit" in our hearts and lives. This is real Christianity. Those words of St. James, should often ring in our ears, "Be ye doers of the word, and not hearers only, deceiving your own selves." (James i. 22.)

Let us not leave these verses without putting to ourselves the important question, "How do we hear?" We live in a Christian country. We go to a place of worship Sunday after Sunday, and hear sermons. In what spirit do we hear them? What effect have they upon our characters? Can we point to anything that deserves the name of "fruit?"

We may rest assured that to reach heaven at last, it needs something more than to go to Church regularly on Sundays, and listen to preachers. The word of God must be received into our hearts, and become the mainspring of our conduct. It must produce practical impressions on our inward man, that shall appear in our outward behaviour. If it does not do this, it will only add to our condemnation in the day of judgment.

MATTHEW XIII. 24—43.

24 Another parable put he forth unto them, saying, The kingdom of heaven is likened unto a man which sowed good seed in his field:

25 But while men slept, his enemy came and sowed tares among the wheat, and went his way.

26 But when the blade was sprung up, and brought forth fruit, then appeared the tares also.

27 So the servants of the householder came and said unto him, Sir, didst not thou sow good seed in thy field? from whence then hath it tares?

28 He said unto them, An enemy hath done this. The servants said unto him, Wilt thou then that we go and gather them up?

29 But he said, Nay; lest while ye

L

gather up the tares, ye root up also the wheat with them.

30 Let both grow together until the harvest: and in the time of harvest I will say to the reapers, Gather ye together first the tares, and bind them in bundles to burn them : but gather the wheat into my barn.

31 Another parable put he forth unto them, saying, The kingdom of heaven is like to a grain of mustard seed, which a man took, and sowed in his field :

32 Which indeed is the least of all seeds : but when it is grown, it is the greatest among herbs, and becometh a tree, so that the birds of the air come and lodge in the branches thereof.

33 Another parable spake he unto them ; The kingdom of heaven is like unto leaven, which a woman took, and hid in three measures of meal, till the whole was leavened.

34 All these things spake Jesus unto the multitude in parables ; and without a parable spake he not unto them :

35 That it might be fulfilled which was spoken by the prophet, saying, I will open my mouth in parables ; I will utter things which have been kept secret from the foundation of the world.

36 Then Jesus sent the multitude away, and went into the house : and his disciples came unto him, saying, Declare unto us the parable of the tares of the field.

37 He answered and said unto them, He that soweth the good seed is the Son of man ;

38 The field is the world ; the good seed are the children of the kingdom ; but the tares are the children of the wicked one ;

39 The enemy that sowed them is the devil ; the harvest is the end of the world ; and the reapers are the angels.

40 As therefore the tares are gathered and burned in the fire ; so shall it be in the end of this world.

41 The Son of man shall send forth his angels, and they shall gather out of his kingdom all things that offend, and them which do iniquity ;

42 And shall cast them into a furnace of fire : there shall be wailing and gnashing of teeth.

43 Then shall the righteous shine forth as the sun in the kingdom of their Father. Who hath ears to hear, let him hear.

THE parable of the wheat and tares, which occupies the chief part of these verses, is one of peculiar importance in the present day.* It is eminently calculated to correct the extravagant expectations in which many Christians indulge, as to the effect of missions abroad, and of preaching the Gospel at home. May we give it the attention which it deserves !

In the first place, this parable teaches us, *that good and evil will always be found together in the professing Church, until the end of the world.*

The visible Church is set before us as a mixed body.

*The consideration of the parables of the mustard seed and the leaven is purposely deferred till a future part of the Exposition.

It is a vast "field" in which "wheat and tares" grow side by side. We must expect to find believers and unbelievers, converted and unconverted, "the children of the kingdom, and the children of the wicked one," all mingled together in every congregation of baptized people.

The purest preaching of the Gospel will not prevent this. In every age of the Church, the same state of things has existed. It was the experience of the early Fathers. It was the experience of the Reformers. It is the experience of the best ministers at the present hour. There has never been a visible Church or a religious assembly, of which the members have been all "wheat." The devil, that great enemy of souls, has always taken care to sow "tares."

The most strict and prudent discipline will not prevent this. Episcopalians, Presbyterians, and Independents, all alike find it to be so. Do what we will to purify a church, we shall never succeed in obtaining a perfectly pure communion. Tares will be found among the wheat. Hypocrites and deceivers will creep in. And, worst of all, if we are extreme in our efforts to obtain purity, we do more harm than good. We run the risk of encouraging many a Judas Iscariot, and breaking many a bruised reed. In our zeal to "gather up the tares," we are in danger of "rooting up the wheat with them." Such zeal is not according to knowledge, and has often done much harm. Those who care not what happens to the wheat, provided they can root up the tares, show little of the mind of Christ. And after all there is deep truth in the charitable saying of Augustine, "Those who are tares to-day, may be wheat to-morrow."

Are we inclined to look for the conversion of the whole world by the labours of missionaries and ministers? Let us place this parable before us, and beware of such an idea. We shall never see all the inhabitants of earth the wheat of God, in the present order of things. The tares and wheat will "grow together till the harvest." The kingdoms of this world will never become the kingdom of Christ, and the millennium begin, until the King Himself returns.

Are we ever tried by the scoffing argument of the infidel, that Christianity can not be a true religion, when there are so many false Christians? Let us call to mind this parable, and remain unmoved. Let us tell the infidel, that the state of things he scoffs at does not surprise us at all. Our Master prepared us for it 1800 years ago. He foresaw and foretold, that His Church would be a field, containing not only wheat, but tares.

Are we ever tempted to leave one Protestant Church for another, because we see many of its members unconverted? Let us remember this parable, and take heed what we do. We shall never find a perfect Church. We may spend our lives in migrating from communion to communion, and pass our days in perpetual disappointment. Go where we will, and worship where we may, we shall always find tares.

In the second place the parable teaches us, *that there is to be a day of separation between the godly and the ungodly members of the visible Church, at the end of the world.*

The present mixed state of things is not to be for ever. The wheat and the tares are to be divided at last. The Lord Jesus shall "send forth his angels" in the day of

His second advent, and gather all professing Christians into two great companies. Those mighty reapers shall make no mistake. They shall discern with unerring judgment between the righteous and the wicked, and place every one in his own lot. The saints and faithful servants of Christ shall receive glory, honour, and eternal life. The worldly, the ungodly, the careless, and the unconverted shall be "cast into a furnace of fire," and receive shame and everlasting contempt.

There is something peculiarly solemn in this part of the parable. The meaning of it admits of no mistake. Our Lord Himself explains it in words of singular clearness, as if He would impress it deeply on our minds. Well may He say at the conclusion, "Who hath ears to hear, let him hear."

Let the ungodly man tremble when he reads this parable. Let him see in its fearful language his own certain doom, unless he repents and is converted. Let him know that he is sowing misery for himself, if he goes on still in his neglect of God. Let him reflect that his end will be to be gathered among the "bundles" of tares, and be burned. Surely such a prospect ought to make a man think. As Baxter truly says, "We must not misinterpret God's patience with the ungodly."

Let the believer in Christ take comfort when he reads this parable. Let him see that there is happiness and safety prepared for him in the great and dreadful day of the Lord. The voice of the archangel and the trump of God will proclaim no terror for him. They will summon him to join what he has long desired to see, a perfect Church and a perfect communion of saints. How beautiful will the whole body of believers appear, when finally separated from the wicked! How fine will the wheat look in the garner of God, when the tares are at length taken away! How brightly will grace shine, when no longer dimmed by incessant contact with the worldly and unconverted! The righteous are little known in the present day. The world sees no beauty in them, even as it saw none in their Master. "The world knoweth us not, because it knew him not." (1 John iii. 1.) But the righteous shall one day "shine forth as the sun in the kingdom of their Father." To use the words of Matthew Henry, "their sanctification will be perfected, and their justification will be published." "When Christ who is our life shall appear, then shall ye also appear with him in glory." (Coloss. iii. 4.)

MATTHEW XIII. 44—50.

44 Again, the kingdom of heaven is like unto treasure hid in a field; the which when a man hath found, he hideth, and for joy thereof goeth and selleth all that he hath, and buyeth that field.

45 Again, the kingdom of heaven is like unto a merchant man, seeking goodly pearls:

46 Who, when he had found one pearl of great price, went and sold all that he had, and bought it.

47 Again, the kingdom of heaven is like unto a net, that was cast into the sea, and gathered of every kind:

48 Which, when it was full, they drew to shore, and sat down, and gathered the good into vessels, but cast the bad away.

49 So shall it be at the end of the world: the angels shall come forth, and sever the wicked from among the just,

50 And shall cast them into the furnace of fire: there shall be wailing and gnashing of teeth.

THE parables of the "treasure hid in a field," and the "merchantman seeking goodly pearls," appear intended to convey one and the same lesson. They vary, no doubt, in one striking particular. The "treasure" was found of one who does not seem to have sought it. The "pearl" was found of one who was actually seeking pearls. But the conduct of the finders, in both cases, was precisely alike. Both "sold all" to make the thing found their own property. And it is exactly at this point that the instruction of both parables agrees.

These two parables are meant to teach us, *that men really convinced of the importance of salvation, will give up everything to win Christ, and eternal life.*

What was the conduct of the two men our Lord describes? The one was persuaded that there was a "treasure hid in a field," which would amply repay him, if he bought the field, however great the price that he might give. The other was persuaded that the "pearl" he had found was so immensely valuable, that it would answer to him to purchase it at any cost. Both were convinced that they had found a thing of great value. Both were satisfied that it was worth a great present sacrifice to make this thing their own. Others might wonder at them. Others might think them foolish for paying such a sum of money for the field and pearl. But they knew what they were about. They were sure that they were making a good bargain.

Behold in this single picture, the conduct of a true Christian explained! He is what he is, and does what he does in his religion, because he is *thoroughly persuaded* that it is worthwhile. He comes out from the world. He puts off the old man. He forsakes the vain companions of his past life. Like Matthew, he gives up everything, and, like Paul, he "counts all things loss" for Christ's sake. And why? Because he is convinced that Christ will make amends to him for all he gives up. He sees in Christ an endless "treasure." He sees in Christ a precious "pearl." To win Christ he will make any sacrifice. This is true faith. This is the stamp of a genuine work of the Holy Ghost.

Behold in these two parables the real clue to the conduct of many unconverted people ! They are what they are in religion, because they are *not fully persuaded* that it is worthwhile to be different. They flinch from decision. They shrink from taking up the cross. They halt between two opinions. They will not commit themselves. They will not come forward boldly on the Lord's side.—And why ? Because they are not convinced that it will answer. They are not sure that "the treasure" is before them. They are not satisfied that "the pearl" is worth so great a price. They cannot yet make up their minds to "sell all," that they may win Christ. And so too often they perish everlastingly ! When a man will venture nothing for Christ's sake, we must draw the sorrowful conclusion that he has not got the grace of God.

The parable of the net let down into the sea, has some points in common with that of the wheat and the tares. It is intended to instruct us on a most important subject, *the true nature of the visible Church of Christ.*

The preaching of the Gospel was the letting down of a large net into the midst of the sea of this world. The professing church which it was to gather together, was to be a mixed body. Within the folds of the net, there were to be fish of every kind, both good and bad. Within the pale of the Church there were to be Christians of various sorts, unconverted as well as converted, false as well as true. The separation of good and bad was sure to come at last, but not before the end of the world. Such was the account which the great Master gave to His disciples of the churches which they were to found.

It is of the utmost importance to have the lessons of this parable deeply graven on our minds. There is hardly any point in Christianity on which greater mistakes exist, than *the nature of the visible Church*. There is none, perhaps, on which mistakes are so perilous to the soul.

Let us learn from this parable, that all congregations of professed Christians ought to be regarded as *mixed bodies*. They are all assemblies containing " good fish and bad," converted and unconverted, children of God and children of the world, and ought to be described and addressed as such. To tell all baptized people, that they are born again, and have the Spirit, and are members of Christ, and are holy, in the face of such a parable as this, is utterly unwarrantable. Such a mode of address may flatter and please. It is not likely to profit or save. It is painfully calculated to promote self-righteousness, and lull sinners to sleep. It overthrows the plain teaching of Christ, and is ruinous to souls. Do we ever hear such doctrine ? If we do, let us remember " the net."

Finally, let it be a settled principle with us, never to be satisfied with mere *outward church-membership*. We may be inside the net, and yet not be in Christ. The waters of baptism are poured on myriads who are never washed in the water of life. The bread and wine are eaten and drunk by thousands at the Lord's table, who never feed on Christ by faith. Are we converted ? Are we among the "good fish?" This is the grand question. It is one which must be answered at last. The net will soon be "drawn to shore." The true character of every man's religion will at length be exposed. There will be an eternal separation between the good fish and the bad. There will be a "furnace of fire" for the wicked. Surely, as Baxter says, "these plain words more need belief and consideration than exposition."

MATTHEW XIII. 51—58.

51 Jesus saith unto them, Have ye understood all these things? They say unto him, Yea, Lord.

52 Then said he unto them, Therefore every Scribe *which is* instructed unto the kingdom of heaven is like unto a man *that is* an householder, which bringeth forth out of his treasure *things* new and old.

53 And it came to pass, *that* when Jesus had finished these parables, he departed thence.

54 And when he was come into his own country, he taught them in their synagogue, insomuch that they were astonished, and said, Whence hath

this *man* this wisdom, and *these* mighty works?

55 Is not this the carpenter's son? is not his mother called Mary? and his brethren, James, and Joses, and Simon, and Judas?

56 And his sisters, are they not all with us? Whence then hath this *man* all these things?

57 And they were offended in him. But Jesus said unto them, A prophet is not without honour, save in his own country, and in his own house.

58 And he did not many mighty works there because of their unbelief.

THE first thing which we ought to notice in these verses, is *the striking question* with which our Lord winds up the seven wonderful parables of this chapter. He said, "Have ye understood all these things?"

Personal application has been called the "soul" of preaching. A sermon without application is like a letter posted without a direction. It may be well-written, rightly dated, and duly signed. But it is useless, because it never reaches its destination. Our Lord's inquiry is an admirable example of real heart-searching application, "Have ye understood?"

The mere form of hearing a sermon can profit no man, unless he comprehends what it means. He might just as well listen to the blowing of a trumpet, or the beating of a drum. He might just as well attend a Roman Catholic service in Latin. His intellect must be set in motion, and his heart impressed. Ideas must be received into his mind. He must carry off the seeds of new thoughts. Without this he hears in vain.

It is of great importance to see this point clearly. There is a vast amount of ignorance about it. There are thousands who go regularly to places of worship, and think they have done their religious duty, but never carry away an idea, or receive an impression. Ask them, when they return home on a Sunday evening, what they have learned, and they cannot tell you a word. Examine them at the end of a year, as to the religious knowledge they have attained, and you will find them as ignorant as the heathen.

Let us watch our souls in this matter. Let us take with us to church, not only our bodies, but our minds, our reason, our hearts, and our consciences. Let us often ask ourselves, "What have I got from this sermon? what have I learned? what truths have been impressed on my mind?" Intellect, no doubt, is not everything in religion. But it does not therefore follow that it is nothing at all.—The heart is unquestionably the main point. But we must never forget that the Holy Ghost generally reaches the heart through the mind.—Sleepy, idle, inattentive hearers, are never likely to be converted.

The second thing which we ought to notice in these

verses, is *the strange treatment which our Lord received in His own country.*

He came to the town of Nazareth, where He had been brought up, and "taught in their synagogue." His teaching, no doubt, was the same as it always was. "Never man spake like this man." But it had no effect on the people of Nazareth. They were "astonished," but their hearts were unmoved. They said, " Is not this the carpenter's son ? Is not his mother called Mary ? " They despised Him, because they were so familiar with Him. "They were offended in him." And they drew from our Lord the solemn remark, "A prophet is not without honour, save in his own country, and in his own house."

Let us see, in this history, a melancholy page of human nature unfolded to our view. We are all apt to despise mercies, if we are accustomed to them, and have them cheap. The Bibles and religious books, which are so plentiful in England, the means of grace of which we have so abundant a supply, the preaching of the Gospel which we hear every week,—all, all are liable to be undervalued. It is mournfully true that in religion, more than in anything else, "familiarity breeds contempt." Men forget that truth is truth, however old and hackneyed it may sound, and despise it because it is old. Alas ! by so doing, they provoke God to take it away.

Do we wonder that the relations, servants, and neighbours of godly people are not always converted ? Do we wonder that the parishioners of eminent ministers of the Gospel are often their hardest and most impenitent hearers ? Let us wonder no more. Let us mark the experience of our Lord at Nazareth, and learn wisdom.

Do we ever fancy that if we had only seen and heard Jesus Christ, we should have been His faithful disciples? Do we think that if we had only lived near Him, and been eyewitnesses of His ways, we should not have been undecided, wavering, and half-hearted about religion? If we do, let us think so no longer. Let us observe the people of Nazareth, and learn wisdom.

The last thing which we ought to notice in these verses is *the ruinous nature of unbelief.* The chapter ends with the fearful words, "He did not many works there, because of their unbelief."

Behold in this single word the secret of the everlasting ruin of multitudes of souls! They perish for ever, because they *will not* believe. There is nothing beside in earth or heaven that prevents their salvation. Their sins, however many, might all be forgiven. The Father's love is ready to receive them. The blood of Christ is ready to cleanse them. The power of the Spirit is ready to renew them. But a great barrier interposes;—they will not believe. "Ye will not come unto me," says Jesus, "that ye might have life." (John v. 40.)

May we all be on our guard against this accursed sin. It is the old root-sin, which caused the fall of man. Cut down in the true child of God by the power of the Spirit, it is ever ready to bud and sprout again. There are three great enemies against which God's children should daily pray,—pride, worldliness, and unbelief. Of these three, none is greater than unbelief

MATTHEW XIV. 1—12.

1 At that time Herod the Tetrarch heard of the fame of Jesus,

2 And said unto his servants, This is John the Baptist; he is risen from the dead; and therefore mighty works do shew forth themselves in him.

3 For Herod had laid hold on John, and bound him, and put *him* in prison for Herodias' sake, his brother Philip's wife.

4 For John said unto him, It is not lawful for thee to have her.

5 And when he would have put him to death, he feared the multitude, because they counted him as a prophet.

6 But when Herod's birthday was kept, the daughter of Herodias danced before them, and pleased Herod.

7 Whereupon he promised with an oath to give her whatsoever she would ask.

8 And she, being before instructed of her mother, said, Give me here John Baptist's head in a charger.

9 And the king was sorry: nevertheless for the oath's sake, and them which sat with him at meat, he commanded *it* to be given *her*.

10 And he sent, and beheaded John in the prison.

11 And his head was brought in a charger, and given to the damsel. and she brought *it* to her mother.

12 And his disciples came, and took up the body, and buried it, and went and told Jesus.

WE have in this passage a page out of God's book of martyrs,—the history of the death of John the Baptist. The wickedness of king Herod, the bold reproof which John gave him, the consequent imprisonment of the faithful reprover, and the disgraceful circumstances of his death, are all written for our learning. "Precious in the sight of the Lord is the death of his saints." (Psalm cxvi. 15.)

The story of John the Baptist's death is told more fully by St. Mark than by St. Matthew. For the present it seems sufficient to draw two general lessons from St. Matthew's narrative, and to fasten our attention exclusively upon them.

Let us learn, in the first place, from these verses, *the great power of conscience.*

King Herod hears of "the fame of Jesus," and says to his servants, "This is John the Baptist: he is risen from the dead." He remembered his own wicked dealings with that holy man, and his heart failed within him.

His heart told him that he had despised his godly counsel, and committed a foul and abominable murder. And his heart told him, that though he had killed John, there would yet be a reckoning day. He and John the Baptist would yet meet again. Well says Bishop Hall, "a wicked man needs no other tormentor, especially for sins of blood, than his own heart."

There is a conscience in all men by nature. Let this never be forgotten. Fallen, lost, desperately wicked as we are all born into the world, God has taken care to leave Himself a witness in our bosoms. It is a poor blind guide, without the Holy Ghost. It can save no one. It leads no one to Christ. It may be seared and trampled under foot. But there is such a thing as conscience in every man, accusing or excusing him; and Scripture and experience alike declare it. (Rom. ii. 15.)

Conscience can make even kings miserable, when they have wilfully rejected its advice. It can fill the princes of this world with fear and trembling, as it did Felix, when Paul preached. They find it easier to imprison and behead the preacher, than to bind his sermon, and silence the voice of his reproof in their own hearts. God's witnesses may be put out of the way, but their testimony often lives and works on long after they are dead. God's prophets live not for ever, but their words often survive them. (2 Tim. ii. 9. Zech. i. 5.)

Let the thoughtless and ungodly remember this, and not sin against their consciences. Let them know that their sins will "surely find them out." They may laugh, and jest, and mock at religion for a little time. They may cry, "Who is afraid? Where is the mighty harm of our ways?" They may depend upon it, they are sowing misery for themselves, and will reap a bitter crop sooner or later. Their wickedness will overtake them one day. They will find, like Herod, that it is an evil thing and bitter to sin against God. (Jerem. ii. 19.)

Let ministers and teachers remember that there is a conscience in men, and work on boldly. Instruction is not always thrown away, because it seems to bear no fruit at the time it is given. Teaching is not always in vain, though we fancy that it is unheeded, wasted, and forgotten. There is a conscience in the hearers of sermons. There is a conscience in the children at our schools. Many a sermon and lesson will yet rise again, when he who preached or taught it is lying, like John the Baptist, in the grave. Thousands know that we are right, and, like Herod, dare not confess it.

Let us learn, in the second place, *that God's children must not look for their reward in this world.*

If ever there was a case of godliness unrewarded in this life, it was that of John the Baptist. Think for a moment what a man he was during his short career, and then think to what an end he came. Behold him, that was the Prophet of the Highest, and greater than any born of woman, imprisoned like a malefactor! Behold him cut off by a violent death, before the age of thirty-four,—the burning light quenched,—the faithful preacher murdered for doing his duty,—and this to gratify the hatred of an adulterous woman, and at the command of a capricious tyrant! Truly there was an event here, if there ever was one in the world, which might make an ignorant man say, "What profit is it to serve God?"

But these are the sort of things which show us, that there will one day be a judgment. The God of the spirits of all flesh shall at last set up an assize, and reward every one according to his works. The blood of John the Baptist, and James the apostle, and Stephen,—the blood of Polycarp, and Huss, and Ridley, and Latimer, shall yet be required. It is all written in God's book. "The earth shall disclose her blood, and no more cover her slain." (Isaiah xxvi. 21.) The world shall yet know, that there is a God that judgeth the earth. "If thou seest the oppression of the poor, and violent perverting of judgment and justice in a province, marvel not at the matter, for he that is higher than the highest regardeth: and there be higher than they." (Eccles. vi. 8.)

Let all true Christians remember, that their best things are yet to come. Let us count it no strange thing, if we have sufferings in this present time. It is a season of probation. We are yet at school. We are learning patience, longsuffering, gentleness, and meekness, which we could hardly learn if we had our good things now. But there is an eternal holiday yet to begin. For this let us wait quietly. It will make amends for all. "Our light affliction which is but for a moment, worketh for us a far more exceeding and eternal weight of glory." (2 Cor. iv. 17.)

MATTHEW XIV. 13—21.

13 When Jesus heard *of it*, he departed thence by ship into a desert place apart : and when the people had heard *thereof*, they followed him on foot out of the cities.

14 And Jesus went forth, and saw a great multitude, and was moved with compassion toward them, and he healed their sick.

15 And when it was evening, his

M

disciples came to him, saying, This is a desert place, and the time is now past; send the multitude away, that they may go into the villages, and buy themselves victuals.

16 But Jesus said unto them, They need not depart; give ye them to eat.

17 And they say unto him, We have here but five loaves, and two fishes.

18 He said, Bring them hither to me.

19 And he commanded the multitude to sit down on the grass, and took the five loaves, and the two fishes, and looking up to heaven, he blessed, and brake, and gave the loaves to *his* disciples, and the disciples to the multitude.

20 And they did all eat, and were filled: and they took up of the fragments that remained twelve baskets full.

21 And they that had eaten were about five thousand men, beside women and children.

THESE verses contain one of our Lord Jesus Christ's greatest miracles, the feeding of "five thousand men, beside women and children," with five loaves and two fishes. Of all the miracles worked by our Lord, not one is so often mentioned in the New Testament as this. Matthew, Mark, Luke, and John, all dwell upon it. It is plain that this event in our Lord's history is intended to receive special attention. Let us give it that attention, and see what we may learn.

In the first place, this miracle is *an unanswerable proof of our Lord's divine power.*

To satisfy the hunger of more than five thousand people with so small a portion of food as five loaves and two fishes, would be manifestly impossible without a supernatural multiplication of the food. It was a thing that no magician, impostor, or false prophet would ever have attempted. Such a person might possibly pretend to cure a single sick person, or raise a single dead body,—and by jugglery and trickery might persuade weak people that he succeeded. But such a person would never attempt such a mighty work as that which is here recorded. He would know well that he could not persuade ten thousand men, women, and children that they were full when they were hungry. He would be exposed as a cheat and impostor on the spot.

Yet this is the mighty work which our Lord actually performed, and by performing it gave a conclusive proof that He was God. He called that into being which did not before exist. He provided visible, tangible, material food for ten thousand people, out of a supply which in itself would not have satisfied fifty. Surely we must be blind if we do not see in this the hand of Him "who provideth food for all flesh," and made the world and all that therein is. To *create* is the peculiar prerogative of God.

We ought to lay firm hold on such passages as this. We should treasure up in our minds every evidence of our Lord's divine power. The cold, orthodox, unconverted man may see little in the story. The true believer should store it in his memory. Let him think of the world, the devil, and his own heart, and learn to thank God that his Saviour, the Lord Jesus Christ, is almighty.

In the second place, this miracle is a *striking example of our Lord's compassion toward men.*

He saw a great company in a desert place, ready to faint for hunger. He knew that many in that company had no true faith and love towards Himself. They followed Him from fashion and curiosity, or some equally low motive. (John vi. 26.) But our Lord had pity upon all. All were relieved. All partook of the food miraculously provided. All were "filled," and none went hungry away.

Let us see in this the heart of our Lord Jesus Christ towards sinners. He is as He was of old, "the Lord, the Lord God, merciful and gracious, longsuffering,

and abundant in goodness and truth." (Exod. xxxiv. 6.)
He does not deal with men according to their sins, or
reward them according to their iniquities. He loads
even His enemies with benefits. None will be so excuse-
less as those who are found impenitent at last. The
Lord's goodness leads them to repentance. (Rom. ii. 4.)
In all His dealings with men on earth, He showed Himself one that "delighteth in mercy." (Micah vii. 18.)
Let us strive to be like Him. "We ought," says Quesnel,
"to have abundance of pity and compassion on diseased
souls."

In the last place, this miracle is a *lively emblem of the
sufficiency of the Gospel to meet the soul-wants of all mankind.*

There can be little doubt that all our Lord's miracles
have a deep figurative meaning, and teach great spiritual
truths. But they must be handled reverently and discreetly. Care must be taken that we do not, like many of
the Fathers, see allegories where the Holy Spirit meant
none to be seen. But perhaps, if there is any miracle
which has a manifest figurative meaning, in addition to
the plain lessons which may be drawn from its surface,
it is that which is now before us.

What does this hungry multitude in a desert place
represent to us? It is an emblem of *all mankind.* The
children of men are a large assembly of perishing sinners,
famishing in the midst of a wilderness world,—helpless,
hopeless, and on the way to ruin. We have all gone
astray like lost sheep. (Isai. liii. 6.) We are by nature
far away from God. Our eyes may not be opened to the
full extent of our danger. But in reality we are wretched,

and miserable, and poor, and blind, and naked. (Rev. iii. 17.) There is but a step between us and everlasting death.

What do these loaves and fishes represent, apparently so inadequate to meet the necessities of the case, but by miracle made sufficient to feed ten thousand people? They are an emblem of *the doctrine of Christ crucified for sinners*, as their vicarious substitute, and making atonement by His death for the sin of the world. That doctrine seems to the natural man weakness itself. Christ crucified was to the Jews a stumbling-block, and to the Greeks foolishness. (1 Cor. i. 23.) And yet Christ crucified has proved the bread of God which cometh down from heaven, and giveth life to the world. (John vi. 33.) The story of the cross has amply met the spiritual wants of mankind wherever it has been preached. Thousands of every rank, age, and nation, are witnesses that it is "the wisdom of God, and the power of God." They have eaten of it and been "filled." They have found it "meat indeed and drink indeed."

Let us ponder these things well. There are great depths in all our Lord Jesus Christ's recorded dealings upon earth, which no one has ever fully fathomed. There are mines of rich instruction in all His words and ways, which no one has thoroughly explored. Many a passage of the Gospels is like the cloud which Elijah's servant saw. (1 Kings xviii. 44.) The more we look at it, the greater it will appear. There is an inexhaustible fulness in Scripture. Other writings seem comparatively threadbare when we become familiar with them. But as to Scripture, the more we read it, the richer we shall find it.

MATTHEW XIV. 22—36.

22 And straightway Jesus constrained his disciples to get into a ship, and to go before him unto the other side, while he sent the multitudes away.

23 And when he had sent the multitudes away, he went up into a mountain apart to pray : and when the evening was come, he was there alone.

24 But the ship was now in the midst of the sea, tossed with waves : for the wind was contrary.

25 And in the fourth watch of the night Jesus went unto them, walking on the sea.

26 And when the disciples saw him walking on the sea, they were troubled, saying, It is a spirit; and they cried out for fear.

27 But straightway Jesus spake unto them, saying, Be of good cheer; it is I; be not afraid.

28 And Peter answered him and said, Lord, if it be thou, bid me come unto thee on the water.

29 And he said, Come. And when

Peter was come down out of the ship, he walked on the water, to go to Jesus.

30 But when he saw the wind boisterous, he was afraid, and beginning to sink, he cried, saying, Lord, save me.

31 And immediately Jesus stretched forth *his* hand, and caught him, and said unto him, O thou of little faith, wherefore didst thou doubt?

32 And when they were come into the ship, the wind ceased.

33 Then they that were in the ship came and worshipped him, saying, Of a truth thou art the Son of God.

34 And when they were gone over, they came into the land of Gennesaret.

35 And when the men of that place had knowledge of him, they sent out into all that country round about, and brought unto him all that were diseased;

36 And besought him that they might only touch the hem of his garment : and as many as touched were made perfectly whole.

THE history contained in these verses, is one of singular interest. The miracle here recorded brings out in strong light the character both of Christ and His people. The power and mercy of the Lord Jesus, and the mixture of faith and unbelief in His best disciples, are beautifully illustrated.

We learn, in the first place, from this miracle, *what absolute dominion our Saviour has over all created things.* We see Him "walking on the sea," as if it was dry land. Those angry waves which tossed the ship of His disciples to and fro, obey the Son of God, and become a solid floor under His feet. That liquid surface, which was agitated by the least breath of wind, bears up the feet of our Redeemer, like a rock. To our poor, weak minds, the whole event is utterly incomprehensible. The picture of two feet walking on the sea, is said by Doddridge to have been the Egyptian emblem of an impossible thing. The man of science will tell us, that for material flesh and blood to walk on water is a physical impossibility. Enough for us to know that it was done. Enough for us to remember, that to Him who created the seas at the beginning, it must have been perfectly easy to walk over their waves when He pleased.

There is encouragement here for all true Christians. Let them know that there is nothing created, which is not under Christ's control. "All things serve Him." He may allow His people to be tried for a season, and tossed to and fro by storms of trouble. He may be later than they wish in coming to their aid, and not draw near till the "fourth watch of the night." But never let them forget that winds, and waves, and storms are all Christ's servants. They cannot move without Christ's permission. "The Lord on high is mightier than the voice of many waters, yea than the mighty waves of the sea." (Psalm xciii. 4.) Are we ever tempted to cry with Jonah, "the floods compassed me about: all thy billows and thy waves passed over me." (Jonah ii. 3.) Let us remember they are "His" billows. Let us wait patiently. We may yet see Jesus coming to us, and "walking on the sea."

We learn, in the second place, from this miracle, *what power Jesus can bestow on them that believe on Him.* We see Simon Peter coming down out of the ship, and walking on the water, like His Lord. What a wonderful proof was this of our Lord's divinity ! To walk on the

sea Himself was a mighty miracle. But to enable a
poor weak disciple to do the same, was a mightier miracle
still.

There is a deep meaning in this part of the history.
It shows us whàt great things our Lord can do for those
that hear His voice, and follow Him. He can enable
them to do things which at one time they would have
thought impossible. He can carry them through difficulties and trials, which without Him they would never have
dared to face. He can give them strength to walk
through fire and water unharmed, and to get the better
of every foe. Moses in Egypt, Daniel in Babylon, the
saints in Nero's household, are all examples of His
mighty power. Let us fear nothing, if we are in the
path of duty. The waters may seem deep. But if
Jesus says, "Come," we have no cause to be afraid.
"He that believeth on me, the works that I do shall he
do also, and greater works than these shall he do."
(John xiv. 12.)

Let us learn, in the third place, from this miracle, *how
much trouble disciples bring upon themselves by unbelief.*
We see Peter walking boldly on the water for a little
way. But by and bye, when he sees "the wind boisterous," he is afraid, and begins to sink. The weak flesh
gets the better of the willing spirit. He forgets the
wonderful proofs of his Lord's goodness and power, which
he had just received. He considered not that the same
Saviour who had enabled him to walk one step, must be
able to hold him up for ever. He did not reflect that he
was nearer to Christ when once on the water, than he
was when he first left the ship. Fear took away his

memory. Alarm confused his reason. He thought of nothing but the winds and waves and his immediate danger, and his faith gave way. "Lord," He cried, "save me."

What a lively picture we have here of the experience of many a believer! How many there are who have faith enough to take the first step in following Christ, but not faith enough to go on as they begun. They take fright at the trials and dangers which seem to be in their way. They look at the enemies that surround them, and the difficulties that seem likely to beset their path. They dwell on them more than on Jesus, and at once their feet begin to sink. Their hearts faint within them. Their hope vanishes away. Their comforts disappear.—And why is all this? Christ is not altered. Their enemies are not greater than they were.—It is just because, like Peter, they have ceased to look to Jesus, and have given way to unbelief. They are taken up with thinking about their enemies, instead of thinking about Christ. May we lay this to heart, and learn wisdom.

Let us learn, in the last place, from this miracle, *how merciful our Lord Jesus Christ is to weak believers.* We see Him stretching forth His hand immediately to save Peter, as soon as Peter cried to Him. He does not leave him to reap the fruit of his own unbelief, and sink in the deep waters. He only seems to consider his trouble, and to think of nothing so much as delivering him from it. The only word He utters, is the gentle reproof, "O thou of little faith, wherefore didst thou doubt?"

Behold in this concluding part of the miracle, the exceeding "gentleness of Christ!" He can bear with much, and forgive much, when He sees true grace in a man's heart. As a mother deals gently with her infant, and does not cast it away because of its little waywardness and frowardness, so does the Lord Jesus deal gently with His people. He loved and pitied them before conversion, and after conversion He loves and pities them still more. He knows their feebleness, and bears long with them. He would have us know that doubting does not prove that a man has no faith, but only that his faith is small. And even when our faith is small, the Lord is ready to help us. "When I said, my foot slippeth, thy mercy, O Lord, held me up." (Psal. xciv. 18.)

How much there is in all this to encourage men to serve Christ! Where is the man that ought to be afraid to begin running the Christian race, with such a Saviour as Jesus? If we fall, He will raise us again. If we err, He will bring us back. But His mercy shall never be altogether taken from us. He has said, "I will never leave thee, nor forsake thee," and He will keep His word. May we only remember, that while we do not despise little faith, we must not sit down content with it. Our prayer must ever be, "Lord, increase our faith."

MATTHEW XV. 1—9.

1 Then came to Jesus Scribes and Pharisees, which were of Jerusalem, saying,

2 Why do thy disciples transgress the tradition of the elders? for they wash not their hands when they eat bread.

3 But he answered and said unto them, Why do ye also transgress the commandment of God by your tradition?

4 For God commanded, saying, Honour thy father and mother : and, He that curseth father or mother, let him die the death.

5 But ye say, Whosoever shall say to *his* father or *his* mother, It *is* a gift, by whatsoever thou mightest be profited by me;

6 And honour not his father or his mother, *he shall be free*. Thus have

ye made the commandment of God of none effect by your tradition.

7 *Ye* hypocrites, well did Esaias prophesy of you, saying,

8 This people draweth nigh unto me with their mouth, and honoureth me with *their* lips; but their heart is far from me.

9 But in vain they do worship me, teaching *for* doctrines the commandments of men.

WE have in these verses a conversation between our Lord Jesus Christ, and certain Scribes and Pharisees. The subject of it may seem, at first sight, of little interest in modern days. But it is not so in reality. The principles of the Pharisees are principles that never die. There are truths laid down here, which are of deep importance.

We learn, for one thing, *that hypocrites generally attach great importance to mere outward things in religion.*

The complaint of the Scribes and Pharisees in this place, is a striking case in point. They brought an accusation to our Lord against His disciples. But what was its nature? It was not that they were covetous or self-righteous. It was not that they were untruthful or uncharitable. It was not that they had broken any part of the law of God. But they "transgressed the traditions of the elders.—They did not wash their hands when they ate bread." They did not observe some rule of mere human authority, which some old Jew had invented! This was the head and front of their offence!

Do we see nothing of the spirit of the Pharisees in the present day? Unhappily we see only too much. There are thousands of professing Christians, who seem to care nothing about the religion of their neighbours, provided that it agrees in outward matters with their own. Does their neighbour worship according to their particular form? Can he repeat their shibboleth, and talk a little about their favourite doctrines? If he can, they are satisfied, though there is no evidence that he is converted. If he cannot, they are always finding fault, and cannot speak peaceably of him, though he may be serving Christ better than themselves. Let us beware of this spirit. It is the very essence of hypocrisy. Let our principle be : "the kingdom of God is not meat and drink, but righteousness and peace, and joy in the Holy Ghost." (Rom. xiv. 17.)

We learn, for another thing, from these verses, *the great danger of attempting to add anything to the word of God.* Whenever a man takes upon him to make additions to the Scriptures, he is likely to end with valuing his own additions above Scripture itself.

We see this point brought out most strikingly in our Lord's answer to the charge of the Pharisees against His disciples. He says, "Why do ye also transgress the commandment of God by your traditions?" He strikes boldly at the whole system of adding anything, as needful to salvation, to God's perfect word. He exposes the mischievous tendency of the system by an example. He shows how the vaunted traditions of the Pharisees were actually destroying the authority of the fifth command- ment. In short, He establishes the great truth, which ought never be forgotten, that there is an inherent tendency in all traditions, to "make the word of God of none effect." The authors of these traditions may have meant no such thing. Their intentions may have been pure. But that there is a tendency in all religious insti- tutions of mere human authority, to usurp the authority of God's word, is evidently the doctrine of Christ. It is a solemn remark of Bucer's, that "a man is rarely to be found, who pays an excessive attention to human inventions in religion, who does not put more trust in them than in the grace of God."

And have we not seen melancholy proof of this truth, in the history of the Church of Christ? Unhappily we have seen only too much. As Baxter says, "men think God's laws too many and too strict, and yet make more of their own, and are precise for keeping them." Have we never read how some have exalted canons, rubrics, and ecclesiastical laws above the word of God, and punished disobedience to them with far greater severity than open sins, like drunkenness and swearing?—Have we never heard of the extravagant importance which the Church of Rome attaches to monastic vows, and vows of celibacy, and keeping feasts and fasts; insomuch that she seems to place them far above family duties, and the ten commandments?—Have we never heard of men who make more ado about eating flesh in Lent, than about gross impurity of life, or murder?—Have we never observed in our own land, how many seem to make adherence to Episcopacy the weightiest matter in Christianity, and to regard "Churchmanship," as they call it, as far outweighing repentance, faith, holiness, and the graces of the Spirit? —These are questions which can only receive one sorrowful answer. The spirit of the Pharisees still lives, after eighteen hundred years. The disposition to "make the word of God of none effect by traditions," is to be found among Christians, as well as among Jews. The tendency practically to exalt man's inventions above God's word, is still fearfully prevalent. May we watch against it, and be on our guard! May we remember that no tradition or man-made institution in religion can ever excuse the neglect of relative duties, or justify disobedience to any plain commandment of God's word.

We learn, in the last place, from these verses, that *the religious worship which God desires, is the worship of the heart.* We find our Lord establishing this by a quotation from Isaiah, "This people draweth near to me with their lips, but their heart is far from me."

The heart is the principal thing in the relation of husband and wife, of friend and friend, of parent and child. The heart must be the principal point to which we attend in all the relations between God and our souls. What is the first thing we need, in order to be Christians? A new heart.—What is the sacrifice God asks us to bring to Him? A broken and a contrite heart.—What is the true circumcision? The circumcision of the heart.—What is genuine obedience? To obey from the heart.—What is saving faith? To believe with the heart.—Where ought Christ to dwell? To dwell in our hearts by faith.—What is the chief request that Wisdom makes to every one? "My son, give me thine heart."

Let us leave the passage with honest self-inquiry as to the state of our own hearts. Let us settle it in our minds, that all formal worship of God, whether in public or private, is utterly in vain, so long as our "hearts are far from Him." The bended knee, the bowed head, the loud amen, the daily chapter, the regular attendance at the Lord's table, are all useless and unprofitable, so long as our affections are nailed to sin, or pleasure, or money, or the world. The question of our Lord must yet be answered satisfactorily, before we can be saved. He says to every one, "lovest thou me?" (John xxii. 17.)

MATTHEW XV. 10—20.

10 And he called the multitude, and said unto them, Hear, and understand;

11 Not that which goeth into the mouth defileth a man; but that which cometh out of the mouth, this defileth a man.

12 Then came his disciples, and said unto him, Knowest thou that the Pharisees were offended, after they heard this saying?

13 But he answered and said, Every plant, which my heavenly Father hath not planted, shall be rooted up.

14 Let them alone: they be blind leaders of the blind. And if the blind lead the blind, both shall fall into the ditch.

15 Then answered Peter and said unto him, Declare unto us this parable.

16 And Jesus said, Are ye also yet without understanding?

17 Do not ye yet understand, that whatsoever entereth in at the mouth goeth into the belly, and is cast out into the draught?

18 But those things which proceed out of the mouth come forth from the heart; and they defile the man.

19 For out of the heart proceed evil thoughts, murders, adulteries, fornications, thefts, false witness, blasphemies:

20 These are *the things* which defile a man: but to eat with unwashen hands defileth not a man.

THERE are two striking sayings of the Lord Jesus in this passage. One respects false doctrine. The other respects the human heart. Both of them deserve the closest attention.

Respecting false doctrine our Lord declares, *that it is a duty to oppose it, that its final destruction is sure, and that its teachers ought to be forsaken.* He says, " Every plant that my heavenly Father hath not planted, shall be rooted up. Let them alone."

It is clear from examination of the passage, that the disciples were surprised at our Lord's strong language about the Pharisees, and their traditions. They had probably been accustomed from their youth to regard them as the wisest and best of men. They were startled to hear their Master denouncing them as hypocrites, and charging them with transgressing the commandment of God. "Knowest thou," they said, "that the Pharisees were offended." To this question we are indebted for our Lord's explanatory declaration,—a declaration which perhaps has never received the notice it deserves.

The plain meaning of our Lord's words is, that false doctrine like that of the Pharisees, was a plant to which no mercy should be shown.—It was a "plant which His heavenly Father had not planted," and a plant which it was a duty to root up, whatever offence it might cause. It was no charity to spare it, because it was injurious to the souls of men.—It mattered nothing that those who planted it were high in office, or learned. If it contradicted the word of God, it ought to be opposed, refuted, and rejected.—His disciples must therefore understand that it was right to resist all teaching that was unscriptural, and to "let alone," and forsake all instructors who persisted in it.—Sooner or later they would find that all false doctrine will be completely overthrown, and put to shame, and nothing shall stand but that which is built on the word of God.

There are lessons of deep wisdom in this saying of our Lord, which serve to throw light on the duty of many a professing Christian. Let us scan them well, and see what they are. It was practical obedience to this saying which produced the blessed Protestant Reformation. Its lessons deserve close attention.

Do we not see here the duty of boldness in resisting false teaching? Beyond doubt we do. No fear of giving offence, no dread of ecclesiastical censure, should make us hold our peace, when God's truth is in peril.

If we are true followers of our Lord, we ought to be out-speaking, unflinching witnesses against error. "Truth," says Musculus, "must not be suppressed because men are wicked and blind."

Do we not see again the duty of forsaking false teachers, if they will not give up their delusions? Beyond doubt we do. No false delicacy, no mock humility should make us shrink from leaving the ministrations of any minister who contradicts God's word. It is at our peril if we submit to unscriptural teaching. Our blood will be on our own heads. To use the words of Whitby, "It never can be right to follow the blind into the ditch."

Do we not see, in the last place, the duty of patience, when we see false teaching abound? Beyond doubt we do. We may take comfort in the thought that it will not stand long. God Himself will defend the cause of His own truth. Sooner or later every heresy "shall be rooted up." We are not to fight with carnal weapons, but wait, and preach, and protest, and pray. Sooner or later, as Wycliffe said, "the truth shall prevail."

Respecting the heart of man, our Lord declares in these verses, *that it is the true source of all sin and defilement.* The Pharisees taught that holiness depended on meats and drinks, on bodily washings and purifications.— They held that all who observed their traditions on these matters were pure and clean in God's sight, and that all who neglected them were impure and unclean. — Our Lord overthrew this miserable doctrine, by showing His disciples that the real fountain of all defilement was not without a man, but within. "Out of the heart," He says, "proceed evil thoughts, murders, adulteries, fornications,

N

thefts, false witnesses, blasphemies : these are the things which defile a man."—He that would serve God aright needs something far more important than bodily washings. He must seek to have "a clean heart."

What an awful picture we have here of human nature, and drawn too by one who knew what was in man! What a fearful catalogue is this of the contents of our own bosoms! What a melancholy list of seeds of evil our Lord has exposed, lying deep down within every one of us, and ready at any time to start into active life! What can the proud and self-righteous say, when they read such a passage as this? This is no sketch of the heart of a robber, or murderer. It is the true and faithful account of the hearts of all mankind. May God grant that we may ponder it well and learn wisdom!

Let it be a settled resolution with us, that in all our religion the state of our hearts shall be the main thing. Let it not content us to go to church, and observe the forms of religion. Let us look far deeper than this, and desire to have a "heart right in the sight of God." (Acts viii. 21.) The right heart is a heart sprinkled with the blood of Christ, and renewed by the Holy Ghost, and purified by faith. Never let us rest till we find within the witness of the Spirit, that God has created in us a clean heart, and made all things new. (Psalm li. 10. 2 Cor. v. 17.)

Finally, let it be a settled resolution with us to "keep our hearts with all diligence," all the days of our lives. (Prov. iv. 23.) Even after renewal they are weak. Even after putting on the new man they are deceitful. Let us never forget that our chief danger is from within. The world and the devil combined, cannot do us so much harm as our own hearts will, if we do not watch and pray. Happy is he who remembers daily the words of Solomon, "He that trusteth in his own heart is a fool." (Prov. xxviii. 26.)

MATTHEW XV. 21—28.

21 Then Jesus went thence, and departed into the coasts of Tyre and Sidon.

22 And, behold, a woman of Canaan came out of the same coasts, and cried unto him, saying, Have mercy on me, O Lord, *thou* Son of David ; my daughter is grievously vexed with a devil.

23 But he answered her not a word. And his disciples came and besought him, saying, Send her away ; for she crieth after us.

24 But he answered and said, I am not sent but unto the lost sheep of the house of Israel.

25 Then came she and worshipped him, saying, Lord, help me.

26 But he answered and said, It is not meet to take the children's bread, and to cast *it* to dogs.

27 And she said, Truth, Lord : yet the dogs eat of the crumbs which fall from their masters' table.

28 Then Jesus answered and said unto her, O woman, great *is* thy faith : be it unto thee even as thou wilt. And her daughter was made whole from that very hour.

ANOTHER of our Lord's miracles is recorded in these verses. The circumstances which attend it are peculiarly full of interest. Let us take them up in order, and see what they are. Every word in these narratives is rich in instruction.

We see, in the first place, *that true faith may sometimes be found, where it might have been least expected.*

A Canaanitish woman cries to our Lord for help, on behalf of her daughter. "Have mercy on me," she says, "O Lord, thou son of David." Such a prayer would have showed great faith, had she lived in Bethany, or Jerusalem. But when we find that she came from the "coasts of Tyre and Sidon," such a prayer may well fill us with surprise. It ought to teach us, that it is grace, not place, which makes people believers. We may live in a prophet's family, like Gehazi, the servant of Elisha, and yet continue impenitent, unbelieving, and fond of the world. We may dwell in the midst of superstition and dark idolatry, like the little maid in Naaman's house, and yet be faithful witnesses for God and His Christ. Let us not despair of any one's soul, merely because his lot is cast in an unfavourable position. It is possible to dwell in the coasts of Tyre and Sidon, and yet sit down in the kingdom of God.

We see, in the second place, *that affliction sometimes proves a blessing to a person's soul.*

This Canaanitish mother no doubt had been sorely tried. She had seen her darling child vexed with a devil, and been unable to relieve her. But yet that trouble brought her to Christ, and taught her to pray. Without it she might have lived and died in careless ignorance, and never seen Jesus at all. Surely it was good for her that she was afflicted. (Psalm cxix. 71.)

Let us mark this well. There is nothing which shows our ignorance so much as our impatience under trouble. We forget that every cross is a message from God, and intended to do us good in the end. Trials are intended to make us think,—to wean us from the world,—to send us to the Bible,—to drive us to our knees. Health is a good thing; but sickness is far better, if it leads us to God. Prosperity is a great mercy; but adversity is a greater one, if it brings us to Christ. Anything, anything is better than living in carelessness, and dying in sin. Better a thousand times be afflicted, like the Canaanitish mother, and like her flee to Christ, than live at ease, like the rich "fool," and die at last without Christ and without hope. (Luke xii. 20.)

We see, in the third place, *that Christ's people are often less gracious and compassionate than Christ Himself.*

The woman about whom we are reading, found small favour with our Lord's disciples. Perhaps they regarded an inhabitant of the coasts of Tyre and Sidon, as unworthy of their Master's help. At any rate they said, "Send her away."

There is only too much of this spirit among many who profess and call themselves believers. They are apt to discourage inquirers after Christ, instead of helping them forward. They are too ready to doubt the reality of a beginner's grace, because it is small, and to treat him as Saul was treated when he first came to Jerusalem after his conversion. "They believed not that he was a disciple." (Acts ix. 26.) Let us beware of giving way to this spirit. Let us seek to have more of the mind that was in Christ. Like Him let us be gentle, and kind, and encouraging in all our treatment of those who are seeking to be saved. Above all, let us tell men continually that they must not judge of Christ by Christians. Let us assure them that there is far more in that gracious Master, than there is in the best of His servants. Peter, and James, and John may say to the afflicted soul, "Send her away." But such a word never came from the lips of Christ. He may sometimes keep us long waiting, as He did this woman. But He will never send us empty away.

We see, in the last place, *what encouragement there is to persevere in prayer, both for ourselves and others.*

It is hard to conceive a more striking illustration of

this truth, than we have in this passage. The prayer of this afflicted mother at first seemed entirely unnoticed: Jesus "answered her not a word." Yet she prayed on. —The saying which by and bye fell from our Lord's lips sounded discouraging: "I am not sent but unto the lost sheep of the house of Israel." Yet she prayed on, "Lord, help me."—The second saying of our Lord was even less encouraging than the first: "It is not meet to take the children's bread, and cast it to the dogs." Yet "hope deferred" did not "make her heart sick." (Prov. xiii. 12.) Even then she was not silenced. Even then she finds a plea for some "crumbs" of mercy to be granted to her. And her importunity obtained at length a gracious reward. "O woman, great is thy faith: be it unto thee even as thou wilt." That promise never yet was broken, "Seek and ye shall find." (Matt. vii. 7.)

Let us remember this history, *when we pray for ourselves.* We are sometimes tempted to think that we get no good by our prayers, and that we may as well give them up altogether. Let us resist the temptation. It comes from the devil. Let us believe, and pray on. Against our besetting sins, against the spirit of the world, against the wiles of the devil, let us pray on, and not faint.—For strength to do duty, for grace to bear our trials, for comfort in every trouble, let us continue in prayer. Let us be sure that no time is so well-spent in every day, as that which we spend upon our knees. Jesus hears us, and in His own good time will give an answer.

Let us remember this history, *when we intercede for others.* Have we children, whose conversion we desire?

Have we relations and friends, about whose salvation we are anxious? Let us follow the example of this Canaanitish woman, and lay the state of their souls before Christ. Let us name their names before Him night and day, and never rest till we have an answer. We may have to wait many a long year. We may seem to pray in vain, and intercede without profit. But let us never give up. Let us believe that Jesus is not changed, and that He who heard the Canaanitish mother, and granted her request, will also hear us, and one day give us an answer of peace.

MATTHEW XV. 29—39.

29 And Jesus departed from thence, and came nigh unto the sea of Galilee; and went up into a mountain, and sat down there.

30 And great multitudes came unto him, having with them *those that were* lame, blind, dumb, maimed, and many others, and cast them down at Jesus' feet; and he healed them:

31 Insomuch that the multitude wondered, when they saw the dumb to speak, the maimed to be whole, the lame to walk, and the blind to see: and they glorified the God of Israel.

32 Then Jesus called his disciples *unto him*, and said, I have compassion on the multitude, because they continue with me now three days, and have nothing to eat: and I will not send them away fasting, lest they faint in the way.

33 And his disciples say unto him,

Whence should we have so much bread in the wilderness, as to fill so great a multitude?

34 And Jesus saith unto them, How many loaves have ye? And they said, Seven, and a few little fishes.

35 And he commanded the multitude to sit down on the ground.

36 And he took the seven loaves and the fishes, and gave thanks, and brake *them*, and gave to his disciples, and the disciples to the multitude.

37 And they did all eat, and were filled: and they took up of the broken *meat* that was left seven baskets full.

38 And they that did eat were four thousand men, beside women and children.

39 And he sent away the multitude, and took ship, and came into the coasts of Magdala.

THE beginning of this passage contains three points which deserve our special attention. For the present let us dwell exclusively on them.

In the first place, let us remark, *how much more pains people take about the relief of their bodily diseases, than about their souls.* We read, that "great multitudes came to Jesus, having with them those that were lame, blind, dumb, maimed, and many others." Many of them, no doubt, had journeyed many miles, and gone through great fatigues. Nothing is so difficult and troublesome, as to move sick people. But the hope of being healed was in sight. Such hope is everything to a sick man.

We know little of human nature, if we wonder, at the conduct of these people. We need not wonder at all. They felt that health was the greatest of earthly blessings. They felt that pain was the hardest of all trials to bear. There is no arguing against sense. A man feels his strength failing. He sees his body wasting, and his face becoming pale. He is sensible that his appetite is leaving him. He knows, in short, that he is ill, and needs a physician. Show him a physician within reach, who is said never to fail in working cures, and he will go to him without delay.

Let us however not forget that our souls are far more diseased than our bodies, and learn a lesson from the conduct of these people. Our souls are afflicted with a malady far more deep-seated, far more complicated, far more hard to cure than any ailment that flesh is heir to. They are in fact plague-stricken by sin. They must be healed, and healed effectually, or perish everlastingly. Do we really know this? Do we feel it? Are we alive to our spiritual disease? Alas! there is but one answer to these questions. The bulk of mankind do not feel it at all. Their eyes are blinded. They are utterly insensible to their danger. For bodily health they crowd the waiting-rooms of doctors. For bodily health they

take long journeys to find purer air. But for their soul's
health they take no thought at all. Happy indeed is that
man or woman who has found out his soul's disease!
Such an one will never rest till he has found Jesus.
Troubles will seem nothing to him. Life, life, eternal
life is at stake. He will count all things loss that he
may win Christ, and be healed.

In the second place, let us remark *the marvellous ease
and power with which our Lord healed all who were brought
to Him.* We read that "the multitude wondered when
they saw the dumb to speak, the maimed to be whole,
the lame to walk, and the blind to see; and they glorified
the God of Israel."

Behold in these words a lively emblem of our Lord
Jesus Christ's power to heal sin-diseased souls! There is
no ailment of heart that He cannot cure. There is no
form of spiritual complaint that He cannot overcome.
The fever of lust, the palsy of the love of the world,
the slow consumption of indolence and sloth, the heart-
disease of unbelief, all, all give way when He sends forth
His Spirit on any one of the children of men. He can
put a new song in a sinner's mouth, and make him speak
with love of that Gospel which he once ridiculed and
blasphemed. He can open the eyes of a man's understanding and make him see the kingdom of God. He
can open the ears of a man and make him willing to hear
His voice, and follow Him whithersoever He goeth. He
can give power to a man who once walked in the broad
way that leadeth unto destruction, to walk in the way of
life. He can make hands that were once instruments of
sin, serve Him and do His will. The time of miracles

is not yet past. Every conversion is a miracle. Have we ever seen a real instance of conversion? Let us know that we saw in it the hand of Christ. We should have seen nothing really greater, if we had seen our Lord making the dumb to speak, and the lame to walk, when He was on earth.

Would we know what to do, if we desire to be saved? Do we feel soul-sick and want a cure? We must just go to Christ by faith and apply to Him for relief. He is not changed. Eighteen hundred years have made no difference in Him. High at the right hand of God He is still the great Physician. He still "receiveth sinners." He is still mighty to heal.

In the third place, let us remark *the abundant compassion of our Lord Jesus Christ.* We read that "He called His disciples and said, I have compassion on the multitude." A great crowd of men and women is always a solemn sight. It should stir our hearts to feel that each is a dying sinner, and each has a soul to be saved. None ever seems to have felt so much when he saw a crowd, as Christ.

It is a curious and striking fact that of all the feelings experienced by our Lord when upon earth, there is none so often mentioned as "compassion." His joy, His sorrow, His thankfulness, His anger, His wonder, His zeal, all are occasionally recorded. But none of these feelings are so frequently mentioned as "compassion." The Holy Spirit seems to point out to us, that this was the distinguishing feature of His character, and the predominant feeling of His mind, when He was among men. Nine times over,—to say nothing of expressions in parables,—nine times over the Spirit has caused that word "compassion" to be written in the Gospels.

There is something very touching and instructive in this circumstance. Nothing is written by chance in the word of God. There is a special reason for the selection of every single expression. That word "compassion," no doubt, was specially chosen for our profit.

It ought to encourage all who are hesitating about beginning to walk in God's ways. Let them remember that their Saviour is full of "compassion." He will receive them graciously. He will forgive them freely. He will remember their former iniquities no more. He will supply all their need abundantly. Let them not be afraid. Christ's mercy is a deep well, of which no one ever found the bottom.

It ought to comfort the saints and servants of the Lord when they feel weary. Let them call to mind that Jesus is full of "compassion." He knows what a world it is in which they live. He knows the body of a man and all its frailties. He knows the devices of their enemy, the devil. And the Lord pities His people. Let them not be cast down. They may feel that weakness, failure, and imperfection are stamped on all they do. But let them not forget that word which says, "His compassions fail not." (Jerem. iii. 22.)

MATTHEW XVI. 1—12.

1 The Pharisees also with the Sadducees came, and tempting desired him that he would shew them a sign from heaven.

2 He answered and said unto them, When it is evening, ye say, *It will be* fair weather: for the sky is red.

3 And in the morning, *It will be* foul weather to day: for the sky is red and lowring. O *ye* hypocrites, ye

can discern the face of the sky ; but can ye not *discern* the signs of the times?

4 A wicked and adulterous generation seeketh after a sign; and there shall no sign be given unto it, but the sign of the prophet Jonas. And he left them, and departed.

5 And when his disciples were come to the other side, they had forgotten to take bread.

6 Then Jesus said unto them, Take heed and beware of the leaven of the Pharisees and of the Sadducees.

7 And they reasoned among themselves, saying, *It is* because we have taken no bread.

8 *Which* when Jesus perceived, he said unto them, O ye of little faith,

why reason ye among yourselves, because ye have brought no bread?

9 Do ye not yet understand, neither remember the five loaves of the five thousand, and how many baskets ye took up?

10 Neither the seven loaves of the four thousand, and how many baskets ye took up?

11 How is it that ye do not understand that I spake *it* not to you concerning bread, that ye should beware of the leaven of the Pharisees and of the Sadducees?

12 Then understood they how that he bade *them* not beware of the leaven of bread, but of the doctrine of the Pharisees and of the Sadducees.

In these verses we find our Lord assailed by the untiring enmity of the Pharisees and Sadducees. As a general rule these two sects were at enmity between themselves. In persecuting Christ, however, they made common cause. Truly it was an unholy alliance! Yet how often we see the same thing in the present day. Men of the most opposite opinions and habits will agree in disliking the Gospel, and will work together to oppose its progress. "There is no new thing under the sun." (Eccles. i. 9.)

The first point in this passage which deserves special notice, *is the repetition which our Lord makes of words used by Him on a former occasion.* He says, "a wicked and adulterous generation seeketh after a sign; and there shall no sign be given unto it, but the sign of the prophet Jonas." If we turn to the twelfth chapter of this Gospel and the 39th verse, we shall find that He had said the very same thing once before.

This repetition may seem a trifling and unimportant matter in the eyes of some. But it is not so in reality.

It throws light on a subject, which has perplexed the
minds of many sincere lovers of the Bible, and ought
therefore to be specially observed.

This repetition shows us that our Lord was in the
habit of *saying the same things over again.* He did not
content Himself with saying a thing once, and afterwards
never repeating it. It is evident that it was His custom
to bring forward certain truths again and again, and thus
to impress them more deeply on the minds of His disciples. He knew the weakness of our memories in spiritual
things. He knew that what we hear twice, we remember
better than what we hear once. He therefore brought
out of His treasury old things as well as new.

Now what does all this teach us? It teaches us that
we need not be so anxious to *harmonize* the narratives
we read in the four Gospels, as many are disposed to be.
It does not follow that the sayings of our Lord, which we
find the same in St. Matthew and St. Luke, were always
used at the same time, or that the events with which
they are connected must necessarily be the same.—St.
Matthew may be describing one event in our Lord's life.
St. Luke may be describing another. And yet the words
of our Lord, on both occasions, may have been precisely
alike.—To attempt to make out the two events to be one
and the same, because of the sameness of the words used,
has often led Bible students into great difficulties. It is
far safer to hold the view here maintained, that at different times our Lord often used the same words.

The second point which deserves special notice in these
verses is, *the solemn warning which our Lord takes occasion
to give to His disciples.* His mind was evidently pained

with the false doctrines which He saw among the
Jews, and the pernicious influence which they exercised.
He seizes the opportunity to utter a caution. "Take
heed, and beware of the leaven of the Pharisees and of the
Sadducees." Let us mark well what those words contain.

To whom was this warning addressed? To the twelve
apostles,—to the first ministers of the Church of Christ,
—to men who had forsaken all for the Gospel's sake!
Even they are warned! The best of men are only men,
and at any time may fall into temptation. "Let him
that thinketh he standeth, take heed lest he fall." If we
love life, and would see good days, let us never think that
we do not need that hint, "take heed, and beware."

Against what does our Lord warn His apostles?
Against the "doctrine" of the Pharisees and of the Saddu-
cees. The Pharisees, we are frequently told in the
Gospels, were self-righteous formalists. The Sadducees
were sceptics, freethinkers, and half infidels. Yet even
Peter, James, and John must beware of their doctrines!
Truly the best and holiest of believers may well be on
his guard!

By what figure does our Lord describe the false
doctrines against which He cautions His disciples? He
calls them *leaven*. Like leaven, they might seem a small
thing compared to the whole body of truth. Like leaven,
once admitted they would work secretly and noiselessly.
Like leaven, they would gradually change the whole
character of the religion with which they were mixed.
How much is often contained in a single word! It was
not merely the open danger of heresy, but "leaven," of
which the apostles were to beware.

There is much in all this that calls loudly for the close attention of all professing Christians. The caution of our Lord in this passage has been shamefully neglected. It would have been well for the Church of Christ, if the warnings of the Gospel had been as much studied as its promises.

Let us then remember that this saying of our Lord's about the "leaven of the Pharisees and Sadducees" was intended for all time. It was not meant only for the generation to which it was spoken. It was meant for the perpetual benefit of the Church of Christ. He who spoke it saw with prophetical eye the future history of Christianity. The Great Physician knew well that Pharisee-doctrines and Sadducee-doctrines would prove the two great wasting diseases of His Church, until the end of the world. He would have us know that there will always be Pharisees and Sadducees in the ranks of Christians. Their succession shall never fail. Their generation shall never become extinct. Their name may change, but their spirit will always remain. Therefore He cries to us, "take heed and beware."

Finally, let us make a personal use of this caution, by keeping up a holy jealousy over our own souls. Let us remember, that we live in a world where Pharisaism and Sadduceeism are continually striving for the mastery in the Church of Christ. Some want to add to the Gospel, and some want to take away from it. Some would bury it, and some would pare it down to nothing. Some would stifle it by heaping on additions, and some would bleed it to death by subtraction from its truths. Both parties agree only in one respect. Both would kill and destroy the life of Christianity, if they succeeded in having their own way. Against both errors let us watch and pray, and stand upon our guard. Let us not add to the Gospel, to please the Roman Catholic Pharisee. Let us not subtract from the Gospel, to please the Neologian Sadducee. Let our principle be "the truth, the whole truth, and nothing but the truth," nothing added to it, and nothing taken away.

MATTHEW XVI. 13—20.

13 When Jesus came into the coasts of Cæsarea Philippi, he asked his disciples, saying, Whom do men say that I the Son of man am?

14 And they said, Some *say that thou art* John the Baptist : some, Elias ; and others, Jeremias, or one of the prophets.

15 He saith unto them, But whom say ye that I am?

16 And Simon Peter answered and said, Thou art the Christ, the Son of the living God.

17 And Jesus answered and said, unto him, Blessed art thou, Simon Bar-jona : for flesh and blood hath not revealed *it* unto thee, but my Father which is in heaven.

18 And I say also unto thee, That thou art Peter, and upon this rock I will build my Church ; and the gates of hell shall not prevail against it.

19 And I will give unto thee the keys of the kingdom of heaven : and whatsoever thou shalt bind on earth shall be bound in heaven : and whatsoever thou shalt loose on earth shall be loosed in heaven.

20 Then charged he his disciples that they should tell no man that he was Jesus the Christ.

THERE are words in this passage which have led to painful differences and divisions among Christians. Men have striven and contended about their meaning, till they have lost sight of all charity, and yet failed to carry conviction to one another's minds. Let it suffice us to glance briefly at the controverted words, and then pass on to more practical lessons.

What then are we to understand, when we read that remarkable saying of our Lord's, "Thou art Peter, and upon this rock I will build my Church." Does it mean that the apostle Peter himself was to be the foundation on which Christ's Church was to be built? Such an interpretation, to say the least, appears exceedingly improbable. To speak of an erring, fallible child of Adam as the foundation of the spiritual temple, is very unlike the ordinary language of Scripture. Above all, no reason can be given why our Lord should not have said, "I will build my church upon *thee*,"—if such had been His meaning,—instead of saying, "I will build my church upon *this rock*."

The true meaning of "the rock" in this passage appears to be the truth of our Lord's Messiahship and divinity, which Peter had just confessed. It is as though our Lord had said, "Thou art rightly called by the name Peter, or stone, for thou hast confessed that mighty truth, on which, as on a rock, I will build my church."*

But what are we to understand, when we read the promise which our Lord makes to Peter, "I will give unto thee the keys of the kingdom of heaven." Do these words mean that the right of admitting souls to heaven was to be placed in Peter's hands? The idea is preposterous. Such an office is the special prerogative of Christ Himself. (Rev. i. 18.) Do the words mean that

* There is nothing modern, or peculiarly Protestant in the view here maintained. It was held by Chrysostom long ago. It was taught by Ferus, a famous Roman Catholic preacher, of the Franciscan order, at Mayence, in the sixteenth century, in his Homilies on St. Matthew.

It may be well to remark, in this place, that it is a complete delusion to suppose that the Scriptures can be interpreted according to the "unanimous consent of the Fathers." There is no such unanimous consent. It is a mere high-sounding phrase, utterly destitute of any foundation in facts. The fathers disagree as much in explaining Scripture, as Whitby and Gill, or Matthew Henry and D'Oyly and Mant.

Peter was to have any primacy or superiority over the rest of the apostles? There is not the slightest proof that such a meaning was attached to the words in the New Testament times, or that Peter had any rank or dignity above the rest of the twelve.

The true meaning of the promise to Peter appears to be, that he was to have the special privilege of first opening the door of salvation, both to the Jews and Gentiles. This was fulfilled to the letter, when he preached on the day of Pentecost to the Jews, and visited the Gentile Cornelius at his own house. On each occasion he used "the keys," and threw open the door of faith. And of this he seems to have been sensible himself: "God," he says, "made choice among us, that by my mouth the Gentiles should hear the word of the Gospel, and believe." (Acts xv. 7.)

Finally, what are we to understand, when we read the words, "Whatsoever thou shalt bind on earth shall be bound in heaven, and whatsoever thou shalt loose on earth shall be loosed in heaven?" Does this mean that the apostle Peter was to have any power of forgiving sins, and absolving sinners? Such an idea is derogatory to Christ's special office, as our Great High Priest. It is a power which we never find Peter, or any of the apostles, once exercising. They always refer men to Christ.

The true meaning of this promise appears to be, that Peter and his brethren, the apostles, were to be specially commissioned to teach with authority the way of salvation. As the Old Testament priest declared authoritatively whose leprosy was cleansed, so the apostles were appointed to "declare and pronounce" authoritatively, whose sins were forgiven.—Beside this, they were to be specially inspired to lay down rules and regulations for the guidance of the Church on disputed questions. Some things they were to "bind" or forbid;—others they were to "loose" or allow. The decision of the council at Jerusalem, that the Gentiles need not be circumcised, was one example of the exercise of this power. (Acts xvi. 19.) But it was a commission specially confined to the apostles. In discharging it they had no successors. With them it began, and with them it expired.

We will leave these controverted words here. Enough perhaps has been said upon them for our personal edification. Let us only remember that, in whatever sense men take them, they have nothing to do with the Church of Rome. Let us now turn our attention to points which more immediately concern our own souls.

In the first place, let us admire *the noble confession which the apostle Peter makes in this passage.* He says, in reply to our Lord's question, "Whom say ye that I am?"—"Thou art the Christ, the Son of the living God."

At first sight a careless reader may see nothing very remarkable in these words of the apostle. He may think it extraordinary that they should call forth such strong commendation from our Lord. But such thoughts arise from ignorance and inconsideration. Men forget that it is a widely different thing to believe in Christ's divine mission, when we dwell in the midst of professing Christians, and to believe in it when we dwell in the midst of hardened and unbelieving Jews. The glory of Peter's confession lies in this, that he made it when few

were with Christ and many against Him. He made it
when the rulers of his own nation, the Scribes, and
Priests, and Pharisees, were all opposed to his Master.
He made it when our Lord was in the "form of a servant,"
without wealth, without royal dignity, without any visible
marks of a King. To make such a confession at such a
time, required great faith and great decision of character.
The confession itself, as Brentius says, "was an epitome
of all Christianity, and a compendium of true doctrine
about religion." Therefore it was that our Lord said,
"Blessed art thou, Simon Bar-jona."

We shall do well to copy that hearty zeal and
affection which Peter here displayed. We are perhaps
too much disposed to underrate this holy man, because of
his occasional instability, and his thrice-repeated denial of
his Lord. This is a great mistake. With all his faults,
Peter was a true-hearted, fervent, single-minded servant
of Christ. With all his imperfections, he has given us a
pattern that many Christians would do wisely to follow.
Zeal like his may have its ebbs and flows, and sometimes lack steadiness of purpose. Zeal like his may be
ill-directed, and sometimes make sad mistakes. But
zeal like his is not to be despised. It awakens the sleeping. It stirs the sluggish. It provokes others to
exertion. Anything is better than sluggishness, luke-
warmness, and torpor, in the Church of Christ. Happy
would it have been for Christendom had there been more
Christians like Peter and Martin Luther, and fewer like
Erasmus.

In the next place, let us take care that *we understand
what our Lord means when He speaks of His Church.*

The Church which Jesus promises to build upon a rock, is the "blessed company of all faithful people." It is not the visible church of any one nation, or country, or place. It is the whole body of believers of every age, and tongue, and people. It is a church composed of all who are washed in Christ's blood, clothed in Christ's righteousness, renewed by Christ's Spirit, joined to Christ by faith, and epistles of Christ in life. It is a church of which every member is baptized with the Holy Ghost, and is really and truly holy. It is a church which is one body. All who belong to it are of one heart and one mind, hold the same truths, and believe the same doctrines as necessary to salvation. It is a church which has only one Head. That Head is Jesus Christ Himself. "He is the head of the body." (Col. i. 18.)

Let us beware of mistakes on this subject. Few words are so much misunderstood as the word "Church." Few mistakes have so much injured the cause of pure religion. Ignorance on this point has been a fertile source of bigotry, sectarianism, and persecution. Men have wrangled and contended about Episcopal, Presbyterian, and Independent Churches, as if it were needful to salvation to belong to some particular party, and as if, belonging to that party, we must of course belong to Christ. And all this time they have lost sight of the one true Church, outside of which there is no salvation at all. It will matter nothing at the last day where we have worshipped, if we are not found members of the true Church of God's elect.

In the last place, let us mark *the glorious promises which our Lord makes to His Church:* He says, "the gates of hell shall not prevail against it."

The meaning of this promise is, that the power of Satan shall never destroy the people of Christ. He that brought sin and death into the first creation, by tempting Eve, shall never bring ruin on the new creation, by over-throwing believers. The mystical body of Christ shall never perish or decay. Though often persecuted, afflicted, distressed, and brought low, it shall never come to an end. It shall outlive the wrath of Pharaohs and Roman Emperors. Visible churches, like Ephesus, may come to nothing. But the true Church never dies. Like the bush that Moses saw, it may burn, but shall not be consumed. *Every* member of it shall be brought safe to glory. In spite of falls, failures, and short-comings,—in spite of the world, the flesh, and the devil,—no member of the true Church shall ever be cast away. (John x. 28.)

MATTHEW XVI. 21—23.

21 From that time forth began Jesus to shew unto his disciples, how that he must go unto Jerusalem, and suffer many things of the elders and Chief Priests and Scribes, and be killed, and be raised again the third day.

22 Then Peter took him, and began to rebuke him, saying, Be it far from thee, Lord: this shall not be unto thee.

23 But he turned, and said unto Peter, Get thee behind me, Satan: thou art an offence unto me: for thou savourest not the things that be of God, but those that be of men.

In the beginning of these verses we find our Lord revealing to His disciples a great and startling truth. That truth was His approaching death upon the cross. For the first time He places before their minds the astounding announcement, that "He must go to Jerusalem, and suffer,—and be killed." He had not come on earth to take a kingdom, but to die. He had not come to reign, and be ministered to, but to shed His blood as a sacrifice, and to give His life as a ransom for many.

It is almost impossible for us to conceive how strange and incomprehensible these tidings must have seemed to His disciples. Like most of the Jews, they could form no idea of a suffering Messiah. They did not understand that the fifty-third chapter of Isaiah must be literally fulfilled. They did not see that the sacrifices of the law were all meant to point them to the death of the true Lamb of God. They thought of nothing but the second glorious coming of Messiah, which is yet to take place at the end of the world. They thought so much of Messiah's crown, that they lost sight of His cross. We shall do well to remember this. A right understanding of this matter throws strong light on the lessons which this passage contains.

We learn, in the first place, from these verses, that *there may be much spiritual ignorance even in a true disciple of Christ.*

We cannot have a clearer proof of this, than the conduct of the apostle Peter in this passage. He tries to dissuade our Lord from suffering on the cross. "Be it far from thee," he says, "this shall not be unto thee." He did not see the full purpose of our Lord's coming into the world. His eyes were blinded to the necessity of our Lord's death. He actually did what he could, to prevent that death taking place at all! And yet we know that Peter was a converted man. He really believed that Jesus was the Messiah. His heart was right in the sight of God.

These things are meant to teach us that we must neither regard good men as infallible, because they are good men, nor yet suppose they have no grace, because their grace is weak and small. One brother may possess singular gifts, and be a bright and shining light in the Church of Christ. But let us not forget that he is a man, and as a man liable to commit great mistakes.—Another brother's knowledge may be scanty. He may fail to judge rightly on many points of doctrine. He may err both in word and deed. But has he faith and love towards Christ? Does he hold the Head? If so, let us deal patiently with him. What he sees not now, he may see hereafter. Like Peter, he may now be in the dark, and yet, like Peter, enjoy one day the full light of the Gospel.

Let us learn, in the second place, from these verses, that *there is no doctrine of Scripture so deeply important as the doctrine of Christ's atoning death.*

We cannot have clearer proof of this, than the language used by our Lord in rebuking Peter. He addresses him by the awful name of "Satan," as if he was an adversary, and doing the devil's work, in trying to prevent His death. He says to him, whom he had so lately called "blessed," "Get thee behind me, thou art an offence unto me." He tells the man whose noble confession he had just commended so highly, "Thou savourest not the things that be of God, but those that be of men." Stronger words than these never fell from our Lord's lips. The error that drew from so loving a Saviour such a stern rebuke to such a true disciple, must have been a mighty error indeed.

The truth is, that our Lord would have us regard the crucifixion as the central truth of Christianity. Right views of His vicarious death, and the benefits resulting from it, lie at the very foundation of Bible-religion. Never let us forget this. On matters of church government, and the form of worship, men may differ from us, and yet reach heaven in safety. On the matter of Christ's atoning death, as the way of peace, truth is only one. If we are wrong here, we are ruined for ever. Error on many points is only a skin disease. Error about Christ's death is a disease at the heart. Here let us take our stand. Let nothing move us from this ground. The sum of all our hopes must be, that " Christ has died for us." (1 Thess. v. 10.) Give up that doctrine, and we have no solid hope at all.

MATTHEW XVI. 24—28.

24 Then said Jesus unto his disciples, If any *man* will come after me, let him deny himself, and take up his cross, and follow me.

25 For whosoever will save his life shall lose it: and whosoever will lose his life for my sake shall find it.

26 For what is a man profited, if he shall gain the whole world, and lose his own soul? or what shall a man give in exchange for his soul?

27 For the Son of man shall come in the glory of his Father with his angels; and then he shall reward every man according to his works.

28 Verily I say unto you, There be some standing here, which shall not taste of death, till they see the Son of man coming in his kingdom.

IN order to see the connection of these verses, we must remember the mistaken impressions of our Lord's disciples as to the purpose of His coming into the world. Like Peter, they could not bear the idea of the crucifixion. They thought that Jesus had come to set up an earthly kingdom. They did not see that He must needs suffer and die. They dreamed of worldly honours and temporal rewards in their Master's service. They did not understand that true Christians, like Christ, must be made perfect through sufferings. Our Lord corrects these misapprehensions in words of peculiar solemnity, which we shall do well to lay up in our hearts.

Let us learn, in the first place, from these verses, *that men must make up their minds to trouble and self-denial, if they follow Christ.*

Our Lord dispels the fond dreams of His disciples, by telling them that His followers must "take up the cross." The glorious kingdom they were expecting, was not about to be set up immediately. They must make up their minds to persecution and affliction, if they intended to be His servants. They must be content to "lose their lives," if they would have their souls saved.

It is good for us all to see this point clearly. We must not conceal from ourselves that true Christianity brings with it a daily cross in this life, while it offers us a crown of glory in the life to come. The flesh must be daily crucified. The devil must be daily resisted. The world must be daily overcome. There is a warfare to be waged, and a battle to be fought. All this is the inseparable accompaniment of true religion. Heaven is not to be won without it. Never was there a truer word than the old saying, "No cross, no crown!" If we never found this out by experience, our souls are in a poor condition.

Let us learn, in the second place, from these verses, *that there is nothing so precious as a man's soul.*

Our Lord teaches this lesson by asking one of the most solemn questions that the New Testament contains. It is a question so well known, and so often repeated, that people often lose sight of its searching character. But it is a question that ought to sound in our ears like a trumpet, whenever we are tempted to neglect our eternal interests : "What shall it profit a man if he gain the whole world and lose his own soul?"

There can only be one answer to this question. There is nothing on earth, or under the earth, that can make amends to us for the loss of our souls. There is nothing that money can buy, or man can give, to be named in comparison with our souls. The world, and all that it contains, is temporal. It is all fading, perishing, and passing away. The soul is *eternal*. That one single word is the key to the whole question. Let it sink down deeply into our hearts. Are we wavering in our religion? Do we fear the cross? Does the way seem too narrow? Let our Master's words ring in our ears, "What shall it profit a man?" and let us doubt no more.

Let us learn, in the last place, *that the second coming of Christ is the time when His people shall receive their rewards.* "The Son of Man shall come in the glory of His Father, and then shall he reward every man according to his works."

There is deep wisdom in this saying of our Lord's, when viewed in connection with the preceding verses. He knows the heart of a man. He knows how soon we are ready to be cast down, and like Israel of old, to be "discouraged by the way." (Num. xxi. 4.) He therefore holds out to us a gracious promise. He reminds us that He has yet to come a second time, as surely as He came the first time. He tells us that this is the time when His disciples shall receive their good things. There will be glory, honour, and reward in abundance one day for all who have served and loved Jesus. But it is to be in the dispensation of the second advent, and not of the first. The bitter must come before the sweet, the cross before the crown. The first advent is the dispensation of the crucifixion. The second advent is the dispensation of the kingdom. We must submit to take part with our Lord in His humiliation, if we mean ever to share in his glory.

And now let us not leave these verses without serious self-inquiry as to the matters which they contain. We have heard of the necessity of taking up the cross, and denying ourselves. Have we taken it up, and are we carrying it daily?—We have heard of the value of the soul. Do we live as if we believed it?—We have heard of Christ's second advent. Do we look forward to it with hope and joy?—Happy is that man who can give a satisfactory answer to these questions.

MATTHEW XVII. 1—13.

1 And after six days Jesus taketh Peter, James, and John his brother, and bringeth them up into an high mountain apart.

2 And was transfigured before them: and his face did shine as the sun, and his raiment was white as the light.

3 And, behold, there appeared unto them Moses and Elias talking with him.

4 Then answered Peter, and said unto Jesus, Lord, it is good for us to be here: if thou wilt, let us make here three tabernacles; one for thee, and one for Moses, and one for Elias.

5 While he yet spake, behold, a bright cloud overshadowed them: and behold a voice out of the cloud, which said, This is my beloved Son, in whom I am well pleased; hear ye him.

6 And when the disciples heard it, they fell on their face, and were sore afraid.

7 And Jesus came and touched them and said, Arise, and be not afraid.

8 And when they had lifted up their eyes, they saw no man, save Jesus only.

9 And as they came down from the mountain, Jesus charged them, saying, Tell the vision to no man, until the Son of man be risen again from the dead.

10 And his disciples asked him, saying, Why then say the Scribes that Elias must first come?

11 And Jesus answered and said unto them, Elias truly shall first come, and restore all things.

12 But I say unto you, That Elias is come already, and they knew him not, but have done unto him whatsoever they listed. Likewise shall also the Son of man suffer of them.

13 Then the disciples understood that he spake unto them of John the Baptist.

THESE verses contain one of the most remarkable events in our Lord's earthly ministry,—the event commonly called the transfiguration. The order in which it is recorded is beautiful and instructive. The latter part of the last chapter showed us the cross. Here we are graciously allowed to see something of the coming reward. The hearts which have just been saddened by a plain statement of Christ's sufferings, are at once gladdened by a vision of Christ's glory. Let us mark this. We often lose much by not tracing the connection between chapter and chapter in the word of God.

There are some mysterious things, no doubt, in the vision here described. It must needs be so. We are yet in the body. Our senses are conversant with gross and material things. Our ideas and perceptions about glorified bodies and dead saints, must necessarily be vague and imperfect. Let us content ourselves with endeavouring to mark out the practical lessons which the transfiguration is meant to teach us.

In the first place, we have in these verses a *striking pattern of the glory in which Christ and His people will appear, when He comes the second time.*

There can be little question that this was one main object of this wonderful vision. It was meant to encourage the disciples, by giving them a glimpse of good things yet to come. That "face shining as the sun," and that "raiment white as the light," were intended to give the disciples some idea of the majesty in which Jesus will appear to the world, when He comes the second time, and all His saints with Him. The corner of the veil was lifted up, to show them their Master's true dignity. They were taught that, if He did not yet appear to the world in the guise of a king, it was only because the time for putting on His royal apparel was not yet come. It is impossible to draw any other conclusion from St. Peter's language, when writing on the subject. He says, with distinct reference to the transfiguration, "We were eye witnesses of his majesty." (2 Peter i. 16.)

It is good for us to have the coming glory of Christ and His people deeply impressed on our minds. We are sadly apt to forget it. There are few visible indications of it in the world.—We see not yet all things put under our Lord's feet. Sin, unbelief, and superstition abound. Thousands are practically saying, "We will not have this man to reign over us."—It doth not yet appear what His people shall be. Their crosses, their tribulations, their weaknesses, their conflicts, are all manifest enough. But there are few signs of their future reward. Let us beware of giving way to doubts in this matter. Let us silence such doubts by reading over the history of the transfiguration. There is laid up for Jesus, and all that believe on Him, such glory as the heart of man never conceived. It is not only promised, but part of it has actually been seen by three competent witnesses. One of them says, "We beheld his glory, the glory as of the only begotten of the Father." (John i. 14.) Surely that which has been seen may well be believed.

In the second place, we have in these verses, *an unanswerable proof of the resurrection of the body, and the life after death.* We are told that Moses and Elijah appeared visibly in glory with Christ. They were seen in a bodily form. They were heard talking with our Lord. Fourteen hundred and eighty years had rolled round, since

Moses died and was buried. More than nine hundred years had passed away, since Elijah "went up by a whirlwind into heaven." Yet here they are seen alive by Peter, James, and John!

Let us lay firm hold on this part of the vision. It deserves close attention. We must all feel, if we ever think at all, that the state of the dead is a wonderful and mysterious subject. One after another we bury them out of our sight. We lay them in their narrow beds, and see them no more, and their bodies become dust. But will they really live again? Shall we really see them any more? Will the grave really give back the dead at the last day? These are questions that will occasionally come across the minds of some, in spite of all the plainest statements in the word of God.

Now we have in the transfiguration the clearest evidence that the dead will rise again. We find two men appearing on earth, in their bodies, who had long been separate from the land of the living,—and in them we have a pledge of the resurrection of all. All that have ever lived upon earth will again be called to life, and render up their account. Not one will be found missing. There is no such thing as annihilation. All that have ever fallen asleep in Christ will be found in safe keeping,—patriarchs, prophets, apostles, martyrs,—down to the humblest servant of God in our own day. Though unseen to us, they all live to God. "He is not a God of the dead, but of the living." (Luke xx. 20.) Their spirits live as surely as we live ourselves, and will appear hereafter in glorified bodies, as surely as Moses and Elijah in the mount. These are indeed solemn thoughts! There is a resurrection, and men like Felix may well tremble. There is a resurrection, and men like Paul may well rejoice.

In the last place, we have in these verses *a remarkable testimony to Christ's infinite superiority over all that are born of woman.*

This is a point which is brought out strongly by the voice from heaven, which the disciples heard. Peter, bewildered by the heavenly vision, and not knowing what to say, proposed to build three tabernacles, one for Christ, one for Moses, and one for Elijah. He seemed in fact to place the law-giver and the prophet side by side with his divine Master, as if all three were equal. At once, we are told, the proposal was rebuked in a marked manner.—A cloud covered Moses and Elijah, and they were no more seen.—A voice at the same time came forth from the cloud, repeating the solemn words, made use of at our Lord's baptism, "This is my beloved Son, in whom I am well pleased: hear ye Him." That voice was meant to teach Peter, that there was one there far greater than Moses or Elijah. Moses was a faithful servant of God. Elijah was a bold witness for the truth. But Christ was far above either one or the other. He was the Saviour to whom law and prophets were continually pointing. He was the true Prophet, whom all were commanded to hear. (Deut. xviii. 15.) Moses and Elijah were great men in their day. But Peter and his companions were to remember, that in nature, dignity, and office, they were far below Christ.—He was the true sun: they were the stars depending daily on His light.—He was the root: they were the branches.—He was the Master:

they were the servants.—Their goodness was all derived:
His was original and His own.—Let them honour Moses
and the prophets, as holy men. But if they would be
saved, they must take Christ alone for their Master, and
glory only in Him. "Hear ye Him."

Let us see in these words a striking lesson to the
whole Church of Christ. There is a constant tendency
in human nature to "hear man." Bishops, priests, deacons, popes, cardinals, councils, presbyterian preachers,
and independent ministers, are continually exalted to a
place which God never intended them to fill, and made
practically to usurp the honour of Christ. Against this
tendency let us all watch, and be on our guard. Let
these solemn words of the vision ever ring in our ears,
"Hear ye Christ."

The best of men are only men at their very best.
Patriarchs, prophets, and apostles,—martyrs, fathers,
reformers, puritans,—all, all are sinners, who need a
Saviour,—holy, useful, honourable in their place,—but
sinners after all. They must never be allowed to stand
between us and Christ. He alone is "the Son, in whom
the Father is well pleased." He alone is sealed and
appointed to give the bread of life. He alone has the
keys in His hands, "God over all, blessed for ever." Let
us take heed that we hear His voice, and follow Him.
Let us value all religious teaching just in proportion as it
leads us to Jesus. The sum and substance of saving
religion is to "hear Christ."

MATTHEW XVII. 14—21.

14 And when they were come to the multitude, there came to him a *certain* man, kneeling down to him, and saying,

15 Lord, have mercy on my son: for he is lunatick, and sore vexed: for ofttimes he falleth into the fire, and oft into the water.

16 And I brought him to thy disciples, and they could not cure him.

17 Then Jesus answered and said, O faithless and perverse generation, how long shall I be with you? how long shall I suffer you? bring him hither to me.

18 And Jesus rebuked the devil; and he departed out of him: and the child was cured from that very hour.

19 Then came the disciples to Jesus apart, and said, Why could not we cast him out?

20 And Jesus said unto them, Because of your unbelief: for verily I say unto you, If ye have faith as a grain of mustard seed, ye shall say unto this mountain, Remove hence to yonder place; and it shall remove; and nothing shall be impossible unto you.

21 Howbeit this kind goeth not out but by prayer and fasting.

WE read in this passage another of our Lord's great miracles. He heals a young man lunatic and possessed with a devil.

The first thing we see in these verses is *a lively emblem of the awful influence sometimes exercised by Satan over the young.* We are told of a certain man's son, who was "lunatic and sore vexed." We are told of the evil spirit pressing him on to the destruction of body and soul. "Oft-times he falleth into the fire, and oft into the water." It was one of those cases of Satanic possession, which, however common in our Lord's times, in our own day is rarely seen. But we can easily imagine that, when they did occur, they must have been peculiarly distressing to the relations of the afflicted. It is painful enough to see the bodies of those we love racked by disease. How much more painful must it have been to see body and mind completely under the influence of the devil. "Out of hell," says Bishop Hall, "there could not be greater misery."

But we must not forget that there are many instances

of Satan's spiritual dominion over young people, which are quite as painful, in their way, as the case described in this passage. There are thousands of young men who seem to have wholly given themselves up to Satan's temptations, and to be led captive at his will. They cast off all fear of God, and all respect for his commandments. They serve divers lusts and pleasures. They run wildly into every excess of riot. They refuse to listen to the advice of parents, teachers, or ministers. They fling aside all regard for health, character, or worldly respectability. They do all that lies in their power to ruin themselves, body and soul, for time and eternity. They are willing bondslaves of Satan.—Who has not seen such young men? They are to be seen in town and in country. They are to be found among rich and among poor. Surely such young men give mournful proof, that although Satan now-a-days seldom has possession of man's body, he still exercises a fearful dominion over some men's souls.

Yet even about such young men as these, be it remembered, we must never despair. We must call to mind the almighty power of our Lord Jesus Christ. Bad as this boy's case was, of whom we read in these verses, he was "cured from the very hour" that he was brought to Christ! Parents, and teachers, and ministers should go on praying for young men, even at their worst. Hard as their hearts seem now, they may yet be softened. Desperate as their wickedness now appears, they may yet be healed. They may yet repent, and be converted, like John Newton, and their last state prove better than their first. Who can tell? Let it be a settled principle with us, when we read our Lord's miracles, never to despair of the conversion of any soul.

In the second place, we see in these verses *a striking example of the weakening effect of unbelief.* The disciples anxiously inquired of our Lord, when they saw the devil yielding to his power, "Why could not we cast him out?" They received an answer full of the deepest instruction,—"because of your unbelief." Would they know the secret of their own sad failure in the hour of need? It was want of faith.

Let us ponder this point well, and learn wisdom. Faith is the key to success in the Christian warfare. Unbelief is the sure road to defeat. Once let our faith languish and decay, and all our graces will languish with it. Courage, patience, long-suffering, and hope, will soon wither and dwindle away. Faith is the root on which they all depend. The same Israelites who at one time went through the Red Sea in triumph, at another time shrunk from danger, like cowards, when they reached the borders of the promised land. Their God was the same who had brought them out of the land of Egypt. Their leader was that same Moses who had wrought so many wonders before their eyes. But their faith was not the same. They gave way to shameful doubts of God's love and power. "They could not enter in because of unbelief." (Heb. iii. 19.)

In the last place, we see in these verses *that Satan's kingdom is not to be pulled down without diligence and pains.* This seems to be the lesson of the verse which concludes the passage we are now considering: "This kind goeth not out but by prayer and fasting." A

gentle rebuke to the disciples appears to be implied in
the words.   Perhaps they had been too much lifted up
by past successes.   Perhaps they had been less careful
in the use of means in their Master's absence, than they
were under their Master's eye.   At any rate they receive
a plain hint from our Lord, that the warfare against
Satan must never be lightly carried on.   They are
warned that no victories are to be won easily over the
prince of this world.   Without fervent prayer, and
diligent self-mortification, they would often meet with
failure and defeat.

The lesson here laid down is one of deep importance.
"I would," says Bullinger, "that this part of the Gospel
pleased us as much as those parts which concede liberty."
We are all apt to contract a habit of doing religious acts
in a thoughtless, perfunctory way.   Like Israel, puffed
up with the fall of Jericho, we are ready to say to ourselves, "The men of Ai are but few;" (Josh. vii. 3.)
"there is no need to put forth all our strength."   Like
Israel, we often learn by bitter experience, that spiritual
battles are not to be won without hard fighting.   The
ark of the Lord must never be handled irreverently.
God's work must never be carelessly done.

May we all bear in mind our Lord's words to His disciples, and make a practical use of them.   In the pulpit, and
on the platform,—in the Sunday school, and in the district,—in our use of family prayers, and in reading our
own Bibles,—let us diligently watch our own spirit.
Whatever we do, let us "do it with our might." (Eccles.
ix. 10.) It is a fatal mistake to underrate our foes. Greater
is He that is for us than he that is against us,—but, for all

that, he that is against us is not to be despised. He is the prince of this world. He is a strong man armed, keeping his house, who will not "go out," and part with his goods without a struggle. We wrestle not against flesh and blood, but against principalities and powers. We have need to take the whole armour of God, and not only to take it, but to use it too. We may be very sure that those who win most victories over the world, the flesh, and the devil, are those who pray most in private, and "keep under their bodies, and bring them into subjection." (1 Cor. ix. 27.)

MATTHEW XVII. 22—27.

22 And while they abode in Galilee, Jesus said unto them, The Son of man shall be betrayed into the hands of men:
23 And they shall kill him, and the third day he shall be raised again. And they were exceeding sorry.
24 And when they were come to Capernaum, they that received tribute *money* came to Peter, and said, Doth not your master pay tribute?
25 He saith, Yes. And when he was come into the house, Jesus prevented him, saying, What thinkest thou, Simon? of whom do the kings of the earth take custom or tribute? of their own children, or of strangers?
26 Peter saith unto him, Of strangers. Jesus saith unto him, Then are the children free.
27 Notwithstanding, lest we should offend them, go thou to the sea, and cast an hook, and take up the fish that first cometh up; and when thou hast opened his mouth, thou shalt find a piece of money: that take, and give unto them for me and thee.

THESE verses contain a circumstance in our Lord's history, which is not recorded by any of the evangelists excepting St. Matthew. A remarkable miracle is worked in order to provide payment of the tribute-money, required for the service of the temple. There are three striking points in the narrative, which deserve attentive observation.

Let us observe, in the first place, *our Lord's perfect knowledge of everything that is said and done in this world.* We are told that those who "received tribute-money came to Peter and said, Doth not your Master pay tribute? He saith, Yes." It is evident that our Lord was not present, when the question was asked and the answer given. And yet no sooner did Peter come into the house than our Lord asked him, "What thinkest thou, Simon? of whom do the kings of the earth take custom or tribute?" He showed that He was as well acquainted with the conversation, as if He had been listening or standing by.

There is something unspeakably solemn in the thought that the Lord Jesus knows all things. There is an eye that sees all our daily conduct. There is an ear that hears all our daily words. All things are naked and opened unto the eyes of Him, with whom we have to do. Concealment is impossible. Hypocrisy is useless. We may deceive ministers. We may impose upon our relations and neighbours. But the Lord sees us through and through. We cannot deceive Christ.

We ought to endeavour to make practical use of this truth. We should strive to live as in the Lord's sight, and, like Abraham, to "walk before him." (Gen. xvii. 1.) Let it be our daily aim to say nothing we would not like Christ to hear, and to do nothing we would not like Christ to see. Let us measure every difficult question as to right and wrong by one simple test, "How would I behave, if Jesus was standing by my side?" Such a standard is not extravagant and absurd. It is a standard that interferes with no duty or relation of life. It interferes with nothing but sin. Happy is he that tries to realize his Lord's presence, and to do all and say all as unto Christ.

Let us observe, in the next place, *our Lord's almighty power over all creation.* He makes a fish his paymaster. He makes a dumb creature bring the tribute-money to meet the collector's demand. Well says Jerome, "I know not which to admire most here, our Lord's foreknowledge or His greatness."

We see here a literal fulfilment of the Psalmist's words, "Thou madest him to have dominion over the works of thine hands; thou hast put all things under His feet;—the fowl of the air and the fish of the sea, and whatsoever passeth through the paths of the seas." (Psalm viii. 6—8.)

Here is one among many proofs of the majesty and greatness of our Lord Jesus Christ. He only who first created, could at His will command the obedience of all His creatures. "By Him were all things created.—By Him all things consist." (Col. i. 16—18.) The believer who goes forth to do Christ's work among the heathen, may safely commit himself to his Master's keeping. He serves one who has all power, even over the beasts of the earth.

How wonderful the thought, that such an Almighty Lord should condescend to be crucified for our salvation! How comfortable the thought that when He comes again the second time, He will gloriously manifest His power over all created things to the whole world: "The wolf and the lamb shall feed together, and the lion shall eat straw like the bullock: and dust shall be the serpent's meat." (Isaiah lxv. 25.)

In the last place, let us observe, in these verses, *our Lord's willingness to make concessions, rather than give offence.* He might justly have claimed exemption from the payment of this tribute-money. He, who was Son of God, might fairly have been excused from paying for the maintenance of His Father's house. He, who was "greater than the temple," might have shown good cause for declining to contribute to the support of the temple. But our Lord does not do so. He claims no exemption. He desires Peter to pay the money demanded. At the same time He declares His reasons. It was to be done, "lest we should offend them." "A miracle is worked," says Bishop Hall, "rather than offend even a tax-collector."

Our Lord's example in this case deserves attention of all who profess and call themselves Christians. There is deep wisdom in those five words, "lest we should offend them." They teach us plainly, that there are matters in which Christ's people ought to sink their own opinions, and submit to requirements which they may not thoroughly approve, rather than give offence and "hinder the Gospel of Christ." God's rights undoubtedly we ought never to give up; but we may sometimes safely give up our own. It may sound very fine and seem very heroic to be always standing out tenaciously for our *rights*. But it may well be doubted, with such a passage as this, whether such tenacity is always wise, and shows the mind of Christ. There are occasions, when it shows more grace in a Christian to submit than to resist.

Let us remember this passage as *citizens and subjects*. We may not like all the political measures of our rulers. We may disapprove of some of the taxes they impose. But the grand question after all is, Will it do any good to the cause of religion to resist the powers that be? Are their measures really injuring our souls? If not, let us hold our peace, "lest we should offend them." "A Christian," says Bullinger, "never ought to disturb the public peace for things of mere temporary importance."

Let us remember this passage as *members of a church*. We may not like every jot and tittle of the forms and ceremonies used in our communion. We may not think that those who rule us in spiritual matters are always wise. But after all, Are the points on which we are dissatisfied really of vital importance? Is any great truth of the Gospel at stake? If not, let us be quiet, "lest we should offend them."

Let us remember this passage as *members of society*. There may be usages and customs in the circle where our lot is cast, which to us, as Christians, are tiresome, useless, and unprofitable. But are they matters of principle? Do they injure our souls? Will it do any good to the cause of religion, if we refuse to comply with them? If not, let us patiently submit, "lest we should offend them."

Well would it be for the church and the world, if these five words of our Lord had been more studied, pondered, and used! Who can tell the damage that has been done to the cause of the Gospel, by morbid scrupulosity, and conscientiousness, falsely so called! May we all remember the example of the great apostle of the Gentiles;—"we suffer all things, lest we should hinder the Gospel of Christ." (1 Cor. ix. 12.)

MATTHEW XVIII. 1—14.

1 At the same time came the disciples unto Jesus, saying, Who is the greatest in the kingdom of heaven?

2 And Jesus called a little child unto him, and set him in the midst of them,

3 And said, Verily I say unto you, Except ye be converted, and become

as little children, ye shall not enter into the kingdom of heaven.

4 Whosoever therefore shall humble himself as this little child, the same is greatest in the kingdom of heaven.

5 And whoso shall receive one such little child in my name receiveth me.

6 But whoso shall offend one of these little ones which believe in me, it were better for him that a millstone were hanged about his neck, and *that* he were drowned in the depth of the sea.

7 Woe unto the world because of offences! for it must needs be that offences come; but woe to that man by whom the offence cometh!

8 Wherefore if thy hand or thy foot offend thee, cut them off, and cast *them* from thee: it is better for thee to enter into life halt or maimed, rather than having two hands or two feet to be cast into everlasting fire.

9 And if thine eye offend thee, pluck it out, and cast *it* from thee: it is better for thee to enter into life with one eye, rather than having two eyes to be cast into hell fire.

10 Take heed that ye despise not one of these little ones; for I say unto you, That in heaven their angels do always behold the face of my Father which is in heaven.

11 For the Son of man is come to save that which was lost.

12 How think ye? if a man have an hundred sheep, and one of them be gone astray, doth he not leave the ninety and nine, and goeth into the mountains, and seeketh that which is gone astray?

13 And if so be that he find it, verily I say unto you, he rejoiceth more of that *sheep*, than of the ninety and nine which went not astray.

14 Even so it is not the will of your Father which is in heaven, that one of these little ones should perish.

THE first thing that we are taught in these verses, is *the necessity of conversion, and of conversion manifested by childlike humility.* The disciples came to our Lord with the question, "Who is the greatest in the kingdom of heaven?" They spoke as men half-enlightened, and full of carnal expectations. They received an answer well calculated to awaken them from their day-dream,—an answer containing a truth which lies at the very foundation of Christianity,—"except ye be converted, and become as little children, ye shall not enter into the kingdom of heaven."

Let these words sink down deeply into our hearts. Without conversion there is no salvation. We all need an entire change of nature. Of ourselves we have neither faith, nor fear, nor love towards God. "We must be born again." Of ourselves we are utterly unfit for dwelling in God's presence. Heaven would be no heaven to us if we were not converted. It is true of all ranks, classes, and orders of mankind. All are born in sin and children of wrath, and all, without exception, need to be born again and made new creatures. A new heart must be given to us, and a new spirit put within us. Old things must pass away, and all things must become new. It is a good thing to be baptized into the Christian Church, and use Christian means of grace. But after all, "are we converted?"

Would we know whether we are really converted? Would we know the test by which we must try ourselves? The surest mark of true conversion is humility. If we have really received the Holy Ghost, we shall show it by a meek and childlike spirit. Like children, we shall think humbly of our own strength and wisdom, and be very dependent on our Father in heaven. Like children, we shall not seek great things in this world; and having food and raiment and a Father's love, we shall be content. Truly this is a heart-searching test! It exposes the unsoundness of many a so-called conversion. It is easy to be a convert from one party to another party, from one sect to another sect, from one set of opinions to another set of opinions. Such conversions save no one's soul. What we all want is a conversion from pride to humility,—from high thoughts of ourselves to lowly thoughts of ourselves,—from self-conceit to self-abasement,—from the mind of the Pharisee to the mind of the Publican.—A conversion of this kind we must experience, if we hope to be saved. These are the conversions that are wrought by the Holy Ghost.

The next thing that we are taught in these verses, is

*the great sin of putting stumblingblocks in the way of
believers.* The words of the Lord Jesus on this subject
are peculiarly solemn. " Woe unto the world because of
offences ! — Woe to that man by whom the offence
cometh."

We put offences or stumblingblocks in the way of
men's souls, whenever we do anything to keep them
back from Christ, — or to turn them out of the way of
salvation, — or to disgust them with true religion. We
may do it directly by persecuting, ridiculing, opposing,
or dissuading them from decided service of Christ. We
may do it indirectly by living a life inconsistent with our
religious profession, and by making Christianity loathsome and distasteful by our own conduct. Whenever we
do anything of the kind, it is clear, from our Lord's
words, that we commit a great sin.

There is something very fearful in the doctrine here laid
down. It ought to stir up within us great searchings of
heart. It is not enough that we wish to do good in this
world. Are we quite sure that we are not doing harm ?
— We may not openly persecute Christ's servants. But are
there none that we are injuring by our ways and our example ? It is awful to think of the amount of harm that can
be done by one inconsistent professor of religion. He gives
a handle to the infidel. He supplies the worldly man
with an excuse for remaining undecided. He checks the
inquirer after salvation. He discourages the saints. He
is, in short, a living sermon on behalf of the devil. The
last day alone will reveal the wholesale ruin of souls,
that " offences " have occasioned in the Church of
Christ. One of Nathan's charges against David was,

"thou hast given great occasion to the enemies of the Lord to blaspheme." (2 Sam. xii. 14.)

The next thing that we are taught in these verses, is *the reality of future punishment after death.* Two strong expressions are used by our Lord on this point. He speaks of being "cast into everlasting fire." He speaks of being "cast into hell fire."

The meaning of these words is clear and unmistakeable. There is a place of unspeakable misery in the world to come, to which all who die impenitent and unbelieving, must ultimately be consigned. There is revealed in Scripture a "fiery indignation," which sooner or later will devour all God's adversaries. (Heb. x. 27.) The same sure word which holds out a heaven to all who repent and are converted, declares plainly that there will be a hell for all the ungodly.

Let no man deceive us with vain words upon this awful subject. Men have arisen in these latter days, who profess to deny the eternity of future punishment, and repeat the devil's old argument, that we "shall not surely die." (Gen. iii. 4.) Let none of their reasonings move us, however plausible they may sound. Let us stand fast in the old paths. The God of love and mercy is also a God of justice. He will surely requite. The flood in Noah's day, and the burning of Sodom, were meant to show us what He will one day do. No lips have ever spoken so clearly about hell as those of Christ himself. Hardened sinners will find out, to their cost, that there is such a thing as the "wrath of the Lamb." (Rev. vi. 17.)

The last thing we are taught in these verses, is *the*

value that God sets on the least and lowest of believers. "It is not the will of your Father in heaven, that one of these little ones should perish."

These words are meant for the encouragement of all true Christians, and not for little children only. The connection in which they are found with the parable of the hundred sheep and one that went astray, seems to place this beyond doubt. They are meant to show us that our Lord Jesus is a Shepherd, who cares tenderly for every soul committed to His charge. The youngest, the weakest, the sickliest of His flock is as dear to Him as the strongest. They shall never perish. None shall ever pluck them out of His hand. He will lead them gently through the wilderness of this world. He will not overdrive them a single day, lest any die. (Gen. xxxiii. 13.) He will carry them through every difficulty. He will defend them against every enemy. The saying which He spoke shall be literally fulfilled : "Of them which thou gavest me have I lost none." (John xviii. 9.) With such a Saviour, who need fear beginning to be a thorough Christian ? With such a Shepherd, who, having once begun, need fear being cast away ?

MATTHEW XVIII. 15—20.

15 Moreover if thy brother shall trespass against thee, go and tell him his fault between thee and him alone : if he shall hear thee, thou hast gained thy brother.

16 But if he will not hear *thee, then* take with thee one or two more, that in the mouth of two or three witnesses every word may be established.

17 And if he shall neglect to hear them, tell *it* unto the Church : but if he neglect to hear the Church, let him be unto thee as a heathen man and a Publican.

18 Verily I say unto you, Whatsoever ye shall bind on earth shall be bound in heaven : and whatsoever ye shall loose on earth shall be loosed in heaven.

19 Again I say unto you, That if

two of you shall agree on earth as touching any thing that they shall ask, it shall be done for them of my Father which is in heaven. | 20 For where two or three are gathered together in my name, there am I in the midst of them.

THESE words of the Lord Jesus contain an expression which has been often misapplied. The command to "hear the church," has been so interpreted as to contradict other passages of God's word. It has been falsely applied to the authority of the whole visible church in matters of doctrine, and so been made an excuse for the exercise of much ecclesiastical tyranny. But the abuse of Scripture truths must not tempt us to neglect the use of them. We must not turn away altogether from any text, because some have perverted it, and made it poison.

Let us notice in the first place, *how admirable are the rules laid down by our Lord, for the healing of differences among brethren.*

If we have unhappily received any injury from a fellow-member of Christ's Church, the first step to be taken is to visit him "alone," and tell him his fault. He may have injured us unintentionally, as Abimelech did Abraham. (Gen. xxi. 26.) His conduct may admit of explanation, like that of the tribes of Reuben, Gad, and Manasseh, when they built an altar, as they returned to their own land. (Joshua xxii. 24.) At any rate, this friendly, faithful, straight-forward way of dealing is the most likely course to win a brother, if he is to be won. "A soft tongue breaketh the bone." (Prov. xxv. 15.) Who can tell but he may say at once, " I was wrong,"— and make ample reparation?

If however this course of proceeding fails to produce any good effect, a second step is to be taken. We are to "take with us one or two" companions, and tell our brother of his fault in their presence and hearing. Who can tell but his conscience may be stricken, when he finds his misconduct made known, and he may be ashamed and repent? If not, we shall at all events have the testimony of witnesses, that we did all we could to bring our brother to a right mind, and that he deliberately refused, when appealed to, to make amends.

Finally, if this second course of proceeding prove useless, we are to refer the whole matter to the Christian *congregation* of which we are members,—we are to "tell it to the church." Who can tell but the heart which has been unmoved by private remonstrances, may be moved by the fear of public exposure? If not, there remains but one view to take of our brother's case,—we must sorrowfully regard him as one who has shaken off all Christian principles, and will be guided by no higher motives than "a heathen man and a publican."

The passage is a beautiful instance of the mingled wisdom and tender consideration of our Lord's teaching. What a knowledge it shows of human nature! Nothing does so much harm to the cause of religion as the quarrels of Christians. No stone should be left unturned, no trouble spared, in order to prevent their being dragged before the public.—What a delicate thoughtfulness it shows for the sensitiveness of poor human nature! Many a scandalous breach would be prevented, if we were more ready to practice the rule of "between thee and him alone." Happy would it be for the Church and the world, if this portion of our Lord's teaching was more carefully studied and obeyed. Differences and divisions there will be, so long as the world stands. But how many of them would be extinguished at once, if the course recommended in these verses was tried.

In the second place, let us observe *what a clear argument we have in these verses for the exercise of discipline in a Christian congregation.*

Our Lord commands disagreements between Christians, which cannot be otherwise settled, to be referred to the decision of the church or Christian assembly to which they belong. "Tell it," he says, "to the church." It is evident from this, that he intends every congregation of professing Christians to take cognizance of the moral conduct of its members, either by the action of the whole body collectively, or of heads and elders to whom its authority may be delegated. It is evident also that He intends every congregation to have the power of excluding disobedient and refractory members from participation in its ordinances. "If he refuse," he says, "to hear the Church, let him be to thee as an heathen man and a publican." He says not a word about temporal punishment, and civil disabilities. Spiritual penalties are the only penalty He permits the Church to inflict, and when rightly inflicted, they are not to be lightly regarded. "Whatsoever ye shall bind on earth shall be bound in heaven." Such appears to be the substance of our Lord's teaching about ecclesiastical discipline.

It is vain to deny that the whole subject is surrounded with difficulties. On no point has the influence of the world weighed so heavily on the action of Churches. On no point have Churches made so many mistakes,— sometimes on the side of sleepy remissness, sometimes on the side of blind severity. No doubt the power of excommunication has been fearfully abused and perverted, and, as Quesnel says, "we ought to be more afraid of our sins than of all the excommunications in the world." Still it is impossible to deny, with such a passage as this before us, that church discipline is according to the mind of Christ, and, when wisely exercised, is calculated to promote a church's health and well-being. It can never be right that all sorts of people, however wicked and ungodly, should be allowed to come to the table of the Lord, no man letting or forbidding. It is the bounden duty of every Christian to use his influence to prevent such a state of things. A perfect communion can never be attained in this world, but purity should be the mark at which we aim. An increasingly high standard of qualification for full church-membership, will always be found one of the best evidences of a prosperous church.

Let us observe, in the last place, *what gracious encouragement Christ holds out to those who meet together in His name.* He says, "Where two or three are gathered together in my name, there am I in the midst of them." That saying is a striking proof of our Lord's divinity. God alone can be in more places than one at the same time.

There is comfort in these words for all who love to meet together for religious purposes. At every assembly for public worship,—at every gathering for prayer and praise,—at every missionary meeting,—at every Bible reading, the King of kings is present,—Christ Himself attends. We may be often disheartened by the small number who are present on such occasions, compared to those who meet for worldly ends. We may sometimes

228 EXPOSITORY THOUGHTS.

find it hard to bear the taunts and ridicule of an ill-natured world, which cries like the enemy of old, "What do these feeble people?" (Nehem. iv. 2.) But we have no reason for despondency. We may boldly fall back on these words of Jesus. At all such meetings we have the company of Christ Himself.

There is solemn rebuke in these words for all who neglect the public worship of God, and never attend meetings for any religious purpose. They turn their backs on the society of the Lord of lords. They miss the opportunity of meeting Christ Himself. It avails nothing to say that the proceedings of religious meetings are marked by weakness and infirmity, or that as much good is got by staying at home as going to church. The words of our Lord should silence such arguments at once. Surely men are not wise when they speak contemptuously of any gathering where Christ is present

May we all ponder these things. If we have met together with God's people for spiritual purposes in times past, let us persevere, and not be ashamed. If we have hitherto despised such meetings, let us consider our ways, and learn wisdom.

MATTHEW XVIII. 21—35.

21 Then came Peter to him, and said, Lord, how often shall my brother sin against me, and I forgive him? till seven times?

22 Jesus saith unto him, I say not unto thee, Until seven times: but, Until seventy times seven.

23 Therefore is the kingdom of heaven likened unto a certain king, which would take account of his servants.

24 And when he had begun to reckon, one was brought unto him, which owed him ten thousand talents.

25 But forasmuch as he had not to pay, his lord commanded him to be sold, and his wife, and children, and all that he had, and payment to be made.

26 The servant therefore fell down, and worshipped him, saying, Lord,

have patience with me, and I will pay thee all.

27 Then the Lord of that servant was moved with compassion, and loosed him, and forgave him the debt.

28 But the same servant went out, and found one of his fellow-servants, which owed him an hundred pence: and he laid hands on him, and took *him* by the throat, saying, Pay me that thou owest.

29 And his fellowservant fell down at his feet, and besought him, saying, Have patience with me, and I will pay thee all.

30 And he would not: but went and cast him into prison till he should pay the debt.

31 So when his fellowservants saw what was done, they were very sorry, and came and told unto their lord all that was done.

32 Then his lord, after that he had called him, said unto him, O thou wicked servant, I forgave thee all that debt, because thou desiredst me:

33 Shouldest not thou also have had compassion on thy fellowservant, even as I had pity on thee?

34 And his lord was wroth, and delivered him to the tormentors, till he should pay all that was due unto him.

35 So likewise shall my heavenly Father do also unto you, if ye from your hearts forgive not every one his brother their trespasses.

In these verses the Lord Jesus deals with a deeply important subject,—the forgiveness of injuries. We live in a wicked world, and it is vain to expect that we can escape ill-treatment, however carefully we may behave. To know how to conduct ourselves, when we are ill-treated, is of great moment to our souls.

In the first place *the Lord Jesus lays it down as a general rule, that we ought to forgive others to the uttermost.* Peter put the question, "How oft shall my brother sin against me and I forgive him? till seven times?" He received for answer, "I say not unto thee till seven times, but until seventy times seven."

The rule here laid down must of course be interpreted with sober-minded qualification. Our Lord does not mean that offences against the law of the land and the good order of society, are to be passed over in silence. He does not mean that we are to allow people to commit thefts, and assaults, with impunity. All that He means is, that we are to study a general spirit of mercy and forgivingness towards our brethren. We are to bear much, and to put up with much, rather than quarrel. We are to look over much, and submit to much, rather than have any strife. We are to lay aside everything like malice, strife, revenge, and retaliation. Such feelings are only fit for heathens. They are utterly unworthy of a disciple of Christ.

What a happy world it would be if this rule of our Lord's was more known and better obeyed! How many of the miseries of mankind are occasioned by disputes, quarrels, lawsuits, and an obstinate tenacity about what men call "their rights!" How many of them might be altogether avoided, if men were more willing to forgive, and more desirous for peace! Let us never forget that a fire cannot go on burning without fuel. Just in the same way it takes two to make a quarrel. Let us each resolve by God's grace, that of these two we'will never be one. Let us resolve to return good for evil, and blessing for cursing, and so melt down enmity, and change our foes into friends. (Rom. xii. 20.) It was a fine feature in Archbishop Cranmer's character, that if you did him an injury, he was sure to be your friend.

In the second place, our Lord supplies us with *two powerful motives for exercising a forgiving spirit.* He tells us a story of a man who owed an enormous sum to his master, and had "nothing to pay." Nevertheless at the time of reckoning his master had compassion on him, and "forgave him all." He tells us that this very man, after being forgiven himself, refused to forgive a fellow servant a trifling debt of a few pence. He actually cast him into prison, and would not abate a jot of his demand. He tells us how punishment overtook this wicked and cruel man, who, after receiving mercy, ought surely to have shown mercy to others. And finally, he concludes the parable with the impressive words, " so likewise shall my heavenly Father do unto you, if ye from your hearts forgive not every one his brother their trespasses."

It is clear from this parable that one motive for forgiving others, ought to be the recollection that we all need forgiveness at God's hands ourselves. Day after day we are coming short in many things, "leaving undone what we ought to do, and doing what we ought not to do." Day after day we require mercy and pardon. Our neighbours' offences against us are mere trifles, compared with our offences against God. Surely it ill becomes poor erring creatures like us, to be extreme in marking what is done amiss by our brethren, or slow to forgive it.

Another motive for forgiving others, ought to be the recollection of the day of judgment, and the standard by which we shall all be tried in that day. There will be no forgiveness in that day for unforgiving people. Such people would be unfit for heaven. They would not be able to value a dwelling-place to which "mercy" is the only title, and in which "mercy" is the eternal subject of song. Surely if we mean to stand at the right hand, when Jesus sits on the throne of His glory, we must learn, while we are on earth, to forgive.

Let these truths sink down deeply into our hearts. It is a melancholy fact that there are few Christian duties so little practised as that of forgiveness. It is sad to see how much bitterness, unmercifulness, spite, hardness, and unkindness there is among men. Yet there are few duties so strongly enforced in the New Testament Scriptures as this duty is, and few the neglect of which so clearly shuts a man out of the kingdom of God.

Would we give proof that we are at peace with God, washed in Christ's blood, born of the Spirit, and made God's children by adoption and grace? Let us remember this passage. Like our Father in heaven, let us be forgiving. Has any man injured us? Let us this day forgive him. As Leighton says, "We ought to forgive ourselves little, and others much."

Would we do good to the world? Would we have any influence on others, and make them see the beauty of true religion? Let us remember this passage. Men who care not for doctrines, can understand a forgiving temper.

Would we grow in grace ourselves, and become more holy in all our ways, words, and works? Let us remember this passage. — Nothing so grieves the Holy Spirit, and brings spiritual darkness over the soul, as giving way to a quarrelsome and unforgiving temper. (Ephes. iv. 30—32.)

MATTHEW XIX. 1—15.

1 And it came to pass, *that* when Jesus had finished these sayings, he departed from Galilee, and came into the coasts of Judæa beyond Jordan;

2 And great multitudes followed him, and he healed them there.

3 The Pharisees also came unto him, tempting him, and saying unto him, Is it lawful for a man to put away his wife for every cause?

4 And he answered and said unto them, Have ye not read, that he which made *them* at the beginning made them male and female,

5 And said, For this cause shall a man leave father and mother, and shall cleave to his wife: and they twain shall be one flesh?

6 Wherefore they are no more twain, but one flesh. What therefore God hath joined together, let not man put asunder.

7 They say unto him, Why did Moses then command to give a writing of divorcement, and to put her away?

8 He saith unto them, Moses because of the hardness of your hearts suffered you to put away your wives: but from the beginning it was not so.

9 And I say unto you, Whosoever

shall put away his wife, except *it be* for fornication, and shall marry another, committeth adultery : and who-so marrieth her which is put away doth commit adultery.

10 His disciples say unto him, If the case of the man be so with *his* wife, it is not good to marry.

11 But he said unto them, All *men* cannot receive this saying, save *they* to whom it is given.

12 For there are some eunuchs, which were so born from *their* mother's womb : and there are some eunuchs which were made eunuchs of men : and there be eunuchs, which have made themselves eunuchs for the kingdom of heaven's sake. He that is able to receive *it*, let him receive *it*.

13 Then were there brought unto him little children, that he should put *his* hands on them, and pray : and the disciples rebuked them.

14 But Jesus said, Suffer little children, and forbid them not, to come unto me : for of such is the kingdom of heaven.

15 And he laid *his* hands on them, and departed thence.

IN these verses we have the mind of Christ declared on two subjects of great moment. One is the relation of husband and wife. The other is the light in which we should regard little children, in the matter of their souls.

It is difficult to overrate the importance of these two subjects. The well-being of nations, and the happiness of society, are closely connected with right views upon them. Nations are nothing but a collection of families. The good order of families depends entirely on keeping up the highest standard of respect for the marriage tie, and on the right training of children. We ought to be thankful, that on both these points, the great Head of the Church has pronounced judgment so clearly.

With respect to marriage, our Lord teaches, that *the union of husband and wife ought never to be broken off, except for the greatest of all causes, namely, actual unfaithfulness.*

In the days when our Lord was upon earth, divorces were permitted among the Jews for the most trifling and frivolous causes. The practice, though tolerated by Moses, to prevent worse evils,—such as cruelty, or murder,—

had gradually become an enormous abuse, and no doubt led to much immorality. (Malachi ii. 14—16.) The remark made by our Lord's disciples shows the deplorably low state of public feeling on the subject. They said, "If the case of the man be so, it is not good to marry." They meant, of course, "if a man may not put away his wife for a slight cause at any time, he had better not marry at all." Such language from the mouths of apostles sounds strange indeed!

Our Lord brings forward a widely different standard for the guidance of his disciples. He first founds His judgment on the original institution of marriage. He quotes the words used in the beginning of Genesis, where the creation of man, and the union of Adam and Eve, are described, as a proof that no relation should be so highly regarded as that of husband and wife. The relation of parent and child may seem very close, but there is one closer still.—"A man shall leave father and mother, and cleave to his wife." He then backs up the quotation by His own solemn words, "What God hath joined together, let not man put asunder."—And finally He brings in the grave charge of breaking the seventh commandment, against marriage contracted after a divorce for light and frivolous causes: "Whosoever shall put away his wife, except it be for fornication, and shall marry another, committeth adultery."

It is clear, from the whole tenor of the passage, that the relation of marriage ought to be highly reverenced and honoured among Christians. It is a relation which was instituted in Paradise, in the time of man's innocency, and is a chosen figure of the mystical union between

Christ and His Church. It is a relation which nothing but death ought to terminate. It is a relation which is sure to have the greatest influence on those whom it brings together, for happiness, or for misery, for good, or for evil. Such a relation ought never to be taken in hand unadvisedly, lightly or wantonly, but soberly, discreetly, and with due consideration. It is only too true, that inconsiderate marriages are one of the most fertile causes of unhappiness, and too often, it may be feared, of sin.

With respect to little children, we find our Lord instructing us in these verses, *both by word and deed, both by precept and example.* " Little children were brought to him, that he should put his hands on them and pray." They were evidently tender infants, too young to receive instruction, but not too young to receive benefit by prayer. The disciples seem to have thought them beneath their Master's notice, and rebuked those that brought them. But this drew forth a solemn declaration from the great Head of the Church,—"Jesus said, Suffer little children, and forbid them not, to come unto me ; for of such is the kingdom of heaven."

There is something deeply interesting both in the language and action of our Lord on this occasion. We know the weakness and feebleness, both in mind and body, of a little infant. Of all creatures born into the world none is so helpless and dependent. We know who it was who here took such notice of infants, and found time, in His busy ministry among grown up men and women, to "put his hands on them and pray." It was the eternal Son of God, the great High Priest, the King of kings, by whom all things consist, "the brightness of the Father's glory, and the express image of His person." What an instructive picture the whole transaction places before our eyes! No wonder that the great majority of the Church of Christ have always seen in this passage, a strong, though indirect, argument in favour of infant baptism.

Let us learn from these verses, that the Lord Jesus cares tenderly for the souls of little children. It is probable that Satan specially hates them. It is certain that Jesus specially loves them. Young as they are, they are not beneath His thoughts, and attention. That mighty heart of his has room for the babe in its cradle, as well as for the king on his throne. He regards each one as possessing within its little body an undying principle, that will outlive the Pyramids of Egypt, and see sun and moon quenched at the last day. With such a passage as this before us, we may surely hope well about the salvation of all who die in infancy. "Of such is the kingdom of heaven."

Finally, let us draw from these verses encouragement to attempt great things in the religious instruction of children. Let us begin from their very earliest years to deal with them as having souls to be lost, or saved, and strive to bring them to Christ. Let us make them acquainted with the Bible, as soon as they can understand anything. Let us pray with them, and pray for them, and teach them to pray for themselves. We may rest assured that Jesus looks with pleasure on such endeavours, and is ready to bless them. We may rest assured that such endeavours are not in vain. The seed sown in infancy, is often found after many days.   Happy is that church whose infant members are cared for as much as the oldest communicants !   The blessing of Him that was crucified will surely be on that church !   He put His hands on little children.   He prayed for them.

MATTHEW XIX. 16—22.

16 And, behold, one came and said unto him, Good Master, what good thing shall I do, that I may have eternal life?

17 And he said unto him, Why callest thou me good? *there is* none good but one, *that is* God : but if thou wilt enter into life, keep the commandments.

18 He saith unto him, Which? Jesus said, Thou shalt do no murder, Thou shalt not commit adultery, Thou shalt not steal, Thou shalt not bear false witness,

19 Honour thy father and *thy* mother : and, Thou shalt love thy neighbour as thyself.

20 The young man saith unto him, All these things have I kept from my youth up : what lack I yet?

21 Jesus said unto him, If thou wilt be perfect, go *and* sell that thou hast, and give to the poor, and thou shalt have treasure in heaven : and come *and* follow me.

22 But when the young man heard that saying, he went away sorrowful : for he had great possessions.

THESE verses detail a conversation between our Lord Jesus Christ and a young man, who came to Him to inquire about the way to eternal life.   Like every conversation recorded in the Gospels, between our Lord and an individual, it deserves special attention.   Salvation is an individual business.   Every one who wishes to be saved, must have private personal dealings with Christ about his own soul.

We see, for one thing, from the case of this young man, *that a person may have desires after salvation, and yet not be saved.*   Here is one who in a day of abounding unbelief comes of his own accord to Christ.   He comes not to have a sickness healed.   He comes not to plead about a child.   He comes about his own soul.   He opens the conference with the frank question, "Good Master, what good thing shall I do, that I may have eternal life?" Surely we might have thought, "this is a promising case : this is no prejudiced ruler or Pharisee: this is a hopeful inquirer." Yet by and bye this very young man "goes away sorrowful;"—and we never read a word to shew that he was converted!

We must never forget that good feelings alone in religion are not the grace of God. We may know the truth intellectually. We may often feel pricked in conscience. We may have religious affections awakened within us, have many anxieties about our souls, and shed many tears. But all this is not conversion. It is not the genuine, saving work of the Holy Ghost.

Unhappily this is not all that must be said on this point. Not only are good feelings alone not grace, but they are even positively dangerous, if we content ourselves with them, and do not *act* as well as *feel*. It is a profound remark of that mighty master on moral questions, Bishop Butler, that passive impressions often repeated, gradually lose all their power. Actions often repeated produce a habit in man's mind. Feelings often indulged in, without leading to corresponding actions, will finally exercise no influence at all.

Let us apply this lesson to our own state. Perhaps we know what it is to feel religious fears, wishes, and desires. Let us beware that we do not rest in them. Let us never be satisfied till we have the witness of the Spirit in our hearts, that we are actually born again and new creatures. Let us never rest till we know that we have really repented, and laid hold on the hope set before us in the

Gospel. It is good to feel. But it is far better to be converted.

We see, for another thing, from this young man's case, *that an unconverted person is often profoundly ignorant on spiritual subjects.* Our Lord refers this inquirer to the eternal standard of right and wrong, the moral law. Seeing that he speaks so boldly about "doing," he tries him by a command well calculated to draw out the real state of his heart, "If thou wilt enter into life, keep the commandments." He even repeats to him the second table of the law.—And at once the young man confidently replies, "All these have I kept from my youth up : what lack I yet?" So utterly ignorant is he of the spirituality of God's statutes, that he never doubts that he has perfectly fulfilled them. He seems thoroughly unaware that the commandments apply to the thoughts and words, as well as to the deeds, and that if God were to enter into judgment with him, he could "not answer Him one of a thousand!" (Job. ix. 3.) How dark must his mind have been as to the nature of God's law! How low must his ideas have been as to the holiness which God requires!

It is a melancholy fact, that ignorance like that of this young man is only too common in the Church of Christ. There are thousands of baptized people, who know no more of the leading doctrines of Christianity than the veriest heathen. Tens of thousands fill churches and chapels weekly, who are utterly in the dark as to the full extent of man's sinfulness. They cling obstinately to the old notion, that in some sort or other their own doings can save them,—and when ministers visit them on their death-beds, they prove as blind as if they had never heard truth at all. So true is it, that the "natural man receiveth not the things of the Spirit of God, for they are foolishness to him." (1 Cor. ii. 14.)

We see, in the last place, from this young man's case, *that one idol cherished in the heart may ruin a soul for ever.* Our Lord, who knew what was in man, at last shews His inquirer his besetting sin. The same searching voice which said to the Samaritan woman, "Go, call thy husband," (John iv. 16,) says to the young man, "Go, sell that thou hast, and give to the poor." At once the weak point in his character is detected. It turns out that, with all his wishes and desires after eternal life, there was one thing he loved better than his soul, and that was his money. He cannot stand the test. He is weighed in the balance and found wanting. And the history ends with the melancholy words, "He went away sorrowful, for he had great possessions."

We have in this history one more proof of the truth, "The love of money is the root of all evil." (1 Tim. vi. 10.) We must place this young man in our memories by the side of Judas, Ananias and Sapphira, and learn to beware of covetousness. Alas! it is a rock on which thousands are continually making shipwreck. There is hardly a minister of the Gospel who could not point to many in his congregation, who, humanly speaking, are "not far from the kingdom of God." But they never seem to make progress. They wish. They feel. They mean. They hope. But there they stick fast! And why? Because they are fond of money.

Let us prove our own selves, as we leave the passage. Let us see how it touches our own souls. Are we honest

and sincere in our professed desire to be true Christians?
Have we given up all our idols? Is there no secret sin
that we are silently clinging to, and refusing to give up?
Is there no thing or person that we are privately loving
more than Christ and our souls? These are questions
that ought to be answered. The true explanation of the
unsatisfactory state of many hearers of the Gospel, is
spiritual idolatry. St. John might well say, "Keep
yourselves from idols." (1 John v. 21.)

MATTHEW XIX. 23—30.

23 Then said Jesus unto his disciples, Verily I say unto you, That a rich man shall hardly enter into the kingdom of heaven.

24 And again I say unto you, It is easier for a camel to go through the eye of a needle, than for a rich man to enter into the kingdom of God.

25 When his disciples heard it, they were exceedingly amazed, saying, Who then can be saved?

26 But Jesus beheld them, and said unto them, With men this is impossible; but with God all things are possible.

27 Then answered Peter and said unto him, Behold, we have forsaken all, and followed thee; what shall we have therefore?

28 And Jesus said unto them, Verily I say unto you, That ye which have followed me, in the regeneration when the Son of man shall sit in the throne of his glory, ye also shall sit upon twelve thrones, judging the twelve tribes of Israel.

29 And every one that hath forsaken houses, or brethren, or sisters, or father, or mother, or wife, or children, or lands, for my name's sake, shall receive an hundred-fold, and shall inherit everlasting life.

30 But many that are first shall be last; and the last shall be first.

THE first thing that we learn in these verses, is *the immense danger which riches bring on the souls of those that possess them.* The Lord Jesus declares, that "A rich man shall hardly enter into the kingdom of heaven." He goes even further. He uses a proverbial saying to strengthen His assertion: "It is easier for a camel to go through the eye of a needle, than for a rich man to enter into the kingdom of God."

Few of our Lord's sayings sound more startling than

R

this. Few run more counter to the opinions and prejudices of mankind. Few are so little believed. Yet this saying is true, and worthy of all acceptation. Riches, which all desire to obtain,—riches, for which men labour and toil, and become gray before their time,—riches are a most perilous possession. They often inflict great injury on the soul. They lead men into many temptations. They engross men's thoughts and affections. They bind heavy burdens on the heart, and make the way to heaven even more difficult than it naturally is.

Let us beware of the love of money. It is possible to use it well, and do good with it. But for one who makes a right use of money, there are thousands who make a wrong use of it, and do harm both to themselves and others. Let the worldly man, if he will, make an idol of money, and count him happiest who has most of it. But let the Christian, who professes to have "treasure in heaven," set his face like a flint against the spirit of the world in this matter. Let him not worship gold. He is not the best man in God's eyes who has most money, but he who has most grace.

Let us pray daily for rich men's souls. They are not to be envied. They are deeply to be pitied. They carry heavy weights in the Christian course. They are of all men the least likely "so to run as to obtain." (1 Cor. ix. 24.) Their prosperity in this world is often their destruction in the world to come. Well may the Litany of the Church of England contain the words, "In all time of our wealth, good Lord, deliver us."

The second thing that we learn in this passage, is *the almighty power of God's grace in the soul.* The disciples were amazed, when they heard our Lord's language about rich men. It was language so subversive of all their notions about the advantages of wealth, that they cried out with surprise, "Who then can be saved?" They drew from our Lord a gracious answer, "With men this is impossible : but with God all things are possible."

The Holy Ghost can incline even the richest of men to seek treasure in heaven. He can dispose even kings to cast their crowns at the feet of Jesus, and count all things but loss for the sake of the kingdom of God. Proof upon proof of this is given to us in the Bible. Abraham was very rich, yet he was the father of the faithful. Moses might have been a prince or king in Egypt, but he forsook all his brilliant prospects for the sake of Him who is invisible. Job was the wealthiest man in the east, yet he was a chosen servant of God. David, Jehoshaphat, Josiah, Hezekiah, were all wealthy monarchs, but they loved God's favour more than their earthly greatness. They all shew us that "nothing is too hard for the Lord," and that faith can grow even in the most unlikely soil.

Let us hold fast this doctrine, and never let it go. No man's place or circumstances shut him out from the kingdom of God. Let us never despair of any one's salvation. No doubt rich people require special grace, and are exposed to special temptations. But the Lord God of Abraham, and Moses, and Job, and David is not changed. He who saved them in spite of their riches, can save others also. When He works, who shall let it? (Isaiah xliii. 13.)

The last thing that we learn in these verses, is *the*

immense encouragement the Gospel offers to those who give up everything for Christ's sake. We are told that Peter asked our Lord what he and the other apostles, who had forsaken their little all for His sake, should receive in return. He obtained a most gracious reply. A full recompence shall be made to all who make sacrifices for Christ's sake: they "shall receive an hundred fold, and shall inherit everlasting life."

There is something very cheering in this promise. Few in the present day, excepting converts among the heathen, are ever required to forsake homes, relations, and lands, on account of their religion. Yet there are few true Christians, who have not much to go through, in one way or another, if they are really faithful to their Lord. The offence of the cross is not yet ceased. Laughter, ridicule, mockery, and family-persecution, are often the portion of an English believer. The favour of the world is often forfeited,—places and situations are often perilled, by a conscientious adherence to the demands of the Gospel of Christ. All who are exposed to trials of this kind may take comfort in the promise of these verses. Jesus foresaw their need, and intended these words to be their consolation.

We may rest assured that no man shall ever be a real loser by following Christ. The believer may seem to suffer loss for a time, when he first begins the life of a decided Christian. He may be much cast down by the afflictions that are brought upon him on account of his religion. But let him rest assured that he will never find himself a loser in the long run. Christ can raise up friends for us who shall more than compensate for those we lose.

Christ can open hearts and homes to us, far more warm and hospitable than those that are closed against us. Above all, Christ can give us peace of conscience, inward joy, bright hopes, and happy feelings, which shall far outweigh every pleasant earthly thing that we have cast away for His sake. He has pledged His royal word that it shall be so. None ever found that word fail. Let us trust it, and not be afraid.

MATTHEW XX. 1—16.

1 For the kingdom of heaven is like unto a man *that is* an householder, which went out early in the morning to hire labourers into his vineyard.

2 And when he had agreed with the labourers for a penny a day, he sent them into his vineyard.

3 And he went out about the third hour, and saw others standing idle in the market-place,

4 And said unto them; Go ye also into the vineyard, and whatsoever is right I will give you. And they went their way.

5 Again he went out about the sixth and ninth hour, and did likewise.

6 And about the eleventh hour he went out, and found others standing idle, and saith unto them, Why stand ye here all the day idle?

7 They say unto him, Because no man hath hired us. He saith unto them, Go ye also into the vineyard; and whatsoever is right, *that* shall ye receive.

8 So when even was come, the lord of the vineyard saith unto his steward, Call the labourers, and give them *their* hire, beginning from the last unto the first.

9 And when they came that *were hired* about the eleventh hour, they received every man a penny.

10 But when the first came, they supposed that they should have received more; and they likewise received every man a penny.

11 And when they had received *it,* they murmured against the goodman of the house,

12 Saying, These last have wrought *but* one hour, and thou hast made them equal unto us, which have borne the burden and heat of the day.

13 But he answered one of them, and said, Friend, I do thee no wrong: didst not thou agree with me for a penny?

14 Take *that* thine *is,* and go thy way: I will give unto this last even as unto thee.

15 Is it not lawful for me to do what I will with mine own? Is thine eye evil, because I am good?

16 So the last shall be first, and the first last: for many be called, but few chosen.

THERE are undeniable difficulties in the parable contained in these verses. The key to the right explanation of them must be sought in the passage which concludes the last chapter. *There* we find the apostle Peter asking our Lord a remarkable question:—"we have forsaken all and followed thee; what shall we have therefore?" *There* we find Jesus giving a remarkable answer. He makes a special promise to Peter and his fellow disciples: —"they should one day sit on twelve thrones, judging the twelve tribes of Israel." He makes a general promise to all who suffer loss for His sake:—"they should receive an hundred-fold, and inherit everlasting life."

Now we must bear in mind that Peter was a Jew. Like most Jews, he had probably been brought up in much ignorance as to God's purposes respecting the salvation of the Gentiles. In fact we know from the Acts, that it required a vision from heaven to take that ignorance away. (Acts x. 28.)—Furthermore we must bear in mind, that Peter and his fellow-disciples were weak in faith and knowledge. They were probably apt to attach a great importance to their own sacrifices for Christ's sake, and inclined to self-righteousness and self-conceit.—Both these points our Lord knew well. He therefore speaks this parable for the special benefit of Peter and his companions. He read their hearts. He saw what spiritual medicine those hearts required, and supplied it without delay. In a word, He checked their rising pride, and taught them humility.

In expounding this parable, we need not inquire closely into the meaning of the "penny," the "market-place," the "steward," or the "hours." Such inquiries often darken counsel by words without knowledge. Well says Calovius, "the theology of parables is not argumentative." The hint of Chrysostom deserves notice. He says, "It is not right to search curiously, and word by word, into all things in a parable; but when we have learned the object for which it was composed, to reap this, and not to busy ourselves about anything further." Two main lessons appear to stand out on the face of the parable, and to embrace the general scope of its meaning. Let us content ourselves with these two.

We learn, in the first place, that *in the calling of nations to the professed knowledge of Himself, God exercises free, sovereign, and unconditional grace.* He calls the families of the earth into the visible church at His own time, and in His own way.

We see this truth wonderfully brought out in the history of God's dealings with the world. We see the children of Israel called and chosen to be God's people in the very beginning of "the day." We see some of the Gentiles called at a later period, by the preaching of the apostles. We see others being called in the present age, by the labours of missionaries. We see others, like the millions of Chinese and Hindoos, still "standing idle, because no man hath hired them."—And why is all this? We cannot tell. We only know that God loves to hide pride from churches, and to take away all occasion of boasting. He will never allow the older branches of His church to look contemptuously on the younger. His Gospel holds out pardon and peace with God through Christ to the heathen of our own times, as fully as it did to St. Paul. The converted inhabitants of Tinnevelly and New Zealand shall be as fully admitted to heaven as the holiest patriarch who died 3500 years ago. The old wall between Jews and Gentiles is removed. There is nothing to prevent the believing heathen being "a fellow-heir and

partaker of the same hope" with the believing Israelite.
The Gentiles converted at "the eleventh hour" of the
world, shall be as really and truly heirs of glory as the Jews.
They shall sit down with Abraham, and Isaac, and
Jacob in the kingdom of heaven, while many of the
children of the kingdom are for ever cast out. "The
last shall indeed be first."

We learn, in the second place, that in *the saving of
individuals, as well as in the calling of nations, God acts as
a sovereign, and gives no account of His matters.* He has
mercy on whom He will have mercy, and that too at
His own time. (Rom. ix. 15.)

This is a truth which we see illustrated on every side
in the church of Christ, as a matter of experience. We
see one man called to repentance and faith in the beginning of his days, like Timothy, and labouring in the
Lord's vineyard for forty or fifty years. We see another
man called "at the eleventh hour," like the thief on the
cross, and plucked like a brand out of the fire,—one day
a hard impenitent sinner, and the next day in paradise.
And yet the whole tenor of the Gospel leads us to believe
that both these men are equally forgiven before God.
Both are equally washed in Christ's blood, and clothed
in Christ's righteousness. Both are equally justified,
both accepted, and both will be found at Christ's right
hand in the last day.

There can be no doubt that this doctrine sounds strange
to the ignorant and inexperienced Christian. It con-
founds the pride of human nature. It leaves the self-
righteous no room to boast. It is a levelling, humbling
doctrine, and gives occasion to many a murmur. But

it is impossible to reject it, unless we reject the whole Bible. True faith in Christ, though it be but a day old, justifies a man before God as completely as the faith of him who has followed Christ for fifty years. The righteousness in which Timothy will stand at the day of judgment, is the same as that of the penitent thief. Both will be saved by grace alone. Both will owe all to Christ.—We may not like this. But it is the doctrine of this parable, and not of this parable only, but of the whole New Testament. Happy is he who can receive the doctrine with humility! Well says Bishop Hall, "If some have cause to magnify God's bounty, none have cause to complain."

Before we leave this parable, let us arm our minds with some necessary cautions. It is a portion of Scripture that is frequently perverted and misapplied. Men have often drawn from it, not milk, but poison.

Let us beware of supposing, from anything in this parable, that salvation is in the slightest degree to be obtained by works. To suppose this is to overthrow the whole teaching of the Bible. Whatever a believer receives in the next world, is a matter of grace, and not of debt. God is never a debtor to us, in any sense whatever. When we have done all, we are unprofitable servants. (Luke xvii. 10.)

Let us beware of supposing, from this parable, that the distinction between Jews and Gentiles is entirely done away by the Gospel. To suppose this is to contradict many plain prophecies, both of the Old Testament and New. In the matter of justification, there is no distinction between the believing Jew and the Greek. Yet

Israel is still a special people, and not "numbered among the nations." God has many purposes concerning the Jews, which are yet to be fulfilled.

Let us beware of supposing, from this parable, that all saved souls will have the same degree of glory. To suppose this, is to contradict many plain texts of Scripture. The title of all believers no doubt is the same,—the righteousness of Christ. But all will not have the same place in heaven. "Every man shall receive his own reward, according to his own labour." (1 Cor. iii. 8.)

Finally, let us beware of supposing from this parable, that it is safe for any one to put off repentance till the end of his days. To suppose this is a most dangerous delusion. The longer men refuse to obey Christ's voice, the less likely they are to be saved. "Now is the accepted time: now is the day of salvation." (2 Cor. vi. 2.) Few are ever saved on their death-beds. One thief on the cross was saved, that none should despair; but only one, that none should presume. A false confidence in those words, "the eleventh hour," has ruined thousands of souls.

MATTHEW XX. 17—23.

17 And Jesus going up to Jerusalem took the twelve disciples apart in the way, and said unto them,

18 Behold, we go up to Jerusalem; and the Son of man shall be betrayed unto the Chief Priests and unto the Scribes, and they shall condemn him to death,

19 And shall deliver him to the Gentiles to mock, and to scourge, and to crucify *him*: and the third day he shall rise again.

20 Then came to him the mother of Zebedee's children with her sons, worshipping *him*, and desiring a certain thing of him.

21 And he said unto her, What wilt thou? She saith unto him, Grant that these my two sons may sit, the one on thy right hand, and the other on the left, in thy kingdom.

22 But Jesus answered and said, Ye know not what ye ask. Are ye able to drink of the cup that I shall drink of, and to be baptized with the baptism that I am baptized with? They say unto him, We are able?

23 And he saith unto them, Ye shall drink indeed of my cup, and be baptized with the baptism that I am baptized with: but to sit on my right hand, and on my left, is not mine to give, but *it shall be given to them* for whom it is prepared of my Father.

THE first thing that we should notice in these verses, is *the clear announcement which the Lord Jesus Christ makes of His own approaching death.* For the third time we find Him telling His disciples the astounding truth, that He, their wonder-working Master, must soon suffer and die.

The Lord Jesus knew from the beginning, all that was before Him. The treachery of Judas Iscariot,—the fierce persecution of chief-priests and scribes,—the unjust judgment,—the delivery to Pontius Pilate,—the mocking,—the scourging,—the crown of thorns,—the cross,—the hanging between two malefactors,—the nails, —the spear,—all, all were spread before His mind like a picture.

How great an aggravation of suffering fore-knowledge is, those know well who have lived in the prospect of some fearful surgical operation. Yet none of these things moved our Lord. He says, "I was not rebellious, neither turned away back. I gave my back to the smiters, and my cheeks to them that plucked off the hair: I hid not my face from shame and spitting." (Isaiah l. 5, 6.) He saw Calvary in the distance all His life through, and yet walked calmly up to it, without turning to the right hand or to the left. Surely there never was sorrow like unto His sorrow, or love like His love.

The Lord Jesus was a voluntary sufferer. When He died on the cross, it was not because He had not power to prevent it. He suffered intentionally, deliberately, and of His own free-will. (John x. 18.) He knew that without shedding of His blood there could be no remission of man's sin. He knew that He was the Lamb of God, who must die to take away the sin of the world. He knew that His death was the appointed sacrifice, which must be offered up to make reconciliation for iniquity. Knowing all this, He went willingly to the cross. His heart was set on finishing the mighty work He came into the world to do. He was well aware that all hinged on His own death, and that, without that death, His miracles and preaching would have done comparatively nothing for the world. No wonder that He thrice pressed on the attention of His disciples that He "must needs" die. Blessed and happy are they who know the real meaning and importance of the sufferings of Christ!

The next thing that we should notice in these verses, *is the mixture of ignorance and faith that may be found, even in true-hearted Christians.* We see the mother of James and John coming to our Lord with her two sons, and preferring on their behalf a strange petition. She asks that they "may sit, one on His right hand, and the other on His left in His kingdom." She seems to have forgotten all He had just been saying about His suffering. Her eager mind can think of nothing but His glory. His plain warnings about the crucifixion, appear to have been thrown away on her sons. Their thoughts were full of nothing but His throne, and the day of His power. There was much of faith in their request, but there was much more of infirmity. There was something to be commended, in that they could see in Jesus of Nazareth a coming king. But there was also much to blame, in that they did not remember that He was to be crucified before He could **reign. Truly the flesh** lusteth against the spirit in all God's children, and Luther well remarks, " the flesh ever seeks to be glorified before it is crucified."

There are many Christians, who are very like this woman and her sons. They see in part, and know in part, the things of God. They have faith enough to follow Christ. They have knowledge enough to hate sin, and come out from the world. And yet there are many truths of Christianity, of which they are deplorably ignorant. They talk ignorantly, they act ignorantly, and commit many sad mistakes. Their acquaintance with the Bible is very scanty. Their insight into their own hearts is very small.—But we must learn from these verses to deal gently with such people, because the Lord has received them. We must not set them down as graceless and godless, because of their ignorance. We must remember that true faith may lie at the bottom of their hearts, though there is much rubbish at the top. We must reflect that the sons of Zebedee, whose knowledge was at one time so imperfect, became at a later period pillars of the Church of Christ. Just so a believer may begin his course in much darkness, and yet prove finally a man mighty in the Scriptures, and a worthy follower of James and John.

The last thing that we should notice in these verses, *is the solemn reproof which our Lord gives to the ignorant request of the mother of Zebedee's children and her two sons.* He says to them, " Ye know not what ye ask." They had asked to share in their Master's reward, but they had not considered that they must first be partakers in their Master's sufferings. (1 Pet. iv. 13.) They had forgotten that those who would stand with Christ in glory, must drink of His cup, and be baptized with His baptism. They did not see that those who carry the cross, and those alone, shall receive the crown. Well might our Lord say, "Ye know not what ye ask."

But do we never commit the same mistake that the sons of Zebedee committed? Do we never fall into their error, and make thoughtless, inconsiderate requests? Do we not often say things in prayer without "counting the cost," and ask for things to be granted to us, without reflecting how much our supplications involve? These are heart-searching questions. It may well be feared that many of us cannot give them a satisfactory answer.

We ask that our souls may be saved and go to heaven, when we die. It is a good request indeed. But are we prepared to take up the cross, and follow Christ? Are we willing to give up the world for His sake? Are we ready to put off the old man, and put on the new,—to fight, to labour, and to run so as to obtain? Are we ready to withstand a taunting world, and endure hardships for Christ's sake?—What shall we say? If we are not so ready, our Lord might say to us also, "Ye know not what ye ask."

We ask that God would make us holy and good. It is a good request indeed. But are we prepared to be sanctified by any process that God in His wisdom may call on us to pass through? Are we ready to be purified by affliction, weaned from the world by bereavements, drawn nearer to God by losses, sicknesses, and sorrow? Alas! these are hard questions. But if we are not, our Lord might well say to us, "Ye know not what ye ask."

Let us leave these verses with a solemn resolution to consider well what we are about, when we draw nigh to God in prayer. Let us beware of thoughtless, inconsiderate, and rash petitions. Well might Solomon say, "Be not rash with thy mouth, and let not thine heart be hasty to utter anything before God." (Eccles. v. 2.)

MATTHEW XX. 24—28.

24 And when the ten heard *it*, they were moved with indignation against the two brethren.

25 But Jesus called them *unto him*, and said, Ye know that the princes of the Gentiles exercise dominion over them, and they that are great exercise authority upon them.

26 But it shall not be so among you: but whosoever will be great among you, let him be your minister;

27 And whosoever will be chief among you, let him be your servant:

28 Even as the Son of man came not to be ministered unto, but to minister, and to give his life a ransom for many.

THESE verses are few in number, but they contain lessons of great importance to all professing Christians. Let us see what they are.

In the first place we learn, that *there may be pride, jealousy, and love of preeminence even among true disciples of Christ.* What saith the Scripture? "When the ten heard" what James and John had asked, "they were moved with indignation against the two brethren."

Pride is one of the oldest and most mischievous of sins. By it the angels fell;—for "they kept not their first estate." (Jude 6.) Through pride Adam and Eve were seduced into eating the forbidden fruit. They were not content with their lot, and thought "they would be as Gods." From pride the saints of God receive their greatest injuries after their conversion. Well says Hooker, "Pride is a vice, which cleaveth so fast unto the hearts of men, that if we were to strip ourselves of all faults, one by one, we should undoubtedly find it the very last and hardest to put off." It is a quaint but true saying of Bishop Hall, that "pride is the inmost coat, which we put off last, and which we put on first."

In the second place we learn, that a *life of self-denying kindness to others is the true secret of greatness in the kingdom of Christ.* What saith the Scripture ? "Whosoever will be great among you, let him be your minister :— Whosoever will be chief among you, let him be your servant."

The standard of the world, and the standard of the Lord Jesus, are indeed widely different. They are more than different. They are flatly contradictory one to the other. Among the children of this world, he is thought the greatest man who has most land, most money, most servants, most rank, and most earthly power. Among the children of God, he is reckoned the greatest who does most to promote the spiritual and temporal happiness of his fellow-creatures. True greatness consists not in receiving, but in giving,—not in selfish absorption of good things, but in imparting good to others,—not in being served, but in serving,—not in sitting still and being ministered to, but in going about and ministering to others. The angels of God see far more beauty in the work of the Missionary, than in the work of the Australian digger for gold. They take far more interest in the labours of men like Howard and Judson, than in the victories of generals, the political speeches of statesmen, or the council-chambers of kings. Let us remember these things. Let us beware of seeking false greatness. Let us aim at that which alone is true. We may be sure there is profound wisdom in that saying of our Lord's, "It is more blessed to give than to receive." (Acts xx. 35.)

In the third place, we learn that *the Lord Jesus Christ is intended to be the example of all true Christians.* What saith the Scripture ? We ought to serve one another, "even as the Son of man came not to be ministered unto, but to minister."

The Lord God has mercifully provided His people with everything necessary to their sanctification. He has given those who follow after holiness the clearest of precepts, the best of motives, and the most encouraging of promises. But this is not all. He has furthermore supplied them with the most perfect pattern and example, even the life of His own Son. By that life He bids us frame our own. In the steps of that life He bids us walk. (1 Peter ii. 21.) It is the model after which we must strive to mould our tempers, our words, and our works, in this evil world.—"Would my Master have spoken in this manner ? Would my Master have behaved in this way ?"—These are the questions by which we ought daily to try ourselves.

How humbling this truth is ! What searchings of heart it ought to raise within us ! What a loud call it is to "lay aside every weight, and the sin which most easily besets us !" What manner of persons ought they to be who profess to copy Christ ! What poor unprofitable religion is that which makes a man content with talking and empty profession, while his life is unholy and unclean ! Alas ! those who know nothing of Christ, as an example, will find at last that He knows nothing of them

s

as His saved people. "He that saith he abideth in Him ought himself also so to walk even as he walked." (1 John ii. 6.)

Finally, let us learn from these verses, *that Christ's death was an atonement for sin.* What saith the Scripture? "The Son of man came to give his life a ransom for many."

This is the mightiest truth in the Bible. Let us take care, that we grasp it firmly, and never let it go. Our Lord Jesus Christ did not die merely as a martyr, or as a splendid example of self-sacrifice and self-denial. Those who can see no more than *that* in His death, fall infinitely short of the truth. They lose sight of the very foundation-stone of Christianity, and miss the whole comfort of the Gospel. Christ died as a sacrifice for man's sin. He died to make reconciliation for man's iniquity. He died to purge our sins by the offering of Himself. He died to redeem us from the curse which we all deserved, and to make satisfaction to the justice of God, which must otherwise have condemned us. Never let us forget this!

We are all by nature debtors. We owe to our holy Maker ten thousand talents, and are not able to pay. We cannot atone for our own transgressions, for we are weak and frail, and only adding to our debts every day. But, blessed be God! what we could not do, Christ came into the world to do for us. What we could not pay, He undertook to pay for us. To pay it He died for us upon the cross. "He offered himself to God." (Heb. ix. 14.) "He suffered for sin, the just for the unjust, that He might bring us to God." (1 Peter iii. 18.) Once more, never let us forget this!

Let us not leave these verses without asking ourselves, where is our humility? what is our idea of true greatness? what is our example? what is our hope?—Life, eternal life, depends on the answer we give to these questions. Happy is that man who is truly humble, strives to do good in his day, walks in the steps of Jesus, and rests all his hopes on the ransom paid for him by Christ's blood. Such a man is a true Christian!

MATTHEW XX. 29—34.

29 And as they departed from Jericho, a great multitude followed him.

30 And, behold, two blind men sitting by the way side, when they heard that Jesus passed by, cried out, saying, Have mercy on us, O Lord, *thou* Son of David.

31 And the multitude rebuked them, because they should hold their peace: but they cried the more, saying, Have mercy on us, O Lord, *thou* Son of David.

32 And Jesus stood still, and called them, and said, What will ye that I shall do unto you?

33 They say unto him, Lord, that our eyes may be opened.

34 So Jesus had compassion *on them*, and touched their eyes: and immediately their eyes received sight, and they followed him.

In these verses we have a touching picture of an event in our Lord's history. He heals two blind men sitting by the way side near Jericho. The circumstances of the event contain several deeply interesting lessons, which all professing Christians would do well to remember.

For one thing, let us mark *what strong faith may sometimes be found, where it might least have been expected.* Blind as these two men were, they believed that Jesus was able to help them. They never saw any of our Lord's miracles. They knew Him only by hear-say, and not face to face. And yet, as soon as they heard that He was passing by, they "cried out, saying, Have mercy on us, O Lord, thou son of David."

Such faith may well put us to shame. With all our books of evidence, and lives of saints, and libraries of divinity, how few know anything of simple, child-like confidence in Christ's mercy and Christ's power. And even among those who are believers, the degree of faith is often strangely disproportionate to the privileges enjoyed. Many an unlearned man, who can only read his New Testament with difficulty, possesses the spirit of unhesitating trust in Christ's advocacy, while deeply-read divines are harassed by questionings and doubts. They who, humanly speaking, ought to be first, are often last, and the last first.

For another thing, let us mark *what wisdom there is in using every opportunity for getting good for our souls.* These blind men sat "by the way-side." Had they not done so, they might never have been healed. Jesus never returned to Jericho, and they might never have met with Him again.

Let us see, in this simple fact, the importance of diligence in the use of means of grace. Let us never neglect the house of God,—never forsake the assembling of ourselves with God's people,—never omit the reading of our Bibles,—never let drop the practice of private prayer. These things, no doubt, will not save us without the grace of the Holy Ghost. Thousands make use of them, and remain dead in trespasses and sins. But it is just in the use of these things that souls are converted and saved. They are the ways in which Jesus walks. It is they who "sit by the way-side" who are likely to be healed. Do we know the diseases of our souls? Do we feel any desire to see the great Physician? If we do, we must not wait in idleness, saying, " If I am to be saved, I shall be saved." We must arise and go to the road where Jesus walks. Who can tell but He will soon pass by for the last time? Let us sit daily by the wayside.

For another thing, let us mark *the value of pains and perseverance in seeking Christ.* These blind men were "rebuked" by the multitude, that accompanied our Lord. Men told them to "hold their peace." But they were not to be silenced in this way. They felt their need of help. They cared nothing for the check which they received. " They cried the more, saying, Have mercy on us, O Lord, thou son of David."

We have in this part of their conduct, a most important example. We are not to be deterred by opposition, or discouraged by difficulties, when we begin to seek the salvation of our souls. We must "pray always, and not faint. (Luke xviii. 1.) We must remember the parable of the importunate widow, and of the friend who came to borrow bread at midnight. Like them we must press our petitions at the throne of grace, and say, "I will not let thee go, except thou bless me." (Gen. xxxii. 26.) Friends, relatives, and neighbours may say unkind things, and reprove our earnestness. We may meet with coldness and want of sympathy, where we might have looked for help. But let none of these things move us. If we feel our diseases, and want to find Jesus, the great Physician,—if we know our sins, and desire to have them pardoned,— let us press on. " The violent take the kingdom by force." (Matt. xi. 12.)

Finally, let us mark *how gracious the Lord Jesus is to*

those who seek Him. "He stood still and called" the blind men. He kindly asked them what it was that they desired. He heard their petition, and did what they requested. He "had compassion on them, and touched their eyes,—and immediately their eyes received sight."

We see here an illustration of that old truth, which we can never know too well, the mercifulness of Christ's heart towards the sons of men. The Lord Jesus is not only a mighty Saviour, but merciful, kind, and gracious to a degree that our minds cannot conceive. Well might the apostle Paul say, that "the love of Christ passeth knowledge." (Ephes. iii. 19.) Like him, let us pray that we may "know" more of that love. We need it when we first begin our Christian course, poor trembling penitents, and babes in grace. We need it afterwards, as we travel along the narrow way, often erring, often stumbling, and often cast down. We shall need it in the evening of our days, when we go down the valley of the shadow of death. Let us then grasp the love of Christ firmly, and keep it daily before our minds. We shall never know, till we wake up in the next world, how much we are indebted to it.

MATTHEW XXI. 1—11.

1 And when they drew nigh unto Jerusalem, and were come to Bethphage, unto the mount of Olives, then sent Jesus two disciples,

2 Saying unto them, Go into the village over against you, and straightway ye shall find an ass tied, and a colt with her: loose *them*, and bring *them* unto me.

3 And if any *man* say ought unto you, ye shall say, The Lord hath need of them; and straightway he will send them.

4 All this was done, that it might be fulfilled which was spoken by the prophet, saying,

5 Tell ye the daughter of Sion, Behold, thy king cometh unto thee, meek, and sitting upon an ass, and a colt the foal of an ass.

6 And the disciples went, and did as Jesus commanded them,

7 And brought the ass, and the colt, and put on them their clothes, and they set *him* thereon.

8 And a very great multitude spread

their garments in the way; others cut down branches from the trees, and strawed *them* in the way.

9 And the multitudes that went before, and that followed, cried, saying, Hosanna to the Son of David: Blessed *is* he that cometh in the name of the Lord; Hosanna in the highest.

10 And when he was come into Jerusalem, all the city was moved, saying, Who is this?

11 And the multitude said, This is Jesus the prophet of Nazareth of Galilee.

THESE verses contain a very remarkable passage in our Lord Jesus Christ's life. They describe His public entry into Jerusalem, when He came there for the last time, before He was crucified.

There is something peculiarly striking in this incident in our Lord's history. The narrative reads like the account of some royal conqueror's return to his own city. "A very great multitude" accompanies him in a kind of triumphal procession. Loud cries and expressions of praise are heard around him. "All the city was moved." The whole transaction is singularly at variance with the past tenor of our Lord's life. It is curiously unlike the ways of Him who did not "cry, nor strive, nor let His voice be heard in the streets,"—who withdrew Himself from the multitude on other occasions,—and said to those He healed, "see thou say nothing to any man." (Mark i. 44.) And yet the whole transaction admits of explanation. The reasons of this public entry are not hard to find out.—Let us see what they were.

The plain truth is, that our Lord knew well that the time of His earthly ministry was drawing to a close. He knew that the hour was approaching when He must finish the mighty work He came to do, by dying for our sins upon the cross. He knew that His last journey had been accomplished, and that there remained nothing now in His earthly ministry, but to be offered as a sacrifice on Calvary. Knowing all this, He no longer, as in time past, sought secrecy. Knowing all this, He thought it good to enter the place where He was to be delivered to death, with peculiar solemnity and publicity. It was not fitting that the Lamb of God should come to be slain on Calvary privately and silently. Before the great sacrifice for the sins of the world was offered up, it was right that every eye should be fixed on the victim. It was suitable that the crowning act of our Lord's life should be done with as much notoriety as possible. Therefore it was that He made this public entry. Therefore it was that He attracted to himself the eyes of the wondering multitude. Therefore it was that all Jerusalem was moved. The atoning blood of the Lamb of God was about to be shed. The deed was not to be "done in a corner." (Acts xxvi. 26.)

It is good to remember these things. The real meaning of our Lord's conduct at this period of His history is not sufficiently considered by many readers of this passage. It remains for us to consider the practical lessons which these verses appear to point out.

In the first place, let us notice in these verses *an example of our Lord Jesus Christ's perfect knowledge.* He sends His two disciples into a village. He tells them that they will there find the ass on which He was to ride. He provides them with an answer to the inquiry of those to whom the ass belonged. He tells them that on giving that answer the ass will be sent. And all happens exactly as He foretells.

There is nothing hid from the Lord's eyes. There are

no secrets with Him.   Alone or in company, by night or by day, in private or in public, He is acquainted with all our ways.   He that saw Nathanael under the fig-tree is unchanged.   Go where we will, and retire from the world as we may, we are never out of sight of Christ.

This is a thought that ought to exercise a restraining and sanctifying effect on our souls.   We all know the influence which the presence of the rulers of this world has upon their subjects.   Nature itself teaches us to put a check on our tongues, and demeanour, and behaviour, when we are under the eye of a king.   The sense of our Lord Jesus Christ's perfect knowledge of all our ways, ought to have the same effect upon our hearts.   Let us do nothing we would not like Christ to see, and say nothing we would not like Christ to hear.   Let us seek to live and move and have our being under a continual recollection of Christ's presence.   Let us behave as we would have done had we walked beside Him, in the company of James and John, by the sea of Galilee.   This is the way to be trained for heaven.   In heaven, "we shall ever be *with the Lord*." (1 Thess. iv. 17.)

In the second place, let us notice in these verses *an example of the manner in which prophecies concerning our Lord's first coming were fulfilled*.   We are told that His public entry fulfilled the words of Zechariah, "Thy King cometh unto thee, meek, and sitting upon an ass."

It appears that this prediction was literally and exactly fulfilled.   The words which the prophet spake by the Holy Ghost received no figurative accomplishment.   As he said, so it came to pass.   As he foretold, so it was done.   Five hundred and fifty years had passed away since the prediction was made,—and then, when the appointed time arrived, the long-promised Messiah did literally ride into Zion on an ass. No doubt the vast majority of the inhabitants of Jerusalem saw nothing in the circumstance. The veil was upon their hearts. But we are not left in doubt as to the fulfilment of the prophecy. We are told plainly, "all this was done that it might be fulfilled."

From the fulfilment of God's word in time past, we are surely intended to gather something as to the manner of its fulfilment in time to come. We have a right to expect that prophecies respecting the *second* advent of Christ, will be as literally fulfilled as those respecting His first advent. He came to this earth literally in person the first time. He will come to this earth literally in person the second time. He came in humiliation once literally to suffer. He will come again in glory literally to reign. Every prediction respecting things accompanying His first advent was literally accomplished. It will be just the same when He returns. All that is foretold about the restoration of the Jews,—the judgments on the ungodly,—the unbelief of the world,—the gathering of the elect,—shall be made good to the letter. Let us not forget this. In the study of unfulfilled prophecy, a fixed principle of interpretation is of the first importance.

Finally, let us notice in these verses *a striking example of the worthlessness of man's favour.* Of all the multitudes who crowded round our Lord as He entered Jerusalem, none stood by Him when He was delivered into the hands of wicked men. Many cried, Hosanna, who four days after cried, "away with Him, crucify Him."

But this is a faithful picture of human nature. This is a proof of the utter folly of thinking more of the praise of man than the praise of God. Nothing in truth is so fickle and uncertain as popularity. It is here to-day and gone to-morrow. It is a sandy foundation, and sure to fail those who build upon it. Let us not care for it. Let us seek the favour of Him who is "the same yesterday, and to-day, and for ever." (Heb. xiii. 8.) Christ never changes. Those whom He loves, He loves to the end. His favour endureth for ever.

MATTHEW XXI. 12—22.

12 And Jesus went into the temple of God, and cast out all them that sold and bought in the temple, and overthrew the tables of the money-changers, and the seats of them that sold doves.

13 And said unto them, It is written, My house shall be called the house of prayer; but ye have made it a den of thieves.

14 And the blind and the lame came to him in the temple; and he healed them.

15 And when the Chief Priests and Scribes saw the wonderful things that he did, and the children crying in the temple, and saying, Hosanna to the Son of David; they were sore displeased,

16 And said unto him, Hearest thou what these say? And Jesus saith unto them, Yea; have ye never read, Out of the mouth of babes and sucklings thou hast perfected praise?

17 And he left them, and went out of the city into Bethany; and he lodged there.

18 Now in the morning as he returned into the city, he hungered.

19 And when he saw a fig tree in the way, he came to it, and found nothing thereon, but leaves only, and said unto it, Let no fruit grow on thee henceforward for ever. And presently the fig tree withered away.

20 And when the disciples saw it, they marvelled, saying, How soon is the fig tree withered away!

21 Jesus answered and said unto them, Verily I say unto you, If ye have faith, and doubt not, ye shall not only do this which is done to the fig tree, but also if ye shall say unto this mountain, Be thou removed, and be thou cast into the sea; it shall be done.

22 And all things, whatsoever ye shall ask in prayer believing, ye shall receive.

WE have in these verses an account of two remarkable events in our Lord's history. In both, there was something eminently figurative and typical. Each was an emblem of spiritual things. Beneath the surface of each, lie lessons of solemn instruction.

The first event that demands our attention, is *our Lord's visit to the temple.* He found His Father's house in a state which too truly shadowed forth the general condition of the whole Jewish church,—everything out of order, and out of course. He found the courts of that holy building disgracefully profaned by worldly transactions. Trading, and buying, and selling, were actually going on within its walls. *There* stood dealers ready to supply the Jew who came from distant countries, with any sacrifice he wanted. *There* sat the money-changer, ready to change his foreign money for the current coin of the land. Bullocks, and sheep, and goats, and pigeons, were there exposed for sale, as if the place had been a market. The jingling of money might there be heard, as if those holy courts had been a bank or an exchange. Such were the scenes that met our Lord's eyes. He saw it all with holy indignation. "He cast out all them that sold and bought." He "overthrew the tables of the money-changers." Resistance there was none, for men knew that He was right. Objection there was none, for all felt that He was only reforming a notorious abuse, which had been basely permitted for the sake of gain. Well might He sound in the ears of the astonished traders, as they fled from the temple : "It is written, my house shall be called the house of prayer ; but ye have made it a den of thieves."

Let us see in our Lord's conduct on this occasion, a striking type of what He will do when He comes again the second time. He will purify His visible church as He purified the temple. He will cleanse it from everything that defiles and works iniquity, and cast every worldly professor out of its pale. He will allow no worshipper of money, or lover of gain, to have a place in that glorious temple, which He will finally exhibit before the world. May we all strive to live in the daily expectation of that coming! May we judge ourselves, that we be not condemned, and cast out in that searching and sifting day! We should often study those words of Malachi: "Who may abide the day of His coming? and who shall stand when He appeareth? for He is like a refiner's fire, and like fuller's soap." (Mal. iii. 2.)

The second event that demands our attention in these verses, *is our Lord's curse upon the fruitless fig-tree.* We are told, that being hungry He came to a fig-tree in the way, and "found nothing thereon, but leaves only, and said unto it, let no fruit grow on thee henceforward for ever. And presently the fig-tree withered away." This is an incident almost without parallel in all our Lord's ministry. It is almost the only occasion on which we find Him making one of His creatures suffer, in order to teach a spiritual truth. There was a heart-searching lesson in that withered fig-tree. It preaches a sermon we shall all do well to hear.

That fig-tree, full of leaves, but barren of fruit, was a striking emblem of the Jewish church, when our Lord was upon earth. The Jewish church had everything to make an outward show. It had the temple, the priesthood, the daily service, the yearly feasts, the Old Testament Scriptures, the courses of the Levites, the morning and evening sacrifice. But beneath these goodly leaves, the Jewish church was utterly destitute of fruit. It had no grace, no faith, no love, no humility, no spirituality, no

real holiness, no willingness to receive its Messiah. (John
i. 11.) And hence, like the fig-tree, the Jewish church
was soon to wither away. It was to be stripped of all its
outward ornaments, and its members scattered over the
face of the earth. Jerusalem was to be destroyed. The
temple was to be burned. The daily sacrifice was to be
taken away. The tree was to wither away to the very
ground. And so it came to pass. Never was there a
type so literally fulfilled. In every wandering Jew we
see a branch of the fig-tree that was cursed.

But we may not stop here. We may find even more
instruction in the event we are now considering. These
things were written for our sakes, as well as for the Jews.

Is not every fruitless branch of Christ's visible church
in awful danger of becoming a withered fig-tree? Beyond doubt it is. High ecclesiastical profession, without
holiness among a people,—overweening confidence in
councils, bishops, liturgies, and ceremonies, while repentance and faith have been neglected,—have ruined
many a visible church in time past, and may yet ruin
many more. Where are the once famous churches of
Ephesus, and Sardis, and Carthage, and Hippo? They
are all gone. They had leaves, but no fruit. Our
Lord's curse came upon them. They became withered
fig-trees. The decree went forth, "Hew them down."
(Dan. iv. 23.) Let us remember this. Let us beware
of Church-pride. Let us not be high-minded, but fear.
(Rom. ii. 20.)

Finally, is not every fruitless professor of Christianity
in awful danger of becoming a withered fig-tree? There
can be no doubt of it. So long as a man is content with

the leaves of religion,—with a name to live while he is dead, and a form of godliness without the power,—so long his soul is in great peril. So long as he is satisfied with going to church or chapel, and receiving the Lord's supper, and being called a Christian, while his heart is not changed, and his sins not forsaken,—so long he is daily provoking God to cut him off without remedy. Fruit, fruit,—the fruit of the Spirit, is the only sure proof that we are savingly united to Christ, and in the way to heaven. May this sink down into our hearts, and never be forgotten!

MATTHEW XXI. 23—32.

23 And when he was come into the temple, the Chief Priests and the elders of the people came unto him as he was teaching, and said, By what authority doest thou these things? and who gave thee this authority?

24 And Jesus answered and said unto them, I also will ask you one thing, which if ye tell me, I in like wise will tell you by what authority I do these things.

25 The baptism of John, whence was it? from heaven, or of men? And they reasoned with themselves, saying, If we shall say, From heaven; he will say unto us, Why did ye not then believe him?

26 But if we shall say, Of men; we fear the people; for all hold John as a prophet.

27 And they answered Jesus, and said, We cannot tell. And he said unto them, Neither tell I you by what authority I do these things.

28 But what think ye? A certain man had two sons; and he came to the first, and said, Son, go work to day in my vineyard.

29 He answered and said, I will not: but afterward he repented, and went.

30 And he came to the second, and said likewise. And he answered and said, I go, sir: and went not.

31 Whether of them twain did the will of his father? They say unto him, The first. Jesus saith unto them, Verily I say unto you, That the Publicans and the harlots go into the kingdom of God before you.

32 For John came unto you in the way of righteousness, and ye believed him not: but the Publicans and the harlots believed him: and ye, when ye had seen it, repented not afterward, that ye might believe him.

THESE verses contain a conversation between our Lord Jesus Christ, and the chief priests and elders of the people. Those bitter enemies of all righteousness saw the sensation which the public entry into Jerusalem, and the cleansing of the temple, had produced. At once they came about our Lord like bees, and endeavoured to find occasion for an accusation against Him.

Let us observe, in the first place, *how ready the enemies of truth are to question the authority of all who do more good than themselves.* The chief priests have not a word to say about our Lord's teaching. They make no charge against the lives or conduct of Himself or His followers. The point on which they fasten is His commission : "By what authority doest thou these things? and who gave thee this authority?"

The same charge has often been made against the servants of God, when they have striven to check the progress of ecclesiastical corruption. It is the old engine by which the children of this world have often laboured to stop the progress of revivals and reformations. It is the weapon which was often brandished in the face of the Reformers, the Puritans, and the Methodists of the last century. It is the poisoned arrow which is often shot at city-missionaries and lay-agents in the present day. Too many care nothing for the manifest blessing of God on a man's work, so long as he is not sent forth by their own sect or party. It matters nothing to them, that some humble labourer in God's harvest can point to numerous conversions of souls through his instrumentality. They still cry, "By what authority doest thou these things?" His success is nothing: they demand his commission. His cures are nothing : they want his diploma. Let us neither be surprised nor moved, when we hear such things. It is the old charge which was brought against

Christ Himself. "There is no new thing under the sun." (Eccles. i. 9.)

Let us observe, in the second place, *the consummate wisdom with which our Lord replied to the question put to Him.* His enemies had asked Him for His authority for doing what He did. They doubtless intended to make His answer a handle for accusing Him. He knew the drift of their inquiry, and said, "I also will ask you one thing, which if ye tell me, I in likewise will tell you by what authority I do these things. The baptism of John, whence was it? from heaven or of men?"

We must distinctly understand, that in this answer of our Lord's there was no evasion. To suppose this is a great mistake. The counter question which He asked, was in reality an answer to His enemies' inquiry. He knew they dared not deny that John the Baptist was a man sent from God. He knew that, this being granted, he needed only to remind them of John's testimony to Himself.—Had not John declared Him to be "the Lamb of God that taketh away the sin of the world?" Had not John pronounced Him to be the Mighty One, who was to "baptize with the Holy Ghost?"—In short, our Lord's question was a home-thrust to the conscience of His enemies. If they once conceded the divine authority of John the Baptist's mission, they must also concede the divinity of His own. If they acknowledged that John came from heaven, they must acknowledge that He Himself was the Christ.

Let us pray that, in this difficult world, we may be supplied with the same kind of wisdom which was here displayed by our Lord. No doubt we ought to act on the

T

injunction of St. Peter, "and be always ready to give a reason of the hope that is in us with meekness and with fear." (1 Peter iii. 15.) We ought to shrink from no inquiry into the principles of our holy religion, and to be ready at any time to defend and explain our practice. But for all this, we must never forget that "wisdom is profitable to direct," and that we should strive to speak wisely in defence of a good cause. The words of Solomon deserve consideration: "Answer not a fool according to his folly, lest thou be like unto him." (Prov. xxvi. 4.)

In the last place, let us observe in these verses, *what immense encouragement our Lord holds out to those who repent.* We see this strikingly brought out in the parable of the two sons. Both were told to go and work in their father's vineyard. One son, like the profligate publicans, for some time flatly refused obedience, but afterwards repented and went. The other, like the formal Pharisees, pretended willingness to go, but in reality went not. "Whether of them twain," says our Lord, "did the will of his father?" Even his enemies were obliged to reply, "the first."

Let it be a settled principle in our Christianity, that the God and Father of our Lord Jesus Christ is infinitely willing to receive penitent sinners.—It matters nothing what a man has been in time past. Does he repent, and come to Christ? Then old things are passed away, and all things are become new.—It matters nothing how high and self-confident a man's profession of religion may be. Does he really give up his sins? If not, his profession is abominable in God's sight, and he himself is still under the curse.—Let us take courage ourselves, if we have been great sinners hitherto. Only let us repent and believe in Christ, and there is hope. Let us encourage others to repent. Let us hold the door wide open to the very chief of sinners. Never will that word fail, "If we confess our sins, he is faithful and just to forgive us our sins, and to cleanse us from all unrighteousness." (1 John i. 9.)

MATTHEW XXI. 33—46.

33 Hear another parable: There was a certain householder, which planted a vineyard, and hedged it round about, and digged a winepress in it, and built a tower, and let it out to husbandmen, and went into a far country:

34 And when the time of the fruit drew near, he sent his servants to the husbandmen, that they might receive the fruits of it.

35 And the husbandmen took his servants, and beat one, and killed another, and stoned another.

36 Again, he sent other servants more than the first: and they did unto them likewise.

37 But last of all he sent unto them his son, saying, They will reverence my son.

38 But when the husbandmen saw the son, they said among themselves, This is the heir; come, let us kill him, and let us sieze on his inheritance.

39 And they caught him, and cast *him* out of the vineyard, and slew *him*.

40 When the lord therefore of the vineyard cometh, what will he do unto those husbandmen?

41 They say unto him, He will miserably destroy those wicked men, and will let out *his* vineyard unto other husbandmen, which shall render him the fruits in their seasons.

42 Jesus saith unto them, Did ye never read in the Scriptures, The stone which the builders rejected, the same is become the head of the corner: this is the Lord's doing, and it is marvellous in our eyes?

43 Therefore say I unto you, The kingdom of God shall be taken from you, and given to a nation bringing forth the fruits thereof.

44 And whosoever shall fall on this stone shall be broken: but on whomsoever it shall fall, it will grind him to powder.

45 And when the Chief Priests and Pharisees had heard his parables, they perceived that he spake of them.

46 But when they sought to lay hands on him, they feared the multitude, because they took him for a prophet.

THE parable contained in these verses was spoken with special reference to the Jews. They are the husbandmen here described. Their sins are set before us here as in a picture. Of this there can be no doubt. It is written, that "He spake of them."

But we must not flatter ourselves that this parable contains nothing for the Gentiles. There are lessons laid down for us, as well as for the Jew. Let us see what they are.

We see, in the first place, *what distinguishing privileges God is pleased to bestow on some nations.*

He chose Israel to be a peculiar people to Himself. He separated them from the other nations of the earth, and bestowed on them countless blessings. He gave them revelations of Himself, while all the rest of the earth was in darkness. He gave them the law, and the covenants, and the oracles of God, while all the world beside was let alone. In short, God dealt with the Jews as a man deals with a piece of land which he fences out and cultivates, while all the fields around are left un-tilled and waste. The vineyard of the Lord was the house of Israel. (Isai. v. 7.)

And have we no privileges? Beyond doubt we have many. We have the Bible, and liberty for every one to read it. We have the Gospel, and permission to every one to hear it. We have spiritual mercies in abundance, of which five hundred millions of our fellow men know nothing at all. How thankful we ought to be! The poorest man in England may say every morning, "There are five hundred millions of immortal souls worse off than I am. Who am I, that I should differ? Bless the Lord, O my soul."

We see, in the next place, *what a bad use nations some-times make of their privileges.*

When the Lord separated the Jews from other people, He had a right to expect that they would serve Him, and obey His laws. When a man has taken pains with a vineyard, he has a right to expect fruit. But Israel rendered not a due return for all God's mercies. They mingled with the heathen, and learned their works. They hardened themselves in sin and unbelief. They turned aside after idols. They kept not God's ordinances. They despised God's temple. They refused to listen to His prophets. They ill-used those whom He sent to call them to repentance. And finally they brought their wickedness to a height, by killing the Son of God Himself, even Christ the Lord.

And what are we doing ourselves with our privileges? Truly that is a serious question, and one that ought to make us think. It may well be feared, that we are not, as a nation, living up to our light, or walking worthy of our many mercies. Must we not confess with shame, that millions amongst us seem utterly without God in the world? Must we not acknowledge, that in many a town, and in many a village, Christ seems hardly to have any disciple, and the Bible seems hardly to be believed? It is vain to shut our eyes to these facts. The fruit that the Lord receives from His vineyard in Great Britain, compared with what it ought to be, is disgracefully small. It may well be doubted whether we are not as provoking to Him as the Jews.

We see, in the next place, *what an awful reckoning God sometimes has with nations and churches, which make a bad use of their privileges.*

A time came when the longsuffering of God towards the Jews had an end. Forty years after our Lord's death, the cup of their iniquity was at length full, and they received a heavy chastisement for their many sins. Their holy city, Jerusalem, was destroyed. Their temple was burned. They themselves were scattered over the face of the earth. "The kingdom of God was taken from them, and given to a nation bringing forth the fruits thereof."

And will the same thing ever happen to us? Will the judgments of God ever come down on this nation of England, because of her unfruitfulness under so many mercies? Who can tell? We may well cry with the prophet, "Lord God, thou knowest." We only know that judgments have come on many a church and nation in the last 1800 years. The kingdom of God has been taken from the African churches. The Mahometan power has overwhelmed most of the churches of the East. At all events it becomes all believers to intercede much on behalf of our country. Nothing offends God so much as neglect of privileges. Much has been given to us, and much will be required.

We see, in the last place, *the power of conscience even in wicked men.*

The chief priests and elders at last discovered that our Lord's parable was specially meant for themselves. The point of its closing words was too sharp to be escaped. "They perceived that he spake of them."

There are many hearers of the Gospel in every congregation, who are exactly in the condition of these unhappy men. They know that what they hear Sunday after Sunday is all true. They know that they are wrong themselves, and that every sermon condemns them. But they have neither will nor courage to acknowledge this. They are too proud and too fond of the world to confess their past mistakes, and to take up the

cross and follow Christ.   Let us all beware of this awful
state of mind.   The last day will prove that there was
more going on in the consciences of hearers than was at
all known to preachers.   Thousands and ten thousands
will be found, like the chief priests, to have been convicted
by their own conscience, and yet to have died unconverted.

<hr>

MATTHEW XXII. 1—14.

1 And Jesus answered and spake unto them again by parables, and said,

2 The kingdom of heaven is like unto a certain king, which made a marriage for his son,

3 And sent forth his servants to call them that were bidden to the wedding : and they would not come.

4 Again, he sent forth other servants, saying, Tell them which are bidden, Behold, I have prepared my dinner : my oxen and *my* fatlings *are* killed, and all things *are* ready : come unto the marriage.

5 But they made light of *it*, and went their ways, one to his farm, another to his merchandise :

6 And the remnant took his servants, and entreated *them* spitefully, and slew *them*.

7 But when the king heard *thereof*, he was wroth : and he sent forth his armies, and destroyed those murderers, and burned up their city.

8 Then saith he to his servants, The wedding is ready, but they which were bidden were not worthy.

9 Go ye therefore into the highways, and as many as ye shall find, bid to the marriage.

10 So those servants went out into the highways, and gathered together all as many as they found, both bad and good : and the wedding was furnished with guests.

11 And when the king came in to see the guests, he saw there a man which had not on a wedding garment :

12 And he saith unto him, Friend, how camest thou in hither not having a wedding garment ? And he was speechless.

13 Then said the king to the servants, Bind him hand and foot, and take him away, and cast *him* into outer darkness ; there shall be weeping and gnashing of teeth.

14 For many are called, but few *are* chosen.

THE parable related in these verses is one of very wide
signification.   In its first application it unquestionably
points to the Jews.   But we may not confine it to them.
It contains heart-searching lessons for all among whom
the Gospel is preached.   It is a spiritual picture which
speaks to us this day, if we have an ear to hear.   The
remark of Olshausen is wise and true, " parables are like

many-sided precious stones, cut so as to cast lustre in more than one direction."

Let us observe, in the first place, that *the salvation of the Gospel is compared to a marriage feast.* The Lord Jesus tell us that "a certain king made a marriage for his son."

There is in the Gospel a complete provision for all the wants of man's soul. There is a supply of everything that can be required to relieve spiritual hunger and spiritual thirst. Pardon, peace with God, lively hope in this world, glory in the world to come, are set before us in rich abundance. It is "a feast of fat things." All this provision is owing to the love of the Son of God, Jesus Christ our Lord. He offers to take us into union with Himself,—to restore us to the family of God as dear children,—to clothe us with His own righteousness,—to give us a place in His kingdom, and to present us faultless before His Father's throne at the last day. The Gospel, in short, is an offer of food to the hungry,—joy to the mourner,—a home to the outcast,—a loving friend to the lost. It is glad tidings. God offers, through His dear Son, to be at one with sinful man. Let us not forget this: "Herein is love, not that we loved God, but that He loved us, and sent His Son to be the propitiation for our sins." (1 John iv. 10.)

Let us observe, in the second place, that *the invitations of the Gospel are wide, full, broad, and unlimited.* The Lord Jesus tells us in the parable, that the king's servants said to those who were bidden, "all things are ready: come unto the marriage."

There is nothing wanting on God's part for the

salvation of sinners' souls.   No one will ever be able to say at last that it was God's fault, if he is not saved. The Father is ready to love and receive.   The Son is ready to pardon and cleanse guilt away.   The Spirit is ready to sanctify and renew.   Angels are ready to rejoice over the returning sinner.   Grace is ready to assist him. The Bible is ready to instruct him.   Heaven is ready to be his everlasting home.   One thing only is needful, and that is, the sinner must be ready and willing himself. Let this also never be forgotten.   Let us not quibble and split hairs upon the point.   God will be found clear of the blood of all lost souls.   The Gospel always speaks of sinners as *responsible* and accountable beings.   The Gospel places an open door before all mankind.   No one is excluded from the range of its offers.   Though efficient only to believers, those offers are sufficient for all the world.   Though few enter the strait gate, all are invited to come in.

Let us observe, in the third place, that *the salvation of the Gospel is rejected by many to whom it is offered.*   The Lord Jesus tells us, that those whom the king's servants bade to the wedding, "made light of it, and went their way."

There are thousands of hearers of the Gospel who derive from it no benefit whatever.   They listen to it Sunday after Sunday, and year after year, and do not believe to the saving of the soul.   They feel no special need of the Gospel.   They see no special beauty in it.   They do not perhaps hate it, or oppose it, or scoff at it, but they do not receive it into their hearts.   They like other things far better.   Their money,—their land,—their business,—

or their pleasures, are all far more interesting subjects to them than their souls.—It is an awful state of mind to be in, but awfully common. Let us search our own hearts, and take heed that it is not our own. Open sin may kill its thousands; but indifference and neglect of the Gospel kill their tens of thousands. Multitudes will find themselves in hell, not so much because they openly broke the ten commandments, as because they made light of the truth. Christ died for them on the cross, but they neglected Him.

Let us observe, in the last place, that *all false professors of religion will be detected, exposed, and eternally condemned at the last day.* The Lord Jesus tells us, that when the wedding was at last furnished with guests, the king came in to see them, and " saw a man which had not on a wedding-garment." He asked him how he came in there without one, and he received no reply. And he then commanded the servants to "bind him hand and foot and take him away."

There will always be some false professors in the Church of Christ, as long as the world stands. In this parable, as Quesnel says, " One single castaway represents all the rest." It is impossible to read the hearts of men. Deceivers and hypocrites will never be entirely excluded from the ranks of those who call themselves Christians. So long as a man professes subjection to the Gospel, and lives an outwardly correct life, we dare not say positively that he is not clothed in the righteousness of Christ. But there will be no deception at the last day. The unerring eye of God will discern who are His own people, and who are not. Nothing but true faith shall abide the fire of His judgment. All spurious Christianity shall be weighed in the balance and found wanting. None but true believers shall sit down at the marriage supper of the Lamb. It shall avail the hypocrite nothing that he has been a loud talker about religion, and had the reputation of being an eminent Christian among men. His triumphing shall be but for a moment. He shall be stripped of all his borrowed plumage, and stand naked and shivering before the bar of God, speechless, self-condemned, hopeless, and helpless. He shall be cast into outer darkness with shame, and reap according as he has sown. Well may our Lord say, " there shall be weeping and gnashing of teeth."

Let us learn wisdom from the solemn pictures of this parable, and give diligence to make our calling and election sure. We ourselves are among those to whom the word is spoken, "All things are ready, come to the marriage." Let us see that we refuse not him that speaketh. Let us not sleep as others do, but watch and be sober. Time hastens on. The King will soon come in to see the guests. Have we or have we not got on the wedding garment? Have we put on Christ? That is the grand question that arises out of this parable. May we never rest till we can give a satisfactory answer! May those heart-searching words daily ring in our ears, "Many are called, but few are chosen!"

MATTHEW XXII. 15—22.

15 Then went the Pharisees, and took counsel how they might entangle him in *his* talk.

16 And they sent out unto him their disciples with the Herodians, saying, Master, we know that thou art true, and teachest the way of God in truth, neither carest thou for any

man : for thou regardest not the person of men.

17 Tell us therefore, What thinkest thou? Is it lawful to give tribute unto Cæsar, or not?

18 But Jesus perceived their wickedness, and said, Why tempt ye me, *ye* hypocrites?

19 Shew me the tribute money. And they brought unto him a penny.

20 And he saith unto them, Whose *is* this image and superscription?

21 They say unto him, Cæsar's. Then saith he unto them, Render therefore unto Cæsar the things which are Cæsar's; and unto God the things that are God's.

22 When they had heard *these words*, they marvelled, and left him, and went their way.

WE see in this passage the first of a series of subtle attacks, which were made on our Lord during the last days of His earthly ministry. His deadly foes, the Pharisees, saw the influence which He was obtaining, both by His miracles and by His preaching. They were determined by some means to silence Him, or put Him to death. They therefore endeavoured to " entangle him in his talk." They sent forth "their disciples with the Herodians," to try Him with a hard question. They wished to entice Him into saying something which might serve as a handle for an accusation against Him. Their scheme, we are told in these verses, entirely failed. They took nothing by their movement, and retreated in confusion.

The first thing which demands our attention in these verses, is *the flattering language with which our Lord was accosted by His enemies.* " Master," they said, "we know that thou art true, and teachest the way of God in truth, neither carest thou for any man; for thou regardest not the person of men." How well these Pharisees and Herodians talked! What smooth and honeyed words were these! They thought, no doubt, that by good words and fair speeches they would throw our Lord off His guard. It might truly be said of them, " the words of his mouth were smoother than butter, but war was in his heart : his

words were softer than oil, yet were they drawn swords."
(Psalm lv. 21.)

It becomes all professing Christians to be much on their
guard against flattery. We mistake greatly if we suppose
that persecution and hard usage are the only weapons in
Satan's armoury. That crafty foe has other engines for
doing us mischief, which he knows well how to work.
He knows how to poison souls by the world's seductive
kindness, when he cannot frighten them by the fiery dart
and the sword. Let us not be ignorant of his devices.
By peace he destroys many.

We are only too apt to forget this truth. We overlook
the many examples which God has given us in Scripture
for our learning. What brought about the ruin of Samson?
Not the armies of the Philistines, but the pretended love
of a Philistine woman.—What led to Solomon's backsliding? Not the strength of outward enemies, but the
blandishment of his numerous wives.—What was the
cause of king Hezekiah's greatest mistake?   Not the
sword of Sennacherib, or the threats cf Rab-shakeh, but
the flattery of the Babylonian ambassadors.—Let us remember these things, and be on our guard. Peace often
ruins nations more than war. Sweet things occasion far
more sicknesses than bitter. The sun makes the traveller
cast off his protective garments far sooner than the north
wind. Let us beware of the flatterer. Satan is never so
dangerous as when he appears as an angel of light. The
world is never so dangerous to the Christian as when it
smiles. When Judas betrayed his Lord, it was with a kiss.
The believer that is proof against the world's frown does
well. But he that is proof against its flattery does better.

The second thing that demands our attention in these verses, is the *marvellous wisdom of the reply which our Lord made to His enemies.* The Pharisees and Herodians asked whether it was lawful to give tribute to Cæsar or not. They doubtless thought, that they had put a question which our Lord could not answer without giving them an advantage.—Had He simply replied that it was, *lawful* to pay tribute, they would have denounced Him to the people as one who dishonoured the privileges of Israel, and considered the children of Abraham no longer free, but subjects to a foreign power.—Had He, on the other hand, replied that it was *not lawful* to pay tribute, they would have denounced Him to the Romans as a mover of sedition, and a rebel against Cæsar, who refused to pay his taxes.—But our Lord's conduct completely baffled them. He demanded to see the tribute-money. He asks them whose head is on that coin. They reply, Cæsar's. They acknowledge that Cæsar has some authority over them, by using money bearing his image and super-scription, since he that coins the current money is ruler of the land where that money is current. And at once they receive an irresistibly conclusive answer to their question,—"Render to Cæsar the things which are Cæsar's, and unto God the things which are God's."

The principle laid down in these well-known words is one of deep importance. There is one obedience owing by every Christian to the civil government under which he lives, in all matters which are temporal, and not purely spiritual. He may not approve of every requirement of that civil government. But he must submit to the laws of the commonwealth, so long as those laws are unrepealed. He must "render unto Cæsar the things that are Cæsar's."—There is another obedience which the Christian owes to the God of the Bible in all matters which are purely spiritual. No temporal loss, no civil disability, no displeasure of the powers that be, must ever tempt him to do things which the Scripture plainly forbids. His position may be very trying. He may have to suffer much for his conscience sake. But he must never fly in the face of unmistakeable requirements of Scripture. If Cæsar coins a new Gospel, he is not to be obeyed. We must "render to God the things that are God's."

The subject unquestionably is one of great difficulty and delicacy. It is certain that the church must not swallow up the state. It is no less certain that the state must not swallow up the church. On no point, perhaps, have conscientious men been so much tried. On no point have good men disagreed so much, as in solving the problem, "where the things of Cæsar end, and the things of God begin." The civil power, on the one side, has often encroached terribly on the rights of conscience,—as the English puritans found to their cost in the unhappy times of the Stewarts. The spiritual power, on the other side, has often pushed its claims to an extravagant extent, so as to take Cæsar's sceptre out of his hands,—as it did when the church of Rome trampled on our own English king John. In order to have a right judgment in all questions of this kind, every true Christian should constantly pray for wisdom from above. The man whose eye is single, and who daily seeks for grace, and practical common sense, will never be allowed greatly to err.

MATTHEW XXII. 23—33.

23 And the same day came to him the Sadducees, which say that there is no resurrection, and asked him,

24 Saying, Master, Moses said, If a man die, having no children, his brother shall marry his wife, and raise up seed unto his brother.

25 Now there were with us seven brethren : and the first, when he had married a wife, deceased, and, having no issue, left his wife unto his brother:

26 Likewise the second also, and the third, unto the seventh.

27 And last of all the woman died also.

28 Therefore in the resurrection whose wife shall she be of the seven? for they all had her.

29 Jesus answered and said unto them, Ye do err, not knowing the Scriptures, nor the power of God.

30 For in the resurrection they neither marry, nor are given in marriage, but are as the angels of God in heaven.

31 But as touching the resurrection of the dead, have ye not read that which was spoken unto you by God, saying,

32 I am the God of Abraham, and the God of Isaac, and the God of Jacob? God is not the God of the dead, but of the living.

33 And when the multitude heard *this*, they were astonished at his doctrine.

THIS passage describes a conversation between our Lord Jesus Christ and the Sadducees. These unhappy men, who said that there was "no resurrection," attempted, like the Pharisees and Herodians, to perplex our Lord with hard questions. Like them, they hoped "to entangle Him in His talk," and to injure His reputation among the people. Like them, they were completely baffled.

Let us observe, in the first place, that *absurd sceptical objections to Bible truths are ancient things*. The Sadducees wished to show the absurdity of the doctrine of the resurrection and the life to come. They therefore came to our Lord with a story which was probably invented for the occasion. They told Him that a certain woman had married seven brothers in succession, who had all died and left no children. They then asked "whose wife" this woman would be in the next world, when all rose again. The object of the question was plain and transparent. They meant, in reality, to bring the whole doctrine of a resurrection into contempt. They meant to insinuate, that there must needs be confusion, and strife, and unseemly disorder, if, after death, men and women were to live again.

It must never surprise us, if we meet with like objections against the doctrines of Scripture, and especially against those doctrines which concern another world. There never probably will be wanting "unreasonable men," who will "intrude" into things unseen, and make imaginary difficulties their excuse for unbelief. *Supposed cases* are one of the favourite strongholds in which an unbelieving mind loves to intrench itself. Such a mind will often set up a shadow of its own imagining, and fight with it, as if it was a truth. Such a mind will often refuse to look at the overwhelming mass of plain evidence by which Christianity is supported, and will fasten down on some one single difficulty, which it fancies is unanswerable. The talk and arguments of people of this character should never shake our faith for a moment. For one thing, we should remember that there must needs be deep and dark things in a religion which comes from God, and that a child may put questions which the greatest philosopher cannot answer.—For another thing, we should remember, that there are countless truths in the Bible, which are clear, and unmistakeable. Let us first attend to them, believe them, and obey them. So doing, we need not doubt that many a thing now unintelligible to us will yet be made plain. So doing, we may be sure that "what we know not now we shall know hereafter."

Let us observe, in the second place, what a *remarkable text our Lord brings forward, in proof of the reality of a life to come.* He places before the Sadducees the words

v

which God spake to Moses in the bush : "I am the God of Abraham, and the God of Isaac, and the God of Jacob." (Exod. iii. 6.) He adds the comment, "God is not the God of the dead, but of the living." At the time when Moses heard these words, Abraham, Isaac, and Jacob had been dead and buried many years. Two centuries had passed away since Jacob, the last of the three, was carried to his tomb. And yet God spoke of them as being still His people, and of Himself as being still their God. He said not, "I *was* their God," but "I *am*."

Perhaps we are not often tempted to doubt the truth of a resurrection, and a life to come. But, unhappily, it is easy to hold truths theoretically, and yet not realize them practically. There are few of us who would not find it good to meditate on the mighty verity which our Lord here unfolds, and to give it a prominent place in our thoughts. Let us settle it in our minds, that the dead are in one sense still alive. From our eyes they have passed away, and their place knows them no more. But in the eyes of God they live, and will one day come forth from their graves to receive an everlasting sentence. There is no such thing as annihilation. The idea is a miserable delusion. The sun, moon, and stars,—the solid mountains, and deep sea, will one day come to nothing. But the weakest babe of the poorest man shall live for evermore, in another world. May we never forget this! Happy is he who can say from his heart the words of the Nicene Creed, "I look for the resurrection of the dead, and the life of the world to come."

Let us observe, in the last place, *the account which our Lord gives of the state of men and women after the resurrec-*

tion. He silences the fancied objections of the Sadducees, by shewing that they entirely mistook the true character of the resurrection state. They took it for granted that it must needs be a gross, carnal existence, like that of mankind upon earth. Our Lord tells them that in the next world we may have a real material body, and yet a body of very different constitution, and different necessities, from that which we have now. He speaks only of the saved, be it remembered. He omits all mention of the lost. He says, "In the resurrection they neither marry nor are given in marriage, but are as the angels of God in heaven."

We know but little of the life to come in heaven. Perhaps our clearest ideas of it are drawn from considering what it will not be, rather than what it will be. It is a state in which we shall hunger no more, nor thirst any more. Sickness, pain, and disease, will not be known. Wasting, old age, and death will have no place. Marriages, births, and a constant succession of inhabitants, will no more be needed. They who are once admitted into heaven shall dwell there for evermore.—And, to pass from negatives to positives, one thing we are told plainly,—we shall be "as the angels of God." Like them, we shall serve God perfectly, unhesitatingly, and unweariedly. Like them, we shall ever be in God's presence. Like them, we shall ever delight to do His will. Like them, we shall give all glory to the Lamb. These are deep things. But they are all true.

Are we ready for this life? Should we enjoy it, if admitted to take part in it? Is the company of God, and the service of God pleasant to us now? Is the occupation of angels one in which we should delight? These are solemn questions. Our hearts must be heavenly on earth, while we live, if we hope to go to heaven when we rise again in another world. (Coloss. iii. 1—4.)

MATTHEW XXII. 34—46.

34 But when the Pharisees had heard that he had put the Sadducees to silence, they were gathered together.

35 Then one of them, *which was* a Lawyer, asked *him a question*, tempting him, and saying,

36 Master, which *is* the great commandment in the law?

37 Jesus said unto him, Thou shalt love the Lord thy God with all thy heart, and with all thy soul, and with all thy mind.

38 This is the first and great commandment.

39 And the second *is* like unto it, Thou shalt love thy neighbour as thyself.

40 On these two commandments hang all the law and the Prophets.

41 While the Pharisees were gathered together, Jesus asked them,

42 Saying, What think ye of Christ? whose son is he? They say unto him, *The Son* of David.

43 He saith unto them, How then doth David in spirit call him Lord, saying,

44 The LORD said unto my Lord, Sit thou on my right hand, till I make thine enemies thy footstool?

45 If David then call him Lord, how is he his son?

46 And no man was able to answer him a word, neither durst any *man* from that day forth ask him any more *questions*.

IN the beginning of this passage we find our Lord replying to the question of a certain lawyer, who asked him which was "the great commandment of the law?" That question was asked in no friendly spirit. But we have reason to be thankful that it was asked at all. It drew from our Lord an answer full of precious instruction. Thus we see how good may come out of evil.

Let us mark *what an admirable summary these verses contain of our duty towards God and our neighbour.* Jesus says, "Thou shalt love the Lord thy God with all thy heart, and with all thy soul, and with all thy mind." He says again, "Thou shalt love thy neighbour as thyself." And He adds, "On these two commandments hang all the law and the prophets."

How simple are these two rules, and yet how comprehensive! How soon the words are repeated, and yet how much they contain! How humbling and condemning they are! How much they prove our daily need of mercy and the precious blood of atonement! Happy would it be for the world, if these rules were more known and more practised!

Love is the grand secret of true obedience to God. When we feel towards Him as children feel towards a dear father, we shall delight to do His will. We shall not find His commandments grievous, and work for Him like slaves under fear of the lash. We shall take pleasure in trying to keep His laws, and mourn when we transgress them. None work so well as they who work for love. The fear of punishment, or the desire of reward, are principles of far less power. They do the will of God best, who do it from the heart. Would we train children right? Let us teach them to love God.

Love is the grand secret of right behaviour towards our fellow men. He who loves his neighbour will scorn to do him any wilful injury, either in person, property, or character.—But he will not rest there. He will desire in every way to do him good. He will strive to promote his comfort and happiness in every way. He will endeavour to lighten his sorrows, and increase his joys. When a man loves us, we feel confidence in him. We know that he will never intentionally do us harm, and that in every time of need he will be our friend. Would we teach children to behave aright towards others? Let us teach them to love everybody as themselves, and do to others as they would have others do to them.

But how shall we obtain this love towards God? It is no natural feeling. We are born in sin, and, as sinners, are afraid of God. How then can we love Him? We can never really love Him till we are at peace with Him through Christ. When we feel our sins forgiven, and ourselves reconciled to our holy Maker, then, and not till then, we shall love Him and have the spirit of adoption. Faith in Christ is the true spring of love to God. They love most who feel most forgiven. "We love him because he first loved us." (1 John iv. 19.)

And how shall we obtain this love towards our neighbour? This also is no natural feeling. We are born selfish, hateful, and hating one another. (Titus iii. 3.) We shall never love our fellow man aright till our hearts are changed by the Holy Ghost. We must be born again. We must put off the old man, and put on the new, and receive the mind that was in Christ Jesus. Then, and not till then, our cold hearts will know true God-like love towards all. "The fruit of the Spirit is love." (Galat. v. 22.)

Let these things sink down into our hearts. There is much vague talk in these latter days about love and charity. Men profess to admire them and desire to see them increased, and yet hate the principles which alone can produce them. Let us stand fast in the old paths. We cannot have fruits and flowers without roots. We cannot have love to God and man without faith in Christ, and without regeneration. The way to spread true love in the world, is to teach the atonement of Christ, and the work of the Holy Ghost.

The concluding portion of the passage, contains *a question put to the Pharisees by our Lord.* After answering with perfect wisdom the inquiries of His adversaries, He at last asks them, "What think ye of Christ? Whose Son is He?" They reply at once, "the son of David." He then asks them to explain, why David in the book of Psalms calls Him Lord. (Psalm cx. 1.) "If David then call him Lord, how is he his son?" At once His enemies were put to silence. "No man was able to answer him a word." The Scribes and Pharisees no doubt were familiar with the Psalm He quoted, but they could not explain its application. It could only be explained by conceding the pre-existence and divinity of the Messiah. This the Pharisees would not concede. Their only idea of Messiah was, that He was to be a man like one of themselves. Their ignorance of the Scriptures, of which they pretended to know more than others, and their low, carnal view of the true nature of Christ, were thus exposed at one and the same time. Well may Matthew say, by the Holy Ghost, "From that day forth durst no man ask him any more questions!"

Let us not leave these verses without making a practical use of our Lord's solemn question, "What think ye of Christ?" What do we think of His person, and His offices? What do we think of His life, and what of His death for us on the cross? What do we think of His resurrection, ascension, and intercession at the right hand of God? Have we tasted that He is gracious? Have we laid hold on Him by faith? Have we found by experience that He is precious to our souls? Can we truly say He is my Redeemer, and my Saviour, my Shepherd, and my Friend?

These are serious inquiries. May we never rest till we can give a satisfactory answer to them. It will not profit us to read about Christ, if we are not joined to Him by living faith. Once more then let us test our religion by this question; "What think we of Christ?"

MATTHEW XXIII. 1—12.

1 Then spake Jesus to the multitude, and to his disciples,

2 Saying, the Scribes and the Pharisees sit in Moses' seat:

3 All therefore whatsoever they bid you observe, *that* observe and do; but do not ye after their works: for they say, and do not.

4 For they bind heavy burdens and grievous to be borne, and lay *them* on men's shoulders; but they *themselves* will not move them with one of their fingers.

5 But all their works they do for to be seen of men: they make broad their phylacteries, and enlarge the borders of their garments,

6 And love the uppermost rooms at feasts, and the chief seats in the synagogues,

7 And greetings in the markets, and to be called of men, Rabbi, Rabbi.

8 But be not ye called Rabbi: for one is your Master, *even* Christ; and all ye are brethren.

9 And call no *man* your father upon the earth: for one is your Father, which is in heaven.

10 Neither be ye called masters: for one is your Master, *even* Christ.

11 But he that is greatest among you shall be your servant.

12 And whosoever shall exalt himself shall be abased; and he that shall humble himself shall be exalted.

WE are now beginning a chapter which in one respect is the most remarkable in the four Gospels. It contains the last words which the Lord Jesus ever spoke within the walls of the temple. Those last words consist of a withering exposure of the Scribes and Pharisees, and a sharp rebuke of their doctrines and practices. Knowing full well that His time on earth was drawing to a close, our Lord no longer keeps back His opinion of the leading teachers of the Jews. Knowing that He would soon leave His followers alone, like sheep among wolves, He warns them plainly against the false shepherds, by whom they were surrounded.

The whole chapter is a signal example of boldness and faithfulness in denouncing error. It is a striking proof that it is possible for the most loving heart to use the language of stern reproof. Above all it is an awful evidence of the guilt of unfaithful teachers. So long as the world stands, this chapter ought to be a warning and a beacon to all ministers of religion. No sins are so sinful as theirs in the sight of Christ.

In the twelve verses which begin the chapter, we see firstly, *the duty of distinguishing between the office of a false teacher and his example.* "The Scribes and Pharisees sat in Moses' seat." Rightly or wrongly, they occupied the position of the chief public teachers of religion among the Jews. However unworthily they filled the place of authority, their office entitled them to respect. But while their office was respected, their bad lives were not to be copied. And although their teaching was to be adhered to, so long as it was Scriptural, it was not to be observed when it contradicted the Word of God. To use the words of Brentius, "They were to be heard when they taught what Moses taught," but no longer. That such was our Lord's meaning is evident from the whole tenor of the chapter we are reading. False doctrine is there denounced as well as false practice.

The duty here placed before us is one of great importance. There is a constant tendency in the human mind to run into extremes. If we do not regard the office of the minister with idolatrous veneration, we are apt to treat it with indecent contempt. Against both these extremes we have need to be on our guard. However much we may disapprove of a minister's practice, or dissent from his teaching, we must never forget to respect his office.—We must show that we can honour the commission, whatever we may think of the officer that holds it. The example of St. Paul on a certain occasion is worthy of notice, "I wist not, brethren, that he was the high priest: for it is written, thou shalt not speak evil of the ruler of thy people." (Acts xxiii. 5.)

We see secondly, in these verses, *that inconsistency, ostentation, and love of pre-eminence, among professors of religion, are specially displeasing to Christ.* As to inconsistency it is remarkable that the very first thing our Lord says of the Pharisees is, that "they say, and do not." They required from others what they did not practice themselves.—As to *ostentation,* our Lord declares that they did all their works "to be seen of men." They had their phylacteries, or strips of parchment, with texts written on them, which many Jews wore on their clothes, made of an excessive size. They had the "borders," or fringes of their garments, which Moses bade Israelites to wear as a remembrance of God, made of an extravagant width. (Num. xv. 38.) And all this was done to attract notice, and to make people think how holy they were.—As to *love of preeminence,* our Lord tells us that the Pharisees loved to have "the chief seats" given them in public places, and to have flattering titles addressed to them. All these things our Lord holds up to reprobation. Against all He would have us watch and pray. They are soul-ruining sins. "How can ye believe which receive honour one of another." (John v. 44.) Happy would it have been for the Church of Christ, if this passage had been more deeply pondered, and the spirit of it more implicitly obeyed. The Pharisees are not the only people who have imposed austerities on others, and affected a sanctity of apparel, and loved the praise of man. The annals of Church history show that only too many Christians have walked closely in their steps. May we remember this and be wise! It is perfectly possible for a baptized Englishman to be in spirit a thorough Pharisee.

We see in the third place, from these verses, that *Christians must never give to any man the titles and honours which are due to God alone and to His Christ.* We are to " call no man Father on earth."

The rule here laid down must be interpreted with proper Scriptural qualification. We are not forbidden to esteem ministers very highly in love for their work's sake. (1 Thess. v. 13.) Even St. Paul, one of the humblest saints, called Titus "his own son in the faith," and says to the Corinthians, " I have begotten you through the gospel." (1 Cor. iv. 15.) But still we must be very careful that we do not insensibly give to ministers a place and an honour which do not belong to them. We must never allow them to come between ourselves and Christ. The very best are not infallible. They are not priests who can atone for us. They are not mediators who can undertake to manage our soul's affairs with God. They are men of like passions with ourselves, needing the same cleansing blood, and the same renewing Spirit, set a-part to a high and holy calling, but still after all only men. Let us never forget these things. Such cautions are always useful. Human nature would always rather lean on a visible minister, than an invisible Christ.

We see in the last place, that *there is no grace which should distinguish the Christian so much as humility.* He that would be great in the eyes of Christ, must aim at a totally different mark from that of the Pharisees. His aim must be, not so much to rule as to serve the Church. Well says Baxter, "church *greatness* consisteth in being *greatly* serviceable." The desire of the Pharisee was to receive honour, and to be called "master." The desire of the Christian must be to do good, and to give himself, and all that he has to the service of others. Truly this is a high standard, but a lower one must never content us. The example of our blessed Lord, the direct command of the apostolic Epistles, both alike require us to be "clothed with humility." (1 Peter v. 5.) Let us seek that blessed grace day by day. None is so beautiful, however much despised by the world. None is such an evidence of saving faith, and true conversion to God. None is so often commended by our Lord. Of all His sayings, hardly any is so often repeated as that which concludes the passage we have now read, "He that shall humble himself shall be exalted."

MATTHEW XXIII. 13—33.

13 But woe unto you, Scribes and Pharisees, hypocrites! for ye shut up the kingdom of heaven against men: for ye neither go in *yourselves*, neither suffer ye them that are entering to go in.

14 Woe unto you, Scribes and Pharisees, hypocrites! for ye devour widows' houses, and for a pretence make long prayer: therefore ye shall receive the greater damnation.

15 Woe unto you, Scribes and Pharisees, hypocrites! for ye compass sea and land to make one proselyte, and when he is made, ye make him twofold more the child of hell than yourselves.

16 Woe unto you, *ye* blind guides, which say, Whosoever shall swear by the temple, it is nothing; but whosoever shall swear by the gold of the temple, he is a debtor!

17 *Ye* fools and blind: for whether is greater, the gold, or the temple that sanctifieth the gold?

18 And, Whosoever shall swear by the altar, it is nothing; but whosoever sweareth by the gift that is upon it, he is guilty.

19 *Ye* fools and blind: for whether *is* greater, the gift, or the altar that sanctifieth the gift?

20 Whoso therefore shall swear by the altar, sweareth by it, and by all things thereon.

21 And whoso shall swear by the temple, sweareth by it, and by him that dwelleth therein.

22 And he that shall swear by heaven, sweareth by the throne of God, and by him that sitteth thereon.

23 Woe unto you, Scribes and Pharisees, hypocrites! for ye pay tithe of mint and anise and cummin, and have omitted the weightier *matters* of the law, judgment, mercy, and faith: these ought ye to have done, and not to leave the other undone.

24 *Ye* blind guides, which strain at a gnat, and swallow a camel.

25 Woe unto you, Scribes and Pharisees, hypocrites! for ye make clean the outside of the cup and of the platter, but within they are full of extortion and excess.

26 *Thou* blind Pharisee, cleanse first that *which is* within the cup and platter, that the outside of them may be clean also.

27 Woe unto you, Scribes and Pharisees, hypocrites! for ye are like unto whited sepulchres, which indeed appear beautiful outward, but are within full of dead *men's* bones, and of all uncleanness.

28 Even so ye also outwardly appear righteous unto men, but within ye are full of hypocrisy and iniquity.

29 Woe unto you, Scribes and Pharisees, hypocrites! because ye build the tombs of the prophets, and garnish the sepulchres of the righteous,

30 And say, If we had been in the days of our fathers, we would not have been partakers with them in the blood of the prophets.

31 Wherefore ye be witnesses unto yourselves, that ye are the children of them which killed the prophets.

32 Fill ye up then the measure of your fathers.

33 *Ye* serpents, *ye* generation of vipers, how can ye escape the damnation of hell?

WE have in these verses the charges of our Lord against the Jewish teachers ranged under eight heads. Standing in the midst of the temple, with a listening crowd around Him, He publicly denounces the main errors of the Scribes and Pharisees in unsparing terms. Eight times He uses the solemn expression, "woe unto you." Seven times He calls them "hypocrites." Twice He speaks of them as blind guides,—twice as "fools and blind,"—once as "serpents and a generation of vipers." Let us mark that language well. It teaches a solemn lesson. It shows how utterly abominable the spirit of the Scribes and Pharisees is in God's sight, in whatever form it may be found.

Let us glance shortly at the eight charges which our Lord brings forward, and then seek to draw from the whole passage some general instruction.

The first "woe" in the list is directed against the systematic opposition of the Scribes and Pharisees to the progress of the Gospel. They "shut up the kingdom of heaven." They would neither go in themselves, nor suffer others to go in. They rejected the warning voice of John the Baptist. They refused to acknowledge Jesus, when He appeared among them, as the Messiah. They tried to keep back Jewish inquirers. They would not believe the Gospel themselves, and they did all in their power to prevent others believing it. This was a great sin.

The second "woe" in the list is directed against the covetousness and self-aggrandizing spirit of the Scribes and Pharisees. They "devoured widows' houses, and for a pretence made long prayer." They imposed on the credulity of weak and unprotected women, by an affectation of great devoutness, until they were regarded as their spiritual directors. They scrupled not to abuse the influence thus unrighteously obtained, to their own temporal advantage, and in a word to make money by their religion. This again was a great sin.

The third "woe" in the list is directed against the zeal of the Scribes and Pharisees for making partisans. They "compassed sea and land to make one proselyte." They laboured incessantly to make men join their party and adopt their opinions. They did this from no desire to benefit men's souls in the least, or to bring them to God. They only did it to swell the ranks of their sect, and to increase the number of their adherents, and their own importance. Their religious zeal arose from sectarianism, and not from the love of God. This also was a great sin.

The fourth "woe" in the list is directed against the doctrines of the Scribes and Pharisees about oaths. They drew subtle distinctions between one kind of oath and another. They taught the jesuitical tenet, that some oaths were binding on men, while others were not. They attached greater importance to oaths sworn "by the gold" offered to the temple, than to oaths sworn "by the temple" itself. By so doing they brought the third commandment into contempt,—and by making men overrate the value of alms and oblations, advanced their own interests. This again was a great sin.*

The fifth "woe" in the list is directed against the practice of the Scribes and Pharisees, to exalt trifles in religion above serious things, to put the last things first, and the first last. They made great ado about tithing "mint," and other garden herbs, as if they could not be too strict in their obedience to God's law. And yet at the same time they neglected great plain duties, such as justice, charity, and honesty. This again was a great sin.

---

* This practice of tampering with oaths, was well known among the heathen, as a feature in the Jewish character. It is a striking fact, that Martial, the Roman poet, specially refers to it.

"Ecce negas, jurasque mihi per templa Tonantis;
    Non credo: Jura, verpe, per Anchialum."—MARTIAL IX. 94.

The sixth and seventh "woes" in the list possess too much in common to be divided. They are directed against a general characteristic of the religion of the Scribes. They set outward purity and decency above inward sanctification and purity of heart. They made it a religious duty to cleanse the "outside" of their cups and platters, but neglected their own inward man. They were like whitened sepulchres, clean and beautiful externally, but within full of all corruption. "Even so they outwardly appeared righteous, but within were full of hypocrisy and iniquity." This also was a great sin.

The last "woe" in the list is directed against the affected veneration of the Scribes and Pharisees for the memory of dead saints. They built the "tombs of the prophets," and garnished "the sepulchres of the righteous." And yet their own lives proved that they were of one mind with those who "killed the prophets." Their own conduct was a daily evidence that they liked dead saints better than living ones. The very men that pretended to honour dead prophets, could see no beauty in a living Christ. This also was a great sin.*

Such is the melancholy picture which our Lord gives of Jewish teachers. Let us turn from the contemplation

---

* A passage from the Berlenberger Bible on this subject is sufficiently striking to deserve insertion.

"Ask in Moses's times, who were the good people, they will be Abraham, Isaac, and Jacob, but not Moses,—he should be stoned. Ask in Samuel's times, who were the good people, they will be Moses and Joshua, but not Samuel. Ask in the times of Christ, who were such, they will be all the former prophets with Samuel, but not Christ and His apostles."

The Latin proverbs "mortui non mordent," and "sit divus, dummodo non vivus," are both illustrative of the same truth.

of it with sorrow and humiliation. It is a fearful exhibition of the morbid anatomy of human nature. It is a picture which unhappily has been reproduced over and over again in the history of the Church of Christ. There is not a point in the character of the Scribes and Pharisees in which it might not be easily shown, that persons calling themselves Christians have often walked in their steps.*

Let us learn from the whole passage how deplorable was the condition of the Jewish nation when our Lord was upon earth. When such were the teachers, what must have been the miserable darkness of the taught! Truly the iniquity of Israel had come to the full. It was high time indeed for the Sun of Righteousness to arise and the Gospel to be preached.

Let us learn from the whole passage how abominable is hypocrisy in the sight of God. These Scribes and Pharisees are not charged with being thieves or murderers, but with being hypocrites to the very core. Whatever we are in our religion, let us resolve never to wear a cloak. Let us by all means be honest and real.

Let us learn from the whole passage how awfully dangerous is the position of an unfaithful minister. It is bad enough to be blind ourselves. It is a thousand times worse to be a blind guide. Of all men none is so

---

*I cannot avoid the opportunity of here expressing my firm conviction, that our Lord's sayings in this chapter are meant to bear a prophetical signification, and to apply to corruptions which He foresaw would spring up in His professing church. Beyond doubt there is a most unhappy similarity between the doctrines and practices of the Scribes and Pharisees, and many of the leading corruptions of the Church of Rome.

W

culpably wicked as an unconverted minister, and none will be judged so severely. It is a solemn saying about such an one, "He resembles an unskilful pilot: he does not perish alone."

Finally, let us beware of supposing from this passage, that the safest course in religion is to make no profession at all. This is to run into a dangerous extreme. It does not follow that there is no such thing as true profession, because some men are hypocrites. It does not follow that all money is bad, because there is much counterfeit coin. Let not hypocrisy prevent our confessing Christ, or move us from our steadfastness, if we have confessed Him. Let us press on, looking unto Jesus, and resting on Him, praying daily to be kept from error, and saying with David, "let my heart be sound in thy statutes." (Psalm cxix. 80.)

MATTHEW XXIII. 34—39.

34 Wherefore, behold, I send unto you prophets, and wise men, and Scribes: and *some* of them ye shall kill and crucify; and *some* of them shall ye scourge in your synagogues, and persecute *them* from city to city:

35 That upon you may come all the righteous blood shed upon the earth, from the blood of righteous Abel unto the blood of Zacharias son of Barachias, whom ye slew between the temple and the altar.

36 Verily I say unto you, All these things shall come upon this generation.

37 O Jerusalem, Jerusalem, *thou* that killest the prophets, and stonest them which are sent unto thee, how often would I have gathered thy children together, even as a hen gathereth her chickens under *her* wings, and ye would not!

38 Behold, your house is left unto you desolate.

39 For I say unto you, Ye shall not see me henceforth, till ye shall say, Blessed *is* he that cometh in the name of the Lord.

THESE verses form the conclusion of our Lord Jesus Christ's address, on the subject of the Scribes and Pharisees. They are the last words which He ever spoke, as a public teacher, in the hearing of the people. The characteristic tenderness and compassion of our Lord, shine forth in a striking manner at the close of His ministry. Though He left His enemies in unbelief, He shows that He loved and pitied them to the last.

We learn, in the first place, from these verses, that *God often takes great pains with ungodly men.* He sent the Jews " prophets and wise men and scribes." He gave them repeated warnings. He sent them message after message. He did not allow them to go on sinning without rebuke. They could never say they were not told when they did wrong.

This is the way in which God generally deals with unconverted Christians. He does not cut them off in their sins without a call to repentance. He knocks at the door of their hearts by sicknesses and afflictions. He assails their consciences by sermons, or by the advice of friends. He summons them to consider their ways by opening the grave under their eyes, and taking away from them their idols. They often know not what it all means. They are often blind and deaf to all His gracious messages. But they will see His hand at last, though perhaps too late. They will find that "God spake once, yea twice, but they perceived it not." (Job. xxxiii. 14.) They will discover that they too, like the Jews, had prophets, and wise men, and scribes, sent to them. There was a voice in every providence, " Turn ye, turn ye, why will ye die ? " (Ezek. xxxiii. 11.)

We learn, in the second place, from these verses, that *God takes notice of the treatment which His messengers and ministers receive, and will one day reckon for it.* The

Jews, as a nation, had often given the servants of God most shameful usage. They had often dealt with them as enemies, because they told them the truth. Some they had persecuted, and some they had scourged, and some they had even killed. They thought perhaps that no account would be required of their conduct. But our Lord tells them they were mistaken. There was an eye that saw all their doings. There was a hand that registered all the innocent blood they shed, in books of everlasting remembrance. The dying words of Zacharias, who was "slain between the temple and the altar," would be found, after eight hundred and fifty years, not to have fallen to the ground.—He said, as he died, "the Lord look upon it and require it." (2 Chron. xxiv. 22.)* Yet a few years, and there would be such an inquisition for blood at Jerusalem as the world had never seen. The holy city would be destroyed. The nation which had murdered so many prophets would itself be wasted by famine, pestilence, and the sword. And even those that escaped would be scattered to the four winds, and become, like Cain the murderer, "fugitives and vagabonds upon earth." We all know how literally these sayings were fulfilled. Well might

---

* It is remarkable that the Zacharias here spoken of, is described in Chronicles as the son of Jehoiada. Our Lord speaks of him as the son of Barachias. This discrepancy has led some to suppose that the Zacharias here spoken of could not be the one who was murdered in the days of Joash, but an entirely different person. But there seems no sufficient reason for this supposition. By far the most satisfactory explanation appears to be, that the father of Zacharias had two names, Jehoiada and Barachias. It was not at all uncommon among the Jews to have two names. Matthew was also called Levi, and Jude Thaddeus.

our Lord say, " Verily all these things shall come upon this generation."

It is good for us all to mark this lesson well. We are too apt to think that " bygones are bygones," and that things which to us are past, and done, and old, will never be raked up again. But we forget that with God " one day is as a thousand years " and that the events of a thousand years ago are as fresh in His sight, as the events of this very hour. God " requireth that which is past," and above all, God will require an account of the treatment of His saints. The blood of the primitive Christians shed by the Roman Emperors,—the blood of the Vallenses and Albigenses, and the sufferers at the massacre of St. Bartholomew,—the blood of the martyrs who were burned at the time of the Reformation, and of those who have been put to death by the Inquisition,—all, all will yet be accounted for. It is an old saying, that "the mill-stones of God's justice grind slowly, but they grind very fine." The world will yet see that " there is a God that judgeth in the earth." (Psalm lviii. 11.)

Let those who persecute God's people in the present day take heed what they are doing. Let them know that all who injure, or ridicule, or mock, or slander others on account of their religion, commit a great sin. Let them know that Christ takes notice of every one who persecutes his neighbour because he is better than himself, or because he prays, reads his Bible, and thinks about his soul. He lives who said, " he that toucheth you, toucheth the apple of mine eye." (Zech. ii. 8.) The judgment day will prove that the King of kings will reckon with all who insult His servants.

We learn, in the last place, from these verses, *that those who are lost for ever, are lost through their own fault.*

The words of our Lord Jesus Christ are very remarkable. He says, "I would have gathered thy children together,—and ye would not."

There is something peculiarly deserving of notice in this expression. It throws light on a mysterious subject, and one which is often darkened by human explanations. It shows that Christ has feelings of pity and mercy for many who are not saved, and that the grand secret of man's ruin is his want of will. Impotent as man is by nature,—unable to think a good thought of himself,—without power to turn himself to faith and calling upon God,—he still appears to have a mighty ability to ruin his own soul. Powerless as he is to good, he is still powerful to evil. We say rightly that a man can do nothing of himself, but we must always remember that the seat of impotence is his *will.* A will to repent and believe no man can give himself, but a will to reject Christ and have his own way, every man possesses by nature, and if not saved at last, that will shall prove to have been his destruction. "Ye *will* not come to me," says Christ, "that ye might have life." (John v. 40.)

Let us leave the subject with the comfortable reflection, that with Christ nothing is impossible. The hardest heart can be made willing in the day of His power. Grace beyond doubt is irresistible. But never let us forget, that the Bible speaks of man as a *responsible* being, and that it says of some, "ye do always resist the Holy Ghost." (Acts vii. 51.) Let us understand that the ruin of those who are lost, is not because Christ was not willing to save them,—nor yet because they wanted to be saved, but could not,—but because they would not come to Christ. Let the ground we take up be always that of the passage we are now considering,—Christ would gather men, but they *will* not to be gathered; Christ would save men, but they *will* not to be saved. Let it be a settled principle in our religion, that man's salvation, if saved, is wholly of God; and that man's ruin, if lost, is wholly of himself. The evil that is in us is all our own. The good, if we have any, is all of God. The saved in the next world will give God all the glory. The lost in the next world will find that they have destroyed themselves. (Hosea xiii. 9.)

MATTHEW XXIV. 1—14.

1 And Jesus went out, and departed from the temple : and his disciples came to *him* for to shew him the buildings of the temple.

2 And Jesus said unto them, See ye not all these things? verily I say unto you, There shall not be left here one stone upon another, that shall not be thrown down.

3 And as he sat upon the mount of Olives, the disciples came unto him privately, saying, Tell us, when shall these things be, and what *shall be* the sign of thy coming, and of the end of the world?

4 And Jesus answered and said unto them, Take heed that no man deceive you.

5 For many shall come in my name, saying, I am Christ; and shall deceive many.

6 And ye shall hear of wars and rumours of wars : see that ye be not troubled : for all *these things* must come to pass, but the end is not yet.

7 For nation shall rise against nation, and kingdom against kingdom : and there shall be famines, and pestilences, and earthquakes, in divers places.

8 All these *are* the beginning of sorrows.

9 Then shall they deliver you up to be afflicted, and shall kill you : and ye shall be hated of all nations for my name's sake.

10 And then shall many be offended, and shall betray one another, and shall hate one another.

11 And many false prophets shall rise, and shall deceive many.

12 And because iniquity shall abound, the love of many shall wax cold.

13 But he that shall endure unto the end, the same shall be saved.

14 And this Gospel of the kingdom shall be preached in all the world for a witness unto all nations; and then shall the end come.

THESE verses begin a chapter full of prophecy,—prophecy

of which a large portion is unfulfilled,—prophecy which ought to be deeply interesting to all true Christians. It is a subject to which the Holy Ghost says, we "do well to take heed." (2 Peter i.)

All portions of Scripture like this, ought to be approached with deep humility, and earnest prayer for the teaching of the Spirit. On no point have good men so entirely disagreed as on the interpretation of prophecy. On no point have the prejudices of one class, the dogmatism of a second, and the extravagance of a third, done so much to rob the church of truths, which God intended to be a blessing. Well says Olshausen, "What does not man see, or fail to see, when it serves to establish his own favourite opinions?"

To understand the drift of the whole chapter, we must carefully keep in view the question which gave rise to our Lord's discourse. On leaving the temple for the last time, the disciples, with the natural feeling of Jews, had called their Master's attention to the splendid buildings of which it was composed. To their surprise and amazement, He tells them that the whole was about to be destroyed. These words appear to have sunk deeply into the minds of the disciples. They came to Him, as He sat upon the Mount of Olives, and asked Him with evident anxiety, "Tell us when shall these things be? and what shall be the sign of thy coming, and of the end of the world?"—In these words we see the clue to the subject of the prophecy now before us. It embraces three points,—one, the destruction of Jerusalem; —another, the second personal advent of Christ;—and a third, the end of the world. These three points are undoubtedly in some parts of the chapter so entwined together, that it is difficult to separate and disentangle them. But all these points appear distinctly in the chapter, and without them it cannot be fairly explained.

The first fourteen verses of the prophecy are taken up with general lessons of wide range and application. They seem to apply with equal force to the close of both Jewish and Christian dispensations, the one event being strikingly typical of the other. They certainly demand special notice from us, on whom the latter ends of the world are come. Let us now see what those lessons are.

The first general lesson before us, is *a warning against deception*. The very first words of the discourse are, "Take heed that no man deceive you."

A more needful warning than this cannot be conceived. Satan knows well the value of prophecy, and has ever laboured to bring the subject into contempt. How many false Christs and false prophets arose before the destruction of Jerusalem, the works of Josephus abundantly prove. In how many ways the eyes of man are continually blinded in the present day, as to things to come, it might easily be shown. Irvingism and Mormonism have been only too successfully used as arguments for rejecting the whole doctrine of the second advent of Christ. Let us watch, and be on our guard.

Let no man deceive us as to the leading *facts* of unfulfilled prophecy, by telling us they are impossible,—or as to the *manner* in which they will be brought to pass, by telling us it is improbable and contrary to past experience. Let no man deceive us as to the *time* when unfulfilled prophecies will be accomplished, either by fixing dates on the one hand, or bidding us wait for the conversion of the world on the other.—On all these points let the plain meaning of Scripture be our only guide, and not the traditional interpretations of men. Let us not be ashamed to say that we expect a literal fulfilment of unfulfilled prophecy. Let us frankly allow that there are many things we do not understand, but still hold our ground tenaciously,—believe much,—wait long,—and not doubt that all will one day be made clear. Above all, let us remember that the first coming of Messiah to *suffer*, was the most improbable event that could have been conceived, and let us not doubt that as He literally came in person to suffer, so He will literally come again in person to *reign*.

The second grand lesson before us, is *a warning against over-sanguine and extravagant expectations as to things which are to happen before the end comes*. It is a warning as deeply important as the preceding one. Happy would it have been for the Church, if it had not been so much neglected.

We are not to expect a reign of universal peace, happiness, and prosperity, before the end comes. If we do, we shall be greatly deceived. Our Lord bids us look for "wars, famines, pestilence," and persecution. It is vain to expect peace until the Prince of Peace returns. Then, and not till then, the swords shall be beaten into ploughshares, and nations learn war no more. Then, and not till then, the earth shall bring forth her increase. (Isai. ii. 4. Psal. lxviii. 6.)

We are not to expect a time of universal purity of

doctrine and practice in the Church of Christ, before the end comes. If we do, we shall be greatly mistaken. Our Lord bids us look for the rising of "false prophets," the "abounding of iniquity," and the "waxing cold of the love of many." The truth will never be received by all professing Christians, and holiness be the rule among men, until the great Head of the Church returns, and Satan is bound. Then, and not till then, there will be a glorious Church, without spot or blemish. (Ephes. v. 27.)

We are not to expect that all the world will be converted before the end comes. If we do, we shall be greatly mistaken. "The Gospel is to be preached in all the world for a witness unto all nations," but we must not think that we shall see it universally believed. It will "take out a people," wherever it is faithfully preached, as witnesses to Christ, but the full gathering of the nations shall never take place until Christ comes. Then, and not till then, shall the earth be full of the knowledge of the Lord, as the waters cover the sea. (Acts xv. 14; Habak. ii. 14.)

Let us lay these things to heart, and remember them well. They are eminently truths for the present times. Let us learn to be moderate in our expectations from any existing machinery in the Church of Christ, and we shall be spared much disappointment. Let us make haste to spread the Gospel in the world, for the time is *short, not long.*—The night cometh when no man can work. Troublous times are a-head. Heresies and persecutions may soon weaken and distract the churches. A fierce war of principles may soon convulse the nations. The doors now open to do good may soon be shut for ever.

Our eyes may yet see the the sun of Christianity go
down like the sun of Judaism, in clouds and storms.
Above all, let us long for our Lord's return.   Oh! for a
heart to pray daily, "Come, Lord Jesus!"

MATTHEW XXIV. 15—28.

15 When ye therefore shall see the abomination of desolation, spoken of by Daniel the prophet, stand in the holy place, (whoso readeth, let him understand :)

16 Then let them which be in Judæa flee into the mountains :

17 Let him which is on the house-top not come down to take any thing out of his house.

18 Neither let him which is in the field return back to take his clothes.

19 And woe unto them that are with child, and to them that give suck in those days !

20 But pray ye that your flight be not in the winter, neither on the sabbath day :

21 For then shall be great tribulation, such as was not since the beginning of the world to this time, no, nor ever shall be.

22 And except those days should be shortened, there should no flesh be saved : but for the elect's sake those days shall be shortened.

23 Then if any man shall say unto you, Lo, here is Christ, or there; believe it not.

24 For there shall arise false Christs, and false prophets, and shall shew great signs and wonders ; insomuch that, if it were possible, they shall deceive the very elect.

25 Behold, I have told you before.

26 Wherefore if they shall say unto you, Behold, he is in the desert; go not forth : behold, he is in the secret chambers; believe it not.

27 For as the lightning cometh out of the east, and shineth even unto the west; so shall also the coming of the Son of man be.

28 For wheresoever the carcase is, there will the eagles be gathered together.

ONE main subject of this part of our Lord's prophecy,
is the taking of Jerusalem by the Romans.   That great
event took place about forty years after the words we
have now read were spoken.   A full account of it is to
be found in the writings of the historian Josephus.   Those
writings are the best comment on our Lord's words.
They are a striking proof of the accuracy of every tittle
of His predictions.*   The horrors and miseries which

---

* These are the words of Josephus. They are the more remarkable when we remember that he was not a Christian. "No

the Jews endured throughout the siege of their city exceed anything on record. It was truly a time of "tribulation, such as was not since the beginning of the world."

It surprises some to find so much importance attached to the taking of Jerusalem. They would rather regard the whole chapter as unfulfilled. Such persons forget that Jerusalem and the temple were the heart of the old Jewish dispensation. When they were destroyed, the old Mosaic system came to an end. The daily sacrifice, the yearly feasts, the altar, the holy of holies, the priesthood, were all essential parts of revealed religion, till Christ came, but no longer. When He died upon the cross, their work was done. They were dead, and it only remained that they should be buried.—But it was not fitting that this thing should be done quietly. The ending of a dispensation given with so much solemnity at Mount Sinai, might well be expected to be marked with peculiar solemnity. The destruction of the holy temple, where so many old saints had seen "shadows of good things to come," might well be expected to form a subject of prophecy. And so it was. The Lord Jesus specially predicts the desolation of "the holy place." The great High Priest describes the end of the dispensation which had been a schoolmaster to bring men to Himself.

But we must not suppose that this part of our Lord's prophecy is exhausted by the first taking of Jerusalem. It is more than probable that our Lord's words have a

other city ever suffered such things. All the calamities which have ever happened to any from the beginning, seem not comparable to those which befel the Jews."

further and deeper application still. It is more than probable that they apply to a *second siege of Jerusalem*, which is yet to take place, when Israel has returned to their own land,—and to a *second tribulation* on the inhabitants thereof, which shall only be stopped by the advent of our Lord Jesus Christ. Such a view of this passage may sound startling to some.* But those who doubt its correctness would do well to study the last chapter of the prophet Zechariah, and the last chapter of Daniel. These two chapters contain solemn things. They throw great light on the verses we are now reading, and their connection with the verses which immediately follow.

It now remains for us to consider the lessons which this passage contains for our own personal edification. These lessons are plain and unmistakeable. In them at least there is no darkness at all.

For one thing, we see that *flight from danger may sometimes be the positive duty of a Christian.* Our Lord Himself commanded his people under certain circumstances "to flee."

The servant of Christ undoubtedly is not to be a coward. He is to confess his master before men. He is to be willing to die, if needful, for the truth. But the servant of Christ is not required to run into danger, unless it comes in the line of duty. He is not to be ashamed to

---

* I think it well to say, that Irenœus, and Hilary among the fathers, and Ferus in the sixteenth century, all refer the fulfilment of this part of our Lord's prophecy to the end of the world, when a personal Antichrist shall appear. Hilary considers that the verse which speaks of "the abomination of desolation standing in the holy place," will be fulfilled by the rise of a mighty personal Antichrist, who shall be worshipped by infidels. In connection with this verse, 2 Thess. ii. 4, deserves attentive study.

use reasonable means to provide for his personal safety, when no good is to be done by dying at his post. There is deep wisdom in this lesson. The true martyrs are not always those who court death, and are in a hurry to be beheaded or burned. There are times when it shows more grace to be quiet, and wait, and pray, and watch for opportunities, than to defy our adversaries, and rush into the battle. May we have wisdom to know how to act in time of persecution! It is possible to be rash, as well as to be a coward,—and to stop our own usefulness by being over hot, as well as by being over cold.

We see, for another thing, that *in delivering this prophecy, our Lord makes special mention of the Sabbath.* "Pray ye," he says, "that your flight be not on the Sabbath day."

This is a fact that deserves special notice. We live in times when the obligation of the Sabbath upon Christians is frequently denied by good men. They tell us that it is no more binding on us than the ceremonial law. It is difficult to see how such a view can be reconciled with our Lord's words on this solemn occasion. He seems intentionally to mention the Sabbath, when He is foretelling the final destruction of the temple and the Mosaic ceremonies, as if to mark the day with honour. He seems to hint that, although His people would be absolved from the yoke of sacrifices and ordinances, there would yet remain the keeping of a Sabbath for them. (Heb. iv. 9.) The friends of a holy Sunday ought carefully to remember this text. It is one which will bear much weight.

We see for another thing, *that God's elect are always special objects of God's care.* Twice in this passage our Lord mentions them. "For the elect's sake the days of tribulation are to be shortened." It will not be possible to deceive the "elect."

Those whom God has chosen to salvation by Christ, are those whom God specially loves in this world. They are the jewels among mankind. He cares more for them than for kings on their thrones, if kings are not converted. He hears their prayers. He orders all the events of nations and the issues of wars for their good, and their sanctification. He keeps them by His Spirit. He allows neither man nor devil to pluck them out of His hand. Whatever tribulation comes on the world, God's elect are safe. May we never rest till we know that we are of this blessed number! There breathes not the man or woman who can prove that he is not one. The promises of the Gospel are open to all. May we give diligence to make our calling and election sure! God's elect are a people who cry unto Him night and day. When Paul saw the faith, and hope, and love of the Thessalonians, then he knew "their election of God." (1 Thess. i. 4. Luke xviii. 7.)

Finally, we see from these verses, that *whenever the second advent of Christ takes place, it will be a very sudden event.* It will be "as the lightning coming out of the east, and shining even to the west."

This is a practical truth that we should ever keep before our minds. That our Lord Jesus will come again in person to this world, we know from Scripture. That He will come in a time of great tribulation, we also know.

But the precise period, the year, the month, the day, the hour, are all hidden things. We only know that it will be a very sudden event. Our plain duty then is to live always prepared for His return. Let us walk by faith, and not by sight. Let us believe in Christ, serve Christ, follow Christ, and love Christ. So living, when ever Christ may return, we shall be ready to meet Him.

MATTHEW XXIV. 29—35.

29 Immediately after the tribulation of those days shall the sun be darkened, and the moon shall not give her light, and the stars shall fall from heaven, and the powers of the heavens shall be shaken :

30 And then shall appear the sign of the Son of man in heaven : and then shall all the tribes of the earth mourn, and they shall see the Son of man coming in the clouds of heaven with power and great glory.

31 And he shall send his angels with a great sound of a trumpet, and they shall gather together his elect from the four winds, from one end of heaven to the other.

32 Now learn a parable of the fig tree ; When his branch is yet tender, and putteth forth leaves, ye know that summer *is* nigh :

33 So likewise ye, when ye shall see all these things, know that it is near, *even* at the doors.

34 Verily I say unto you, This generation shall not pass till all these things be fulfilled.

35 Heaven and earth shall pass away, but my words shall not pass away.

In this part of our Lord's prophecy, He describes His own second coming, to judge the world. This, at all events, seems the natural meaning of the passage. To take any lower view appears to be a violent straining of Scripture language. If the solemn words here used mean nothing more than the coming of the Roman armies to Jerusalem, we may explain away any thing in the Bible. The event here described is one of far greater moment than the march of any earthly army. It is nothing less than the closing act of this dispensation, the second personal advent of Jesus Christ.

x

These verses teach us, in the first place, *that when the Lord Jesus returns to this world, He shall come with peculiar glory and majesty.* He shall come " in the clouds of heaven with power and great glory." Before His presence the very sun, moon, and stars shall be darkened, and " the powers of heaven shall be shaken."

The second personal coming of Christ shall be as different as possible from the first. He came the first time as a man of sorrows and acquainted with grief. He was born in the manger of Bethlehem, in lowliness and humiliation. He took on Him the form of a servant, and was despised and rejected of men. He was betrayed into the hands of wicked men, condemned by an unjust judgment, mocked, scourged, crowned with thorns, and at last crucified between two thieves.—He shall come the second time as the King of all the earth, with all royal majesty. The princes and great men of this world, shall themselves stand before His throne to receive an eternal sentence. Before Him every mouth shall be stopped, and every knee bow, and every tongue shall confess that Jesus Christ is Lord. May we all remember this. Whatever ungodly men may do now, there will be no scoffing, no jesting at Christ, no infidelity at the last day. The servants of Jesus may well wait patiently. Their master shall one day be acknowledged King of kings by all the world.

These verses teach us, in the second place, *that when Christ returns to this world, He will first take care of His believing people.* He shall " send his angels," and " gather together his elect."

In the day of judgment true Christians shall be perfectly safe. Not a hair of their heads shall fall to the ground. Not one bone of Christ's mystical body shall be broken. There was an ark for Noah, in the day of the flood. There was a Zoar for Lot, when Sodom was destroyed. There shall be a hiding-place for all believers in Jesus, when the wrath of God at last bursts on this wicked world. Those mighty angels who rejoiced in heaven when each sinner repented, shall gladly catch up the people of Christ to meet their Lord in the air. That day no doubt will be an awful day, but believers may look forward to it without fear.

In the day of judgment true Christians shall at length be gathered together. The saints of every age, and every tongue shall be assembled out of every land. All shall be there, from righteous Abel down to the last soul that is converted to God,—from the oldest patriarch down to the little infant that just breathed and died. Let us think what a happy gathering that will be, when all the family of God are at length together. If it has been pleasant to meet one or two saints occasionally on earth, how much more pleasant will it be to meet a "multitude that no man can number!" Surely we may be content to carry the cross, and put up with partings for a few years. We travel on towards a day, when we shall meet to part no more.

These verses teach us, in the third place, that *until Christ returns to this earth, the Jews will always remain a separate people.* Our Lord tells us, "This generation shall not pass, till all these things be fulfilled." *

---

* I see no other interpretation of these much controverted words, "this generation," which is in the least satisfactory, and is not

The continued existence of the Jews as a distinct nation, is undeniably a great miracle. It is one of those evidences of the truth of the Bible which the Infidel can never overthrow. Without a land, without a king, without a government, scattered and dispersed over the world for eighteen hundred years, the Jews are never absorbed among the people of the countries where they live, like Frenchmen, Englishmen, and Germans, but "dwell alone." Nothing can account for this but the finger of God. The Jewish nation stands before the world, a crushing answer to infidelity, and a living book of evidence that the Bible is true. But we ought not to regard the Jews only as witnesses of the truth of Scripture. We should see in them a continual pledge, that the Lord Jesus is coming again one day. Like the sacrament of the Lord's supper, they witness to the reality of the second advent, as well as of the first. Let us remember this. Let us see in every wandering Jew a proof that the Bible is true, and that Christ will one day return.

Finally, these verses teach us, *that our Lord's predictions will certainly be fulfilled.* He says, "heaven and earth shall pass away, but my words shall not pass away."

Our Lord knew well the natural unbelief of human

open to very serious objections. The word "generation" admits of the sense in which I have taken it, and seems to me to be used in that sense in Matt. xii. 45, xvii. 17, and xxiii. 36; Luke xvi. 8, and xvii. 25; and Philipp. ii. 15. The view that I have propounded is not new. It is adopted by Mede, Parœus, Flacius Illyricus, Calovius, Jansenius, Du Veil, Adam Clarke, and Stier.

Chrysostom, Origen and Theophylact consider "this generation" to mean "true believers."

nature. He knew that scoffers would arise in the last days, saying, where is the promise of His coming ? (2 Pet. iii. 4.) He knew that when He came, faith would be rare on the earth. He foresaw how many would contemptuously reject the solemn predictions He had just been delivering as improbable, unlikely, and absurd. He warns us all against such sceptical thoughts, with a caution of peculiar solemnity. He tells us that, whatever man may say or think, His words shall be fulfilled in their season, and shall not " pass away," unaccomplished. May we all lay to heart His warning. We live in an unbelieving age. Few believed the report of our Lord's first coming, and few believe the report of His second. (Isaiah liii. 1.) Let us beware of this infection, and believe to the saving of our souls. We are not reading cunningly devised fables, but deep and momentous truths. May God give us a heart to believe them.

MATTHEW XXIV. 36—51.

36 But of that day and hour knoweth no *mun*, no, not the angels of heaven, but my Father only.

37 But as the days of Noe *were*, so shall also the coming of the Son of man be.

38 For as in the days that were before the flood they were eating and drinking, marrying and giving in marriage, until the day that Noe entered into the ark,

39 And knew not until the flood came, and took them all away; so shall also the coming of the Son of man be.

40 Then shall two be in the field; the one shall be taken, and the other left.

41 Two *women shall be* grinding at the mill; the one shall be taken, and the other left.

42 Watch therefore : for ye know not what hour your Lord doth come.

43 But know this, that if the goodman of the house had known in what watch the thief would come, he would have watched, and would not have suffered his house to be broken up.

44 Therefore be ye also ready : for in such an hour as ye think not the Son of man cometh.

45 Who then is a faithful and wise servant, whom his lord hath made ruler over his household, to give them meat in due season ?

46 Blessed *is* that servant whom his lord when he cometh shall find so doing.

47 Verily I say unto you, That he shall make him ruler over all his goods.

48 But and if that evil servant shall say in his heart, My lord delayeth his coming;

49 And shall begin to smite *his* fellow-servants, and to eat and drink with the drunken;

50 The lord of that servant shall come in a day when he looketh not for *him*, and in an hour that he is not aware of,

51 And shall cut him asunder, and appoint *him* his portion with the hypocrites : there shall be weeping and gnashing of teeth.

THERE are verses in this passage which are often much misapplied. "The coming of the Son of man" is often spoken of as being the same thing as death. The texts which describe the uncertainty of His coming are often used in epitaphs, and thought suitable to the tomb. But there is really no solid ground for such an application of this passage. Death is one thing, and the coming of the Son of man is quite another. The subject of these verses is not death, but the second advent of Jesus Christ. Let us remember this. It is a serious thing to wrest Scripture out of its true meaning.

The first thing that demands our attention in these verses, *is the awful account that they give of the state of the world, when the Lord Jesus comes again.*

The world will not be converted when Christ returns. It will be found in the same condition that it was in the day of the flood. When the flood came, men were found "eating and drinking, marrying and given in marriage," absorbed in their worldly pursuits, and utterly regardless of Noah's repeated warnings. They saw no likelihood of a flood. They would not believe there was any danger. But at last the flood came suddenly and "took them all away." All that were not with Noah in the ark were drowned. They were all swept away to their last account, unpardoned, unconverted, and unprepared to meet God. And our Lord says, "so shall also the coming of the Son of man be."

Let us mark this text, and store it up in our minds. There are many strange opinions current on this subject, even among good men. Let us not flatter ourselves that the heathen will all be converted, and the earth filled with the knowledge of God, before the Lord comes. Let us not dream that the end of all things cannot be at hand, because there is yet much wickedness both in the Church and in the world. Such views receive a flat contradiction in the passage now before us. The days of Noah are the true type of the days when Christ shall return. Millions of professing Christians will be found thoughtless, unbelieving, Godless, Christless, worldly, and unfit to meet their Judge. Let us take heed that we are not found amongst them.

The second thing that demands our attention, is *the awful separation that will take place, when the Lord Jesus comes again.* We read twice over, that " one shall be taken and the other left."

The godly and the ungodly, at present, are all mingled together. In the congregation and in the place of worship,—in the city and in the field,—the children of God, and the children of the world, are all side by side. But it shall not be so always. In the day of our Lord's return, there shall at length be a complete division. In a moment, in the twinkling of an eye, at the last trumpet, each party shall be separated from the other for evermore. Wives shall be separated from husbands,—parents from children,— brothers from sisters,— masters from servants,—preachers from hearers. There shall be no

time for parting words, or a change of mind, when the
Lord appears.   All shall be taken as they are, and reap
according as they have sown. Believers shall be caught up
to glory, honour, and eternal life. Unbelievers shall be left
behind to shame and everlasting contempt.   Blessed and
happy are they who are of one heart in following Christ!
Their union alone shall never be broken.   It shall last
for evermore.   Who can describe the happiness of those
who are taken, when the Lord returns?   Who can
imagine the misery of those who are left behind?   May
we think on these things and consider our ways.

The last thing that demands our attention in these
verses, is *the practical duty of watchfulness in the prospect
of Christ's second coming.* "Watch," says our Lord, "for
ye know not what hour your Lord doth come." "Be ye
ready, for in such an hour as ye think not, the Son of
man cometh."

This is a point which our blessed Master frequently
presses upon our notice. We hardly ever find Him
dwelling on the second advent without adding an injunction to "watch." He knows the sleepiness of our
nature. He knows how soon we forget the most solemn
subjects in religion. He knows how unceasingly Satan
labours to obscure the glorious doctrine of His coming
again. He arms us with heartsearching exhortations
to keep awake, if we would not be ruined for evermore.
May we all have an ear to hear them.

True Christians ought to live like watchmen. The
day of the Lord so cometh as a thief in the night. They
should strive to be always on their guard. They should
behave like the sentinel of an army in an enemy's land.

They should resolve by God's grace not to sleep at their post. That text of St. Paul's deserves many a thought: "let us not sleep as do others; but let us watch and be sober." (1 Thess. v. 6.)

True Christians ought to live like good servants, whose master is not at home. They should strive to be always ready for their master's return. They should never give way to the feeling, "my Lord delayeth his coming." They should seek to keep their hearts in such a frame, that whenever Christ appears, they may at once give Him a warm and loving reception. There is a vast depth in that saying, "Blessed is that servant, whom his Lord when he cometh shall find so doing." We may well doubt whether we are true believers in Jesus, if we are not ready at any time to have our faith changed into sight.

Let us close the chapter with solemn feelings. The things we have just been reading call, loudly for great searchings of heart. Let us seek to make sure that we are in Christ, and have an ark of safety when the day of wrath breaks on the world. Let us strive so to live that we may be pronounced "blessed" at the last, and not cast off for evermore. Not least, let us dismiss from our minds the common idea that unfulfilled prophecy is a speculative and not a practical thing. If the things we have been considering are not practical, there is no such thing as practical religion at all. Well might St. John say, "Every man that hath *this hope in him* purifieth himself, even as he is pure." (1 John iii. 2.)

MATTHEW XXV. 1—13.

1 Then shall the kingdom of heaven be likened unto ten virgins, which took their lamps, and went forth to meet the bridegroom.

2 And five of them were wise, and five *were* foolish.

3 They that *were* foolish took their lamps, and took no oil with them:

4 But the wise took oil in their vessels with their lamps.

5 While the bridegroom tarried, they all slumbered and slept.

6 And at midnight there was a cry made, Behold, the bridegroom cometh; go ye out to meet him.

7 Then all those virgins arose, and trimmed their lamps.

8 And the foolish said unto the wise, Give us of your oil; for our lamps are gone out.

9 But the wise answered, saying, *Not so ;* lest there be not enough for us and you: but go ye rather to them that sell, and buy for yourselves.

10 And while they went to buy, the bridegroom came; and they that were ready went in with him to the marriage: and the door was shut.

11 Afterward came also the other virgins, saying, Lord, Lord, open to us.

12 But he answered and said, Verily I say unto you, I know you not.

13 Watch therefore, for ye know neither the day nor the hour wherein the Son of man cometh.

THE chapter we have now begun is a continuation of our Lord's prophetical discourse on the Mount of Olives. The time to which it all refers is plain and unmistakeable. From first to last, there is a continual reference to the second advent of Christ, and the end of the world. The whole chapter contains three great divisions. In the first, our Lord uses his own second coming as an argument for watchfulness and heart-religion. This He does by the parable of the ten virgins.—In the second, He uses His own second coming as an argument for diligence and faithfulness. This He does by the parable of the talents.—In the third, He winds up all by a description of the great day of judgment, a passage which for majesty and beauty stands unequalled in the New Testament.

The parable of the ten virgins, which we have now read, contains lessons peculiarly solemn and awakening. Let us see what they are.

We see for one thing, that *the second coming of Christ*

will find His Church a mixed body, containing evil as well as good.

The professing Church is compared to " ten virgins, who took their lamps and went forth to meet the bridegroom." All of them had lamps, but only five had oil in their vessels to feed the flame. All of them professed to have one object in view, but five only were truly wise, and the rest were foolish. The visible Church of Christ is just in the same condition. All its members are baptized in the name of Christ, but not all really hear His voice and follow Him. All are called Christians, and profess to be of the Christian religion, but not all have the grace of the Spirit in their hearts, and really are what they profess to be. Our own eyes tell us that it is so now. The Lord Jesus tells us that it will be so, when He comes again.*

Let us mark well this description. It is a humbling picture. After all our preachings and prayings,—after

---

* I think it fair to say, that a different view of this parable is held by some interpreters. They consider that the ten virgins represent true believers, and that the five foolish ones are believers that fall away,—or believers that are only shut out from certain privileges at the Lord's return, and are finally saved.

I cannot admit the correctness of this view. It appears to me to do great violence to the plain meaning of the conclusion of the parable, to be out of keeping with the general tenor of our Lord's discourse in this place, and to contradict many texts of Scripture.

I believe that the ten virgins represent the two great classes which compose the visible Church of Christ,—the converted and the unconverted,—the false professors and the real Christians,—the hypocrites and the true believers,—the foolish builders and the wise builders,—the good fish and the bad,—the living and the dead,—the wheat and the tares.

This view is neither new nor uncommon. It is held, in the main, by the following commentators:—Bullinger, Brentius, Gualter, Pellican, Beza, Ferus, Parœus, Piscator, Musculus, Leigh, Baxter, Quesnel, Poole, Manton, Henry, Burkitt, Doddridge, Gill, and Scott.

all our visiting and teaching,—after all our missionary exertions abroad, and means of grace at home, many will be found at last " dead in trespasses and sins ! " The wickedness and unbelief of human nature, is a subject about which we have all much to learn.

We see, for another thing, that *Christ's second coming, whenever it may be, will take men by surprise.*

This is a truth which is set before us in the parable, in a very striking manner.   At midnight, when the virgins were slumbering and sleeping, there was a cry, " The bridegroom cometh, go ye forth to meet Him."   It will be just the same, when Jesus returns to the world.   He will find the vast majority of mankind utterly unbelieving and unprepared.   He will find the bulk of His believing people in a sleepy and indolent state of soul.   Business will be going on in town and country, just as it does now. Politics, trades, farming, buying, selling, pleasure-seeking, will be taking up men's attention, just as they do now.   Rich men will still be faring sumptuously, and poor men murmuring and complaining.   Churches will still be full of divisions, and wrangling about trifles, and theological controversies will be still raging.   Ministers will still be calling men to repent, and congregations still putting off the day of decision.—In the midst of all this, the Lord Jesus Himself shall suddenly appear.   In an hour when no man thinketh, the startled world shall be summoned to break off all its employments, and to stand before its lawful King.   There is something unspeakably awful in the idea.   But thus it is written and thus it shall be.   Well might a dying minister say, " we are none of us more than half-awake."

We see, in the next place, that *when the Lord comes again, many will find out the value of saving religion too late.*

The parable tells us that when the bridegroom came, the foolish virgins said unto the wise, "give us of your oil; for our lamps are gone out." It tells us further, that as the wise had no oil to spare, the foolish went to "buy for themselves." It tells us finally, that they came when the door was shut, and asked in vain for admission. "Lord, Lord," they cried, "open unto us." All these expressions are striking emblems of things to come. Let us take heed that we do not find them true by experience, to our own eternal ruin.

We may settle it in our minds, that there will be an entire change of opinion one day as to the necessity of decided Christianity. At present, we must all be aware, the vast majority of professing Christians care nothing at all about it. They have no sense of sin. They have no love towards Christ. They know nothing of being born again. Repentance, and faith, and grace, and holiness, are mere words and names to them. They are subjects which they either dislike, or about which they feel no concern. But all this state of things shall one day come to an end. Knowledge, conviction, the value of the soul, the need of a Saviour, shall all burst on men's minds one day like a flash of lightning. But alas! it will be too late. It will be too late to be buying oil, when the Lord returns. The mistakes that are not found out till that day are irretrievable.

Are we ever mocked and persecuted and thought foolish because of our religion? Let us bear it patiently, and pray for those who persecute us. They know not what they are doing. They will certainly alter their minds one day. We may yet hear them confessing, that we were wise and they were foolish. The whole world shall one day acknowledge, that the saints of God made a wise choice.

We see, lastly, in this parable, *that when Christ returns, true Christians shall receive a rich reward for all they have suffered for their Master's sake.* We are told that when the bridegroom came, "they that were ready went in with Him to the marriage: and the door was shut."

True Christians shall alone be found ready at the second advent. Washed in the blood of atonement, clothed in Christ's righteousness, renewed by the Spirit, they shall meet their Lord with boldness, and sit down at the marriage supper of the Lamb, to go out no more. Surely this is a blessed prospect.

They shall be with their Lord,—with Him who loved them and gave Himself for them,—with Him who bore with them, and carried them through their earthly pilgrimage,—with Him, whom they loved truly and followed faithfully on earth, though with much weakness, and many a tear. Surely this also is a blessed prospect.

The door shall be shut at last,—shut on all pain and sorrow,—shut on an illnatured and wicked world,—shut on a tempting devil,—shut on all doubts and fears,— shut, to be opened again no more. Surely, we may again say, this is a blessed prospect.

Let us remember these things. They will bear meditation. They are all true. The believer may have much tribulation, but he has before him abounding consolations.   Heaviness may endure for a night, but joy cometh in the morning.   The day of Christ's return shall surely make amends for all.

Let us leave this parable with a settled determination, never to be content with anything short of indwelling grace in our hearts.   The lamp and the name of Christian, —the profession and the ordinances of Christianity, are all well in their way, but they are not the one thing needful.   Let us never rest till we know that we have the oil of the Spirit in our hearts.

MATTHEW XXV. 14—30.

14 For *the kingdom of heaven is* as a man travelling into a far country, *who* called his own servants, and delivered unto them his goods.

15 And unto one he gave five talents, to another two, and to another one; to every man according to his several ability; and straightway took his journey.

16 Then he that had received the five talents went and traded with the same, and made *them* other five talents.

17 And likewise he that *had received* two, he also gained other two.

18 But he that had received one went and digged in the earth, and hid his lord's money.

19 After a long time the lord of those servants cometh, and reckoneth with them.

20 And so he that had received five talents came and brought other five talents, saying, Lord, thou deliveredst unto me five talents: behold, I have gained beside them five talents more.

21 His lord said unto him, Well done, *thou* good and faithful servant: thou hast been faithful over a few things, I will make thee ruler over many things: enter thou into the joy of thy lord.

22 He also that had received two talents came and said, Lord thou deliveredst unto me two talents: behold, I have gained two other talents beside them.

23 His lord said unto him, Well done, good and faithful servant; thou hast been faithful over a few things, I will make thee ruler over many things : enter thou into the joy of thy Lord.

24 Then he which had received the one talent came and said, Lord, I knew thee that thou art an hard man, reaping where thou hast not sown, and gathering where thou hast not strawed:

25 And I was afraid, and went and hid thy talent in the earth : lo, *there* thou hast *that is* thine.

26 His lord answered and said unto him, *Thou* wicked and slothful servant, thou knewest that I reap where I sowed not, and gather where I have not strawed :

27 Thou oughtest therefore to have put my money to the exchangers, and *then* at my coming I should have received mine own with usury.

28 Take therefore the talent from him, and give *it* unto him which hath ten talents.

29 For unto every one that hath shall be given, and he shall have abundance: but from him that hath not shall be taken away even that which he hath.

30 And cast ye the unprofitable servant into outer darkness: there shall be weeping and gnashing of teeth.

THE parable of the talents which we have now read is near akin to that of the ten virgins. Both direct our minds to the same important event, the second advent of Jesus Christ. Both bring before us the same persons, the members of the professing Church of Christ. The virgins and the servants are one and the same people,—but the same people regarded from a different point, and viewed on different sides. The practical lesson of each parable is the main point of difference. Vigilance is the key note of the first parable, diligence that of the second. The story of the virgins calls on the Church to watch, the story of the talents calls on the Church to work.

We learn, in the first place, from this parable, *that all professing Christians have received something from God.* We are all God's "servants." We have all "talents" entrusted to our charge.

The word "talents" is an expression that has been curiously turned aside from its original meaning. It is generally applied to none but people of remarkable ability or gifts. They are called "talented" people. Such an use of the expression is a mere modern invention. In the sense in which our Lord used the word in this parable, it applies to all baptized persons without distinction. We have all talents in God's sight. We are all talented people.

Anything whereby we may glorify God is a talent.

Our gifts, our influence, our money, our knowledge, our health, our strength, our time, our senses, our reason, our intellect, our memory, our affections, our privileges as members of Christ's Church, our advantages as possessors of the Bible,—all, all are talents. Whence came these things? What hand bestowed them? Why are we what we are? Why are we not the worms that crawl on the earth? There is only one answer to these questions. All that we have is a loan from God. We are God's stewards. We are God's debtors. Let this thought sink deeply into our hearts.

We learn in the second place, that *many make a bad use of the privileges and mercies they receive from God.* We are told in the parable of one who "digged in the earth and hid his Lord's money." That man represents a large class of mankind.

To hide our talent is to neglect opportunities of glorifying God, when we have them. The Bible-despiser, the prayer-neglecter, and the Sabbath-breaker,—the unbelieving, the sensual, and the earthly-minded,—the trifler, the thoughtless, and the pleasure-seeker,—the money-lover, the covetous, and the self-indulgent,—all, all are alike burying their Lord's money in the ground. They have all light that they do not use. They might all be better than they are. But they are all daily robbing God. He has lent them much and they make Him no return. The words of Daniel to Belshazzar, are strictly applicable to every unconverted person: "the God in whose hand thy breath is, and whose are all thy ways, hast thou not glorified." (Dan. v. 23.)

We learn in the third place, *that all professing Chris-*

Y

tians must one day have a reckoning with God. The parable tells us that "after a long time the lord of those servants came, and reckoned with them."

There is a judgment before us all. Words have no meaning in the Bible, if there is none. It is mere trifling with Scripture to deny it. There is a judgment before us according to our works, certain, strict, and unavoidable. High or low, rich or poor, learned or unlearned, we shall all have to stand at the bar of God and to receive our eternal sentence. There will be no escape. Concealment will be impossible. We and God must at last meet face to face. We shall have to render an account of every privilege that was granted to us, and of every ray of light that we enjoyed. We shall find that we are dealt with as accountable and responsible creatures, and that to whomsoever much is given, of them much will be required. Let us remember this every day we live. Let us "judge ourselves that we be not condemned of the Lord."

We learn, in the fourth place, *that true Christians will receive an abundant reward in the great day of reckoning.* The parable tells us that the servants who had used their Lord's money well, were commended as "good and faithful," and told to "enter into the joy of their Lord."

These words are full of comfort to all believers, and may well fill us with wonder and surprise. The best of Christians is a poor frail creature, and needs the blood of atonement every day that he lives. But the least and lowest of believers will find that he is counted among Christ's servants, and that his labour has not been in vain in the Lord. He will discover to his amazement, that his Master's eye saw more beauty in his efforts to please Him, than he ever saw himself. He will find that every hour spent in Christ's service, and every word spoken on Christ's behalf, has been written in a book of remembrance. Let believers remember these things and take courage.—The cross may be heavy now, but the glorious reward shall make amends for all. Well says Leighton, "Here some drops of joy enter into us, but there we shall enter into joy."

We learn in the last place, that all *unfruitful members of Christ's Church will be condemned and cast away in the day of judgment*. The parable tells us that the servant who buried his master's money, was condemned as "wicked," "slothful," and "unprofitable," and cast into "outer darkness." And our Lord adds the solemn words, " there shall be weeping and gnashing of teeth."

There will be no excuse for an unconverted Christian at the last day. The reasons with which he now pretends to satisfy himself will prove useless and vain. The Judge of all the earth will be found to have done right. The ruin of the lost soul will be found to be his own fault. Those words of our Lord, "thou knewest," are words that ought to ring loudly in many a man's ears, and prick him to the heart. Thousands are living at this day without Christ and without conversion, and yet pretending that they cannot help it. And all this time they know in their own conscience that they are guilty. They are burying their talent. They are not doing what they can. Happy are they who find this out betimes. It will all come out at the last day.

Let us leave this parable with a solemn determination,

by God's grace, never to be content with a profession of Christianity without practice. Let us not only talk about religion, but act. Let us not only feel the importance of religion, but do something too. We are not told that the unprofitable servant was a murderer, or a thief, or even a waster of his Lord's money But he *did nothing*,— and this was his ruin. Let us beware of a do-nothing Christianity. Such Christianity does not come from the Spirit of God. "To do no harm," says Baxter, "is the praise of a stone, not of a man."

MATTHEW XXV. 31—46.

31 When the Son of man shall come in his glory, and all the holy angels with him, then shall he sit upon the throne of his glory:

32 And before him shall be gathered all nations: and he shall separate them one from another, as a shepherd divideth *his* sheep from the goats:

33 And he shall set the sheep on his right hand, but the goats on the left.

34 Then shall the king say unto them on his right hand, Come, ye blessed of my Father, inherit the kingdom prepared for you from the foundation of the world:

35 For I was an hungered, and ye gave me meat: I was thirsty, and ye gave me drink: I was a stranger, and ye took me in:

36 Naked, and ye clothed me: I was sick, and ye visited me: I was in prison, and ye came unto me.

37 Then shall the righteous answer him, saying, Lord, when saw we thee an hungered, and fed *thee?* or thirsty, and gave *thee* drink?

38 When saw we thee a stranger, and took *thee* in? or naked, and clothed *thee?*

39 Or when saw we thee sick, or in prison, and came unto thee?

40 And the King shall answer and say unto them, Verily I say unto you, Inasmuch as ye have done *it* unto one of the least of these my brethren, ye have done *it* unto me.

41 Then shall he say also unto them on the left hand, Depart from me, ye cursed, into everlasting fire, prepared for the devil and his angels:

42 For I was an hungered, and ye gave me no meat: I was thirsty, and ye gave me no drink:

43 I was a stranger, and ye took me not in: naked, and ye clothed me not: sick, and in prison, and ye visited me not.

44 Then shall they also answer him, saying, Lord, when saw we thee an hungred, or athirst, or a stranger, or naked, or sick, or in prison, and did not minister unto thee?

45 Then shall he answer them, saying, Verily I say unto you, Inasmuch as ye did *it* not to one of the least of these, ye did *it* not to me.

46 And these shall go away into everlasting punishment: but the righteous into life eternal.

In these verses our Lord Jesus Christ describes the judgment-day, and some of its leading circumstances.

There are few passages in the whole Bible more solemn and heart-searching than this. May we read it with the deep and serious attention which it deserves.

Let us mark in the first place, *who will be the Judge in the last day.* We read that it will be "the Son of Man," Jesus Christ Himself.

That same Jesus who was born in the manger of Bethlehem, and took upon Him the form of a servant,— who was despised and rejected of men, and often had not where to lay His head,—who was condemned by the princes of this world, beaten, scourged, and nailed to the cross,—that same Jesus shall Himself judge the world, when He comes in His glory. To Him the Father hath committed all judgment. (John v. 22.) To Him at last every knee shall bow, and every tongue confess that He is Lord. (Philip. ii. 10, 11.)

Let believers think of this, and take comfort. He that sits upon the throne in that great and dreadful day will be their Saviour, their Shepherd, their High Priest, their elder Brother, their Friend. When they see Him, they will have no cause to be alarmed.

Let unconverted people think of this, and be afraid. Their judge will be that very Christ, whose Gospel they now despise, and whose gracious invitations they refuse to hear. How great will be their confusion at last, if they go on in unbelief and die in their sins! To be condemned in the day of judgment by any one would be awful. But to be condemned by Him who would have saved them will be awful indeed. Well may the Psalmist say, "Kiss the Son lest he be angry." (Psalm. ii. 12.)

Let us mark, in the second place, *who will be judged in*

the last day. We read that before Christ "shall be gathered all nations."

All that have ever lived shall one day give account of themselves at the bar of Christ. All must obey the summons of the great King, and come forward to receive their sentence. Those who would not come to worship Christ on earth, will find they must come to His great assize, when He returns to judge the world.

All that are judged will be divided into two great classes. There will no longer be any distinction between kings and subjects, or masters and servants, or dissenters and churchmen. There will be no mention of ranks and denominations, for the former things will have passed away. Grace or no grace, conversion or unconversion, faith or no faith, will be the only distinctions at the last day. All that are found in Christ will be placed among the sheep at His right hand. All that are not found in Christ will be placed among the goats at His left. Well says Sherlock, "Our separations will avail us nothing, unless we take care to be found in the number of Christ's sheep, when He comes to judgment."

Let us mark, in the third place, *in what manner the judgment will be conducted in the last day.* We read of several striking particulars on this point. Let us see what they are.

The last judgment will be a judgment according to evidence. The works of men are the witnesses which will be brought forward, and above all their works of charity. The question to be ascertained will not merely be what we said, but what we did,—not merely what we professed, but what we practised. Our works unquestionably will not justify us. We are justified by faith without the deeds of the law. But the truth of our faith will be tested by our lives. Faith which hath not works is dead, being alone. (James ii. 11.)

The last judgment will be a judgment that will bring joy to all true believers. They will hear those precious words, "Come, ye blessed of my Father, inherit the kingdom." They will be owned and confessed by their Master before His Father and the holy angels. They shall find that the wages He gives to His faithful servants are nothing less than "a kingdom." The least, and lowest, and poorest of the family of God, shall have a crown of glory, and be a king.

The last judgment will be a judgment that will bring confusion on all unconverted people. They will hear those awful words, "Depart, ye cursed, into everlasting fire." They will be disowned by the great Head of the Church before the assembled world. They will find that as they would sow to the flesh, so of the flesh they must reap corruption. They would not hear Christ, when He said "Come unto me, and I will give you rest," and now they must hear Him say, "Depart, into everlasting fire." They would not carry His cross, and so they can have no place in His kingdom.

The last judgment will be a judgment that will strikingly bring out the characters both of the lost and saved. They on the right hand, who are Christ's sheep, will still be "clothed with humility." They will marvel to hear any work of theirs brought forward and commended.—They on the left hand, who are not Christ's, will still be blind and self-righteous. They will not be sensible of any neglect of Christ, "Lord," they say, "when saw we thee,—and did not minister unto thee?" Let this thought sink down into our hearts. Characters on earth will prove an everlasting possession in the world to come. With the same heart that men die, with that heart they will rise again.

Let us mark, in the last place, *what will be the final results of the judgment day.* We are told this in words that ought never to be forgotten, "the wicked shall go away into everlasting punishment: but the righteous into life eternal."

The state of things after the judgment is changeless and without end. The misery of the lost, and the blessedness of the saved, are both alike for ever. Let no man deceive us on this point. It is clearly revealed in Scripture. The eternity of God, and heaven, and hell, all stand on the same foundation. As surely as God is eternal, so surely is heaven an endless day without night, and hell an endless night without day.

Who shall describe the blessedness of eternal life? It passes the power of man to conceive. It can only be measured by contrast and comparison. An eternal rest, after warfare and conflict,—the eternal company of saints, after buffeting with an evil world,—an eternally glorious and painless body, after struggling with weakness and infirmity,—an eternal sight of Jesus face to face, after only hearing and believing,—all this is blessedness indeed. And yet the half of it remains untold.

Who shall describe the misery of eternal punishment? It is something utterly indescribable and inconceivable. The eternal pain of body,—the eternal sting of an accusing conscience,—the eternal society of none but the wicked, the devil and his angels,—the eternal remembrance of opportunities neglected and Christ despised,—the eternal prospect of a weary, hopeless future,—all this is misery indeed. It is enough to make our ears tingle, and our blood run cold. And yet this picture is nothing, compared to the reality.

Let us close these verses with serious self-inquiry. Let us ask ourselves on which side of Christ we are likely to be at the last day. Shall we be on the right hand, or shall we be on the left? Happy is he who never rests till he can give a satisfactory answer to this question.

MATTHEW XXVI. 1—13.

1 And it came to pass, when Jesus had finished all these sayings, he said unto his disciples,

2 Ye know that after two days is *the feast of* the Passover, and the Son of man is betrayed to be crucified.

3 Then assembled together the Chief Priests, and the Scribes, and the elders of the people, unto the palace of the High Priest, who was called Caiaphas,

4 And consulted that they might take Jesus by subtilty, and kill *him*.

5 But they said, Not on the feast *day*, lest there be an uproar among the people.

6 Now when Jesus was in Bethany, in the house of Simon the leper,

7 There came unto him a woman having an alabaster box of very precious ointment, and poured it on his head, as he sat *at meat*.

8 But when his disciples saw *it*, they had indignation, saying, To what purpose *is* this waste?

9 For this ointment might have been sold for much, and given to the poor.

10 When Jesus understood *it*, he said unto them, Why trouble ye the woman? for she hath wrought a good work upon me.

11 For ye have the poor always with you; but me ye have not always.

12 For in that she hath poured this ointment on my body, she did *it* for my burial.

13 Verily I say unto you, Wheresoever this Gospel shall be preached in the whole world, *there* shall also this, that this woman hath done, be told for a memorial of her.

WE now approach the closing scene of our Lord Jesus Christ's earthly ministry. Hitherto we have read of His sayings and doings: we are now about to read of His sufferings and death. Hitherto we have seen Him as the great Prophet : we are now about to see Him as the great High Priest.

It is a portion of Scripture which ought to be read with peculiar reverence and attention. The place whereon we stand is holy ground. Here we see how the Seed of the woman bruised the Serpent's head. Here we see the great sacrifice to which all the sacrifices of the Old Testament had long pointed. Here we see how the blood was shed which " cleanseth from all sin," and the Lamb slain who " taketh away the sin of the world." We see in the death of Christ, the great mystery revealed, how God can be just, and yet justify the ungodly. No wonder that all the four Gospels contain a full account of this wonderful event. On other points in our Lord's history, we often find, that when one evangelist speaks, the other three are silent. But when we come to the crucifixion, we find it minutely described by all four.

In these verses we have now read, let us first observe *how careful our Lord is to recall the attention of His disciples to His own death.* He said to them, "Ye know that after two days is the feast of the passover, and the Son of Man is betrayed to be crucified."

The connexion of these words with the preceding chapter is exceedingly striking. Our Lord had just been dwelling on His own second coming in power and glory, at the end of the world. He had been describing the last judgment, and all its awful accompaniments. He had been speaking of Himself as the Judge, before whose throne all nations would be gathered. And then at once, without pause or interval, He goes on to speak of His crucifixion. While the marvellous predictions of His final glory were yet ringing in the ears of His disciples, He tells them once and again of His coming sufferings. He reminds them that He must die as a sin-offering before He reigned as a king,—that He must make atonement on the cross, before He took the crown.

We can never attach too much importance to the atoning death of Christ. It is the leading fact in the word of God, on which the eyes of our soul ought to be ever fixed. Without the shedding of His blood, there is no remission of sin. It is the cardinal truth on which the whole system of Christianity hinges. Without it the Gospel is an arch without a key-stone, a fair building without a foundation, a solar system without a sun. Let us make much of our Lord's incarnation and example, His miracles and His parables, His works and His words, but above all let us make much of His death. Let us delight in the hope of His second personal coming and millennial reign, but let us not think more even of these blessed truths, than of the atonement on the cross. This, after all, is the master-truth of Scripture, that "Christ died for our sins." To this let us daily return. On this let us daily feed our souls. Some, like the Greeks of old, may sneer at the doctrine, and call it "foolishness." But let us never be ashamed to say with Paul, "God forbid that I should glory save in the cross of our Lord Jesus Christ." (Gal. vi. 14.)

Let us observe, in the second place, in these verses, *what honour Christ loves to put on those that honour Him.*

We are told that when He was "in the house of Simon the leper," a certain woman came, while He sat at meat, and poured a box of precious ointment on His head. She did it, no doubt, out of reverence and affection. She had received soul-benefit from Him, and she thought no mark of honour too costly to be bestowed on Him in return. But this deed of hers called forth disapprobation from some who saw it. They called it "waste." They said it might have been better to sell the ointment, and give the money to the poor. At once our Lord rebuked these cold-hearted fault-finders. He tells them that the woman has "wrought a good work," and one that He accepts and approves. And He goes on to make a striking prediction, "Wheresoever this Gospel is preached in the whole world, there shall also this that this woman hath done be told for a memorial of her."

We see, in this little incident, how perfectly our Lord knew things to come, and how easy it is for Him to confer honour. This prophecy of His about this woman is receiving a fulfilment every day before our eyes. Wherever the Gospel of St. Matthew is read, the deed that she did is known. The deeds and titles of many a king, and emperor, and general, are as completely forgotten, as if written in the sand. But the grateful act of one humble Christian woman is recorded in one hundred and fifty different languages, and is known all over the globe. The praise of man is but for a few days. The praise of Christ endureth for ever. The pathway to lasting honour, is to honour Christ.

Last, but not least, we see in this incident a blessed foretaste of things that will yet take place in the day of judgment. In that great day no honour done to Christ on earth shall be found to have been forgotten. The

speeches of parliamentary orators, the exploits of warri-
ors, the works of poets and painters, shall not be
mentioned in that day. But the least work that the
weakest Christian woman has done for Christ, or His
members, shall be found written in a book of everlasting
remembrance. Not a single kind word or deed. not a
cup of cold water, or a box of ointment, shall be omitted
from the record. Silver and gold she may have had
none,—rank, power, and influence she may not have
possessed,—but if she loved Christ, and confessed Christ,
and worked for Christ, her memorial shall be found on
high. She shall be commended before assembled worlds.

Do we know what it is to work for Christ? If we do,
let us take courage, and work on. What greater encouragement can we desire than we see here? We may
be laughed at and ridiculed by the world. Our motives
may be misunderstood. Our conduct may be misrepresented. Our sacrifices for Christ's sake may be called
"waste,"—waste of time, waste of money, waste of strength.
Let none of these things move us. The eye of Him who
sat in Simon's house in Bethany is upon us. He notes
all we do, and is well-pleased. Let us be "steadfast,
unmovable, always abounding in the work of the Lord,
forasmuch as we know that our labour is not in vain in
the Lord." (1 Cor. xv. 58.)

MATTHEW XXVI. 14—25.

14 Then one of the twelve, called Judas Iscariot, went unto the Chief Priests,

15 And said *unto them,* What will ye give me, and I will deliver him unto you? And they covenanted with him for thirty pieces of silver.

16 And from that time he sought opportunity to betray him.

17 Now the first *day* of the *feast*

of unleavened bread the disciples came to Jesus, saying unto him, Where wilt thou that we prepare for thee to eat the Passover?

18 And he said, Go into the city to such a man, and say unto him, The Master saith, My time is at hand; I will keep the Passover at thy house with my disciples.

19 And the disciples did as Jesus had appointed them; and they made ready the Passover.

20 Now when the even was come, he sat down with the twelve.

21 And as they did eat, he said, Verily I say unto you, that one of you shall betray me.

22 And they were exceeding sorrowful, and began every one of them to say unto him, Lord, is it I?

23 And he answered and said, He that dippeth *his* hand with me in the dish, the same shall betray me.

24 The Son of man goeth as it is written of him : but woe unto that man by whom the Son of man is betrayed! it had been good for that man if he had not been born.

25 Then Judas, which betrayed him, answered and said, Master, is it I? He said unto him, Thou hast said.

WE read in the beginning of this passage, how our Lord Jesus Christ was betrayed into the hands of His deadly enemies. The priests and scribes, however anxious to put Him to death, were at a loss how to effect their purpose, from fear of an uproar among the people. At this juncture a fitting instrument for carrying out their designs, offered himself to them, in the person of Judas Iscariot. That false apostle undertook to deliver his Master into their hands, for thirty pieces of silver.

There are few blacker pages in all history, than the character and conduct of Judas Iscariot. There is no more awful evidence of the wickedness of man. A poet of our own has said, that "sharper than a serpent's tooth is a thankless child." But what shall we say of a disciple who could betray his own Master,—an apostle who could sell Christ? Surely this was not the least bitter part of the cup of suffering which our Lord drank.

Let us learn, in the first place, from these verses, *that a man may enjoy great privileges, and make a great religious profession, and yet his heart all the time may not be right before God.*

Judas Iscariot had the highest possible religious privileges. He was a chosen apostle, and companion of
Christ. He was an eye-witness of our Lord's miracles,
and a hearer of His sermons. He saw what Abraham
and Moses never saw, and heard what David and Isaiah
never heard. He lived in the society of the eleven
apostles. He was a fellow-labourer with Peter, James,
and John. But for all this his heart was never changed.
He clung to one darling sin.

Judas Iscariot made a reputable profession of religion.
There was nothing but what was right, and proper, and
becoming in his outward conduct. Like the other apostles, he appeared to believe and to give up all for Christ's
sake. Like them he was sent forth to preach and work
miracles. No one of the eleven appears to have suspected him of hypocrisy. When our Lord said, "One
of you shall betray me," no one said, "Is it Judas?"
Yet all this time his heart was never changed.

We ought to observe these things. They are deeply
humbling and instructive. Like Lot's wife, Judas is
intended to be a beacon to the whole church. Let us
often think about him, and say, as we think, "Search
me, O Lord, and try my heart, and see if there be any
wicked way in me." Let us resolve, by God's grace,
that we will never be content with anything short of
sound, thorough, heart conversion.

Let us learn, in the second place, from these verses,
that the love of money is one of the greatest snares to a
man's soul. We cannot conceive a clearer proof of this,
than the case of Judas. That wretched question, "What
will ye give me?" reveals the secret sin which was his

ruin. He had given up much for Christ's sake, but he had not given up his covetousness.

The words of the apostle Paul should often ring in our ears, "the love of money is the root of all evil." (2 Tim. vi. 10.) The history of the Church abounds in illustrations of this truth. For money Joseph was sold by his brethren. For money Samson was betrayed to the Philistines. For money Gehazi deceived Naaman, and lied to Elisha. For money Ananias and Sapphira tried to deceive Peter. For money the Son of God was delivered into the hands of wicked men. Wonderful indeed does it seem that the cause of so much evil should be loved so well.

Let us all be on our guard against the love of money. The world is full of it in our days. The plague is abroad. Thousands who would abhor the idea of worshipping Juggernaut, are not ashamed to make an idol of gold. We are all liable to the infection, from the least to the greatest. We may love money without having it, just as we may have money without loving it. It is an evil that works very deceitfully. It carries us captives before we are aware of our chains. Once let it get the mastery, and it will harden, palsy, sear, freeze, blight, and wither our souls. It overthrew an apostle of Christ. Let us take heed that it does not overthrow us. One leak may sink a ship. One unmortified sin may ruin a soul.

We ought frequently to call to mind the solemn words, "What shall it profit a man if he gain the whole world, and lose his own soul?" "We brought nothing into this world, and it is certain we can carry nothing out." Our daily prayer should be, "Give me neither poverty nor riches: feed me with food convenient for me." (Prov. xxx. 8.) Our constant aim should be to be rich in grace. They that "*will* be rich" in worldly possessions often find at last that they have made the worst of bargains. Like Esau, they have bartered an eternal portion for a little temporary gratification. Like Judas Iscariot, they have sold themselves to everlasting perdition.

Let us learn, in the last place, from these verses, *the hopeless condition of all who die unconverted.* The words of our Lord on this subject are peculiarly solemn. He says of Judas, "It had been good for that man, if he had not been born."

This saying admits of only one interpretation. It teaches plainly, that it is better never to live at all, than to live without faith, and to die without grace. To die in this state is to be ruined for evermore. It is a fall from which there is no rising. It is a loss which is utterly irretrievable. There is no change in hell. The gulf between hell and heaven is one that no man can pass.

This saying could never have been used, if there was any truth in the doctrine of universal salvation. If it really was true that all would sooner or later reach heaven, and hell sooner or later be emptied of inhabitants, it never could be said that it would have been "good for a man not to have been born." Hell itself would lose its terrors, if it had an end. Hell itself would be endurable, if after millions of ages there was a hope of freedom and of heaven. But universal salvation will find no foot-hold in Scripture. The teaching of the word of God is plain and express on the subject. There is a worm that never dies, and a fire that is not quenched. (Mark ix. 44.) "Except a man be born again," he will wish one day he had never been born at all. "Better," says Burkitt, "have no being, than not have a being in Christ."

Let us grasp this truth firmly, and not let it go. There are always persons who dislike the reality and eternity of hell. We live in a day when a morbid charity induces many to exaggerate God's mercy, at the expense of His justice, and when false teachers are daring to talk of a "love of God, lower even than hell." Let us resist such teaching with a holy jealousy, and abide by the doctrine of Holy Scripture. Let us not be ashamed to walk in the old paths, and to believe that there is an eternal God, an eternal heaven, and an eternal hell. Once depart from this belief, and we admit the thin edge of the wedge of scepticism, and may at last deny any doctrine of the Gospel. We may rest assured that there is no firm standing ground between a belief in the eternity of hell, and downright infidelity.

MATTHEW XXVI. 26—35.

26 And as they were eating, Jesus took bread, and blessed *it*, and brake *it*, and gave *it* to the disciples, and said, Take, eat; this is my body.

27 And he took the cup, and gave thanks, and gave *it* to them, saying, Drink ye all of it;

28 For this is my blood of the new testament, which is shed for many for the remission of sins.

29 But I say unto you, I will not drink henceforth of this fruit of the vine, until that day when I drink it new with you in my Father's kingdom.

30 And when they had sung an hymn, they went out into the mount of Olives.

31 Then saith Jesus unto them, All ye shall be offended because of me this night; for it is written, I will smite the shepherd, and the sheep of the flock shall be scattered abroad.

32 But after I am risen again, I will go before you into Galilee.

33 Peter answered and said unto him, Though all *men* shall be offended because of thee, *yet* will I never be offended.

34 Jesus said unto him, Verily I say unto thee, That this night, before the cock crow, thou shalt deny me thrice.

35 Peter said unto him, Though I should die with thee, yet will I not deny thee. Likewise also said all the disciples.

THESE verses describe the appointment of the sacrament of the Lord's Supper. Our Lord knew well the things that were before Him, and graciously chose the last quiet evening that He could have before His crucifixion, as an occasion for bestowing a parting gift on His church. How precious must this ordinance have afterwards appeared to His disciples, when they remembered the events of that night. How mournful is the thought, that no ordinance has led to such fierce controversy, and been so grievously misunderstood, as the ordinance of the Lord's Supper. It ought to have united the church, but our sins have made it a cause of division. The thing which should have been for our welfare, has been too often made an occasion of falling.

The first thing that demands our notice in these verses, *is the right meaning of our Lord's words, "this is my body, this is my blood."*

It is needless to say, that this question has divided the visible church of Christ. It has caused volumes of controversial theology to be written. But we must not shrink from having decided opinions upon it, because theologians have disputed and differed. Unsoundness on this point has given rise to many deplorable superstitions.

The plain meaning of our Lord's words appears to be this,—" This bread represents my body. This wine represents my blood." He did not mean that the bread He gave to His disciples was really and literally His body. He did not mean that the wine He gave to His disciples was really and literally His blood. Let us lay firm hold on this interpretation. It may be supported by several grave reasons.*

* " Bishop Law has remarked that there is no term in the

The conduct of the disciples at the Lord's Supper forbids us to believe that the bread they received was Christ's body, and the wine they received was Christ's blood. They were all Jews, taught from their infancy to believe that it was sinful to eat flesh with the blood. (Deut. xii. 23—25.) Yet there is nothing in the narrative to shew that they were startled by our Lord's words. They evidently perceived no change in the bread and wine.

Our own senses at the present day forbid us to believe that there is any change in the bread and wine in the Lord's Supper. Our own taste tells us that they are really and literally what they appear to be. Things above our reason the Bible requires us to believe. But we are never bid to believe that which contradicts our senses.

The true doctrine about our Lord's human nature forbids us to believe that the bread in the Lord's Supper can be His body, or the wine His blood. The natural body of Christ cannot be at one time in more places than one.—If our Lord's body could sit at table, and at the same time be eaten by the disciples, it is perfectly clear that it was not a human body like our own. But this we must never allow for one moment. It is the glory of Christianity that our Redeemer is perfect man as well as perfect God.

Hebrew language, which expresses to *signify* or *denote;* and that the Greek here naturally takes the impress of the Hebrew or Syriac idiom, *it is* being used for *it signifies.* Hence the similar use of the verb in various passages; "The three branches *are* three days." Gen. xl. 12. "The seven kine *are* seven years." Gen xli. 26. "The ten horns *are* ten kings." Dan. vii. 24. "The field *is* the world." Matt. xiii. 38. "The seven stars *are* the angels of the seven churches, and the seven candlesticks which thou sawest *are* the seven churches." Rev. i. 20." *Watson on Matthew. p.* 386.

Finally, the genius of the language in which our Lord spoke at the Lord's Supper, makes it entirely unnnecessary to interpret His words literally. The Bible is full of expressions of a similar kind, to which no one thinks of giving any but a figurative meaning. Our Lord speaks of Himself as the "door" and the "vine," and we know that He is using emblems and figures, when He so speaks. There is therefore no inconsistency in supposing that He used figurative language when He appointed the Lord's Supper; and we have the more right to say so, when we remember the grave objections which stand in the way of a literal view of His words.

Let us lay up these things in our minds, and not forget them. In a day of abounding heresy, it is good to be well armed. Ignorant and confused views of the meaning of Scripture language, are one great cause of religious error.

The second thing which demands our notice in these verses, is *the purpose and object for which the Lord's Supper was appointed.*

This is a subject again on which great darkness prevails. The ordinance of the Lord's Supper has been regarded as something mysterious and past understanding. Immense harm has been done to Christianity by the vague and high-flown language, in which many writers have indulged in treating of the sacrament. There is certainly nothing to warrant such language in the account of its original institution. The more simple our views of its purpose, the more Scriptural they are likely to be.

The Lord's Supper is not a sacrifice. There is no

oblation in it,—no offering up of anything but our prayers, praises, and thanksgivings. From the day that Jesus died there needed no more offering for sin. By one offering He perfected for ever them that are sanctified. (Heb. x. 14.) Priests, altars, and sacrifices, all ceased to be necessary, when the Lamb of God offered up Himself. Their office came to an end. Their work was done.

The Lord's Supper has no power to confer benefit on those who come to it, if they do not come to it with faith. The mere formal act of eating the bread and drinking the wine is utterly unprofitable, unless it is done with a right heart. It is eminently an ordinance for the living soul, not for the dead,—for the converted, not for the unconverted.

The Lord's Supper was ordained for a continual remembrance of the sacrifice of Christ's death, until He comes again. The benefits it confers, are spiritual, not physical. Its effects must be looked for in our inward man. It was intended to remind us, by the visible, tangible emblems of bread and wine, that the offering of Christ's body and blood for us on the cross, is the only atonement for sin, and the life of a believer's soul. It was meant to help our poor weak faith to closer fellowship with our crucified Saviour, and to assist us in spiritually feeding on Christ's body and blood. It is an ordinance for redeemed sinners, and not for unfallen angels. By receiving it we publicly declare our sense of guilt, and need of a Saviour,—our trust in Jesus, and our love to Him,—our desire to live upon Him, and our hope to live with Him. Using it in this spirit, we shall find our repentance deepened, our faith increased, our hope brightened, and our love enlarged,—our besetting sins weakened, and our graces strengthened. It will draw us nearer to Christ.

Let us bear these things in mind. They need to be remembered in these latter days. There is nothing in our religion which we are so ready to pervert and misunderstand as those parts which approach our senses. Whatever we can touch with our hand, and see with our eyes, we are apt to exalt into an idol, or to expect good from it as a mere charm. Let us specially beware of this tendency in the matter of the Lord's Supper. Above all, "let us take heed," in the words of the Homily, "lest of the memory it be made a sacrifice."

The last thing which deserves a brief notice in this passage, is *the character of the first communicants.* It is a point full of comfort and instruction.

The little company to which the bread and wine were first administered by our Lord, was composed of the apostles, whom He had chosen to accompany Him during His earthly ministry. They were poor and unlearned men, who loved Christ, but were weak alike in faith and knowledge. They knew but little of the full meaning of their Master's sayings and doings. They knew but little of the frailty of their own hearts. They thought they were ready to die with Jesus, and yet that very night they all forsook Him and fled. All this our Lord knew perfectly well. The state of their hearts was not hid from Him. And yet He did not keep back from them the Lord's Supper.

There is something very teaching in this circumstance. It shows us plainly that we must not make great knowledge, and great strength of grace, an indispensable qualification for communicants. A man may know but little, and be no better than a child in spiritual strength, but he is not on that account to be excluded from the Lord's table.—Does he really feel his sins? Does he really love Christ? Does he really desire to serve Him? If this be so, we ought to encourage and receive him. Doubtless we must do all we can to exclude unworthy communicants. No graceless person ought to come to the Lord's Supper. But we must take heed that we do not reject those whom Christ has not rejected. There is no wisdom in being more strict than our Lord and His apostles.

Let us leave the passage with serious self-inquiry as to our own conduct with respect to the Lord's Supper. Do we turn away from it, when it is administered? If so, how can we justify our conduct?—It will not do to say it is not a necessary ordinance. To say so is to pour contempt on Christ Himself, and declare that we do not obey Him.—It will not do to say that we feel unworthy to come to the Lord's table. To say so is to declare that we are unfit to die, and unprepared to meet God. These are solemn considerations. All non-communicants should ponder them well.

Are we in the habit of coming to the Lord's table? If so, in what frame of mind do we come? Do we draw near intelligently, humbly, and with faith? Do we understand what we are about? Do we really feel our sinfulness and need of Christ? Do we really desire to live a Christian life, as well as profess the Christian faith? Happy is that soul who can give a satisfactory answer to these questions. Let him go forward, and persevere.

MATTHEW XXVI. 36—46.

36 Then cometh Jesus with them unto a place called Gethsemane, and saith unto the disciples, Sit ye here, while I go and pray yonder.

37 And he took with him Peter and the two sons of Zebedee, and began to be sorrowful and very heavy.

38 Then saith he unto them, My soul is exceeding sorrowful, even unto death : tarry ye here, and watch with me.

39 And he went a little farther, and fell on his face, and prayed, saying, O my Father, if it be possible, let this cup pass from me : nevertheless not as I will, but as thou *wilt*.

40 And he cometh unto the disciples, and findeth them asleep, and saith unto Peter, What, could ye not watch with me one hour ?

41 Watch and pray, that ye enter not into temptation : the spirit indeed *is* willing, but the flesh *is* weak.

42 He went away again the second time, and prayed, saying, O my Father, if this cup may not pass away from me, except I drink it, thy will be done.

43 And he came and found them asleep again : for their eyes were heavy.

44 And he left them, and went away again, and prayed the third time, saying the same words.

45 Then cometh he to his disciples, and saith unto them, Sleep on now, and take *your* rest : behold, the hour is at hand, and the Son of man is betrayed into the hands of sinners.

46 Rise, let us be going : behold, he is at hand that doth betray me.

THE verses we have now read, describe what is commonly called Christ's agony at Gethsemane. It is a passage which undoubtedly contains deep and mysterious things. We ought to read it with reverence and wonder, for there is much in it which we cannot fully comprehend.

Why do we find our Lord so "sorrowful and very heavy," as He is here described? What are we to make of His words, "my soul is exceeding sorrowful, even unto death?" Why do we see Him going apart from His disciples, and falling on His face, and crying to His Father with strong cries, and thrice-repeated prayer? Why is the Almighty Son of God, who had worked so many miracles, so heavy and disquieted? Why is Jesus, who came into the world to die, so like one ready to faint at the approach of death? Why is all this?

There is but one reasonable answer to these questions. The weight that pressed down our Lord's soul, was not the fear of death, and its pains. Thousands have endured the most agonizing sufferings of body, and died without a groan, and so, no doubt, might our Lord. But the real weight that bowed down the heart of Jesus, was the weight of the sin of the world, which seems to have now pressed down upon Him with peculiar force. It was the burden of our guilt imputed to Him, which was now laid on Him, as on the head of the scape goat. How great that burden must have been, no heart of man can conceive. It is known only to God. Well may the Greek Litany speak of the "unknown sufferings of Christ." The words of Scott on this subject are probably correct;—"Christ at this time endured as much misery, of the same kind with that of condemned spirits, as could possibly consist with a pure conscience, perfect love of God and man, and an assured confidence of a glorious event." *

* I believe that the view maintained in this exposition, is the only reasonable solution that can be given of our Lord's agony. How any Socinian, or any divine who denies the imputation of man's sin to Christ, and the vicarious nature of Christ's sufferings, can account satisfactorily for the agony, I am totally at a loss to conceive.—Upon the principle of the Socinian, who utterly denies the doctrine of atonement, and says that our Lord was only a man, and not God, He was one who shewed less firmness in suffering than many men have shown.—Upon the principle of some modern divines, who say that our Lord's death was not a propitiation and expiation for sin, but only a great example of self-sacrifice, the intense agony of body and mind here described is equally unaccountable.—Both views appear to me alike dishonouring to our Lord Jesus Christ, and utterly unscriptural and unsatisfactory. I believe the agony in the garden to be a knot that nothing can untie, but the old doctrine of our sin being really *imputed* to Christ, and Christ being made sin and a curse for us.

There are deep things in this passage of Scripture, containing the account of the agony, which I purposely leave untouched. They are too deep for man's line to fathom. The extent to which Satan was allowed to tempt our Lord in this hour,—the degree of suffering, both mental and bodily, which an entirely sinless person, like our Lord, would endure in bearing the sin of all mankind,—

But however mysterious this part of our Lord's history may seem to us, we must not fail to observe the precious lessons of practical instruction, which it contains. Let us now see what those lessons are.

Let us learn, in the first place, that *prayer is the best practical remedy that we can use in time of trouble.* We see that Christ Himself prayed, when His soul was sorrowful. All true Christians ought to do the same.

Trouble is a cup that all must drink in this world of sin. We are "born to trouble as the sparks fly upward." (Job v. 7.) We cannot avoid it. Of all creatures, none is so vulnerable as man. Our bodies, our minds, our families, our business, our friends, are all so many doors through which trial will come in. The holiest saints can claim no exemption from it. Like their Master, they are often "men of sorrow."

But what is the first thing to be done in time of trouble ? We must pray.—Like Job, we must fall down and worship. (Job i. 20.) Like Hezekiah, we must spread our matters before the Lord. (2 Kings xix. 14.) The first person we must turn to for help, must be our God. We must tell our Father in heaven all our sorrow. We must believe confidently that nothing is too trivial or minute to be laid before Him, so long as we do it with entire submission to His will. It is the mark of faith to keep nothing back from our best Friend. So doing, we may be sure we shall have an answer. "If it be possible," and the thing we

the manner in which the human and divine wills both operated in our Lord's experience, since He was at all times as really man as God,—all these are points which I prefer to leave alone. It is easy on such questions to "darken counsel by words without knowledge."

ask is for God's glory, it shall be done. The thorn in the flesh will either be removed, or grace to endure it will be given to us, as it was to St. Paul. (2 Cor. xii. 9.) May we all store up this lesson against the day of need. It is a true saying, that "prayers are the leeches of care."

Let us learn, in the second place, that *entire submission of will to the will of God should be one of our chief aims in this world.* The words of our Lord are a beautiful example of the spirit that we should follow after in this matter. He says, "Not as I will, but as thou wilt." He says again, "Thy will be done."

A will unsanctified and uncontrolled, is one great cause of unhappiness in life. It may be seen in little infants. It is born with us. We all like our own way. We wish and want many things, and forget that we are entirely ignorant what is for our good, and unfit to choose for ourselves. Happy is he who has learned to have no wishes, and in every state to be content. It is a lesson which we are slow to learn, and like St. Paul, we must learn it not in the school of mortal man, but of Christ. (Phil. iv. 11.)

Would we know whether we are born again, and growing in grace? Let us see how it is with us in the matter of our wills. Can we bear disappointment? Can we put up patiently with unexpected trials and vexations? Can we see our pet plans, and darling schemes crossed without murmuring and complaint? Can we sit still, and suffer calmly, as well as go up and down and work actively? These are the things that prove whether we have the mind of Christ. It ought never to be forgotten, that warm feelings and joyful

frames are not the truest evidences of grace. A morti-
fied will is a far more valuable possession. Even our
Lord Himself did not always rejoice; but He could
always say, "Thy will be done."

Let us learn, in the last place, that there is *great
weakness, even in true disciples of Christ, and that they
have need to watch and pray against it.* We see Peter,
James, and John, those three chosen apostles, sleeping
when they ought to have been watching and praying.
And we find our Lord addressing them in these solemn
words, "Watch and pray, that ye enter not into temptation : the spirit indeed is willing, but the flesh is weak.".

There is a double nature in all believers. Converted,
renewed, sanctified as they are, they still carry about
with them a mass of indwelling corruption, a body of sin.
St. Paul speaks of this, when he says, "I find a law,
that, when I would do good, evil is present with me.
For I delight in the law of God after the inward man :
But I see another law in my members, warring against
the law of my mind." (Rom. vii. 21—23.) The experience of all true Christians in every age confirms this.
They find within two contrary principles, and a continual strife between the two. To these two principles
our Lord alludes when he addresses His half-awakened
disciples. He calls the one flesh, and the other spirit.
He says, "the spirit is willing, but the flesh is weak."

But does our Lord excuse this weakness of his disciples? Be it far from us to think so. Those who draw
this conclusion mistake His meaning. He uses that
very weakness as an argument for watchfulness and
prayer. He teaches us that the very fact that we are

encompassed with infirmity, should stir us up continually to "watch and pray."

If we know anything of true religion, let us never forget this lesson. If we desire to walk with God comfortably, and not fall, like David or Peter, let us never forget to watch and pray. Let us live like men on enemy's ground, and be always on our guard. We cannot walk too carefully. We cannot be too jealous over our souls. The world is very ensnaring. The devil is very busy. Let our Lord's words ring in our ears daily like a trumpet. Our spirits may sometimes be very willing. But our flesh is always very weak. Then let us always watch and always pray.

MATTHEW XXVI. 47—56.

47 And while he yet spake, lo, Judas, one of the twelve, came, and with him a great multitude with swords and staves, from the Chief Priests and elders of the people.

48 Now he that betrayed him gave them a sign, saying, Whomsoever I shall kiss, that same is he : hold him fast.

49 And forthwith he came to Jesus, and said, Hail, master ; and kissed him.

50 And Jesus said unto him, Friend, wherefore art thou come ? Then came they, and laid hands on Jesus, and took him.

51 And, behold, one of them which were with Jesus stretched out *his* hand, and drew his sword, and struck a servant of the High Priest's, and smote off his ear.

52 Then said Jesus unto him, Put up again thy sword into his place : for all they that take the sword shall perish with the sword.

53 Thinkest thou that I cannot now pray to my Father, and he shall presently give me more than twelve legions of angels ?

54 But how then shall the Scriptures be fulfilled, that thus it must be ?

55 In that same hour said Jesus to the multitudes, Are ye come out as against a thief with swords and staves for to take me ? I sat daily with you teaching in the temple, and ye laid no hold on me.

56 But all this was done, that the Scriptures of the prophets might be fulfilled. Then all the disciples forsook him, and fled.

WE see in these verses the cup of our Lord Jesus Christ's sufferings beginning to be filled. We see Him betrayed by one of His disciples, forsaken by the rest, and taken prisoner by His deadly enemies. Never surely was there sorrow like His sorrow! Never may we forget, as we read this part of the Bible, that our sins were the cause of these sorrows! Jesus was "delivered for our offences." (Rom. iv. 25.)

Let us notice, for one thing, in these verses, *what gracious condescension marked our Lord's intercourse with His disciples.*

We have this point proved by a deeply touching circumstance at the moment of our Lord's betrayal. When Judas Iscariot undertook to guide the multitude to the place where his Master was, he gave them a sign by which they might distinguish Jesus in the dim moonlight from his disciples. He said, "Whomsoever I shall kiss, that same is he." And so, when he came to Jesus, he said, "Hail! master, and kissed him." That simple fact reveals the affectionate terms on which the disciples associated with our Lord. It is an universal custom in Eastern countries, when friend meets friend, to salute one another with a kiss. (Exod. xviii. 7; 1 Sam. xx. 41.) It would seem therefore, that when Judas kissed our Lord, he only did that which all the apostles were accustomed to do, when they met their Master after an absence.

Let us draw comfort from this little circumstance for our own souls. Our Lord Jesus Christ is a most gracious and condescending Saviour. He is not an "austere man," repelling sinners, and keeping them at a distance. He is not a being so different from us in nature, that we must regard Him with awe rather than affection. He would have us rather regard Him as an elder Brother, and a beloved Friend. His heart in heaven is still the same that it was upon earth.   He is ever meek, merciful, and condescending to men of low estate.   Let us trust Him and not be afraid.

Let us notice for another thing, *how our Lord condemns those who think to use carnal weapons in defence of Him and His cause.*   He reproves one of His disciples for striking a servant of the high priest.   He bids him "put up his sword into his place."   And he adds a solemn declaration of perpetual significance, " all they that take the sword shall perish by the sword."

The sword has a lawful office of its own.   It may be used righteously in the defence of nations against oppression.   It may become positively necessary to use it, to prevent confusion, plunder, and rapine upon earth.   But the sword is not to be used in the propagation and maintenance of the Gospel.   Christianity is not to be enforced by bloodshed, and belief in it extorted by force.   Happy would it have been for the Church if this sentence had been more frequently remembered!   There are few countries in Christendom, where the mistake has not been made, of attempting to change men's religious opinions by compulsion, penalties, imprisonment, and death.   And with what effect?   The pages of history supply an answer.   No wars have been so bloody as those which have arisen out of the collision of religious opinions.   Often, mournfully often, the very men who have been most forward to promote those wars, have themselves been slain.   May we never forget this!   The weapons of the Christian warfare are not carnal, but spiritual.   (2 Cor. x. 4.)

Let us notice for another thing, *how our Lord submitted*

to be made a prisoner of His own free will. He was not taken captive because He could not escape. It would have been easy for Him to scatter His enemies to the winds, if He had thought fit. "Thinkest thou," He says to a disciple," "that I cannot pray to my Father, and he shall presently give me more than twelve legions of angels? But how then shall the Scriptures be fulfilled, that thus it must be."

We see in those words the secret of His voluntary submission to His foes. He came on purpose to fulfil the types and promises of Old Testament Scriptures, and by fulfilling them to provide salvation for the world. He came intentionally to be the true Lamb of God, the Passover Lamb. He came to be the Scape-goat on whom the iniquities of the people were to be laid. His heart was set on accomplishing this great work. It could not be done without the "hiding of his power" for a time. To do it he became a willing sufferer. He was taken, tried, condemned, and crucified entirely of His own free will.

Let us observe this. There is much encouragement in it. The willing sufferer will surely be a willing Saviour. The almighty Son of God, who allowed men to bind Him and lead Him away captive, when He might have prevented them with a word, must surely be full of readiness to save the souls that flee to Him. Once more then let us learn to trust Him, and not be afraid.

Let us notice, in the last place, *how little Christians know the weakness of their own hearts, until they are tried.* We have a mournful illustration of this in the conduct of our Lord's apostles. The verses we have read conclude with the words, "Then all the disciples forsook him, and fled." They forgot their confident assertions made a few hours before. They forgot that they had declared their willingness to die with their Master. They forgot everything but the danger that stared them in the face. The fear of death overcame them. They "forsook him, and fled."

How many professing Christians have done the same! How many, under the influence of excited feelings, have promised that they would never be ashamed of Christ! They have come away from the communion table, or the striking sermon, or the Christian meeting, full of zeal and love, and ready to say to all who caution them against backsliding, "Is thy servant a dog that he should do this thing?" And yet in a few days these feelings have cooled down and passed away. A trial has come and they have fallen before it. They have forsaken Christ.

Let us learn from the passage lessons of humiliation and self-abasement. Let us resolve by God's grace to cultivate a spirit of lowliness, and self-distrust. Let us settle it in our minds, that there is nothing so bad that the best of us may not do it, unless he watches, prays, and is held up by the grace of God. And let it be one of our daily prayers, "Hold thou me up, and I shall be safe." (Psalm cxix. 117.)

MATTHEW XXVI. 57—68.

57 And they that had laid hold on Jesus led *him* away to Caiaphas the High Priest, where the Scribes and the elders were assembled.

58 But Peter followed him afar off unto the High Priest's palace, and went in, and sat with the servants, to see the end.

59 Now the Chief Priests, and elders, and all the council, sought false

witness against Jesus, to put him to death;

60 But found none: yea, though many false witnesses came, *yet* found they none. At the last came two false witnesses,

61 And said, This *fellow* said, I am able to destroy the temple of God, and to build it in three days.

62 And the High Priest arose, and said unto him, Answerest thou nothing? what *is it which* these witness against thee?

63 But Jesus held his peace. And the High Priest answered and said unto him, I adjure thee by the living God, that thou tell us whether thou be the Christ, the Son of God.

64 Jesus saith unto him, Thou hast said: nevertheless I say unto you, Hereafter shall ye see the Son of man sitting on the right hand of power, and coming in the clouds of heaven.

65 Then the High Priest rent his clothes, saying, He hath spoken blasphemy; what further need have we of witnesses? behold, now ye have heard his blasphemy.

66 What think ye? They answered and said, He is guilty of death.

67 Then did they spit in his face, and buffeted him; and others smote *him* with the palms of their hands.

68 Saying, Prophesy unto us, thou Christ, Who is he that smote thee?

WE read in these verses how our Lord Jesus Christ was brought before Caiaphas the high priest, and solemnly pronounced guilty. It was fitting that it should be so. The great day of atonement was come. The wondrous type of the scape-goat was about to be completely fulfilled. It was only suitable that the Jewish high priest should do his part, and declare sin to be upon the head of the victim, before He was led forth to be crucified. May we ponder these things and understand them. There was a deep meaning in every step of our Lord's passion.

Let us observe in these verses, that *the chief priests were the principal agents in bringing about our Lord's death.* It was not so much the Jewish people, we must remember, who pushed forward this wicked deed, as Caiaphas and his companions, the chief priests.

This is an instructive fact, and deserves notice. It is a clear proof that high ecclesiastical office exempts no man from gross errors in doctrine, and tremendous sins in practice. The Jewish priests could trace up their pedigree to Aaron, and were his lineal successors. Their

office was one of peculiar sanctity, and entailed peculiar
responsibilities.   And yet these very men were the murderers of Christ !

Let us beware of regarding any minister of religion as
infallible.   His orders, however regularly conferred, are
no guarantee that he may not lead us astray, and even
ruin our souls.   The teaching and conduct of all ministers
must be tried by the Word of God.   They are to be
followed so long as they follow the Bible, but no longer.
The maxim laid down in Isaiah must be our guide : "To
the law and the testimony : if they speak not according
to this word, it is because there is no light in them."
(Isai. viii. 20.)

Let us observe, in the second place, *how fully our Lord
declared to the Jewish council His own Messiahship, and
His future coming in glory.*

The unconverted Jew can never tell us at the present
day, that his forefathers were left in ignorance that Jesus
was the Messiah.   Our Lord's answer to the solemn ad-
juration of the high priest is a sufficient reply.   He tells
the council plainly that He is " the Christ, the Son of
God."   He goes on to warn them that though He had
not yet appeared in glory, as they expected Messias
would have done, a day would come when He would do
so.   " Hereafter ye shall see the Son of Man sitting on
the right hand of power, and coming in the clouds of
heaven."   They would yet see that very Jesus of Nazareth, whom they had arraigned at their bar, appear in all
majesty as King of kings. (Rev. i. 7.)

It is a striking fact which we should not fail to notice,
that almost the last word spoken by our Lord to the

Jews, was a warning prediction about His own second advent. He tells them plainly that they would yet see Him in glory. No doubt He referred to the seventh chapter of Daniel, in the language that he used. But He spoke to deaf ears. Unbelief, prejudice, self-righteousness covered them like a thick cloud. Never was there such an instance of spiritual blindness. Well may the Church of England litany contain the prayer, "From all blindness,—and from hardness of heart, Good Lord deliver us."

Let us observe, in the last place, *how much our Lord endured before the council, from false witness and mockery.*

Falsehood and ridicule are old and favourite weapons of the devil. "He is a liar, and the father of it." (John viii. 44.) All through our Lord's earthly ministry we see these weapons continually employed against Him. He was called a glutton, a winebibber, and a friend of publicans and sinners. He was held up to contempt as a Samaritan. The closing scene of His life was only in keeping with all the past tenor of it. Satan stirred up His enemies to add insult to injury. No sooner was He pronounced guilty, than every sort of mean indignity was heaped upon Him. "They spit in his face, and buffeted him." "They smote him with the palms of their hands." They said mockingly, "Prophesy unto us, thou Christ, who is he that smote thee?"

How wonderful and strange it all sounds! How wonderful that the Holy Son of God should have voluntarily submitted to such indignities, to redeem such miserable sinners as we are! How wonderful, not least, that every tittle of these insults was foretold seven hundred years before they were inflicted! Seven hundred years before, Isaiah had written down the words, " I hid not my face from shame and spitting." (Isai. l. 6.)

Let us draw from the passage one practical conclusion. Let it never surprise us, if we have to endure mockery, and ridicule, and false reports, because we belong to Christ. The disciple is not greater than His Master, nor the servant than His Lord. If lies and insults were heaped upon our Saviour, we need not wonder if the same weapons are constantly used against His people. It is one of Satan's great devices to blacken the characters of godly men, and bring them into contempt. The lives of Luther, Cranmer, Calvin, and Wesley supply abundant examples of this. If we are ever called upon to suffer in this way, let us bear it patiently. We drink the same cup that was drunk by our beloved Lord. But there is one great difference. At the worst, we only drink a few bitter drops. He drank the cup to the very dregs.

MATTHEW XXVI. 69—75.

69 Now Peter sat without in the palace: and a damsel came unto him, saying, Thou also wast with Jesus of Galilee.

70 But he denied before *them* all, saying, I know not what thou sayest.

71 And when he was gone out into the porch, another *maid* saw him, and said unto them that were there, This *fellow* was also with Jesus of Nazareth.

72 And again he denied with an oath, I do not know the man.

73 And after a while came unto *him* they that stood by, and said to Peter, Surely thou also art *one* of them; for thy speech bewrayeth thee.

74 Then began he to curse and to swear, *saying*, I know not the man. And immediately the cock crew.

75 And Peter remembered the word of Jesus, which said unto him, Before the cock crow, thou shalt deny me thrice. And he went out, and wept bitterly.

THESE verses relate a remarkable and deeply instructive event, the apostle Peter's denial of Christ. It is one of those events, which indirectly prove the truth of the Bible.

If the Gospel had been a mere invention of man, we should never have been told that one of its principal preachers was once so weak and erring, as to deny His Master.

The first thing that demands our notice, is *the full nature of the sin of which Peter was guilty.*

It was a great sin. We see a man, who had followed Christ for three years, and been forward in professing faith and love towards Him,—a man who had received boundless mercies, and loving-kindness, and been treated by Christ as a familiar friend,—we see this man denying three times that he knows Jesus!—This was bad.—It was a sin committed under circumstances of great aggravation. Peter had been warned plainly of his danger, and had heard the warning. He had just been receiving the bread and wine at our Lord's hand, and declaring loudly that though he died with Him, he would not deny Him!—This also was bad.—It was a sin committed under apparently small provocation. Two weak women make the remark that he was with Jesus. They that stood by say, "Surely thou art one of them." No threat seems to have been used. No violence seems to have been done. But it was enough to overthrow Peter's faith. He denies before all. He denies with an oath. He curses and swears.—Truly it is a humbling picture !

Let us mark this history, and store it up in our minds. It teaches us plainly that the best of saints are only men, and men encompassed with many infirmities. A man may be converted to God, have faith, and hope, and love towards Christ, and yet be overtaken in a fault, and have awful falls. It shews us the necessity of humility.

So long as we are in the body, we are in danger. The flesh is weak, and the devil is active. We must never think, "I cannot fall." It points out to us the duty of charity towards erring saints. We must not set down men as graceless reprobates, because they occasionally stumble and err. We must remember Peter, and "restore them in the spirit of meekness." (Gal. vi. 1.)

The second thing that demands our notice, is *the series of steps by which Peter was led to deny his Lord.*

These steps are mercifully recorded for our learning. The Spirit of God has taken care to have them written down for the perpetual benefit of the Church of Christ. Let us trace them out one by one.

The first step to Peter's fall, was self-confidence. He said, "though all men should be offended, yet will I never be offended."—The second step was indolence. His Master told him to watch and pray. Instead of doing so, he slept.—The third step was cowardly compromising. Instead of keeping close to his Master, he first forsook Him, and then "followed him afar off."—The last step was needless venturing into evil company. He went into the priest's palace, and "sat with the servants," like one of themselves.—And then came the final fall,—the cursing, the swearing, and the three-fold denial. Startling as it appears, his heart had been preparing for it. It was the fruit of seeds which he himself had sown. "He ate the fruit of his own ways."

Let us remember this part of Peter's history. It is deeply instructive to all who profess and call themselves Christians. Great illnesses seldom attack the body, without a previous train of premonitory symptoms. Great

falls seldom happen to a saint, without a previous course of
secret backsliding. The church and the world are sometimes
shocked by the sudden misconduct of some great professor of religion. Believers are discouraged and stumbled
by it. The enemies of God rejoice and blaspheme. But
if the truth could be known, the explanation of such
cases would generally be found to have been private
departure from God. Men fall in private, long before
they fall in public. The tree falls with a great crash,
but the secret decay which accounts for it, is often not
discovered till it is down on the ground.

The last thing that demands our notice is *the sorrow
which Peter's sin brought upon him.* We read at the end
of the chapter, "He went out and wept bitterly."

These words deserve more attention than they generally receive. Thousands have read the history of Peter's
sin, who have thought little of Peter's tears, and Peter's
repentance. May we have an eye to see, and a heart to
understand!

We see in Peter's tears, the close connection between
unhappiness and departure from God. It is a merciful
arrangement of God, that in one sense holiness shall
always be its own reward. A heavy heart, and an
uneasy conscience, a clouded hope, and an abundant crop
of doubts, will always be the consequence of backsliding
and inconsistency. The words of Solomon describe the
experience of many an inconsistent child of God, "The
backslider in heart shall be filled with his own ways."
(Prov. xiv. 14.) Let it be a settled principle in our
religion, that if we love inward peace, we must walk
closely with God.

We see in Peter's bitter tears, the grand mark of difference between the hypocrite and the true believer. When the hypocrite is overtaken by sin, he generally falls to rise no more. He has no principle of life within him to raise him up.—When the child of God is overtaken, he rises again by true repentance, and by the grace of God amends his life.—Let no man flatter himself that he may sin with impunity, because David committed adultery, and because Peter denied his Lord. No doubt these holy men sinned greatly. But they did not continue in their sin. They repented greatly. They mourned over their falls. They loathed and abhorred their own wickedness. Well would it be for many, if they would imitate them in their repentance, as well as in their sins. Too many are acquainted with their fall, but not with their recovery. Like David and Peter, they have sinned, but they have not, like David and Peter, repented.

The whole passage is full of lessons that ought never to be forgotten. Do we profess to have a hope in Christ? Let us mark the weakness of a believer, and the steps that lead to a fall.—Have we unhappily backslidden, and left our first love? Let us remember that the Saviour of Peter still lives. There is mercy for us as well as for him. But we must repent, and seek that mercy, if we would find it. Let us turn unto God, and He will turn to us. His compassions fail not. (Lam. iii. 22.)

MATTHEW XXVII. 1—10.

1 When the morning was come, all the Chief Priests and elders of the people took counsel against Jesus to put him to death:

2 And when they had bound him, they led *him* away, and delivered him to Pontius Pilate the governor.

3 Then Judas, which had betrayed him, when he saw that he was condemned, repented himself, and brought again the thirty pieces of silver to the Chief Priests and elders,

4 Saying, I have sinned in that I have betrayed the innocent blood. And they said, What *is that* to us? see thou *to that*.

5 And he cast down the pieces of silver in the temple, and departed, and went and hanged himself.

6 And the Chief Priests took the silver pieces, and said, It is not lawful for to put them into the treasury, because it is the price of blood.

7 And they took counsel, and bought with them the potter's field, to bury strangers in.

8 Wherefore that field was called, The field of blood, unto this day.

9 Then was fulfilled that which was spoken by Jeremy the prophet, saying, And they took the thirty pieces of silver, the price of him that was valued, whom they of the children of Israel did value;

10 And gave them for the potter's field, as the Lord appointed me.

THE opening of this chapter describes the delivery of our Lord Jesus Christ into the hands of the Gentiles. The chief priests and elders of the Jews led Him away to Pontius Pilate, the Roman governor. We may see in this incident the finger of God. It was ordered by His providence, that Gentiles as well as Jews should be concerned in the murder of Christ. It was ordered by His providence, that the priests should publicly confess that the "sceptre had departed from Judah." They were unable to put any one to death, without going to the Romans. The words of Jacob were therefore fulfilled. The Messiah, "Shiloh, had indeed come." (Gen. xlix. 10.)

The subject that principally occupies the verses we have read, is the melancholy end of the false apostle, Judas Iscariot. It is a subject full of instruction. Let us mark well what it contains.

We see in the end of Judas *a plain proof of our Lord's innocence of every charge laid against Him.*

If there was any living witness who could give evidence against our Lord Jesus Christ, Judas Iscariot was the man. A chosen apostle of Jesus, a constant companion in all His journeyings, a hearer of all His teaching, both in public and private,—he must have known well if our Lord had done any wrong, either in word or deed. A deserter from our Lord's company, a betrayer of Him into the hands of His enemies, it was his interest for his own character's sake, to prove Jesus guilty. It would extenuate and excuse his own conduct, if he could make out that His former master was an offender, and an impostor.

Why then did not Judas Iscariot come forward? Why did he not stand forth before the Jewish council, and specify his charges, if he had any to make? Why did he not venture to accompany the chief priests to Pilate, and prove to the Romans that Jesus was a malefactor?— There is but one answer to these questions. Judas did not come forward as a witness, because his conscience would not let him. Bad as he was, he knew he could prove nothing against Christ. Wicked as he was, he knew well that his Master was holy, harmless, innocent, blameless, and true. Let this never be forgotten. The absence of Judas Iscariot at our Lord's trial, is one among many proofs that the Lamb of God was without blemish,—a sinless man.

We see, for another thing, in the end of Judas, *that there is such a thing as repentance which is too late.* We are told plainly that "Judas repented himself." We are even told that he went to the priests, and said, "I have sinned." And yet it is clear that he did not repent unto salvation.

This is a point which deserves special attention. It is a common saying, "that it is never too late to repent."

The saying, no doubt, is true, if repentance be true ; but unhappily late repentance is often not genuine. It is possible for a man to feel his sins, and be sorry for them, —to be under strong convictions of guilt, and express deep remorse,—to be pricked in conscience, and exhibit much distress of mind,—and yet, for all this, not repent with his heart. Present danger, or the fear of death, may account for all his feelings, and the Holy Ghost may have done no work whatever on his soul.

Let us beware of trusting to a late repentance. "Now is the accepted time. To-day is the day of salvation." One penitent thief was saved in the hour of death, that no man might despair, but only one, that no man might presume. Let us put off nothing that concerns our souls, and above all not put off repentance, under the vain idea that it is a thing in our own power. The words of Solomon on this subject are very fearful. He speaks of men who " shall call upon God, but he will not answer ; who shall seek him early, and not find him." (Prov. i. 28.)

Let us see, for another thing, in the end of Judas, *how little comfort ungodliness brings a man at the last.* We are told that he cast down the thirty pieces of silver for which he had sold his Master, in the temple, and went away in bitterness of soul. That money was dearly earned. It brought him no pleasure, even when he had it.* The "treasures of wickedness profit nothing." (Prov. x. 2.)

---

*It is a great and undeniable difficulty, that the words quoted as having been used by "Jeremy the prophet," are not to be found in any writings of Jeremiah that we possess, and that they are found in the prophet Zechariah. The following solutions of the difficulty have been suggested.

Sin is, in truth, the hardest of all masters. In its service there is plenty of fair promises, but an utter dearth of performance. Its pleasures are but for a season. Its wages are sorrow, remorse, self-accusation, and too often death. They that sow to the flesh, do indeed reap corruption.

Are we tempted to commit sin? Let us remember the

1. Some think that the prophecy quoted by Matthew was really delivered by Jeremiah, though not written, and only handed down and recorded by Zechariah. In favour of this view, we must remember that we have a saying of our Lord's at Acts xx. 35, which is not recorded in the Gospels, and a prophecy of Enoch's in Jude. (Jude 14.)

2. Some think that the name of Jeremiah was applied by the Jews to all that portion of the Old Testament Scripture containing prophecies, and that Matthew did not really mean that Jeremy had delivered the prophecy. This is the view of Lightfoot.

3. Some think that Matthew originally wrote the words "The prophet," without quoting the name of any one in particular, and that the word "Jeremy" was inserted by an ignorant transcriber. In favour of this view, it is fair to say that the Syriac version, one of the oldest extant, simply says "the prophet," and omits Jeremy's name. The Persian version also omits it.

4. Some think that Matthew originally wrote the words "Zechariah the prophet," and that some ignorant transcriber changed the word into Jeremiah. In favour of this view, it must fairly be remembered that in manuscripts, names were often written short, and that IOU,—and ZOU, are not very unlike.

I offer no opinion on these solutions of the difficulty. A question of this sort, which has puzzled so many interpreters, is not likely to be settled at this period of the world.

One solution of the difficulty I only mention in order to enter my protest against it. That solution was propounded by Augustine, and is adopted by many modern divines. It is simply this, that "Matthew forgot what he was doing and made a blunder. He quoted from memory, and inaccurately. He meant Zechariah and not Jeremiah." I can only say that at this rate we must give up the inspiration of Scripture altogether! If writers of the Bible could make blunders like this, we never know where we are in quoting a text. To use such an argument is putting a sword into the hands of Arians and Socinians, which they know well how to use. Once give up the verbal inspiration of Scripture and we stand on a quicksand.

words of Scripture, "Your sin will find you out," and
resist the temptation. Let us be sure that sooner or
later, in this life or in the life to come, in this world or in
the judgment-day, sin and the sinner will meet face to
face, and have a bitter reckoning. Let us be sure that
of all trades sin is the most unprofitable. Judas, Achan,
Gehazi, Ananias and Sapphira, all found it so to their
cost. Well might St. Paul say, "What fruit had ye
in those things whereof ye are now ashamed?" (Rom.
vi. 21.)

Finally, let us see in the case of Judas, *to what a
miserable end a man may come, if he has great privileges,
and does not use them rightly.* We are told that this
unhappy man "departed and went and hanged himself."
What an awful death to die ! An apostle of Christ, a
former preacher of the Gospel, a companion of Peter and
John, commits suicide, and rushes into God's presence
unprepared and unforgiven.

Let us never forget that no sinners are so sinful as
sinners against light and knowledge. None are so provoking to God. None, if we look at Scripture, have been
so often removed from this world by sudden and fearful
visitations. Let us remember Lot's wife, Pharaoh,
Korah, Dathan, and Abiram, and Saul king of Israel.
They are all cases in point. It is a solemn saying of
Bunyan, "that none fall so deep into the pit, as those
who fall backward." It is written in Proverbs, " he that
being often reproved hardeneth his neck, shall suddenly
be destroyed, and that without remedy." (Prov. xxix. 1.)
May we all strive to live up to our light. There is such
a thing as sin against the Holy Ghost. Clear knowledge

of truth in the head, combined with deliberate love of sin in the heart, go a long way towards it.

And now what is the state of our hearts? Are we ever tempted to rest on our knowledge and profession of religion? Let us remember Judas, and beware.—Are we disposed to cling to the world, and give money a prominent place in our minds? Again, let us remember Judas, and beware.—Are we trifling with any one sin, and flattering ourselves we may repent by and bye? Once more, let us remember Judas, and beware.—He is set up before us as a beacon. Let us look well at him, and not make shipwreck.

MATTHEW XXVII. 11—26.

11 And Jesus stood before the governor: and the governor asked him, saying, Art thou the King of the Jews? And Jesus said unto him, Thou sayest.

12 And when he was accused of the Chief Priests and elders, he answered nothing.

13 Then said Pilate unto him, Hearest thou not how many things they witness against thee?

14 And he answered him to never a word; insomuch that the governor marvelled greatly.

15 Now at *that* feast the governor was wont to release unto the people a prisoner, whom they would.

16 And they had then a notable prisoner, called Barabbas.

17 Therefore when they were gathered together, Pilate said unto them, Whom will ye that I release unto you? Barabbas, or Jesus which is called Christ?

18 For he knew that for envy they had delivered him.

19 When he was set down on the judgment seat, his wife sent unto him, saying, Have thou nothing to do with that just man: for I have suffered many things this day in a dream because of him.

20 But the Chief Priests and elders persuaded the multitude that they should ask Barabbas, and destroy Jesus.

21 The governor answered and said unto them, Whether of the twain will ye that I release unto you? They said, Barabbas.

22 Pilate saith unto them, What shall I do then with Jesus which is called Christ? *They* all say unto him, Let him be crucified.

23 And the governor said, Why, what evil hath he done? But they cried out the more, saying, Let him be crucified.

24 When Pilate saw that he could prevail nothing, but *that* rather a tumult was made, he took water, and washed *his* hands before the multitude, saying, I am innocent of the blood of this just person: see ye *to it*.

25 Then answered all the people, and said, His blood *be* on us, and on our children.

26 Then released he Barabbas unto them: and when he had scourged Jesus, he delivered *him* to be crucified.

THESE verses describe our Lord's appearance before Pontius Pilate, the Roman governor. That sight must have been wonderful to the angels of God. He who will one day judge the world allowed himself to be judged and condemned, though " he had done no violence, neither was any deceit in his mouth." (Isaiah liii. 9.) He from whose lips Pilate and Caiaphas will one day receive their eternal sentence, suffered silently an unjust sentence to be passed upon him. Those silent sufferings fulfilled the words of Isaiah, "as a sheep before her shearers is dumb, so he openeth not his mouth." (Isaiah liii. 7.) To those silent sufferings believers owe all their peace and hope.— Through them they will have boldness in the day of judgment, who in themselves would have nothing to say.

Let us learn from the conduct of Pilate, *how pitiful is the condition of an unprincipled great man.*

Pilate appears to have been inwardly satisfied that our Lord had done nothing worthy of death. We are told distinctly, that "he knew that for envy they had delivered him." Left to the exercise of his own unbiassed judgment, he would probably have dismissed the charges against our Lord, and let Him go free.

But Pilate was the governor of a jealous and turbulent people. His great desire was to procure favour with them and please them. He cared little how much he sinned against God and conscience, so long as he had the praise of man. Though willing to save our Lord's life, he was afraid to do it, if it offended the Jews. And so, after a feeble attempt to divert the fury of the people from Jesus to Barabbas,—and a feebler attempt to satisfy his own conscience, by washing his hands publicly before the people,

—he at last condemned one whom he himself called a "just person." He rejected the strange and mysterious warning which his wife sent to him after her dream. He stifled the remonstrances of his own conscience. He "delivered Jesus to be crucified."

Behold in this miserable man a lively emblem of many a ruler of this world! How many there are, who know well that their public acts are wrong, and yet have not the courage to act up to their knowledge. They fear the people! They dread being laughed at! They cannot bear being unpopular! Like dead fish, they float with the tide. The praise of man is the idol before which they bow down, and to that idol they sacrifice conscience, inward peace, and an immortal soul.

Whatever our position in life may be, let us seek to be guided by principle, and not by expediency. The praise of man is a poor, feeble, uncertain thing. It is here to-day, and gone to-morrow. Let us strive to please God, and then we may care little who else is pleased. Let us fear God, and then there is none else of whom we need be afraid.

Let us learn from the conduct of the Jews described in these verses, *the desperate wickedness of human nature.*

The behaviour of Pilate afforded the chief priests and elders an occasion of reconsidering what they were about. The difficulties he raised about condemning our Lord, gave time for second thoughts. But there were no second thoughts in the minds of our Lord's enemies. They pressed on their wicked deed. They rejected the compromise that Pilate offered. They actually preferred having a wretched felon, named Barabbas, set at liberty rather than Jesus. They clamoured loudly for our Lord's crucifixion. And they wound up all by recklessly taking on themselves all the guilt of our Lord's death, in words of portentous meaning, "His blood be on us and our children."

And what had our Lord done, that the Jews should hate Him so? He was no robber, or murderer. He was no blasphemer of their God, or reviler of their prophets. He was one whose life was love. He was one who "went about doing good, and healing all that were oppressed of the devil." (Acts x. 38.) He was innocent of any transgression against the law of God or man. And yet the Jews hated Him, and never rested till He was slain! They hated Him, because He told them the truth. They hated Him, because He testified of their works that they were evil. They hated the light, because it made their own darkness visible. In a word, they hated Christ, because He was righteous and they were wicked,—because He was holy and they were unholy,—because He testified against sin, and they were determined to keep their sins and not let them go.

Let us observe this. There are few things so little believed and realized as the corruption of human nature. Men fancy that if they saw a perfect person, they would love and admire him. They flatter themselves that it is the inconsistency of professing Christians which they dislike, and not their religion. They forget that when a really perfect man was on earth, in the person of the Son of God, He was hated and put to death. That single fact goes far to prove the truth of Edwards' remark,—"unconverted men would kill God, if they could get at Him."

Let us never be surprised at the wickedness there is in the world. Let us mourn over it, and labour to make it less, but let us never be surprised at its extent. There is nothing which the heart of man is not capable of conceiving, or the hand of man of doing. As long as we live, let us mistrust our own hearts. Even when renewed by the Spirit, they are still "deceitful above all things and desperately wicked." (Jer. xvii. 9.)

MATTHEW XXVII. 27—44.

27 Then the soldiers of the governor took Jesus into the common hall, and gathered unto him the whole band *of soldiers.*

28 And they stripped him, and put on him a scarlet robe.

29 And when they had platted a crown of thorns, they put *it* upon his head, and a reed in his right hand: and they bowed the knee before him, and mocked him, saying, Hail, King of the Jews!

30 And they spit upon him, and took the reed, and smote him on the head.

31 And after that they had mocked him, they took the robe off from him, and put his own raiment on him, and led him away to crucify *him.*

32 And as they came out, they found a man of Cyrene, Simon by name: him they compelled to bear his cross.

33 And when they were come unto a place called Golgotha, that is to say, a place of a skull,

34 They gave him vinegar to drink mingled with gall: and when he had tasted *thereof,* he would not drink.

35 And they crucified him, and parted his garments, casting lots: that it might be fulfilled which was spoken by the prophet, They parted my garments among them, and upon my vesture did they cast lots.

36 And sitting down they watched him there;

37 And set up over his head his accusation written, THIS IS JESUS THE KING OF THE JEWS.

38 Then were there two thieves crucified with him, one on the right hand, and another on the left.

39 And they that passed by reviled him, wagging their heads,

40 And saying, Thou that destroyest the temple, and buildest *it* in three days, save thyself. If thou be the Son of God, come down from the cross.

41 Likewise also the Chief Priests mocking *him,* with the Scribes and elders, said,

42 He saved others; himself he cannot save. If he be the King of Israel, let him now come down from the cross, and we will believe him.

43 He trusted in God; let him deliver him now, if he will have him: for he said, I am the Son of God.

44 The thieves also, which were crucified with him, cast the same in his teeth.

THESE verses describe the sufferings of our Lord Jesus Christ after His condemnation by Pilate,—His sufferings in the hands of the brutal Roman soldiers, and His final sufferings on the cross. They form a marvellous record. They are marvellous when we remember the sufferer, the eternal Son of God! They are marvellous when we remember the persons for whom these sufferings were endured. We and our sins were the cause of all this sorrow. He " died for our sins." (1 Cor. xv. 3.)

Let us observe in the first place, *the extent and reality of our Lord's sufferings.*

The catalogue of all the pains endured by our Lord's body, is indeed a fearful one. Seldom has such suffering been inflicted on one body in the last few hours of a life. The most savage tribes, in their refinement of cruelty, could not have heaped more agonizing tortures on an enemy than were accumulated on the flesh and bones of our beloved Master. Never let it be forgotten that He had a real human body, a body exactly like our own, just as sensitive, just as vulnerable, just as capable of feeling intense pain. And then let us see what that body endured.

Our Lord, we must remember, had already passed a night without sleep, and endured excessive fatigue. He had been taken from Gethsemane to the Jewish council, and from the council to Pilate's judgment hall. He had been twice placed on His trial, and twice unjustly condemned. He had been already scourged and beaten cruelly with rods. And now, after all this suffering, He was delivered up to the Roman soldiers, a body of men no doubt expert in cruelty, and of all people least likely to behave with delicacy or compassion.—These hard men at once proceeded to work their will. They "gathered together the whole band." They stripped our Lord of His raiment, and put on Him, in mockery, a scarlet robe. They platted a crown of sharp thorns, and in derision placed it on His head. They then bowed the knee before Him in mockery, as nothing better than a pretended king. They spit upon Him. They smote Him on the head. And finally having put His own robe on Him, they led Him out of the city, to a place called Golgotha, and there crucified Him between two thieves.

But what was a crucifixion? Let us try to realize it, and understand its misery. The person crucified was laid on His back on a piece of timber, with a cross-piece nailed to it near one end,—or on the trunk of a tree with branching arms, which answered the same purpose. His hands were spread out on the cross-piece, and nails driven through each of them, fastening them to the wood. His feet in like manner were nailed to the upright part of the cross. And then, the body having been securely fastened, the cross was raised up, and fixed firmly in the ground. And there hung the unhappy sufferer, till pain and exhaustion brought him to his end,—not dying suddenly, for no vital part of him was injured,—but enduring the most excruciating agony from his hands and feet, and unable to move. Such was the death of the cross. Such was the death that Jesus died for us! For six long hours He hung there before a gazing crowd, naked, and bleeding from head to foot,—His head pierced with thorns,—His back lacerated with scourging,—His hands and feet torn with nails,—and mocked and reviled by His cruel enemies to the very last.

Let us meditate frequently on these things. Let us often

read over the story of Christ's cross and passion. Let us remember, not least, that all these horrible sufferings were borne without a murmur. No word of impatience crossed our Lord's lips. In His death, no less than in His life, He was perfect. To the very last, Satan found nothing in Him. (John xiv. 30.)

Let us observe, in the second place, that *all our Lord Jesus Christ's sufferings were vicarious.* He suffered not for His own sins, but for our's. He was eminently our substitute in all His passion.

This is a truth of the deepest importance. Without it the story of our Lord's sufferings, with all its minute details, must always seem mysterious and inexplicable. It is a truth, however, of which the Scriptures speak frequently, and that too with no uncertain sound. We are told that Christ "bare our sins in his own body on the tree,"—that He " suffered for sin, the just for the unjust,"—that " He was made sin for us, who knew no sin, that we might be made the righteousness of God in him,"—that " He was made a curse for us,"—that " He was offered to bear the sins of many,"—that " He was wounded for our transgressions, and bruised for our iniquities,"—and that " the Lord hath laid on Him the iniquity of us all." (1 Peter ii. 22, and iii. 18. 2 Cor. v. 21. Gal. iii. 13. Heb. ix. 28. Isaiah liii. 5, 6.) May we all remember these texts well. They are among the foundation stones of the Gospel.

But we must not be content with a vague general belief, that Christ's sufferings on the cross were vicarious. We are intended to see this truth in every part of His passion. We may follow Him all through, from the bar of Pilate,

to the minute of His death, and see Him at every step as
our mighty Substitute, our Representative, our Head, our
Surety, our Proxy,—the Divine Friend who undertook
to stand in our stead, and by the priceless merit of
His sufferings, to purchase our redemption.—Was He
scourged ?   It was that " through His stripes we might
be healed."—Was He condemned, though innocent ?   It
was that we might be acquitted, though guilty.—Did He
wear a crown of thorns ?   It was that we might wear the
crown of glory.—Was He stripped of His raiment ?   It
was that we might be clothed in everlasting righteousness.
—Was He mocked and reviled ?   It was that we might
be honoured and blessed.—Was He reckoned a malefactor, and numbered among transgressors ?   It was that
we might be reckoned innocent, and justified from all sin.
—Was he declared unable to save Himself ?   It was
that He might be able to save others to the uttermost.—
Did He die at last, and that the most painful and disgraceful of deaths ?   It was that we might live for
evermore, and be exalted to the highest glory.—Let us
ponder these things well.   They are worth remembering.
The very key to peace is a right apprehension of the
vicarious sufferings of Christ.

Let us leave the story of our Lord's passion with
feelings of deep thankfulness.   Our sins are many and
great.   But a great atonement has been made for them.
There was an infinite merit in all Christ's sufferings.
They were the sufferings of One who was God as well as
man.   Surely it is meet, right, and our bounden duty, to
praise God daily because Christ has died.

Last, but not least, let us ever learn from the story of

the passion, to hate sin with a great hatred. Sin was the cause of all our Saviour's suffering. Our sins platted the crown of thorns. Our sins drove the nails into His hands and feet. On account of our sins His blood was shed. Surely the thought of Christ crucified should make us loathe all sin. Well says the Homily of the Passion, "Let this image of Christ crucified be always printed in our hearts. Let it stir us up to the hatred of sin, and provoke our minds to the earnest love of Almighty God."

MATTHEW XXVII. 45—56.

45 Now from the sixth hour there was darkness over all the land unto the ninth hour.

46 And about the ninth hour Jesus cried with a loud voice, saying, Eli, Eli, lama sabachthani? that is to say, My God, my God, why hast thou forsaken me?

47 Some of them that stood there, when they heard *that*, said, This *man* calleth for Elias.

48 And straightway one of them ran, and took a spunge, and filled *it* with vinegar, and put *it* on a reed, and gave him to drink.

49 The rest said, Let be, let us see whether Elias will come to save him.

50 Jesus, when he had cried again with a loud voice, yielded up the ghost.

51 And, behold, the veil of the temple was rent in twain from the top to the bottom; and the earth did quake, and the rocks rent;

52 And the graves were opened; and many bodies of the saints which slept arose,

53 And came out of the graves after his resurrection, and went into the holy city, and appeared unto many.

54 Now when the centurion, and they that were with him, watching Jesus, saw the earthquake, and those things that were done, they feared greatly, saying, Truly this was the Son of God.

55 And many women were there beholding afar off, which followed Jesus from Galilee, ministering unto him:

56 Among which was Mary Magdalene, and Mary the mother of James and Joses, and the mother of Zebedee's children.

IN these verses we read the conclusion of our Lord Jesus Christ's passion. After six hours of agonizing suffering, He became obedient even unto death, and "yielded up the ghost." Three points in the narrative demand a special notice. To them let us confine our attention.

Let us observe, in the first place, *the remarkable words*

which Jesus uttered shortly before His death, " My God, my God, why hast thou forsaken me ! "

There is a deep mystery in these words, which no mortal man can fathom. No doubt they were not wrung from our Lord by mere bodily pain. Such an explanation is utterly unsatisfactory, and dishonourable to our blessed Saviour. They were meant to express the real pressure on His soul of the enormous burden of a world's sins. They were meant to show how truly and literally He was our substitute, was made sin, and a curse for us, and endured God's righteous anger against a world's sin in His own person. At that awful moment, the iniquity of us all was laid upon Him to the uttermost. It pleased the Lord to bruise Him, and put Him to grief. (Isaiah liii. 10.) He bore our sins. He carried our transgressions. Heavy must have been that burden, real and literal must have been our Lord's substitution for us, when He, the eternal Son of God, could speak of Himself as for a time " forsaken."

Let the expression sink down into our hearts, and not be forgotten. We can have no stronger proof of the sinfulness of sin, or of the vicarious nature of Christ's sufferings, than His cry, " My God, my God, why hast thou forsaken me." It is a cry that should stir us up to hate sin, and encourage us to trust in Christ.*

* The following quotations deserve notice, and throw light on this peculiarly solemn portion of Scripture.

" Our Lord said this, under a deep sense of His Father's wrath unto mankind, in whose stead He now underwent that which was due for the sins of the whole world. When He said ' Why hast thou forsaken me,' He implied that God had for the time withdrawn from Him the sense and vision of His comfortable presence. When He said, ' My God,' He implied the strength of His faith whereby

Let us observe, in the second place, *how much is contained in the words which describe our Lord's end.* We are simply told, " He yielded up the ghost."

There never was a last breath drawn, of such deep import as this. There never was an event on which so much depended. The Roman soldiers, and the gaping crowd around the cross, saw nothing remarkable. They only saw a person dying as others die, with all the usual agony and suffering, which attend a crucifixion. But they knew nothing of the eternal interests which were involved in the whole transaction.

That death discharged in full the mighty debt which sinners owe to God, and threw open the door of life to every believer. That death satisfied the righteous claims of God's holy law, and enabled God to be just, and yet the justifier of the ungodly. That death was no mere example of self-sacrifice, but a complete atonement and propitiation for man's sin, affecting the condition and prospects of all mankind. That death solved the hard problem, how God could be perfectly holy, and yet perfectly merciful. It opened to the world a fountain for all sin and uncleanness.—It was a complete victory over Satan, and spoiled him openly. It finished the transgression, made reconciliation for iniquity, and brought in everlasting righteousness.—It proved the sinfulness of sin, when it needed such a sacrifice to atone for it.—It proved the

He did firmly apprehend the sure and gracious aid of His eternal Father."—*Bishop Hall.*

"All the wailings and howlings of the damned to all eternity, will fall infinitely short of expressing the evil and bitterness of sin with such emphasis as these few words, 'My God, my God, why hast thou forsaken me.'"—*Jamieson.*

love of God to sinners, when He sent His own Son to
make the atonement. Never, in fact, was there, or could
there be again, such a death. No wonder that the earth
quaked, when Jesus died, in our stead, on the accursed
tree. The solid frame of the world might well tremble
and be amazed, when the soul of Christ was made an
offering for sin. (Isaiah liii. 10.)

Let us observe, in the last place, *what a remarkable
miracle occurred at the hour of our Lord's death, in the
very midst of the Jewish temple.* We are told that " the
veil of the temple was rent in twain." The curtain
which separated the holy of holies from the rest of the
temple, and through which the high priest alone might
pass, was split from top to bottom.

Of all the wonderful signs which accompanied our
Lord's death, none was more significant than this. The
mid-day darkness, for three hours, must needs have been
a startling event. The earthquake, which rent the rocks,
must have been a tremendous shock. But there was a
meaning in the sudden rending of the veil from top to
bottom, which must have pricked the heart of any intelligent Jew. The conscience of Caiaphas, the high priest,
must have been hard indeed, if the tidings of that rent
veil did not fill him with dismay.

That rending of the veil proclaimed the termination
and passing away of the ceremonial law. It was a sign
that the old dispensation of sacrifices and ordinances
was no longer needed. Its work was done. Its occupation was gone, from the moment that Christ died.
There was no more need of an earthly high priest, and a
mercy seat, and a sprinkling of blood, and an offering up of

incense, and a day of atonement. The true High Priest had at length appeared. The true Lamb of God had been slain. The true mercy seat was at length revealed. The figures and shadows were no longer wanted. May we all remember this! To set up an altar, and a sacrifice, and a priesthood *now*, is to light a candle at noon-day.

That rending of the veil proclaimed the opening of the way of salvation to all mankind. The way into the presence of God was unknown to the Gentile, and only seen dimly by the Jew, until Christ died. But Christ having now offered up a perfect sacrifice, and obtained eternal redemption, the darkness and mystery were to pass away. All were to be invited now to draw near to God with boldness, and approach Him with confidence, by faith in Jesus. A door was thrown open, and a way of life set before the whole world. May we all remember this! From the time that Jesus died, the way of peace was never meant to be shrouded in mystery. There was to be no reserve. The Gospel was the revelation of a mystery, which had been hid from ages and generations. To clothe religion *now* with mystery, is to mistake the grand characteristic of Christianity.

Let us turn from the story of the crucifixion, every time we read it, with hearts full of praise. Let us praise God for the confidence it gives us, as to the ground of our hope of pardon. Our sins may be many and great, but the payment made by our Great Substitute far outweighs them all.—Let us praise God for the view it gives us of the love of our Father in heaven. He that spared not His own Son, but delivered Him up for us all, will surely with Him give us all things.—Not least, let us praise God for the view it gives us of the sympathy of Jesus with all His believing people. He can be touched with the feeling of our infirmities. He knows what suffering is. He is just the Saviour that an infirm body, with a weak heart, in an evil world, requires.

MATTHEW XXVII. 57—66.

57 When the even was come, there came a rich man of Arimathæa, named Joseph, who also himself was Jesus' disciple:

58 He went to Pilate, and begged the body of Jesus. Then Pilate commanded the body to be delivered.

59 And when Joseph had taken the body, he wrapped it in a clean linen cloth,

60 And laid it in his own new tomb, which he had hewn out in the rock: and he rolled a great stone to the door of the sepulchre, and departed.

61 And there was Mary Magdalene, and the other Mary, sitting over against the sepulchre.

62 Now the next day, that followed the day of the preparation, the Chief Priests and Pharisees came together unto Pilate,

63 Saying, Sir, we remember that that deceiver said, while he was yet alive, After three days I will rise again.

64 Command therefore that the sepulchre be made sure until the third day, lest his disciples come by night, and steal him away, and say unto the people, He is risen from the dead: so the last error shall be worse than the first.

65 Pilate said unto them, Ye have a watch: go your way, make *it* as sure as ye can.

66 So they went, and made the sepulchre sure, sealing the stone, and setting a watch.

THESE verses contain the history of our Lord Jesus Christ's burial. There was yet one thing needful, in order to make it certain that our Redeemer accomplished that great work of redemption which He undertook. That holy body, in which He bore our sins on the cross, must actually be laid in the grave, and rise again. His resurrection was to be the seal and head-stone of all the work.

The infinite wisdom of God foresaw the objections of unbelievers and infidels, and provided against them.—Did the Son of God really die? Did He really rise again? Might there not have been some delusion as to the reality of His death? Might there not have been imposition or deception, as to the reality of His resurrection?—All these, and many more objections, would doubtless have been raised, if opportunity had been given. But He who knows the end from the beginning, prevented the possibility of such objections being made. By His over-ruling providence, He ordered things so that the death and burial of Jesus were placed beyond a doubt.—Pilate gives consent to His burial. A loving disciple wraps the body in linen, and lays it in a new tomb hewn out of a rock, "wherein was never man yet laid." The chief priests themselves set a guard over the place where His body was deposited. Jews and Gentiles, friends and enemies, all alike testify to the great fact, that Christ did really and actually die, and was laid in a grave. It is a fact that can never be questioned.—He was really "bruised." He really "suffered." He really "died." He was really "buried." Let us mark this well. It deserves recollection.

Let us learn, for one thing, from these verses, that *our Lord Jesus Christ has friends of whom little is known.*

We cannot have a more striking example of this truth, than we see in the passage now before us. A man named Joseph of Arimathæa comes forward, when our Lord was dead, and asks permission to bury Him. We have never heard of this man at any former period of our Lord's earthly ministry. We never hear of him again. We know nothing, but that he was a disciple who loved Christ, and did Him honour. At a time when the apostles had forsaken our Lord,—at a time when it was a dangerous thing to confess regard for Him,—at a time when there seemed to be no earthly advantage to be gained by confessing His discipleship,—at such a time as this Joseph comes boldly forward, and begs the body of Jesus, and lays it in his own new tomb.

This fact is full of comfort and encouragement. It shews us that there are some quiet, retiring souls on earth, who know the Lord, and the Lord knows them, and yet they are little known by the Church. It shows us that there are diversities of gifts among Christ's people. There are some who glorify Christ passively, and some who glorify Him actively. There are some whose vocation it is to build the Church, and fill a public place, and there are some who only come forward, like Joseph, in times of special need. But each and all are led by one Spirit, and each and all glorify God in their several ways.

Let these things teach us to be more hopeful. Let us believe that many shall yet come from the east and west, and sit down with Abraham, and Isaac, and Jacob, in the kingdom of heaven. There may be in some dark corners of Christendom many, who, like Simeon, and Anna, and Joseph of Arimathæa, are at present little known, who shall shine brightly among the Lord's jewels in the day of His appearing.

Let us learn, for another thing, from these verses, *that God can make the devices of wicked men work round to His own glory.*

We are taught that lesson in a striking manner, by the conduct of the priests and Pharisees, after our Lord was buried. The restless enmity of these unhappy men could not sleep, even when the body of Jesus was in the grave. They called to mind the words, which they remembered He had said, about "rising again." They resolved, as they thought, to make His rising again impossible. They went to Pilate. They obtained from him a guard of Roman soldiers. They set a watch over the tomb of our Lord. They placed a seal upon the stone. In short, they did all they could to "make the sepulchre sure."

They little thought what they were doing. They little thought that unwittingly they were providing the most complete evidence of the truth of Christ's coming resurrection. They were actually making it impossible to prove that there was any deception or imposition. Their seal, their guard, their precautions, were all to become witnesses, in a few hours, that Christ had risen. They might as well have tried to stop the tides of the sea, or to prevent the sun rising, as to prevent Jesus coming forth from the tomb. They were taken in their own craftiness. (1 Cor. iii. 19.) Their own devices became instruments to show forth God's glory.

The history of the Church of Christ is full of examples of a similar kind. The very things that have seemed most unfavourable to God's people, have often turned out to be for their good. What harm did the "persecution which arose about Stephen" do to the Church of Christ? They that were scattered went every where, preaching the word. (Acts vii. 4.)—What harm did imprisonment do St. Paul? It gave him time to write many of those Epistles, which are now read all over the world.—What real harm did the persecution of bloody Mary do to the cause of the English Reformation? The blood of the Martyrs became the seed of the Church.—What harm does persecution do the people of God at this very day? It only drives them nearer to Christ. It only makes them cling more closely to the throne of grace, the Bible, and prayer.

Let all true Christians lay these things to heart, and take courage. We live in a world where all things are ordered by a hand of perfect wisdom, and where all things are working together continually for the good of the body of Christ. The powers of this world are only tools in the hand of God. He is ever using them for His own purposes, however little they may be aware of it.—They are the instruments by which He is ever squaring and polishing the living stones of His spiritual temple, and all their schemes and plans will only turn to His praise. Let us be patient in days of trouble and darkness, and look forward. The very things which now seem against us, are all working together for God's glory. We see but half now.—Yet a little, we shall see all. And we shall then discover that all the persecution we now endure was, like the seal and the guard, tending to God's glory. God can make the "wrath of man praise him." (Psalm. lxxvii. 10.)

MATTHEW XXVIII. 1—10.

1 In the end of the sabbath, as it began to dawn toward the first *day* of the week, came Mary Magdalene and the other Mary to see the sepulchre.

2 And, behold, there was a great earthquake: for the angel of the Lord descended from heaven, and came and rolled back the stone from the door, and sat upon it.

3 His countenance was like lightning, and his raiment white as snow:

4 And for fear of him the keepers did shake, and became as dead *men*.

5 And the angel answered and said unto the women, Fear not ye: for I know that ye seek Jesus, which was crucified.

6 He is not here: for he is risen, as he said. Come, see the place where the Lord lay.

7 And go quickly, and tell his disciples that he is risen from the dead: and, behold, he goeth before you into Galilee; there shall ye see him: lo, I have told you.

8 And they departed quickly from the sepulchre with fear and great joy; and did run to bring his disciples word.

9 And as they went to tell his disciples, behold, Jesus met them, saying, All hail. And they came and held him by the feet, and worshipped him.

10 Then said Jesus unto them, Be not afraid: go tell my brethren that they go into Galilee, and there shall they see me.

THE principal subject of these verses is the resurrection of our Lord Jesus Christ from the dead. It is one of those truths which lie at the very foundation of Christianity, and has therefore received special attention in the four Gospels. All four evangelists describe minutely how our Lord was crucified. All four relate with no less clearness, that He rose again.

We need not wonder that so much importance is attached to our Lord's resurrection. It is the seal and headstone of the great work of redemption, which He came to do. It is the crowning proof that He has paid the debt which He undertook to pay on our behalf, won the battle which He fought to deliver us from hell, and is accepted as our Surety and our Substitute by our Father in heaven. Had He never come forth from the prison of the grave, how could we ever have been sure that our ransom had been fully paid? (1 Cor. xv. 17.) Had He never risen from His conflict with the last enemy, how could we have felt confident, that He has overcome death, and him that had the power of death, that is the devil? (Heb. ii. 14.) But thanks be unto God, we are not left in doubt. The Lord Jesus really "rose again for our justification." True Christians are "begotten again unto a lively hope by the resurrection of Jesus Christ from the dead." They may boldly say with Paul, "Who is he that condemneth: it is Christ that died, yea rather that is risen again." (Rom. viii. 34. Rom. iv. 25. 1 Peter i. 3.)

We have reason to be very thankful, that this wonderful truth of our religion is so clearly and fully proved. It is a striking circumstance, that of all the facts of our Lord's earthly ministry, none are so incontrovertibly established as the fact that He rose again. The wisdom of God, who knows the unbelief of human nature, has provided a great cloud of witnesses on the subject. Never was there a fact which the friends of God were so slow to believe, as the resurrection of Christ. Never was there a fact which the enemies of God were so anxious to disprove. And yet, in spite of the unbelief of friends, and the enmity of foes, the fact was thoroughly established. Its evidences will always appear to a fair and impartial mind unanswerable. It would be impossible to prove any thing in the world, if we refuse to believe that Jesus rose again.

Let us notice in these verses, *the glory and majesty with which Christ rose from the dead*. We are told that "there was a great earthquake." We are told that "the angel of the Lord descended from heaven, and came and rolled back the stone from the door of the sepulchre, and sat upon it." We need not suppose that our blessed Lord needed the help of any angel, when He came forth from the grave. We need not for a moment doubt that He rose again by His own power. But it pleased God, that His resurrection should be accompanied and followed by signs and wonders. It seemed good that the earth should shake, and a glorious angel appear, when the Son of God arose from the dead as a conqueror.

Let us not fail to see in the manner of our Lord's resurrection, a type and pledge of the resurrection of His believing people. The grave could not hold Him beyond the appointed time, and it shall not be able to hold them. —A glorious angel was a witness of His rising, and glorious angels shall be the messengers who shall gather believers when they rise again.—He rose with a renewed body, and yet a body, real, true, and material, and so also shall His people have a glorious body, and be like their Head.—"When we see him we shall be like him." (1 John iii. 2.)

Let us take comfort in this thought. Trial, sorrow, and persecution are often the portion of God's people. Sickness, weakness, and pain often hurt and wear their poor earthly tabernacle. But their good time is yet to come. Let them wait patiently, and they shall have a glorious resurrection. When we die, and where we are buried, and what kind of a funeral we have, matters little. The great question to be asked is this, "how shall we rise again?"

Let us notice in the next place, *the terror which Christ's enemies felt at the period of His resurrection.* We are told that, at the sight of the angel, "the keepers did shake and became as dead men." Those hardy Roman soldiers, though not unused to dreadful sights, saw a sight which made them quail. Their courage melted at once at the appearance of one angel of God.

Let us again see in this fact, a type and emblem of things yet to come. What will the ungodly and the wicked do at the last day, when the trumpet shall sound, and Christ shall come in glory to judge the world? What will they do, when they see *all* the dead, both small and great, coming forth from their graves, and *all* the angels of God assembled round the great white throne?

What fears and terrors will possess their souls, when they find they can no longer avoid God's presence, and must at length meet Him face to face? Oh! that men were wise, and would consider their latter end! Oh! that they would remember that there is a resurrection and a judgment, and that there is such a thing as the wrath of the Lamb!

Let us notice in the next place, *the words of comfort which the angel addressed to the friends of Christ.* We read that he said, " Fear not ye: for I know that ye seek Jesus, that was crucified."

These words were spoken with a deep meaning. They were meant to cheer the hearts of believers in every age, in the prospect of the resurrection. They were intended to remind us, that true Christians have no cause for alarm, whatever may come on the world. The Lord shall appear in the clouds of heaven, and the earth be burned up. The graves shall give up the dead that are in them, and the last day come. The judgment shall be set, and the books shall be opened. The angels shall sift the wheat from the chaff, and divide between the good fish and the bad. —But in all this there is nothing that need make believers afraid. Clothed in the righteousness of Christ, they shall be found without spot and blameless. Safe in the one true ark, they shall not be hurt when the flood of God's wrath breaks on the earth. Then shall the words of the Lord receive their complete fulfilment: " when these things begin to come to pass, lift up your heads, for your redemption draweth nigh." Then shall the wicked and unbelieving see how true was that word, " blessed are the people whose God is the Lord." (Psalm xxxiii. 12.)

Let us notice, finally, *the gracious message which the Lord sent to the disciples after His resurrection.* He appeared in person to the women who had come to do honour to His body. Last at the cross and first at the tomb, they were the first privileged to see Him after He rose. And to them He gives commission to carry tidings to His disciples. His first thought is for His little scattered flock. "Go, tell my brethren."

There is something deeply touching in those simple words, "my brethren." They deserve a thousand thoughts. Weak, frail, erring as the disciples were, Jesus still calls them His "brethren." He comforts them, as Joseph did his brethren who had sold him, saying, "I am your brother Joseph." Much as they had come short of their profession,—sadly as they had yielded to the fear of man,—they are still His "brethren." Glorious as He was in Himself,—a conqueror over death, and hell, and the grave, the Son of God is still "meek and lowly of heart." He calls His disciples " brethren."

Let us turn from the passage with comfortable thoughts, if we know anything of true religion. Let us see in these words of Christ, an encouragement to trust and not be afraid. Our Saviour is one who never forgets His people. He pities their infirmities. He does not despise them. He knows their weakness, and yet does not cast them away. Our great High Priest is also our elder brother.

MATTHEW XXVIII. 11—20.

11 Now when they were going, behold, some of the watch came into the city, and shewed unto the Chief Priests all the things that were done.

12 And when they were assembled with the elders, and had taken counsel, they gave large money unto the soldiers,

13 Saying, Say ye, His disciples came by night, and stole him *away* while we slept.

14 And if this come to the governor's ears, we will persuade him and secure you.

15 So they took the money, and did as they were taught: and this saying is commonly reported among the Jews until this day.

16 Then the eleven disciples went away into Galilee, into a mountain where Jesus had appointed them.

17 And when they saw him, they worshipped him: but some doubted.

18 And Jesus came and spake unto them, saying, All power is given unto me in heaven and in earth.

19 Go ye therefore, and teach all nations, baptizing them in the name of the Father, and of the Son, and of the Holy Ghost:

20 Teaching them to observe all things whatsoever I have commanded you: and, lo, I am with you alway, *even* unto the end of the world. Amen.

THESE verses form the conclusion of the Gospel of St. Matthew. They begin by showing us what absurdities blind prejudice will believe, rather than believe the truth. They go on to show us what weakness there is in the hearts of some disciples, and how slow they are to believe. They finish by telling us some of the last words spoken by our Lord upon earth,—words so remarkable that they demand and deserve all our attention.

Let us observe, in the first place, *the honour which God has put on our Lord Jesus Christ.* Our Lord says, "all power is given unto me, in heaven and earth."

This is a truth which is declared by St. Paul to the Philippians, "God hath highly exalted Him and given Him a name, which is above every name." (Phil. ii. 9.) It is a truth which in nowise takes away from the true notion of Christ's divinity, as some have ignorantly supposed. It is simply a declaration, that, in the counsels of the eternal Trinity, Jesus, as Son of man, is appointed heir of all things,—that He is the Mediator between God and man,—that the salvation of all who are saved is laid upon Him,—and that He is the great fountain of mercy, grace, life, and peace. It was for this "joy set before Him that He endured the cross." (Heb. xii. 2.)

Let us embrace this truth reverently, and cling to it

firmly. Christ is He who has the keys of death and hell. Christ is the anointed Priest, who alone can ab- solve sinners. Christ is the fountain of living waters, in whom alone we can be cleansed. Christ is the Prince and Saviour, who alone can give repentance and remission of sins. In Him all fulness dwells. He is the way, the door, the light, the life, the Shepherd, the altar of refuge. He that hath the Son hath life,—and he that hath not the Son hath not life. May we all strive to understand this. No doubt men may easily think too little of God the Father, and God the Spirit; but no man ever thought too much of Christ.

Let us observe, in the second place, *the duty which Jesus lays on His disciples.* He bids them " go and teach all nations." They were not to confine their knowledge to themselves, but communicate it to others. They were not to suppose that salvation was revealed only to the Jews, but to make it known to all the world. They were to strive to make disciples of all nations, and to tell the whole earth that Christ had died for sinners.

Let us never forget that this solemn injunction is still in full force. It is still the bounden duty of every disciple of Christ to do all he can in person, and by prayer, to make others acquainted with Jesus. Where is our faith, if we neglect this duty? Where is our charity? It may well be questioned whether a man knows the value of the Gospel himself, if he does not desire to make it known to all the world.

Let us observe, in the third place, *the public profession which Jesus requires of those who believe His Gospel.* He tells His apostles to " baptize " those whom they received as disciples.

It is very difficult to conceive when we read this last command of our Lord's, how men can avoid the conclusion that baptism is necessary, when it may be had. It seems impossible to explain the word that we have here of any but an outward ordinance, to be administered to all who join His Church.—That outward baptism is not absolutely necessary to salvation, the case of the penitent thief plainly shows. He went to paradise unbaptized.— That outward baptism alone often confers no benefit, the case of Simon Magus plainly shows. Although baptized he remained "in the gall of bitterness and bond of iniquity." (Acts viii. 23.)—But that baptism is a matter of entire indifference, and need not be used at all, is an assertion which seems at variance with our Lord's words in this place.*

The plain practical lesson of the words is the necessity of a public confession of faith in Christ. It is not enough to be a secret disciple. We must not be ashamed to let men see whose we are, and whom we serve. We must not behave as if we did not like to be thought Christians, but take up our cross and confess our Master before the world. His words are very solemn, "Whosoever shall be ashamed of me,—of him shall the Son of man be ashamed, when he cometh in the glory of his Father, with the holy angels." (Mark viii. 38.)

* I purposely abstain from saying anything on the subject of infant baptism.

There is nothing in this text which can be fairly used either way in settling this much-vexed controversy.

It is certain that the missionaries of the Church of England carry out the meaning of this text as fully and thoroughly as the missionaries of Baptist Churches.

The point settled by the text is not so much what ought to be done with the *children* of Christians, as what ought to be done with heathens when converted.

Let us observe, in the fourth place, the *obedience which Jesus requires of all who profess themselves His disciples.* He bids the apostles "teach them to observe all things, whatsoever He has commanded them."

This is a searching expression. It shows the uselessness of a mere name and form of Christianity. It shows that they only are to be counted true Christians who live in a practical obedience to His word, and strive to do the things that He has commanded. The water of baptism, and the bread and wine of the Lord's Supper alone will save no man's soul. It profits nothing that we go to a place of worship and hear Christ's ministers, and approve of the Gospel, if our religion goes no further than this.—What are our lives? What is our daily conduct, at home and abroad? Is the Sermon on the Mount our rule and standard? Do we strive to copy Christ's example? Do we seek to do the things that He commanded?—These are questions that must be answered in the affirmative, if we would prove ourselves born again and children of God. Obedience is the only proof of reality. Faith without works is dead, being alone. "Ye are my friends," says Jesus, "if ye do whatsoever I command you." (John xv. 14.)

Let us observe, in the fifth place, the *solemn mention of the blessed Trinity which our Lord makes in these verses.* He bids the apostles to baptize "in the name of the Father, and of the Son, and of the Holy Ghost."

This is one of those great plain texts which directly teach the mighty doctrine of the Trinity. It speaks of Father, Son, and Holy Ghost as Three distinct persons, and speaks of all Three as co-equal. Such as the

Father is, such is the Son, and such is the Holy Ghost. And yet these Three are One.

This truth is a great mystery. Let it be enough to receive and believe it, and let us ever abstain from all attempts at explanation. It is childish folly to refuse assent to things that we do not understand. We are poor crawling worms of a day, and know little at our best about God and eternity. Suffice it for us to receive the doctrine of the Trinity in Unity, with humility and reverence, and to ask no vain questions. Let us believe that no sinful soul could be saved without the work of all three Persons in the blessed Trinity, and let us rejoice that Father, Son, and Holy Ghost, who co-operated to make man, do also co-operate to save him. Here let us pause. We may receive practically what we cannot explain theoretically.

Finally, let us observe in these verses, *the gracious promise with which Jesus closes His words.* He says to His disciples "I am with you always even to the end of the world."

It is impossible to conceive words more comforting, strengthening, cheering, and sanctifying than these. Though left alone, like orphan children in a cold unkind world, the disciples were not to think they were deserted. Their Master would be ever "with them." Though commissioned to do a work as hard as that of Moses when sent to Pharaoh, they were not to be discouraged. Their Master would certainly be "with them." No words could be more suited to the position of those to whom they were first spoken. No words could be imagined more consolatory to believers in every age of the world.

Let all true Christians lay hold on these words and keep them in mind. Christ is "with us" always. Christ is "with us" wherever we go. He came to be "Emmanuel, God with us," when He first came into the world. He declares that He is ever Emmanuel, "with us", when He comes to the end of His earthly ministry and is about to leave the world. He is with us daily to pardon and forgive,—with us daily to sanctify and strengthen,—with us daily to defend and keep,—with us daily to lead and to guide,—with us in sorrow, and with us in joy,—with us in sickness, and with us in health,—with us in life, and with us in death,—with us in time, and with us in eternity.

What stronger consolation could believers desire than this? Whatever happens, they at least are never completely friendless and alone. Christ is ever with them. They may look into the grave, and say with David, "though I walk through the valley of the shadow of death I will fear no evil, for thou art with me." They may look forward beyond the grave, and say with Paul, "we shall ever be with the Lord." (Psalm xxiii. 4. 1 Thes. iv. 17.) He has said it, and He will stand to it, "I am with you always, even to the end of the world." "I will never leave you and never forsake you."—We could ask nothing more. Let us go on believing, and not be afraid. It is everything to be a real Christian. None have such a King, such a Priest, such a constant Companion, and such an unfailing Friend, as the true servants of Christ.

RYLE'S Expository Thoughts ON THE Gospels

By
J. C. RYLE

Anniversary Edition

MARK

Zondervan Publishing House
GRAND RAPIDS, MICHIGAN

MARK I. 1—8.

1 THE beginning of the Gospel of Jesus Christ, the Son of God;

2 As it is written in the prophets, Behold, I send my messenger before thy face, which shall prepare thy way before thee.

3 The voice of one crying in the wilderness, Prepare ye the way of the Lord, make his paths straight.

4 John did baptize in the wilderness, and preach the baptism of repentance for the remission of sins.

5 And there went out unto him all the land of Judea, and they of Jerusalem, and were all baptized of him in the river of Jordan, confessing their sins.

6 And John was clothed with camel's hair, and with a girdle of a skin about his loins; and he did eat locusts and wild honey;

7 And preached, saying, There cometh one mightier than I after me, the latchet of whose shoes I am not worthy to stoop down and unloose.

8 I indeed have baptized you with water: but he shall baptize you with the Holy Ghost.

THE Gospel of St. Mark, which we now begin, is in some respects unlike the other three Gospels. It tells us nothing about the birth and early life of our Lord Jesus Christ. It contains comparatively few of His sayings and discourses. Of all the four inspired histories of our Lord's earthly ministry, this is by far the shortest.

But we must not allow these peculiarities to make us undervalue St. Mark's Gospel. It is a Gospel singularly full of precious facts about the Lord Jesus, narrated in a simple, terse, pithy, and condensed style. If it tells us few of our Lord's sayings, it is eminently rich in its catalogue of His doings. It often contains minute historical

B

details of deep interest, which are wholly omitted in Matthew, Luke, and John.   In short, it is no mere abridged copy of St. Matthew, as some have rashly asserted, but the independent narrative of an independent witness, who was inspired to write a history of our Lord's *works*, rather than of His *words*.   Let us read it with holy reverence.   Like all the rest of Scripture, every word of St. Mark is "given by inspiration of God," and every word is "profitable." *

Let us observe, in these verses, *what a full declaration we have of the dignity of our Lord Jesus Christ's person.* The very first sentence speaks of Him as "the Son of God."

These words, "the Son of God," conveyed far more to Jewish minds than they do to ours.   They were nothing less than an assertion of our Lord's divinity. They were a declaration that Jesus was Himself very God, and "equal with God."   (John v. 18.)

There is a beautiful fitness in placing this truth in the very beginning of a Gospel.   The divinity of Christ is the citadel and keep of Christianity.   Here lies the infinite value of the satisfaction He made upon the cross. Here lies the peculiar merit of His atoning death for sinners.   That death was not the death of a mere man,

---

* "St. Mark has a special gift of terse brevity and of graphic painting in wonderful combination.   While on every occasion he compresses the discourses, works, and history into the simplest possible kernel, he on the other hand, unfolds the scenes more clearly than St. Matthew does, who excels in the discourses.   Not only do single incidents become in his hands complete pictures, but even when he is very brief, he often gives, with one pencil stroke, something new and peculiarly his own."—*Stier's Words of the Lord Jesus.*

like ourselves, but of one who is "over all, God blessed
for ever." (Rom. ix. 5.) We need not wonder that the
sufferings of one person were a sufficient propitiation
for the sin of a world, when we remember that He who
suffered was "the Son of God."

Let believers cling to this doctrine with jealous watchfulness. With it, they stand upon a rock. Without it,
they have nothing solid beneath their feet. Our hearts
are weak. Our sins are many. We need a Redeemer
who is able to save to the uttermost, and deliver from
the wrath to come. We have such a Redeemer in Jesus
Christ. He is "the mighty God." (Isa. ix. 6.)

Let us observe, in the second place, *how the beginning
of the Gospel was a fulfilment of Scripture.* John the
Baptist began his ministry, "as it is written in the
Prophets."

There was nothing unforeseen and suddenly contrived
in the coming of Jesus Christ into the world. In the
very beginning of Genesis we find it predicted that "the
seed of the woman shall bruise the serpent's head." (Gen.
iii. 15.) All through the Old Testament we find the same
event foretold with constantly increasing clearness. It
was a promise often renewed to patriarchs, and repeated
by prophets, that a Deliverer and Redeemer should one
day come. His birth, His character, His life, His death,
His resurrection, His forerunner, were all prophesied of
long before He came. Redemption was worked out and
accomplished in every step, just "as it was written."

We should always read the Old Testament with a
desire to find something in it about Jesus Christ. We
study this portion of the Bible with little profit, if we

can see in it nothing but Moses, and David, and Samuel, and the Prophets. Let us search the books of the Old Testament more closely. It was said by Him whose words can never pass away, "These are they which testify of Me." (John v. 40.)

Let us observe, in the third place, *how great were the effects which the ministry of John the Baptist produced for a time on the Jewish nation.* We are told that "there went out to him all the land of Judæa, and they of Jerusalem, and were all baptized of him in the river of Jordan."

The fact here recorded is one that is much overlooked. We are apt to lose sight of him who went before the face of our Lord, and to see nothing but the Lord Himself. We forget the morning star in the full blaze of the Sun. And yet it is clear that John's preaching arrested the attention of the whole Jewish people, and created an excitement all over Palestine. It aroused the nation from its slumbers, and prepared it for the ministry of our Lord, when He appeared. Jesus Himself says, "He was a burning and a shining light:—ye were willing to rejoice for a season in his light." (John v. 35.)

We ought to remark here how little dependence is to be placed on what is called "popularity." If ever there was one who was a popular minister for a season, John the Baptist was that man. Yet of all the crowds who came to his baptism, and heard his preaching, how few, it may be feared, were converted! Some, we may hope, like Andrew, were guided by John to Christ. But the vast majority, in all probability, died in their sins. Let us remember this whenever we see a crowded church.

A great congregation no doubt is a pleasing sight. But the thought should often come across our minds, "How many of these people will reach heaven at last?" It is not enough to hear and admire popular preachers. It is no proof of our conversion that we always worship in a place where there is a crowd. Let us take care that we hear the voice of Christ Himself, and follow Him.

Let us observe, in the last place, *what clear doctrine characterized John the Baptist's preaching.* He exalted Christ: "There cometh one mightier than I after me." He spoke plainly of the Holy Ghost: "He shall baptize you with the Holy Ghost."

These truths had never been so plainly proclaimed before by mortal man. More important truths than these are not to be found in the whole system of Christianity at this day. The principal work of every faithful minister of the Gospel, is to set the Lord Jesus fully before His people, and to show them His fulness and His power to save.—The next great work he has to do, is to set before them the work of the Holy Ghost, and the need of being born again, and inwardly baptized by His grace.—These two mighty truths appear to have been frequently on the lips of John the Baptist. It would be well for the church and the world, if there were more ministers like him.

Let us ask ourselves, as we leave the passage, How much we know by practical experience of the truths which John preached? What think we of Christ? Have we felt our need of Him, and fled to Him for peace? Is He king over our hearts, and all things to our souls?—What think we of the Holy Ghost? Has

He wrought any work in our hearts? Has He renewed, and changed them? Has he made us partakers of the divine nature? Life or death depend on our answer to these questions. "If any man have not the Spirit of Christ he is none of His." (Rom. viii. 9.)

MARK I. 9—20.

9 And it came to pass in those days, that Jesus came from Nazareth of Galilee, and was baptized of John in Jordan.

10 And straightway coming up out of the water, he saw the heavens opened, and the Spirit like a dove descending upon him:

11 And there came a voice from heaven, *saying*, Thou art my beloved Son, in whom I am well pleased.

12 And immediately the spirit driveth him into the wilderness.

13 And he was there in the wilderness forty days, tempted of Satan; and was with the wild beasts; and the angels ministered unto him.

14 Now after that John was put in prison, Jesus came into Galilee, preaching the Gospel of the kingdom of God,

15 And saying, The time is fulfilled, and the kingdom 'of God is at hand: repent ye, and believe the Gospel.

16 Now as he walked by the sea of Galilee, he saw Simon and Andrew his brother casting a net into the sea: for they were fishers.

17 And Jesus said unto them, Come ye after me, and I will make you to become fishers of men.

18 And straightway they forsook their nets, and followed him.

19 And when he had gone a little farther thence, he saw James the *son* of Zebedee, and John his brother, who also were in the ship mending their nets.

20 And straightway he called them: and they left their father Zebedee in the ship with the hired servants, and went after him.

THIS passage is singularly full of matter. It is a striking instance of that brevity of style, which is the peculiar characteristic of St. Mark's Gospel. The baptism of our Lord, His temptation in the wilderness, the commencement of His preaching, and the calling of His first disciples, are all related here in eleven verses.

Let us notice, in the first place, *the voice from heaven which was heard at our Lord's baptism.* We read, "There came a voice from heaven, saying, Thou art my beloved Son, in whom I am well pleased."

That voice was the voice of God the Father. It

declared the wondrous and ineffable love which has
existed between the Father and the Son from all eternity.
"The Father loveth the Son, and hath given all things
into His hand." (John iii. 35.) It proclaimed the Father's
full and complete approbation of Christ's mission to seek
and save the lost. It announced the Father's acceptance
of the Son as the Mediator, Substitute, and Surety of the
new covenant.

There is a rich mine of comfort in these words, for all
Christ's believing members. In themselves, and in their
own doings, they see nothing to please God. They are
daily sensible of weakness, shortcoming, and imperfection in all their ways. But let them recollect that
the Father regards them as members of His beloved Son
Jesus Christ. He sees no spot in them. (Cant. iv. 7.)
He beholds them as "in Christ," clothed in His righteousness, and invested with His merit. They are
"accepted in the Beloved," and when the holy eye of
God looks at them, He is "well pleased."

Let us notice, in the second place, *the nature of Christ's
preaching.* We read that He came saying, "Repent ye,
and believe the Gospel."

This is that old sermon which all the faithful witnesses
of God have continually preached, from the very beginning of the world. From Noah down to the present
day the burden of their address has been always the
same : "Repent and believe."

The Apostle Paul told the Ephesian elders, when he
left them for the last time, that the substance of his teaching among them had been "repentance toward God, and
faith toward our Lord Jesus Christ." (Acts xx. 21.)

He had the best of precedents for such teaching. The Great Head of the Church had given him a pattern. Repentance and faith were the foundation stones of Christ's ministry.—Repentance and faith must always be the main subjects of every faithful minister's instruction.

We need not wonder at this, if we consider the necessities of human nature. All of us are by nature born in sin and children of wrath, and all need to repent, be converted, and born again, if we would see the kingdom of God.—All of us are by nature guilty and condemned before God, and all must flee to the hope set before us in the Gospel, and believe in it, if we would be saved. All of us, once penitent, need daily stirring up to deeper repentance. All of us, though believing, need constant exhortation to increased faith.

Let us ask ourselves what we know of this repentance and faith. Have we felt our sins, and forsaken them? Have we laid hold on Christ, and believed? We may reach heaven without learning, or riches, or health, or worldly greatness. But we shall never reach heaven, if we die impenitent and unbelieving. A new heart, and a lively faith in a Redeemer are absolutely needful to salvation. May we never rest till we know them by experience, and can call them our own! With them all true Christianity begins in the soul. In the exercise of them consists the life of religion. It is only through the possession of them, that men have peace at the last. Churchmembership and priestly absolution alone save no one. They only die in the Lord who "repent and believe."

Let us notice, in the third place, *the occupation of those*

who were first called to be Christ's disciples. We read
that our Lord called Simon and Andrew, when they
were "casting a net into the sea," and James and John
while they were "mending their nets."

It is clear from these words, that the first followers
of our Lord were not the great of this world. They
were men who had neither riches, nor rank, nor power.
But the kingdom of Christ is not dependent on such
things as these. His cause advances in the world, "not
by might, nor by power, but by my Spirit, saith the
Lord of hosts." (Zech. iv. 6.) The words of St. Paul
will always be found true: "Not many wise men after
the flesh, not many mighty, not many noble, are called.
But God hath chosen the foolish things of the world to
confound the wise; and God hath chosen the weak
things of the world to confound the things which are
mighty." (1 Cor. i. 26, 27.) The Church which began
with a few fishermen, and yet overspread half the world,
must have been founded by God.

We must beware of giving way to the common notion,
that there is anything disgraceful in being poor, and in
working with our own hands. The Bible contains many
instances of special privileges conferred on working men.
Moses was keeping sheep, when God appeared to him in
the burning bush. Gideon was thrashing wheat, when
the angel brought him a message from heaven. Elisha
was ploughing, when Elijah called him to be a prophet
in his stead. The Apostles were fishing, when Jesus called
them to follow Him. It is disgraceful to be covetous, or
proud, or a cheat, or a gambler, or a drunkard, or a glutton,
or unclean. But it is no disgrace to be poor. The labourer

who serves Christ faithfully is far more honourable in God's eyes, than the nobleman who serves sin.

Let us notice, in the last place, *the office to which our Lord called His first disciples.* We read that He said, "Come ye after Me, and I will make you to become fishers of men."

The meaning of this expression is clear and unmistakable. The disciples were to become fishers for souls. They were to labour to draw men out of darkness into light, and from the power of Satan to God. They were to strive to bring men into the net of Christ's Church, that so they might be saved alive, and not perish everlastingly.

We ought to mark this expression well. It is full of instruction. It is the oldest name by which the ministerial office is described in the New Testament. It lies deeper down than the name of bishop, elder, or deacon. It is the first idea which should be before a minister's mind. He is not to be a mere reader of forms, or administrator of ordinances. He is to be a "fisher" of souls. The minister who does not strive to live up to this name, has mistaken his calling.

Does the fisherman strive to catch fish? Does he use all means, and grieve if unsuccessful? The minister ought to do the same.—Does the fisherman have patience? Does he toil on day after day, and wait, and work on in hope? Let the minister do the same.—Happy is that man, in whom the fisher's skill, and diligence, and patience, are all combined!

Let us resolve to pray much for ministers. Their office is no light one if they do their duty. They need the help of many intercessions from all praying people. They have not only their own souls to care for, but the souls of others. No wonder that St. Paul cries, "Who is sufficient for these things?" (2 Cor. ii. 16.) If we never prayed for ministers before, let us begin to do it this day.

MARK I. 21—34.

21 And they went into Capernaum; and straightway on the sabbath day he entered into the synagogue, and taught.

22 And they were astonished at his doctrine: for he taught them as one that had authority, and not as the Scribes.

23 And there was in their synagogue a man with an unclean spirit; and he cried out,

24 Saying, Let *us* alone; what have we to do with thee, thou Jesus of Nazareth? art thou come to destroy us? I know thee who thou art, the Holy One of God.

25 And Jesus rebuked him, saying, Hold thy peace, and come out of him.

26 And when the unclean spirit had torn him, and cried with a loud voice, he came out of him.

27 And they were all amazed, insomuch that they questioned among themselves, saying, What thing is this? what new doctrine is this? for with authority commandeth he even the unclean spirits, and they do obey him.

28 And immediately his fame spread abroad throughout all the region round about Galilee.

29 And forthwith, when they were come out of the synagogue, they entered into the house of Simon and Andrew, with James and John.

30 But Simon's wife's mother lay sick of a fever, and anon they tell him of her.

31 And he came and took her by the hand, and lifted her up; and immediately the fever left her, and she ministered unto them.

32 And at even, when the sun did set, they brought unto him all that were diseased, and them that were possessed with devils.

33 And all the city was gathered together at the door.

34 And he healed many that were sick of divers diseases, and cast out many devils; and suffered not the devils to speak, because they knew him.

THESE verses begin the long list of miracles which St. Mark's Gospel contains. They tell us how our Lord cast out devils in Capernaum, and healed Peter's wife's mother of a fever.

We learn, in the first place, from these verses, the *uselessness of a mere intellectual knowledge of religion.* Twice we are specially told that the unclean spirits knew our Lord. In one place it says, "they knew Him." In another, the devil cries out, "I know Thee who Thou art, the Holy one of God." They knew Christ, when Scribes were ignorant of Him, and Pharisees would not acknowledge Him. And yet their knowledge was not unto salvation !

The mere belief of the facts and doctrines of Christianity will never save our souls. Such belief is no better than the belief of devils. They all believe and know that Jesus is the Christ. They believe that He will one day judge the world, and cast them down to endless torment in hell. It is a solemn and sorrowful thought, that on these points some professing Christians have even less faith than the devil. There are some who doubt the reality of hell and the eternity of punishment. Such doubts as these find no place except in the hearts of self-willed men and women. There is no infidelity among devils. "They believe and tremble." (James ii. 19.)

Let us take heed that our faith be a faith of the heart as well as of the head. Let us see that our knowledge has a sanctifying influence on our affections and our lives. Let us not only know Christ but love Him, from a sense of actual benefit received from Him. Let us not only believe that He is the Son of God and the Saviour of the world, but rejoice in Him, and cleave to Him with purpose of heart. Let us not only be acquainted with Him by the hearing of the ear, but by daily personal application to Him for mercy and grace. "The life of Christianity," says Luther, "consists in possessive pronouns." It is one thing to say "Christ is a Saviour." It is quite another to say "He is my Saviour and my

Lord." The devil can say the first. The true Christian alone can say the second.*

We learn, in the second place, *to what remedy a Christian ought to resort first, in time of trouble.* He ought to follow the example of the friends of Simon's wife's mother. We read that when she "lay sick of a fever," they "told Jesus of her."

There is no remedy like this. Means are to be used diligently, without question, in any time of need. Doctors are to be sent for in sickness. Lawyers are to be consulted when property or character needs defence. The help of friends is to be sought. But still, after all, the first thing to be done is to cry to the Lord Jesus Christ for help. None can relieve us so effectually as He can. None is so compassionate, and so willing to relieve. When Jacob was in trouble, He turned to his God first: "Deliver me, I pray Thee, from the hand of Esau." (Gen. xxxii. 11.) When Hezekiah was in trouble, he first spread Sennacherib's letter before the Lord: "I beseech Thee, save Thou us out of his hand." (2 Kings xix. 19.) When Lazarus fell sick, his sisters sent immediately to Jesus: "Lord," they said, "he whom Thou lovest is sick." (John xi. 2.) Now let us do likewise. "Cast thy burden upon the Lord, and He shall sustain thee." "Casting all your care upon Him." "In everything by prayer

---

* "Rest not in an historical knowledge or faith. If thou do, it will not save thee; for if it would it would save the devils: for they have their literal knowledge and general belief of the Word. Dost thou think it enough to know and believe that Christ lived and died for sinners? The devil and his angels know and believe as much. Labour then to outstrip them, and to get a better faith than is in them."—*Petter on Mark.* 1661.

and supplication with thanksgiving, let your requests be made known to God." (Psa. lv. 22; 1 Pet. v. 7; Phil. iv. 6.)

Let us not only remember this rule, but practice it too. We live in a world of sin and sorrow. The days of darkness in a man's life are many. It needs no prophet's eye to foresee that we shall all shed many a tear, and feel many a heart-wrench, before we die. Let us be armed with a receipt against despair, before our troubles come. Let us know what to do, when sickness, or bereavement, or cross, or loss, or disappointment breaks in upon us like an armed man. Let us do as they did in Simon's house at Capernaum. Let us at once "tell Jesus."

We learn, in the last place, from these verses, *what a complete and perfect cure the Lord Jesus makes, when He heals.* He takes the sick woman by the hand, and lifts her up, and "immediately the fever left her." But this was not all. A greater miracle remained behind. At once we are told "she ministered unto them." That weakness and prostration of strength which, as a general rule, a fever leaves behind it, in her case was entirely removed. The fevered woman was not only made well in a moment, but in the same moment made strong and able to work.*

---

* Let us not fail to observe here, that Peter, one of our Lord's principal apostles, had a wife. Yet he was called to be a disciple, and afterwards chosen to be an apostle. More than this, we find St. Paul speaking of him as a married man, in his Epistle to the Corinthians, many years after this. (1 Cor. ix. 5.)

How this fact can be reconciled with the compulsory celibacy of the clergy, which the Church of Rome enforces and requires, it is for the friends and advocates of the Roman Catholic Church to explain. To a plain reader, it seems a plain proof that it is not

We may see in this case a lively emblem of Christ's dealing with sin-sick souls. That blessed Saviour not only gives mercy and forgiveness ;—He gives renewing grace besides. To as many as receive Him as their Physician, He gives power to become the sons of God. He cleanses them by His Spirit, when He washes them in His precious blood. Those whom He justifies, He also sanctifies. When He bestows an absolution, He also bestows a new heart. When He grants free forgiveness for the past, He also grants strength to "minister" to Him for the time to come. The sin-sick soul is not merely cured, and then left to itself. It is also supplied with a new heart and a right spirit, and enabled so to live as to please God.

There is comfort in this thought for all who feel a desire to serve Christ, but at present are afraid to begin. There are many in this state of mind. They fear that if they come forward boldly, and take up the cross, they shall by and by fall away. They fear that they shall not be able to persevere, and shall bring discredit on their profession. Let them fear no longer. Let them know that Jesus is an Almighty Saviour, who never forsakes those who once commit themselves to Him. Once raised by His mighty hand from the death of sin, and washed in His precious blood, they shall go on "ministering to Him" to their life's end. They shall have power to overcome the world, and crucify the flesh, and resist

wrong for ministers to be married men. And when we add to this striking fact, that St. Paul, when writing to Timothy, says, that "a bishop should be the husband of one wife" (1 Tim. iii. 2), it is clear that the whole Romish doctrine of clerical celibacy is utterly opposed to Holy Scripture.

the devil. Only let them begin, and they shall go on. Jesus knows nothing of half-cured cases and half-finished work. Let them trust in Jesns and go forward. The pardoned soul shall always be enabled to serve Christ.

There is comfort here for all who are really serving Christ, and are yet cast down by a sense of their own infirmity. There are many in such case. They are oppressed by doubts and anxieties. They sometimes think they shall never reach heaven after all, but be cast away in the wilderness. Let them fear no longer. Their strength shall be according to their day. The difficulties they now fear shall vanish out of their path. The lion in the way which they now dread, shall prove to be chained. The same gracious hand which first touched and healed, shall uphold, strengthen, and lead them to the last. The Lord Jesus will never lose one of His sheep. Those whom He loves and pardons, He loves unto the end. Though sometimes cast down, they shall never be cast away. The healed soul shall always go on "ministering to the Lord." Grace shall always lead to glory.

MARK I. 35—39.

35 And in the morning, rising up a great while before day, he went out and departed into a solitary place, and there prayed.

36 And Simon and they that were with him followed after him.

37 And when they had found him, they said unto him, All *men* seek for thee.

38 And he said unto them, Let us go into the next towns, that I may preach there also: for therefore came I forth.

39 And he preached in their synagogues throughout all Galilee, and cast out devils.

EVERY fact in our Lord's life on earth, and every word which fell from His lips, ought to be deeply interesting to a true Christian.   We see a fact and a saying in the passage we have just read, which deserve close attention.

We see, for one thing, *an example of our Lord Jesus Christ's habits about private prayer*.   We are told, that "in the morning, rising up a great while before day, He went out, and departed into a solitary place, and there prayed."

We shall find the same thing often recorded of our Lord in the Gospel history.   When He was baptized, we are told that He was "praying." (Luke iii. 21.) When He was transfigured, we are told, that "as He prayed, the fashion of His face was altered." (Luke ix. 29.)   Before He chose the twelve Apostles, we are told that "He continued all night in prayer to God." (Luke vi. 12.)   When all men spoke well of Him, and would fain have made Him a King, we are told that "He went up into a mountain apart to pray." (Mark xiv. 23.) When tempted in the garden of Gethsemane, He said, "Sit ye here, while I shall pray." (Mark xiv. 34.)   In short, our Lord prayed always, and did not faint.   Sinless as He was, He set us an example of diligent communion with His Father.   His Godhead did not render Him independent of the use of all means as a man.   His very perfection was a perfection kept up through the exercise of prayer.

We ought to see in all this the immense importance of private devotion.   If He who was "holy, harmless, undefiled, and separate from sinners," thus prayed continually, how much more ought we who are compassed with infirmity ?   If He found it needful to offer up supplications with strong crying and tears, how much more needful is it for us, who in many things offend daily?

What shall we say to those who never pray at all, in the face of such a passage as this? There are many such, it may be feared, in the list of baptized people,—many who rise up in the morning without prayer, and without prayer lie down at night,—many who never speak one word to God. Are they Christians? It is impossible to say so. A praying master, like Jesus, can have no prayer-less servants. The Spirit of Adoption will always make a man call upon God. To be prayerless is to be Christ-less, Godless, and in the high road to destruction.

What shall we say to those who pray, yet give but little time to their prayers? We are obliged to say that they show at present very little of the mind of Christ. Asking little, they must expect to have little. Seeking little, they cannot be surprised if they possess little. It will always be found that when prayers are few, grace, strength, peace, and hope are small.*

We shall do well to watch our habits of prayer with a holy watchfulness. Here is the pulse of our Christianity. Here is the true test of our state before God. Here true religion begins in the soul, when it does begin. Here it decays and goes backward, when a man backslides from

* "Ministers must pray much, if they would be successful. The Apostles spent their time this way. (Acts vi. 3.) Yea, our Lord Jesus preached all day, and continued all night alone in prayer to God. Ministers should be much in prayer. They use to reckon how many hours they spend in reading and study. It were far better both for ourselves and the Church of God, if more time was spent in prayer. Luther's spending three hours daily in secret prayer, and Bradford's studying on his knees, and other instances of men in our time, are talked of rather than imitated."—*Traill,* 1696.

God.   Let us walk in the steps of our blessed Master in
this respect as well as in every other.   Like Him, let us
be diligent in our private devotion.   Let us know what
it is to "depart into solitary places and pray."

We see, for another thing, in this passage, *a remarkable
saying of our Lord as to the purpose for which He came
into the world.*   We find Him saying, "Let us go into
the next towns, that I may preach there also : for therefore came I forth."

The meaning of these words is plain and unmistakable.
Our Lord declares that He came on earth to be a preacher
and a teacher.   He came to fulfil the prophetical office,
to be the "Prophet greater than Moses," who had been so
long foretold. (Deut. xviii. 15.)   He left the glory which
He had from all eternity with the Father, to do the work
of an evangelist.   He came down to earth to show to man
the way of peace, to proclaim deliverance to the captives,
and recovering of sight to the blind.   One principal part
of His work on earth was to go up and down and publish glad tidings, to offer healing to the broken-hearted,
light to them that sat in darkness, and pardon to the
chief of sinners.   "Therefore," He says, "came I forth."

We ought to observe here, what infinite honour the
Lord Jesus puts on the office of the preacher.   It is an
office which the eternal Son of God Himself undertook.
He might have spent His earthly ministry in instituting
and keeping up ceremonies, like Aaron.   He might have
ruled and reigned as a king, like David.   But he chose
a different calling.   Until the time when He died as a
sacrifice for our sins, His daily, and almost hourly work
was to preach.   "Therefore," He says, "came I forth."

Let us never be moved by those who cry down the preacher's office, and tell us that sacraments and other ordinances are of more importance than sermons. Let us give to every part of God's public worship its proper place and honour, but let us beware of placing any part of it above preaching. By preaching, the Church of Christ was first gathered together and founded, and by preaching, it has ever been maintained in health and prosperity. By preaching, sinners are awakened. By preaching, inquirers are led on. By preaching, saints are built up. By preaching, Christianity is being carried to the heathen world.—There are many now who sneer at missionaries, and mock at those who go out into the high-ways of our own land, to preach to crowds in the open air. But such persons would do well to pause, and consider calmly what they are doing. The very work which they ridicule is the work which turned the world upside down, and cast heathenism to the ground. Above all, it is the very work which Christ Himself undertook. The King of kings and Lord of lords Himself was once a preacher. For three long years He went to and fro proclaiming the Gospel. Sometimes we see Him in a house, sometimes on the mountain side, sometimes in a Jewish synagogue, sometimes in a boat on the sea. But the great work He took up was always one and the same. He came always preaching and teaching. "Therefore," He says, "came I forth."

Let us leave the passage with a solemn resolution never to "despise prophesying." (1 Thess. v. 20.) The minister we hear may not be highly gifted. The sermons that we listen to may be weak and poor. But

after all, preaching is God's grand ordinance for converting and saving souls.   The faithful preacher of the
Gospel is handling the very weapon which the Son of
God was not ashamed to employ.   This is the work of
which Christ has said, "Therefore came I forth."

MARK I. 40—45.

40 And there came a leper to him, beseeching him, and kneeling down to him, and saying unto him, If thou wilt, thou canst make me clean.

41 And Jesus, moved with compassion, put forth *his* hand, and touched him, and saith unto him, I will; be thou clean.

42 And as soon as he had spoken, immediately the leprosy departed from him, and he was cleansed.

43 And he straitly charged him, and forthwith sent him away;

44 And saith unto him, See thou say nothing to any man: but go thy way, shew thyself to the priest, and offer for thy cleansing those things which Moses commanded, for a testimony unto them.

45 But he went out, and began to publish *it* much, and to blaze abroad the matter, insomuch that Jesus could no more openly enter into the city, but was without in desert places: and they came to him from every quarter.

WE read in these verses how our Lord Jesus Christ
healed a leper.   Of all our Lord's miracles of healing
none were probably more marvellous than those performed on leprous people.   Two cases only have been
fully described in the Gospel history.   Of these two, the
case before us is one.

Let us try to realize, in the first place, *the dreadful
nature of the disease which Jesus cured.*

Leprosy is a complaint of which we know little or
nothing in our northern climate.   In Bible lands it is far
more common.   It is a disease which is utterly incurable.
It is no mere skin affection, as some ignorantly suppose.
It is a radical disease of the whole man.   It attacks, not
merely the skin, but the blood, the flesh, and the bones,
until the unhappy patient begins to lose his extremities,
and to rot by inches.—Let us remember beside this,

that amongst the Jews the leper was reckoned unclean, and was cut off from the congregation of Israel and the ordinances of religion. He was obliged to dwell in a separate house. None might touch him or minister to him. Let us remember all this, and then we may have some idea of the remarkable wretchedness of a leprous person. To use the words of Aaron, when he interceded for Miriam, he was, "as one dead, of whom the flesh is half consumed." (Numbers xii. 12.)

But is there nothing like leprosy among ourselves? Yes: indeed there is! There is a foul soul-disease which is engrained into our very nature, and cleaves to our bones and marrow with deadly force. That disease is the plague of sin. Like leprosy, it is a deep-seated disease, infecting every part of our nature, heart, will, conscience, understanding, memory, and affections. Like leprosy, it makes us loathsome and abominable, unfit for the conpany of God, and unmeet for the glory of heaven. Like leprosy, it is incurable by any earthly physician, and is slowly but surely dragging us down to the second death. And worst of all, far worse than leprosy, it is a disease from which no mortal man is exempt. "We are all," in God's sight, "as an unclean thing." (Isaiah lxiv. 6.)

Do we know these things? Have we found them out? Have we discovered our own sinfulness, guilt, and corruption? Happy indeed is that person who has been really taught to feel that he is a "miserable sinner," and that there is "no health in him!" Blessed indeed is he who has learned that he is a spiritual leper, and a bad, wicked, sinful creature! To know our disease is one step towards a cure. It is the misery and the ruin of many souls that they never yet saw their sins and their need.

Let us learn, in the second place, from these verses, *the wondrous and almighty power of the Lord Jesus Christ.*

We are told that the unhappy leper came to our Lord, "beseeching Him, and kneeling down, and saying, If thou wilt, thou canst make me clean." We are told that "Jesus, moved with compassion, put forth His hand and touched him, and said to him, I will; be thou clean." At once the cure was effected. That very instant the deadly plague departed from the poor sufferer, and he was healed. It is but a word, and a touch, and there stands before our Lord, not a leper, but a sound and healthy man.

Who can conceive the greatness of the change in the feelings of this leper, when he found himself healed? The morning sun rose upon him, a miserable being, more dead than alive, his whole frame a mass of sores and corruption, his very existence a burden. The evening sun saw him full of hope and joy, free from pain, and fit for the society of his fellow-men. Surely the change must have been like life from the dead.

Let us bless God that the Saviour with whom we have to do is almighty. It is a cheering and comfortable thought that with Christ nothing is impossible. No heart-disease is so deep-seated but He is able to cure it. No plague of soul is so virulent but our Great Physician can heal it. Let us never despair of any one's salvation, so long as he lives. The worst of spiritual lepers may yet be cleansed. No cases of spiritual leprosy could be worse than those of Manasseh, Saul, and, Zacchæus, yet

they were all cured: Jesus Christ made them whole.
The chief of sinners may yet be brought nigh to God by
the blood and Spirit of Christ. Men are not lost, because they are too bad to be saved, but because they
will not come to Christ that He may save them.

Let us learn, in the last place, from these verses, that
*there is a time to be silent about the work of Christ, as well
as a time to speak.*

This is a truth which is taught us in a remarkable
way. We find our Lord strictly charging this man to
tell no one of his cure, to "say nothing to any man."
We find this man in the warmth of his zeal disobeying
this injunction, and publishing and "blazing abroad" his
cure in every quarter. And we are told that the result
was that Jesus "could no more enter into the city, but
was without in desert places."

There is a lesson in all this of deep importance, however difficult it may be to use it rightly. It is clear that
there are times when our Lord would have us work for
Him quietly and silently, rather than attract public
attention by a noisy zeal. There is a zeal which is "not
according to knowledge," as well as a zeal which is
righteous and praiseworthy. Everything is beautiful in
its season. Our Master's cause may on some occasions
be more advanced by quietness and patience than in
any other way. We are not to "give that which is holy
to dogs," nor "cast pearls before swine." By forgetfulness of this we may even do more harm than good, and
retard the very cause we want to assist.

The subject is a delicate and difficult one, without
doubt. Unquestionably the majority of Christians are far

more inclined to be silent about their glorious Master than to confess Him before men, and do not need the bridle so much as the spur.   But still it is undeniable that there is a time for all things; and to know the time should be one great aim of a Christian.   There are good men who have more zeal than discretion, and even help the enemy of truth by unseasonable acts and words.*

Let us all pray for the Spirit of wisdom and of a sound mind.   Let us seek daily to know the path of duty, and ask daily for discretion and good sense.   Let us be bold as a lion in confessing Christ, and not be afraid to " speak of Him before princes," if need be.   But let us never forget that " Wisdom is profitable to direct " (Eccles. x. 11), and let us beware of doing harm by an ill-directed zeal.

* It would not be wise for a speaker at an English public meeting to proclaim the names of the families in Italy where the Bible is read, and to point out the streets and houses where these families resided.   Such a speaker might be well-meaning, and full of zeal. He might really desire to glorify Christ, and publish the triumphs of His grace.   But he would be guilty of a sad indiscretion, and show great ignorance of the very lesson which the verses before us contain. The words of an old commentator on this subject deserve notice :

"In that our Saviour forbids this leper to publish this miracle at this unseasonable time, we learn that all truths are not fit to be professed or uttered at all times.   Though we must never deny any truth, being demanded of it, or lawfully enjoined to profess it, yet there is a wise concealment of the truth, which is sometimes to be used.   (Eccles. iii. 7.)

"When are we to conceal the truth? 1. When the case stands so that the uttering of it may bring hurt to the truth itself, as here the publishing of this miracle was like to stop Christ's ministry. 2. When we are in the company of such persons as are more likely to cavil and scoff at the truth, than to make any good use of it. 3. When we are in the company of malicious enemies of the truth." (Matt. vii. 6.)—*Petter on Mark.* 1661.

MARK II. 1—12.

1 And again he entered into Capernaum after, *some* days; and it was noised that he was in the house.

2 And straightway many were gathered together, insomuch that there was no room to receive *them*, no, not so much as about the door: and he preached the word unto them.

3 And they come unto him, bringing one sick of the palsy, which was borne of four.

4 And when they could not come nigh unto him for the press, they uncovered the roof where he was: and when they had broken *it* up, they let down the bed wherein the sick of the palsy lay.

5 When Jesus saw their faith, he said unto the sick of the palsy, Son, thy sins be forgiven thee.

6 But there were certain of the scribes sitting there, and reasoning in their hearts,

7 Why doth this *man* thus speak blasphemies? who can forgive sins but God only?

8 And immediately when Jesus perceived in his spirit that they so reasoned within themselves, he said unto them, Why reason ye these things in your hearts?

9 Whether is it easier to say to the sick of the palsy, *Thy* sins be forgiven thee; or to say, Arise, and take up thy bed, and walk?

10 But that ye may know that the Son of man hath power on earth to forgive sins, (he saith to the sick of the palsy,)

11 I say unto thee, Arise, and take up thy bed, and go thy way into thine house.

12 And immediately he arose, took up the bed, and went forth before them all; insomuch that they were all amazed, and glorified God, saying, We never saw it on this fashion.

THIS passage shows us our Lord once more at Capernaum. Once more we find Him doing His accustomed work, preaching the Word, and healing those that were sick.

We see, in these verses, *what great spiritual privileges some persons enjoy, and yet make no use of them.*

This is a truth which is strikingly illustrated by the history of Capernaum. No city in Palestine appears to have enjoyed so much of our Lord's presence, during His earthly ministry, as did this city. It was the place where He dwelt, after He left Nazareth. (Matt. iv. 13.) It was the place where many of His miracles were worked, and many of His sermons delivered. But nothing that Jesus said or did seems to have had any effect on the hearts of the inhabitants. They crowded to hear Him, as we read in this passage, "till there was no room about the door." They were amazed. They

were astonished.   They were filled with wonder at His
mighty works.   But they were not converted.   They
lived in the full noon-tide blaze of the Sun of Righteousness, and yet their hearts remained hard.   And they
drew from our Lord the heaviest condemnation that He
ever pronounced against any place, except Jerusalem:
"Thou, Capernaum, which are exalted unto heaven,
shalt be brought down to hell: for if the mighty works,
which have been done in thee, had been done in Sodom,
it would have remained until this day.   But I say unto
you, That it shall be more tolerable for the land of
Sodom in the day of judgment, than for thee." (Matt.
xi. 23, 24.)

It is good for us all to mark well this case of Capernaum.   We are all too apt to suppose that it needs
nothing but the powerful preaching of the Gospel to
convert people's souls, and that if the Gospel is only
brought into a place everybody *must* believe.   We forget
the amazing power of unbelief, and the depth of man's
enmity against God.   We forget that the Capernaites
heard the most faultless preaching, and saw it confirmed
by the most surprising miracles, and yet remained dead
in trespasses and sins.   We need reminding that the
same Gospel which is the savour of life to some, is the
savour of death to others, and that the same fire which
softens the wax will also harden the clay.   Nothing in
fact seems to harden man's heart so much as to hear the
Gospel regularly, and yet deliberately prefer the service
of sin and the world.   Never was there a people so
highly favoured as the people of Capernaum, and never
was there a people who appear to have become so hard.

Let us beware of walking in their steps. We ought often to use the prayer of the Litany, "From hardness of heart, Good Lord, deliver us."

We see, in the second place, from these verses, *how great a blessing affliction may prove to a man's soul.*

We are told that one sick of the palsy was brought to our Lord, at Capernaum, in order to be healed. Helpless and impotent, he was carried in his bed by four kind friends, and let down into the midst of the place where Jesus was preaching. At once the object of the man's desire was gained. ·The great Physician of soul and body saw him, and gave him speedy relief. He restored him to health and strength. He granted him the far greater blessing of forgiveness of sins. In short the man who had been carried from his house that morning weak, dependent, and bowed down both in body and soul, returned to his own house rejoicing.

Who can doubt that to the end of his days this man would thank God for this palsy? Without it he might probably have lived and died in ignorance, and never seen Christ at all. Without it, he might have kept his sheep on the green hills of Galilee all his life long, and never been brought to Christ, and never heard these blessed words, "Thy sins be forgiven thee." That palsy was indeed a blessing. Who can tell but it was the beginning of eternal life to his soul?

How many in every age can testify that this palsied man's experience has been their own! They have learned wisdom by affliction. Bereavements have proved mercies. Losses have proved real gains. Sicknesses have led them to the great Physician of souls, sent them to the Bible, shut out the world, shown them their own foolishness, taught them to pray. Thousands can say like David, "It is good for me that I was afflicted, that I might learn thy statutes." (Psal. cxix. 71.)

Let us beware of murmuring under affliction. We may be sure there is a needs-be for every cross, and a wise reason for every trial. Every sickness and sorrow is a gracious message from God, and is meant to call us nearer to Him. Let us pray that we may learn the lesson that each affliction is appointed to convey. Let us see that we "refuse not Him that speaketh."

We see, in the last place, in these verses, *the priestly power of forgiving sins, which is possessed by our Lord Jesus Christ.*

We read that our Lord said to the sick of the palsy, "Son, thy sins be forgiven thee." He said these words with a meaning. He knew the hearts of the Scribes by whom He was surrounded. He intended to show them that He laid claim to be the true High Priest, and to have the power of absolving sinners, though at present the claim was seldom put forward. But that He had the power He told them expressly. He says, "The Son of man hath power on earth to forgive sins." In saying "thy sins be forgiven thee," He had only exercised His rightful office.

Let us consider how great must be the authority of Him who has the power to forgive sins! This is the thing that none can do but God. No angel in heaven, no man upon earth, no Church in council, no minister of any denomination, can take away from the sinner's conscience the load of guilt, and give him

peace with God.   They may point to the Fountain open
for all sin.   They may declare with authority whose sins
God is willing to forgive.   But they cannot absolve by
their own authority.   They cannot put away transgressions.   This is the peculiar prerogative of God, and a
prerogative which He has put in the hands of His Son
Jesus Christ.

Let us think for a moment how great a blessing it is
that Jesus is our great High Priest, and that we know
where to go for absolution! We must have a Priest and
a sacrifice between ourselves and God.   Conscience demands an atonement for our many sins.   God's holiness
makes it absolutely needful.   Without an atoning Priest
there can be no peace of soul.   Jesus Christ is the very
Priest that we need, mighty to forgive and pardon,
tender-hearted and willing to save.

And now let us ask ourselves whether we have yet
known the Lord Jesus as our High Priest?   Have we
applied to Him?   Have we sought absolution?   If not,
we are yet in our sins.   May we never rest till the Spirit
witnesses with our spirit that we have sat at the feet of
Jesus and heard His voice, saying, "Son, thy sins be forgiven thee."

MARK II. 13—22.

13 And he went forth again by the sea side; and all the multitude resorted unto him, and he taught them.

14 And as he passed by, he saw Levi the *son* of Alphæus sitting at the receipt of custom, and said unto him, Follow me.   And he arose and followed him.

15 And it came to pass, that, as Jesus sat at meat in his house, many publicans and sinners sat also together with Jesus and his disciples: for there were many, and they followed him.

16 And when the scribes and Pharisees saw him eat with publicans and sinners, they said unto his disciples, How is it that he eateth and drinketh with publicans and sinners?

17 When Jesus heard *it*, he saith unto them, They that are whole have no need of the physician, but they that are sick: I came not to call the

righteous, but sinners to repentance.

18 And the disciples of John and of the Pharisees used to fast: and they come and say unto him, Why do the disciples of John and of the Pharisees fast, but thy disciples fast not?

19 And Jesus said unto them, Can the children of the bridechamber fast, while the bridegroom is with them? as long as they have the bridegroom with them, they cannot fast.

20 But the days will come, when the bridegroom shall be taken away from them, and then shall they fast in those days.

21 No man also seweth a piece of new cloth on an old garment: else the new piece that filled it up taketh away from the old, and the rent is made worse.

22 And no man putteth new wine into old bottles: else the new wine doth burst the bottles, and the wine is spilled, and the bottles will be marred: but new wine must be put into new bottles.

THE person who is called Levi, at the beginning of this passage, is the same person who is called Matthew in the first of the four Gospels. Let us not forget this. It is no less than an Apostle and an Evangelist, whose early history is now before our eyes.

We learn from these verses, *the power of Christ to call men out from the world, and make them His disciples.* We read that He said to Levi, when "sitting at the receipt of custom, Follow me." And at once "he arose and followed Him." From a publican he became an Apostle, and a writer of the first book in that New Testament which is now known all over the world.

This is a truth of deep importance. Without a divine call no one can be saved. We are all so sunk in sin, and so wedded to the world, that we should never turn to God and seek salvation, unless He first called us by His grace. God must speak to our hearts by His Spirit, before we shall ever speak to Him. Those who are sons of God, says the 17th Article, are "called according to God's purpose by His Spirit working in due season." Now how blessed is the thought that this calling of sinners is committed to so gracious a Saviour as Christ.

When the Lord Jesus calls a sinner to be His servant,

He acts as a Sovereign; but He acts with infinite mercy. He often chooses those who seem most unlikely to do His will, and furthest off from His kingdom. He draws them to Himself with almighty power, breaks the chains of old habits and customs, and makes them new creatures. As the loadstone attracts the iron, and the south wind softens the frozen ground, so does Christ's calling draw sinners out from the world, and melt the hardest heart. "The voice of the Lord is mighty in operation." Blessed are they, who, when they hear it, harden not their hearts!

We ought never to despair entirely of any one's salvation, when we read this passage of Scripture. He who called Levi, still lives and still works. The age of miracles is not yet past. The love of money is a powerful principle, but the call of Christ is more powerful. Let us not despair even about those who "sit at the receipt of custom," and enjoy abundance of this world's good things. The voice which said to Levi, "Follow me," may yet reach their hearts. We may yet see them arise, and take up the cross and follow Christ. Let us hope continually, and pray for others. Who can tell what God may be going to do for any one around us? No one is too bad for Christ to call. Let us pray for all.

We learn, for another thing, from these verses, that *one of Christ's principal offices is that of a Physician.* The Scribes and Pharisees found fault with Him for eating and drinking with publicans and sinners. But "when Jesus heard it, He saith unto them, They that are whole have no need of the physician, but they that are sick."

The Lord Jesus did not come into the world, as some suppose, to be nothing more than a lawgiver, a king, a teacher, and an example. Had this been all the purpose of His coming there would have been small comfort for man. Diet-tables and rules of living are all very well for the convalescent,˙but not suitable to the man labouring under a mortal disease. A teacher and an example might be sufficient for an unfallen being, like Adam in the garden of Eden. But fallen sinners, like ourselves, want healing first, before we can value rules.

The Lord Jesus came into the world to be a physician as well as a teacher. He knew the necessities of human nature. He saw us all sick of a mortal disease, stricken with the plague of sin, and dying daily. He pitied us, and came down to bring divine medicine for our relief. He came to give health and cure to the dying, to heal the broken hearted, and to offer strength to the weak. No sin-sick soul is too far gone for Him. It is His glory to heal and restore to life the most desperate cases. For unfailing skill, for unwearied tenderness, for long experience of man's spiritual ailments, the great Physician of souls stands alone. There is none like Him.

But what do we know ourselves of this special office of Christ? Have we ever felt our spiritual sickness and applied to Him for relief? We are never right in the sight of God until we do. We know nothing aright in religion if we think the sense of sin should keep us back from Christ. To feel our sins and know our sickness is the beginning of real Christianity. To be sensible of our corruption and abhor our own transgressions is the first symptom of spiritual health. Happy, indeed,

D

are they who have found out their soul's disease! Let them know that Christ is the very Physician they require, and let them apply to Him without delay.

We learn, in the last place, from these verses, that *in religion it is worse than useless to attempt to mix things which essentially differ.* "No man," he tells the Pharisees, "seweth a piece of new cloth on an old garment." "No man putteth new wine into old bottles."

These words, we must of course see, were a parable. They were spoken with a special reference to the question which the Pharisees had just raised: "Why do the disciples of John fast, but Thy disciples fast not?" Our Lord's reply evidently means, that to enforce fasting among His disciples would be inexpedient and unseasonable. His little flock was as yet young in grace, and weak in faith, knowledge, and experience. They must be led on softly, and not burdened at this early stage with requirements which they were not able to bear. Fasting, moreover, might be suitable to the disciples of him who was only the Bridegroom's friend, who lived in the wilderness, preached the baptism of repentance, was clothed in camel's hair, and ate locusts and wild honey. But fasting was not equally suitable to the disciples of Him who was the Bridegroom Himself, brought glad tidings to sinners, and came living like other men. In short, to require fasting of His disciples at present would be putting "new wine into old bottles." It would be trying to mingle and amalgamate things that essentially differed.

The principle laid down in these little parables is one of great importance. It is a kind of proverbial saying, and admits of a wide application. Forgetfulness of it has frequently done great harm in the Church. The evils that have arisen from trying to sew the new patch on the old garment, and put the new wine into old bottles, have neither been few nor small.

How was it with the Galatian Church? It is recorded in St. Paul's Epistle. Men wished in that Church to reconcile Judaism with Christianity, and to circumcise as well as baptize. They endeavoured to keep alive the law of ceremonies and ordinances, and to place it side by side with the Gospel of Christ. In fact they would fain have put the "new wine into old bottles." And in so doing they greatly erred.

How was it with the early Christian Church, after the Apostles were dead? We have it recorded in the pages of Church history. Some tried to make the Gospel more acceptable by mingling it with Platonic philosophy. Some laboured to recommend it to the heathen by borrowing forms, processions, and vestments from the temples of heathen gods. In short, they "sewed the new patch on the old garment." And in so doing they scattered broadcast the seeds of enormous evil. They paved the way for the whole Romish apostasy.

How is it with many professing Christians in the present day? We have only to look around us and see. There are thousands who are trying to reconcile the service of Christ and the service of the world, to have the name of Christians and yet live the life of the ungodly,—to keep in with the servants of pleasure and sin, and yet be the followers of the crucified Jesus at the same time. In a word, they are trying to enjoy the

"new wine," and yet to cling to the "old bottles." They
will find one day that they have attempted that which
cannot be done.

Let us leave the passage in a spirit of serious self-
inquiry. It is one that ought to raise great searchings
of heart in the present day. Have we never read what
the Scripture says? "No man can serve two masters."
"Ye cannot serve God and mammon." Let us place
side by side with these texts the concluding words of
our Lord in this passage: "New wine must be put into
new bottles."*

MARK II. 23—28.

23 And it came to pass, that he went through the corn fields on the sabbath day; and his disciples began, as they went, to pluck the ears of corn.

24 And the Pharisees said unto him, Behold, why do they on the sabbath day that which is not lawful?

25 And he said unto them, Have ye never read what David did, when he had need, and was an hungred, he, and they that were with him?

26 How he went into the house of God in the days of Abiathar the high priest, and did eat the shewbread, which is not lawful to eat but for the priests, and gave also to them which were with him?

27 And he said unto them, The sabbath was made for man, and not man for the sabbath;

28 Therefore the Son of man is Lord also of the Sabbath.

THESE verses set before us a remarkable scene in our
Lord Jesus Christ's earthly ministry. We see our blessed
Master and His disciples going "through the corn fields
on the Sabbath day." We are told that His disciples,
"as they went began to pluck the ears of corn." At
once we hear the Pharisees accusing them to our Lord,
as if they had committed some great moral offence.

---

* It must always be remembered that the "bottle" here spoken
of was not a bottle of glass or of earthenware, but of leather. Unless
this is kept in view, the parable is unintelligible to an English
mind. A similar remark applies to David's words, "I am become
like a bottle in the smoke." (Psalm cxix. 83.)

"Why do they on the Sabbath day that which is not lawful?" They received an answer full of deep wisdom, which all should study well, who desire to understand the subject of Sabbath observance.

We see from these verses, *what extravagant importance is attached to trifles by those who are mere formalists in religion.*

The Pharisees were mere formalists, if there ever were any in the world. They seem to have thought exclusively of the outward part, the husk, the shell, and the ceremonial of religion. They even added to these externals by traditions of their own. Their godliness was made up of washings and fastings and peculiarities in dress and will-worship, while repentance and faith and holiness were comparatively overlooked.

The Pharisees would probably have found no fault if the disciples had been guilty of some offence against the moral law. They would have winked at covetousness, or perjury, or extortions, or excess, because they were sins to which they themselves were inclined. But no sooner did they see an infringement of their man-made traditions about the right way of keeping the Sabbath, than they raised an outcry, and found fault.

Let us watch and pray, lest we fall into the error of the Pharisees. There are never wanting Christians who walk in their steps. There are thousands at the present day who plainly think more of the mere outward ceremonial of religion than of its doctrines. They make more ado about keeping saints' days, and turning to the East in the creed, and bowing at the name of Jesus, than about repentance, or faith, or separation from the

world.   Against this spirit let us ever be on our guard.
It can neither comfort, satisfy, nor save.

It ought to be a settled principle in our minds that a
man's soul is in a bad state when he begins to regard
man-made rites and ceremonies as things of superior
importance, and exalts them above the preaching of the
Gospel.   It is a symptom of spiritual disease.   There is
mischief within.   It is too often the resource of· an
uneasy conscience.   The first steps of apostasy from
Protestantism to Romanism have often been in this
direction.   No wonder that St. Paul said to the Gala-
tians, " Ye observe days, and months, and times, and
years.   I am afraid of you, lest I have bestowed on you
labour in vain."   (Gal. iv. 10, 11.)

We see, in the second place, from these verses, *the
value of a knowledge of Holy Scripture.*

Our Lord replies to the accusation of the Pharisees by
a reference to Holy Scripture.   He reminds His enemies
of the conduct of David, when "he had need and was
an hungred."   "Have ye never read what David did ? "
They could not deny that the writer of the book of
Psalms, and the man after God's own heart, was not
likely to set a bad example.   They knew in fact that he
had not turned aside from God's commandment, all the
days of his life, "save only in the matter of Uriah the
Hittite."   (1 Kings xv. 5.)   Yet what had David done ?
He had gone into the house of God, when pressed by
hunger, and eaten the "shewbread, which is not lawful
to eat but for the priests."*   He had thus shown that

* There is some difficulty in this passage in the mention of
Abiathar as " the High Priest."   In the book of Samuel it appears

some requirements of God's laws might be relaxed in case of necessity. To this Scripture example our Lord refers His adversaries. They found nothing to reply to

that Abimelech was the High Priest, when the circumstance here referred to took place. (1 Sam. xxi. 6.)

The explanations of this difficulty are various. They are as follows :—

1. Beza says that both Abiathar and Abimelech had each two names, and that Abiathar was frequently called Abimelech, and Abimelech Abiathar. (See in proof of this, 2 Sam. viii. 17 : 1 Chron. viii. 16, and xxiv. 3.)

2. Lightfoot would translate the words, "in the days of Abiathar, the son of the High Priest," and says he is named rather than his father, because he brought the Ephod to David, and by him inquiry was made by Urim and Thummim. He also says, that the Jews by "Abiathar" understood the Urim and Thummim, and to say that the thing was done "under Abiathar" would show that it was done by Divine direction.

3. Whitby thinks that by "the High Priest" here, we are not to understand him who was strictly so called, but only one who was an eminent man of the order. He quotes as examples, Matt. ii. 4; xxvi. 3; xxvii. 62 : John xi. 47 : Mark xiv. 10, 43.

4. Some think that both Abimelech and Abiathar officiated as High Priests at the same time. That there was nothing altogether unusual in there being two Chief Priests at once is shown by 1 Sam. viii. 17, where two names are given as "the Priests."

5. Some think that there has been a mistake made in transcribing the original words of St. Mark in this place, and some words have been inserted, or wrongly written. Beza's manuscript omits the words translated, "in the time of Abiathar the High Priest," altogether. The St. Gall manuscript and the Gothic version have the word "Priest" simply, and not "High Priest." The Persian version has "Abimelech" instead of "Abiathar." However, it is only fair to say that the evidence of the great majority of manuscripts and versions is in favour of the text as it stands.

Some of these solutions of the difficulty are evidently more probable than others. But any one of them is far more reasonable and deserving of belief than to suppose, as some have asserted, that St. Mark made a blunder ! Such a theory destroys the whole principle of the inspiration of Scripture. Transcribers of the Bible have possibly made occasional mistakes. The original writers were inspired in the writing of every word, and therefore could not err.

it. The sword of the Spirit was a weapon which they could not resist. They were silenced, and put to shame.

Now the conduct of our Lord on this occasion ought to be a pattern to all His people. Our grand reason for our faith and practice, should always be, "Thus it is written in the Bible." "What saith the Scripture?" We should endeavour to have the Word of God on our side in all debatable questions. We should seek to be able to give a Scriptural answer for our behaviour in all matters of dispute. We should refer our enemies to the Bible as our rule of conduct. We shall always find a plain text the most powerful argument we can use. In a world like this we must expect our opinions to be attacked, if we serve Christ, and we may be sure that nothing silences adversaries so soon as a quotation from Scripture.

Let us however remember that if we are to use the Bible as our Lord did we must know it well, and be acquainted with its contents. We must read it diligently, humbly, perseveringly, prayerfully, or we shall never find its texts coming to our aid in the time of need. To use the sword of the Spirit effectually, we must be familiar with it, and have it often in our hands. There is no royal road to the knowledge of the Bible. It does not come to man by intuition. The book must be studied, pondered, prayed over, searched into, and not left always lying on a shelf, or carelessly looked at now and then. It is the students of the Bible, and they only, who will find it a weapon ready to hand in the day of battle.

We see, in the last place, from these verses, the *true principle by which all questions about the observance of the Sabbath ought to be decided.* "The Sabbath," says our

Lord, "was made for man, and not man for the Sabbath."

There is a mine of deep wisdom in those words. They deserve close attention, and the more so because they are not recorded in any Gospel but that of St. Mark. Let us see what they contain.

"The Sabbath was made for man." God made it for Adam in paradise, and renewed it to Israel on Mount Sinai. It was made for all mankind : not for the Jew only, but for the whole family of Adam. It was made for man's benefit and happiness. It was for the good of his body, the good of his mind, and the good of his soul. It was given to him as a boon and a blessing, and not as a burden. This was the original institution.

But "man was not made for the Sabbath." The observance of the day of God was never meant to be so enforced as to be an injury to his health, or to interfere with his necessary wants. The original command to "keep holy the Sabbath Day," was not intended to be so interpreted as to do harm to his body, or prevent acts of mercy to his fellow-creatures. This was the point that the Pharisees had forgotten, or buried under their traditions.

There is nothing in all this to warrant the rash assertion of some, that our Lord has done away with the fourth commandment. On the contrary, He manifestly speaks of the Sabbath Day as a privilege and a gift, and only regulates the extent to which its observance should be enforced. He shows that works of necessity and mercy may be done on the Sabbath Day ; but He says not a word to justify the notion that Christians need not "remember the day to keep it holy."

Let us be jealous over our own conduct in the matter of observing the Sabbath. There is little danger of the day being kept too strictly in the present age. There is far more danger of its being profaned and forgotten entirely. Let us contend earnestly for its preservation among us in all its integrity. We may rest assured that national prosperity and personal growth in grace are intimately bound up in the maintenance of a holy Sabbath.*

---

* The concluding words of the passage now expounded are remarkable: "The Son of man is Lord also of the Sabbath." They have received some rather strange interpretations, which it may be well to notice.

1. Chrysostom, Grotius, Calovius, and others, think that the "son of man" in this place means "any man," any one naturally born of the family of Adam, and not Christ Himself. To say nothing of the objections that might be brought against the doctrines involved in such a sense, it is an unanswerable objection that the expression "son of man" is never used in this way in the New Testament. Whitby says that it occurs eighty-eight times, and always applies to Christ.

2. Others say that our Lord's meaning is, to assert His own right to dispense with the observance of the fourth commandment. This, however, seems a very unsatisfactory interpretation. Our Lord declares plainly in one place, that He came "not to destroy the law, but to fulfil." He challenges the Jews in another place to convict Him of any breach of the law: "which of you convinceth me of sin?" His enemies, when they brought Him at last before Caiaphas, did not charge Him with breaking the fourth commandment. No doubt they would have done so had He given them occasion, either by His teaching or practice.

The true meaning appears to be, that our Lord claims the right to dispense with all the traditional rules, and man-made laws about the Sabbath, with which the Pharisees had overloaded the day of rest. As Son of man, who came not to destroy, but to save, He asserts His power to set free the blessed Sabbath from the false and superstitious notions with which the Rabbins had clogged and poisoned it, and to restore it to its proper meaning and use. He declares that the Sabbath is His day,—His by creation and institution, since He first gave it in Paradise and at Sinai,—and proclaims His determination to defend and purify His day from

MARK III. 1—12.

1 And he entered again into the synagogue; and there was a man there which had a withered hand.

2 And they watched him, whether he would heal him on the sabbath day; that they might accuse him.

3 And he saith unto the man which had the withered hand, Stand forth.

4 And he saith unto them, Is it lawful to do good on the sabbath days, or to do evil? to save life, or to kill? But they held their peace.

5 And when he had looked round about on them with anger, being grieved for the hardness of their hearts, he saith unto the man, Stretch forth thine hand. And he stretched *it* out: and his hand was restored whole as the other.

6 And the Pharisees went forth, and straightway took counsel with the Herodians against him, how they might destroy him.

7 But Jesus withdrew himself with his disciples to the sea: and a great multitude from Galilee followed him, and from Judæa,

8 And from Jerusalem, and from Idumæa, and *from* beyond Jordan; and they about Tyre and Sidon, a great multitude, when they had heard what great things he did, came unto him.

9 And he spake to his disciples, that a small ship should wait on him because of the multitude, lest they should throng him.

10 For he had healed many; insomuch that they pressed upon him for to touch him, as many as had plagues.

11 And unclean spirits, when they saw him, fell down before him, and cried, saying, Thou art the Son of God.

12 And he straitly charged them that they should not make him known.

THESE verses show us our Lord again working a miracle. He heals a man in the synagogue, "which had a withered hand." Always about His Father's business,—always doing good,—doing it in the sight of enemies as well as

Jewish imposition, and to give it to His disciples as a day of blessing, comfort, and benefit, according to its original intention.

Two things are implied in our Lord's words. One is His own divinity. The "Lord of the Sabbath day" could be no less than God himself. It is like the expression, "In this place is one greater than the temple." (Matt. xii. 6.) The other is His intention of altering the day of rest from the seventh day of the week to the first. At the time that He spoke neither of these things doubtless were apparent to the Jews, and probably not to His disciples. After His ascension they "would remember His words."

A passage in Mayer's Commentary is worth reading. "It is certain that Christ being a perfect pattern of doctrine in all things, did not transgress, or maintain any transgression against any law of God. Wherefore it is to be held that all His speech here tendeth to nothing else but to convince the Pharisees of blindness and ignorance touching the right keeping of the Sabbath according to the commandment, it being never required to rest so strictly as they thought." —*Mayer's Commentary.* 1631.

of friends,—such was the daily tenor of our Lord's earthly ministry. And He "left us an example that we should follow His steps." (1 Peter ii. 21.) Blessed indeed are those Christians who strive, however feebly, to imitate their Master!

Let us observe in these versss, *how our Lord Jesus Christ was watched by His enemies.* We read that "they watched Him, whether He would heal him on the Sabbath Day, that they might accuse Him."

What a melancholy proof we have here of the wickedness of human nature! It was the Sabbath Day when these things happened. It was in the synagogue, where men were assembled to hear the Word and worship God. Yet even on the day of God, and at the time of worshipping God, these wretched formalists were plotting mischief against our Lord. The very men who pretended to such strictness and sanctity in little things, were full of malicious and angry thoughts in the midst of the congregation. (Prov. v. 14.)

Christ's people must not expect to fare better than their Master. They are always watched by an ill-natured and spiteful world. Their conduct is scanned with a keen and jealous eye. Their ways are noted and diligently observed. They are marked men. They can do nothing without the world noticing it. Their dress, their expenditure, their employment of time, their conduct in all the relations of life, are all rigidly and closely remarked. Their adversaries wait for their halting, and if at any time they fall into an error, the ungodly rejoice.

It is good for all Christians to keep this before their minds. Wherever we go, and whatever we do, let us remember that, like our Master, we are "watched." The thought should make us exercise a holy jealousy over all our conduct, that we may do nothing to cause the enemy to blaspheme. It should make us diligent to avoid even the "appearance of evil." Above all, it should make us pray much, to be kept in our tempers, tongues, and daily public demeanour. That Saviour who was "watched" Himself, knows how to sympathize with His people, and to supply grace to help in time of need.

Let us observe, in the second place, *the great principle that our Lord lays down about Sabbath observance.* He teaches that it is lawful "to do good" on the Sabbath.

The principle is taught by a remarkable question. He asks those around Him, whether it was "lawful to do good or evil on the Sabbath day, to save life, or to kill?" Was it better to heal this poor sufferer before Him with the withered hand, or to leave him alone? Was it more sinful to restore a person to health on the Sabbath, than to plot murder, and nourish hatred against an innocent person, as they were doing at that moment against Himself? Was He to be blamed for saving a life on the Sabbath? Were they blameless who were desirous to kill? No wonder that before such a question as this our Lord's enemies "held their peace."

It is plain, from these words of our Lord, that no Christian need ever hesitate to do a really good work on the Sunday. A real work of mercy, such as ministering to the sick, or relieving pain, may always be done without scruple. The holiness with which the fourth commandment invests the Sabbath Day is not in the least degree invaded by anything of this kind.

But we must take care that the principle here laid down by our Lord is not abused and turned to bad account. We must not allow ourselves to suppose that the permission to "do good," implied that every one might find his own pleasure on the Sabbath. The permission to "do good," was never meant to open the door to amusements, worldly festivities, travelling, journeying, and sensual gratification. It was never intended to license the Sunday railway train, or the Sunday steamboat, or the Sunday exhibition. These things do good to none, and do certain harm to many. They rob many a servant of his seventh day's rest. They turn the Sunday of thousands into a day of hard toil. Let us beware of perverting our Lord's words from their proper meaning. Let us remember what kind of "doing good" on the Sabbath His blessed example sanctioned. Let us ask ourselves whether there is the slightest likeness between our Lord's works on the Sabbath, and those ways of spending the Sabbath for which many contend, who yet dare to appeal to our Lord's example. Let us fall back on the plain meaning of our Lord's words, and take our stand on them. He gives us a liberty to "do good" on Sunday, but for feasting, sight-seeing, party-giving, and excursions, He gives no liberty at all.

Let us observe, in the last place, *the feelings which the conduct of our Lord's enemies called forth in His heart.* We are told that "He looked round about on them with anger, being grieved for the hardness of their hearts."

This expression is very remarkable, and demands special attention. It is meant to remind us that our Lord Jesus Christ was a man like ourselves in all things, sin only excepted. Whatever sinless feelings belong to the constitution of man, our Lord partook of, and knew by experience. We read that He "marvelled," that He "rejoiced," that He "wept," that He "loved," and here we read that He felt "anger."

It is plain from these words that there is an "anger" which is lawful, right, and not sinful. There is an indignation which is justifiable, and on some occasions may be properly manifested. The words of Solomon and St. Paul both seem to teach the same lesson. "The north wind driveth away rain, so doth an angry countenance a backbiting tongue." "Be ye angry and sin not." (Prov. xxv. 23; Ephes. iv. 26.)

Yet it must be confessed that the subject is full of difficulty. Of all the feelings that man's heart experiences there is none perhaps which so soon runs into sin as the feeling of anger. There is none which once excited seems less under control. There is none which leads on to so much evil. The length to which ill-temper, irritability, and passion, will carry even godly men, all must know. The history of "the contention" of Paul and Barnabas at Antioch, and the story of Moses being provoked till he "spake unadvisedly with his lips," are familiar to every Bible reader. The awful fact that passionate words are a breach of the sixth commandment is plainly taught in the Sermon on the Mount. And yet here we see that there is an anger which is lawful.

Let us leave this subject with an earnest prayer that we may all be enabled to take heed to our spirit in the matter of anger. We may rest assured that there is no human feeling which needs so much cautious guarding

as this. A sinless wrath is a very rare thing. The
wrath of man is seldom for the glory of God. In every
case a righteous indignation should be mingled with
grief and sorrow for those who cause it, even- as it
was in the case of our Lord. And this, at all events, we
may be sure of,—it is better never to be angry, than to
be angry and sin.*

MARK III. 13—21.

13 And he goeth up into a mountain, and calleth *unto him* whom he would: and they came unto him.
14 And he ordained twelve, that they should be with him, and that he might send them forth to preach,
15 And to have power to heal sicknesses, and to cast out devils:
16 And Simon he surnamed Peter;
17 And James the *son* of Zebedee, and John the brother of James; and he surnamed them Boanerges, which is, The sons of thunder:

18 And Andrew, and Philip, and Bartholomew, and Matthew, and Thomas, and James the *son* of Alphæus, and Thaddæus, and Simon the Canaanite,
19 And Judas Iscariot, which also betrayed him: and they went into an house.
20 And the multitude cometh together again, so that they could not so much as eat bread.
21 And when his friends heard *of it,* they went out to lay hold on him: for they said, He is beside himself.

THE beginning of this passage describes the appointment of the twelve Apostles. It is an event in our Lord's
earthly ministry which should always be read with deep
interest. What a vast amount of benefit these few men
have conferred on the world! The names of a few Jewish
fishermen are know and loved by millions all over the

---

* In connection with this subject, Bishop Butler's Sermon on
Resentment deserves perusal. He says at the conclusion of it:
"That passion, from whence men take occasion to run into the dreadful sins of malice and revenge, even that passion, as implanted in
our nature by God, is not only innocent but a generous movement
of mind. It is in itself, and in its original, no more than indignation against injury and wickedness,—that which is the only defor-
mity in the creation, and the only reasonable object of abhorrence
and dislike."—*Bishop Butler.*

globe, while the names of many Kings and rich men are lost and forgotten. It is they who do good to souls who are had "in everlasting remembrance." (Psalm cxii. 6.)

Let us notice in these verses, *how many of the twelve who are here named, had been called to be disciples before they were ordained Apostles.*

There are six, at least, out of the number, whose first call to follow Christ is specially recorded. These six are Peter and Andrew, James and John, Philip and Matthew. In short there can be little doubt that eleven of our Lord's Apostles were converted before they were ordained.

It ought to be the same with all ministers of the Gospel. They ought to be men who have been first called by the Spirit, before they are set apart for the great work of teaching others. The rule should be the same with them as with the Apostles,—"first converted, then ordained."

It is impossible to overrate the importance of this to the interests of true religion. Bishops and presbyteries can never be too strict and particular in the inquiries they make about the spiritual character of candidates for orders. An unconverted minister is utterly unfit for his office. How can he speak experimentally of that grace which he has never tasted himself? How can he commend that Saviour to his people whom he himself only knows by name? How can he urge on souls the need of that conversion and new birth, which he himself has not experienced? Miserably mistaken are those parents, who persuade their sons to become clergymen, in order to obtain a good living, or follow a

E

respectable profession! What is it but persuading them to say what is not true, and to take the Lord's name in vain? None do such injury to the cause of Christianity, as unconverted, worldly ministers. They are a support to the infidel, a joy to the devil, and an offence to God.

Let us notice, in the second place, *the nature of the office to which the Apostles were ordained.* They were to " be with Christ." They were to be " sent forth to preach." They were to have " power to heal sicknesses." They were to " cast out devils."

These four points deserve attention. They contain much instruction. Our Lord's twelve Apostles, beyond doubt, were a distinct order of men. They had no successors when they died. Strictly and literally speaking, there is no such thing as apostolical succession. No man can be really called a " successor of the Apostles," unless he can work miracles, and teach infallibly, as they did. But still, in saying this, we must not forget, that in many things the Apostles were intended to be patterns and models for all ministers of the Gospel. Bearing this in mind, we may draw most useful lessons from this passage, as to the duties of a faithful minister.

Like the Apostles, the faithful minister ought to keep up close communion with Christ. He should be much " with Him." His fellowship should be " with the Son." (1 John i. 3.) He should abide in Him. He should be separate from the world, and daily sit, like Mary, at Jesus' feet, and hear His Word. He should study Him, copy Him, drink into His Spirit, and walk in His steps. He should strive to be able to say, when he enters the pulpit, "That which we have seen and heard, declare we unto you." (1 John i. 3.)

Like the Apostles, the faithful minister ought to be a preacher. This must ever be his principal work, and receive the greatest part of his thoughts. He must place it above the administration of the sacraments. (1 Cor. i. 17.) He must exalt it above the reading of forms. An unpreaching minister is of little use to the Church of Christ. He is a lampless light-house, a silent trumpeter, a sleeping watchman, a painted fire.

Like the Apostles, the faithful minister must labour to do good in every way. Though he cannot heal the sick, he must seek to alleviate sorrow, and to increase happiness among all with whom he has to do. He must strive to be known as the comforter, the counsellor, the peacemaker, the helper, and the friend of all. Men should know him, not as one who rules and domineers, but as one who is "their servant for Jesus' sake." (2 Cor. iv. 5.)

Like the Apostles, the faithful minister must oppose every work of the devil. Though not called now to cast out evil spirits from the body, he must be ever ready to resist the devil's devices, and to denounce his snares for the soul. He must expose the tendency of races, theatres, balls, gambling, drunkenness, Sabbath-profanation, and sensual gratifications. Every age has its own peculiar temptations. Many are the devices of Satan. But whatever be the direction in which the devil is most busy, there ought the minister to be, ready to confront and withstand him.

How great is the responsibility of ministers! How heavy their work, if they do their duty! How much they need the prayers of all praying people, in order to support and strengthen their hands! No wonder that St. Paul says so often to the Churches, " Pray for us."

Let us notice, in the last place, how *our Lord Jesus Christ's zeal was misunderstood by His enemies.* We are told that they "went out to lay hold of Him, for they said, He is beside Himself."

There is nothing in this fact that need surprise us. The prophet who came to anoint Jehu was called a " mad fellow." (2 Kings ix. 11.) Festus told Paul that he was "mad." Few things show the corruption of human nature more clearly than man's inability to understand zeal in religion. Zeal about money, or science, or war, or commerce, or business, is intelligible to the world. But zeal about religion is too often reckoned foolishness, fanaticism, and the sign of a weak mind. If a man injures his health by study, or excessive attention to business, no fault is found: " He is a diligent man." But if he wears himself out with preaching, or spends his whole time in doing good to souls, the cry is raised, " He is an enthusiast and righteous over much." The world is not altered. The " things of the Spirit " are always "foolishness to the natural man." (1 Cor. ii. 14.)

Let it not shake our faith if we have to drink of the same cup as our blessed Lord. Hard as it may be to flesh and blood to be misunderstood by our relations, we must recollect it is no new thing. Let us call to mind our Lord's words, " He that loveth father and mother more than Me, is not worthy of Me." Jesus knows the bitterness of our trials. Jesus feels for us. Jesus will give us help.

Let us bear patiently the unreasonableness of unconverted men, even as our Lord did. Let us pity their
blindness and want of knowledge, and not love them
one whit the less. Above all, let us pray that God
would change their hearts. Who can tell but the very
persons who now try to turn us away from Christ, may
one day become new creatures, see all things differently,
and follow Christ themselves?

MARK III. 22—30.

22 And the Scribes which came down from Jerusalem said, He hath Beelzebub, and by the prince of the devils casteth he out devils.

23 And he called them *unto him*, and said unto them in parables, How can Satan cast out Satan?

24 And if a kingdom be divided against itself, that kingdom cannot stand.

25 And if a house be divided against itself, that house cannot stand.

26 And if Satan rise up against himself, and be divided, he cannot stand, but hath an end.

27 No man can enter into a strong man's house, and spoil his goods, except he will first bind the strong man; and then he will spoil his house.

28 Verily I say unto you, All sins shall be forgiven unto the sons of men, and blasphemies wherewith soever they shall blaspheme:

29 But he that shall blaspheme against the Holy Ghost hath never forgiveness, but is in danger of eternal damnation:

30 Because they said, He hath an unclean spirit.

WE all know how painful it is to have our conduct
misunderstood and misrepresented, when we are doing
right. It is a trial which our Lord Jesus Christ had to
endure continually, all through His earthly ministry.
We have an instance in the passage before us. The
"Scribes which came down from Jerusalem" saw the
miracles which He worked. They could not deny their
reality. What then did they do? They accused our
blessed Saviour of being in league and union with the
devil. They said, "He hath Beelzebub, and by the
prince of the devils casteth He out devils."

In our Lord's solemn answer to this wicked accusation, there are expressions which deserve special attention. Let us see what lessons they contain for our use.

We ought to notice, in the first place, *how great is the evil of dissensions and divisions.*

This is a lesson which is strongly brought out in the beginning of our Lord's reply to the Scribes. He shows the absurdity of supposing that Satan would " cast out Satan," and so help to destroy his own power. He appeals to the notorious fact, which even His enemies must allow, that there can be no strength where there is division. " If a kingdom be divided against itself, that kingdom cannot stand."

This truth is one which does not receive sufficient consideration. On no point has the abuse of the right of private judgment produced so much evil. The divisions of Christians are one great cause of the weakness of the visible Church. They often absorb energy, time, and power, which might have been well bestowed on better things. They furnish the infidel with a prime argument against the truth of Christianity. They help the devil. Satan, indeed, is the chief promoter of religious divisions. If he cannot extinguish Christianity, he labours to make Christians quarrel with one another, and to set every man's hand against his neighbour. None knows better than the devil, that " to divide is to conquer."

Let us resolve, so far as in us lies, to avoid all differences, dissensions, and disputes in religion. Let us loathe and abhor them as the plague of the Churches. We cannot be too jealous about all saving truths. But it is easy to mistake morbid scrupulosity for conscientiousness, and zeal about mere trifles for zeal about the truth. Nothing justifies separation from a Church but the separation of that Church from the Gospel. Let us be ready to concede much, and make many sacrifices for the sake of unity and peace.

We ought to notice, in the second place, *what a glorious declaration our Lord makes in these verses about the forgiveness of sins.* He says, " All sins shall be forgiven to the sons of men, and blasphemies wherewith soever they shall blaspheme."

These words fall lightly on the ears of many persons. They see no particular beauty in them. But to the man who is alive to his own sinfulness and deeply sensible of his need of mercy, these words are sweet and precious. "All sins shall be forgiven." The sins of youth and age, —the sins of head, and hand, and tongue, and imagination,—the sins against all God's commandments,—the sins of persecutors, like Saul,—the sins of idolaters, like Manasseh,—the sins of open enemies of Christ, like the Jews who crucified Him,—the sins of backsliders from Christ, like Peter,—all, all may be forgiven. The blood of Christ can cleanse all away. The righteousness of Christ can cover all, and hide all from God's eyes.

The doctrine here laid down is the crown and glory of the Gospel. The very first thing it proposes to man is free pardon, full forgiveness, complete remission, without money and without price. " Through this man is preached unto you the forgiveness of sins; and by Him all that believe are justified from all things." (Acts xiii. 39.)

Let us lay hold on this doctrine without delay, if we never received it before. It is for us, as well as for others.

We too, this very day, if we come to Christ, may be completely forgiven. "Though our sins have been as scarlet, they shall be white as snow." (Isaiah i. 18.)

Let us cleave firmly to this doctrine, if we have received it already. We may sometimes feel faint, and unworthy, and cast down. But if we have really come to Jesus by faith, our sins are clean forgiven. They are cast behind God's back,—blotted out of the book of His remembrance,—sunk into the depths of the sea. Let us believe and not be afraid.

We ought to notice, in the last place, that *it is possible for a man's soul to be lost for ever in hell.* The words of our Lord are distinct and express. He speaks of one who "hath never forgiveness, but is in danger of eternal damnation."

This is an awful truth, beyond doubt. But it is a truth, and we must not shut our eyes against it. We find it asserted over and over again in Scripture. Figures of all kinds are multiplied, and language of every sort is employed, in order to make it plain and unmistakable. In short, if there is no such thing as "eternal damnation," we may throw the Bible aside, and say that words have no meaning at all.

We have great need to keep this awful truth steadily in view in these latter days. Teachers have risen up, who are openly attacking the doctrine of the eternity of punishment, or labouring hard to explain it away. Men's ears are being tickled with plausible sayings about "the love of God," and the impossibility of a loving God permitting an everlasting hell. The eternity of punishment is spoken of as a mere "speculative question," about which men may believe anything they please.—In the midst of all this flood of false doctrine, let us hold firmly the old truths. Let us not be ashamed to believe that there is an eternal God,—an eternal heaven,—and an eternal hell. Let us recollect that sin is an infinite evil. It needed an atonement of infinite value to deliver the believer from its consequences,—and it entails an infinite loss on the unbeliever who rejects the remedy provided for it. Above all, let us fall back on plain Scriptural statements, like that before us this day. One plain text is worth a thousand abstruse arguments.

Finally, if it be true that there is an " eternal damnation," let us give diligence that we ourselves do not fall into it. Let us escape for our lives and not linger. (Gen. xix. 16, 17.) Let us flee for refuge to the hope set before us in the Gospel, and never rest till we know and feel that we are safe. And never, never let us be ashamed of seeking safety. Of sin, worldliness, and the love of pleasure, we may well be ashamed. But we never need be ashamed of seeking to be delivered from an eternal hell.*

* There is an expression in the passage now expounded, which appears to demand special notice. It is confessedly one of the hard things of Scripture, and has often troubled the hearts of Bible readers. I refer to the saying of our Lord, "He that blasphemeth against the Holy Ghost hath never forgiveness." It seems that there is such a thing as an *unpardonable sin.*

Some interpreters have endeavoured to cut the knot of the difficulty, by maintaining that the sin here referred to was entirely confined to the time when our Lord was on earth. They say that when the Scribes and Pharisees saw the evidence of our Lord's miracles, and yet refused to believe in Him as the Messiah, they committed the unpardonable sin. Their assertion that our Lord worked miracles through Beelzebub, was blasphemy against the Holy Ghost.

There might be something in this view, if the passage under consideration stood entirely alone,—though even then he would be a

MARK III. 31—35.

31 There came then his brethren and his mother, and, standing without, sent unto him, calling him.

32 And the multitude sat about him, and they said unto him, Behold, thy mother and thy brethren without seek for thee.

33 And he answered them, saying,

Who is my mother, or my brethren?

34 And he looked round about on them which sat about him, and said, Behold my mother and my brethren!

35 For whosoever shall do the will of God, the same is my brother, and my sister, and mother.

IN the verses which immediately precede this passage, we see our blessed Lord accused by the Scribes of being in league with the devil. They said, "He hath Beelzebub, and by the prince of the devils casteth He out devils."

In the verses we have now read, we find that this absurd charge of the Scribes was not all that Jesus had to endure at this time. We are told that "His brethren

bold man who would assert that there were no hardened Scribes and Pharisees among the 3000 converted and forgiven on the day of Pentecost. But unfortunately for this theory, the doctrine here laid down is to be found in other places of Scripture beside this. I allude of course to the well-known passages, Heb. vi. 4—6, Heb. x. 26, and 1 John v. 17. In all these places there seems a reference to a sin which is not forgiven.

What then is the unpardonable sin? It must be frankly confessed that its precise nature is nowhere defined in Holy Scripture. The most probable view is, that it is a combination of clear intellectual knowledge of the Gospel, with deliberate rejection of it, and wilful choice of sin. It is an union of light in the head, and hatred in the heart. Such was the case of Judas Iscariot. We must not flatter ourselves that none have walked in his steps. In the absence of any definition in Scripture, we shall probably not get much nearer to the mark than this. Yet even this view must be carefully handled. The limits which knowledge combined with unbelief must pass, in order to become the unpardonable sin, are graciously withheld from us. It is mercifully ordered of God, that man can never decide positively of any brother, that he has committed a sin which cannot be forgiven.

But although it is difficult to define what the unpardonable sin is, it is far less difficult to point out what it is not. A few words on this point may possibly help to relieve tender consciences.

We may lay it down as nearly certain, that those who are troubled with fears that they have sinned the unpardonable sin, and His mother came, and, standing without, sent unto Him, calling Him." They could not yet understand the beauty and usefulness of the life that our Lord was living. Though they doubtless loved Him well, they would fain have persuaded Him to cease from His work, and "spare Himself." Little did they know what they were doing! Little had they observed or understood our Lord's words when He was only twelve years old : " Wist ye not that I must be about my Father's business ? " *   (Luke ii. 49.)

It is interesting to remark the quiet, firm perseverance

are the very people who have not sinned it.   The very fact that they are afraid and anxious about it, is the strongest possible evidence in their favour.   A troubled conscience,—an anxiety about salvation, and a dread of being cast away,—a concern about the next world, and a desire to escape from the wrath of God,—will probably never be found in the heart of that person who has sinned the sin for which there is no forgiveness.   It is far more probable that the general marks of such a person will be utter hardness of conscience,—a seared heart,—an absence of any feeling,—a thorough insensibility to spiritual concern.   The subject may safely be left here.   There is such a thing as a sin which is never forgiven.   But those who are troubled about it, are most unlikely to have committed it.

The following quotation from Thomas Fuller deserves attention :

" The sin against the Holy Ghost is ever attended with these two symptoms,—absence of all contrition, and of all desire of forgiveness. Now, if thou canst truly say that thy sins are a burden to thee,— that thou dost desire forgiveness, and wouldst give anything to attain it, be of good comfort ; thou hast not yet, and, by God's grace, never shall commit that unpardonable offence.   I will not define how near thou hast been unto it.   As David said to Jonathan, 'there is but a step between me and death,'—so, may be, thou hast missed it very narrowly ; but assure thyself thou art not as yet guilty thereof."—*Fuller's Cause and Cure of a Wounded Conscience.*

* The remarks of Scott on the conduct of our Lord's mother on this occasion, are worth quoting : "It is plain that many of these intimations were suited, and doubtless prophetically intended, to be a Scriptural protest against the idolatrous honour, to this day, by vast multitudes, rendered to Mary the mother of Jesus.   She

of our Lord, in the face of all discouragements. None of these things moved Him. The slanderous suggestions of enemies, and the well-meant remonstrances of ignorant friends, were alike powerless to turn Him from His course. He had set His face as a flint towards the cross and the crown. He knew the work He had come into the world to do. He had a baptism to be baptized, and was straitened till it was accomplished. (Luke xii. 50.)

So let it be with all true servants of Christ. Let nothing turn them for a moment out of the narrow way, or make them stop and look back. Let them not heed the ill-natured remarks of enemies. Let them not give way to the well-intentioned but mistaken entreaties of unconverted relations and friends. Let them reply, in the words of Nehemiah, "I am doing a great work, and I cannot come down." (Neh. vi. 3.) Let them say, "I have taken up the cross, and I will not cast it away."

was, no doubt, an excellent and honourable character, but evidently not perfect. She is entitled to great estimation, and high veneration, but surely not to religious confidence and worship."

It is difficult to mention any doctrine more completely destitute of Scriptural foundation, than the Romish doctrine of the efficacy of the Virgin Mary's intercession, or the utility of addressing our prayers to her. As to the doctrine of the immaculate conception of the Virgin Mary, which has been lately accredited by the Romish Church, it is a mere man-made figment, without a single word of Scripture to support it. Holy and full of grace as the Virgin Mary was, it is plain that she regarded herself as one "born in sin," and needing a Saviour. We have her own remarkable words in evidence of this last point : "My spirit hath rejoiced in God my Saviour." (Luke i. 47.)

As to the opinion of the Fathers on the conduct of the mother of our Lord in this place, Whitby has collected some curious expressions :—"Theophylact taxes her with vain-glory and guilt, in endeavouring to draw Jesus from teaching the Word. Tertullian pronounceth her guilty of incredulity,—Chrysostom of vain-glory, infirmity and madness, for this very thing."

We learn from these verses one mighty lesson. We learn, *who they are that are reckoned the relations of Jesus Christ.* They are they who are His disciples, and "do the will of God." Of such the great Head of the Church says, "the same is my brother, and sister, and mother."

How much there is in this single expression! What a rich mine of consolation it opens to all true believers! Who can conceive the depth of our Lord's love towards Mary the mother that bare Him, and on whose bosom He had been nursed? Who can imagine the breadth of His love towards His brethren according to the flesh, with whom the tender years of His childhood had been spent? Doubtless no heart ever had within it such deep well-springs of affection as the heart of Christ. Yet even He says, of all who "do the will of God," that each "is His brother, and sister, and mother."

Let all true Christians drink comfort out of these words. Let them know that there is One at least who knows them, loves them, cares for them, and reckons them as His own family. What though they be poor in this world? They have no cause to be ashamed, when they remember that they are the brethren and sisters of the Son of God. What though they be persecuted and ill-treated in their own homes because of their religion? They may remember the words of David, and apply them to their own case, "When my father and mother forsake me, then the Lord will take me up." (Psalm xxvii. 10.)

Finally, let all who persecute and ridicule others

because of their religion, take warning by these words, and repent? Whom are they persecuting and ridiculing? The relations of Jesus the Son of God! The family of the King of kings and Lord of lords! Surely they would do wisely to hold their peace, and consider well what they are doing. Those whom they persecute have a mighty Friend. "Their Reedeemer is mighty: He shall plead their cause." (Prov. xxiii. 11.)

MARK IV. 1—20.

1 And he began again to teach by the sea side: and there was gathered unto him a great multitude, so that he entered into a ship, and sat in the sea: and the whole multitude was by the sea on the land.

2 And he taught them many things by parables, and said unto them in his doctrine,

3 Hearken; Behold, there went out a sower to sow:

4 And it came to pass, as he sowed, some fell by the way side, and the fowls of the air came and devoured it up.

5 And some fell on stony ground, where it had not much earth; and immediately it sprang up, because it had no depth of earth:

6 But when the sun was up, it was scorched; and because it had no root, it withered away.

7 And some fell among thorns, and the thorns grew up, and choked it, and it yielded no fruit.

8 And other fell on good ground, and did yield fruit that sprang up and increased; and brought forth, some thirty, and some sixty, and some an hundred.

9 And he said unto them, He that hath ears to hear, let him hear.

10 And when he was alone, they that were about him with the twelve asked of him the parable.

11 And he said unto them, Unto you it is given to know the mystery of the kingdom of God: but unto them that are without, all *these* things are done in parables;

12 That seeing they may see, and not perceive; and hearing they may hear, and not understand; lest at any time they should be converted, and *their* sins should be forgiven them.

13 And he said unto them, Know ye not this parable? and how then will ye know all parables?

14 The sower soweth the word.

15 And these are they by the way side, where the word is sown; but when they have heard, Satan cometh immediately, and taketh away the word that was sown in their hearts.

16 And these are they likewise which are sown on stony ground; who, when they have heard the word, immediately receive it with gladness,

17 And have no root in themselves, and so endure but for a time: afterward, when affliction or persecution ariseth for the word's sake, immediately they are offended.

18 And these are they which are sown among thorns; such as hear the word,

19 And the cares of this world, and the deceitfulness of riches, and the lusts of other things entering in, choke the word, and it becometh unfruitful.

20 And these are they which are sown on good ground; such as hear the word, and receive *it*, and bring forth fruit, some thirty-fold, some sixty, and some an hundred.

THESE verses contain the parable of the sower. Of all the parables spoken by our Lord, none is probably so

well-known as this. There is none which is so easily
understood by all, from the gracious familiarity of the
figures which it contains.* There is none which is of
such universal and perpetual application. So long as
there is a Church of Christ and a congregation of
Christians, so long there will be employment for this
parable.

The language of the parable requires no explanation.
To use the words of an ancient writer, "it needs application, not exposition." Let us now see what it teaches.

We are taught, in the first place *that there are some
hearers of the Gospel, whose hearts are like the way-side in
a field.*

These are they who hear sermons, but pay no attention to them. They go to a place of worship, for form,
or fashion, or to appear respectable before men. But
they take no interest whatever in the preaching. It
seems to them a mere matter of words, and names, and
unintelligible talk. It is neither money, nor meat, nor

---

* "Our Saviour borroweth His comparisons from easy and familiar things, such as the sower, the seed, the ground, the growth,
the withering, the answering or failing of the sower's expectations,
all of them things well known, and by all these would teach us some
spiritual instruction. For there is no earthly thing, which is not
fitted to put us in mind of some heavenly. Christ cannot look upon
the sun, the wind, fire, water, a hen, a little grain of mustard seed ;
nor upon ordinary occasions, as the penny given for the day's work,
the wedding-garment and ceremonies of the Jews about it, nor the
waiting of servants at their master's table, or children asking bread
and fish at their father's table, but He applies all to some special use
of edification in grace.

"Earthly things must remind us of heavenly. We must translate
the book of nature into the book of grace."—*Thomas Taylor on the
Parable of the Sower.* 1634.

drink, nor clothes, nor company ;—and as they sit under
the sound of it, they are taken up with thinking of other
things.   It matters nothing whether it is law or Gospel.
It produces no more effect on them than water on a
stone.   And at the end they go away, knowing no more
than when they came in.

There are myriads of professing Christians in this
state of soul.   There is hardly a church or chapel where
scores of them are not to be found.   Sunday after Sunday they allow the devil to catch away the good seed
that is sown on the face of their hearts.   Week after
week they live on, without faith, or fear, or knowledge,
or grace,—feeling nothing, caring nothing, taking no
more interest in religion than if Christ had never died
on the cross at all.   And in this state they often die and
are buried, and are lost for ever in hell.   This is a
mournful picture, but only too true.

We are taught, in the second place, *that there are
some hearers of the Gospel, whose hearts are like the stony
ground in a field.*

These are they on whom preaching produces temporary impressions, but no deep, lasting, and abiding
effect.   They take pleasure in hearing sermons in which
the truth is faithfully set forth.   They can speak with
apparent joy and enthusiasm about the sweetness of the
Gospel, and the happiness which they experience in listening to it.   They can be moved to tears by the appeals
of preachers, and talk with apparent earnestness of their
own inward conflicts, hopes, struggles, desires, and fears.
But unhappily there is no stability about their religion.
They have no root in themselves, and so endure but for

a time." There is no real work of the Holy Ghost within their hearts. Their impressions are like Jonah's
gourd, which came up in a night and perished in a
night. They fade as rapidly as they grow. No sooner
does "affliction and persecution arise for the Word's
sake," than they fall away. Their goodness proves as
"the morning cloud, and the early dew." (Hosea vi. 4.)
Their religion has no more life in it than the cut flower.
It has no root, and soon withers away.

There are many in every congregation which hears the
Gospel, who are just in this state of soul. They are not
careless and inattentive hearers, like many around them,
and are therefore tempted to think well of their own
condition. They feel a pleasure in the preaching to
which they listen, and therefore flatter themselves they
must have grace in their hearts. And yet they are thoroughly deceived. Old things have not yet passed away.
There is no real work of conversion in their inward man.
With all their feelings, affections, joys, hopes, and desires,
they are actually on the high road to destruction.*

We are taught, in the third place, *that there are some
hearers of the Gospel whose hearts are like the thorny
ground in a field.*

These are they who attend to the preaching of Christ's
truth, and to a certain extent obey it. Their understanding assents to it. Their judgment approves of it.

---

* All who wish to understand the character of the "stony-ground
hearers," should study the treatise of Jonathan Edwards, on the
Religious Affections. Few Christians, who have not looked into the
subject, have any idea of the lengths to which a person may go in
religious feelings, while he is at the same time utterly destitute of
the grace of God.

Their conscience is affected by it.   Their affections are in favour of it.   They acknowledge that it is all right, and good, and worthy of all reception.   They even abstain from many things which the Gospel condemns, and adopt many habits which the Gospel requires.   But here unhappily they stop short.   Something appears to chain them fast, and they never get beyond a certain point in their religion.   And the grand secret of their condition is the world.   "The cares of the world, and the deceitfulness of riches, and the lusts of other things," prevent the Word having its full effect on their souls. With everything apparently that is promising and favourable in their spiritual state, they stand still.   They never come up to the full standard of New Testament Christianity.   They bring no fruit to perfection.

There are few faithful ministers of Christ who could not point to cases like these.   Of all cases they are the most melancholy.   To go so far and yet go no further, to see so much and yet not see all, to approve so much and yet not give Christ the heart,—this is indeed most deplorable!   And there is but one verdict that can be given about such people.   Without a decided change they will never enter the kingdom of heaven.   Christ will have all our hearts.   "If any man will be a friend of the world, he is the enemy of God."   (James iv. 4.)

We are taught in the last place, *that there are some hearers of the Gospel whose hearts are like the good ground in a field.*

These are they who really receive Christ's truth into the bottom of their hearts, believe it implicitly, and obey it thoroughly.   In these the fruits of that truth will be seen,—uniform, plain, and unmistakable results in heart and life. Sin will be truly hated, mourned over, resisted, and renounced. Christ will be truly loved, trusted in, followed, and obeyed. Holiness will show itself in all their conversation, in humility, spiritual-mindedness, patience, meekness, and charity. There will be something that can be seen. The true work of the Holy Ghost cannot be hid.

There will always be some persons in this state of soul, where the Gospel is faithfully preached. Their numbers may very likely be few, compared to the worldly around them. Their experience and degree of spiritual attainment may differ widely, some bringing forth thirty, some sixty, and some a hundred fold. But the fruit of the seed falling into good ground will always be of the same kind. There will always be visible repentance, visible faith in Christ, and visible holiness of life. Without these things there is no saving religion.

And now let us ask ourselves, What are we? Under which class of hearers ought we to be ranked? With what kind of hearts do we hear the Word? Never, never may we forget that there are three ways of hearing without profit, and only one way of hearing aright! Never, never may we forget that there is only one infallible mark of being a right-hearted hearer! That mark is to bear fruit. To be without fruit, is to be in the way to hell.

MARK IV. 21—25.

21 And he said unto them, Is a candle brought to be put under a bushel, or under a bed, and not to be set on a candlestick?

22 For there is nothing hid, which shall not be manifested; neither was anything kept secret, but that it should come abroad.

23 If any man have ears to hear, let him hear.

24 And he said unto them, Take heed what ye hear: with what measure ye mete, it shall be measured to you: and unto you that hear shall more be given.

25 For he that hath, to him shall be given: and he that hath not, from him shall be taken even that which he hath.

THESE verses seem intended to enforce the parable of the sower on the attention of those who heard it. They are remarkable for the succession of short, pithy, proverbial sayings which they contain. Such sayings are eminently calculated to arrest an ignorant hearer. They often strike and stick in the memory, when the main subject of the sermon is forgotten.*

We learn from these verses, *that we ought not only to receive knowledge, but to impart it to others.*

A candle is not lighted in order to be hidden and concealed, but to be set on a candlestick and used. Religious light is not given to a man for himself alone, but for the benefit of others. We are to try to spread and diffuse our knowledge. We are to display to others the precious treasure that we have fonnd, and persuade them to seek it for themselves. We are to tell them of the

* The passage now under consideration is one among many proofs that our Lord used the same words and the same ideas on many different occasions. The proverbial saying sbout the "candlestick under a bushel," will be found in the Sermon on the Mount. So also the saying, "there is nothing hid that shall not be manifested," —and the saying, "with what measure ye mete, it shall be measured to you again,"—are both to be found in the Gospel of St Matthew, but in both cases in an entirely different connection from the passage in St. Mark, now before us. (Matt. x. 26, and Matt. vii. 2.)

The subject is one that deserves attention. The needless difficulties that have been created by attempting to harmonize the Gospels, and to make out that our Lord never said the same thing more than once, are neither few nor small.

good news that we have heard, and endeavour to make them believe it, and value it themselves.

We shall all have to give account of our use of knowledge one day. The books of God in the day of judgment will show what we have done. If we have buried our talent in the earth,—if we have been content with a lazy, idle, do-nothing Christianity, and cared nothing what happened to others, so long as we went to heaven ourselves,—there will be a fearful exposure at last : "There is nothing hid, which shall not be manifested."

It becomes all Christians to lay these things to heart. It is high time that the old tradition, that the clergy alone ought to teach and spread religious knowledge, should be exploded and cast aside for ever. To do good and diffuse light is a duty for which all members of Christ's Church are responsible, whether ministers or laymen. Neighbours ought to tell neighbours, if they have found an unfailing remedy in time of plague. Christians ought to tell others that they have found medicine for their souls, if they see them ignorant, and dying for want of it. What saith the Apostle Peter ? "As every man hath received the gift, even so minister the same one to another." (1 Peter iv. 10.) They will be happy days for the Church when that text is obeyed.

We learn, in the second place, from these verses, *the importance of hearing, and of considering well what we hear.*

This is a point to which our Lord evidently attaches great weight. We have seen it already brought out in the parable of the sower. We see it here enforced in two remarkable expressions. " If any man have an ear to hear, let him hear."   " Take heed what ye hear." Hearing the truth is one principal avenue through which grace is conveyed to the soul of man. " Faith cometh by hearing."   (Rom. x. 17.)   One of the first steps towards conversion is to receive from the Spirit a hearing ear. Seldom. are men brought to repentance and faith in Christ without " hearing."   The general rule is that of which St. Paul reminds the Ephesians, " Ye also trusted, after that ye heard the word of truth."   (Eph. i. 13.)

Let us bear this in mind when we hear preaching decried as a means of grace. There are never wanting men who seek to cast it down from the high place which the Bible gives it. There are many who proclaim loudly that it is of far more importance to the soul to hear liturgical forms read, and to receive the Lord's Supper, than to hear God's Word expounded. Of all such notions let us beware. Let it be a settled principle with us that " hearing the Word " is one of the foremost means of grace that God has given to man. Let us give to every other means and ordinance its proper value and proportion. But never let us forget the words of St. Paul, " Despise not prophecyings ; " and his dying charge to Timothy, " Preach the Word." *   (1 Thess. v. 20 ; 2 Tim. iv. 2.)

* " Public and continual preaching of God's Word is the ordinary means and instrument of the salvation of mankind. St. Paul calleth it the ministry of reconciliation of man unto God. By preaching of God's Word, the glory of God is enlarged, faith is nourished, and charity increased. By it the ignorant is instructed, the negligent exhorted and invited, the stubborn rebuked, the weak conscience comforted, and to all those that sin of malicious wickedness, the wrath of God is threatened. By preaching, due obedience to Christian princes and magistrates is planted in the hearts of subjects : for obedience proceedeth of conscience, con-

We learn, in the last place, from these verses, *the importance of a diligent use of religious privileges.* What says our Lord ? " Unto you that hear shall more be given. He that hath, to him shall be given : and he that hath not, from him shall be taken even that which he hath."

This is a principle which we find continually brought forward in Scripture. All that believers have is undoubtedly of grace. Their repentance, faith, and holiness, all are the gift of God. But the degree to which a believer attains in grace, is ever set before us as closely connected with his own diligence in the use of means, and his own faithfulness in living fully up to the light and knowledge which he possesses. Indolence and laziness are always discouraged in God's Word. Labour and pains in hearing, reading, and prayer, are always represented as bringing their own reward. "The soul of the diligent shall be made fat." (Prov. xiii. 4.) "An idle soul shall suffer hunger." (Prov. xix. 15.)

Attention to this great principle is the main secret of spiritual prosperity. The man who makes rapid progress in spiritual attainments,—who grows visibly in grace, and knowledge, and strength, and usefulness,—will always be found to be a diligent man. He leaves no stone unturned to promote his soul's well-doing. He is diligent over his Bible, diligent in his private devotions, diligent as a hearer of sermons, diligent in his attendance at the Lord's table. And he reaps according as he sows. Just

science is grounded upon the Word of God, the Word of God worketh his effect by preaching. So as generally when preaching wanteth obedience faileth."—*Archbishop Grindal's Letter to Queen Elizabeth.*

as the muscles of the body are strengthened by regular exercise, so are the graces of the soul increased by diligence in using them.

Do we wish to grow in grace? Do we desire to have stronger faith, brighter hope, and clearer knowledge? Beyond doubt we do, if we are true Christians. Then let us live fully up to our light, and improve every opportunity. Let us never forget our Lord's words in this passage. "With what measure we mete" to our souls, "it shall be measured to us again." The more we do for our souls, the more shall we find God does for them.

MARK IV. 26—29.

26 And he said, So is the kingdom of God, as if a man should cast seed into the ground;
27 And should sleep, and rise night and day, and the seed should spring and grow up, he knoweth not how.
28 For the earth bringeth forth fruit of herself; first the blade, then the ear, after that the full corn in the ear.
29 But when the fruit is brought forth, immediately he putteth in the sickle, because the harvest is come.

THE parable contained in these verses is short, and only recorded in St. Mark's Gospel. But it is one that ought to be deeply interesting to all who have reason to hope that they are true Christians. It sets before us the history of the work of grace in an individual soul. It summons us to an examination of our own experience in divine things.

There are some expressions in the parable which we must not press too far. Such are the "sleeping and rising" of the husbandman, and the "night and day." In this, as in many of our Lord's parables, we must carefully keep in view the main scope and object of the whole story, and not lay too much stress on lesser points. In the case before us the main thing taught is the close resemblance between some familiar operations in the culture of corn, and the work of grace in the heart. To this let us rigidly confine our attention.

We are taught, firstly, that, as in the growth of corn, so in the work of grace, *there must be a sower.*

The earth, as we all know, never brings forth corn of itself. It is a mother of weeds, but not of wheat. The hand of man must plough it, and scatter the seed, or else there would never be a harvest.

The heart of man, in like manner, will never of itself turn to God, repent, believe, and obey. It is utterly barren of grace. It is entirely dead towards God, and unable to give itself spiritual life. The Son of man must break it up by His Spirit, and give it a new nature. He must scatter over it, by the hand of His labouring ministers, the good seed of the Word.

Let us mark this truth well. Grace in the heart of man is an exotic. It is a new principle from without, sent down from heaven and implanted in his soul. Left to himself, no man living would ever seek God. And yet in communicating grace, God ordinarily works by means. To despise the instrumentality of teachers and preachers, is to expect corn where no seed has been sown.

We are taught, secondly, that, as in the growth of corn, so in the work of grace, *there is much that is beyond man's comprehension and control.*

The wisest farmer on earth can never explain all that takes place in a grain of wheat, when he has sown it. He knows the broad fact that unless he puts it into the land, and covers it up, there will not be an ear of corn in time of harvest. But he cannot command the prosperity of each grain. He cannot explain why some grains come up and others die. He cannot specify the hour or the minute when life shall begin to show itself. He cannot define what that life is. These are matters he must leave alone. He sows his seed, and leaves the growth to God. "God giveth the increase."* (1 Cor. iii. 7.)

The workings of grace in the heart in like manner, are utterly mysterious and unsearchable. We cannot explain why the Word produces effects on one person in a congregation, and not upon another. We cannot explain why, in some cases,—with every possible advantage, and in spite of every entreaty,—people reject the Word, and continue dead in trespasses and sins. We cannot explain why in other cases,—with every possible difficulty, and with no encouragement,—people are born again, and become decided Christians. We cannot define the manner in which the Spirit of God conveys life to a soul, and the exact process by which a believer receives a new nature. All these are hidden things to us. We see certain results, but we can go no further. "The wind

* "A grain of corn, committed to the ground by the hand of man, will sprout and shoot; the shoot will disclose the stem, the stem the ear, and the ear the fruit: and were the most illiterate and unphilosophical person to be asked why all this should necessarily follow from the mere act of burying a seed in the earth, he might be disposed to laugh at the apparent simplicity of the question. Yet no human wisdom was ever able to return the answer to this question,—no human sagacity ever yet could penetrate into the true causes of this effect; and no human knowledge, upon such subjects, has ever gone further than the mere discovery, by a regular and constant experience, that such and such consequences will uniformly follow from such and such previous acts."—*Greswell on the Parables.* Vol. 2; p. 132.

bloweth where it listeth, and thou hearest the sound thereof, but canst not tell whence it cometh, and whither it goeth : so is every one that is born of the Spirit." (John iii. 10.)

Let us mark this truth also, for it is deeply instructive. It is humbling no doubt to ministers, and teachers of others. The highest abilities, the most powerful preaching, the most diligent working, cannot command success. God alone can give life. But it is a truth, at the same time, which supplies an admirable antidote to over-carefulness and despondency. Our principal work is to sow the seed. That done, we may wait with faith and patience for the result. "We may sleep, and rise night and day," and leave our work with the Lord. He alone can, and, if He thinks fit, He will give success.

We are taught, thirdly, that, as in the growth of corn, so in the work of grace, *life manifests itself gradually.*

There is a true proverb which says, "Nature does nothing at a bound." The ripe ear of wheat does not appear at once, as soon as the seed bursts forth into life. The plant goes through many stages, before it arrives at perfection : "first the blade, then the ear, then the full corn in the ear." But in all these stages one great thing is true about it,—even at its weakest, it is a living plant.

The work of grace, in like manner, goes on in the heart by degrees. The children of God are not born perfect in faith, or hope, or knowledge, or experience. Their beginning is generally a "day of small things." They see in part their own sinfulness, and Christ's fulness, and the beauty of holiness. But for all that, the weakest child in God's family is a true child of God. With all

his weakness and infirmity he is alive. The seed of
grace has really come up in his heart, though at present
it be only in the blade. He is "alive from the dead."
And the wise man says, " A living dog is better than a
dead lion." (Eccles. ix. 4.)

Let us mark this truth also, for it is full of consolation.
Let us not despise grace because it is weak, or think
people are not converted because they are not yet as
strong in the faith as St. Paul. Let us remember that
grace, like everything else, must have a beginning. The
mightiest oak was once an acorn. The strongest man
was once a babe. Better a thousand times have grace
in the blade than no grace at all.

We are taught, lastly, that, as in the growth of corn,
so in the work of grace, *there is no harvest until the seed
is ripe.*

No farmer thinks of cutting his wheat when it is
green. He waits till the sun, and rain, and heat, and
cold, have done their appointed work, and the golden
ears hang down. Then, and not till then, he puts in
the sickle, and gathers the wheat into his barn.

God deals with His work of grace exactly in the same
way. He never removes His people from this world till
they are ripe and ready. He never takes them away till
their work is done. They never die at the wrong time,
however mysterious their deaths appear sometimes to
man. Josiah, and James the brother of John, were both
cut off in the midst of usefulness. Our own King Edward
the Sixth was not allowed to reach man's estate. But
we shall see in the resurrection morning that there was a
needs-be. All was done well about their deaths, as well

as about their births. The Great Husbandman never
cuts His corn till it is ripe.

Let us leave the parable with this truth on our minds,
and take comfort about the death of every believer. Let
us rest satisfied, that there is no chance, no accident, no
mistake about the decease of any of God's children.
They are all "God's husbandry," and God knows best
when they are ready for the harvest.

MARK IV. 30—34.

30 And he said, Whereunto shall we liken the kingdom of God? or with what comparison shall we compare it?

31 *It is* like a grain of mustard seed, which, when it is sown in the earth, is less than all the seeds that be in the earth:

32 But when it is sown, it groweth up, and becometh greater than all herbs, and shooteth out great branches; so that the fowls of the air may lodge under the shadow of it.

33 And with many such parables spake he the word unto them, as they were able to hear *it*.

34 But without a parable spake he not unto them: and when they were alone, he expounded all things to his disciples.

THE parable of the mustard seed is one of those parables
which partake of the character both of history and
prophecy. It seems intended to illustrate the history of
Christ's visible Church on earth, from the time of the
first advent down to the judgment day. The seed cast
into the earth, in the preceding parable, showed us the
work of grace in a heart. The mustard seed shows us
the progress of professing Christianity in the world.

We learn, in the first place, that, like the grain of
mustard seed, *Christ's visible Church was to be small and
weak in its beginnings.*

A grain of mustard seed was a proverbial expression
among the Jews for something very small and insignifi-

cant. Our Lord calls it "less than all the seeds that
be in the earth." Twice in the Gospels we find our
Lord using the figure as a word of comparison, when
speaking of a weak faith. (Matt. xvii. 20 ; Luke xvii. 6.)
The idea was doubtless familiar to a Jewish mind, however strange it may sound to us. Here, as in other
places, the Son of God shows us the wisdom of using
language familiar to the minds of those whom we address.

It would be difficult to find an emblem which more
faithfully represents the history of the visible Church
of Christ than this grain of mustard seed.

Weakness and apparent insignificance were undoubtedly the characteristics of its beginning. How did its
Head and King come into the world ? He came as a
feeble infant, born in a manger at Bethlehem, without
riches, or armies, or attendants, or power.—Who were
the men that the Head of the Church gathered round
Himself, and appointed His Apostles ? They were poor
and unlearned persons,—fishermen, publicans, and men
of like occupations, to all appearance the most unlikely
people to shake the world.—What was the last public
act of the earthly ministry of the great Head of the
Church ? He was crucified, like a malefactor, between
two thieves, after having been forsaken by nearly all His
disciples, betrayed by one, and denied by another.—What
was the doctrine which the first builders of the Church
went forth from the upper chamber in Jerusalem to preach
to mankind ? It was a doctrine which to the Jews was
a stumbling-block, and to the Greeks foolishness. It
was a proclamation that the great Head of their new
religion had been put to death on a cross, and that

notwithstanding this, they offered life through His death to the world!—In all this the mind of man can perceive nothing but weakness and feebleness. Truly the emblem of the grain of mustard seed was verified and fulfilled to the very letter. To the eyes of man the beginning of the visible Church was contemptible, insignificant, powerless, and small.

We learn, in the second place, that, like the mustard seed, *the visible Church, once planted, was to grow and greatly increase.*

"The grain of mustard seed," says our Lord, "when it is sown, groweth up and becometh greater than all herbs." These words may sound startling to an English ear. We are not accustomed to such a growth in our cold northern climate. But to those who know eastern countries, there is nothing surprising in it. The testimony of well-informed and experienced travellers is distinct, that such an increase is both possible and probable.*

No figure could be chosen more strikingly applicable to the growth and increase of Christ's visible Church in the world. It began to grow from the day of Pentecost, and grew with a rapidity, which nothing can account for but the finger of God. It grew wonderfully when three

---

* To show the size to which the mustard plant will grow in eastern countries, Lightfoot quotes the following passages from Rabbinical writers. "There was a stalk of mustard in Sichim, from which sprang out three boughs, one of which was broken off, and covered the tent of a potter, and produced three cabs of mustard." Rabbi Simeon Ben Chalaphta said, "A stalk of mustard seed was in my field, into which I was wont to climb, as men are wont to climb into a fig-tree."

The enormous size to which the rhododendron, the heath, and the fern will grow, in some climates which suit them better than ours, should be remembered by an English reader of this parable.

thousand souls, were converted at once, and five thousand more in a few days afterwards. It grew wonderfully, when at Antioch, and Ephesus, and Philippi, and Corinth, and Rome, congregations were gathered together, and Christianity firmly established. It grew wonderfully, when at last the despised religion of Christ overspread the greater part of Europe, and Asia Minor, and North Africa, and, in spite of fierce persecution and opposition, supplanted heathen idolatry, and became the professed creed of the whole Roman empire. Such growth must have been marvellous in the eyes of many. But it was only what our Lord foretold in the parable before us. "The kingdom of God is like a grain of mustard seed."

The visible Church of Christ has not yet done growing. Notwithstanding the melancholy apostacy of some of its branches, and the deplorable weakness of others, it is still extending and expanding over the world. New branches have continually been springing up in America, in India, in Australia, in Africa, in China, in the Islands of the South Seas, during the last fifty years. Evils undoubtedly there are many. False profession and corruption abound. But still, on the whole, heathenism is waning, wearing out, and melting away. In spite of all the predictions of Voltaire and Payne, in spite of foes without and treachery within, the visible Church progresses,—the mustard plant still grows.

And the prophecy, we may rest assured, is not yet exhausted. A day shall yet come, when the great Head of the Church shall take to Himself His power, and reign, and put down every enemy under His feet. The earth shall yet be filled with the knowledge of God, as the waters cover the sea. (Isa. ii. 2.) Satan shall yet be bound. The heathen shall yet be our Lord's inheritance, and the utmost parts of the earth His possession. And then this parable shall receive its full accomplishment. The little seed shall become " a great tree," and fill the whole earth. (Dan. iii. 35.)

Let us leave the parable with a resolution never to despise any movement or instrumentality in the Church of Christ, because at first it is weak and small. Let us remember the manger of Bethlehem, and learn wisdom. The name of Him who lay there, a helpless infant, is now known all over the globe. The little seed which was planted in the day when Jesus was born, has become a great tree, and we ourselves are rejoicing under its shadow. Let it be a settled principle in our religion, never to "despise the day of small things." (Zech. iv. 10.) One child may be the beginning of a flourishing school, —one conversion, the beginning of a mighty Church,— one word, the beginning of some blessed Christian enterprise,—one seed, the beginning of a rich harvest of saved souls.*

---

* It is fair to say that the view which I have adopted of the meaning of this parable, is not the view which is held by some interpreters.

Some think that the parable, is intended to show the progress of the work of grace in the heart of an individual believer. I am not prepared to say that this may not have been in our Lord's mind, in speaking the parable. I think it quite possible that the parable admits of a double interpretation; for the experience of a believer and the experience of the whole Church are much the same. My principal objection to this view is, that it does not appear to suit the language of the parable so well as that which I have maintained.

Some few interpreters think that the mustard seed signifies the principle of evil and corruption, and that the main object of the

MARK IV. 35—41.

35 And the same day, when the even was come, he saith unto them, Let us pass over unto the other side.

36 And when they had sent away the multitude, they took him even as he was in the ship. And there were also with him other little ships.

37 And there arose a great storm of wind, and the waves beat into the ship, so that it was now full.

38 And he was in the hinder part of the ship, asleep on a pillow; and they awake him, and say unto him,

Master, carest thou not that we perish?

39 And he arose, and rebuked the wind, and said unto the sea, Peace, be still. And the wind ceased, and there was a great calm.

40 And he said unto them, Why are ye so fearful? how is it that ye have no faith?

41 And they feared exceedingly, and said one to another, What manner of man is this, that even the wind and the sea obey him?

THESE verses describe a storm on the Sea of Galilee, when our Lord and His disciples were crossing it, and a miracle performed by our Lord in calming the storm in a moment. Few miracles recorded in the Gospel were so likely to strike the minds of the disciples as this. Four of them at least were fishermen. Peter, Andrew, James, and John, had probably known the Sea of Galilee, and its storms, from their youth. Few events in our Lord's

parable is to show how insidiously apostacy would begin in the Church, and how completely it would at last overgrow and fill the whole body. I own that I cannot for a moment see the soundness of this interpretation. To say nothing of other reasons, there seems an excessive harshness in this sense, when we consider the opening words of the parable, "Wherewith shall we liken the kingdom of God?" One would rather expect the question to have been, "Wherewith shall we liken the kingdom of the devil?" if the whole parable is occupied with describing the progress of evil.

I confess that I think the meaning of "the fowls of the air," is a point which admits of some question. Many think that it signifies the number of converts to Christianity, who, as the Church increased, joined themselves to it, and came "as doves to the windows." (Isaiah lx. 8.) Some think that it signifies the number of worldly and false professors who joined the Church from mere carnal motives, when it began to be great and prosperous, as in the days of Constantine. When we remember that the "fowls of the air," in the parable of the sower (Mark iv. 4—15), are declared by our Lord Himself to mean "Satan," we must admit that there is considerable force in this interpretation.

journeyings to and fro upon earth, contain more rich instruction than the one related in this passage.

Let us learn, in the first place, *that Christ's service does not exempt His servants from storms.* Here were the twelve disciples in the path of duty. They were obediently following Jesus, wherever He went. They were daily attending on His ministry, and hearkening to His word. They were daily testifying to the world, that, whatever Scribes and Pharisees might think, they believed on Jesus, loved Jesus, and were not ashamed to give up all for His sake. Yet here we see these men in trouble, tossed up and down by a tempest, and in danger of being drowned.

Let us mark well this lesson. If we are true Christians, we must not expect everything smooth in our journey to heaven. We must count it no strange thing, if we have to endure sicknesses, losses, bereavements, and disappointments, just like other men. Free pardon and full forgiveness, grace by the way, and glory at the end,—all this our Saviour has promised to give. But He has never promised that we shall have no afflictions. He loves us too well to promise that. By affliction He teaches us many precious lessons, which without it we should never learn. By affliction He shows us our emptiness and weakness, draws us to the throne of grace, purifies our affections, weans us from the world, makes us long for heaven. In the resurrection morning we shall all say, "It is good for me that I was afflicted." We shall thank God for every storm.

Let us learn, in the second place, *that our Lord Jesus Christ was really and truly man.* We are told in these

verses, that when the storm began, and the waves beat
over the ship, he was in the hinder part "asleep." He
had a body exactly like our own,—a body that could
hunger, and thirst, and feel pain, and be weary, and
need rest. No wonder that His body needed repose at
this time. He had been diligent in His Father's business
all the day. He had been preaching to a great multitude in the open air. No wonder that "when the even
was come," and His work finished, He fell "asleep."

Let us mark this lesson also attentively. The Saviour
in whom we are bid to trust, is as really man as He is
God. He knows the trials of a man, for He has experienced them. He knows the bodily infirmities of a
man, for He has felt them. He can well understand
what we mean, when we cry to Him for help in this
world of need. He is just the very Saviour that men
and women, with weary frames and aching heads, in a
weary world, require for their comfort every morning
and night. "We have not an high priest which cannot be touched with the feeling of our infirmities."
(Heb. iv. 15.)

Let us learn, in the third place, *that our Lord Jesus
Christ as God, has almighty power.* We see Him in
these verses doing that which is proverbially impossible.
He speaks to the winds, and they obey Him. He speaks
to the waves, and they submit to His command. He
turns the raging storm into a calm with a few words,—
"Peace, be still." Those words were the words of Him
who first created all things. The elements knew the
voice of their Master, and like obedient servants, were
quiet at once.

Let us mark this lesson also, and lay it up in our minds. With the Lord Jesus Christ nothing is impossible. No stormy passions are so strong but He can tame them. No temper is so rough and violent but He can change it. No conscience is so disquieted, but He can speak peace to it, and make it calm. No man ever need despair, if he will only bow down his pride, and come as a humbled sinner to Christ. Christ can do miracles upon his heart.—No man ever need despair of reaching his journey's end, if he has once committed his soul to Christ's keeping. Christ will carry him through every danger. Christ will make him conqueror over every foe.—What though our relations oppose us? What though our neighbours laugh us to scorn? What though our place be hard? What though our temptations be great? It is all nothing, if Christ is on our side, and we are in the ship with Him. Greater is He that is for us, than all they that are against us.

Finally, we learn from this passage, *that our Lord Jesus Christ is exceedingly patient and pitiful in dealing with His own people.* We see the disciples on this occasion showing great want of faith, and giving way to most unseemly fears. They forgot their Master's miracles and care for them in days gone by. They thought of nothing but their present peril. They awoke our Lord hastily, and cried, "Carest thou not that we perish?" We see our Lord dealing most gently and tenderly with them. He gives them no sharp reproof. He makes no threat of casting them off, because of their unbelief. He

simply asks the touching question, " Why are ye so fearful ?   How is it that ye have no faith ? "

Let us mark well this lesson. The Lord Jesus is very
pitiful and of tender mercy.   " As a father pitieth his
children, even so the Lord pitieth them that fear Him."
(Psalm ciii. 13.)   He does not deal with believers
according to their sins, nor reward them according to
their iniquities. He sees their weakness. He is aware
of their short-comings. He knows all the defects of
their faith, and hope, and love, and courage. And yet
He will not cast them off. He bears v.ith them continually. He loves them even to the end. He raises
them when they fall. He restores them when they err.
His patience, like His love, is a patience that passeth
knowledge. When he sees a heart right, it is His
glory to pass over many a short-coming.

Let us leave these verses with the comfortable recollection that Jesus is not changed. His heart is still the
same that it was when He crossed the sea of Galilee
and stilled the storm. High in heaven at the right hand
of God, Jesus is still sympathizing,—still almighty,—
still pitiful and patient towards His people.—Let us be
more charitable and patient towards our brethren in the
faith. They may err in many things, but if Jesus has
received them and can bear with them, surely we may
bear with them too.—Let us be more hopeful about ourselves. We may be very weak, and frail, and unstable ;
but if we can truly say that we do come to Christ and
believe on Him, we may take comfort. The question
for conscience to answer is not, "Are we like the angels ?

are we perfect as we shall be in heaven?" The question is, "Are we real and true in our approaches to Christ? Do we truly repent and believe?" *

MARK V. 1—17.

1 And they came over unto the other side of the sea, into the country of the Gadarenes.

2 And when he was come out of the ship, immediately there met him out of the tombs a man with an unclean spirit,

3 Who had *his* dwelling among the tombs; and no man could bind him, no, not with chains:

4 Because that he had been often bound with fetters and chains, and the chains had been plucked asunder by him, and the fetters broken in pieces: neither could any *man* tame him.

5 And always, night and day, he was in the mountains, and in the tombs, crying, and cutting himself with stones.

6 But when he saw Jesus afar off, he ran and worshipped him.

7 And cried with a loud voice, and said, What have I to do with thee, Jesus, *thou* Son of the most high God? I adjure thee by God, that thou torment me not.

8 For he said unto him, Come out of the man, *thou* unclean spirit.

9 And he asked him, What *is* thy name? And he answered, saying, My name *is* Legion: for we are many.

10 And he besought him much that he would not send them away out of the country.

11 Now there was there nigh unto the mountains a great herd of swine feeding.

12 And all the devils besought him, saying, Send us into the swine, that we may enter into them.

13 And forthwith Jesus gave them leave. And the unclean spirits went out, and entered into the swine: and the herd ran violently down a steep place into the sea, (they were about two thousand;) and were choked in the sea.

14 And they that fed the swine fled, and told *it* in the city, and in the country. And they went out to see what it was that was done.

15 And they come to Jesus, and see him that was possessed with the devil, and had the legion, sitting, and clothed, and in his right mind: and they were afraid.

16 And they that saw *it* told them how it befell to him that was possessed with the devil, and *also* concerning the swine.

17 And they began to pray him to depart out of their coasts.

THESE verses describe one of those mysterious miracles which the Gospels frequently record,—the casting out of a devil. Of all the cases of this kind in the New

---

* The Sea of Galilee, or Tiberias, on which the circumstances recorded in this passage took place, is an inland lake, through which the river Jordan flows, about fifteen miles long and six broad. It lies in a deep valley, much depressed below the level of the sea,— its surface being 652 feet below that of the Mediterranean,—and is surrounded on most sides by steep hills. Owing to these last circumstances, sudden squalls or storms are reported by all travellers to be very common on the lake.

The Sea of Galilee and the country surrounding it, were favoured

Testament, none is so fully described as this one. Of all the three Evangelists who relate the history, none give it so fully and minutely as St. Mark.

We see, in the first place, in these verses, *that the possession of a man's body by the devil, was a real and true thing in the time of our Lord's earthly ministry.*

It is a painful fact, that there are never wanting professing Christians who try to explain away our Lord's miracles. They endeavour to account for them by natural causes, and to show that they were not worked by any extraordinary power. Of all miracles, there are none which they assault so strenuously as the casting out of devils. They do not scruple to deny Satanic possession entirely. They tell us that it was nothing more than lunacy, or frenzy, or epilepsy, and that the idea of the devil inhabiting a man's body is absurd.

The best and simplest answer to such sceptical objections, is a reference to the plain narratives of the

with more of our blessed Lord's presence, during His earthly ministry, than any other part of Palestine. Capernaum, Tiberias, Bethsaida, and the country of the Gergesenes were all on its shores, or in the immediate neighbourhood of this lake. It was on the Sea of Galilee that our Lord walked. It was on its shore that He appeared to His disciples after His resurrection. Sitting in a boat on its waters, and in a house hard by, He delivered the seven parables recorded in the 13th chapter of St. Matthew. On its banks, He called Peter, and Andrew, James and John. From it, He commanded His disciples to draw the miraculous draught of fishes. Within sight of it, He twice fed the multitude with a few loaves and fishes. On its shore, He healed the man possessed with devils ; and into it the two thousand swine plunged headlong after that miracle had been wrought.

Few localities in the Holy Land were so immediately connected with our Lord's ministry as the Sea of Galilee and the country round it.

Gospels, and especially to the one before us at this moment. The facts here detailed are utterly inexplicable, if we do not believe Satanic possession. It is notorious that lunacy, and frenzy, and epilepsy are not infectious complaints, and at any rate cannot be communicated to a herd of swine! And yet men ask us to believe, that as soon as this man was healed, two thousand swine ran violently down a steep place into the sea, from a sudden impulse, without any apparent cause to account for their so doing! Such reasoning is the height of credulity. When men can satisfy themselves with such explanations, they are in a pitiable state of mind.

Let us beware of a sceptical and incredulous spirit in all matters relating to the devil. No doubt there is much in the subject of Satanic possession which we do not understand, and cannot explain. But let us not therefore refuse to believe it. The Eastern King who would not believe in the possibility of ice, because he lived in a hot country, and had never seen it, was not more foolish than the man who refuses to believe in Satanic possession, because he never saw a case himself, and cannot understand it. We may be sure, that upon the subject of the devil and his power, we are far more likely to believe too little than too much. Unbelief about the existence and personality of Satan, has often proved the first step to unbelief about God.

We see, in the second place, in these verses, *what an awfully cruel, powerful, and malicious being Satan is.* On all these three points, the passage before us is full of instruction.

The *cruelty* of Satan appears in the miserable condition of the unhappy man, of whose body he had possession. We read that he dwelt "among the tombs,"—that "no man could bind him, no, not with chains,"—that no man could "tame him,"—and that he was "always night and day in the mountains, and in the tombs, crying, and cutting himself with stones," naked, and without clothing. Such is the state to which the devil would bring us all, if he only had the power. He would rejoice to inflict upon us the utmost misery, both of body and mind. Cases like this are faint types of the miseries of hell.

The *power* of Satan appears in the awful words which the unclean spirit used, when our Lord asked, "What is thy name?" He answered, saying, "My name is Legion: for we are many." We probably have not the faintest idea of the number, subtlety, and activity of Satan's agents. We forget that he is King over an enormous host of subordinate spirits who do his will. We should probably find, if our eyes were opened to see spirits, that they are about our path, and about our bed, and observing all our ways, to an extent of which we have no conception. In private and in public, in church and in the world, there are busy enemies ever near us, of whose presence we are not aware.

The *malice* of Satan appears in the strange petition, "Send us into the swine." Cast forth from the man, whose body they had so long inhabited and possessed, they still thirsted to do mischief. Unable to injure any more an immortal soul, they desired leave to injure the dumb beasts which were feeding near. Such is the true character of Satan. It is the bent of his nature to do harm, to kill, and to destroy. No wonder that he is called Apollyon, the destroyer.

Let us beware of giving way to the senseless habit of jesting about the devil. It is a habit which furnishes awful evidence of the blindness and corruption of human nature, and one which is far too common. When it is seemly in the condemned criminal to jest about his executioner, then, and not till then, it will be seemly for mortal man to talk lightly about Satan. Well would it be for us all if we strove more to realize the power and presence of our great spiritual enemy, and prayed more to be delivered from him. It was a true saying of an eminent Christian, now gone to rest, "No prayer is complete which does not contain a petition to be kept from the devil."

We see, in the last place, from these verses, *how complete is our Lord's power and authority over the devil.* We see it in the cry of the unclean spirit, " I adjure Thee by God, that Thou torment me not." We see it in the command, " Come out of the man, thou unclean spirit," and the immediate obedience that followed. We see it in the blessed change that at once took place in him that was possessed : he was found " sitting, and clothed, and in his right mind." We see it in the petition of all the devils,—" Send us into the swine," confessing their consciousness that they could do nothing without leave. All these things show that one mightier than Satan was there. Strong as the great enemy of man was, he was in the presence of One stronger than he. Numerous as his hosts were, he was confronted with One who could command more than twelve legions of angels.

"Where the word of the King is, there is power."
(Eccles. viii. 4.)

The truth here taught is full of strong consolation for
all true Christians. We live in a world full of difficulties and snares. We are ourselves weak and compassed
with infirmity. The awful thought that we have a
mighty spiritual enemy ever near us, subtle, powerful,
and malicious as Satan is, might well disquiet us, and
cast us down. But, thanks be unto God, we have in
Jesus an almighty Friend, who is "able to save us to
the uttermost." He has already triumphed over Satan
on the cross. He will ever triumph over him in the
hearts of all believers, and intercede for them that their
faith fail not. And He will finally triumph over Satan
completely, when He shall come forth at the second
advent, and bind him in the bottomless pit.

And now, are we ourselves delivered from Satan's
power? This, after all, is the grand question that concerns our souls. He still reigns and rules in the hearts of
all who are children of disobedience. (Ephes. ii. 3.) He
is still a King over the ungodly. Have we, by grace,
broken his bonds, and escaped his hand? Have we really
renounced him and all his works? Do we daily resist him
and make him flee? Do we put on the whole armour
of God and stand against his wiles? May we never rest
till we can give satisfactory answers to these questions.*

---

* The whole subject of the demoniacs, or cases of Satanic possession recorded in the New Testament, is unquestionably full of deep
mystery. The miserable sufferings of the unhappy people possessed,
—their clear knowledge that our Lord was the Son of God,—their
double consciousness, sometimes the spirit speaking, sometimes the
man,—all these are deep mysteries. And it can hardly be otherwise.

MARK V. 18—20.

18 And when he was come into the ship, he that had been possessed with the devil prayed him that he might be with him.

19 Howbeit Jesus suffered him not, but saith unto him, Go home to thy friends, and tell them how great things the Lord hath done for thee, and hath had compassion on thee.

20 And he departed, and began to publish in Decapolis how great things Jesus had done for him: and all *men* did marvel.

The after-conduct of those whom our Lord Jesus Christ healed and cured when upon earth, is a thing which is not often related in the Gospels. The story often describes the miraculous cure, and then leaves the after history of the person cured in obscurity, and passes on to other things.

But there are some deeply interesting cases, in which the after-conduct of persons cured is described; and the

We know little of beings that we cannot see and touch. We know nothing of the manner in which a spirit operates on the mind of a creature with flesh and bones like ourselves. We can see plainly that there were many persons possessed with devils during our Lord's earthly ministry. We can see plainly that bodily possession was something distinct from possession of heart and soul. We can conjecture the reason of their permitted possession,—to make it plain that our Lord came to destroy the works of the devil. But we must stop here. We can go no further.

Let us, however, beware of supposing that Satanic possession was entirely confined to our Lord's time, and that there is no such thing in our own days. This would be a rash and unwarrantable conclusion. Awful as the thought is, there are sometimes cases in asylums for the insane, which, if they are not cases of Satanic possession, approach as nearly to it as possible.—In short, I believe the opinion of not a few eminent physicians is clear and decided that Satanic possession still continues, though cases are exceedingly rare.

Of course it would be presumption to handle so fearful a doctrine lightly, and to pronounce positively of any particular person that "he had a devil." But if such things have been,—and the New Testament puts this beyond question,—no good reason can be assigned why they should not be again. Human nature is not changed since our Lord was on earth. Satan is not yet bound. Satanic possession is therefore neither impossible nor improbable, though limits may be set to the frequency of it, through the mercy of God.

man from whom the devil was cast out in the country of the Gadarenes is one. The verses before us tell the story. Few as they are, they are full of precious instruction.

We learn from these verses, that *the Lord Jesus knows better than His people, what is the right position for them to be in.* We are told that when our Lord was on the point of leaving the country of the Gadarenes, the man "that had been possessed with the devil, prayed Him that he might be with Him." We can well understand that request. He felt grateful for the blessed change that had taken place in himself. He felt full of love towards his Deliverer. He thought he could not do better than follow our Lord, and go with Him as His companion and disciple. He was ready to give up home and country, and go after Christ. And yet, strange as it appears at first sight, the request was refused. "Jesus suffered him not." Our Lord had other work for him to do. Our Lord saw better than he did in what way he could glorify God most. "Go home to thy friends," He says, "and tell them how great things the Lord hath done for thee, and hath had compassion on thee."

There are lessons of profound wisdom in these words. The place that Christians wish to be in, is not always the place which is best for their souls. The position that they would choose, if they could have their own way, is not always that which Jesus would have them occupy.

There are none who need this lesson so much as believers newly converted to God. Such persons are often very poor judges of what is really for their good. Full of the new views which they have been graciously taught, excited with the novelty of their present position, seeing everything around them in a new light, knowing little yet of the depths of Satan and the weakness of their own hearts,—knowing only that a little time ago they were blind, and now, through mercy, they see,—of all people they are in the greatest danger of making mistakes. With the best intentions, they are apt to fall into mistakes about their plans in life, their choices, their moves, their professions. They forget that what we like best is not always best for our souls, and that the seed of grace needs winter as well as summer, cold as well as heat, to ripen it for glory.

Let us pray that God would guide us in all our ways after conversion, and not allow us to err in our choices, or to make hasty decisions. That place and position is most healthful for us in which we are kept most humble, —most taught our own sinfulness,—drawn most to the Bible and prayer,—led most to live by faith and not by sight. It may not be quite what we like. But if Christ by His providence has placed us in it, let us not be in a hurry to leave it. Let us therein abide with God. The great thing is to have no will of our own, and to be where Jesus would have us be.*

---

* I cannot help remarking, in connection with our Lord's words in this passage, that it admits of question, whether men do not *sometimes* act unadvisedly in giving up a secular calling, in order to enter the ministry of the Gospel. In plain words, I doubt whether men, who have been suddenly converted to God in the army, the navy, the law, or the merchant's office, do not *sometimes* forsake their professions with undue precipitation, in order to become clergymen.

It seems to be forgotten that conversion alone is no proof that we are called and qualified to become teachers of others. God may be glorified as really and truly in the secular calling as in the pulpit. Converted men can be eminently useful as landlords, magistrates, soldiers, sailors, barristers, or merchants. We want witnesses for

We learn, for another thing, from these verses, that *a believer's own home has the first claims on his attention.* We are taught that in the striking words which our Lord addresses to the man who had been possessed with the devil. "Go home," He says, "to thy friends, and tell them how great things the Lord hath done for thee." The friends of this man had probably not seen him for some years, excepting under the influence of Satan. Most likely he had been as one dead to them, or worse than dead, and a constant cause of trouble, anxiety, and sorrow. Here then was the path of duty. Here was the way by which he could most glorify God. Let him go home and tell his friends what Jesus had done for him. Let him be a living witness before their eyes of the compassion of Christ. Let him deny himself the pleasure of being in Christ's bodily presence, in order to do the higher work of being useful to others.

Christ in all these professions. Colonel Gardiner and Capt. Vicars have probably done more for the cause of Christ, as military men, than they would ever have done if they had left the army and become clergymen.

In steering our course through life, we should carefully look for the call of *providence* as well as the call of *inclination.* The position that we choose for ourselves is often that which is the worst for our souls. When two conflicting paths of duty lie before a believer, the path which has least of the cross, and is most agreeable to his own taste, is seldom the right one.

I write all this with a due recollection of many eminent Christians who began in a secular profession, and left it for the office of the minister. John Newton and Edward Bickersteth are instances. But I apprehend such cases are exceptions. I apprehend moreover that in every such case there would be found to have been a remarkable call of *providence* as well as an inward call of the Holy Ghost. As a general rule, I believe that the rule of St. Paul ought to be carefully observed: "Let every man, wherein he is called, therein abide with God." (1 Cor. vii. 24.)

How much there is in these simple words of our Lord! What thoughts they ought to stir up in the hearts of all true Christians!—" Go home and tell thy friends." Home is the place above all others where the child of God ought to make his first endeavours to do good. Home is the place where he is most continually seen, and where the reality of his grace ought most truly to appear. Home is the place where his best affections ought to be concentrated. Home is the place where he should strive daily to be a witness for Christ. Home is the place where he was daily doing harm by his example, so long as he served the world. Home is the place where he is specially bound to be a living epistle of Christ, so soon as he has been mercifully taught to serve God. May we all remember these things daily! May it never be said of us, that we are saints abroad, but wicked by our own fireside,—talkers about religion abroad, but worldly and ungodly at home!

But, after all, have we anything to tell others? Can we testify to any work of grace in our hearts? Have we experienced any deliverance from the power of the world, the flesh, and the devil? Have we ever tasted the graciousness of Christ? These are indeed serious questions. If we have never yet been born again, and made new creatures, we can, of course, have nothing to " tell."

If we have anything to tell others about Christ, let us resolve to tell it. Let us not be silent if we have found peace and rest in the Gospel. Let us speak to our relations, and friends, and families, and neighbours, according as we have opportunity, and tell them what the Lord has done for our souls. All are not called to be ministers. All are not intended to preach. But all can walk in the

H

steps of the man of whom we have been reading, and
in the steps of Andrew, and Philip, and the Samaritan
woman. (John i. 41, 45 ; iv. 29.) Happy is he who is
not ashamed to say to others, "Come and hear what the
Lord hath done for my soul." (Psa. lxvi. 16.)

MARK V. 21—34.

21 And when Jesus was passed over again by ship unto the other side, much people gathered unto him : and he was nigh unto the sea.

22 And, behold, there cometh one of the rulers of the synagogue, Jairus by name ; and when he saw him, he fell at his feet,

23 And besought him greatly, saying, My little daughter lieth at the point of death : *I pray thee*, come and lay thy hands on her, that she may be healed ; and she shall live.

24 And *Jesus* went with him ; and much people followed him, and thronged him.

25 And a certain woman, which had an issue of blood twelve years,

26 And had suffered many things of many physicians, and had spent all that she had, and was nothing bettered, but rather grew worse,

27 When she had heard of Jesus, came in the press behind, and touched his garment.

28 For she said, If I may touch but his clothes, I shall be whole.

29 And straightway the fountain of her blood was dried up ; and she felt in her body that she was healed of that plague.

30 And Jesus, immediately knowing in himself that virtue had gone out of him, turned him about in the press, and said, Who touched my clothes ?

31 And his disciples said unto him, Thou seest the multitude thronging thee, and sayest thou, Who touched me ?

32 And he looked round about to see her that had done this thing.

33 But the woman fearing and trembling, knowing what was done in her, came and fell down before him, and told him all the truth.

34 And he said unto her, Daughter, thy faith hath made thee whole ; go in peace, and be whole of thy plague.

THE main subject of these verses is the miraculous
healing of a sick woman. Great is our Lord's experience
in cases of disease ! Great is His sympathy with His
sick and ailing members ! The gods of the heathen are
generally represented as terrible and mighty in battle,
delighting in bloodshed, the strong man's patrons, and
the warrior's friends. The Saviour of the Christian is
always set before us as gentle, and easy to be entreated,
the healer of the broken-hearted, the refuge of the weak
and helpless, the comforter of the distressed, the sick

man's best friend. And is not this just the Saviour that human nature needs? The world is full of pain and trouble. The weak on earth are far more numerous than the strong.

Let us mark, in these verses, *what misery sin has brought into the world*. We read of one who had had a most painful disease "for twelve years." She had "suffered many things of many physicians, and had spent all that she had, and was nothing bettered, but rather grew worse." Means of every kind had been tried in vain. Medical skill had proved unable to cure. Twelve long weary years had been spent in battling with disease, and relief seemed no nearer than at first. "Hope deferred" might well "make her heart sick." (Proverbs xiii. 12.)

How marvellous it is that we do not hate sin more than we do! Sin is the cause of all the pain and disease in the world. God did not create man to be an ailing and suffering creature. It was sin, and nothing but sin, which brought in all the ills that flesh is heir to. It was sin to which we owe every racking pain, and every loathsome infirmity, and every humbling weakness to which our poor bodies are liable. Let us keep this ever in mind. Let us hate sin with a godly hatred.

Let us mark, in the second place, *how different are the feelings with which people draw near to Christ*. We are told, in these verses, that "much people followed" our Lord, "and thronged Him." But we are only told of one person who "came in the press behind," and touched Him with faith, and was healed. Many followed Jesus from curiosity, and derived no benefit from Him.

One, and only one, followed under a deep sense of her need, and of our Saviour's power to relieve her, and that one received a mighty blessing.

We see the same thing going on continually in the Church of Christ at the present day.   Multitudes go to our places of worship, and fill our pews.   Hundreds come up to the Lord's table, and receive the bread and wine. But of all these worshippers and communicants how few really obtain anything from Christ!   Fashion, custom, form, habit, the love of excitement, or an itching ear, are the true motives of the vast majority.   There are but a few here and there who touch Christ by faith, and go home "in peace."   These may seem hard sayings. But they are unhappily too true!

Let us mark, in the third place, *how immediate and instantaneous was the cure which this woman received.* No sooner did she touch our Lord's clothes than she was healed.   The thing that she had sought in vain for twelve years, was done in a moment.   The cure that many physicians could not effect, was wrought in an instant of time.   She felt in her body that she was healed of that plague.

We need not doubt that we are meant to see here an emblem of the relief that the Gospel confers on souls. The experience of many a weary conscience has been exactly like that of this woman with her disease.   Many a man has spent sorrowful years in search of peace with God, and failed to find it.   He has gone to earthly remedies, and obtained no relief.   He has wearied himself in going from place to place, and church to church, and has felt after all "nothing bettered, but rather worse."   But

at last he has found rest.—And where has he found it?—
He has found it where this woman found hers, in Jesus
Christ. He has ceased from his own works. He has
given over looking to his own endeavours and doings for
relief. He has come to Christ Himself, as a humble
sinner, and committed himself to His mercy. At once
the burden has fallen from off his shoulders. Heaviness
is turned to joy, and anxiety to peace.—One touch of
real faith can do more for the soul than a hundred
self-imposed austerities. One look at Jesus is more effi-
cacious than years of sack-cloth and ashes. May we
never forget this to our dying day! Personal application
to Christ is the real secret of peace with God.

Let us mark, in the fourth place, *how much it becomes
Christians to confess before men the benefits they receive from
Christ.* We see that this woman was not allowed to
go home, when cured, without her cure being noticed.
Our Lord inquired who had touched Him, and "looked
round about to see her that had done this thing." No
doubt He knew perfectly the name and history of the
woman. He needed not that any should tell Him. But
He desired to teach her, and all around Him, that healed
souls should make public acknowledgment of mercies
received.

There is a lesson here which all true Christians
would do well to remember. We are not to be ashamed
to confess Christ before men, and to let others know
what He has done for our souls. If we have found
peace through His blood, and been renewed by His
Spirit, we must not shrink from avowing it on every
proper occasion. It is not necessary to blow a trumpet

in the streets, and force our experience on every body's notice. All that is required is a willingness to acknowledge Christ as our Master, without flinching from the ridicule or persecution, which by so doing we may bring on ourselves. More than this is not required; but less than this ought not to content us. If we are ashamed of Jesus before men, He will one day be ashamed of us before His Father and the angels.

Let us mark, in the last place, *how precious a grace is faith.* " Daughter," says our Lord to the woman who was healed, " thy faith hath made thee whole : go in peace."

Of all the Christian graces, none is so frequently mentioned in the New Testament as faith, and none is so highly commended.—No grace brings such glory to Christ. Hope brings an eager expectation of good things to come. Love brings a warm and willing heart. Faith brings an empty hand, receives everything, and can give nothing in return.—No grace is so important to the Christian's own soul. By faith we begin. By faith we live. By faith we stand. We walk by faith and not by sight. By faith we overcome. By faith we have peace. By faith we enter into rest.—No grace should be the subject of so much self-inquiry. We should often ask ourselves, Do I really believe ? Is my faith true, genuine, and the gift of God ?

May we never rest till we can give a satisfactory answer to these questions ! Christ is not changed since the day when this woman was healed. He is still gracious and still mighty to save. There is but one thing needful if we want salvation. That one thing is the hand of faith.   Let a man only "touch" Jesus, and he shall be made whole. *

MARK V. 35—43.

35 While he yet spake, there came from the ruler of the synagogue's *house certain* which said, Thy daughter is dead : why troublest thou the Master any further ?

36 As soon as Jesus heard the word that was spoken, he saith unto the ruler of the synagogue, Be not afraid, only believe.

37 And he suffered no man to follow him, save Peter, and James, and John the brother of James.

38 And he cometh to the house of the ruler of the synagogue, and seeth the tumult, and them that wept and wailed greatly.

39 And when he was come in, he saith unto them, Why make ye this ado, and weep ? the damsel is not dead, but sleepeth.

40 And they laughed him to scorn. But when he had put them all out, he taketh the father and the mother of the damsel, and them that were with him, and entereth in where the damsel was lying.

41 And he took the damsel by the hand, and said unto her, Talitha cumi : which is, being interpreted, Damsel, I say unto thee, arise.

42 And straightway the damsel arose, and walked ; for she was *of the age* of twelve years   And they were astonished with a great astonishment.

43 And he charged them straitly that no man should know it ; and commanded that something should be given her to eat.

A GREAT miracle is recorded in these verses.   A dead girl is restored to life.   Mighty as the "King of terrors" is, there is One mightier than he.   The keys of death are in our Lord Jesus Christ's hands.   He will one day "swallow up death in victory."   (Isaiah xxv. 8.)

Let us learn from these verses, that *rank places no*

---

* Some remarks of Melancthon's on this woman's case are worth reading.   We are doubtless to be careful that we do not hastily attach an allegorical and mystical sense to the words of Scripture. Yet we must not forget the depth of meaning which lies in all the acts of our Lord's earthly ministry ; and at any rate there is much beauty in the thought which the good Reformer expresses.   He says, "This woman doth aptly represent the Jewish synagogue vexed a long time with many mischiefs and miseries, especially tortured with unconscionable princes, and unskilful priests, or physicians of the soul, the Pharisees and Sadducees, on whom she had wasted all her goods ; and yet she was not a whit better, but rather much worse, till the blessed Lord of Israel in His own person came to 'visit and redeem her.'"

man beyond the reach of sorrow. Jairus was a "ruler;" yet sickness and trouble came to his house. Jairus probably had wealth, and all the medical help that wealth can command; yet money could not keep death away from his child. The daughters of rulers are liable to sickness as well as the daughters of poor men. The daughters of rulers must die.

It is good for us all to remember this. We are too apt to forget it. We often think and talk as if the possession of riches was the great antidote to sorrow, and as if money could secure us against sickness and death. But it is the very extreme of blindness to think so. We have only to look around us and see a hundred proofs to the contrary. Death comes to halls and palaces as well as to cottages,—to landlords as well as to tenants, —to rich as well as to poor. It stands on no ceremony. It tarries no man's leisure or convenience. It will not be kept out by locks and bars. "It is appointed unto men once to die, but after this the judgment." (Heb. ix. 27.) All are going to one place,—the grave.

We may be sure there is far more equality in the portions appointed to men than at first sight appears. Sickness is a great leveller. It makes no distinction. Heaven is the only place where "the inhabitant shall not say, I am sick." (Isa. xxiii. 24.) Happy are they who set their affections on things above! They, and they only, have a treasure which is incorruptible. Yet a little while, and they will be where they shall hear no more evil tidings. All tears shall be wiped from their faces. They shall put on mourning no more. Never again shall they hear those sorrowful words,

"thy daughter,—thy son,—thy wife,—thy husband,—
is dead." The former things will have passed away.

Let us learn, for another thing, *how almighty is the
power of our Lord Jesus Christ.* That message which
pierced the ruler's heart, telling him that his child was
dead, did not stop our Lord for a moment. At once He
cheered the father's fainting spirits with these gracious
words, "Be not afraid, only believe." He comes•to the
house, where many are weeping and wailing, and enters
the room where the damsel is lying. He takes her by
the hand, and says, "Damsel, I say unto thee, arise."
At once the heart begins to beat again, and the breath
returns to the lifeless body. "The damsel arose and
walked." No wonder that we read the words, "They
were astonished with a great astonishment."

Let us think for a moment how wonderful was the
change which took place in that house. From weeping
to rejoicing,—from mourning to congratulation,—from
death to life,—how great and marvellous must have
been the transition! They only can tell that who have
seen death face to face, and had the light of their
households quenched, and felt the iron entering into
their own souls. They, and they only, can conceive
what the family of Jairus must have felt, when they
saw their beloved one given back once more into their
bosom by the power of Christ.—There must have been
a happy family gathering that night!

Let us see in this glorious miracle a proof of what
Jesus can do for dead souls. He can raise our children
from the death of trespasses and sins, and make them
walk before Him in newness of life. He can take our

sons and daughters by the hand, and say to them,
"Arise," and bid them live not to themselves, but to Him
that died for them and rose again.   Have we a dead
soul in our family?   Let us call on the Lord to come
and quicken him. (Eph. ii. 1.)   Let us send to Him
message after message, and entreat Him to help.   He
that came to the succour of Jairus is still plenteous in
mercy, and mighty in power.

Finally, let us see in this miracle a blessed pledge
of what our Lord will do in the day of His second appearing.   He will call His believing people from their
graves.   He will give them a better, more glorious, and
more beautiful body, than they had in the days of their
pilgrimage.   He will gather together His elect from
north, and south, and east, and west, to part no more,
and die no more.   Believing parents shall once more
see believing children.   Believing husbands shall once
more see believing wives.   Let us beware of sorrowing
like those who have no hope, over friends who fall
asleep in Christ.   The youngest and loveliest believer
can never die before the right time.   Let us look forward.   There is a glorious resurrection morning yet to
come.   "Them which sleep in Jesus will God bring
with Him." (1 Thess. iv. 14.)   Those words shall one
day receive a complete fulfilment.   "I will ransom them
from the power of the grave: I will redeem them from
death: O death, I will be thy plagues: O grave, I will
be thy destruction." (Hosea xiii. 14.)   He that raised
the daughter of Jairus still lives.   When He gathers
His flock around Him at the last day, not one lamb
shall be found missing.

MARK VI. 1—6.

1 And he went out from thence, and came into his own country: and his disciples follow him.

2 And when the sabbath day was come, he began to teach in the synagogue: and many hearing *him* were astonished, saying, From whence hath this *man* these things? and what wisdom *is* this which is given unto him, that even such mighty works are wrought by his hands?

3 Is not this the carpenter, the son of Mary, the brother of James, and Joses, and of Juda, and Simon? and are not his sisters here with us? And they were offended at him.

4 But Jesus said unto them, A prophet is not without honour, but in his own country, and among his own kin, and in his own house.

5 And he could there do no mighty work, save that he laid his hands upon a few sick folk, and healed *them.*

6 And he marvelled because of their unbelief. And he went round about the villages, teaching.

THIS passage shows us our Lord Jesus Christ in "His own country," at Nazareth. It is a melancholy illustration of the wickedness of man's heart, and deserves special attention.

We see, in the first place, *how apt men are to undervalue things with which they are familiar.* The men of Nazareth "were offended" at our Lord. They could not think it possible that one who had lived so many years among themselves, and whose brethren and sisters they knew, could deserve to be followed as a public teacher.

Never had, any place on earth such privileges as Nazareth. For thirty years the Son of God resided in this town, and went to and fro in its streets. For thirty years he walked with God before the eyes of its inhabitants, living a blameless, perfect life. But it was all lost upon them. They were not ready to believe the Gospel, when the Lord came among them, and taught in their synagogue. They would not believe that one whose face they knew so well, and who had lived so long, eating, and drinking, and dressing like one of themselves, had any right to claim their attention. They were "offended at Him."

There is nothing in all this that need surprise us. The same thing is going on around us every day, in our own land. The holy Scriptures, the preaching of the Gospel, the public ordinances of religion, the abundant means of grace that England enjoys, are continually undervalued by English people. They are so accustomed to them, that they do not know their privileges. It is an awful truth, that in religion, more than in anything else, familiarity breeds contempt.

There is comfort in this part of our Lord's experience, for some of the Lord's people. There is comfort for faithful ministers of the Gospel, who are cast down by the unbelief of their parishioners or regular hearers. There is comfort for true Christians, who stand alone in their families, and see all around them cleaving to the world. Let both remember that they are drinking the same cup as their beloved Master. Let them remember that He too was despised most by those who knew Him best. Let them learn that the utmost consistency of conduct will not make others adopt their views and opinions, any more than it did the people of Nazareth. Let them know that the sorrowful words of their Lord will generally be fulfilled in the experience of His servants, "A prophet is not without honour, but in his own country, and among his own kin, and in his own house."

We see, in the second place, *how humble was the rank of life which our Lord condescended to occupy, before He began His public ministry.* The people of Nazareth said of Him, in contempt, " Is not this the carpenter ? "

This is a remarkable expression, and is only found in the Gospel of St. Mark. It shows us plainly that for the

first thirty years of His life, our Lord was not ashamed
to work with his own hands. There is something marvellous and overwhelming in the thought! He who
made heaven, and earth, and sea, and all that therein is,
—He, without whom nothing was made that was made,
—the Son of God Himself, took on Him the form of a
servant, and "in the sweat of His face ate bread," as a
working man. This is indeed that "love of Christ that
passeth knowledge." Though He was rich yet for our
sakes He became poor. Both in life and death He
humbled Himself, that through Him sinners might live
and reign for evermore.

Let us remember, when we read this passage, that there
is no sin in poverty. We never need be ashamed of
poverty, unless our own sins have brought it upon us.
We never ought to despise others because they are poor.
It is disgraceful to be a gambler, or a drunkard, or a
coveteous man, or a liar ; but it is no disgrace to work
with our own hands, and earn our bread by our own
labour. The thought of the carpenter's shop at Nazareth
should cast down the high thoughts of all who make an
idol of riches. It cannot be dishonourable to occupy
the same position as the Son of God and Saviour of
the world.

We see, in the last place, *how exceedingly sinful is the
sin of unbelief.* Two remarkable expressions are used in
teaching this lesson. One is, that our Lord "could do
no mighty work" at Nazareth, by reason of the hardness
of the people's hearts. The other is, that "He marvelled
because of their unbelief." The one shows us that unbelief has a power to rob men of the highest blessings.

The other shows that it is so suicidal and unreasonable a sin that even the Son of God regards it with surprise.

We can never be too much on our guard against unbelief. It is the oldest sin in the world. It began in the garden of Eden, when Eve listened to the devil's promises, instead of believing God's words: "Ye shall die."—It is the most ruinous of all sins in its consequences. It brought death into the world: it kept Israel for forty years out of Canaan. It is the sin which specially fills hell. "He that believeth not shall be damned."—It is the most foolish and inconsistent of all sins. It makes a man refuse the plainest evidence, shut his eyes against the clearest testimony, and yet believe lies.—Worst of all, it is the commonest sin in the world. Thousands are guilty of it on every side. In profession they are Christians. They know nothing of Paine and Voltaire. But in practice they are really unbelievers. They do not implicitly believe the Bible, and receive Christ as their Saviour.

Let us watch our own hearts carefully in the matter of unbelief. The heart, and not the head, is the seat of its mysterious power. It is neither the want of evidence, nor the difficulties of Christian doctrine, that make men unbelievers.—It is want of will to believe. They love sin. They are wedded to the world. In this state of mind they never lack specious reasons to confirm their will. The humble, child-like heart is the heart that believes.

Let us go on watching our hearts, even after we have believed. The root of unbelief is never entirely destroyed. We have only to leave off watching and

praying, and a rank crop of unbelief will soon spring up
No prayer is so important as that of the disciples: "Lord,
increase our faith." *

MARK VI. 7—13.

7 And he called *unto him* the twelve, and began to send them forth by two and two; ;and gave them power over unclean spirits;

8 And commanded them that they should take nothing for *their* journey, save a staff only; no scrip, no bread, no money in *their* purse:

9 But *be* shod with sandals; and not put on two coats.

10 And he said unto them, In what place soever ye enter into an house, there abide till ye depart from that place.

11 And whosoever shall not receive you, nor hear you, when ye depart thence, shake off the dust under your feet for a testimony against them. Verily I say unto you, It shall be more tolerable for Sodom and Gomorrha in the day of judgment, than for that city.

12 And they went out, and preached that men should repent.

13 And they cast out many devils, and anointed with oil many that were sick, and healed *them*.

THESE verses describe the first sending forth of the Apostles to preach. The great Head of the Church made proof of His ministers, before He left them alone in the world. He taught them to try their own powers of teaching, and to find out their own weaknesses, while He was yet with them. Thus, on the one hand, He was enabled to correct their mistakes. Thus, on the other, they were

* There is a peculiar expression in this passage, which deserves notice. I refer to the words which say, that our Lord "*could* do no mighty work there, because of their unbelief."

This expression, of course, cannot mean that it was "impossible" for our Lord to do a mighty work there, and that although He had the will to do mighty works, He was stopped and prevented by a power greater than His own. Such a view would be dishonouring to our Lord, and in fact would be a practical denial of His divinity. With Jesus nothing is impossible. If He had willed to do works, He had the power.

The meaning evidently must be, that our Lord "*would*" not do any mighty work there, because of the unbelief that He saw. He was prevented by what He perceived was the state of the people's hearts. He would not waste signs and wonders on an unbelieving and hardened generation. He "*could not*" do a mighty work, trained for the work they were one day to do, and were not novices, when finally left to themselves.—Well would it be for the Church, if all ministers of the Gospel were prepared for their duty in like manner, and did not so often take up their office untried, unproved, and inexperienced.

Let us observe, in these verses, *how our Lord Jesus*

without departing from His rule,—"According to your faith be it unto you." He had the power in His hands, but He did not will to use it.

The distinction I have attempted to draw is doubly useful, because of the light it throws on another Scriptural expression, which is often grievously misunderstood. I refer to the expression, "No man can come to Me, except the Father which hath sent Me draw him." (John iv. 44.) The words, "no man *can* come," are often much misapprehended.

The text is a plain declaration of man's natural corruption and helpless impotence. Man is dead in sin. He cannot come to Christ, except the Father draws him. In a word, he is *unable* to come. But what is the precise nature of his inability? This is the very point on which misapprehension exists.

Once for all, let us clearly understand that man's inability to come to Christ is not physical. It is utterly untrue to say that a man can have a strong decided will to come to Christ, and yet be stopped by some mysterious physical obstacle,—that he can really and honestly have a will to come, and yet have no power. Such a doctrine entirely overthrows man's responsibility, and leads in many cases, to wicked continuance in sin. Thousands of ignorant people will tell you that "they wish to believe, and wish to come to Christ, and wish to be saved,"—and yet say that "though they have the will they have not the power." It is a fatal delusion, and ruinous to many souls.

The truth is, that man's inability to come to Christ, and impotence to that which is good, is *moral*, and not physical. It is not true that he has the will to come to Christ, but is unable. He is 'unable, doubtless, and has no power; but it is simply *because* he has no will. His will is the principal cause of his unconverted state, and until his will is changed by the Holy Ghost, he will never alter. He may not like this. But it is true. The fault of his condition is his own will. Say what he pleases, the blame lies there. He may pretend to have many good wishes, but in reality he has no honest, sincere WILL to be better. He "will not come to Christ that he may have life."

Christ sent forth His Apostles "two and two."—St. Mark is the only Evangelist who mentions this fact. It is one that deserves special notice.

There can be no doubt that this fact is meant to teach us the advantages of Christian company to all who work for Christ. The wise man had good reason for saying, "Two are better than one." (Eccles. iv. 9.) Two men together will do more work than two men singly. They will help one another in judgment, and commit fewer mistakes. They will aid one another in difficulties, and less often fail of success. They will stir one another up when tempted to idleness, and less often relapse into indolence and indifference. They will comfort one another in times of trial, and be less often cast down. "Woe to him that is alone when he falleth; for he hath not another to help him up." (Eccles. iv. 11.)

It is probable that this principle is not sufficiently remembered in the Church of Christ in these latter days. The harvest is undoubtedly great all over the world, both at home and abroad. The labourers are unquestionably few, and the supply of faithful men far less than the demand. The arguments for sending out men "one by one," under existing circumstances, are undeniably strong and weighty. But still the conduct of our Lord in this place is a striking fact. The fact that there is hardly a single case in the Acts where we find Paul or any other Apostle working entirely alone is another remarkable circumstance. It is difficult to avoid the conclusion, that if the rule of going forth "two and two" had been more strictly observed, the missionary field would have yielded larger results than it has.

I

One thing at all events is clear, and that is the duty of all workers for Christ to work together and help one another whenever they can. " As iron sharpeneth iron, so doth the countenance of a man his friend." Ministers and missionaries, and district visitors, and Sunday-school teachers, should make opportunities for meeting, and taking sweet counsel together. The words of St. Paul contain a truth which is too much forgotten: "Consider one another, to provoke unto love and good works; not forsaking the assembling of yourselves together." (Heb. x. 24, 25.)

Let us observe, in the second place, *what solemn words our Lord uses about those who will not receive nor hear His ministers.* He says, "it shall be more tolerable for Sodom and Gomorrah in the day of judgment than for that city."

This is a truth which we find very frequently laid down in the Gospels. It is painful to think how entirely it is overlooked by many. Thousands appear to suppose, that so long as they go to church, and do not murder, or steal, or cheat, or openly break any of God's commandments, they are in no great danger. They forget that it needs something more than mere abstinence from outward irregularities to save a man's soul. They do not see that one of the greatest sins a man can commit in the sight of God, is to hear the Gospel of Christ and not believe it,—to be invited to repent and believe, and yet remain careless and unbelieving. In short, to reject the Gospel will sink a man to the lowest place in hell.

Let us never turn away from a passage like this without asking ourselves, What are we doing with the Gospel? We live in a Christian land. We have the Bible in our houses. We hear of the salvation of the Gospel frequently every year. But have we received it into our hearts? Have we really obeyed it in our lives? Have we, in short, laid hold on the hope set before us, taken up the cross, and followed Christ?—If not, we are far worse than the heathen, who bow down to stocks and stones. We are far more guilty than the people of Sodom and Gomorrah. They never heard the Gospel, and therefore never rejected it. But as for us, we hear the Gospel, and yet will not believe. May we search our own hearts, and take heed that we do not ruin our own souls!

Let us observe, in the last place, *what was the doctrine which our Lord's Apostles preached.* We read that "they went out and preached that men should repent."

The necessity of repentance may seem at first sight a very simple and elementary truth. And yet volumes might be written to show the fulness of the doctrine, and the suitableness of it to every age and time, and to every rank and class of mankind. It is inseparably connected with right views of God, of human nature, of sin, of Christ, of holiness, and of heaven. All have sinned and come short of the glory of God. All need to be brought to a sense of their sins,—to a sorrow for them,—to a willingness to give them up,—and to a hunger and thirst after pardon. All, in a word, need to be born again and to flee to Christ. This is repentance unto life. Nothing less than this is required for the salvation of any man. Nothing less than this ought to be pressed on men, by every one who professes to teach Bible religion. We must bid men repent, if we would walk in the steps of the Apostles, and when they have repented, we must bid them repent more and more to their last day.

Have we ourselves repented? This, after all, is the question that concerns us most. It is well to know what the Apostles taught. It is well to be familiar with the whole system of Christian doctrine. But it is far better to know repentance by experience, and to feel it inwardly in our own hearts. May we never rest till we know and feel that we have repented! There are no impenitent people in the kingdom of heaven. All who enter in there have felt, mourned over, forsaken, and sought pardon for sin. This must be our experience, if we hope to be saved. *

MARK VI. 14—29.

14 And king Herod heard *of him;* (for his name was spread abroad:) and he said, That John the Baptist was risen from the dead, and therefore mighty works do shew forth themselves in him.

15 Others said, That it is Elias. And others said, That it is a prophet, or as one of the prophets.

16 But when Herod heard *thereof*, he said, It is John, whom I beheaded: he is risen from the dead.

* The concluding verse in this passage, together with one in the Epistle of James (Jas. v. 14) is generally quoted by Roman Catholics in support of their pretended sacrament of extreme unction. A moment's reflection will show that neither this text nor the other referred to, is any proof at all.

In both cases, the anointing with oil is expressly connected with the *healing* of those anointed. Extreme unction, on the contrary, is an anointing administered to a *dying* person, when there is no hope of his recovery.

This discrepancy between the anointing of the Apostolic times and the anointing practised by the Church of Rome, is so glaring, that some of the ablest Romish controversialists have been obliged to acknowledge that "extreme unction" is founded on Church authority, and not on the authority of Scripture.—Lombardus, Bonaventura, Bellarmine, Jansenius, and Tirinus, are all mentioned by Calovius as being of this opinion.

17 For Herod himself had sent forth and laid hold upon John, and bound him in prison for Herodias' sake, his brother Philip's wife: for he had married her.

18 For John had said unto Herod, It is not lawful for thee to have thy brother's wife.

19 Therefore Herodias had a quarrel against him, and would have killed him; but she could not:

20 For Herod feared John, knowing that he was a just man and an holy, and observed him; and when he heard him, he did many things, and heard him gladly.

21 And when a convenient day was come, that Herod on his birthday made a supper to his lords, high captains, and chief *estates* of Galilee;

22 And when the daughter of the said Herodias came in, and danced, and pleased Herod and them that sat with him, the king said unto the damsel, Ask of me whatsoever thou wilt, and I will give *it* thee.

23 And he sware unto her, Whatsoever thou shalt ask of me, I will give *it* thee, unto the half of my kingdom.

24 And she went forth, and said unto her mother, What shall I ask? And she said, The head of John the Baptist.

25 And she came in straightway with haste unto the king, and asked, saying, I will that thou give me by and by in a charger the head of John the Baptist.

26 And the king was exceeding sorry: *yet* for his oath's sake, and for their sakes which sat with him, he would not reject her

27 And immediately the king sent an executioner, and commanded his head to be brought: and he went and beheaded him in the prison,

28 And brought his head in a charger, and gave it to the damsel: and the damsel gave it to her mother.

29 And when his disciples heard *of it*, they came and took up his corpse, and laid it in a tomb.

THESE verses describe the death of one of the most eminent saints of God. They relate the murder of John the Baptist. Of all the Evangelists none tells this melancholy story so fully as St. Mark. Let us see what practical lessons the passage contains for our own souls.

We see, in the first place, *the amazing power of truth over the conscience.* Herod "fears" John the Baptist while he lives, and is troubled about him after he dies. A friendless, solitary preacher, with no other weapon than God's truth, disturbs and terrifies a King.

Every body has a conscience. Here lies the secret of a faithful minister's power. This is the reason why Felix "trembled," and Agrippa was "almost persuaded," when Paul the prisoner spoke before them. God has not left Himself without witness in the hearts of unconverted people. Fallen and corrupt as man is, there are thoughts within him accusing or excusing, according as he lives,—thoughts that will not be shut out,—thoughts that can make even Kings, like Herod, restless and afraid.

None ought to remember this so much as ministers and teachers. If they teach and preach Christ's truth, they may rest assured that their work is not in vain. Children may seem inattentive in schools. Hearers may seem careless in congregations. But in both cases there is often far more going on in the conscience than our eyes see. Seeds often spring up and bear fruit, when the sower, like John the Baptist, is dead or gone.

We see, in the second place, *how far people may go in religion, and yet miss salvation by yielding to one master-sin.*

King Herod went further than many. He " feared John." He " knew that he was a just man and a holy." He " observed " him. He " heard him, and did many things " in consequence. He even " heard him gladly." But there was one thing Herod would not do. He would not cease from adultery. He would not give up Herodias. And so he ruined his soul for evermore.

Let us take warning from Herod's case. Let us keep back nothing,—cleave to no favourite vice,—spare nothing that stands between us and salvation. Let us often look within, and make sure that there is no darling lust or pet transgression, which, Herodias-like, is murdering our souls. Let us rather cut off the right hand, and pluck out the right eye, than go into hell-fire. Let us not be content with admiring favourite preachers, and

gladly hearing evangelical sermons. Let us not rest till
we can say with David, "I esteem all Thy commandments concerning all things to be right, and I hate
every false way." (Psalm cxix. 128.)

We see, in the third place, *how boldly a faithful
minister of God ought to rebuke sin.* John the Baptist
spoke plainly to Herod about the wickedness of his life.
He did not excuse himself under the plea that it was
imprudent, or impolitic, or untimely, or useless to speak
out. He did not say smooth things, and palliate the
King's ungodliness by using soft words to describe his
offence. He told his royal hearer the plain truth, regardless of all consequences : " It is not lawful for thee
to have thy brother's wife."

Here is a pattern that all ministers ought to follow.
Publicly and privately, from the pulpit and in private
visits, they ought to rebuke all open sin, and deliver a
faithful warning to all who are living in it. It may
give offence. It may entail immense unpopularity. With
all this they have nothing to do. Duties are theirs.
Results are God's.

No doubt it requires great grace and courage to do
this. No doubt a reprover, like John the Baptist, must
go to work wisely and lovingly in carrying out his
Master's commission, and rebuking the wicked. But it
is a matter in which his character for faithfulness and
charity are manifestly at stake. If he believes a man
is injuring his soul, he ought surely to tell him so. If
he loves him truly and tenderly, he ought not to let him
ruin himself unwarned. Great as the present offence
may be, in the long run the faithful reprover will

generally be respected. "He that rebuketh a man afterwards shall find more favour than he that flattereth him with his tongue." (Prov. xxviii. 23.)

We see, in the fourth place, *how bitterly people hate a reprover, when they are determined to keep their sins.* Herodias, the King's unhappy partner in iniquity, seems to have sunk even deeper in sin than Herod. Hardened and seared in conscience by her wickedness, she hated John the Baptist for his faithful testimony, and never rested till she had procured his death.

We need not wonder at this. When men and women have chosen their line, and resolved to have their own wicked way, they dislike any one who tries to turn them. They would fain be let alone. They are irritated by opposition. They are angry when they are told the truth. The prophet Elijah was called a "man that troubled Israel." The prophet Micaiah was hated by Ahab, "because he never prophesied good of him, but evil." The prophets and faithful preachers of every age have been treated in like manner. They have been hated by some, as well as not believed.

Let it never surprise us when we hear of faithful ministers of the Gospel being spoken against, hated, and reviled. Let us rather remember that they are ordained to bear witness against sin, the world, and the devil, and that if they are faithful they cannot help giving offence. It is no disgrace to a minister's character to be disliked by the wicked and ungodly. It is no real honour to a minister to be thought well of by everybody. Those words of our Lord are not enough considered: "Woe unto you when all men speak well of you."

We see, in the fifth place, *how much sin may sometimes follow from feasting and revelling.* Herod keeps his birth-day with a splendid banquet. Company, drinking, danc-ing, fill up the day. In a moment of excitement, he grants a wicked girl's request to have the head of John the Baptist cut off. Next day, in all probability, he repented bitterly of his conduct. But the deed was done. It was too late.

This is a faithful picture of what often results from feasting and merry-making. People do things at such seasons from heated feelings, which they afterwards deeply repent. Happy are they who keep clear of temptations, and avoid giving occasion to the devil! Men never know what they may do, when they once venture off safe ground. Late hours and crowded rooms, and splendid entertainments, and mixed com-pany, and music, and dancing may seem harmless to many people. But the Christian should never forget that to take part in these things is to open a wide door to temptation.

We see, finally, in these verses, *how little reward some of God's best servants receive in this world.* An unjust imprisonment and a violent death, were the last fruit that John the Baptist reaped, in return for his labour. Like Stephen, and James, and others, of whom the world was not worthy, he was called to seal his testi-mony with his blood.

Histories like these are meant to remind us that the true Christian's best things are yet to come. His rest, his crown, his wages, his reward, are all on the other side of the grave. Here, in this world, he must

walk by faith and not by sight; and if he looks for the
praise of man, he will be disappointed.   Here, in this
life, he must sow, and labour, and fight, and endure persecution; and if he expects a great earthly reward, he
expects what he will not find.—But this life is not all.
There is to be a day of retribution.   There is a glorious
harvest yet to come.   Heaven will make amends for all.
Eye hath not seen, and ear hath not heard the glorious
things that God has laid up for all that love Him.   The
value of real religion is not to be measured by the things
seen, but the things unseen.   "The sufferings of this
present time are not worthy to be compared with the
glory which shall be revealed."   "Our light affliction,
which is but for a moment, worketh for us a far more
exceeding and eternal weight of glory."   (Rom. viii. 18;
2 Cor. iv. 17.)

MARK IV. 30—34.

30 And the apostles gathered themselves together unto Jesus, and told him
all things, both what they had done,
and what they had taught.

31 And he said unto them, Come ye
yourselves apart into a desert place,
and rest a while: for there were many
coming and going, and they had no
leisure so much as to eat.

32 And they departed into a desert
place by ship privately.

33 And the people saw them departing, and many knew him, and ran afoot
thither out of all cities, and outwent
them, and came together unto him.

34 And Jesus, when he came out, saw
much people, and was moved with compassion toward them, because they were
as sheep not having a shepherd: and he
began to teach them many things.

LET us mark, in this passage, *the conduct of the Apostles
when they returned from their first mission as preachers.*
We read that they "gathered themselves together unto
Jesus, and told Him all things, both what they had done,
and what they had taught."

These words are deeply instructive. They are a bright example to all ministers of the Gospel, and to all labourers in the great work of doing good to souls. All such should daily do as the Apostles did on this occasion. They should tell all their proceedings to the great Head of the Church. They should spread all their work before Christ, and ask of Him counsel, guidance, strength and help.

Prayer is the main secret of success in spiritual business. It moves Him who can move heaven and earth. It brings down the promised aid of the Holy Ghost, without whom the finest sermons, the clearest teaching, and the most diligent working, are all alike in vain. It is not always those who have the most eminent gifts who are most successful labourers for God. It is generally those who keep up closest communion with Christ and are most instant in prayer. It is those who cry with the prophet Ezekiel, "Come from the four winds, O breath, and breathe upon these slain, that they may live." (Ezek. xxxvii. 9.) It is those who follow most exactly the Apostolic model, and "give themselves to prayer and the ministry of the word." (Acts vi. 4.) Happy is that Church which has a praying as well as a preaching ministry! The question we should ask about a new minister is not merely, "Can he preach well?" but, "Does he pray much for his people and his work?"

Let us mark, in the second place, *the words of our Lord to the Apostles, when they returned from their first public ministry.* "He said unto them, Come ye apart yourselves into a desert place, and rest a while."

These words are full of tender consideration. Our

Lord knows well that His servants are flesh as well as spirit, and have bodies as well as souls. He knows that at best they have a treasure in earthen vessels, and are themselves compassed with many infirmities. He shows them that He does not expect from them more than their bodily strength can do. He asks for what we *can* do, and not for what we cannot do. "Come ye apart," He says, "and rest awhile."

These words are full of deep wisdom. Our Lord knows well that His servants must attend to their own souls as well as the souls of others. He knows that a constant attention to public work is apt to make us forget our own private soul-business, and that while we are keeping the vineyards of others we are in danger of neglecting our own. (Cant. i. 6.) He reminds us that it is good for ministers to withdraw occasionally from public work, and look within. "Come ye apart," He says, "into a desert place."

There are few unhappily in the Church of Christ, who need these admonitions. There are but few in danger of overworking themselves, and injuring their own bodies and souls by excessive attention to others. The vast majority of professing Christians are indolent and slothful, and do nothing for the world around them. There are few comparatively who need the bridle nearly so much as the spur.—Yet these few ought to lay to heart the lessons of this passage. They should economize their health as a talent, and not squander it away like gamblers. They should be content with spending their daily income of strength, and should not draw recklessly on their principal. They should remember that to do a

little, and do it well, is often the way to do most in the
long run.   Above all they should never forget to watch
their own hearts jealously, and to make time for regular
self-examination and calm meditation.   The prosperity
of a man's ministry and public work is intimately bound
up with the prosperity of his own soul.   Occasional retirement is one of the most useful ordinances.

Finally, let us mark the *feelings of our Lord Jesus
Christ towards the people who came together to Him.*   We
read that He " was moved with compassion toward them,
because they were as sheep without a shepherd."   They
were destitute of teachers.   They had no guides but the
blind Scribes and Pharisees.   They had no spiritual food
but man-made traditions.   Thousands of immortal souls
stood before our Lord, ignorant, helpless, and on the high-
road to ruin.   It touched the gracious heart of our Lord
Jesus Christ.   He was " moved with compassion toward
them.   He began to teach them many things."

Let us never forget that our Lord is the same yesterday, to-day, and for ever.   He never changes.   High in
heaven, at God's right hand, He still looks with compassion on the children of men.   He still pities the
ignorant, and them that are out of the way.   He is still
willing to " teach them many things."   Special as His
love is towards His own sheep who hear His voice, He
still has a mighty general love towards all mankind,—a
love of real pity, a love of compassion.   We must not
overlook this.   It is a poor theology which teaches that
Christ cares for none except believers.   There is warrant in Scripture for telling the chief of sinners that
Jesus pities them and cares for their souls, that Jesus is

willing to save them, and invites them to believe and be saved.

Let us ask ourselves, as we leave the passage; whether we know anything of the mind of Christ? Are we like Him, tenderly concerned about the souls of the unconverted? Do we, like Him, feel deep compassion for all who are yet as sheep without a shepherd? Do we care about the impenitent and ungodly near our own doors? Do we care about the heathen, the Jew, the Mahometan, and the Roman Catholic in foreign lands? Do we use every means, and give our money willingly, to spread the Gospel in the world? These are serious questions and demand a serious reply. The man who cares nothing for the souls of other people is not like Jesus Christ. It may well be doubted whether he is converted himself, and knows the value of his own soul.

MARK VI. 35—46.

35 And when the day was now far spent, his disciples came unto him, and said, This is a desert place, and now the time is far passed:

36 Send them away, that they may go into the country round about, and into the villages, and buy themselves bread: for they had nothing to eat.

37 He answered and said unto them, Give ye them to eat. And they say unto him, Shall we go and buy two hundred penny worth of bread, and give them to eat?

38 He saith unto them, How many loaves have ye? go and see. And when they knew, they say, Five, and two fishes.

39 And he commanded them to make all sit down by companies upon the green grass.

40 And they sat down in ranks, by hundreds, and by fifties.

41 And when he had taken the five loaves and the two fishes, he looked up to heaven, and blessed, and brake the loaves, and gave *them* to his diciples to set before them; and the two fishes divided he among them all.

42 Andt hey did all eat, and were filled.

43 And they took up twelve baskets full of the fragments, and of the fishes.

44 And they that did eat of the loaves were about five thousand men.

45 And straightway he constrained his disciples to get into the ship, and to go to the other side before unto Bethsaida, while he sent away the people

46 And when he had sent them away, he departed into a mountain to pray.

OF all our Lord Jesus Christ's miracles, none is so frequently described in the Gospels as that which we have

now read.   Each of the four Evangelists was inspired to
record it.   It is evident that it demands a more than
ordinary attention from every reader of God's Word.

Let us observe, for one thing, in this passage, *what an
example this miracle affords of our Lord Jesus Christ's
almighty power.*   We are told that He fed five thousand
men, with five loaves and two fishes.   We are distinctly
told that this multitude had nothing to eat.   We are no
less distinctly told that the whole provision for their
sustenance consisted of only five loaves and two fishes.
And yet we read that our Lord took these loaves and
fishes, blessed, brake, and gave them to His disciples to
set before the people.   And the conclusion of the narrative tells us, that "they did all eat, and were filled,"
and that "twelve baskets full of fragments" were taken
up.

Here was creative power beyond all question.   Something real, solid, substantial, must manifestly have been
called into being, which did not before exist.   There is
no room left for the theory, that the people were under
the influence of an optical delusion, or a heated imagination.   Five thousand hungry people would never have
been satisfied, if they had not received into their mouths
material bread.   Twelve baskets full of fragments would
never have been taken up, if the five loaves had not
been miraculously multiplied.   In short, it is plain that
the hand of Him who made the world out of nothing
was present on this occasion.   None but He who at the
first created all things, and sent down manna in the
desert, could thus have " spread a table in the wilderness."

It becomes all true Christians to store up facts like

these in their minds, and to remember them in time of
need. We live in the midst of an evil world, and see
few with us, and many against us. We carry within
us a weak heart, too ready at any moment to turn aside
from the right way. We have near us, at every moment,
a busy devil, watching continually for our halting, and
seeking to lead us into temptation. Where shall we
turn for comfort? What shall keep faith alive, and
preserve us from sinking in despair?—There is only one
answer. We must look to Jesus. We must think on
His almighty power, and His wonders of old time. We
must call to mind how He can create food for His
people out of nothing, and supply the wants of those
who follow Him, even in the wilderness.—And as we
think these thoughts, we must remember that this Jesus
still lives, never changes, and is on our side.

Let us observe, for another thing, in this passage, *our
Lord Jesus Christ's conduct, when the miracle of feeding
the multitude had been performed.* We read, that " when
He had sent them away, He departed into a mountain
to pray."

There is something deeply instructive in this circumstance. Our Lord sought not the praise of man. After
one of His greatest miracles we find Him immediately
seeking solitude and spending His time in prayer. He
practised what He had taught elsewhere, when He said,
"Enter into thy closet, and shut thy door, and pray to
thy Father which is in secret." None ever did such
mighty works as He did. None ever spake such words.
None ever was so instant in prayer.

Let our Lord's conduct in this respect be our example.

We cannot work miracles as He did; in this He stands alone. But we can walk in His steps in the matter of private devotion. If we have the Spirit of adoption, we can pray. Let us resolve to pray more than we have done hitherto. Let us strive to make time, and place, and opportunity for being alone with God. Above all, let us not only pray before we attempt to work for God, but pray also after our work is done.

It would be well for us all if we examined ourselves more frequently as to our habits about private prayer. What time do we give to it in the twenty-four hours of the day? What progress can we mark, one year with another, in the fervency, fulness, and earnestness of our prayers? What do we know by experience of "labouring fervently in prayer"? (Colos. iv. 12.) These are humbling inquiries, but they are useful for our souls. There are few things, it may be feared, in which Christians come so far short of Christ's example as they do in the matter of prayer. Our Master's strong crying and tears, His continuing all night in prayer to God, His frequent withdrawal to private places to hold close communion with the Father, are things more talked of and admired than imitated. We live in an age of hurry, bustle, and so-called activity. Men are tempted continually to cut short their private devotions, and abridge their prayers. When this is the case, we need not wonder that the Church of Christ does little in proportion to its machinery. The Church must learn to copy its Head more closely. Its members must be more in their closets. "We have little," because little is asked. (James iv. 2.)

K

MARK VI. 47—56.

47 And when even was come, the ship was in the midst of the sea, and he alone on the land.

48 And he saw them toiling in rowing; for the wind was contrary unto them: and about the fourth watch of the night he cometh unto them, walking upon the sea, and would have passed by them.

49 But when they saw him walking upon the sea, they supposed it had been a spirit, and cried out:

50 For they all saw him, and were troubled. And immediately he talked with them, and saith unto them, Be of good cheer: it is I; be not afraid.

51 And he went up unto them into the ship; and the wind ceased: and they were sore amazed in themselves beyond measure, and wondered.

52 For they considered not *the miracle* of the loaves: for their heart was hardened.

53 And when they had passed over, they came into the land of Gennesaret, and drew to the shore.

54 And when they were come out of the ship, straightway they knew him.

55 And ran through that whole region round about, and began to carry about in beds those that were sick, where they heard he was.

56 And whithersoever he entered, into villages, or cities, or country, they laid the sick in the streets, and besought him that they might touch if it were but the border of his garment: and as many as touched him were made whole.

THE event first recorded in these verses is a beautiful emblem of the position of all believers, between the first and second advents of Jesus Christ. Like the disciples, we are now tossed to and fro by storms, and do not enjoy the visible presence of our Lord. Like the disciples, we shall see our Lord face to face again, though it may be a time of great extremity, when He returns. Like the disciples, we shall see all things changed for the better, when our Master comes to us. We shall no longer be buffeted by storms. There will be a great calm.

There is nothing fanciful in such an application of the passage. We need not doubt that there is a deep meaning in every step of His life, who was "God manifest in the flesh." For the present, however, let us confine ourselves to the plain practical lessons which these verses contain.

Let us notice, in the first place, how *our Lord sees the troubles of His believing people, and in due time will help them.* We read that when "the ship was in the midst of the sea, and He alone on the land," He " saw His disciples toiling in rowing," came to them walking on the sea, cheered them with the gracious words, " It is I ; be not afraid," and changed the storm into a calm.

There are thoughts of comfort here for all true believers. Wherever they may be, or whatsoever their circumstances, the Lord Jesus sees them. Alone or in company, in sickness or in health, by sea or by land, in perils in the city, in perils in the wilderness,—the same eye which saw the disciples tossed on the lake, is ever looking at us. We are never beyond the reach of His care. Our way is never hid from Him. He knows the path that we take, and is still able to help. He may not come to our aid at the time we like best, but He will never allow us utterly to fail. He that walked upon the water never changes. He will always come at the right time to uphold His people. Though He tarry, let us wait patiently. Jesus sees us, and will not forsake us.

Let us notice, in the second place, *the fears of the disciples, when they first saw our Lord walking upon the sea.* We are told that "they supposed it had been a spirit, and cried out: for they all saw Him, and were troubled."

What a faithful picture of human nature we have in these words ! How many thousands in the present day, if they had seen what the disciples saw, would have behaved in the same manner ! How few, if they were on board a ship in a storm at midnight and suddenly saw one walking on the water and drawing near to the ship, —how few would preserve their composure, and be altogether free from fears ! Let men laugh, if they please, at the superstitious fears of these unlearned disciples. Let them boast, if they like, of the march of intellect, and the spread of knowledge, in these latter times. There are few, we may confidently assert, who, placed in the same position as the Apostles, would have shown more courage than they. The boldest sceptics have sometimes proved the greatest cowards when appearances have been seen at night which they could not explain.

The truth is there is an instinctive feeling in all men which makes them shrink from anything which seems to belong to another world. There is a consciousness, which many try in vain to conceal by affected carelessness, that there are beings unseen, as well as seen, and that the life which we now live in the flesh is not the only life in which man has a portion. The common stories about ghosts and apparitions are undoubtedly foolish and superstitious : they are almost always traceable to the fears and imaginations of weak-minded people; yet the universal currency which such stories obtain, all over the world, is a fact that deserves notice. It is an indirect evidence of latent belief in unseen things, just as counterfeit coin is an evidence that there is true money. It forms a peculiar testimony which the infidel would find it hard to explain away. It proves that there is something within men which testifies of a world beyond the grave, and that when men feel it they are afraid.

The plain duty of the true Christian is to live provided with an antidote against all fears of the great unseen world. That antidote is faith in an unseen Saviour,

and constant communion with Him. Armed with that
antidote, and seeing Him who is invisible, nothing need
make us afraid. We travel on towards a world of spirits.
We are surrounded even now by many dangers. But
with Jesus for our Shepherd, we have no cause for alarm.
With Him for our Shield, we are safe.

Let us notice, in the conclusion of the chapter, *what
a bright example we have of our duty to one another.* We
are told that when our Lord came into the land of Gennesaret, the people " ran through that whole region,"
and brought to Him in beds " those that were sick." We
read that " whithersoever He entered, into villages, or
cities, or country, they laid the sick in the streets, and
besought Him that they might touch if it were but the
border of His garment."

Let us see here a pattern for ourselves. Let us go and
do likewise. Let us strive to bring all around us who
are in need of spiritual medicine, to Jesus the great Physician, that they may be healed. Souls are dying every
day. Time is short. Opportunities are rapidly passing
away. The night cometh when no man can work. Let
us spare no pains in labouring to bring men and women
to the knowledge of Jesus Christ, that they may be
saved. It is a comfortable thought, that " as many as
touch Him will be made whole."

MARK VII. 1—13.

1 Then came together unto him the
Pharisees, and certain of the scribes,
which came from Jerusalem.

2 And when they saw some of his
disciples eat bread with defiled, that is
to say, with unwashen hands, they
found fault.

3 For the Pharisees, and all the Jews,
except they wash *their* hands oft, eat
not, holding the tradition of the elders.

4 And *when they come* from the market,
except they wash, they eat not. And
many other things there be, which they
have received to hold, *as* the washing of

cups, and pots, brazen vessels, and of tables.

5 Then the Pharisees and scribes asked him, Why walk not thy disciples according to the tradition of the elders, but eat bread with unwashen hands?

6 He answered and said unto them, Well hath Esaias prophesied of you hypocrites, as it is written, This people honoureth me with their lips, but their heart is far from me.

7 Howbeit in vain do they worship me, teaching *for* doctrines the commandments of men.

8 For laying aside the commandment of God, ye hold the tradition of men, *as* the washing of pots and cups: and many

other such like things ye do.

9 And he said unto them, Full well ye reject the commandment of God, that ye may keep your own tradition.

10 For Moses said, Honour thy father and thy mother; and, Whoso curseth father or mother, let him die the death:

11 But ye say, If a man shall say to his father or mother, *It is* Corban, that is to say, a gift, by whatsoever thou mightest be profited by me; *he shall be free.*

12 And ye suffer him no more to do ought for his father or his mother;

13 Making the word of God of none effect through your tradition, which ye have delivered: and many such like things do ye.

THIS passage contains a humbling picture of what human nature is capable of doing in religion. It is one of those Scriptures which ought to be frequently and diligently studied by all who desire the prosperity of the Church of Christ.

The first thing, which demands our attention in these verses, is *the low and degraded condition of Jewish religion, when our Lord was upon earth.* What can be more deplorable than the statement now before us? We find the principal teachers of the Jewish nation finding fault, " because our Lord's disciples ate bread with unwashen hands!" We are told that they attached great importance to the " washing of cups, and pots, and brazen vessels, and tables!" In short, the man who paid most rigid attention to mere external observances of human invention was reckoned the holiest man!

The nation, be it remembered, in which this state of things existed, was the most highly favoured in the world. To it was given the law on Mount Sinai, the service of God, the priesthood, the covenants, and the promises. Moses, and Samuel, and David, and the Prophets, lived and died among its people. No nation upon earth ever had so many spiritual privileges.   No nation ever misused its privileges so fearfully, and so thoroughly forsook its own mercies.   Never did fine gold become so dim! From the religion of the books of Deuteronomy and Psalms, to the religion of washing hands, and pots, and cups, how great was the fall!   No wonder that, in the time of our Lord's earthly ministry, He found the people like sheep without a shepherd.   External observances alone feed no consciences and sanctify no hearts.

Let the history of the Jewish Church be a warning to us never to trifle with false doctrine.   If we once tolerate it we never know how far it may go, or into what degraded state of religion we may at last fall.   Once leave the King's highway of truth, and we may end with washing pots and cups, like Pharisees and scribes.   There is nothing too mean, trifling, or irrational for a man, if he once turns his back on God's Word.   There are branches of the Church of Christ at this day in which the Scriptures are never read, and the Gospel never preached,— branches in which the only religion now remaining consists in using a few unmeaning forms and keeping certain man-made fasts and feasts,—branches which began well, like the Jewish Church, and like the Jewish Church have now fallen into utter barrenness and decay.   We can never be too jealous about false doctrine.   A little leaven leaveneth the whole lump.   Let us earnestly contend for the whole faith once delivered to the saints.*

---

* Absurd and ridiculous as the customs and traditions of the Pharisees appear at first sight, it is a humbling fact that the Pharisees have never wanted imitators and successors. Zeal about

The second thing that demands our attention, is *the uselessness of mere lip-service in the worship of God.* Our Lord enforces this lesson by a quotation from the Old Testament: "Well hath Esaias prophesied of you hypocrites, This people honoureth me with their lips, but their heart is far from me."

The heart is the part of man which God chiefly notices in religion. The bowed head and the bended knee, the grave face and the rigid posture, the regular response and the formal Amen,—all these together do not make up a spiritual worshipper. The eyes of God look further and deeper. He requires the worship of the heart. "My son," He says to every one of us, "Give Me thy heart."

Let us remember this in the public congregation. It must not content us to take our bodies to church, if we leave our hearts at home. The eye of man may detect no flaw in our service. Our minister may look at us with approbation. Our neighbours may think us patterns of

washing pots, and cups, and tables, may seem almost ludicrous, and worthy of none but children; but we need not look far to find an exact parallel near home. What can we say to the gravity and seriousness with which men argue on behalf of chasubles, albs, tunicles, piscinas, sedilia, credence-tables, rood-screens, and the like, in the present day?—What can we say to the exaggerated attention paid by many to ceremonies, ornaments, gestures, and postures, in the worship of God, about which it is enough to say that Scripture is totally silent?—What is it all but Pharisaism over again?—What is it but a melancholy repetition of disproportioned zeal about men's traditional usages? What single argument can be used in defence of these things that the Pharisees might not have used with equal force? Eighteen hundred years have passed away, and yet the generation that made so much ado about washing pots, cups, and tables, is still amongst us. The succession of the Pharisees has never ceased.

what a Christian ought to be.   Our voice may be heard
foremost in the praise and prayer.   But it is all worse
than nothing in God's sight if our hearts are far away.
It is only wood, hay, and stubble before Him who dis-
cerns thoughts, and reads the secrets of the inward man.

Let us remember this in our private devotions.   It
must not satisfy us to say good words, if our heart and
our lips do not go together.   What does it profit us to
be fluent and lengthy, if our imaginations are roving far
away, while we are upon our knees?—It profits us
nothing at all.   God sees what we are about, and rejects
our offering.   Heart-prayers are the prayers He loves to
hear.   Heart-prayers are the only prayers that He will
answer.   Our petitions may be weak, and stammering,
and mean in our eyes.   They may be presented with no
fine words, or well-chosen language, and might seem
almost unintelligible, if they were written down.   But
if they come from a right heart, God understands them.
Such prayers are His delight.

The last thing that demands' our attention in these
verses, is *the tendency of man's inventions in religion to
supplant God's Word.*   Three times we find this charge
brought forward by our Lord against the Pharisees.
"Laying aside the commandments of God, ye hold the
traditions of men."—"Full well ye reject the commandment of God, that ye may keep your own traditions."
—"Making the Word of God of none effect through
your traditions."—The first step of the Pharisees was to
add their traditions to the Scriptures, as useful supple-
ments.   The second was to place them on a level with
the Word of God, and give them equal authority.   The

last was to honour them above the Scripture, and to degrade Scripture from its lawful position. This was the state of things which our Lord found when He was upon earth. Practically, the traditions of man were everything, and the Word of God was nothing at all. Obedience to the traditions constituted true religion. Obedience to the Scriptures was lost sight of altogether.

It is a mournful fact that Christians have far too often walked in the steps of Pharisees in this matter. The very same process has taken place over and over again. The very same consequences have resulted. Religious observances of man's invention, have been pressed on the acceptance of Christians,—observances to all appearance useful, and at all events well-meant, but observances nowhere commanded in the Word of God. These very observances have by and by been enjoined with more vigour than God's own commandments, and defended with more zeal than the authority of God's own Word. We need not look far for examples. The history of our own Church will supply them.*

Let us beware of attempting to add anything to the Word of God, as a necessary to salvation. It provokes

---

* The persecution of the Puritans in the time of the Stewarts, on account of canons and rubrics, was, in too many cases, neither more nor less than zeal for traditions. An enormous amount of zeal was expended in enforcing conformity to the Church of England, while drunkenness, swearing, and open sin were comparatively let alone. Obedience to man-made ecclesiastical rules was required, on pain of fine or imprisonment, while open disobedience to God's ten commandments was overlooked. Experience supplies painful proof, that traditions once called into being are first called *useful*. Then they become *necessary*. At last they are too often made *idols*, and all must bow down to them, or be punished.

God to give us over to judicial blindness. It is as good as saying that His Bible is not perfect, and that we know better than He does what is necessary for man's salvation. It is just as easy to destroy the authority of God's Word by addition as by subtraction, by burying it under man's inventions as by denying its truth. The whole Bible, and nothing but the Bible, must be our rule of faith,—nothing added and nothing taken away.

Finally, let us draw a broad line of distinction between those things in religion which have been devised by man, and those which are plainly commanded in God's Word. What God commands is necessary to salvation. What man commands is not. What man devises may be useful and expedient for the times; but salvation does not hinge on obedience to it. What God requires is essential to life eternal. He that wilfully disobeys it ruins his own soul.*

* The subtle way in which the Pharisees evaded the requirements of the fifth commandment, to which our Lord refers in this passage, calls for a few words of explanation.

We must remember that the Pharisees did not openly deny the obligation of the fifth commandment. In all probability they professed to attach as much importance to it as any men. And yet they contrived to make it void ! How did they effect this ?

They taught that a man might dedicate to God's service, as sacred, any part of his property which might be applied to the relief of his parents, and so discharge himself from any further expense about them. He had only to say that all his money was "corban,"—that is, given over to holy purposes,—and no further claim could be made upon him for his father's or mother's support. Under pretence of giving God a prior claim, he set himself free from the burden of maintaining them for ever. He did not flatly deny his duty to minister of his wordly substance to his parents' necessities. But he evaded it by setting up a human tradition, and asserting a higher call of duty, even duty to God.

The likeness between the traditions and sophistries of the Phari-

MARK VII. 14—23.

14 And when he had called all the people *unto him*, he said unto them, Hearken unto me every one *of you*, and understand:

15 There is nothing from without a man, that entering into him can defile him: but the things which come out of him, those are they that defile the man.

16 If any man have ears to hear, let him hear.

17 And when he was entered into the house from the people, his disciples asked him concerning the parable.

18 And he saith unto them, Are ye so without understanding also? Do ye not perceive, that whatsoever thing from without entereth into the man, *it* cannot defile him;

19 Because it entereth not into his heart, but into the belly, and goeth out into the draught, purging all meats?

20 And he said, That which cometh out of the man, that defileth the man.

21 For from within, out of the heart of men, proceed evil thoughts, adulteries, fornications, murders,

22 Thefts, covetousness, wickedness, deceit, lasciviousness, an evil eye, blasphemy, pride, foolishness:

23 All these evil things come from within, and defile the man.

WE see in the beginning of this passage, *how slow of understanding men are in spiritual things.* "Hearken," says our Lord to the people, "hearken unto Me every one of you, and understand."—"Are ye so without understanding?" He says to His disciples,—"Do ye not perceive?"

sees, making void God's Word under a pretended zeal for God's glory, and those of the Jesuits, and other advocates of the Roman Catholic Church, is painfully striking. The following passage from an old commentator is worth reading.

"The Scriptures teach that there is no difference to be put between meats, in regard of holiness, but that every creature of God is good. This the Papists make void by teaching that it is matter of religion and conscience to abstain from flesh meats at certain seasons.—The Scripture teaches that we should pray to God alone. This they make void by their manifold prayers to saints departed.—The Scripture teacheth Christ alone to be our Mediator, both of redemption and intercession. This they make void by making saints intercessors.—The Scripture teacheth Christ to be the only Head of the Church. This they abrogate by their doctrine of the Pope's supremacy.—The Scripture teacheth that every soul should be subject to the higher power. This they abrogate by exempting the Pope and popish clergy from subjection to the civil power of princes and magistrates.—Lastly, to instance in the same kind as our Saviour here against the Pharisees, whereas the Word of God commands children to honour their parents, the Papists teach that if the child have vowed a monastical life he is exempted from duty to parents."—*Petter on St. Mark.*

The corruption of human nature is an universal dis-ease. It affects not only a man's heart, will, and con-science, but his mind, memory, and understanding. The very same person who is quick and clever in worldly things, will often utterly fail to comprehend the simplest truths of Christianity. He will often be unable to take in the plainest reasonings of the Gospel. He will see no meaning in the clearest statements of evangelical doctrine. They will sound to him either foolish or mysterious. He will listen to them like one listening to a foreign language, catching a word here and there, but not seeing the drift of the whole. "The world by wisdom knows not God." (1 Cor. i. 21.) It hears, but does not understand.

We must pray daily for the teaching of the Holy Ghost if we would make progress in the knowledge of divine things. Without Him the mightiest intellect and the strongest reasoning powers will carry us but a little way. In reading the Bible and hearing sermons, every-thing depends on the spirit in which we read and hear. A humble, teachable, child-like frame of mind is the grand secret of success. Happy is he who often says with David, "Teach me Thy statutes." (Psalm cxix. 64.) Such an one will understand as well as hear.

We see, in the second place, from this passage, *that the heart is the chief source of defilement and impurity in God's sight.* Moral purity does not depend on washing or not washing, touching things or not touching them, eating things or not eating them, as the Scribes and Pharisees taught. "There is nothing from without a man, that entering into him can defile him : but the things which come out of him, these are they that defile the man."

There is a deep truth in these words which is frequently overlooked. Our original sinfulness and natural inclination to evil are seldom sufficiently considered. The wickedness of men is often attributed to bad examples, bad company, peculiar temptations, or the snares of the devil. It seems forgotten that every man carries within him a fountain of wickedness. We need no bad company to teach us, and no devil to tempt us, in order to run into sin. We have within us the beginning of every sin under heaven.

We ought to remember this in the training and education of children. In all our management we must never forget that the seeds of all mischief and wickedness are in their hearts. It is not enough to keep boys and girls at home, and shut out every outward temptation. They carry within them a heart ready for any sin, and until that heart is changed they are not safe, whatever we do. When children do wrong it is a common practice to lay all the blame on bad companions. But it is mere ignorance, blindness, and foolishness to do so. Bad companions are a great evil no doubt, and an evil to be avoided as much as possible. But no bad companion teaches a boy or girl half as much sin as their own hearts will suggest to them, unless they are renewed by the Spirit. The beginning of all wickedness is within. If parents were half as diligent in praying for their children's conversion, as they are in keeping them from bad company, their children would turn out far better than they do.*

---

* The common arguments against "public-school" education, appear to me based on forgetfulness of our Lord's teaching about the

We see, in the last place, from this passage, *what a black catalogue of evils the human heart contains.* "Out of the heart of men," says our Lord, "proceed evil thoughts, adulteries, fornications, murders, thefts, covetousness, an evil eye, blasphemy, pride, foolishness : all these evil things come from within."

Let us distinctly understand, when we read these words, that our Lord is speaking of the human heart generally. He is not speaking only of the notorious profligate, or the prisoner in the jail. He is speaking of all mankind. All of us, whether high or low, rich or poor, masters or servants, old or young, learned or un-learned,—all of us have by nature such a heart as Jesus here describes. The seeds of all the evils here mentioned lie hid within us all. They may lie dormant all our lives. They may be kept down by the fear of consequences, the restraint of public opinion, the dread of discovery, the desire to be thought respectable, and, above all, by the almighty grace of God. But every man has within him the root of every sin.

How humble we ought to be, when we read these verses ! "We are all as an unclean thing" in God's

heart. Unquestionably there are many evils in "public schools," however carefully conducted. It must needs be so. We must ex-pect it. But it is no less true that there are great dangers in private education, and dangers in their kind quite as formidable as any which beset a boy at public school. Of course no universal rule can be laid down. Regard must be had to individual character and temperament. But to suppose, as some seem to do, that boys educated at public schools must turn out ill, and boys educated at home must turn out well, is surely not wise. It is forgetting our Lord's doctrine, that the heart is the principal source of evil. Without a change of heart a boy may be kept at home, and yet learn all manner of sin.

sight. (Isa. lxiv. 6.) He sees in each one of us countless evils, which the world never sees at all, for He
reads our hearts. Surely of all sins to which we are
liable, self-righteousness is the most unreasonable and
unbecoming.

How thankful we ought to be for the Gospel, when
we read these verses! That Gospel contains a complete
provision for all the wants of our poor defiled natures.
The blood of Christ can "cleanse us from all sin." The
Holy Ghost can change even our sinful hearts, and
keep them clean, when changed. The man that does
not glory in the Gospel can surely know little of the
plague that is within him.

How watchful we ought to be, when we remember
these verses! What a careful guard we ought to keep
over our imaginations, our tongues, and our daily behaviour! At the head of the black list of our heart's
contents, stand "evil thoughts." Let us never forget
that. Thoughts are the parents of words and deeds.
Let us pray daily for grace to keep our *thoughts* in order,
and let us cry earnestly and fervently, "Lead us not into
temptation."

MARK VII. 24—30.

24 And from thence he arose, and went into the borders of Tyre and Sidon, and entered into an house, and would have no man know *it:* but he could not be hid.

25 For a *certain* woman, whose young daughter had an unclean spirit, heard of him, and came and fell at his feet:

26 The woman was a Greek, a Syrophenician by nation; and she besought him that he would cast forth the devil out of her daughter.

27 But Jesus said unto her, Let the children first be filled: for it is not meet to take the children's bread, and to cast *it* unto the dogs.

28 And she answered and said unto him, Yes, Lord: yet the dogs under the table eat of the children's crumbs.

29 And he said unto her, For this saying go thy way; the devil is gone out of thy daughter.

30 And when she was come to her house, she found the devil gone out, and her daughter laid upon the bed.

WE know nothing of the woman who is here mentioned, beyond the facts that we here read. Her name, her former history, the way in which she was led to seek our Lord, though a Gentile, and dwelling in the borders of Tyre and Sidon,—all these things are hidden from us. But the few facts that are related about this woman are full of precious instruction. Let us observe them, and learn wisdom.

In the first place, *this passage is meant to encourage us to pray for others.* The woman who came to our Lord, in the history now before us, must doubtless have been in deep affliction. She saw a beloved child possessed by an unclean spirit. She saw her in a condition in which no teaching could reach the mind, and no medicine could heal the body,—a condition only one degree better than death itself. She hears of Jesus, and beseeches Him to "cast forth the devil out of her daughter." She prays for one who could not pray for herself, and never rests till her prayer is granted. By prayer she obtains the cure which no human means could obtain. Through the prayer of the mother the daughter is healed. On her own behalf that daughter did not speak a word ; but her mother spoke for her to the Lord, and did not speak in vain. Hopeless and desperate as her case appeared, she had a praying mother, and where there is a praying mother there is always hope.

The truth here taught is one of deep importance. The case here recorded is one that does not stand alone. Few duties are so strongly recommended by Scriptural example, as the duty of intercessory prayer. There is a long catalogue of instances in Scripture, which show the benefits that may be conferred on others by praying for them. The nobleman's son at Capernaum, the centurion's servant, the daughter of Jairus, are all striking examples. Wonderful as it may seem, God is pleased to do great things for souls, when friends and relations are moved to pray for them. "The effectual fervent prayer of a righteous man availeth much." (James v. 16.)

Fathers and mothers are especially bound to remember the case of this woman. They cannot give their children new hearts. They can give them Christian education, and show them the way of life; but they cannot give them a will to choose Christ's service, and a mind to love God. Yet there is one thing they can always do: they can pray for them. They can pray for the conversion of profligate sons, who will have their own way, and run greedily into sin. They can pray for the conversion of worldly daughters, who set their affections on things below, and love pleasure more than God. Such prayers are heard on high. Such prayers will often bring down blessings. Never, never let us forget that the children for whom many prayers have been offered seldom finally perish. Let us pray more for our sons and daughters. Even when they will not let us speak to them about religion, they cannot prevent us speaking for them to God.

In the second place, *this passage is meant to teach us to persevere in praying for others.* The woman whose history we are now reading, appeared at first to obtain nothing by her application to our Lord. On the contrary, our Lord's reply was discouraging. Yet she did not give up in despair. She prayed on, and did not faint.

She pressed her suit with ingenious arguments. She would take no refusal. She pleaded for a few " crumbs " of mercy, rather than none at all. And through this holy importunity she succeeded. She heard at last these joyful words : " For this saying go thy way ; the devil is gone out of thy daughter."

Perseverance in prayer is a point of great moment. Our hearts are apt to become cool and indifferent, and to think that it is no use to draw near to God. Our hands soon hang down, and our knees wax faint. Satan is ever labouring to draw us off from our prayers, and filling our minds with reasons why we may give them up.—These things are true with respect to all prayers, but they are especially true with respect to intercessory prayer. It is always far more meagre than it ought to be. It is often attempted for a little season, and then left off. We see no immediate answer to our prayers. We see the persons for whose souls we pray, going on still in sin. We draw the conclusion that it is useless to pray for them, and allow our intercession to come to an end.

In order to arm our minds with arguments for perseverance in intercessory prayer, let us often study the case of this woman. Let us remember how she prayed on, and did not faint in the face of great discouragement. Let us mark how at last she went home rejoicing, and let us resolve, by God's grace, to follow her example.

Do we know what it is to pray for ourselves ? This, after all, is the first question for self-inquiry. The man who never speaks to God about his own soul, can know nothing of praying for others. He is as yet

Godless, Christless, and hopeless, and has to learn the very rudiments of religion. Let him awake, and call upon God.

But do we pray for ourselves ? Then let us take heed that we pray for others also. Let us beware of selfish prayers,—prayers which are wholly taken up with our own affairs, and in which there is no place for other souls beside our own. Let us name all whom we love before God continually. Let us pray for all,—the worst, the hardest, and the most unbelieving. Let us continue praying for them year after year, in spite of their continued unbelief. God's time of mercy may be a distant one. Our eyes may not see an answer to our intercessions. The answer may not come for ten, fifteen, or twenty years. It may not come till we have exchanged prayer for praise, and are far away from this world. But while we live, let us pray for others. It is the greatest kindness we can do to any one, to speak for him to our Lord Jesus Christ. The day of judgment will show that one of the greatest links in drawing some souls to God, has been the intercessory prayer of friends.

MARK VII. 31—37.

31 And again, departing from the coasts of Tyre and Sidon, he came unto the sea of Galilee, through the midst of the coasts of Decapolis.

32 And they bring unto him one that was deaf, and had an impediment in his speech ; and they beseech him to put his hand upon him.

33 And he took him aside from the multitude, and put his fingers into his ears, and he spit, and touched his tongue ;

34 And looking up to heaven, he sighed, and said unto him, Ephphatha, that is, Be opened.

35 And straightway his ears were opened, and the string of his tongue was loosed, and he spake plain.

36 And he charged them that they should tell no man : but the more he charged them, so much the more a great deal they published *it* ;

37 And were beyond measure astonished, saying, He hath done all things well : he maketh both the deaf to hear, and the dumb to speak.

THE first thing that demands our notice in these verses,

is *the mighty miracle which is here recorded.* We read that they brought unto our Lord "one that was deaf and had an impediment in his speech," and besought Him that He would "put His hand upon him." At once the petition is granted, and the cure is wrought. Speech and hearing are instantaneously given to the man by a word and a touch. "Straightway his ears were opened, and the string of his tongue was loosed, and he spake plain."

We see but half the instruction of this passage, if we only regard it as an example of our Lord's divine power. It is such an example, beyond doubt, but it is something more than that. We must look further, deeper, and lower than the surface, and we shall find in the passage precious spiritual truths.

Here we are meant to see our Lord's power to heal the spiritually deaf. He can give the chief of sinners a hearing ear. He can make him delight in listening to the very Gospel which he once ridiculed and despised.

Here also we are meant to see our Lord's power to heal the spiritually dumb. He can teach the hardest of transgressors to call upon God. He can put a new song in the mouth of him whose talk was once only of this world. He can make the vilest of men speak of spiritual things, and testify the Gospel of the grace of God.

When Jesus pours forth His Spirit, nothing is impossible. We must never despair of others. We must never regard our own hearts as too bad to be changed. He that healed the deaf and dumb still lives. The cases which moral philosophy pronounces hopeless, are not incurable if they are brought to Christ.

The second thing which demands our notice in these verses, is.*the peculiar manner in which our Lord thought good to work the miracle here recorded.* We are told that when the deaf and dumb person was brought to Jesus, " He took him aside from the multitude, and put His fingers into his ears, and He spit and touched his tongue ; and looking up to heaven, He sighed,"—and then, and not till then, came the words of commanding power : " Ephphatha, that is, be opened."

There is undoubtedly much that is mysterious in these actions. We know not why they were used. It would have been as easy to our Lord to speak the word, and command health to return at once, as to do what He here did. His reasons for the course He adopted are not recorded. We only know that the result was the same as on other occasions : the man was cured.

But there is one simple lesson to be learned from our Lord's conduct on this occasion. That lesson is, that Christ was not tied to the use of any one means in doing His works among men. Sometimes He thought fit to work in one way, sometimes in another. His enemies were never able to say that unless He employed certain invariable agency He could not work at all.

We see the same thing going on still in the Church of Christ. We see continual proof that the Lord is not tied to the use of any one means exclusively in convey- ing grace to the soul. Sometimes He is pleased to work by the Word preached publicly, sometimes by the Word read privately. Sometimes He awakens people by sickness and affliction, sometimes by the rebukes or counsel of friends. Sometimes He employs means of

grace to turn people out of the way of sin.   Sometimes
He arrests their attention by some providence, without
any means of grace at all.   He will not have any means
of grace made an idol and exalted, to the disparagement
of other means.   He will not have any means despised
as useless, and neglected as of no value.   All are good
and valuable.   All are in their turn employed for the
same great end,—the conversion of souls.   All are in the
hands of Him who "giveth not account of His matters,"
and knows best which to use, in each separate case that
He heals.

The last thing which demands our notice in these
verses, is *the remarkable testimony which was borne by
those who saw the miracle here recorded.*   They said of
our Lord, "He hath done all things well!"

It is more than probable that those who said these
words were little sensible of their full meaning, when
applied to Christ.   Like Caiaphas, they "spoke not of
themselves." (John xi. 51.)   But the truth to which
they gave utterance is full of deep and unspeakable
comfort, and ought to be daily remembered by all true
Christians.

Let us remember it as we look back over the days
past of our lives, from the hour of our conversion.
" Our Lord hath done all things well."   In first bringing
us out of darkness into marvellous light,—in humbling
us and teaching us our weakness, guilt, and folly,—in
stripping us of our idols, and choosing all our portions,
—in placing us where we are, and giving us what we
have,—how well everything has been done!   How great
the mercy that we have not had our own way!

Let us remember it as we look forward to the days yet to come. We know not what they may be, bright or dark, many or few. But we know that we are in the hands of Him who "doeth all things well." He will not err in any of His dealings with us. He will take away and give, He will afflict and bereave, He will move and He will settle with perfect wisdom, at the right time, in the right way. The great Shepherd of the sheep makes no mistakes. He leads every lamb of His flock by the right way to the city of habitation.

We shall never see the full beauty of these words till the resurrection morning. We shall then look back over our lives, and know the meaning of everything that happened from first to last. We shall remember all the way by which we were led, and confess that all was "well done." The why and the wherefore, the causes and the reasons of every thing which now perplexes, will be clear and plain as the sun at noon-day. We shall wonder at our own past blindness, and marvel that we could ever have doubted our Lord's love. "Now we see through a glass darkly, but then face to face. Now we know in part, but then shall we know even as we are know." *   (1 Cor. xiii. 13.)

---

* The reason why our Lord made use of the previous actions recorded in this miracle,—spitting, looking up to heaven, and sighing,—is a question that has often perplexed commentators. Some observations of Luther, quoted by Stier, are worth reading:

"This sigh was not drawn from Christ on account of the single tongue and ear of this poor man; but it is a common sigh over all tongues and ears, yea over all hearts, bodies, and souls, and over all men, from Adam to his last descendant.

MARK VIII. 1—13.

1 In those days the multitude being very great, and having nothing to eat, Jesus called his disciples *unto him*, and saith unto them,

2 I have compassion on the multitude, because they have now been with me three days, and have nothing to eat:

3 And if I send them away fasting to their own houses, they will faint by the way: for divers of them came from far.

4 And his disciples answered him, From whence can a man satisfy these *men* with bread here in the wilderness?

5 And he asked them, How many loaves have ye? And they said, Seven.

6 And he commanded the people to sit down on the ground: and he took the seven loaves, and gave thanks, and brake, and gave to his disciples to set before *them;* and they did set *them* before the people.

7 And they had a few small fishes: and he blessed, and commanded to set them also before *them*.

8 So they did eat, and were filled: and they took up of the broken *meat* that was left seven baskets.

9 And they that had eaten were about four thousand: and he sent them away.

10 And straightway he entered into a ship with his disciples, and came into the parts of Dalmanutha.

11 And the Pharisees came forth, and began to question with him, seeking of him a sign from heaven, tempting him.

12 And he sighed deeply in his spirit, and saith, Why doth this generation seek after a sign? verily I say unto you, There shall no sign be given unto this generation.

13 And he left them, and entering into the ship again departed to the other side.

ONCE more we see our Lord feeding a great multitude with a few loaves and fishes. He knew the heart of man. He foresaw the rise of cavillers and sceptics, who would question the reality of the wonderful works He performed. By repeating the mighty miracle here recorded, He stops the mouth of all who are not wilfully blind to evidence. Publicly, and before four thousand witnesses, He shows His almighty power a second time.

Let us observe, in this passage, *how great is the kindness and compassion of our Lord Jesus Christ.* He saw around Him a "very great multitude," who had nothing to eat. He knew that the great majority were following

"Our beloved Lord saw well what an amount of suffering and sorrow would be occasioned by tongues and ears. For the greatest mischief which has been inflicted on Christianity has not arisen from tyrants (with persecution, murder, and pride against the word), but from that little bit of flesh which abides between the jaws. This it is that inflicts the greatest injury upon the kingdom of God."

Him from no other motive than idle curiosity, and had no claim whatever to be regarded as His disciples. Yet when He saw them hungry and destitute, He pitied them: "I have compassion on the multitude, because they have now been with me three days, and have nothing to eat."

The feeling heart of our Lord Jesus Christ appears in these words. He has compassion even on those who are not His people,—the faithless, the graceless, the followers of this world. He feels tenderly for them, though they know it not. He died for them, though they care little for what He did on the cross. He would receive them graciously, and pardon them freely, if they would only repent and believe on Him. Let us ever beware of measuring the love of Christ by any human measure. He has a special love, beyond doubt, for His own believing people. But He has also a general love of compassion, even for the unthankful and the evil. His love "passeth knowledge." (Eph. iii. 19.)

Let us strive to make Jesus our pattern in this, as well as in everything else. Let us be kind and compassionate, and pitiful, and courteous to all men. Let us be ready to do good to all men, and not only to friends and the household of faith. Let us carry into practice our Lord's injunction: "Love your enemies, bless them that curse you, do good to them that hate you." (Matt. v. 44.) This is to show the mind of Christ. This is the right way to heap coals of fire on an enemy's head, and to melt foes into friends. (Rom. xii. 20.)

Let us observe, in the second place, from this passage, *that with Christ nothing is impossible.* The disciples said.

"From whence can a man satisfy these men with bread here in the wilderness?" They might well say so. Without the hand of Him who first made the world out of nothing, the thing could not be. But in the almighty hand of Jesus seven loaves and a few fishes were made sufficient to satisfy four thousand men. Nothing is too hard for the Lord.

We must never allow ourselves to doubt Christ's power to supply the spiritual wants of all His people. He has "bread enough and to spare" for every soul that trusts in Him. Weak, infirm, corrupt, empty as believers feel themselves, let them never despair, while Jesus lives. In Him there is a boundless store of mercy and grace, laid up for the use of all His believing members, and ready to be bestowed on all who ask in prayer. "It pleased the Father that in Him should all fulness dwell." (Col. i. 19.)

Let us never doubt Christ's providential care for the temporal wants of all His people. He knows their circumstances. He is acquainted with all their necessities. He will never allow them to lack anything that is really for their good. His heart is not changed since He ascended up on high, and sat down on the right hand of God. He still lives who had compassion on the hungry crowd in the wilderness, and supplied their need. How much more, may we suppose, will He supply the need of those who trust Him? He will supply them without fail. Their faith may occasionally be tried. They may sometimes be kept waiting, and be brought very low. But the believer shall never be left entirely destitute. "Bread shall be given him; his water shall be sure." (Isaiah xxxiii. 16.)

Let us observe, in the last place, *how much sorrow unbelief occasions to our Lord Jesus Christ.* We are told that when "the Pharisees began to question with Him, seeking of Him a sign from heaven, tempting Him, He sighed deeply in His spirit." There was a deep meaning in that sigh! It came from a heart which mourned over the ruin which these wicked men were bringing on their own souls. Enemies as they were, Jesus could not behold them hardening themselves in unbelief without sorrow.

The feeling which our Lord Jesus Christ here expressed, will always be the feeling of all true Christians. Grief over the sins of others is one leading evidence of true grace. The man who is really converted, will always regard the unconverted with pity and concern. This was the mind of David : " I beheld the transgressors, and was grieved." (Psalm cxix. 158.) This was the mind of the godly in the days of Ezekiel : " They sighed and cried for the abominations done in the land." (Ezek. ix. 4.) This was the mind of Lot : " He vexed his righteous soul with the unlawful deeds " of those around him. (2 Peter ii. 8.) This was the mind of Paul : " I have great heaviness and continual sorrow for my brethren." (Rom. ix. 2.) In all these cases we see something of the mind of Christ. As the great Head feels, so feel the members. They all grieve when they see sin.

Let us leave the passage with solemn self-inquiry. Do we know anything of likeness to Christ, and fellow-feeling with Him? Do we feel hurt, and pained, and sorrowful, when we see men continuing in sin and unbelief? Do we feel grieved and concerned about the state of the unconverted? These are heart-searching questions, and demand serious consideration. There are few surer marks of an unconverted heart than carelessness and indifference about the souls of others.

Finally, let us never forget that unbelief and sin are just as great a cause of grief to our Lord now, as they were eighteen hundred years ago. Let us strive and pray that we may not add to that grief by any act or deed of ours. The sin of grieving Christ is one which many commit continually without thought or reflection. He that sighed over the unbelief of the Pharisees is still unchanged. Can we doubt that when He sees some persisting in unbelief at the present day, He is grieved? From such sin may we be delivered.

MARK VIII. 14—21.

14 Now *the disciples* had forgotten to take bread, neither had they in the ship with them more than one loaf.

15 And he charged them, saying, Take heed, beware of the leaven of the Pharisees, and *of* the leaven of Herod.

16 And they reasoned among themselves, saying, *It is* because we have no bread.

17 And when Jesus knew *it*, he saith unto them, Why reason ye, because ye have no bread? perceive ye not yet, neither understand? have ye your heart yet hardened?

18 Having eyes, see ye not? and having ears, hear ye not? and do ye not remember?

19 When I brake the five loaves among five thousand, how many baskets full of fragments took ye up? They say unto him, Twelve.

20 And when the seven among four thousands, how many baskets full of fragments took ye up? And they said, Seven.

21 And he said unto them, How is it that ye do not understand?

LET us notice *the solemn warning* which our Lord gives to His disciples at the beginning of this passage. He says, "Take heed, beware of the leaven of the Pharisees, and of the leaven of Herod."

We are not left to conjecture the meaning of this

warning.   This is made clear by the parallel passage in
St. Matthew's Gospel.   We there read that Jesus did
not mean the leaven of "bread," but the leaven of
"doctrine."   The self-righteousness and formalism of
the Pharisees, the worldliness and scepticism of the
courtiers of Herod, were the objects of our Lord's caution.   Against both He bids His disciples be on their
guard.

Such warnings are of deep importance.   It would be
well for the Church of Christ if they had been more
remembered.   The assaults of persecution from without
have never done half so much harm to the Church as
the rise of false doctrines within.   False prophets and
false teachers within the camp have done far more mischief in Christendom than all the bloody persecutions of
the Emperors of Rome.   The sword of the foe has never
done such damage to the cause of truth as the tongue
and the pen.

The doctrines which our Lord specifies, are precisely
those which have always been found to inflict most
injury on the cause of Christianity.   Formalism, on the
one hand, and scepticism, on the other, have been
chronic diseases in the professing Church of Christ.   In
every age multitudes of Christians have been infected
by them.   In every age men need to watch against them,
and be on their guard.

The expression used by our Lord in speaking of false
doctrine is singularly forcible and appropriate.   He calls
it "leaven."   No word more suitable could have been
employed.   It exactly describes the small beginnings of
false doctrine,—the subtle quiet way in which it insen-

sibly pervades a man's religion,—the deadly power with which it changes the whole character of his Christianity. Here, in fact, lies the great danger of false doctrine. If it approached us under its true colours, it would do little harm. The great secret of its success is its subtlety and likeness to truth. Every error in religion has been said to be a truth abused.

Let us often examine "ourselves whether we be in the faith," and "beware of leaven." Let us no more trifle with a little false doctrine than we would trifle with a little immorality, or a little lie. Once admit it into our hearts, and we never know how far it may lead us astray. The beginning of departure from the pure truth is like the letting out of waters,—first a drop, and at last a torrent. "A little leaven leaveneth the whole lump." (Gal. v. 9.)

Let us notice *the dull understanding of the disciples*, when our Lord gave the warning of this passage. They thought that the "leaven" of which He spoke must be the leaven of bread. It never struck them that He was speaking of doctrine. They drew from Him the sharp reproof, "Perceive ye not yet, neither understand? have ye your heart yet hardened? How is it that ye do not understand?" Believers, converted, renewed, as the disciples were, they were still dull of apprehension in spiritual things. Their eyes were still dim, and their perception slow in the matters of the kingdom of God.

We shall find it useful to ourselves to remember what is here recorded of the disciples. It may help to correct the high thoughts which we are apt to entertain of our own wisdom, and to keep us humble and lowly minded.

We must not fancy that we know everything as soon as we are converted. Our knowledge, like all our graces, is always imperfect, and never so far from perfection as at our first beginning in the service of Christ. There is more ignorance in our hearts than we are at all aware of. "If any man think that he knoweth anything, he knoweth nothing yet as he ought to know." (1 Cor. viii. 2.)

Above all, we shall find it useful to remember what is here recorded, in dealing with young Christians. We must not expect perfection in a new convert. We must not set him down as graceless, and godless, and a false professor, because at first he sees but half the truth, and commits many mistakes. His heart may be right in the sight of God, and yet, like the disciples, he may be very slow of understanding in the things of the Spirit. We must bear with him patiently, and not cast him aside. We must give him time to grow in grace and knowledge, and his latter end may find him ripe in wisdom, like Peter and John. It is a blessed thought that Jesus, our Master in heaven, despises none of His people. Marvellous and blameworthy as their slowness to learn undoubtedly is, His patience never gives way. He goes on teaching them, "line upon line, precept upon precept." Let us do likewise. Let it be a rule with us never to despise the weakness and dulness of young Christians. Wherever we see a spark of true grace, however dim and mixed with infirmity, let us be helpful and kind. Let us do as we would be done by.

MARK VIII. 22—26.

22 And he cometh to Bethsaida; and they bring a blind man unto him, and besought him to touch him.

23 And he took the blind man by the hand, and led him out of the town; and when he had spit on his eyes, and put his hands upon him, he asked him if he saw ought.

24 And he looked up, and said, I see men as trees, walking.

25 After that he put *his* hands again upon his eyes, and made him look up : and he was restored, and saw every man clearly.

26 And he sent him away to his house, saying, Neither go into the town, nor tell *it* to any in the town.

WE do not know the reason of the peculiar means employed by our Lord Jesus Christ in working the miracle recorded in these verses. We see a blind man miraculously healed. We know that a word from our Lord's mouth, or a touch of His hand would have been sufficient to effect a cure. But we see Jesus taking this blind man by the hand,—leading him out of the town,—spitting on his eyes,—putting His hands on him, and then, and not till then, restoring his sight. And the meaning of all these actions the passage before us leaves entirely unexplained.

But it is well to remember, in reading passages of this kind, that the Lord is not tied to the use of any one means. In the conversion of men's souls there are diversities of operation, but it is the same Spirit which converts. So also in the healing of men's bodies there were varieties of agency employed by our Lord, but it was the same Divine power that effected the cure. In all His works God is a sovereign. He giveth not account of any of His matters.

One thing in the passage demands our special observation. That thing is the gradual nature of the cure which our Lord performed on this blind man. He did not deliver him from his blindness at once, but by degrees. He might have done it in a moment, but He

M

chose to do it step by step. First the blind man said that he only saw "men as trees walking." Afterwards his eyesight was restored completely, and he "saw every man clearly." In this respect the miracle stands entirely alone.

We need hardly doubt that this gradual cure was meant to be an emblem of spiritual things. We may be sure that there was a deep meaning in every word and work of our Lord's earthly ministry, and here, as in other places, we shall find a useful lesson.

Let us see then in this gradual restoration to sight, a vivid illustration of *the manner in which the Spirit frequently works in the conversion of souls.* We are all naturally blind and ignorant in the matters which concern our souls. Conversion is an illumination, a change from darkness to light, from blindness to seeing the kingdom of God. Yet few converted people see things distinctly at first. The nature and proportion of doctrines, practices, and ordinances of the Gospel are dimly seen by them, and imperfectly understood. They are like the man before us, who at first saw men as trees walking. Their vision is dazzled and unaccustomed to the new world into which they have been introduced. It is not till the work of the Spirit has become deeper and their experience been somewhat matured, that they see all things clearly, and give to each part of religion its proper place. This is the history of thousands of God's children. They begin with seeing men as trees walking,—they end with seeing all clearly. Happy is he who has learned this lesson well, and is humble and distrustful of his own judgment.

Finally, let us see in the gradual cure of this blind man, a striking picture of *the present position of Christ's believing people in the world,* compared with that which is to come. We see in part and know in part in the present dispensation. We are like those that travel by night. We know not the meaning of much that is passing around us. In the providential dealings of God with His children, and in the conduct of many of God's saints, we see much that we cannot understand,—and cannot alter. In short, we are like him that saw "men as trees walking."

But let us look forward and take comfort. The time comes when we shall see all "clearly." The night is far spent. The day is at hand. Let us be content to wait, and watch, and work, and pray. When the day of the Lord comes, our spiritual eyesight will be perfected. We shall see as we have been seen, and know as we have been known.

MARK VIII. 27—33.

27 And Jesus went out, and his disciples, into the towns of Cæsarea Philippi: and by the way he asked his disciples, saying unto them, Whom do men say that I am?

28 And they answered, John the Baptist: but some *say,* Elias; and others, One of the prophets.

29 And he saith unto them, But whom say ye that I am? And Peter answereth and saith unto him, Thou art the Christ.

30 And he charged them that they should tell no man of him.

31 And he began to teach them, that the Son of man must suffer many things, and be rejected of the elders, and *of* the chief priests, and scribes, and be killed, and after three days rise again.

32 And he spake that saying openly. And Peter took him, and began to rebuke him.

33 But when he had turned about and looked on his disciples, he rebuked Peter, saying, Get thee behind me, Satan: for thou savourest not the things that be of God, but the things that be of men.

THE circumstances here recorded are of great importance. They took place during a journey, and arose out

of a conversation " by the way." Happy are those journeys, in which time is not wasted on trifles, but redeemed as far as possible for the consideration of
serious things.

Let us observe *the variety of opinions about Christ*,
which prevailed among the Jews. Some said that He
was John the Baptist,—some Elias,—and others one of
the Prophets. In short, every kind of opinion appears to
have been current, excepting that one which was true.

We may see the same thing on every side at the
present day. Christ and His Gospel are just as little
understood in reality, and are the subject of just as
many different opinions as they were eighteen hundred
years ago. Many know the name of Christ, acknowledge
Him as One who came into the world to save sinners,
and regularly worship in buildings set apart for His
service. Few thoroughly realize that He is very God,—
the one Mediator,—the one High Priest,—the only source
of life and peace,—their own Shepherd and their own
Friend. Vague ideas about Christ are still very common.
Intelligent experimental acquaintance with Christ is still
very rare. May we never rest till we can say of Christ,
" My beloved is mine, and I am His." (Cant. ii. 16.)
This is saving knowledge. This is life eternal.

Let us observe *the good confession of faith which the
Apostle Peter witnessed.* He replied to our Lord's question,
"Whom say ye that I am ?" "Thou art the Christ."

This was a noble answer, when the circumstances
under which it was made are duly considered. It was
made when Jesus was poor in condition, without honour,
majesty, wealth, or power. It was made when the

heads of the Jewish nation, both in Church and State, refused to receive Jesus as the Messiah.   Yet even then Simon Peter says, "Thou art the Christ."   His strong faith was not stumbled by our Lord's poverty and low estate.   His confidence was not shaken by the opposition of scribes and pharisees, and the contempt of rulers and priests.   None of these things moved Simon Peter.   He believed that He whom he followed, Jesus of Nazareth, was the promised Saviour, the true Prophet greater than Moses, the long-predicted Messiah.   He declared it boldly and unhesitatingly, as the creed of himself and his few companions: "Thou art the Christ."

There is much that we may profitably learn from Peter's conduct on this occasion.   Erring and unstable as he sometimes was, the faith he exhibited in the passage now before us is well worthy of imitation. Such bold confessions as his are the truest evidence of living faith, and are required in every age, if men will prove themselves to be Christ's disciples.   We too must be ready to confess Christ, even as Peter did.   We shall never find our Master and His doctrine popular.   We must be prepared to confess Him, with few on our side, and many against us.   But let us take courage and walk in Peter's steps, and we shall not fail of receiving Peter's reward.   Jesus takes notice of those who confess Him before men, and will one day confess them as His servants before an assembled world.

Let us observe *the full declaration which our Lord makes of His own coming death and resurrection.*   We read that "He began to teach them, that the Son of man must suffer many things, and be rejected of the elders, and of the chief priests, and scribes, and be killed, and after three days rise again."

The events here announced must have sounded strange to the disciples.   To be told that their beloved Master, after all His mighty works, would soon be put to death, must have been heavy tidings, and past their understanding   But the words which convey the announcement are scarcely less remarkable than the event : " He *must* suffer,—He *must* be killed,—He *must* rise again."

Why did our Lord say " must " ?   Did He mean that He was unable to escape suffering,—that He must die by compulsion of a stronger power than His own? Impossible.   This could not have been His meaning.— Did He mean that He must needs die to give a great example to the world of self-sacrifice and self-denial, and that this, and this alone, made His death necessary ? Once more it may be replied, " Impossible."—There is a far deeper meaning in the word " must " suffer and be killed.   He meant that His death and passion were necessary in order to make atonement for man's sin. Without shedding His blood, there could be no remission. Without the sacrifice of His body on the cross, there could be no satisfaction to God's holy law.   He " must " suffer to make reconciliation for iniquity.   He " must " die because without His death as a propitiatory offering sinners could never have life.   He " must " suffer, because without His vicarious sufferings, our sins could never be taken away.   In a word, He " must " be delivered for our offences, and raised again for our justification.

Here is the centre truth of our Bible.   Let us never forget that.   All other truths compared to this are of

secondary importance. Whatever views we hold of religious truth, let us see that we have a firm grasp upon
the atoning efficacy of Christ's death. Let the truth so
often proclaimed by our Lord to His disciples, and so
diligently taught by the disciples to the world, be the
foundation truth in our Christianity. In life and in
death, in health and in sickness, let us lean all our
weight on this mighty fact,—that though we have sinned,
Christ hath died for sinners, and that though we deserve
nothing, Christ hath suffered on the cross for us, and
by that suffering purchased heaven for all that believe
in Him.

Finally, let us observe in this passage, *the strange
mixture of grace and infirmity which may be found in
the heart of a true Christian.* We see that very Peter
who had just witnessed so noble a confession, presuming
to rebuke his Master because He spoke of suffering
and dying. We see him drawing down on himself the
sharpest rebuke which ever fell from our Lord's lips
during His earthly ministry: "Get thee behind Me,
Satan: thou savourest not the things that be of God,
but the things that be of man."

We have here a humbling proof that the best of saints
is a poor fallible creature.—Here was *ignorance* in
Simon Peter. He did not understand the necessity of
our Lord's death, and would have actually prevented
His sacrifice on the cross.—Here was *self-conceit* in
Simon Peter. He thought he knew what was right
and fitting for his Master better than his Master himself,
and actually undertook to show the Messiah a more
excellent way.—And last, but not least, Simon Peter

did it all with the *best intentions!*   He meant well.
His motives were pure.   But zeal and earnestness are no
excuse for error.   A man may mean well and yet fall
into tremendous mistakes.

Let us learn humility from the facts here recorded.
Let us beware of being puffed up with our own spiritual
attainments, or exalted by the praise of others.   Let
us never think that we know everything and are not
likely to err.   We see that it is but a little step from
making a good confession to being a "Satan" in Christ's
way.   Let us pray daily, "Hold Thou me up,—keep
me,—teach me,—let me not err."

Lastly, let us learn charity towards others, from the
facts here recorded.   Let us not be in a hurry to cast off
our brother as graceless because of errors and mistakes.
Let us remember that his heart may be right in the
sight of God, like Peter's, though like Peter he may for
a time turn aside.   Rather let us call to mind St. Paul's
advice and act upon it.   "If a man be overtaken in a
fault, ye which are spiritual, restore such an one in the
spirit of meekness ; considering thyself, lest thou also be
tempted."   (Gal. vi. 1.)

MARK VIII. 34—38.

34 And when he had called the people *unto him* with his disciples also, he said unto them, Whosoever will come after me, let him deny himself, and take up his cross, and follow me.

35 For whosoever will save his life shall lose it; but whosoever shall lose his life for my sake and the gospel's, the same shall save it.

36 For what shall it profit a man, if he shall gain the whole world, and lose his own soul ?

37 Or what shall a man give in exchange for his soul ?

38 Whosoever therefore shall be ashamed of me and of my words in this adulterous and sinful generation ; of him also shall the Son of man be ashamed, when he cometh in the glory of his Father with the holy angels.

THE words of our Lord Jesus Christ in this passage are

peculiarly weighty and solemn. They were spoken to correct the mistaken views of His disciples, as to the nature of His kingdom. But they contain truths of the deepest importance to Christians in every age of the Church. The whole passage is one which should often form the subject of private meditation.

We learn, for one thing, from these verses, *the absolute necessity of self-denial, if we would be Christ's disciples, and be saved.* What saith our Lord? "Whosoever will come after Me, let him deny himself, and take up his cross, and follow Me."

Salvation is undoubtedly all of grace. It is offered freely in the Gospel to the chief of sinners, without money and without price. "By grace are ye saved through faith, and that not of yourselves; it is the gift of God: not of works, lest any man should boast." (Ephes. ii. 8, 9.) But all who accept this great salvation must prove the reality of their faith by carrying the cross after Christ. They must not think to enter heaven without trouble, pain, suffering, and conflict on earth. They must be content to take up the cross of doctrine, and the cross of practice,—the cross of holding a faith which the world despises, and the cross of living a life which the world ridicules as too strict and righteous overmuch. They must be willing to crucify the flesh, to mortify the deeds of the body, to fight daily with the devil, to come out from the world, and to lose their lives, if needful, for Christ's sake and the Gospel's.—These are hard sayings, but they admit of no evasion. The words of our Lord are plain and unmistakable. If we will not carry the cross, we shall never wear the crown.

Let us not be deterred from Christ's service by fear of the cross. Heavy as that cross may seem, Jesus will give us grace to bear it. "I can do all things through Christ which strengtheneth me." (Phil. iv. 13.) Thousands and tens of thousands have borne it before us, and have found Christ's yoke easy, and Christ's burden light. No good thing on earth was ever attained without trouble. We cannot surely expect that without trouble we can enter the kingdom of God. Let us go forward boldly, and allow no difficulty to keep us back. The cross by the way is but for a few years. The glory at the end is for evermore.

Let us often ask ourselves whether our Christianity costs us anything? Does it entail any sacrifice? Has it the true stamp of heaven? Does it carry with it any cross?—If not, we may well tremble and be afraid. We have everything to learn. A religion which costs nothing, is worth nothing. It will do us no good in the life that now is. It will lead to no salvation in the life to come.

We learn, for another thing, from these verses, *the unspeakable value of the soul*. What saith our Lord? "What shall it profit a man, if he shall gain the whole world, and lose his own soul?" These words were meant to stir us up to exertion and self-denial. They ought to ring in our ears like a trumpet, every morning when we rise from our beds, and every night when we lie down. May they be deeply graven in our memories, and never effaced by the devil and the world!

We have all souls that will live for evermore. Whether we know it or not, we all carry about with us something which will live on when our bodies are mouldering in the grave.   We have all souls, for which we shall have to give account to God.   It is an awful thought, when we consider how little attention most men give to anything except this world : but it is true.

Any man may lose his own soul.   He cannot save it : Christ alone can do that.   But he can lose it, and that in many different ways.—He may murder it, by loving sin and cleaving to the world.—He may poison it, by choosing a religion of lies and believing man-made superstitions.—He may starve it, by neglecting all means of grace and refusing to receive into his heart the Gospel. —Many are the ways that lead to the pit. Whatever way a man takes, he, and he alone, is accountable for it. Weak, corrupt, fallen, impotent as human nature is, man has a mighty power of destroying, ruining, and losing his own soul.

The whole world cannot make up to a man the loss of his soul.   The possession of all the treasures that the world contains would not compensate for eternal ruin. They would not satisfy us, and make us happy while we had them.   They could only be enjoyed for a few years, at best, and must then be left for evermore. Of all un- profitable and foolish bargains that man can make, the worst is that of giving up his soul's salvation for the sake of this present world. It is a bargain of which thousands, like Esau, who sold his birthright for a mess of pottage, have repented,—but many, unhappily, like Esau, have repented too late.

Let these sayings of our Lord sink deep into our hearts. Words are inadequate to express their importance. May we remember them in the hour of temptation, when the soul seems a small and unimportant thing, and the world seems very bright and great. May we remember them in the hour of persecution, when we are tried by the fear of man, and half inclined to forsake Christ. In hours like these let us call to mind this mighty question of our Lord, and repeat it to ourselves: " What shall it profit a man, if he gain the whole world, and lose his own soul ? "

We learn, in the last place, from these verses *the great danger of being ashamed of Christ.* What saith our Lord ? " Whosoever shall be ashamed of Me and of my words in this adulterous and sinful generation, of him also shall the Son of Man be ashamed, when He cometh in the glory of His Father with the holy angels."

When can it be said of any one, that he is ashamed of Christ? We are guilty of it when we are ashamed of letting people see that we believe and love the doctrines of Christ, that we desire to live according to the commandment of Christ, and that we wish to be reckoned among the people of Christ. Christ's doctrine, laws, and people were never popular, and never will be. The man who boldly confesses that he loves them, is sure to bring on himself ridicule and persecution. Whosoever shrinks from this confession from fear of this ridicule and persecution, is ashamed of Christ, and comes under the sentence of the passage before us.

Perhaps there are few of our Lord's sayings which are more condemning than this. " The fear of man " does indeed " bring a snare." (Prov. xxix. 25.) There are thousands of men who would face a lion, or storm a breach, if duty called them, and fear nothing,—and yet would be ashamed of being thought "religious," and would not dare to avow that they desired to please Christ rather than man. Wonderful indeed is the power of ridicule! Marvellous is the bondage in which men live to the opinion of the world!

Let us all pray daily for faith and courage to confess Christ before men. Of sin, or worldliness, or unbelief, we may well be ashamed. We ought never to be ashamed of Him who died for us on the cross. In spite of laughter, mockery, and hard words, let us boldly avow that we serve Christ. Let us often look forward to the day of His second coming, and remember what He says in this place. Better a thousand times confess Christ now, and be despised by man, than be disowned by Christ before His Father in the day of judgment.

MARK IX. 1—13.

1 And he said unto them, Verily I say unto you, That there be some of them that stand here, which shall not taste of death, till they have seen the kingdom of God come with power.

2 And after six days Jesus taketh *with him* Peter, and James, and John, and leadeth them up into an high mountain apart by themselves: and he was transfigured before them.

3 And his raiment became shining, exceeding white as snow; so as no fuller on earth can white them.

4 And there appeared unto them Elias with Moses: and they were talking with Jesus.

5 And Peter answered and said to Jesus, Master, it is good for us to be here: and let us make three tabernacles; one for thee, and one for Moses, and one for Elias.

6 For he wist not what to say; for they were sore afraid.

7 And there was a cloud that overshadowed them: and a voice came out of the cloud, saying, This is my beloved Son: hear him.

8 And suddenly, when they had looked round about, they saw no man any more, save Jesus only with themselves.

9 And as they came down from the mountain, he charged them that they should tell no man what things they had seen, till the Son of man were risen from the dead.

10 And they kept that saying with themselves, questioning one with another what the rising from the dead should mean.

11 And they asked him, saying, Why say the scribes that Elias must first come?

12 And he answered and told them, Elias verily cometh first, and restoreth all things; and how it is written of the Son of man, that he must suffer many things, and be set at nought.

13 But I say unto you, That Elias is indeed come, and they have done unto him whatsoever they listed, as it is written of him.

THE connection of this passage with the end of the last chapter ought never to be overlooked. Our Lord had been speaking of His own coming death and passion,—of the necessity of self-denial, if men would be His disciples,—of the need of losing our lives, if we would have them saved.—But in the same breath He goes on to speak of His future kingdom and glory. He takes off the edge of His " hard sayings," by promising a sight of that glory to some of those who heard Him. And in the history of the transfiguration, which is here recorded, we see that promise fulfilled.

The first thing which demands our notice in these verses, is *the marvellous vision they contain of the glory which Christ and His people shall have at His second coming.*

There can be no doubt that this was one of the principal purposes of the transfiguration. It was meant to teach the disciples, that though their Lord was lowly and poor in appearance now, He would one day appear in such royal majesty as became the son of God. It was meant to teach them, that when their Master came the second time, His saints, like Moses and Elias, would appear with Him. It was meant to remind them, that though reviled and persecuted now, because they belonged to Christ, they would one day be clothed with honour, and be partakers of their Master's glory.*

* The analogy between the glory assumed by our Lord at His transfiguration, and the glory which the saints shall receive at His resurrection, is well pointed out by Victor Antiochenus in a passage quoted by Du Veil. He says, "We must not suppose that there is to be any change of the natural form of man in the kingdom of heaven. For as the appearance of Christ was not in

We have reason to thank God for this vision. We are often tempted to give up Christ's service, because of the cross and affliction which it entails. We see few with us, and many against us. We find our names cast out as evil, and all manner of evil said of us, because we believe and love the Gospel. Year after year we see our companions in Christ's service removed by death, and we feel as if we knew little about them, except that they are gone to an unknown world, and that we are left alone. All these things are trying to flesh and blood. No wonder that the faith of believers sometimes languishes, and their eyes fail while they look for their hope.

Let us see in the story of the transfiguration, a remedy for such doubting thoughts as these. The vision of the holy mount is a gracious pledge that glorious things are in store for the people of God. Their crucified Saviour shall come again in power and great glory. His saints shall all come with Him, and are in safe keeping until that happy day. We may wait patiently. "When Christ, who is our life shall appear, then shall ye also appear with Him in glory." (Coloss. iii. 4.)

The second thing which demands our notice in this passage, is *the strong expression of the Apostle Peter, when he saw his Lord transfigured.* "Master," he said, "it is good for us to be here."

No doubt there was much in this saying, which cannot be commended. It showed an ignorauce of the purpose

itself changed, but only illumined (or glorified),—so, also, the just who will be conformed to His glorious body, will not be changed as to their outward form. Their bodies will only receive a certain accession of splendour and light, which St. Paul calls a change (1 Cor. xv. 52), but the Evangelists a transfiguration."

for which Jesus came into the world, to suffer and to die. It showed a forgetfulness of his brethren, who were not with him, and of the dark world which so much needed his Master's presence. Above all, the proposal which he made at the same time, to "build three tabernacles," for Moses, Elias, and Christ, showed a low view of his Master's dignity, and implied that he did not know that a greater than Moses and Elias was there. In all these respects the Apostle's exclamation is not to be praised, but to be blamed.

But having said this, let us not fail to remark what joy and happiness this glorious vision conferred on this warm-hearted disciple.* Let us see in his fervent cry, "It is good to be here," what comfort and consolation the sight of glory can give to a true believer. Let us look forward, and try to form some idea of the pleasure which the saints shall experience, when they shall at last meet the Lord Jesus at His second coming, and meet to part no more. A vision of a few minutes was sufficient to warm and stir Peter's heart. The sight of two saints in glory was so cheering and quickening, that he would fain have enjoyed more of it. What then shall we say, when we see our Lord appear at the last day with all His saints? What shall we say, when we ourselves are

---

* The remark of Brentius on the glorious nature of the whole vision of the transfiguration is well worth quoting. Like most of that admirable commentator's expositions, it contains much in few words.

"No Synod on earth was ever more gloriously attended than this. No assembly was ever more illustrious. Here is God the Father, God the Son, and God the Holy Ghost. Here are Moses and Elias, the chief of the Prophets. Here are Peter, James, and John, the chief of the Apostles."

allowed to share in His glory, and join the happy company
and feel that we shall go out no more from the joy of our
Lord ? These are questions that no man can answer.
The happiness of that great day of gathering together is
one that we cannot now conceive. The feelings of which
Peter had a little foretaste, will then be ours in full experience. We shall all say with one heart and one voice, when
we see Christ and all His saints, " It is good to be here."

The last thing which demands our notice in this
passage is *the distinct testimony which it bears to Christ's
office and dignity, as the promised Messiah.* We see this
testimony first in the appearance of Moses and Elias,
the representatives of the law and the prophets. They
appear as witnesses that Jesus is He of whom they spoke
in old times, and of whom they wrote that He would
come. They disappear after a few minutes, and leave
Jesus alone, as though they would show that they were
only witnesses, and that our Master having come, the
servants resign to Him the chief place.—We see this
testimony, secondly, in the miraculous Voice from heaven,
saying, " This is my beloved Son : hear Him." The same
Voice of God the Father which was heard at our Lord's
baptism, was heard once more at His transfiguration.
On both occasions there was the same solemn declaration :
" This is my beloved Son." On this last occasion, there
was an addition of two most important words : " Hear
Him."

The whole conclusion of the vision was calculated to
leave a lasting impression on the minds of the three
disciples. It taught them in the most striking manner,
that their Lord was as far above them and the prophets,

N

as the master of the house is above the servants, and that they must in all things believe, follow, obey, trust, and hear Him.

Finally, the last words of the Voice from heaven, are words that should be ever before the minds of all true Christians. They should " *hear Christ.*" He is the great Teacher : they that would be wise must learn of Him. He is the Light of the world : they that would not err must follow Him. He is the Head of the Church : they that would be living members of His mystical body must ever look to Him. The grand question that concerns us all is not so much what man says or ministers say, what the Church says or what councils say, but—What says Christ ? Him let us hear. In Him let us abide. On Him let us lean. To Him let us look. He and He only will never fail us, never disappoint us, and never lead us astray. Happy are they who know experimentally the meaning of the text, " My sheep hear my voice, and I know them, and they follow Me : and I give unto them eternal life ; and they shall never perish, neither shall any man pluck them out of my hand." *   (John x. 27, 28.)

* The coming of Elias, or Elijah, which forms the topic of conversation between our Lord and His disciples in the latter part of the passage now expounded, is a deep and mysterious subject.

(1) According to one class of interpreters, the ministry of John the Baptist was the coming of Elias. They consider that the prophecy of Malachi (Mal. iv. 5, 6), that Elijah the Prophet should be sent before the great and dreadful day of the Lord, was completely accomplished in John the Baptist, and that no other coming of Elias is to be expected. This is the view maintained by the great majority of Protestant commentators, both English and foreign, from the time of the Reformation to the present day.

(2) According to another class of interpreters, a literal coming of

MARK IX. 14—29.

14 And when he came to *his* disciples, he saw a great multitude about them, and the scribes questioning with them.

15 And straightway all the people, when they beheld him, were greatly amazed, and running to *him* saluted him.

16 And he asked the scribes, What question ye with them? .

17 And one of the multitude answered and said, Master, I have brought unto thee my son, which hath a dumb spirit;

18 And wheresoever he taketh him, he teareth him: and he foameth, and gnasheth with his teeth, and pineth away: and I spake to thy disciples that they should cast him out; and they could not.

19 He answereth him, and saith, O faithless generation, how long shall I be with you? how long shall I suffer you? bring him unto me.

20 And they brought him unto him: and when he saw him, straightway the spirit tare him; and he fell on the ground, and wallowed foaming.

21 And he asked his father, How long is it ago since this came unto him? And he said, Of a child.

22 And ofttimes it hath cast him into the fire, and into the waters, to destroy him: but if thou canst do any thing, have compassion on us, and help us.

23 Jesus said unto him, If thou canst believe, all things *are* possible to him that believeth.

24 And straightway the father of the child cried out, and said with tears, Lord, I believe; help thou mine unbelief.

25 When Jesus saw that the people came running together, he rebuked the foul spirit, saying unto him, *Thou* dumb and deaf spirit, I charge thee, come out of him, and enter no more into him.

26 And *the spirit* cried, and rent him sore, and came out of him: and he was as one dead; insomuch that many said, He is dead.

27 But Jesus took him by the hand, and lifted him up; and he arose.

28 And when he was come into the house, his disciples asked him privately, Why could not we cast him out?

29 And he said unto them, This kind can come forth by nothing, but by prayer and fasting.

THE contrast between these verses and those which precede them in the chapter is very striking. We pass from the mount of transfiguration to a melancholy history of the work of the devil. We come down from the vision

Elias is yet to take place. They consider that John the Baptist only went before our Lord in the "spirit and power of Elias" (Luke i. 17), and that the words of Malachi are yet to be fulfilled. This is the view maintained by nearly all the Fathers, by the great majority of the Roman Catholic commentators, and by not a few modern Protestant divines, both English and Continental, at the present time.

If I must express an opinion, when great and learned divines differ so widely, I must honestly confess that I decidedly incline to the second of the two interpretations above given. I believe that a literal appearing of Elijah the Prophet before the second coming of Christ may be expected. Dark and incomprehensible as the subject is, the scriptural arguments in favour of this view appear to me unanswerable. Any other view seems to do violence to the plain meaning of the words of Malachi iv. 5, 6; Matt. xvii. 11; John i. 21. There seems no reason why there should not be a double "coming of glory, to a conflict with Satanic possession. We change the blessed company of Moses and Elias, for the rude intercourse of unbelieving scribes. We leave the foretaste of millennial glory, and the solemn voice of God the Father testifying to God the Son, and return once more to a scene of pain, weakness, and misery,—a boy in agony of body, a father in deep distress, and a little band of feeble disciples baffled by Satan's power, and unable to give relief.—The contrast, we must all feel, is very great. Yet it is but a faint emblem of the change of scene that Jesus voluntarily undertook to witness when He first laid aside His glory and came into the world. And it is, after all, a vivid picture of the life of all true Christians. With them, as with their Master, work, conflict, and scenes of weakness and sorrow will always be the rule. With them, too, visions of glory, foretastes of heaven, seasons on the mount, will always be the exception.

Let us learn from these verses, *how dependent Christ's disciples are on the company and help of their Master.*

We see this truth brought out in a striking manner in

of Elias : " the first " in spirit and power," when John the Baptist preached ; the second, "literal and in person," when He shall come at the end of the world, immediately before the great and dreadful day of the Lord.

The whole question is undoubtedly surrounded with difficulties, whatever view we adopt. I can only say that after patient and calm investigation, I see much fewer difficulties in the way of the interpretation to which I lean, than in the way of the other. I hold, with Augustine, Jerome, Chrysostom, Hilary, Jansenius, Brentius, Greswell, Alford, and Stier, that Malachi iv. 5, 6, is not yet completely fulfilled, and that Elijah the Prophet will yet come. Those who can read Greek will find an interesting note on this subject in Cramer's Catena on St. Mark.

the scene which meets our Lord's eyes when He came
down from the mount. Like Moses, when he came down
from Mount Sinai, He finds His little flock in confusion.
He sees His nine Apostles beset by a party of malicious
scribes, and baffled in an attempt to heal one who had
been brought to them possessed with a devil. The very
same disciples who a short time before had done many
miracles and "cast out many devils," had now met with
a case too hard for them. They were learning by
humbling experience the great lesson, "Without Me ye
can do nothing." (John xv. 5.)—It was a useful lesson,
no doubt, and over-ruled to their spiritual good. It would
probably be remembered all the days of their lives. The
things that we learn by smarting experience abide in our
memories, while truths heard with the ear are often forgotten. But we may be sure it was a bitter lesson at the
time.—We do not love to learn that we can do nothing
without Christ.

We need not look far to see many illustrations of this
truth in the history of Christ's people in every age. The
very men who at one time have done great exploits in
the cause of the Gospel, at another time have failed
entirely, and proved weak and unstable as water. The
temporary recantations of Cranmer and Jewell are
striking examples. The holiest and best of Christians
has nothing to glory of. His strength is not his own.
He has nothing but what he has received. He has only
to provoke the Lord to leave him for a season, and he
will soon discover that his power is gone. Like Samson when his hair was shorn, he is weak as any other
man.

Let us learn a lesson of humility from the failure of
the disciples.   Let us strive to realize every day our
need of the grace and presence of Christ.   With Him we
may do all things.   Without Him we can do nothing
at all.   With Him we may overcome the greatest temptations.   Without Him the least may overcome us.   Let
our cry be every morning, " Leave us not to ourselves :
we know not what a day may bring forth.   If Thy presence go not with us we cannot go up."

Let us learn, in the second place, from these verses,
how early in life we are liable to be injured by Satan.   We
read a fearful description of the miseries inflicted by
Satan on the young man whose case is here recorded.
And we are told that he had been under this awful visi-
tation from his very infancy.   It came to him "of a child."

There is a lesson of deep importance here, which we
must not overlook.   We must labour to do good to our
children, even from their earliest years.   If Satan begins
so early to do them harm, we must not be behind him
in diligence to lead them to God.   How soon in life a
child becomes responsible and accountable, is a difficult
question to solve.   Perhaps far sooner than many of us
suppose.   One thing, at all events, is very clear : it is never
too soon to strive and pray for the salvation of the souls
of children,—never too soon to speak to them as moral
beings, and tell them of God and Christ, and right and
wrong.   The devil, we may be quite sure, loses no time
in endeavouring to influence the minds of young people.
He begins with them even "of a child."   Let us work
hard to counteract him.   If young hearts can be filled
by Satan, they can also be filled with the Spirit of God.

Let us learn, in the third place, from these verses, *how faith and unbelief can be mixed together in the same heart.* The words of the child's father set this truth before us in a touching way. "Lord," he cried, "I believe; help thou mine unbelief."

We see in those words a vivid picture of the heart of many a true Christian. Few indeed are to be found among believers, in whom trust and doubt, hope and fear do not exist side by side. Nothing is perfect in a child of God so long as he is in the body. His knowledge, and love, and humility, are all more or less defective, and mingled with corruption. And as it is with his other graces, so it is with his faith. He believes, and yet has about him a remainder of unbelief.

What shall we do with our faith? We must *use* it. Weak, trembling, doubting, feeble as it may be, we must use it. We must not wait until it is great, perfect, and mighty, but like the man before us turn it to account, and hope that one day it will be more strong. "Lord," he said, "I believe."

What shall we do with our unbelief. We must *resist it*, and pray against it. We must not allow it to keep us back from Christ. We must take it to Christ, as we take all other sins and infirmities, and cry to Him for deliverance. Like the man before us, we must cry, "Lord, help mine unbelief."

These are experimental truths. Happy are they who know something of them. The world is ignorant of them. Faith and unbelief, doubts and fears, are all foolishness to the natural man. But let the true Christian study these things well, and thoroughly understand them. It is of the utmost importance to our comfort to know that a true believer may be known by his inward warfare, as well as by his inward peace.

Let us mark, in the last place, *the complete dominion which our Lord exercises over Satan and all his agents.* The spirit who was too strong for the disciples, is at once ˙cast out by the Master. He speaks with mighty authority, and Satan at once is obliged to obey. "I charge thee, come out of him, and enter no more into him."

We may leave the passage with comfortable feelings. Greater is He that is for us than all they that are against us. Satan is strong, busy, active, malicious. But Jesus is able to save to the uttermost all that come unto God by Him,—from the devil, as well as from sin,—from the devil, as well as from the world. Let us possess our souls in patience. Jesus still lives, and will not let Satan pluck us out of His hand. Jesus still lives, and will soon come again to deliver us entirely from the fiery darts of the wicked one. The great chain is pre-- pared. (Rev. xx. 1.) Satan shall one day be bound. The God of peace shall bruise Satan under our feet shortly.* (Rom. xvi. 20.)

MARK IX. 30—37.

30 And they departed thence, and passed through Galilee; and he would not that any man should know *it.*

31 For he taught his disciples, and said unto them, The Son of man is delivered into the hands of men, and they shall kill him; and after that he is killed, he shall rise the third day.

32 But they understood not that saying, and were afraid to ask him.

33 And he came to Capernaum; and being in the house he asked them,

* The expression, "greatly amazed," in the fifteenth verse of the passsage now expounded, deserves some notice. The Greek word

What was it that ye disputed among yourselves by the way ?

34 But they held their peace : for by the way they had disputed among themselves, who *should be* the greatest.

35 And he sat down, and called the twelve, and saith unto them, If any man desire to be first, *the same* shall be last of all, and servant of all.

36 And he took a child, and set him in the midst of them : and when he had taken him in his arms, he said unto them,

37 Whosoever shall receive one of such children in my name, receiveth me : and whosoever shall receive me, receiveth not me, but him that sent me.

LET us mark, in these verses, *our Lord's renewed announcement of His own coming death and resurrection.* "He taught His disciples, and said unto them, The Son of man is delivered into the hands of men, and they shall kill Him ; and after that He is killed, He shall rise the third day."

The dullness of the disciples in spiritual things appears once more as soon as this announcement was made. There was good in the tidings as well as seeming evil, —sweet as well as bitter,—life as well as death,—the resurrection as well as the cross. But it was all darkness to the bewildered twelve. "They understood not that saying, and were afraid to ask." Their minds were still full of their mistaken ideas of their Master's reign upon earth. They thought that His earthly kingdom was immediately to appear. Never are we so slow to understand as when prejudice and pre-conceived opinions darken our eyes.

The immense importance of our Lord's death and resurrection comes out strongly in this fresh announce-

is exceedingly strong, and implies a feeling much beyond that which the English word "amazed" conveys to our minds. It certainly seems as if some traces of visible glory, or, at any rate, some expression of extraordinary majesty appeared in our Lord's countenance after the transfiguration. It reminds us of the face of Moses shining when he came down from the mount.

ment which He makes. It is not for nothing that He reminds us again that He must die. He would have us know that His death was the great end for which He came into the world. He would remind us that by that death the great problem was to be solved, how God could be just and yet justify sinners. He did not come upon earth merely to teach, and preach, and work miracles. He came to make satisfaction for sin, by His own blood and suffering on the cross. Let us never forget this. The incarnation, and example, and words of Christ are all of deep importance. But the grand object which demands our notice in the history of His earthly ministry, is His death on Calvary.

Let us mark, in the second place, in these verses, *the ambition and love of pre-eminence which the Apostles exhibited.* "By the way they disputed among themselves who should be greatest."

How strange this sounds! Who would have thought that a few fishermen and publicans could have been overcome by emulation and the desire of supremacy? Who would have expected that poor men, who had given up all for Christ's sake, would have been troubled by strife and dissension, as to the place and precedence which each one deserved? Yet so it is. The fact is recorded for our learning. The Holy Ghost has caused it to be written down for the perpetual use of Christ's Church. Let us take care that it is not written in vain.

It is an awful fact, whether we like to allow it or not, that pride is one of the commonest sins which beset human nature. We are all born Pharisees. We all naturally think far better of ourselves than we ought.

We all naturally fancy that we deserve something better than we have.—It is an old sin. It began in the garden of Eden, when Adam and Eve thought they had not got everything that their merits deserved.—It is a subtle sin. It rules and reigns in many a heart without being detected, and can even wear the garb of humility.—It is a most soul-ruining sin. It prevents repentance, keeps men back from Christ, checks brotherly love, and nips in the bud spiritual anxiety.—Let us watch against it, and be on our guard. Of all garments, none is so graceful, none wears so well, and none is so rare, as true humility.

Let us mark, in the third place, *the peculiar standard of true greatness which our Lord sets before His disciples.* He says to them, "If any man desire to be first, the same shall be last of all, and servant of all."

These words are deeply instructive. They show us that the maxims of the world are directly contrary to the mind of Christ. The world's idea of greatness is to rule, but Christian greatness consists in serving. The world's ambition is to receive honour and attention, but the desire of the Christian should be to give rather than receive, and to attend on others rather than be attended on himself. In short, the man who lays himself out most to serve his fellow-men, and to be useful in his day and generation, is the greatest man in the eyes of Christ. *

Let us strive to make a practical use of this heart-searching maxim. Let us seek to do good to our fellow-

---

* The words of Augustine on this point are worth reading. He says,—

"A Bishop's office is a name of labour rather than of honour : so that he who coveteth pre-eminence rather than usefulness, may understand that he is not a bishop."—*De Civit. Dei.*

men, and to mortify that self-pleasing and self-indulgence
to which we are all so prone.   Is there any service that
we can render to our fellow-Christians?   Is there any
kindness that we can do them, to help them and promote
their happiness?   If there is, let us do it without delay.
Well would it be for Christendom if empty boasts of
Churchmanship and orthodoxy were less frequent, and
practical attention to our Lord's words in this passage
more common.   The men who are willing to be last of
all, and servants of all, for Christ's sake, are always
few.   Yet these are the men who do good, break down
prejudices, convince infidels that Christianity is a reality,
and shake the world.

Let us mark, in the last place, *what encouragement our
Lord gives us to show kindness to the least and lowest who
believe in His name.*   He teaches this lesson in a very
touching manner.   He took a child in His arms, and
said to His disciples, "Whosoever shall receive one of
such children in my name, receiveth Me, and whosoever
shall receive Me, receiveth Him that sent Me."

The principle here laid down is a continuation of that
which we have just considered.   It is one which is foolishness to the natural man.   Flesh and blood can see no
other way to greatness than crowns, and rank, and
wealth, and high position in the world.   The Son of God
declares that the way lies in devoting ourselves to the
care of the weakest and lowest of His flock.   He enforces
His declaration by marvellous words, which are often
read and heard without thought.   He tells us that to
"receive one child in His name, is to receive Christ, and
to receive Christ is to receive God."

There is rich encouragement here for all who devote themselves to the charitable work of doing good to neglected souls.   There is encouragement for every one who labours to restore the outcast to a place in society,—to raise the fallen,—to gather together the ragged children whom no man cares for,—to pluck the worst of characters from a life of sin, like brands from the burning,—and to bring the wanderers home.   Let all such take comfort when they read these words.   Their work may often be hard and discouraging.   They may be mocked, ridiculed, and held up to scorn by the world.   But let them know that the Son of God marks all they do, and is well pleased.   Whatever the world may think, these are they whom Jesus will delight to honour at the last day.

MARK IX. 38—50.

38 And John answered him, saying, Master, we saw one casting out devils in thy name, and he followeth not us: and we forbad him, because he followeth not us.

39 But Jesus said, Forbid him not: for there is no man which shall do a miracle in my name, that can lightly speak evil of me.

40 For he that is not against us is on our part.

41 For whosoever shall give you a cup of water to drink in my name, because ye belong to Christ, verily I say unto you, he shall not lose his reward.

42 And whosoever shall offend one of these little ones that believe in me, it is better for him that a millstone were hanged about his neck, and he were cast into the sea.

43 And if thy hand offend thee, cut it off: it is better for thee to enter into life maimed, than having two hands to go into hell, into the fire that never shall be quenched:

44 Where their worm dieth not, and the fire is not quenched.

45 And if thy foot offend thee, cut it off: it is better for thee to enter halt into life, than having two feet to be cast into hell, into the fire that never shall be quenched:

46 Where their worm dieth not, and the fire is not quenched.

47 And if thine eye offend thee, pluck it out: it is better for thee to enter into the kingdom of God with one eye, than having two eyes to be cast into hell fire:

48 Where their worm dieth not, and the fire is not quenched.

49 For every one shall be salted with fire, and every sacrifice shall be salted with salt.

50 Salt is good: but if the salt have lost his saltness, wherewith will ye season it? Have salt in yourselves, and have peace one with another.

WE see in these verses, *the mind of Christ on the great subject of toleration in religion.*   The Apostle John said

to Him, "Master, we saw one casting out devils in Thy
name, and he followeth not us: and we forbad him,
because he followeth not us." The man was doing a
good work without doubt. He was warring on the same
side as the Apostles, beyond question. But this did not
satisfy John. He did not work in the company of the
Apostles. He did not fight in line with them. And
therefore John had forbidden him.—But let us hear now
what the great Head of the Church decides! "Jesus
said, Forbid him not; for there is no man which shall
do a miracle in my name that can lightly speak evil of
Me. For he that is not against us, is on our part."

Here is a golden rule indeed, and one that human
nature sorely needs, and has too often forgotten. Men of
all branches of Christ's Church are apt to think that no
good can be done in the world unless it is done by their
own party and denomination. They are so narrow-
minded that they cannot conceive the possibility of
working on any other pattern but that which they follow.
They make an idol of their own peculiar ecclesiastical
machinery, and can see no merit in any other. They are
like him who cried when Eldad and Medad prophesied
in the camp, "My lord Moses, forbid them." (Num.
xi. 28.)

To this intolerant spirit we owe some of the blackest
pages of Church history. Christians have repeatedly
persecuted Christians for no better reason than that
which is here given by John. They have practically
proclaimed to their brethren, "You shall either follow
us, or not work for Christ at all."

Let us be on our guard against this feeling. It is

only too near the surface of all our hearts.   Let us study to realize that liberal, tolerant spirit which Jesus here recommends, and be thankful for good works wheresoever and by whomsoever done.   Let us beware of the slightest inclination to stop and check others, merely because they do not choose to adopt our plans, or work by our side. We may think our fellow-Christians mistaken in some points.   We may fancy that more would be done for Christ if they would join us, and if all worked in the same way.   We may see many evils arising from religious dissensions and divisions.—But all this must not prevent us rejoicing if the works of the devil are destroyed and souls are saved.   Is our neighbour warring against Satan ? Is he really trying to labour for Christ?   This is the grand question.   Better a thousand times that the work should be done by other hands than not done at all. Happy is he who knows something of the spirit of Moses, when he said, "Would God that all the Lord's people were prophets;"—and of Paul, when he says, "If Christ is preached, I rejoice, yea, and will rejoice." *   (Numb. xi. 29 ; Phil. i. 18.)

* The remarks of Quesnel on this passage are interesting,—and doubly so when we remember that the writer was a Roman Catholic. He says, "That which John here does, is an example of an indiscreet zeal for the interests of Christ.   The most holy persons have sometimes occasion to secure themselves from secret emulations. We very easily mingle our own interests with those of God ; and our vanity uses the glory of His name only as a veil.   A preacher sometimes imagines that his only desire is that men should follow Christ and adhere to His word ; and it is himself whom he desires they should follow, and to whom he is very glad to find them adhere."

"Christ suffers many things in His Church, which are done without His mission ; but He makes them contribute to the

We see, for another thing, in these verses, *the need of giving up anything that stands between us and the salvation of our souls.* The "hand" and the "foot" are to be cut off, and the "eye" to be plucked out, if they offend, or are occasions of falling. The things that are dear to us, as eye, foot, or hand, are to be cast off and given up, if they injure our souls, whatever pain the sacrifice may cost us.

This is a rule that sounds stern and harsh at first sight. But our loving Master did not give the rule without cause. Compliance with it is absolutely necessary, since neglect of it is the sure way to hell. Our bodily senses are the channels through which many of our most formidable temptations approach us. Our bodily members are ready instruments of evil, but slow to that which is good. The eye, the hand and the foot are good servants, when under right direction. But they need daily watching, lest they lead us into sin.

Let us resolve by God's grace to make a practical use of our Lord's solemn injunction in this place. Let us regard it as the advice of a wise physician, the counsel of a tender father, the warning of a faithful friend. However men may ridicule us for our strictness and preciseness, let us habitually "crucify our flesh with its affections and lusts." Let us deny ourselves any enjoyment, rather than incur peril of sinning against God. Let us walk in Job's steps : He says, "I made a covenant with mine eyes." (Job xxxi. 1.) Let us remember Paul : He says, "I keep

establishment of His kingdom. Whatever reason we may have to fear that some persons will not persevere in goodness, we must notwithstanding suffer them to continue their endeavours when they appear to be any ways useful. God Himself authorizes such persons, since it is He who performs the good in them."

under my body, and bring it into subjection : lest that by any means, when I have preached to others, I myself should be a castaway." (1 Cor. ix. 27.)

We see, in the last place, in these verses, *the reality, awfulness, and eternity of future punishment.* Three times the Lord Jesus speaks of " hell." Three times He mentions the " worm that never dies." Three times He says that " the fire is not quenched."

These are awful expressions. They call for reflection rather than exposition. They should be pondered, considered, and remembered by all professing Christians. It matters little whether we regard them as figurative and emblematic. If they are so, one thing at least is very clear. The worm and the fire are emblems of real things. There is a real hell, and that hell is eternal.

There is no mercy in keeping back from men the subject of hell. Fearful and tremendous as it is, it ought to be pressed on all, as one of the great truths of Christianity. Our loving Saviour speaks frequently of it. The Apostle John, in the Book of Revelation, often describes it. The servants of God in these days must not be ashamed of confessing their belief in it. Were there no boundless mercy in Christ for all that believe in Him, we might well shrink from the awful topic. Were there no precious blood of Christ able to cleanse away all sin, we might well keep silence about the wrath to come. But there is mercy for all who ask in Christ's name. There is a fountain open for all sin. Let us then boldly and unhesitatingly maintain that there is a hell, and beseech men to flee from it, before it be too late. " Knowing the terrors of the Lord," the worm, and the fire, let us " per-

o

suade men." (1 Cor. v. 11.) It is not possible to say too much about Christ. But it is quite possible to say too little about hell.

Let the concluding words of our Lord ring in our ears, as we leave the passage : "Have salt in yourselves, and have peace one with another." Let us make sure that we have in our hearts the saving grace of the Holy Ghost, sanctifying, purifying, preserving from corruption, our whole inward man. Let us watch the grace given to us with daily watchfulness, and pray to be kept from carelessness and sin, lest we be overtaken in faults, bring misery on our consciences, and discredit on our profession. Above all let us live in peace one with another,—not seeking great things, or striving for the preeminence, but clothed with humility, and loving all who love Christ in sincerity. These seem simple things. But in attending to them is great reward.*

---

* The last verse but one in the passage now expounded, appears to baffle all the commentators. I allude of course to the words, "Every one shall be salted with fire, and every sacrifice shall be salted with salt." The true meaning of these words and their connection with the context, are problems which seem not yet solved. At all events, not one of the many interpretations which have been hitherto proposed is entirely satisfactory. We must confess that it is one of those knots which are yet untied in the exposition of Scripture.

1. Some think that our Lord is speaking only of the wicked and their future punishment, and that He means,—"Every lost soul shall be salted with the fire of hell, even as every sacrifice under the law of Moses is salted with salt." This appears to be the view held by Whitby.

2. Some think that our Lord is speaking only of the righteous and their fiery trials in this life, by which they are purified and preserved from corruption, and that He means,—"Every true disciple of mine shall be as it were salted and passed through the fire of tribulation, even as every sacrifice is salted with salt." Of those

MARK X. 1—12.

1 And he arose from thence, and cometh into the coasts of Judæa, by the farther side of Jordan : and the people resort unto him again; and, as he was wont, he taught them again.

2 And the Pharisees came to him, and asked him, Is it lawful for a man to put away *his* wife ? tempting him.

3 And he answered and said unto them, What did Moses command you ?

4 And they said, Moses suffered to write a bill of divorcement, and to put *her* away.

5 And Jesus answered and said unto them, For the hardness of your heart he wrote you this precept.

6 But from the beginning of the creation God made them male and female.

7 For this cause shall a man leave his father and mother, and cleave to his wife;

8 And they twain shall be one flesh : so then they are no more twain, but one flesh.

9 What therefore God hath joined together, let not man put asunder.

10 And in the house his disciples asked him again of the same *matter*.

11 And he saith unto them, Whosoever shall put away his wife, and marry another, committeth adultery against her.

12 And if a woman shall put away her husband, and be married to another, she committeth adultery.

THE opening verse of this passage shows us *the patient perseverance of our Lord Jesus Christ as a teacher.* We who think that our Lord speaks only of the righteous, some think that the "fire" means not tribulation, and some the work of the Holy Spirit. Cartwright holds the last of these opinions, Junius the first.

3. Some think that in the first clause of the verse, our Lord is speaking of all members of His Church, both good and bad, and that His meaning is the same as that of St. Paul, where he says "The fire shall try every man's work of what sort it is." (1 Cor. iii. 13.) The second clause, they think, describes the preserving effect of grace on the hearts of true believers. According to this view, the meaning of the verse would be,—"Every one shall be finally salted, tried, and tested by the fire of the last day : and every one who has offered himself as a living sacrifice to God, shall be salted with grace, and so finally preserved from death and corruption."

4. Some think that in the first clause of the verse, our Lord is speaking of the wicked, and in the second clause of the righteous. According to this view, the sense would be,—"Every wicked man shall be salted with fire and punished for evermore ; and every living sacrifice to God, or godly man, shall be salted with grace, kept from the power of death, and saved for evermore."—This is the view of Hammond and Manton.

I offer no opinion and make no comment on any of the above views. The objections which might be made against every one of them are neither few nor small. Whether these objections are insuperable or not, is a point on which learned theologians differ widely, and a conclusion will perhaps never be attained until the Lord appears. My own conviction is, that we must wait for more light, and regard the text at present as one of the "deep things" of God.

are told that He came " into the coasts of Judæa by the
farther side of Jordan : and the people resort unto Him
again : and as He was wont, He taught them again."

Wherever our Lord went, He was always about His
Father's business, preaching, teaching, and labouring to
do good to souls.   He threw away no opportunity.   In
the whole history of His earthly ministry we never read
of an idle day.   Of Him it may be truly said, that He
" sowed beside all waters," and that " in the morning He
sowed His seed, and in the evening withheld not His
hand."   (Isaiah xxxii. 20.   Eccles. xi. 6.)

And yet our Lord knew the hearts of all men. He knew
perfectly well that the great proportion of His hearers
were hardened and unbelieving. He knew, as He spoke,
that most of His words fell to the ground uncared for
and unheeded, and that so far as concerned the salvation
of souls, most of His labour was in vain.   He knew all
this, and yet He laboured on.

Let us see in this fact a standing pattern to all who try
to do good to others, whatever their office may be. Let it
be remembered by every minister and every missionary,—
by every schoolmaster and every Sunday-school teacher,
—by every district visitor and every lay agent,—by every
head of a house who has family prayers, and by every
nurse who has the charge of children.   Let all such
remember Christ's example, and resolve to do likewise.
We are not to give up teaching, because we see no good
done.   We are not to relax our exertions, because we see
no fruit of our toil.   We are to work on steadily, keeping before us the great principle, that duty is our's and
results are God's.   There must be ploughmen and sowers,

as well as reapers and binders of sheaves. The honest master pays his labourers according to the work they do, and not according to the crops that grow on his land. Our Master in heaven will deal with all His servants at the last day in like manner. He knows that success is not in their hands. He knows that they cannot change hearts. He will reward them according to their labour, and not according to the fruits which have resulted from their labour. It is not "the good and *successful* servant," but the "good and *faithful* servant," to whom He will say, "Enter thou into the joy of thy Lord." * (Matt. xxv. 21.)

The greater portion of this passage is meant to show us *the dignity and importance of the relation of marriage.* It is plain that the prevailing opinions of the Jews upon this subject, when our Lord was upon earth, were lax and low in the extreme. The binding character of the marriage tie was not recognized. Divorce for slight and

---

* Some remarks of Bishop Latimer on this point are well worth reading. They occur in a passage in one of his sermons on the parable of the wedding garment. He says, "the man who had not the wedding garment was blamed because he professed one thing, and was indeed another. Why did not the King blame the preachers? There was no fault in them, they did their duties : they had no further commandment but to call men to the marriage. The garment he should have provided himself. Therefore he quarrelleth not with the preachers, 'What doth this fellow here? why suffered ye him to enter?' For their commission extended no further, but only to call him. Many are grieved that there is so little fruit of their preaching. And when they are asked, 'Why do you not preach, having so great gifts given you of God?' 'I would preach,' say they, 'but I see so little fruit, so little amendment of life, that it maketh me weary :' a naughty answer: a very naughty answer. Thou art troubled with that which God gave thee no charge of : and leavest undone that which thou art charged with."—*Latimer's Works. Parker Society. Vol. I., p. 286.*

trivial causes was allowable and common.* The duties of husbands towards wives, and of wives towards husbands, as a natural consequence, were little understood. To correct this state of things our Lord sets up a high and holy standard of principles. He refers to the original institution of marriage at the creation, as the union of one man and one woman. He quotes and endorses the solemn words used at the marriage of Adam and Eve, as words of perpetual significance : "A man shall leave his father and mother, and cleave to his wife : and they twain shall be one flesh." He adds a solemn comment to these words : "What God hath joined together, let not man put asunder." And finally, in reply to the inquiry of His disciples, He declares that divorce followed by re-marriage, except for the cause of unfaithfulness, is a breach of the seventh commandment. †

* The extent to which the Jews allowed divorce for absurd and frivolous causes, would be almost incredible, if we had not the evidence of their own Rabbinical writings on the subject. A full account of the matter will be found in Lightfoot's Horæ Hebraicæ on St. Matthew v. 31. One passage quoted by him will be sufficient to give the reader an idea of Jewish customs about divorce : "The school of Hillel saith, If the wife cooks her husband's food ill by over-salting it, or over-roasting it, she is to be put away."

† I am aware that the opinions I have expressed at the close of this paragraph are contrary to that of some learned divines. I can only say that I have arrived at them deliberately, after calm investigation of the parallel passage in Matt. xix. 9, and of the words of our Lord in Matt. v. 32. I decidedly believe that the re-marriage forbidden by Christ, is re-marriage after a divorce for trivial and frivolous causes, and that His words do not apply to re-marriage after divorce on account of unfaithfulness. Re-marriage after divorce for frivolous causes is clearly adultery, for one simple reason ;—the divorce never ought to have taken place, and the divorced party is still a married person in the sight of God.—Re-marriage after divorce for unfaithfulness, by the same process of reasoning, is not adultery. Unfaithfulness dissolves the marriage tie altogether, and place the

The importance of the whole subject, on which our Lord here pronounces judgment, can hardly be overrated. We ought to be very thankful that we have so clear and full an exposition of His mind upon it. The marriage relation lies at the very root of the social system of nations. The public morality of a people, and the private happiness of the families which compose a people, are deeply involved in the whole question of the law of marriage. The experience of all nations confirms the wisdom of our Lord's decision in this passage, in the most striking manner. It is a fact clearly ascertained, that polygamy, and permission to obtain divorce on slight grounds, have a direct tendency to promote immorality. In short, the nearer a nation's laws about marriage approach to the law of Christ, the higher has the moral tone of that nation always proved to be.

It becomes all those who are married, or purpose marriage, to ponder well the teaching of our Lord Jesus Christ in this passage. Of all relations of life, none ought to be regarded with such reverence, and none taken in hand so cautiously as the relation of husband and wife. In no relation is such earthly happiness to be found, if it be entered upon discreetly, advisedly, and in the fear of God. In none is so much misery seen to follow, if it be taken in hand unadvisedly, lightly, wantonly, and without thought.—From no step in life does so much benefit come to the soul, if people marry "in the Lord." From none does the soul take so much harm, if fancy, passion, or any mere worldly motive is the only cause which produce the union. Solomon was

husband and wife once more in the position of unmarried people, or of a widower or widow.

the wisest of men. "Nevertheless even him did out-
landish women cause to sin." (Neh. xiii. 26.)

There is, unhappily, only too much necessity for im-
pressing these truths upon people. It is a mournful fact,
that few steps in life are generally taken with so much
levity, self-will, and forgetfulness of God as marriage.
Few are the young couples who think of inviting Christ
to their wedding! It is a mournful fact that unhappy
marriages are one great cause of the misery and sorrow
of which there is so much in the world. People find out
too late, that they have made a mistake, and go in bitterness all their days. Happy are they, who in the matter of
marriage observe three rules. The *first* is to marry only
in the Lord, and after prayer for God's approval and
blessing. The *second* is not to expect too much from their
partners, and to remember that marriage is, after all, the
union of two sinners, and not of two angels. The *third*
rule is to strive first and foremost for one another's sanctification. The more holy married people are, the happier
they are. "Christ loved the Church, and gave Himself
for it, that He might *sanctify* it." * (Eph. v. 25, 26.)

* There is an expression in this passage which claims special
observation. The Pharisees told our Lord, that "Moses suffered to
write a bill of divorcement, and to put her away." The answer of
our Lord is very remarkable. He says, " *For the hardness of your
hearts he wrote you this precept.*" And He then goes on to show that
this permission to divorce was a proof that their forefathers had fallen
below the original standard of marriage, and were dealt with as being
in a weak and diseased state of soul. For, He says, "But from the
beginning of the creation God made them male and female."

The expression throws much light on some portions of the civil
law of Moses. It shows us that it was an institution which in
some of its requirements was specially adapted to the state of mind
in which the Israelites were, on first leaving the land of Egypt. It
was not intended in all its minute particulars to be a code of
perpetual obligation. It was meant to lead on to something better

MARK X. 13—16.

13 And they brought young children to him, that he should touch them : and *his* disciples rebuked those that brought *them.*

14 But when Jesus saw *it,* he was much displeased, and said unto them, Suffer the little children to come unto me, and forbid them not ; for of such is the kingdom of God.

15 Verily I say unto you, Whosoever shall not receive the kingdom of God as a little child, he shall not enter therein.

16 And he took them up in his arms, put *his* hands upon them, and blessed them.

THE scene brought before us in these four verses is deeply interesting.—We see young children brought to Christ, " that He should touch them," and the disciples rebuking those that brought them.   We are told that when Jesus saw this He was "much displeased," and rebuked His disciples in words of a very remarkable tenor.   And finally we are told, that " He took them up in His arms, put His hands upon them and blessed them."

and higher, when the people were able to bear it.   The possession of it was undoubtedly a great privilege, and one of which the Jews might justly glory.   Yet in glorying they were to remember also, that their law contained some grounds for humiliation.   Its very permission to obtain divorce on light grounds, was a standing witness of the hardness and cruelty of the people.   It was thought better to tolerate such divorces, than to have the nation filled with murder, adultery, cruelty, and desertion.   In short, the very law of which the Jew boasted, was shown by our Lord to contain permissive statutes, which were in reality written to his shame.

The expression throws light on the position of God's people in this world of sin.   It shows us that there may be things *tolerated* and permitted by God, both in Churches and States, not because they are the best things, but because they are the things best suited to the Church or State in which they are found.   It is vain to expect perfection in any Government, or in any Church.   If we have the essentials of justice in the one, and of truth in the other, we may be content.   God tolerated many things in the goverment of Israel, until the time of reformation.   Surely we may tolerate many things too.   To spend our lives in searching after an imaginary state of perfection, either civil or ecclesiastical, is at best a waste of time.   If God was pleased to suffer some things in Israel "for the hardness of their hearts," we may well endure some things in Churches and States which we do not quite like.   There is a balance of evil in every position in the world.   There are imperfections everywhere.   The state of perfection is yet to come.

Let us learn, for one thing, from this passage, *how much attention the souls of children should receive from the Church of Christ.* The Great Head of the Church found time to take special notice of children. Although His time on earth was precious, and grown up men and women were perishing on every side for lack of knowledge, He did not think little boys and girls of small importance. He had room in His mighty heart even for them. He declared by His outward gesture and deed, His good will toward them. And not least, He has left on record words concerning them, which His Church should never forget: "Of such is the kingdom of God."

We must never allow ourselves to suppose that little children's souls may be safely let alone. Their characters for life depend exceedingly on what they see and hear during their first seven years. They are never too young to learn evil and sin. They are never too young to receive religious impressions. They think in their childish way about God, and their souls, and a world to come, far sooner and far more deeply than most people are aware. They are far more ready to respond to appeals to their feeling of right and wrong than many suppose. They have each a conscience. God has mercifully not left Himself without a witness in their hearts, fallen and corrupt as their natures are. They have each a soul which will live for ever in heaven or in hell. We cannot begin too soon to endeavour to bring them to Christ.

These truths ought to be diligently considered by every branch of the Church of Christ. It is the bounden duty of every Christian congregation to make provision for the

spiritual training of its children.   The boys and girls of
every family should be taught as soon as they can learn,—
should be brought to public worship as soon as they can
behave with propriety,—should be regarded with affectionate interest as the future congregation, which will fill
our places when we are dead. We may confidently expect
Christ's blessing on all attempts to do good to children.
No Church can be regarded as being in a healthy state
which neglects its younger members, and lazily excuses
itself on the plea, that "young people will be young,"
and that it is useless to try to do them good.   Such a
Church shows plainly that it has not the mind of Christ.
A congregation which consists of none but grown up
people, whose children are idling at home or running
wild in the streets or fields, is a most deplorable and unsatisfactory sight.   The members of such a congregation
may pride themselves on their numbers, and on the
soundness of their own views. They may content themselves with loud assertions that they cannot change their
children's hearts, and that God will convert them some
day if He thinks fit.   But they have yet to learn that
Christ regards them as neglecting a solemn duty, and
that Christians who do not use every means to bring
children to Christ are committing a great sin.

Let us learn, for another thing, from this passage, *how
much encouragement there is to bring young children to be
baptized.* Of course it is not pretended that there is any
mention of baptism, or even any reference to it in the
verses before us.   All we mean to say is, that the expressions and gestures of our Lord in this passage, are a
strong indirect argument in favour of infant baptism. It

is on this account that the passage occupies a prominent place in the baptismal service of the Church of England.

The subject of infant baptism is undoubtedly a delicate and difficult one. Holy and praying men are unable to see alike upon it. Although they read the same Bible, and profess to be led by the same Spirit, they arrive at different conclusions about this sacrament. The great majority of Christians hold that infant baptism is Scriptural and right. A comparatively small section of the Protestant Church, but one containing many eminent saints among its members, regards infant baptism as unscriptural and wrong. The difference is a melancholy proof of the blindness and infirmity which remain, even in the saints of God.

But the difference now referred to must not make members of the Church of England shrink from holding decided opinions on the subject. That Church has declared plainly in its Articles, that "the baptism of young children is in any wise to be retained, as most agreeable with the institution of Christ." To this opinion we need not be afraid to adhere.

It is allowed on all sides that infants may be elect and chosen of God unto salvation,—may be washed in Christ's blood, born again of the Spirit, have grace, be justified, sanctified, and enter heaven. If these things be so, it is hard to see why they may not receive the outward sign of baptism.

It is allowed furthermore that infants are members of Christ's visible Church, by virtue of their parents' Christianity. What else can we make of St. Paul's words: "Now are they holy." (1 Cor. vii. 14.) If this be so, it is difficult to understand why an infant may not receive the outward sign of admission into the Church, just as the Jewish child received the outward sign of circumcision.

The objection that baptism ought only to be given to those who are old enough to repent and believe, does not appear a convincing one. We read in the New Testament that the "houses" of Lydia and Stephanas were baptized, and that the jailer of Philippi and "all his" were baptized. It is very difficult to suppose that in no one of these three cases were there any children. (Acts xvi. 15, 33. 1 Cor. i. 16.)

The objection that our Lord Jesus Christ Himself never directly commanded infants to be baptized is not a weighty one. The Church of the Jews, to which He came, had always been accustomed to admit children into the Church by the sign of circumcision. The very fact that Jesus says nothing about the age for baptizing goes far to prove that He intended no change to be made.*

* In considering the arguments in favour of infant baptism, there are two facts which ought to be duly pondered. They are extra-scriptural facts, and I have therefore purposely omitted them in the Expository Thoughts on this passage. But they are weighty facts, and may help some minds in coming to a conclusion.

1.   One fact is the testimony of history to the almost universal practice of infant baptism in the early Church. The proof of this is to be found in Wall's History of Infant Baptism. If infant baptism is so entirely opposed to the mind of Christ, as some say that it is, it is at least a curious circumstance that the early Church should have been so ignorant on the subject.

2.   The other fact is the notorious practice of baptizing the infant children of proselytes in the Jewish Church. The proof of this is to be found in Lightfoot's Horæ Hebraicæ on St. Matthew iii. 6. He says, for instance, "The Anabaptists object, 'It is not commanded to baptize infants,—therefore they are not to be baptized.' to whom I answer, 'It is not forbidden to baptize infants,—therefore they are to be baptized.' And the reason is plain. For when

The subject may be safely left here. Few controversies have done so much harm, and led to so little spiritual fruit as the controversy about baptism. On none has so much been said and written without producing conviction. On none does experience seem to show that Christians had better leave each other alone, and agree to differ.

The baptism that it concerns us all to know is not so much the baptism of water as the baptism of the Holy Ghost. Thousands are washed in baptismal waters who are never renewed by the Spirit. Have we been born again? Have we received the Holy Spirit, and been made new creatures in Jesus Christ? If not, it matters little when, and where, and how we have been baptized; we are yet in our sins. Without a new birth there can be no salvation. May we never rest till we know and feel that we have passed from death to life, and are indeed born of God.

Pædobaptism in the Jewish Church was so known, usual and frequent in the admission of proselytes, there was no need to strengthen it with any precept, when baptism passed into an evangelical sacrament. For Christ took baptism into His own hands, and into evangelical use, as He found it; this only added, that He might promote it to a worthier end, and larger use. The whole nation knew well enough that little children used to be baptized: there was no need of a precept for that which had ever, by common use, prevailed.

"On the other hand, there was need of a plain and open prohibition, that infants and little children should not be baptized, if our Saviour would not have had them baptized. For since it was most common, in all ages foregoing, that little children should be baptized, if Christ had minded to abolish the custom He would have openly forbidden it. Therefore His silence and the silence of Scripture confirms Pædobaptism, and continues it unto all ages."— *Lightfoot's Works.* *Vol.* xi. *p.* 59. *Pitman's edition.*

MARK X. 17—27.

17 And when he was gone forth into the way, there came one running, and kneeled to him, and asked him, Good Master, what shall I do that I may inherit eternal life?

18 And Jesus said unto him, Why callest thou me good? *there is* none good but one, *that is,* God.

19 Thou knowest the commandments, Do not commit adultery, Do not kill, Do not steal, Do not bear false witness, Defraud not, Honour thy father and mother.

20 And he answered and said unto him, Master, all these have I observed from my youth.

21 Then Jesus beholding him loved him, and said unto him, One thing thou lackest: go thy way, sell whatsoever thou hast, and give to the poor, and thou shalt have treasure in heaven: and come, take up the cross, and follow me.

22 And he was sad at that saying, and went away grieved: for he had great possessions.

23 And Jesus looked round about, and saith unto his disciples, How hardly shall they that have riches enter into the kingdom of God!

24 And the disciples were astonished at his words. But Jesus answereth again, and saith unto them, Children, how hard is it for them that trust in riches to enter into the kingdom of God!

25 It is easier for a camel to go through the eye of a needle, than for a rich man to enter into the kingdom of God.

26 And they were astonished out of measure, saying among themselves, Who then can be saved?

27 And Jesus looking upon them saith, With men *it is* impossible, but not with God: for with God all things are possible.

THE story we have now read is recorded no less than three times in the New Testament. Matthew, Mark, and Luke were all inspired by one Spirit to write it for our learning. There is, no doubt, a wise purpose in this three-fold repetition of the same simple facts. It is intended to show us that the lessons of the passage deserve particular notice from the Church of Christ.

Let us learn, for one thing, from this passage, *the self-ignorance of man.*

We are told of one who "came running" to our Lord, "and kneeled to Him, and asked" the solemn question, "What shall I do that I may inherit eternal life?" At first sight there was much that was promising in this man's case. He showed anxiety about spiritual things, while most around him were careless and indifferent. He showed a disposition to reverence our Lord, by kneeling to Him, while Scribes and Pharisees despised Him. Yet all this time this man was profoundly ignorant of his own heart. He hears our Lord recite those commandments which make up our duty to our neighbour, and at once declares, " All these have I observed from my youth." The searching nature of the moral law, its application to our thoughts, and words, as well as actions, are matters with which he is utterly unacquainted.

The spiritual blindness here exhibited is unhappily most common. Myriads of professing Christians at the present day have not an idea of their own sinfulness and guilt in the sight of God. They flatter themselves that they have never done anything very wicked : "They have never murdered, or stolen, or committed adultery, or borne false witness. They cannot surely be in much danger of missing heaven."—They forget the holy nature of that God with whom they have to do. They forget how often they break His law in temper, or imagination, even when their outward conduct is correct. They never study such portions of Scripture as the fifth chapter of St. Matthew, or at any rate they study it with a thick veil over their hearts, and do not apply it to themselves. The result is, that they are wrapped up in self-righteousness. Like the Church of Laodicea, they are "rich and increased with goods, and have need of nothing." (Rev. iii. 17.) Self-satisfied they live, and self-satisfied too often they die.

Let us beware of this state of mind. So long as we think that we can keep the law of God, Christ profits us nothing. Let us pray for self-knowledge. Let us ask for the Holy Spirit to convince us of sin, to show us our own hearts, to show us God's holiness, and so to show us our need of Christ. Happy is he who has learned by experience the meaning of St. Paul's words: "I was alive without the law once; but when the commandment came, sin revived, and I died." (Rom. vii. 9.) Ignorance of the Law and ignorance of the Gospel will generally be found together. He whose eyes have really been opened to the spirituality of the commandments, will never rest till he has found Christ.

Let us learn, for another thing, from this passage, *the love of Christ towards sinners.*

This is a truth which is brought out in the expression used by St. Mark, when in his account of this man's story, he says that "Jesus beholding him, loved him." That love, beyond doubt, was a love of pity and compassion. Our Lord beheld with pity the strange mixture of earnestness and ignorance whch the case before Him presented. He saw with compassion a soul struggling with all the weakness and infirmity entailed by the fall; the conscience ill at ease, and sensible that it wanted relief,—the understanding sunk in darkness, and blinded as to the first principles of spiritual religion. Just as we look with sorrow at some noble ruin, roofless, and shattered, and unfit for man's use, yet showing many a mark of the skill with which it was designed and reared at first, so may we suppose that Jesus looked with tender concern at this man's soul.

We must never forget that Jesus feels love and compassion for the souls of the ungodly. Without controversy He feels a peculiar love for those who hear His voice and follow Him. They are His sheep, given to

Him by the Father, and watched with a special care.
They are His bride, joined to Him in an everlasting
covenant, and dear to Him as part of Himself. But the
heart of Jesus is a wide heart. He has abundance of
pity, compassion, and tender concern even for those who
are following sin and the world. He who wept over
unbelieving Jerusalem is still the same : He would still
gather into His bosom the ignorant and self-righteous,
the faithless and impenitent, if they were only willing
to be gathered. (Matt. xxiii. 37.) We may boldly tell
the chief of sinners that Christ loves him. Salvation is
ready for the worst of men, if they will only come to
Christ. If men are lost, it is not because Jesus does not
love them, and is not ready to save. His own solemn
words unravel the mystery : "Men love darkness rather
than light." "Ye will not come unto Me that ye might
have life." (John iii. 19 ; v. 40.)

Let us learn, in the last place, from this passage, *the
immense danger of the love of money.* This is a lesson
which is twice enforced on our notice. Once it comes
out in the conduct of the man whose history is here related. With all his professed desire after eternal life, he
loved his money better than his soul : "He went away
grieved."—Once it comes out in the solemn words of our
Lord to His disciples : "How hard it is for them that
have riches to enter into the kingdom of God." "It is
easier for a camel to go through the eye of a needle than
for a rich man to enter into the kingdom of God." The
last day alone will fully prove how true these words are.

Let us watch against the love of money. It is a snare
to the poor as well as to the rich. It is not so much

the having money, as the trusting in it, which ruins the soul. Let us pray for contentment with such things as we have. The highest wisdom is to be of one mind with St. Paul: "I have learned, in whatsoever state I am, therewith to be content." (Phil. iv. 11.)

MARK X. 28—34.

28 Then Peter began to say unto him, Lo, we have left all, and have followed thee,

29 And Jesus answered and said, Verily I say unto you, There is no man that hath left house, or brethren, or sisters, or father, or mother, or wife, or children, or lands, for my sake, and the Gospel's,

30 But he shall receive an hundred-fold now in this time, houses, and brethren, and sisters, and mothers, and children, and lands, with persecutions; and in the world to come eternal life.

31 But many *that are* first shall be last; and the last first.

32 And they were in the way going up to Jerusalem; and Jesus went before them: and they were amazed; and as they followed, they were afraid. And he took again the twelve, and began to tell them what things should happen unto him,

33 *Saying*, Behold, we go up to Jerusalem; and the Son of man shall be delivered unto the chief priests, and unto the scribes; and they shall condemn him to death, and shall deliver him to the Gentiles:

34 And they shall mock him, and shall scourge him, and shall spit upon him, and shall kill him: and the third day he shall rise again.

THE first thing which demands our attention in these verses is *the glorious promise which they contain*. The Lord Jesus says to His Apostles, "Verily I say unto you, There is no man that hath left house, or brethren, or sisters, or father, or mother, or wife, or children, or lands, for My sake, and the Gospel's, but he shall receive an hundred-fold now in this time, houses, and brethren, and sisters, and mothers, and children, and lands, with persecutions; and in the world to come eternal life."

There are few wider promises than this in the Word of God. There is none certainly in the New Testament which holds out such encouragement for the life that now is. Let every one that is fearful and faint-hearted in Christ's service look at this promise. Let all who are enduring hardness and tribulation for Christ's sake, study this promise well, and drink out of it comfort.

To all who make sacrifices on account of the Gospel, Jesus promises "an hundred-fold now in this time." They shall have not only pardon and glory in the world to come; they shall have even here upon earth, hopes, and joys, and sensible comforts sufficient to make up for all that they lose. They shall find in the communion of saints, new friends, new relations, new companions, more loving, faithful, and valuable than any they had before their conversion. Their introduction into the family of God shall be an abundant recompense for exclusion from the society of this world. This may sound startling and incredible to many ears. But thousands have found by experience that it is true.

To all who make sacrifices on account of the Gospel Jesus promises "eternal life in the world to come." As soon as they put off their earthly tabernacle, they shall enter upon a glorious existence, and in the morning of the resurrection shall receive such honour and joy as pass man's understanding. Their light affliction for a few years shall end in an everlasting reward. Their fights and sorrows while in the body, shall be exchanged for perfect rest and a conqueror's crown. They shall dwell in a world where there is no death, no sin, no devil, no cares, no weeping, no parting, for the former things will have passed away. God has said it, and it shall all be found true.

Where is the saint who will dare to say in the face of these glorious promises, that there is no encouragement to serve Christ? Where is the man or woman whose hands are beginning to hang down, and whose knees are beginning to faint in the Christian race? Let all such ponder this passage, and take fresh courage. The time is short. The end is sure. Heaviness may endure for a night, but joy cometh in the morning. Let us wait patiently on the Lord.

The second thing which demands our attention in these verses is *the solemn warning which they contain.*

The Lord Jesus saw the secret self-conceit of His Apostles. He gives them a word in season to check their high thoughts. " Many that are first shall be last, and the last first."

How true were these words, when applied to the twelve Apostles! There stood among those who heard our Lord speak, a man who at one time seemed likely to be one of the foremost of the twelve. He was one who appeared more careful and trustworthy than any. He had the charge of the bag, and kept what was put in it. And yet that man fell away and came to a disgraceful end. His name was Judas Iscariot.—Again, there did not stand among our Lord's hearers that day one who at a later period did more for Christ than any of the twelve. At the time when our Lord spoke he was a young Pharisee, brought up at the feet of Gamaliel, and zealous for nothing so much as the Law. And yet that young man in the end was converted to the faith of Christ, was not behind the chiefest Apostles, and laboured more abundantly than all. His name was Saul. Well might our Lord say, "The first shall be last; and the last first."

How true were these words, when we apply them to

the history of Christian Churches! There was a time when Asia Minor, and Greece, and Northern Africa, were full of professing Christians, while England and America were heathen lands. Sixteen hundred years have made a mighty change. The Churches of Africa and Asia have fallen into complete decay. The English and American Churches are labouring to spread the Gospel over the world. Well might our Lord say, "The first shall be last, and the last first."

How true these words appear to believers, when they look back over their own lives, and remember all they have seen from the time of their own conversion! How many began to serve Christ at the same time with themselves, and seemed to run well for a season. But where are they now? The world has got hold of one. False doctrine has beguiled another. A mistake in marriage has spoiled a third. Few indeed are the believers who cannot call to mind many such cases. Few have failed to discover, by sorrowful experience, that "the last are often first, and the first last."

Let us learn to pray for humility, when we read texts like this. It is not enough to begin well. We must persevere, and go on, and continue in well-doing. We must not be content with the fair blossoms of a few religious convictions, and joys, and sorrows, and hopes, and fears. We must bear the good fruit of settled habits of repentance, faith, and holiness. Happy is he who counts the cost, and resolves, having once begun to walk in the narrow way, by God's grace never to turn aside.

The last thing that demands our attention in this passage is *our Lord's clear foreknowledge of His own sufferings and death.*   Calmly and deliberately He tells His disciples of His coming passion at Jerusalem.   One after another He describes all the leading circumstances which would attend His death.   Nothing is reserved. Nothing is kept back.

Let us mark this well.   There was nothing involuntary and unforeseen in our Lord's death.   It was the result of His own free, determinate, and deliberate choice. From the beginning of His earthly ministry He saw the cross before Him, and went to it a willing sufferer. He knew that His death was the needful payment that must be made to reconcile God and man.   That payment He had covenanted and engaged to make at the price of His own blood.   And so, when the appointed time came, like a faithful surety He kept His word, and died for our sins on Calvary.

Let us ever bless God that the Gospel sets before us such a Saviour, so faithful to the terms of the covenant, —so ready to suffer,—so willing to be reckoned sin, and a curse in our stead.   Let us not doubt that He who fulfilled His engagement to suffer, will also fulfil His engagement to save all who come to Him.   Let us not only accept Him gladly as our Redeemer and Advocate, but gladly give ourselves, and all we have, to His service.   Surely if Jesus cheerfully died for us, it is a small thing to require Christians to live for Him.

MARK X. 35—45.

35 And James and John, the sons of Zebedee, come unto him, saying, Master, we would that thou shouldest do for us whatsoever we shall desire.

36 And he said unto them, What would ye that I should do for you?

37 They said unto him, Grant unto us, that we may sit, one on thy right hand, and the other on thy left hand, in thy glory.

38 But Jesus said unto them, Ye know not what ye ask: can ye drink of the cup that I drink of? and be baptized with the baptism that I am baptized with?

39 And they said unto him, We can. And Jesus said unto them, Ye shall indeed drink of the cup that I drink of; and with the baptism that I am baptized withal shall ye be baptized:

40 But to sit on my right hand and on my left hand is not mine to give; but *it shall be given to them* for whom it is prepared.

41 And when the ten heard *it*, they began to be much displeased with James and John.

42 But Jesus called them *to him*, and saith unto them, Ye know that they which are accounted to rule over the Gentiles exercise lordship over them; and their great ones exercise authority upon them.

43 But so shall it not be among you: but whosoever will be great among you, shall be your minister:

44 And whosoever of you will be the chiefest, shall be servant of all.

45 For even the Son of man came not to be ministered unto, but to minister, and to give his life a ransom for many.

LET us mark, in this passage, *the ignorance of our Lord's disciples.* We find James and John petitioning for the first places in the kingdom of glory. We find them confidently declaring their ability to drink of their Master's cup, and be baptized with their Master's baptism. In spite of all the plain warnings of our Lord, they clung obstinately to the belief that Christ's kingdom on earth was immediately going to appear. Notwithstanding their many shortcomings in Christ's service, they had no misgivings as to their power to endure anything which might come upon them. With all their faith and grace and love to Jesus, they neither knew their own hearts nor the nature of the path before them. They still dreamed of temporal crowns and earthly rewards. They still knew not what manner of men they were.

There are few true Christians who do not resemble James and John, when they first begin the service of Christ. We are apt to expect far more present enjoyment from our religion than the Gospel warrants us to expect. We are apt to forget the cross, and the tribulation, and to think only of the crown. We form an incorrect estimate of our own patience and power of endurance. We misjudge our own ability to stand temptation and trial. And the result of all is that we often buy wisdom dearly, by bitter experience, after many disappointments, and not a few falls.

Let the case before us teach us the importance of a solid and calm judgment in our religion. Like James and John, we are right in coveting the best gifts, and in telling all our desires to Christ. Like them we are right in believing that Jesus is King of kings, and will one day reign upon the earth. But let us not, like them, forget that there is a cross to be borne by every Christian, and that "through much tribulation we must enter into the kingdom of God." (Acts xiv. 22.) Let us not, like them, be over-confident in our own strength, and forward in professing that we can do anything that Christ requires. Let us, in short, beware of a boastful spirit when we first begin to run the Christian course. If we remember this it may save us many a humbling fall.

Let us mark, secondly, in this passage, *what praise our Lord bestows on lowliness, and devotion to the good of others.* It seems that the ten were much displeased with James and John, because of the petition which they made to their Master. Their ambition and love of preeminence were once more excited at the idea of any one being placed above themselves. Our Lord saw their feelings, and like a wise physician proceeded at once to supply a corrective medicine. He tells them that their ideas of greatness were built on a mistaken foundation. He repeats with renewed emphasis the lesson already laid down in the preceding chapter "Whosoever of you will be the chiefest shall be servant of all." And He backs up all by the overwhelming argument of His own example: "Even the Son of man came not to be ministered unto, but to minister." *

Let all who desire to please Christ, watch and pray against self-esteem. It is a feeling which is deeply rooted in our hearts. Thousands have come out from the world, taken up the cross, professed to forsake their own righteousness and believe in Christ, who have felt irritated and annoyed when a brother has been more honoured than themselves. These things ought not so to be. We ought often to ponder the words of St. Paul: "Let nothing be done through strife or vain glory; but in lowliness of mind let each esteem others better than themselves." (Philipp. ii. 3.) Blessed is that man who

---

* The remarks of Quesnel on this passage are worth reading. He says, "The ambition of clergymen is a great scandal in the Church, and is frequently an occasion of emulations, enmities, divisions, schisms, and wars; of all which the displeasure of the Apostles gives us an imperfect shadow and resemblance. If Apostles, trained up in the school of humility and charity, are not free from this vice, what effects will not ambition produce in souls wholly immersed in flesh and blood, which have no motion but from their passions, no law but that of their own desires?

"Men strangely forget themselves, when, as a ministry appointed only for the sake of heaven, they are contending with the great ones of the earth in haughtiness and grandeur. It is very difficult to support equally the double character of a spiritual pastor and a temporal prince; and to join humility with grandeur, meekness with dominion, and the constant application of a pastor with the care of secular affairs.

"The greatest prelate in the Church is he who is most conformable to the example of Christ, by humility, charity, and continual attendance on his flock, and who looks on himself as a servant to the children of God."

can sincerely rejoice when others are exalted, though he himself is overlooked and passed by !

Above all, let all who desire to walk in Christ's steps, labour to be useful to others. Let them lay themselves, out to do good in their day and generation. There is always a vast field for doing it, if men have the will and inclination. Let them never forget that true greatness does not consist in being an admiral, or a general, a statesman, or an artist. It consists in devoting ourselves, body and soul and spirit, to the blessed work of making our fellow-men more holy and more happy. It is those who exert themselves by the use of Scripture means to lessen the sorrow and increase the joy of all around them,—the Howards, the Wilberforces, the Martyns, the Judsons of a country,—who are truly great in the sight of God. While they live they are laughed at, mocked, ridiculed, and often persecuted. But their memorial is on high. Their names are written in heaven. Their praise endureth for ever. Let us remember these things, and while we have time, do good unto all men and be servants of all for Christ's sake. Let us strive to leave the world better, holier, happier than it was when we were born. A life spent in this way is truly Christlike, and brings its own reward.

Let us mark, lastly, in this passage, *the language which our Lord uses in speaking of His own death.* He says, "The Son of man came to give His life a ransom for many."

This is one of those expressions which ought to be carefully treasured up in the minds of all true Christians. It is one of the texts which prove incontrovertibly the atoning character of Christ's death. That death was no common death, like the death of a martyr, or of other holy men. It was the public payment by an Almighty Representative of the debts of sinful man to a holy God. It was the ransom which a Divine Surety undertook to provide, in order to procure liberty for sinners tied and bound by the chain of their sins. By that death Jesus made a full and complete satisfaction for man's countless transgressions. He bore our sins in His own body on the tree. The Lord laid on Him the iniquity of us all. When He died, He died for us. When He suffered, He suffered in our stead. When He hung on the cross, He hung there as our Substitute. When His blood flowed, it was the price of our souls.

Let all who trust in Christ take comfort in the thought that they build on a sure foundation. It is true that we are sinners, but Christ has borne our sins. It is true that we are poor helpless debtors, but Christ has paid our debts. It is true that we deserve to be shut up for ever in the prison of hell. But, thanks be to God, Christ hath paid a full and complete ransom for us. The door is wide open. The prisoners may go free. May we all know this privilege by heartfelt experience, and walk in the blessed liberty of the children of God.*

---

* The manner in which our Lord uses the word baptism in the passage now expounded, deserves careful notice. He says to two disciples, who were already baptized with water, "Can ye be baptized with the baptism that I am baptized with?" The expression is very remarkable. It is a clear proof that in the New Testament a sacramental dipping or sprinkling with water is not always necessarily implied by the word baptism. It establishes the fact that there is such a thing as being baptized, in a certain sense, without the use of any outward ordinance at all.

MARK X. 46—52.

46 And they came to Jericho: and as he went out of Jericho with his disciples and a great number of people, blind Bartimæus, the son of Timæus, sat by the highway side begging.

47 And when he heard that it was Jesus of Nazareth, he began to cry out, and say, Jesus, *thou* Son of David, have mercy on me.

48 And many charged him that he should hold his peace: but he cried the more a great deal, *Thou* Son of David, have mercy on me.

49 And Jesus stood still, and commanded him to be called. And they call the blind man, saying unto him, Be of good comfort, rise; he calleth thee.

50 And he, casting away his garment, rose, and came to Jesus.

51 And Jesus answered and said unto him, What wilt thou that I should do unto thee? The blind man said unto him, Lord, that I might receive my sight.

52 And Jesus said unto him, Go thy way; thy faith hath made thee whole. And immediately he received his sight, and followed Jesus in the way.

WE read in these verses an account of one of our Lord's miracles. Let us see in it, as we read, a vivid emblem of spiritual things. We are not studying a history which concerns us personally any more than the exploits of Cæsar or Alexander. We have before us a picture which ought to be deeply interesting to the soul of every Christian.

This is a point that ought to be remembered in interpreting some of the passages in the Epistles where the words "baptism" and "baptized" are used. In such texts, for instance, as "baptism doth save us" (1 Peter iii. 21), or, "as many as have been baptized into Christ have put on Christ" (Gal. iii. 27), it is clear that something more is contained than any mere outward ordinance. In both cases, the baptism of water is undoubtedly meant, but it is no less evident that something is implied also of deeper moment than any ordinance administered by man. In both cases it is a baptism which is accompanied by true faith, and a heart-reception of Christ, such as was the baptism of the Philippian jailor. To quote such texts, in support of what is commonly called the baptismal regeneration of infants, is to wrest and pervert them from their proper meaning. The conclusion of the text in St. Peter, for example, seems to place this beyond question. He emphatically warns us not to suppose that he means nothing more than the washing of water, or bodily reception of a sacrament, by the word baptism.

It has been a wise act on the part of translators of the New Testament to adhere to the Greek words "baptize" and "baptism," in rendering the Bible into the vernacular tongue of each nation. No other words could possibly imply all that the two Greek words

In the first place we have here *an example of strong faith.* We are told that as Jesus went out of Jericho, a blind man, named Bartimæus, " sat by the wayside begging. And when he heard that it was Jesus of Nazareth, he began to cry out, and say, Jesus, thou Son of David, have mercy on me."

Bartimæus was blind in body, but not in soul. The eyes of his understanding were open. He saw things which Annas and Caiaphas, and hosts of letter-learned Scribes and Pharisees, never saw at all. He saw that Jesus of Nazareth, as our Lord was contemptuously called,—Jesus, who had lived for thirty years in an obscure Galilean village,—this very Jesus was the Son of David,—the Messiah of whom prophets had prophecied long ago. He had witnessed none of our Lord's mighty miracles. He had not had the opportunity of beholding dead people raised with a word, and lepers healed by a touch. Of all these privileges his blindness totally deprived him. But he had heard the report of our Lord's mighty works, and hearing had believed. He was satisfied from mere hearsay, that He, of whom such wonderful things were reported, must be the promised Saviour, and must be able to heal him. And so when

convey. All other expressions would either weaken the sense of the inspired writers or convey a false impression to the mind of the reader. To take one solitary instance, what could be more meagre or unsatisfactory than to render the passage now before us in the following way, " Can ye be sprinkled with the sprinkling, or dipped with the dipping, that I am sprinkled or dipped with ? "—The firmness of the British and Foreign Bible Society on this point, ought to be cause of thankfulness to all the Protestant Churches. In resolving to use the Greek words "baptize" and "baptism," in all their versions, they have exercised a wise discretion.

our Lord drew near, he cried, "Jesus, thou Son of David, have mercy on me."

Let us strive and pray that we may have like precious faith. We, too, are not allowed to see Jesus with our bodily eyes. But we have the report of His power, and grace, and willingness to save, in the Gospel. We have exceeding great promises from His own lips, written down for our encouragement. Let us trust those promises implicitly, and commit our souls to Christ unhesitatingly. Let us not be afraid to repose all our confidence on His own gracious words, and to believe that what He has engaged to do for sinners He will surely perform. What is the beginning of all saving faith, but a soul's venture on Christ? What is the life of saving faith, when once begun, but a continual leaning on an unseen Saviour's word? What is the first step of a Christian, but a crying, like Bartimæus, "Jesus have mercy on me?" What is the daily course of a Christian, but keeping up the same spirit of faith? "Though now we see Him not, yet believing, we rejoice with joy unspeakable and full of glory." (1 Peter i. 8.)

We have, in the second place, in these verses, *an example of determined perseverance in the face of difficulties.* We are told that when Bartimæus begun to cry out, "Jesus, thou Son of David, have mercy on me," he met with little encouragement from those who were near him. On the contrary, "many charged him that he should hold his peace." But he was not to be stopped. If others did not know the misery of blindness, he did. If others did not think it worth while to take such trouble, in order to obtain relief, he, at any rate, knew better. He cared

not for the rebukes of unfeeling bystanders. He heeded
not the ridicule which his importunity probably brought
on him. "He cried the more a great deal," and so crying obtained his heart's desire, and received his sight.

Let all who wish to be saved, mark well this conduct
of Bartimæus, and walk diligently in his steps. Like
him, we must care nothing what others think and say
of us, when we seek the healing of our souls. There
never will be wanting people who will tell us that it is
"too soon," or "too late,"—that we are going "too fast,"
or "too far,"—that we need not pray so much, or read
our Bibles so much, or be so anxious about salvation.
We must give no heed to such people. Like Bartimæus,
we must cry the more, "Jesus, have mercy on me."

What is the reason that men are so half-hearted in
seeking Christ? Why are they so soon deterred, and
checked, and discouraged in drawing near to God? The
answer is short and simple. They do not feel sufficiently
their own sins. They are not thoroughly convinced of
the plague of their own hearts, and the disease of their
own souls. Once let a man see his own guilt, as it really
is, and he will never rest till he has found pardon and
peace in Christ. It is they who, like Bartimæus, really
know their own deplorable condition, who persevere,
like Bartimæus, and are finally healed.

In the last place, we have in these verses, *an example of
the constraining influence which gratitude to Christ ought
to have upon our souls.* Bartimæus did not return home
as soon as he was restored to sight. He would not leave
Him from whom he had received such mercy. At once
he devoted the new powers which his cure gave him, to

the Son of David who had worked the cure. His history concludes with the touching expression, He "followed Jesus in the way."

Let us see in these simple words a lively emblem of the effect that the grace of Christ ought to have on every one who tastes it. It ought to make him a follower of Jesus in his life, and to draw him with mighty power into the way of holiness. Freely pardoned, he ought to give himself freely and willingly to Christ's service. Bought at so mighty a price as the blood of Christ, he ought to devote himself heartily and thoroughly to Him who redeemed him. Grace, really experienced, will make a man feel daily, "What shall I render to the Lord for all His benefits?" It did so for the Apostle Paul : He says, "The love of Christ constraineth us." (2 Cor. v. 14.) It will do so for all true Christians at the present day. The man who boasts of having an interest in Christ, while he does not follow Christ in his life, is a miserable self-deceiver, and is ruining his own soul. "As many as are led by the Spirit of God, they," and they only, "are the sons of God." (Rom. viii. 14.)

Have we had our eyes opened by the Spirit of God? Have we yet been taught to see sin, and Christ, and holiness, and heaven, in their true light? Can we say, "One thing I know, that, whereas I was blind, now I see"? If so, we shall know the things of which we have been reading by experience. If not, we are yet in the broad way that leadeth to destruction, and have everything to learn.

Q

MARK XI. 1—11.

1 And when they came nigh to Jerusalem, unto Bethphage and Bethany, at the mount of Olives, he sendeth forth two of his disciples,

2 And saith unto them, Go your way into the village over against you: and as soon as ye be entered into it, ye shall find a colt tied, whereon never man sat; loose him and bring *him*.

3 And if any man say unto you, Why do ye this? say ye that the Lord hath need of him; and straightway he will send him hither.

4 And they went their way, and found the colt tied by the door without in a place where two ways met; and they loose him.

5 And certain of them that stood there said unto them, What do ye, loosing the colt?

6 And they said unto them even as Jesus had commanded: and they let them go.

7 And they brought the colt to Jesus, and cast their garments on him; and he sat upon him.

8 And many spread their garments in the way: and others cut down branches off the trees, and strawed *them* in the way.

9 And they that went before, and they that followed, cried, saying, Hosanna; Blessed *is* he that cometh in the name of the Lord:

10 Blessed *be* the kingdom of our father David, that cometh in the name of the Lord: Hosanna in the highest.

11 And Jesus entered into Jerusalem, and into the temple: and when he had looked round about upon all things, and now the eventide was come, he went out unto Bethany with the twelve.

THE event described in these verses is a singular exception in the history of our Lord's earthly ministry. Generally speaking, we see Jesus withdrawing Himself from public notice, often passing His time in the remote parts of Galilee, not unfrequently abiding in the wilderness,—and so fulfilling the prophecy, that He should " not cry, nor strive, nor let His voice be heard in the streets." Here, and here only, our Lord appears to drop His private character, and of His own choice to call public attention to Himself. He deliberately makes a public entry into Jerusalem, at the head of His disciples. He voluntarily rides into the holy city, surrounded by a vast multitude, crying, Hosanna, like King David returning to his palace in triumph. (2 Sam. xix. 40.) All this, too, was done at a time when myriads of Jews were gathered out of every land to Jerusalem to keep the Passover. We may well believe that the holy city rang with the tidings of our Lord's arrival. It is probable there was not a house in Jerusalem in which the entry of the Prophet of Nazareth was not known and talked of that night.

These things should always be remembered in reading this portion of our Lord's history. It is not for nothing that this entry into Jerusalem is four times related in the New Testament. It is evident that it is a scene in the earthly life of Jesus which Christians are intended to study with special attention. Let us study it in that spirit, and see what practical lessons we may learn from the passage for our own souls.

Let us observe, in the first place, *how public our Lord purposely made the last act of His life.* He came to Jerusalem to die, and He desired that all Jerusalem should know it. When He taught the deep things of the Spirit, He often spoke to none but His apostles. When He delivered His parables, He often addressed none but a multitude of poor and ignorant Galileans. When He worked His miracles, He was generally at Capernaum, or in the land of Zebulon and Napthali. But when the time came that He should die, He made a public entry into Jerusalem. He drew the attention of rulers and priests and elders and Scribes and Greeks and Romans to Himself. He knew that the most wonderful event that ever happened in this world was about to take place. The eternal Son of God was about to suffer in the stead of sinful men,—the great Sacrifice for sin about to be offered up,—the great Passover Lamb about to be slain,—the great Atonement for a world's sin about to be made. He therefore ordered it so that His death was eminently a public death. He over-ruled things in such a way that the eyes of all Jerusalem were fixed upon Him, and when He died, He died before many witnesses.

Let us see here one more proof of the unspeakable importance of the death of Christ. Let us treasure up His gracious sayings. Let us strive to walk in the steps of His holy life. Let us prize His intercession. Let us long for His second coming. But never let us forget that the crowning fact in all we know of Jesus Christ, is His death upon the cross. From that death flow all our hopes. Without that death we should have nothing solid beneath our feet. May we prize that death more and more every year we live; and in all our thoughts about Christ, rejoice in nothing so much as the great fact that He died for us!

Let us observe, in the second place, in this passage, *the voluntary poverty which our Lord underwent when He was upon earth.* How did He enter Jerusalem when He came to it on this remarkable occasion? Did He come in a royal chariot, with horses, soldiers, and a retinue around Him, like the kings of this world? We are told nothing of the kind. We read that He borrowed the colt of an ass for the occasion, and sat upon the garments of His disciples for lack of a saddle. This was in perfect keeping with all the tenor of His ministry. He never had any of the riches of this world. When He crossed the sea of Galilee, it was in a borrowed boat. When He rode into the holy city, it was on a borrowed beast. When He was buried, it was in a borrowed tomb.

We have, in this simple fact, an instance of that marvellous union of weakness * and power, riches and

* I use the word "weakness" in this passage advisedly. There

poverty, the godhead, and the manhood, which may be so often traced in the history of our blessed Lord. Who that reads the Gospels carefully can fail to observe, that He who could feed thousands with a few loaves, was Himself sometimes hungry,—and He who could heal the sick and infirm, was Himself sometimes weary,—that He who could cast out devils with a word, was Himself tempted,—and He who could raise the dead, could Himself submit to die? We see the very same thing in the passage before us. We see the power of our Lord in His bending the wills of a vast multitude to conduct Him into Jerusalem in triumph. We see the poverty of our Lord in His borrowing an ass, to carry Him when He made His triumphal entry. It is all wonderful, but there is a fitness in it all. It is meet and right that we should never forget the union of the divine and human natures in our Lord's person. If we saw His divine acts only, we might forget that He was man. If we saw His

is scriptural warrant for it in the text: "He was crucified through weakness." (2 Cor. xiii. 4.) Nevertheless I wish it to be distinctly understood, that I utterly disclaim the idea of there being any *moral weakness* in the human nature of Christ. The only weakness I mean is that sinless infirmity, which is inseparably connected with flesh and blood, and from which Adam before the fall was not exempt. Of all such weakness I believe our Lord was partaker to the fullest extent.

Whether or not our Lord's riding upon an ass instead of a horse, was a mark of humiliation, is a point on which opinions differ widely. Some dwell on the fact that the ass in Oriental countries was an animal that even kings rode, and refer to Judges v. 10: "Speak, ye that ride on white asses," etc. Others think that the choice of an ass was purposely made as emblematic of our Lord's lowly nature. Gerhardt in his Commentary refers to a saying of Tertullian, that the Gentiles called Christians "asinarii," in ridicule because they believed in Christ who rode on an ass, and even calumniously charged them with worshipping an ass's head!

seasons of poverty and weakness only, we might forget that He was God. But we are intended to see in Jesus, divine strength and human weakness united in one person. We cannot explain the mystery; but we may take comfort in the thought, "this is our Saviour, this is our Christ: one able to sympathize, because He is man; but one Almighty to save, because He is God."

Finally, let us see in the simple fact that our Lord rode on a borrowed ass, one more proof that poverty is in itself no sin. The causes which occasion much of the poverty there is around us are undoubtedly very sinful. Drunkenness, extravagance, profligacy, dishonesty, idleness, which produce so much of the destitution in the world, are unquestionably wrong in the sight of God. But to be born a poor man, and to inherit nothing from our parents, to work with our own hands for our bread and to have no land of our own,—all this is nót sinful at aH. The honest poor man is as honourable in the sight of God as the richest king. The Lord Jesus Christ Himself was poor. Silver and gold He had none. He had often nowhere to lay His head. Though He was rich, yet for our sakes He became poor. To be like Him in circumstances cannot be in itself wrong. Let us do our duty in that state of life to which God has called us, and if He thinks fit to keep us poor let us not be ashamed. The Saviour of sinners cares for us as well as for others. The Saviour of sinners knows what it is to be poor.

MARK XI. 12—21.

12 And on the morrow, when they were come from Bethany, he was hungry:

13 And seeing a fig tree afar off having leaves, he came, if haply he might find any thing thereon: and when he came to it, he found nothing but leaves; for the time of figs was not *yet*.

14 And Jesus answered and said unto it, No man eat fruit of thee hereafter for ever. And his disciples heard *it*.

15 And they come to Jerusalem: and Jesus went into the temple, and began to cast out them that sold and bought in the temple, and overthrew the tables of the moneychangers, and the seats of them that sold doves;

16 And would not suffer that any man should carry *any* vessel through the temple.

17 And he taught, saying unto them, Is it not written, My house shall be called of all nations the house of prayer? but ye have made it a den of thieves.

18 And the scribes and chief priests heard *it*, and sought how they might destroy him: for they feared him, because all the people was astonished at his doctrine.

19 And when even was come, he went out of the city.

20 And in the morning, as they passed by, they saw the fig tree dried up from the roots.

21 And Peter calling to remembrance saith unto him, Master, behold, the fig tree which thou cursedst is withered away.

WE see, in the beginning of this passage, *one of the many proofs that our Lord Jesus Christ was really man.* We read that " He was hungry." He had a nature and bodily constitution like our own in all things, sin only excepted. He could weep and rejoice and suffer pain. He could be weary and need rest. He could be thirsty and need drink. He could be hungry and need food.

Expressions like this should teach us the condescension of Christ. How wonderful they are when we reflect upon them! He who is the eternal God,—He who made the world and all that it contains,—He from whose hand the fruits of the earth, the fish of the sea, the fowls of the air, the beasts of the field, all had their beginning, —He, even He was pleased to suffer hunger, when He came into the world to save sinners. This is a great mystery. Kindness and love like this pass man's understanding. No wonder that St. Paul speaks of the " unsearchable riches of Christ." (Ephes. iii. 8.)

Expressions like this should teach us Christ's power to sympathize with His believing people on earth. He

knows their sorrows by experience. He can be touched
with the feeling of their infirmities. He has had experience of a body and its daily wants. He has suffered
Himself the severe sufferings that the body of man is
liable to. He has tasted pain, and weakness, and weariness, and hunger, and thirst. When we tell Him of
these things in our prayers, He knows what we mean,
and is no stranger to our troubles. Surely this is just
the Saviour and Friend that poor aching, groaning,
human nature requires!

We learn, in the second place, from these verses, *the
great danger of unfruitfulness and formality in religion.*
This is a lesson which our Lord teaches in a remarkable
typical action. We are told that coming to a fig tree in
search of fruit, and finding on it "nothing but leaves,"
He pronounced on it the solemn sentence, "No man eat
fruit of thee hereafter for ever." And we are told that
the next day the fig tree was found "dried up from the
roots." We cannot doubt for a moment that this whole
transaction was an emblem of spiritual things. It was
a parable in deeds, as full of meaning as any of our
Lord's parables in words.*

But who were they to whom this withered fig tree was
intended to speak? It was a sermon of three-fold appli-

---

* There are two difficulties connected with the story of the withered
fig tree, which weigh considerably on some minds, and therefore
deserve notice.

1. It is a difficulty with some persons that our Lord should have
pronounced any curse at all on the fig tree. They say that it looks
like a needless destruction of an innocent and unoffending creature,
and out of keeping with the spirit of Deut. xx. 19.

Such objectors appear to forget that the withering of the fig tree
was not a mere empty exhibition of power, like the pretended miracles

cation, a sermon that ought to speak loudly to the consciences of all professing Christians. Though withered
and dried up, that fig tree yet speaks. There was a
voice in it for the Jewish Church. Rich in the leaves
of a formal religion, but barren of all fruits of the Spirit,
that Church was in fearful danger at the very time when
this withering took place. Well would it have been for
the Jewish Church if it had had eyes to see its peril!

of Mahomet and other false prophets. It was a mighty typical act,
teaching deep spiritual lessons, lessons of such importance as might
well justify the destruction of one of God's unintelligent creatures
in order to convey them. Remembering this, we have no more
right to object to it than to object to the daily offering of a lamb
under the Mosaic law. In that offering the life of an innocent and
unoffending creature was daily taken away. But the great end of
daily setting before the eyes of man the One Sacrifice for sin, justified the taking away the life of the lamb. Just in the same way we
may justify our Lord's taking away the life of the tree.

2. It is a difficulty with some persons that the account of St.
Mark contains the words, "the time of figs was not yet." They ask
to be told why our Lord should have gone to the tree seeking fruit
when the season for figs had not yet arrived?

The answers to this difficulty are various. The simplest of them
appears to be as follows. "The time of figs, as a general rule, had
not yet come. But our Lord seeing a fig tree covered with leaves,
unlike the other fig trees, had a right to suppose that figs were to be
found on it, and therefore came to it." It is no small recommen-
dation of this view that it supplies an exact illustration of the state
of the Jewish Church when our Lord was upon earth. The time
of figs was not yet,—that is, the nations of the earth were all in
darkness, and bore no fruit to the glory of God. But among the nations, there was one covered with leaves,—that is the Jewish Church,
full of light, knowledge, privileges and high profession. Seeing this
fig tree full of leaves, our Lord came to it seeking fruit,—that is, He
came to the Jews justly expecting them to have fruit according to
their outward profession. But when our Lord came to this leafy
Jewish fig tree, He found it utterly destitute of fruit, faithless, and
unbelieving; and the end was that He pronounced sentence on it:
gave it over to be destroyed by the Romans, and scattered the Jews
over the earth.

There was a voice in the fig tree for all the branches of Christ's visible Church, in every age and every part of the world. There was a warning against an empty profession of Christianity unaccompanied by sound doctrine and holy living, which some of those branches would have done well to lay to heart.—But above all there was a voice in that withered fig tree for all carnal, hypocritical, and false-hearted Christians. Well would it be for all who are content with a name to live while in reality they are dead, if they would only see their own faces in the glass of this passage.

Let us take care that we each individually learn the lesson that this fig tree conveys. Let us always remember that baptism, and church-membership, and reception of the Lord's supper, and a diligent use of the outward forms of Christianity, are not sufficient to save our souls. They are leaves, nothing but leaves, and without fruit will add to our condemnation. Like the fig leaves of which Adam and Eve made themselves garments, they will not hide the nakedness of our souls from the eye of an all-seeing God, or give us boldness when we stand before Him at the last day. No : we must bear fruit, or be lost for ever! There must be fruit in our hearts and fruit in our lives—the fruit of repentance toward God, and faith toward our Lord Jesus Christ,—and true holiness in our conversation. Without such fruits as these a profession of Christianity will only sink us lower into hell.

We learn, in the last place, from this passage, *how reverently we ought to use places which are set apart for public worship*. This is a truth which is taught us in a striking manner by our Lord Jesus Christ's conduct when He went into the temple.   We are told that "He cast out them that sold and bought in the temple, and overthrew the tables of the money-changers, and the seats of them that sold doves."   And we are told that He enforced this action by warrant of Scripture, saying, "Is it not written, My house shall be called of all nations the house of prayer? but ye have made it a den of thieves."

We need not doubt that there was deep meaning in this action of our Lord on this occasion.   Like the cursing of the fig tree, the whole transaction was eminently typical.   But in saying this we must not allow ourselves to lose sight of one simple and obvious lesson which lies on the surface of the passage.   That lesson is the sinfulness of careless and irreverent behaviour in the use of buildings set apart for the public service of God. It was not so much as the house of sacrifice, but as the "house of prayer," that our Lord purified the temple. His action clearly indicates the feeling with which every "house of prayer" should be regarded.   A Christian place of worship no doubt is in no sense so sacred as the Jewish tabernacle, or temple.   Its arrangements have no typical meaning.   It is not built after a divine model, and intended to serve as an example of heavenly things. But it does not follow because these things are so, that a Christian place of worship is to be used with no more reverence than a private dwelling, or a shop, or an inn. There is surely a decent reverence, which is due to a place where Christ and His people regularly meet together, and public prayer is offered up,—a reverence which it is foolish and unwise to brand as superstitious, and confound with Popery. There is a certain feeling of sanctity and solemnity which ought to belong to all places where Christ is preached, and souls are born again, a feeling which does not depend on any consecration of man, and ought to be encouraged rather than checked. At all events the mind of the Lord Jesus in this passage seems very plain. He takes notice of men's behaviour in places of worship, and all irreverence or profanity is an offence in His sight.

Let us remember these verses whenever we go to the house of God, and take heed that we go in a serious frame, and do not offer the sacrifice of fools. Let us call to mind where we are, what we are doing, what business we are about, and in whose Presence we are engaged. Let us beware of giving God a mere formal service, while our hearts are full of the world. Let us leave our business and money at home, and not carry them with us to church. Let us beware of allowing any buying and selling in our hearts, in the midst of our religious assemblies. The Lord still lives who cast out buyers and sellers from the temple, and when He sees such conduct He is much displeased.

MARK XI. 22—26.

22 And Jesus answering saith unto them, Have faith in God.

23 For verily I say unto you, That whosoever shall say unto this mountain, Be thou removed, and be thou cast into the sea; and shall not doubt in his heart, but shall believe that those things which he saith shall come to pass; he shall have whatsoever he saith.

24 Therefore I say unto you, What things soever ye desire, when ye pray, believe that ye receive *them*, and ye shall have *them*.

25 And when ye stand praying, forgive, if ye have ought against any: that your Father also which is in heaven may forgive you your trespasses.

26 But if ye do not forgive, neither will your Father which is in heaven forgive your trespasses.

LET us learn from these words of our Lord Jesus Christ, *the immense importance of faith.*

This is a lesson which our Lord teaches first by a proverbial saying. Faith shall enable a man to accomplish works and overcome difficulties as great and formidable as the "removing of a mountain, and casting it into the sea."* Afterwards the lesson is impressed upon us still further, by a general exhortation to exercise faith when we pray. "What things soever ye desire, when ye pray, believe that ye receive them, and ye shall have them." This promise must of course be taken with a reasonable qualification. It assumes that a believer will ask things which are not sinful, and which are in accordance with the will of God. When He asks such things, he may confidently believe that his prayer will be answered. To use the words of St. James, "Let him ask in faith, nothing wavering." (James i. 6.)

The faith here commended must be distinguished

---

* It is clear that a promise like this of "removing mountains" must be taken in a figurative sense. It appears to be a proverbial expression, and to be used as such by St. Paul. (2 Cor. xiii. 11.) Moreover it is a promise that must be interpreted with sober and reasonable limitations. We have no right to expect that whatever we take into our heads to ask of God shall at once be done for us, whether it be for His glory and our sanctification or not. We have no warrant for presuming that in every difficulty and trouble God will at once work a miracle, and deliver us from our anxiety as soon as we make it a subject of prayer. The things about which we pray must be things having special reference to our own vocation and providential position. Moses at the head of the twelve tribes of Israel, Elijah on Mount Carmel, Paul in the Philippian prison, might confidently expect miraculous interpositions in answer to prayer, in a way that private individuals may not expect in our days. Above all, we must not think to prescribe to God the time and way in which He shall "remove mountains" for us.

from that faith which is essential to justification. In principle undoubtedly all true faith is one and the same. It is always trust or belief. But in the object and operations of faith there are diversities which it is useful to understand. Justifying faith is that act of the soul by which a man lays hold on Christ and has peace with God. Its special object is the atonement for sin which Jesus made on the cross.—The faith spoken of in the passage now before us is a grace of more general signification, the fruit and companion of justifying faith, but still not to be confounded with it. It is rather a general confidence in God's power, wisdom, and goodwill towards believers. And its special objects are the promises, the word, and the character of God in Christ.

Confidence in God's power and will to help every believer in Christ, and in the truth of every word that God has spoken, is the grand secret of success and prosperity in our religion. In fact, it is the very root of saving Christianity. "By it the elders obtained a good report." "He that cometh unto God must believe that He is, and that He is a rewarder of them that diligently seek Him." To know the full worth of it in the sight of God we should often study the eleventh chapter of the Epistle to the Hebrews.

Do we desire to grow in grace, and in the knowledge of our Lord Jesus Christ? Do we wish to make progress in our religion, and become strong Christians, and not mere babes in spiritual things? Then let us pray daily for more faith, and watch our faith with most jealous watchfulness. Here is the corner-stone of our religion. A flaw or weakness here will affect the whole condition

of our inner man. According to our faith will be the
degree of our peace, our hope, our joy, our decision in
Christ's service, our boldness in confession, our strength
in work, our patience in trial, our resignation in trouble,
our sensible comfort in prayer. All, all will hinge on the
proportion of our faith. Happy are they who know how
to rest their whole weight continually on a covenant
God, and to walk by faith, not by sight. "He that
believeth shall not make haste." (Isai. xxviii. 16.)

Let us learn, for another thing, from these verses, *the
absolute necessity of a forgiving spirit towards others.* This
lesson is here taught us in a striking way. There is no
immediate connection between the importance of faith,
of which our Lord has just been speaking, and the subject
of forgiving injuries. But the connecting link is prayer.
First we are told that faith is essential to the success
of our prayers. But then it is added, no prayer can
be heard which do not come from a forgiving heart.
"When ye stand praying, forgive, if ye have ought
against any, that your Father also which is in heaven
may forgive you your trespasses."

The value of our prayers, we can all understand,
depends exceedingly on the state of mind in which we
offer them. But the point before us is one which
receives far less attention than it deserves. Our prayers
must not only be earnest, fervent, and sincere, and in
the name of Christ. They must contain one more
ingredient besides. They must come from a forgiving
heart. We have no right to look for mercy if we are not
ready to extend mercy to our brethren. We cannot
really feel the sinfulness of the sins we ask to have

pardoned if we cherish malice towards our fellow-men. We must have the heart of a brother toward our neighbour on earth if we wish God to be our Father in heaven. We must not flatter ourselves that we have the Spirit of adoption if we cannot bear and forbear.

This is a heart-searching subject. The quantity of malice, bitterness, and party-spirit among Christians is fearfully great. No wonder that so many prayers seem to be thrown away and unheard. It is a subject which ought to come home to all classes of Christians. All have not equal gifts of knowledge and utterance in their approaches to God. But all can forgive their fellow-men. It is a subject which our Lord Jesus Christ has taken special pains to impress on our minds. He has given it a prominent place in that pattern of prayers, the Lord's prayer. We are all familiar from our infancy with the words, "forgive us our trespasses as we forgive them that trespass against us." Well would it be for many; if they would consider what those words mean!

Let us leave the passage with serious self-inquiry. Do we know what it is to be of a forgiving spirit? Can we look over the injuries that we receive from time to time in this evil world? Can we pass over a transgression and pardon an offence? If not, where is our Christianity? If not, why should we wonder that our souls do not prosper?—Let us resolve to amend our ways in this matter. Let us determine by God's grace to forgive, even as we hope to be forgiven. This is the nearest approach we can make to the mind of Christ Jesus. This is the character which is most suitable to a poor sinful child of Adam. God's free forgiveness of sins

is our highest privilege in this world.   God's free forgiveness will be our only title to eternal life in the world
to come.   Then let us be forgiving during the few years
that we are here upon earth.*

MARK XI. 27—33.

27 And they come again to Jerusalem : and as he was walking in the
temple, there come to him the chief
priests, and the scribes, and the elders,
28 And say unto him, By what authority doest thou these things? and
who gave thee this authority to do these
things?
29 And Jesus answered and said unto
them, I will also ask of you one question,
and answer me, and I will tell you by
what authority I do these things.
30 The baptism of John, was *it* from
heaven, or of men? answer me.
31 And they reasoned with themselves,
saying, If we shall say, From heaven :
he will say, Why then did ye not believe
him?
32 But if we shall say, Of men : they
feared the people : for all *men* counted
John, that he was a prophet indeed.
33 And they answered and said unto
Jesus, We cannot tell.   And Jesus answering saith unto them, Neither do I
tell you by what authority I do these
things.

LET us observe in these verses *how much spiritual
blindness may be in the hearts of those who hold high ecclesiastical office.*   We see "the chief priest and scribes
and elders" coming to our Lord Jesus, and raising
difficulties and objections in the way of His work.

These men, we know, were the accredited teachers and

---

* The expression "when ye stand praying," in this passage, ought
not to be overlooked.   It is one of those forms of speech in the Bible,
which ought to teach all Christians not to be dogmatical in laying
down minute rules about the externals of religion, and especially
about the precise manner, gesture, or posture in which a believer
ought to pray.   If a man is fully persuaded that he can hold closer
communion with God, and pour out his heart more freely and without distraction, in the attitude of standing than in that of kneeling,
I dare not tell him that he is wrong.   The great point to insist on is
the absolute necessity of praying with the heart.   The last words of
Sir Walter Raleigh to his executioner on the scaffold are a beautiful
illustration of the right view of the question : "Friend, it matters
little how a man's head lies, if his heart be right in the sight of
God."

R

rulers of the Jewish Church.   They were regarded by
the Jews as the fountain and spring-head of religious
knowledge.   They were, most of them, regularly ordained to the position they held, and could trace their
orders by regular descent from Aaron.   And yet we find
these very men, at the time when they ought to have
been instructors of others, full of prejudice against the
truth, and bitter enemies of the Messiah! *

These things are written to show Christians, that they
must beware of depending too much on ordained men.
They must not look up to ministers as Popes, or regard
them as infallible.   The orders of no Church confer
infallibility, whether they be Episcopal, Presbyterian,
or Independent.   Bishops, priests, and deacons, at their
best, are only flesh and blood, and may err both in
doctrine and practice, as well as the chief priests and
elders of the Jews.   Their acts and teaching must always
be tested by the Word of God.   They must be followed
so far as they follow Scripture, and no further.   There
is only one Priest and Bishop of souls, who makes no

* The following remarks from Gerhard's Commentary are worth
reading :—

"The Church is not tied to those teachers who are in the regular
succession, for they frequently err from the path of truth.   In such
cases the Church ought not to follow their errors, but to embrace
the truth as set forth in the Word.   Thus, Aaron setting up the
golden calf,—Urijah the high priest in the time of Ahaz, building a
new altar,—Pashur and the other priests in Jeremiah's time, all erred
most grievously.   And in this very passage, the priests sitting in
Moses' seat reject the Messiah Himself, and impugn His authority.
But if those who succeeded Aaron in the divinely appointed priesthood of the Old Testament, could err, and in fact, did occasionally
err, how much more likely to err are the Popes of Rome, who cannot
prove from God's Word that the Pope's office has been instituted by
Christ in the New Testament."

mistakes.   That one is the Lord Jesus Christ.   In Him alone is no weakness, no failure, no shadow of infirmity. Let us learn to lean more entirely on Him.   Let us "call no man father on earth." (Matt. xxiii. 9.)   So doing, we shall never be disappointed.

Let us observe, in the second place, *how envy and un-belief make men throw discredit on the commission of those who work for God.*   These chief priests and elders could not deny the reality of our Lord's miracles of mercy. They could not say that His teaching was contrary to Holy Scripture, or that His life was sinful.   What then did they do?   They attacked His claim to attention, and demanded His authority: "By what authority doest thou these things? and who gave thee this authority?"*

There can be no doubt whatever that, as a general

---

* Brentius has some sensible remarks on the unreasonableness of the Chief Priests and Pharisees, who would neither keep the temple from the encroachments of the buyers and sellers, nor let others do it for them.   They would neither exercise the lawful authority which was in their hands, nor allow of our Lord exercising it for them.   He shows the similarity of their conduct to that of the Greek and Roman Churches, and to that of a foolish head of a family, who neither corrects his children himself, nor likes any one to correct them for him.   And he concludes by saying, "Let us learn that every one should do his own duty, or else yield up his place to another. Let us not be like the dog in the manger, who would neither eat the hay himself, nor yet allow the ox to eat it."   The history of the Church of Christ contains only too much of the dog in the manger! Ministers and teachers have often neglected the souls of their people shamefully, and yet found fault with any one who has tried to do good, and haughtily demanded his authority!

The reflections of the Roman Catholic writer, Quesnel, on this subject are remarkable: "Those who find themseles vanquished by truth, generally endeavour to reject authority.   There are no persons more forward to demand of others a reason for their actions than those who think they may do everything themselves without control."

principle, all who undertake to teach others should be regularly appointed to the work.   St. Paul himself declares that this was the case with our Lord, in the matter of the priestly office : "No man taketh this honour unto himself, but he that is called of God, as was Aaron." (Heb. v. 4.) And even now, when the office of the sacrificing priest no longer exists, the words of the twenty-third Article of the Church of England are wise and scriptural : "It is not lawful for any man to take upon him the office of public preaching, or ministering the sacraments in the congregation, before he be lawfully called and sent to execute the same." But it is one thing to maintain the lawfulness of an outward call to minister in sacred things, and quite another to assert that it is the one thing needful, without which no work for God can be done.   This is the point on which the Jews evidently erred in the time of our Lord's earthly ministry, and on which many have unhappily followed them down to the present day.

Let us beware of this narrow spirit, and specially in these last ages of the world.   Unquestionably we must not undervalue order and discipline in the Church.   It is just as valuable there as it is in an army.   But we must not suppose that God is absolutely tied to the use of ordained men.   We must not forget that there may be an inward call of the Holy Ghost without any outward call of man, no less than an outward call of man without any inward call of the Holy Ghost.   The first question after all is this: "Is a man for Christ, or against Him ?   What does he teach ?   How does he live ?   Is he doing good ?"   If questions like these can be answered satisfactorily, let us thank God and be content. We must remember that a physician is useless, however high his degree and diploma, if he cannot cure diseases, and a soldier useless, however well dressed and drilled, if he will not face the enemy in the day of battle. The best doctor is the man who can cure, and the best soldier the man who can fight.

Let us observe, in the last place, *what dishonesty and equivocation unbelievers may be led into by prejudice against the truth.* The chief priests and elders dared not answer our Lord's question about John's baptism. They dared not say, it was " of men," because they feared the people. They dared not confess that it was " of heaven," because they saw our Lord would say, " Why did ye not believe him? He testified plainly of Me." What then did they do? They told a direct lie. They said, " We cannot tell."

It is a melancholy fact, that dishonesty like this is far from being uncommon among unconverted people. There are thousands who evade appeals to their conscience by answers which are not true. When pressed to attend to their souls, they say things which they know are not correct. They love the world and their own way, and like our Lord's enemies, are determined not to give them up, but like them also are ashamed to say the truth. And so they answer exhortations to repentance and decision by false excuses. One man pretends that he " cannot understand" the doctrines of the Gospel. Another assures us that he really "tries" to serve God, but makes no progress. A third declares that he has every wish to serve Christ, but " has no time." All these are often nothing better than miserable equivocations. As a general rule, they are as worthless as the chief priest's answer : "We cannot tell."

The plain truth is that we ought to be very slow to give credit to the unconverted man's professed reasons for not serving Christ. We may be tolerably sure that when he says, "I cannot," the real meaning of his heart is, "I will not." A really honest spirit in religious matters is a mighty blessing. Once let a man be willing to live up to his light, and act up to his knowledge, and he will soon know of the doctrine of Christ, and come out from the world. (John vii. 17.) The ruin of thousands is simply this, that they deal dishonestly with their own souls. They allege pretended difficulties as the cause of their not serving Christ, while in reality they "love darkness rather than light," and have no honest desire to change. (John iii. 19.)

MARK XII. 1—12.

1 And he began to speak unto them by parables. A *certain* man planted a vineyard, and set an hedge about *it*, and digged *a place for* the winefat, and built a tower, and let it out to husbandmen, and went into a far country.

2 And at the season he sent to the husbandmen a servant, that he might receive from the husbandmen of the fruit of the vineyard.

3 And they caught *him*, and beat him, and sent *him* away empty.

4 And again he sent unto them another servant; and at him they cast stones, and wounded *him* in the head, and sent *him* away shamefully handled.

5 And again he sent another; and him they killed, and many others; beating some, and killing some.

6 Having yet therefore one son, his well-beloved, he sent him also last unto them, saying, They will reverence my son.

7 But those husbandmen said among themselves, This is the heir; come, let us kill him, and the inheritance shall be our's.

8 And they took him, and killed *him*, and cast *him* out of the vineyard.

9 What shall therefore the lord of the vineyard do ? he will come and destroy the husbandmen, and will give the vineyard unto others.

10 And have ye not read this Scripture; The stone which the builders rejected is become the head of the corner:

11 This was the Lord's doing, and it is marvellous in our eyes?

12 And they sought to lay hold on him, but feared the people : for they knew that he had spoken the parable against them : and they left him, and went their way.

THE verses before us contain an historical parable. The history of the Jewish nation, from the day that Israel left Egypt down to the time of the destruction of Jerusalem, is here set before us as in a glass. Under the figure of the vineyard and the husbandmen, the Lord Jesus tells the story of God's dealings with His people for fifteen hundred years. Let us study it attentively, and apply it to ourselves.

Let us observe, in the first place, *God's special kindness to the Jewish Church and nation.* He gave to them peculiar privileges. He dealt with them as a man deals with a piece of land which he separates and hedges in for "a vineyard." He gave them good laws and ordinances. He planted them in a goodly land, and cast out seven nations before them. He passed by greater and mightier nations to show them favour. He let alone Egypt, and Assyria, and Greece, and Rome, and showered down mercies on a few millions of people in Palestine. The vineyard of the Lord was the house of Israel. No family under heaven ever received so many signal and distinguishing privileges as the family of Abraham.

And we, too, who live in Great Britain, can we say that we have received no special mercies from God? We cannot say so. Why are we not a heathen country, like China? Why are we not a land of idolaters, like Hindostan? We owe it all to the distinguishing favour of God. It is not for our goodness and worthiness, but of God's free grace that England is what England is among the nations of the earth. Let us be thankful for our mercies, and know the hand from which they come. Let us not be high-minded, but humble, lest we provoke

God to take our mercies away. If Israel had peculiar national privileges, so also has England. Let Englishmen mark this well, and take heed, lest that which happened to Israel should happen also to them.

Let us observe, in the second place, *God's patience and longsuffering towards the Jewish nation.* What is their whole history as recorded in the Old Testament, but a long record of repeated provocations and repeated pardons? Over and over again we read of prophets being sent to them, and warnings being delivered, but too often entirely in vain. One servant after another came to the vineyard of Israel, and asked for fruit.—One servant after another was "sent away empty" by the Jewish husbandmen, and no fruit borne by the nation to the glory of God. "They mocked the messengers of God, and despised His words, and misused His prophets." (2 Chron. xxxvi. 16.) Yet hundreds of years passed away before "the wrath of the Lord arose against His people, till there was no remedy." Never was there a people so patiently dealt with as Israel.

And we, too, who dwell in Great Britain, have we no longsuffering of God to be thankful for? Beyond doubt we have abundant cause to say that our Lord is patient. He does not deal with us according to our sins, or reward us according to our iniquities. We have often provoked Him to take our candlestick away, and to deal with us as He has dealt with Tyre, and Babylon, and Rome. Yet His longsuffering and loving-kindness continue still. Let us beware that we do not presume on His goodness too far. Let us hear in His mercies a loud call to us to bear fruit, and let us strive to abound in that righteousness, which alone exalteth a nation. (Prov. xiv. 34.) Let every family in the land feel its responsibility to God, and then the whole nation will be seen showing forth His praise.

Let us observe, in the third place, *the hardness and wickedness of human nature, as exemplified in the history of the Jewish people.*

It is difficult to imagine a more striking proof of this truth, than the summary of Israel's dealings with God's messengers, which our Lord sketches in this parable. Prophet after prophet was sent to them in vain. Miracle after miracle was wrought among them, without any lasting effect. The Son of God Himself, the well-beloved, at last came down to them, and was not believed. God Himself was manifest in the flesh, dwelling among them, and "they took Him and killed Him."

There is no truth so little realized and believed as the " desperate wickedness " of the human heart. Let the parable before us this day be always reckoned among the standing proofs of it. Let us see in it what men and women can do, in the full blaze of religious privileges,— in the midst of prophecies and miracles,—in the presence of the Son of God Himself. " The carnal mind is enmity against God." (Rom. viii. 7.) Men never saw God face to face but once, when Jesus became a man, and lived upon earth. They saw Him holy, harmless, undefiled, going about doing good. Yet they would not have Him, rebelled against Him, and at last killed Him. Let us dismiss from our minds the idea that there is any innate goodness, or natural rectitude in our hearts. Let us put away the common notion that seeing and knowing what is good is enough to make a man a Christian. The great experiment has been made in the instance of the Jewish nation. We, too, like Israel, might have among us miracles, prophets, and the company of Christ Himself in the flesh, and, yet, like Israel, have them in vain. Nothing but the Spirit of God can change the heart. "We must be born again." (John iii. 7.)

Let us observe, in the last place, *that men's consciences may be pricked, and yet they may continue impenitent.* The Jews, to whom our Lord addressed the solemn historical parable which we have been reading, saw clearly that it applied to themselves. They felt that they and their forefathers were the husbandmen to whom the vineyard was let, and who ought to have rendered fruit to God. They felt that they and their forefathers were the wicked labourers, who had refused to give the Master of the vineyard His dues, and had " shamefully handled " His servants, beating some, and killing some." Above all, they felt that they themselves were planning the last crowning act of wickedness, which the parable described. There were about to kill the well-beloved Son, and " cast Him out of the vineyard." All this they knew perfectly well. " They knew that He had spoken the parable against them." Yet, though they knew it, they would not repent. Though convicted by their own consciences, they were hardened in sin.

Let us learn from this awful fact, that knowledge and conviction alone save no man's soul. It is quite possible to know that we are wrong, and be unable to deny it, and yet to cleave to our sins obstinately, and perish miserably in hell. The thing that we all need, is a

change of heart and will. For this let us pray earnestly.
Till we have this, let us never rest. Without this, we
shall never be real Christiáns, and reach heaven. Without it we may live all our lives, like the Jews, knowing
inwardly that we are wrong, and yet, like the Jews,
persevere in our own way, and die in our sins.

MARK XII. 13—17.

13 And they send unto him certain of the Pharisees and of the Herodians, to catch him in *his* words.

14 And when they were come, they say unto him, Master, we know that thou art true, and carest for no man: for thou regardest not the person of men, but teachest the way of God in truth: Is it lawful to give tribute to Cæsar or not?

15 Shall we give, or shall we not give? But he, knowing their hypoc-risy, said unto them, Why tempt ye me? bring me a penny, that I may see *it.*

16 And they brought *it.* And he saith unto them, Whose is this image and superscription? And they said unto him, Cæsar's.

17 And Jesus answering said unto them, Render to Cæsar the things that are Cæsar's, and to God the things that are God's. And they marvelled at him.

LET us observe in the beginning of this passage, *how men
of different religious opinions can unite in opposing Christ.*
We read of " Pharisees and Herodians " coming together
to " catch our Lord in His words," and perplex Him
with a hard question. The Pharisee was a superstitious
formalist, who cared for nothing but the outward ceremonies of religion. The Herodian was a mere man of
the world, who despised all religion, and cared more for
pleasing men than God. Yet when there came among
them a mighty Teacher who assailed the ruling passions
of both alike, and spared neither formalist nor world-
ling, we see them making common cause, and uniting in
a common effort to stop His mouth.

It has always been so from the beginning of the world.
We may see the same thing going on at the present day.

Worldly men and formalists have little real sympathy with one another. They dislike one another's principles, and despise one another's ways. But there is one thing which they both dislike even more, and that is the pure Gospel of Jesus Christ. And hence, whenever there is a chance of opposing the Gospel, we shall always see the worldly man and the formalist combine and act together. We must expect no mercy from them : they will show none. We must never reckon on their divisions : they will always patch up an alliance to resist Christ.

Let us observe, for another thing, in this passage, *the exceeding subtlety of the question propounded to our Lord.* His enemies asked Him, " Is it lawful to give tribute to Cæsar, the Roman Emperor, or not? Shall we give, or shall we not give ? " Here was a question, which it seemed at first sight impossible to answer without peril. If our Lord had replied, " Give," the Pharisees would have accused Him before the priests as one who regarded the Jewish nation as under subjection to Rome.—If our Lord had replied, " Do not give," the Herodians would have accused Him before Pilate, as a seditious person who taught rebellion against the Roman government. The trap was indeed well planned. Surely we may see in it the cunning hand of one greater than man. That old serpent the devil was there.

We shall do well to remember that of all questions which have perplexed Christians, none have ever proved so intricate and puzzling as the class of questions which the Pharisees and Herodians here propounded.*

---

* " Nothing is more likely to ensnare ministers, than bringing them to meddle with controversies about civil rights, and to settle

What are the dues of Cæsar and what are the dues of
God, where the rights of the Church end and where
the rights of the State begin, what are lawful civil
claims and what are lawful spiritual claims,—all these
are hard knots and deep problems, which Christians
have often found it difficult to untie and almost impossible to solve. Let us pray to be delivered from them.
Never does the cause of Christ suffer so much as when
the devil succeeds in bringing Churches into collisions
and law-suits with the civil power. In such collisions
precious time is wasted,—energies are misapplied,—
ministers are drawn off from their proper work,—the
souls of people suffer, and a Church's victory often proves
only one degree better than defeat. " Give peace in our
time, O Lord," is a prayer of wide meaning, and one
that should often be on a Christian's lips.

Let us observe, in the last place, *the marvellous wisdom
which our Lord showed in His answer to His enemies.*

Their flattering words did not deceive Him. He " knew
their hypocrisy." His all-seeing eye detected the " pot-
sherds covered with silver dross" which stood before Him.
(Prov. xxvi. 23.) He was not imposed upon, as too many
of His people are, by glowing language and fine speeches.

He made the daily practice of His own enemies supply
Him with an answer to their cunning question. He tells
them to bring Him a penny, a common coin which they
themselves were in the habit of using. He asks them
"whose image and superscription" are stamped upon that

landmarks between the prince and the subjects, which it is fit should
be done, while it is not at all fit that they should have the doing of
it."—*Matthew Henry.*

penny? They were obliged to reply, "Cæsar's." They were themselves using a Roman coin, issued and circulated by the Roman government. By their own confession they were in some way under the power of the Romans, or this Roman money would not have been current among them. At once our Lord silences them by the memorable words, " Render unto Cæsar the things that are Cæsar's, and unto God the things that are God's." He bids them pay tribute to the Roman government in temporal things, for by using its money they allowed themselves bound to do so. Yet He bids them give obedience to God in spiritual things, and not to suppose that duty to an earthly Sovereign and a heavenly Sovereign are incapable of being reconciled one with the other. In short, He bids the proud Pharisee not to refuse his dues to Cæsar, and the worldly Herodian not to refuse his dues to God·

Let us learn from this masterly decision the great principle, that true Christianity was never meant to interfere with a man's obedience to the civil power. So far from this being the case it ought to make him a quiet, loyal, and faithful subject. He ought to regard the powers that be as "ordained of God," and to submit to their rules and regulations, so long as the law is enforced, though he may not thoroughly approve of them. If the law of the land and the law of God come in collision, no doubt his course is clear,—he must obey God rather than man. Like the three children, though he serves a heathen King, he must not bow down to an idol. Like Daniel, though he submits to a tyrannical government, he must not give over praying in order to please the ruling powers.*

* Sibelius quotes a passage from Augustine on the Psalms, which

Let us often pray for a larger measure of that spirit of wisdom which dwelt so abundantly in our blessed Lord. Many are the evils which have arisen in the Church of Christ, from a morbid and distorted view of the relative positions of the civil government and of God. Many are the rents and divisions which have been occasioned by lack of sound judgment as to their comparative claims. Happy is he who remembers our Lord's decision in this passage, understands it rightly, and makes a practical application of it to his own times.

MARK XII. 18—27.

18 Then came unto him the Sadducees, which say there is no resurrection ; and they asked him, saying,

19 Master, Moses wrote unto us, If a man's brother die, and leave *his* wife *behind him*, and leave no children, that his brother should take his wife, and raise up seed unto his brother.

20 Now there were seven brethren : and the first took a wife, and dying left no seed.

21 And the second took her, and died, neither left he any seed : and the third likewise.

22 And the seven had her, and left no seed : last of all the woman died also.

23 In the resurrection therefore, when they shall rise, whose wife shall she be of them? for the seven had her to wife.

24 And Jesus answering said unto them, Do ye not therefore err, because ye know not the Scriptures, neither the power of God ?

25 For when they shall rise from the dead, they neither marry, nor are given in marriage ; but are as the angels which are in heaven.

26 And as touching the dead, that they rise ; have ye not read in the book of Moses, how in the bush God spake unto him, saying, I *am* the God of Abraham, and the God of Isaac, and the God of Jacob.

27 He is not the God of the dead, but the God of the living : ye therefore do greatly err.

is worth reading, as an illustration of the subject now before us. "Julian was an unbelieving Emperor. He was an apostate, a wicked man, and an idolater. And yet Christian men served as soldiers under this unbelieving Emperor. When the cause of Christ was concerned, they acknowledged no commander but Him that was in heaven. When the Emperor wished them to worship idols or burn incense to them, they preferred honouring God before him. But when he said, 'Draw out in order of battle : march against that nation,' they obeyed him. They drew a distinction between their eternal Master, and their temporal master ; and yet were submissive to their temporal master for their eternal Master's sake."

THESE verses relate a conversation between our Lord
Jesus Christ and the Sadducees. The religion of these
men, we know, was little better than infidelity. They
said there was "no resurrection." They too, like the
Pharisees, thought to entangle and perplex our Lord with
hard questions. The Church of Christ must not expect
to fare better than its Master. Formalism on one side
and infidelity on another, are two enemies for whose
attacks we must always be prepared.

We learn from this passage, *how much unfairness may
often be detected in the arguments of infidels.*

The question propounded by the Sadducees is a striking
illustration of this. They tell him of a woman who
married seven brothers in succession, had no children, had
outlived her seven husbands. They ask "whose wife" of
all the seven the woman would be "in the resurrection"?
It may well be surmised that the case was a supposed and
not a real one. On the face of it, there is the strongest
appearance of improbability. The chances against such
a case occurring in reality, any actuary would tell us, are
almost infinite. But that was nothing to the Sadducees.
All they cared for was to raise a difficulty, and if possible
to put our Lord to silence. The doctrine of the resurrection they had not the face manfully to deny. The
possible consequences of the doctrine were the ground
which they chose to take up.

There are three things which we shall do well to remember, if unhappily we have at any time to argue with
infidels.—For one thing, let us remember that an infidel
will always try to press us with the difficulties and abstruse things of religion, and especially with those which

are connected with the world to come. We must avoid this mode of argument as far as possible. It is leaving the open field to fight in a jungle. We must endeavour, as far as we can, to make our discussion turn on the great plain facts and evidences of Christianity.—For another thing, let us remember we must be on our guard against unfairness and dishonesty in argument. It may seem hard and uncharitable to say this. But experience proves that it is needful. Thousands of professed infidels have confessed in their latter days that they had never studied the Bible which they pretended to deny, and though well read in the works of unbelievers and sceptics, had never calmly examined the foundations of Christianity. Above all, let us remember that every infidel has a conscience. To this we may always appeal confidently. The very men who talk most loudly and disdainfully against religion, are often feeling conscious, even while they talk, that they are wrong. The very arguments which they have sneered at and ridiculed, will often prove at last not to have been thrown away.

We learn, in the second place, from this passage, *how much of religious error may be traced to ignorance of the Bible.* Our Lord's first words in reply to the Sadducees declare this plainly. He says, "Do ye not err, because ye know not the Scriptures?"

The truth of the principle here laid down, is proved by facts in almost every age of Church history. The reformation in Josiah's day was closely connected with the discovery of the Book of the Law. The false doctrines of the Jews in our Lord's time were the result of neglecting the Scriptures. The dark ages of Christendom were

s

times when the Bible was kept back from the people. The Protestant Reformation was mainly effected by translating and circulating the Bible. The Churches which are most flourishing at this day, are Churches which honour the Bible. The nations which enjoy most moral light, are nations in which the Bible is most known. The parishes in our land where there is most true religion, are those in which the Bible is most studied. The godliest families are Bible-reading families. The holiest men and women are Bible-reading people. These are simple facts which cannot be denied.

Let these things sink deeply into our hearts, and bear fruit in our lives. Let us not be ignorant of the Bible, lest we fall into some deadly error. Let us rather read it diligently, and make it our rule of faith and practice. Let us labour to spread the Bible over the world. The more the book is known, the better the world will be. Not least, let us teach our children to value the Bible. The very best portion we can give them is a knowledge of the Scriptures.

We learn, in the last place, from this passage, *how different will be the state of things after the resurrection, from the state in which we live now.* Our Lord tells us that "when they shall rise from the dead, they neither marry, nor are given in marriage; but are as the angels which are in heaven."

It would be foolish to deny that there are many difficulties connected with the doctrine of the life to come. It must needs be so. The world beyond the grave is a world unseen by mortal eye, and therefore unknown. The conditions of existence there are necessarily hidden from us, and if more were told we should probably not understand it. Let it suffice us to know that the bodies of the saints shall be raised, and, though glorified, shall be like their bodies on earth; so like, that those who knew them once shall know them again. But though raised with a real body, the risen saint will be completely freed from everything which is now an evidence of weakness and infirmity. There shall be nothing like Mahomet's gross and sensual Paradise in the Christian's future existence. Hunger and thirst being no more,—there shall be no need of food. Weariness and fatigue being no more,—there shall be no need of sleep. Death being no more,—there shall be no need of births to supply the place of those who are removed. Enjoying the full presence of God and His Christ,—men and women shall no more need the marriage union in order to help one another. Able to serve God without weariness, and attend on Him without distraction,—doing His will perfectly, and seeing His face continually,—clothed in a glorious body,—they shall be "as the angels which are in heaven."

There is comfort in all this for the true Christian. In the body that he now has he often "groans, being burdened," from a daily sense of weakness and imperfection. (2 Cor. v. 4.) He is now tried by many cares about this world,—what to eat, and what to drink, and what to put on,—how to manage his affairs, where to live, and what company to choose. In the world to come, all shall be changed. Nothing shall be lacking to make his happiness complete.

One thing only we must carefully bear in mind. Let us take heed that we rise again in "the resurrection of life," and not in "the resurrection of condemnation."

(John v. 29.) To the believer in the Lord Jesus, the resurrection will be the greatest of blessings. To the worldly, the godless, and the profane, the resurrection will be a misery and a curse. Let us never rest till we are one with Christ and Christ in us, and then we may look forward with joy to a life to come.*

* The text by which our Lord silenced the Sadducees, and proved the resurrection to be a Scriptural doctrine, has been a cause of surprise to many Bible readers. Some have wondered that our Lord should have chosen this text, when others far more plain might have been adduced. Some have been unable to see the force and cogency of the text as any proof at all of the resurrection of the body.

As to the particular fitness of the text, as a proof, compared to others, we are perhaps very poor judges. It may well be suspected that there is a fulness of meaning in some texts of Scripture which, in our hasty and superficial reading, we have not yet fathomed. At any rate it is clear that, to a Jewish hearer of the Lord, the argument was so forcible as to be unanswerable. This quotation and the famous one in John x. 34, go far to show that the Jewish mind saw a depth of meaning in Scriptural expressions, which many of us in modern times have not at all seen yet. It is a matter in which we have much to learn.

As to the text, "I am the God of Abraham," etc., being a convincing proof of the resurrection of the body, there is a passage in Bishop Pearson which is worth reading. He says of this text, as quoted by our Lord, "With the force of this argument the multitude was astonished, and the Sadducees silenced. For under the name of God was understood a great benefactor, a God of promise; and to be '*their* God,' was to bless them and reward them; as in them to be 'His servants,' and 'His people' was to believe in Him and obey Him. Now Abraham, Isaac, and Jacob had not received the promise which they expected : and therefore God, after their death, desiring still to be called 'their God,' He thereby acknowledgeth that He had a blessing and a reward for them still, and consequently that He will raise them to another life, in which they may receive it. So that the argument of our Saviour is the same which the Jews have drawn from another place of Moses. (Exod. vi. 3, 4.) 'I appeared unto Abraham, unto Isaac, and unto Jacob by the name of God Almighty : but by my name Jehovah was I not made known to them. Nevertheless I have established my covenant with them, to give them the land of Canaan.' It is not said, 'to give their sons,' but 'to give *them* the land;' and, therefore, because while they lived here they enjoyed it not, they must rise again that they may receive the promise."

MARK XII. 28—34.

28 And one of the scribes came, and having heard them reasoning together, and perceiving that he had answered them well, asked him, Which is the first commandment of all?

29 And Jesus answered him, The first of all the commandments is, Hear, O Israel: The Lord our God is one Lord:

30 And thou shalt love the Lord thy God with all thy heart, and with all thy soul, and with all thy mind, and with all thy strength: this is the first commandment.

31 And the second is like, namely this, Thou shalt love thy neighbour as thyself. There is none other command-ment greater than these.

32 And the scribe said unto him, Well, Master, thou hast said the truth: for there is one God; and there is none other but he:

33 And to love him with all the heart, and with all the understanding, and with all the soul, and with all the strength, and to love his neighbour as himself, is more than all whole burnt offerings and sacrifices.

34 And when Jesus saw that he answered discreetly, he said unto him, Thou art not far from the kingdom of God. And no man after that durst any him any question.

THESE verses contain a conversation between our Lord Jesus Christ and "one of the scribes." For the third time in one day we see our Lord tried by a hard question. Having put to silence the Pharisees and Sadducees, He is asked to decide a point on which much difference of opinion prevailed among the Jews: "Which is the first commandment of all?" We have reason to bless God that so many hard questions were propounded to our Lord. Without them the marvellous words of wisdom which His three answers contain, might never have been spoken at all. Here, as in many other cases, we see how God can bring good out of evil. He can make the most malicious assaults of His enemies work round to the good of His Church, and redound to His own praise. He can make the enmity of Pharisees and Sadducees and Scribes minister instruction to His people. Little did the three questioners in this chapter think what benefit their crafty questions would confer on all Christendom. "Out of the eater came forth meat." (Judges xiv. 14.)

Let us observe in these verses, *how high is our Lord Jesus Christ's standard of duty to God and man.*

The question that the scribe propounded was a very wide one: "Which is the first commandment of all?" The answer he received was probably very unlike what he expected. At any rate, if he thought that our Lord would commend to him the observance of some outward form or ceremony, he was mistaken. He hears these solemn words: "Thou shalt love the Lord thy God with all thy heart, and with all thy soul, and with all thy mind, and with all thy strength: this is the first commandment. And the second is like, namely this, Thou shalt love thy neighbour as thyself."

How striking is our Lord's description of the *feeling* with which we ought to regard both God and our neighbour! We are not merely to obey the one, or to abstain from injuring the other. In both cases we are to give far more than this. We are to give love, the strongest of all affections, and the most comprehensive. A rule like this includes everything. It makes all petty details unnecessary. Nothing will be intentionally lacking where there is love.

How striking again is our Lord's description of the *measure* in which we should love God and our neighbour! We are to love God better than ourselves, with all the powers of our inward man. We cannot love Him too well. We are to love our neighbour as ourselves, and to deal with him in all respects as we would like him to deal with us. The marvellous wisdom of this distinction is clear and plain. We may easily err in our affections towards others, either by thinking too little or too much of them.

We therefore need the rule to love them as ourselves, neither more nor less. We cannot err in our affections towards God in the matter of excess. He is worthy of all we can give Him. We are therefore to love Him with all our heart.

Let us keep these two grand rules continually before our minds, and use them daily in our journey through life. Let us see in them a summary of all that we ought to aim at in our practice, both as regards God and man. By them let us try every difficulty of conscience that may happen to beset us, as to right and wrong. Happy is that man who strives to frame his life according to these rules.

Let us learn from this brief exposition of the true standard of duty, how great is the need in which we all naturally stand of the atonement and mediation of our Lord Jesus Christ. Where are the men or women who can say with truth, that they have perfectly loved God and perfectly loved man? Where is the person on earth who must not plead "Guilty," when tried by such a law as this? No wonder that the Scripture says, "There is none righteous, no, not one." "By the deeds of the law shall no flesh be justified." (Rom. iii. 10, 20.) It is only gross ignorance of the requirements of God's law which makes people undervalue the Gospel. The man who has the clearest view of the moral law, will always be the man who has the highest sense of the value of Christ's atoning blood.

Let us observe, for another thing, in these verses, *how far a man may go in religion, and yet not be a true disciple of Christ.*

The scribe, in the passage now before us, was evidently a man of more knowledge than most of his equals. He saw things which many scribes and Pharisees never saw at all. His own words are a strong proof of this. "There is one God: and there is none other but He: and to love Him with all the heart, and with all the understanding, and with all the soul, and with all the strength, and to love his neighbour as himself, is more than all whole burnt offerings and sacrifices." These words are remarkable in themselves, and doubly remarkable when we remember who the speaker was, and the generation amongst whom he lived. No wonder that we read next that our Lord said, "Thou art not far from the kingdom of God."

But we must not shut our eyes to the fact that we are nowhere told that this man became one of our Lord's disciples. On this point there is a mournful silence. The parallel passage in St. Matthew throws not a gleam of light on his case. The other parts of the New Testament tell us nothing about him. We are left to draw the painful conclusion that, like the rich young man, he could not make up his mind to give up all and follow Christ; or that, like the chief rulers, elsewhere mentioned. he "loved the praise of men more than the praise of God." (John xii. 43.) In short, though "not far from the kingdom of God," he probably never entered into it, and died outside.

Cases like that of this scribe, are unhappily far from being uncommon. There are thousands on every side, who, like him, see much and know much of religious truth, and yet live and die undecided. There are few things which are so much overlooked as the length to which people may go in religious attainments, and yet never be converted, and never saved. May we all mark well this man's case, and take care !

Let us beware of resting our hopes of salvation on mere intellectual knowledge. We live in days when there is great danger of doing so. Education makes children acquainted with many things in religion, of which their parents were once utterly ignorant. But education alone will never make a Christian in the sight of God. We must not only know the leading doctrines of the Gospel with our heads, but receive them into our hearts, and be guided by them in our lives. May we never rest till we are inside the kingdom of God, till we have truly repented, really believed, and have been made new creatures in Christ Jesus. If we rest satisfied with being "not far from the kingdom," we shall find at last that we are shut out for evermore.

MARK XII. 35—44.

35 And Jesus answered and said, while he taught in the temple, How say the scribes that Christ is the Son of David ?

36 For David himself said by the Holy Ghost, The LORD said to my Lord, Sit thou on my right hand, till I make thine enemies thy footstool.

37 David therefore himself calleth him Lord; and whence is he *then* his son ? And the common people heard him gladly.

38 And he said unto them in his doctrine, Beware of the scribes, which love to go in long clothing, and *love* salutations in the marketplaces,

39 And the chief seats in the synagogues, and the uppermost rooms at feasts :

40 Which devour widows' houses, and for a pretence make long prayers : these shall receive greater damnation.

41 And Jesus sat over against the treasury, and beheld how the people cast money into the treasury : and many that were rich cast in much.

42 And there came a certain poor widow, and she threw in two mites, which make a farthing.

43 And he called *unto him* his disciples, and saith unto them, Verily I say unto you, That this poor widow hath cast more in, than all they which have cast into the treasury :

44 For all *they* did cast in of their abundance; but she of her want did cast in all that she had, *even* all her living.

WE have seen in the former part of this chapter how the

enemies of our Lord endeavoured to "catch Him in His words." We have seen how the Pharisees, the Sadducees, and the scribes successively propounded to Him hard questions,—questions, we can hardly fail to observe, more likely to minister strife than edification. The passage before us begins with a question of a very different character. Our Lord Himself propounds it. He asks His enemies about Christ and the meaning of Holy Scripture. Such questions are always truly profitable. Well would it be for the Church if theological discussions were less about trifles, and more about weighty matters, and things necessary to salvation.

Let us learn, in the first place, from these verses, *how much there is about Christ in the Old Testament Scriptures.* Our Lord desires to expose the ignorance of the Jewish teachers about the true nature of the Messiah. He does it by referring to a passage in the book of Psalms, and showing that the scribes did not rightly understand it. And in so doing He shows us that one subject about which David was inspired by the Holy Ghost to write, was Christ.

We know, from our Lord's own words in another place, that the Old Testament Scriptures "testify of Christ." (John v. 39.) They were intended to teach men about Christ by types and figures and prophecy, till He Himself should appear on earth. We should always keep this in mind in reading the Old Testament, but never so much as in reading the Psalms. Christ is undoubtedly to be found in every part of the Law and the Prophets, but nowhere is He so much to be found as in the book of Psalms. His experience and sufferings at His first coming into the world,—His future glory, and His final triumph at His second coming,—are the chief subjects of many a passage in that wonderful part of God's Word. It is a true saying, that we should look for Christ quite as much as David, in reading the Psalms.

Let us beware of undervaluing, or despising the Old Testament. In its place and proportion the Old Testament is just as valuable as the New. There are probably many rich passages in that part of the Bible which have never yet been fully explored. There are deep things about Jesus in it, which many walk over like hidden gold mines, and know not the treasures beneath their feet. Let us reverence *all* the Bible. All is given by inspiration, and all is profitable. One part throws light upon another, and no part can ever be neglected without loss and damage to our souls. A boastful contempt for the Old Testament Scriptures has often proved the first step towards infidelity.

Let us learn, in the second place, from these verses, *how odious is the sin of hypocrisy in the sight of Christ.* This is a lesson which is taught us by our Lord's warning against the scribes. He exposes some of their notorious practices,—their ostentatious manner of dressing,—their love of the honour and praise of man rather than God, —their love of money, disguised under a pretended concern for widows,—their long-protracted public devotions, intended to make men think them eminently godly. And He winds up all by the solemn declaration, "These shall receive greater damnation."

Of all the sins into which men can fall, none seem so exceedingly sinful as false profession and hypocrisy. At all events, none have drawn from our Lord's mouth such strong language, and such heavy denunciations. It is bad enough to be led away captive by open sin, and to serve divers lusts and pleasures. But it is even worse to pretend to have a religion, while in reality we serve the world. Let us beware of falling into this abominable sin. Whatever we do in religion, let us never wear a cloak. Let us be real, honest, thorough, and sincere in our Christianity. We cannot deceive an all-seeing God. We may take in poor short-sighted man by a little talk and profession, and a few cant phrases, and an affectation of devoutness. But God is not mocked. He is a discerner of the thoughts and intents of the heart. His all-seeing eye pierces through the paint, and varnish, and tinsel, which cover the unsound heart. The day of judgment will soon be here. The "joy of the hypocrite is but for a moment." (Job xx. 5.) His end will be shame and everlasting contempt.

One thing, however, must never be forgotten in connection with the subject of hypocrisy. Let us not flatter ourselves because some make a false profession of religion, that others need not make any profession at all. This is a common delusion, and one against which we must carefully guard. It does not follow, because some bring Christianity into contempt by professing what they do not really believe and feel, that we should run into the other extreme, and bring it into contempt by a cowardly silence, and by keeping our religion out of sight. Let us rather be doubly careful to adorn our doctrine by our lives. Let us prove our sincerity by the consistency of our conversation. Let us show the world that there is true coin, as well as counterfeit coin, and that the visible Church contains Christians who can witness a good confession, as well as Pharisees and scribes. Let us confess our Master modestly and humbly, but firmly and decidedly, and show the world that although some men may be hypocrites, there are others who are honest and true.

Let us learn, in the last place, from these verses, *how pleasing to Christ is self-denying liberality in giving.* This is a lesson which is taught us in a striking manner by our Lord's commendation of a certain poor widow. We are told that He "beheld how the people cast in" their voluntary contributions for God's service into the public collecting box or "treasury." He saw "many that were rich casting in much." At last He saw this poor widow cast in all that she had for her daily maintenance. And then we hear Him pronounce the solemn word, "This poor woman hath cast more in than they all,"— more in the sight of Him who looks not merely at the amount given, but at the ability of the giver,—not merely at the quantity contributed, but at the motive and heart of the contributor.

There are few of our Lord's sayings so much overlooked as this. There are thousands who remember all His doctrinal discourses, and yet contrive to forget this little incident in His earthly ministry. The proof of this is to be seen in the meagre and sparing contributions which are yearly made by Christ's Church to do good in the world. The proof is to be seen in the miserably small incomes of all the Missionary Societies, in proportion to the wealth of the Churches. The proof is to be seen in the long annual list of self-complacent guinea subscribers, of whom many could easily give hundreds of pounds. The stinginess of professing Christians in all matters which concern God and religion, is one of the crying sins of the day, and one of the worst signs of the times. The givers to Christ's cause are but a small section of the visible Church. Not one baptized person in twenty, probably, knows anything of being "rich towards God." (Luke xii. 21.) The vast majority spend pounds on themselves, and give not even pence to Christ.

Let us mourn over this state of things, and pray God to amend it. Let us pray Him to open men's eyes, and awake men's hearts, and stir up a spirit of liberality. Above all, let us each do our own duty, and give liberally and gladly to every Christian object, while we can. There will be no giving when we are dead. Let us give as those who remember that the eyes of Christ are upon us. He still sees exactly what each gives, and knows exactly how much is left behind. Above all, let us give as the disciples of a crucified Saviour, who gave Himself for us, body and soul, on the cross. Freely we have received. Let us freely give.*

---

* It is probable, according to Arias Montanus and Brentius, that the words "all her living," mean "all her daily income," and not all her property.

It may be well to remark in this connection, that nothing can be more absurd than to say, as some do, that they contribute "their mite" to an object, when they probably contribute some trifling sum which they do not miss, and which bears not the most remote proportion to the widow's scale of liberality.—A man contributes "his mite" when he contributes half his daily income, and not till then.   all!

MARK XIII. 1—8.

1 And as he went out of the temple, one of his disciples saith unto him, Master, see what manner of stones and what buildings *are here !*

2 And Jesus answering said unto him, Seest thou these great buildings ? there shall not be left one stone upon another, that shall not be thrown down.

3 And as he sat upon the mount of Olives over against the temple, Peter and James and John and Andrew asked him privately ;

4 Tell us, when shall these things be ? and what *shall be* the sign when all these things shall be fulfilled ?

5 And Jesus answering them began to say, Take heed lest any *man* deceive you :

6 For many shall come in my name, saying, I am *Christ ;* and shall deceive many.

7 And when ye shall hear of wars and rumours of wars, be ye not troubled : for *such things* must needs be ; but the end *shall* not *be* yet.

8 For nation shall rise against nation, and kingdom˙ against kingdom : and there shall be earthquakes in divers places, and there shall be famines and troubles : these *are* the beginnings of sorrows.

THE chapter we have now begun is full of prophecy,— prophecy of which part has been fulfilled, and part remains to be accomplished. Two great events form the subject of this prophecy. One is the destruction of Jerusalem, and the consequent end of the Jewish dispensation. The other is the second coming of our Lord Jesus Christ, and the winding up of the state of things under which we now live. The destruction of Jerusalem was an event which happened only forty years after our Lord was crucified. The second coming of Christ is an event which is yet to come, and we may yet live to see it with our own eyes." *

---

* I think it right to repeat here what I said in commenting on the report of our Lord's prophecy given by St. Matthew, respecting the destruction of Jerusalem. I believe that in the prophecy now under consideration, our Lord had in view a *second* siege of Jerusalem and a *second* tribulation accompanying that siege, as well as the first siege and tribulation when the city was taken by Titus. That such a siege is to be expected, the fourteenth chapter of Zechariah appears to me to be unanswerable proof.

I see no other way of explaining the close connection which appears in the prophecy, between the "affliction" here foretold, and the "coming of the Son of Man in the clouds with power and great glory." To interpret that "coming of the Son of Man," as the

Chapters like this ought to be deeply interesting to every true Christian. No history ought to receive so much of our attention as the past and future history of the Church of Christ. The rise and fall of worldly empires are events of comparatively small importance in the sight of God. Babylon and Greece and Rome and France and England, are as nothing in His eyes by the side of the mystical body of Christ. The march of armies and the victories of conquerors are mere trifles in comparison with the progress of the Gospel and the final triumph of the Prince of Peace. May we remember this in reading prophetical Scripture! "Blessed is he that readeth." (Rev. i. 3.)

The first thing that demands our attention in the verses before us, is *the prediction of our Lord concerning the temple at Jerusalem.*

The disciples, with the natural pride of Jews, had called their Master's attention to the architectural splendour of the temple. "See," they said, "what manner of stones and what buildings are here!"* They re-

coming of the Roman army in judgment on the Jews, appears to me positive trifling with Scripture.

The view that our Lord is prophesying of *two* sieges of Jerusalem, and *two* tremendous tribulations which would fall especially on the Jews, and of His own second coming as an event which would immediately follow the second siege, makes the whole chapter plain and intelligible.

All these events ought to be deeply interesting to believers : and would be especially so to Jewish believers, like the Apostles, in whose time the temple was yet standing, the Jewish dispensation not yet put aside, and Jerusalem not yet destroyed.

* It may be well to remark that the temple here spoken of, was in a certain sense, the third temple in order which had been built at Jerusalem. The first was built by Solomon, and destroyed by

ceived an answer from the Lord very different from what they expected, a heart-saddening answer, and one well calculated to stir up inquisitive thoughts in their minds. No word of admiration falls from His lips. He expresses no commendation of the design or workmanship of the gorgeous structure before Him. He appears to lose sight of the form and comeliness of the material building, in His concern for the wickedness of the nation to which it belonged. "Seest thou," He replies, "these great buildings? There shall not be left one stone upon another, that shall not be cast down."

Let us learn from this solemn saying, that the true glory of a Church does not consist in its buildings for public worship, but in the faith and godliness of its members. The eyes of our Lord Jesus Christ could find no pleasure in looking at the very temple which contained the holy of holies, and the golden candlestick, and the altar of burnt offering. Much less, may we suppose, can He find pleasure in the most splendid place of worship among professing Christians, if His Word and His Spirit are not honoured in it.

We shall all do well to remember this. We are naturally inclined to judge things by the outward appearance, like children who value poppies more than corn. We are too apt to suppose that where there is a stately ecclesiastical building and a magnificent ceremonial,—carved

Nebuchadnezzar. The second was built by Ezra and Nehemiah. The third, if it may be so called, was enlarged and almost re-built about the time of our Lord Jesus Christ's birth, by Herod. The enormous size of the stones used in building it, and the general magnificence of the whole fabric, are attested not only by Josephus, but by heathen writers.

stone and painted glass,—fine music and gorgeously-dressed ministers, there must be some real religion. And yet there may be no religion at all. It may be all form, and show, and appeal to the senses. There may be nothing to satisfy the conscience,—nothing to cure the heart. It may prove on inquiry that Christ is not preached in that stately building, and the Word of God not expounded. The ministers may perhaps be utterly ignorant of the Gospel, and the worshippers may be dead in trespasses and sins. We need not doubt that God sees no beauty in such a building as this. We need not doubt the Parthenon had no glory in God's sight compared to the dens and caves where the early Christians worshipped, or that the meanest room where Christ is preached at this day, is more honourable in His eyes than the Cathedral of St. Peter's at Rome.

Let us however not run into the absurd extreme of supposing that it matters not what kind of building we set apart for God's service. There is no Popery in making a church handsome. There is no true religion in having a dirty, mean, shabby, and disorderly place of worship. "Let all things be done decently and in order." (1 Cor. xiv. 40.) But let it be a settled principle in our religion, however beautiful we make our churches, to regard pure doctrine and holy practice as their principal ornaments. *Without* these two things, the noblest ecclesiastical edifice is radically defective. It has no glory if God is not there. *With* these two things, the humblest brick cottage where the Gospel is preached, is lovely and beautiful. It is consecrated by Christ's own presence, and the Holy Spirit's own blessing.

The second thing that demands our attention in these verses, is *the remarkable manner in which our Lord commences the great prophecy of this chapter.*

We are told that four of His disciples, aroused no doubt by His warning prediction about the temple, applied to Him for further information. " Tell us," they said, " when shall these things be ? and what shall be the sign when all these things shall be fulfilled ? "

The answer which our Lord gives to these questions, begins at once with a prediction of coming false doctrine and coming wars. If His disciples thought He would promise them immediate success and temporal prosperity in this world, they were soon undeceived. So far from bidding them expect a speedy victory of truth, He tells them to look out for the rise of error. " Take heed lest any man deceive you.—Many shall come in my Name, saying, I am Christ." So far from bidding them expect a general reign of peace and quietness, He tells them to prepare for wars and troubles. " Nation shall rise against nation, and kingdom against kingdom.—There shall be earthquakes in divers places, and there shall be famines and troubles : these are the beginnings of sorrows."

There is something deeply instructive in this opening of our Lord's prophetical discourse. It seems like the key note of what His Church is to expect between His first and second advents. It looks as if it were specially intended to correct the mistaken views, not only of His Apostles, but of the vast body of professing Christians in every age. It looks as if our Lord knew well that man is always catching at the idea of a "good time coming," and as if He would give us plain notice that there will be no "good time" till He returns. It may not be pleasant to us to hear such tidings. But it is in strict accordance with what we read in the prophet Jeremiah : "The prophets that have been before, prophesied of war, and of evil, and of pestilence. The prophet which prophesieth of peace, when the word of the prophet shall come to pass, then shall the prophet be known, that the Lord hath truly sent him." (Jer. xxviii. 8, 9.)

Let us learn, from our Lord's opening prediction, to be moderate in our expectations. Nothing has created so much disappointment in the Church of Christ, as the extravagant expectations in which many of its members have indulged, Let us not be carried away by the common idea, that the world will be converted before the Lord Jesus returns, and the earth filled with the knowledge of the Lord. It will not be so. There is nothing in Scripture to justify such expectations. Let us cease to expect a reign of peace. Let us rather look for wars. Let us cease to expect all men to be made holy by any existing instrumentality,—schools, missions, preaching, or anything of the kind. Let us rather look for the rise of Antichrist himself. Let us understand that we live in a day of election, and not of universal conversion. There will be no universal peace till the Prince of Peace appears. There will be no universal holiness till Satan is bound. It may cost us much to hold such opinions as these. But there is not a Church or congregation on earth, whose state does not show that these opinions are true, and that while "many are called, few are chosen." It may bring on us the unkind remarks and the unfavourable judgment of many. But the end will prove

who is right and who is wrong. For that end let us
wait patiently. Let us labour and teach and work
and pray. But let it not surprise us if we find our
Lord's word strictly true: "Narrow is the way which
leadeth unto life, and few there be that find it." (Matt.
v. 14.)

MARK XIII. 9—13.

9 But take heed to yourselves: for they shall deliver you up to councils; and in the synagogues ye shall be beaten: and ye shall be brought before rulers and kings for my sake, for a testimony against them.

10 And the Gospel must first be published among all nations.

11 But when they shall lead *you*, and deliver you up, take no thought beforehand what ye shall speak, neither do ye premeditate; but whatsoever shall be given you in that hour, that speak ye: for it is not ye that speak, but the Holy Ghost.

12 Now the brother shall betray the brother to death, and the father the son; and children shall rise up against *their* parents, and shall cause them to be put to death.

13 And ye shall be hated of all *men* for my name's sake: but he that shall endure unto the end, the same shall be saved.

IN reading the prophecies of the Bible concerning Christ's
Church, we shall generally find judgment and mercy
blended together. They are seldom all bitter without
any sweet,—seldom all darkness without any light. The
Lord knows our weakness and readiness to faint, and has
taken care to mingle consolations with threatenings,—
kind words with hard words, like warp and woof in a
garment. We may remark this throughout the book of
Revelation. We may see it all through the prophecy
we are now considering. We may note it in the few
verses which we have just read.

Let us observe, in the first place, *what troubles our
Lord bids His people expect between the time of His
first and second comings.* Trouble, no doubt, is the
portion of all men, since the day that Adam fell. It
came in with the thorns and thistles. "Man is born

to trouble as the sparks fly upwards." (Job. v. 7.)
But there are special troubles to which believers in
Jesus Christ are liable, and of these our Lord gives
them plain warning.

They must expect trouble *from the world.* They
must not look for the help of "rulers and kings." They
will find their ways and their doctrines bring them no
favour in high places.   On the contrary, they will often
be imprisoned, beaten, and brought before judgment
seats as malefactors, for no other reason than their
adherence to the Gospel of Christ.

They must expect trouble from *their own relations.*
"Brother shall betray brother to death, and the father
the son." Their own flesh and blood will often forget to
love them, from hatred to their religion. They will find
sometimes that the enmity of the carnal mind against
God is stronger than even the ties of family and blood.

We shall do well to lay these things to heart, and to
"count the cost" of being a Christian. We must think it
no strange thing if our religion brings with it some bitter
things.   Our lot, no doubt, is cast in favourable times.
The lines of a British Christian are fallen in pleasant
places.   We have no reason to be afraid of death or
imprisonment, if we serve Christ.   But, for all that, we
must make up our minds to endure a certain proportion of
hardship, if we are real, thorough, and decided Christians.
We must be content to put up with laughter, ridicule,
mockery, slander, and petty persecution. We must even
bear hard words and unkindness from our nearest and
dearest relations. The offence "of the cross" is not ceased.
"The natural man receiveth not the things of the Spirit of

God." They that are " born after the flesh " will persecute those that are " born after the Spirit." (1 Cor. ii.
14 ; Gal. iv. 29.) The utmost consistency of life will
not prevent it. If we are converted, we must never be
surprised to find that we are hated for Christ's sake.

Let us observe, in the second place, *what rich encouragement the Lord Jesus holds out to His persecuted
people.* He sets before them three rich cordials to cheer
their souls.

For one thing, He tells us that " the Gospel must first
be preached among all nations." It must be, and it shall
be. In spite of men and devils, the story of the cross
of Christ shall be told in every part of the world. The
gates of hell shall not prevail against it. Notwithstanding
persecution, imprisonment, and death, there never shall be
wanting a succession of faithful men, who shall proclaim
the glad tidings of salvation by grace. Few may believe
them. Many of their hearers may continue hardened in
sin. But nothing shall prevent the Gospel being preached.
The Word shall never be bound, though those who preach
it may be imprisoned and slain. (2 Tim. ii. 9.)

For another thing, our Lord tells us, that those who
are placed in special trial for the Gospel's sake, shall
have special help in their time of need. The Holy Ghost
shall assist them in making their defence. They shall
have a mouth and wisdom which their adversaries shall
not be able to gainsay or resist. As it was with Peter
and John and Paul, when brought before Jewish and
Roman councils, so shall it be with all true-hearted disciples. How thoroughly this promise has been fulfilled,
the histories of Huss, and Luther, and Latimer, and

Ridley, and Baxter, abundantly prove. Christ has been faithful to His word.

For another thing, our Lord tells us that patient perseverance shall result in final salvation. "He that shall endure unto the end, the same shall be saved." Not one of those who endure tribulation shall miss his reward. All shall at length reap a rich harvest. Though they sow in tears, they shall reap in joy. Their light affliction, which is but for a moment, shall lead to an eternal weight of glory.

Let us gather comfort from these comfortable promises for all true-hearted servants of Christ. Persecuted, vexed, and mocked as they are now, they shall find at length they are on the victorious side. Beset, perplexed, tried, as they sometimes are, they shall never find themselves entirely forsaken. Though cast down, they shall not be destroyed. Let them possess their souls in patience. The end of all that they see going on around them is certain, fixed and sure. The kingdoms of this world shall yet become the kingdoms of their God and of his Christ. And when the scoffers and ungodly, who so often insulted them, are put to shame, believers shall receive a crown of glory that fadeth not away.*

* There is a promise in the passage now expounded which is often much perverted. I allude to the implied promise contained in the words, "Take no thought before hand what ye shall speak, neither do ye premeditate : but whatsoever shall be given you in that time, that speak ye."

The perversion I mean, consists in supposing that this passage warrants ministers in getting up to preach unprepared every Sunday, and in expecting special help of the Holy Ghost in addressing regular congregations, when they have neither meditated, read, nor taken pains about their subject.

MARK XIII. 14—23.

14 But when ye shall see the abomination of desolation, spoken of by Daniel the prophet, standing where it ought not, (let him that readeth understand,) then let them that be in Judæa flee to the mountains:

15 And let him that is on the house-top not go down into the house, neither enter *therein*, to take anything out of his house:

16 And let him that is in the field not turn back again for to take up his garment.

17 But woe to them that are with child, and to them that give suck in those days!

18 And pray ye that your flight be not in the winter.

19 For *in* those days shall be affliction, such as was not from the beginning of the creation which God created unto this time, neither shall be.

20 And except that the Lord had shortened those days, no flesh should be saved: but for the elect's sake, whom he hath chosen, he hath shortened the days.

21 And then if any man shall say to you, Lo, here *is* Christ; or, Lo, *he is* there; believe *him* not:

22 For false Christs and false prophets shall rise, and shall show signs and wonders, to seduce, if it *were* possible, even the elect.

23 But take ye heed: behold, I have foretold you all things.

WE are taught in these verses *the lawfulness of using means to provide for our own personal safety.* The language of our Lord Jesus Christ on the subject is clear and unmistakeable: "Let them that be in Judæa flee to the mountains:—let him that is on the house-top not go down into the house;—let him that is in the field not turn back again:—pray ye that your flight be not in the winter." Not a word is said to make us suppose that flight from danger, in certain circumstances, is unworthy of a Christian. As to the time prophesied of in the passage before us, men may differ widely. But as to the lawfulness of taking measures to avoid peril, the teaching of the passage is plain.

A moment's reflection must show any reader that such an application of the passage before us is utterly unjustifiable. The passage has no reference whatever to the regular Sabbath sermon of a minister, and only holds out the promise of special help in special times of need.

It would be well for the Church if this was more remembered than it is. At present it may be feared this promise is not unfrequently made an excuse for ministerial idleness, and undigested sermons. Men seem to forget, when they enter the pulpit, that what costs nothing is worth nothing, and that the "foolishness of preaching," and foolish preaching, are widely different things.

The lesson is one of wide application, and of much usefulness. A Christian is not to neglect the use of means, because he is a Christian, in the things of this life any more than in the things of the life to come. A believer is not to suppose that God will take care of him, and provide for his wants, if he does not make use of means and the common sense which God has given him, as well as other people. Beyond doubt he may expect the special help of his Father in heaven, in every time of need. But he must expect it in the diligent use of lawful means. To profess to trust God, while we idly sit still and do nothing, is nothing better than enthusiasm and fanaticism, and brings religion into contempt.

The Word of God contains several instructive examples on this subject, to which we shall do well to take heed. The conduct of Jacob, when he went to meet his brother Esau, is a striking case in point. He first prays a most touching prayer, and then sends his brother a carefully arranged present. (Gen. xxxii. 9—13.) The conduct of Hezekiah, when Sennacherib came against Jerusalem. is another case. "With us," he tells the people, "is the Lord our God, to fight our battles." And yet, at the same time, he built up the walls of the city, and made darts and shields. (2 Chron. xxxii. 5.)—The conduct of St. Paul is another case. Frequently we read of his fleeing from one place to another, to preserve life. Once we see him let down from the walls of Damascus by a basket. Once we hear him telling the soldiers on board the Alexandrian corn ship, "Except the shipmen abide in the ship, ye cannot be saved." (Acts xxvii. 31.) We know the great Apostle's faith and confidence. We know his courage and reliance on his Master. And yet we see that even he never despised the use of means. Let us not be ashamed to do likewise.

One thing only let us bear in mind. Let us not rest upon means while we use them. Let us look far beyond them to the blessing of God. It is a great sin to be like Asa, and seek not to the Lord but to the physicians. To use all means diligently, and then leave the whole event in the hand of God, is the mark at which a true believer ought to aim.

We are taught, for another thing, in these verses, *the great privileges of God's elect.* Twice in the passage our Lord uses a remarkable expression about them. He says of the great tribulation, "Except that the Lord had shortened those days, no flesh should be saved; but for the elect's sake, whom He hath chosen, He hath shortened the days." He says again of the false Christs and false prophets, that they "shall show signs and wonders, to deceive, if it were possible, the elect."

It is plain from this, and other passages in the Bible, that God has an elect people in the world. They are those, according to the seventeenth Article of our Church, whom "He has constantly decreed by His counsel, secret to us, to deliver from curse and damnation; those whom He hath chosen in Christ out of mankind, and decreed to bring by Christ to everlasting salvation, as vessels made to honour." To them, and them only, belong the great privileges of justification, sanctification, and final glory. They, and they only, are "called by the Spirit in due season." They, and they only, "obey the calling. They are made sons of God by adoption.

They are made like the image of God's only begotten
Son, Jesus Christ. They walk religiously in good works,
and at length, by God's mercy, attain to everlasting
felicity." To them belong the precious promises of the
Gospel. They are the bride, the Lamb's wife. They
are the Holy Catholic Church, which is Christ's body.
They are those whom God especially cares for in the
world. Kings, princes, noblemen, rich men, are all
nothing in God's eyes, compared to His elect. These
things are plainly revealed in Scripture. The pride of
man may not like them. But they cannot be gainsaid.

The subject of election is, no doubt, deep and mysterious. Unquestionably it has been often sadly perverted
and abused. But the misuse of truths must not prevent
us from using them. Rightly used, and fenced with
proper cautions, election is a doctrine "full of sweet,
pleasant, and unspeakable comfort." Before we leave
the subject, let us see what these cautions are.

For one thing, we must never forget that God's election does not destroy man's responsibility and accounta-
bleness for his own soul. The same Bible which speaks
of election, always addresses men as free agents, and
calls on them to repent, to believe, to seek, to pray, to
strive, to labour. "In our doings," most wisely says the
seventeenth Article, "that will of God is to be followed,
which we have expressly declared unto us in the Word
of God."

For another thing, let us never forget that the great
thing we have to do, is to repent and believe the Gospel.
We have no right to take any comfort from God's election, unless we can show plain evidence of repentance

and faith. We are not to stand still, troubling ourselves with anxious speculations whether we are elect or not, when God commands us plainly to repent and believe. (Acts xvii. 30; 1 John iii. 23.) Let us cease to do evil. Let us learn to do well. Let us break off from sin. Let us lay hold on Christ. Let us draw near to God in prayer. So doing, we shall soon know and feel whether we are God's elect. To use the words of an old divine, we must begin at the *grammar school* of repentance and faith, before we go to the *university* of election. It was when Paul remembered the faith and hope and love of the Thessalonians, that he said, "I know your election of God." * (1 Thess. i. 4.)

MARK XIII. 24—31.

24 But in those days, after that tribulation, the sun shall be darkened, and the moon shall not give her light,

25 And the stars of heaven shall fall, and the powers that are in heaven shall be shaken.

26 And then shall they see the Son of man coming in the clouds with great power and glory.

27 And then shall he send his angels, and shall gather together his elect from the four winds, from the uttermost part of the earth to the uttermost part of heaven.

28 Now learn a parable of the fig tree; When her branch is yet tender, and putteth forth leaves, ye know that summer is near:

29 So ye in like manner, when ye shall see these things come to pass, know that it is nigh, *even* at the doors.

30 Verily I say unto you, that this generation shall not pass, till all these things be done.

31 Heaven and earth shall pass away: but my words shall not pass away.

* The meaning of the "abomination of desolation," in this passage, has always perplexed the commentators. The most common view undoubtedly is, that it signifies the Roman armies, who executed God's judgment on the Jewish nation.

It may be questioned whether this interpretation completely fulfils the prophecy. I venture, though with much diffidence, to suggest that a more complete and literal accomplishment yet remains to come. The remarkable words of St. Paul to the Thessalonians appear to me scarcely to have received yet a complete fulfilment: "He, as God, sitteth in the temple of God, showing Himself that He is God." (2 Thess. ii. 4.) I own that it seems to me by no means improbable that a personal anti-christ, yet to be revealed at

THIS part of our Lord's prophecy on the Mount of Olives is entirely unfulfilled. The events described in it are all yet to take place. They may possibly take place in our own day. The passage therefore is one which we ought always to read with peculiar interest.

Let us observe, in the first place, *what solemn majesty will attend our Lord Jesus Christ's second coming to this world.* The language that is used about the sun, moon, and stars, conveys the idea of some universal convulsion of the universe at the close of the present dispensation. It reminds us of the Apostle Peter's words: "The heavens shall pass away with a great noise, and the elements shall melt with fervent heat." (2 Peter iii. 10.) At such a time as this, amidst terror and confusion, exceeding all that even earthquakes or hurricanes are known to produce, men "shall see the Son of man coming in the clouds with great power and glory."

The second coming of Christ shall be utterly unlike the first. He came the first time in weakness, a tender infant, born of a poor woman in the manger at Bethlehem, unnoticed, unhonoured, and scarcely known. He shall come the second time in royal dignity, with the armies of heaven around Him, to be known, recognized, and feared, by all the tribes of the earth. He came the first time to suffer,—to bear our sins,—to be reckoned a curse,—to be despised, rejected, unjustly condemned, and slain. He shall come the second time to reign,—to put down every enemy beneath His feet,—to take the king-

Jerusalem, may prove the final accomplishment of these words. I desire to avoid dogmatism on the subject. I only suggest it as a possible and probable thing.

doms of this world for His inheritance,—to rule them with righteousness,—to judge all men, and to live for evermore.

How vast the difference ! How mighty the contrast! How startling the comparison between the second advent and the first ! How solemn the thoughts that the subject ought to stir up in our minds! Here are *comfortable* thoughts for Christ's friends. Their own King will soon be here. They shall reap according as they have sown. They shall receive a rich reward for all that they have endured for Christ's sake. They shall exchange their cross for a crown. Here are *confounding* thoughts for Christ's foes. That same Jesus of Nazareth, whom they have so long despised and rejected, shall at length have the pre-eminence. That very Christ whose Gospel they have refused to believe shall appear as their Judge, and helpless, hopeless, and speechless, they will have to stand before His bar. May we all lay these things to heart, and learn wisdom !

Let us observe, in the next place, that *the first event after the Lord's second coming, shall be the gathering of His elect.* " He shall send His angels and gather together His elect from the four winds."

The safety of the Lord's people shall be provided for, when judgment falls upon the earth. He will do nothing till He has placed them beyond the reach of harm. The flood did not begin till Noah was safe in the ark. The fire did not fall on Sodom till Lot was safe within the walls of Zoar. The wrath of God on unbelievers shall not be let loose till believers are hidden and secure.

The true Christian may look forward to the advent of

Christ without fear.   However terrible the things that shall come upon the earth, his Master will take care that no harm comes to him.—He may well bear patiently the partings and separations of this present time.   He shall have a joyful meeting, by-and-by, with all his brethren in the faith, of every age and country and people and tongue.   Those who meet in that day, shall meet to part no more.—The great gathering is yet to come.   (2 Thess. ii. 1.)

Let us observe, in the next place, *how important it is to note the signs of our own times.*   Our Lord bids His disciples "learn a parable of the fig-tree."   Just as its budding leaves tell men that summer is near, so the fulfilment of events in the world around us should teach us that the Lord's coming "is nigh, even at the doors."

It becomes all true Christians to observe carefully the public events of their own day.   It is not only a duty to do this, but a sin to neglect it.   Our Lord reproved the Jews for "not discerning the signs of the, times."   (Matt. xvi. 3.)   They did not see that the sceptre was passing away from Judah, and the weeks of Daniel running out.   Let us beware of falling into their error.   Let us rather open our eyes, and look at the world around us.   Let us mark the drying up of the Turkish power, and the increase of missionary work in the world.   Let us mark the revival of Popery, and the rise of new and subtle forms of infidelity. Let us mark the rapid spread of lawlessness and contempt for authority.   What are these things but the budding of the fig-tree ?   They show us that this world is wearing out, and needs a new and better dynasty.   It needs its rightful king, even Jesus.   May we watch and keep our garments, and live ready to meet our Lord!   (Rev. xvi. 15.)

Let us observe, lastly, in these verses, *how carefully our Lord asserts the certainty of His predictions being fulfilled.* He speaks as though He foresaw the incredulity and scepticism of these latter days.   He warns us emphatically against it: "Heaven and earth shall pass away, but my words shall not pass away."

We ought never to allow ourselves to suppose that any prophecy is improbable or unlikely to be fulfilled, merely because it is contrary to past experience.   Let us not say, "Where is the likelihood of Christ coming again?   Where is the likelihood of the world being burned up?"   We have nothing to do with "likely or unlikely" in such matters.   The only question is, "What is written in God's Word?"   The words of St. Peter should never be forgotten: "There shall come in the last days scoffers, walking after their own lusts, saying, Where is the promise of His coming?"   (2 Peter iii. 3, 4.)

We shall do well to ask ourselves what we should have thought if we had lived on earth two thousand years ago.   Should we have thought it more probable that the Son of God would come on earth as a poor man and die, or that He would come on earth as a King and reign? Should we not have said at once, that if He came at all, He would come to reign and not to die?   Yet we know that He did come as "a Man of Sorrows," and died on the cross.   Then let us not doubt that He will come the second time in glory, and reign as a King for evermore.

v

Let us leave the passage with a thorough conviction of the truth of every jot of. its predictions.   Let us believe that every word of it shall prove at last to have been fully accomplished.   Above all, let us strive to live under an abiding sense of its truth, like good servants ready to meet their master.   Then, whatever be the fulfilment of it, or however soon, we shall be safe.*

MARK XIII. 32—37.

32 But of that day and *that* hour knoweth no man, no, not the angels which are in heaven, neither the Son, but the Father.

33 Take ye heed, watch and pray: for ye know not when the time is.

34 *For the Son of man is* as a man taking a far journey, who left his house, and gave authority to his servants, and to every man his work, and commanded the porter to watch.

35 Watch ye therefore: for ye know not when the master of the house cometh, at even, or at midnight, or at the cockcrowing, or in the morning:

36 Lest coming suddenly he find you sleeping.

37 And what I say unto you I say unto all, Watch.

THESE verses conclude St. Mark's report of our Lord's prophecy on the Mount of Olives.   They ought to form

* I am aware that some interpreters of the passage now expounded, explain its language very differently from myself.   Many regard the "sun, moon, and stars" as emblems of kings and rulers,—the "coming of the Son of man," as a general expression signifying any great exhibition of Divine power,—and the "sending forth of His angels," as nothing more than the sending of ministers and messengers of the Gospel to gather together the people of God.

I will only say that I can see no ground or warrant for such interpretations   They appear to me to be a dangerous tampering with the plain literal meaning of Scripture, and to give a great handle to the Arian, and Socinian, and the Jew, in the arguments that they respectively bring forward in support of their own peculiar views.

I take this opportunity of expressing my decided opinion, that the word "generation" in the verse,—"this generation shall not pass away," can only mean "this nation or people—the Jewish nation—shall not pass away."

The view that it means "the generation of men which is alive now while I am speaking," would make our Lord to say that which a personal application of the whole discourse to our consciences.

We learn from these verses that *the exact time of our Lord Jesus Christ's second advent is purposely withheld from His Church.* The event is certain. The precise day and hour are not revealed. "Of that day and hour knoweth no man, no, not the angels which are in heaven." *

was not true. His words were in no sense completely fulfilled when the generation to which He spoke had passed away.

The view that it means "the same generation which is alive when these things begin, shall also see them accomplished," appears to me untenable for one simple reason : it is not the natural meaning of the Greek words from which our translation is made.

* There is undoubtedly some difficulty in the words of our Lord, "Of that day and hour knoweth no man, no, not the angels which are in heaven, neither the Son." The question has often been raised, "How can the Lord Jesus be ignorant of anything, since He is very God, and says Himself, 'I and my Father are one'? How can the expression be reconciled with the saying, 'In Him are hid all the treasures of wisdom and knowledge'?" (Col. ii. 3.)

The answer to these questions is to be found in our deep ignorance of the great mystery of the union of two natures in one Person. That our Lord Jesus Christ was at the same time perfect God and perfect man, we know. That these two distinct natures were both found together in His Person, we also know. But how, and in what way, and to what extent the Divine nature did not always operate in Him so as to overshadow the human nature, I believe it to be impossible for mortal man to explain.—Enough for us to know that we sometimes see in our Lord's words and actions the "man Christ Jesus," and sometimes see the "God over all blessed for ever." But though we see clearly, and admire, we cannot explain. We can only say, in the present instance, that our Lord spake as a man, and not as God

Bullinger, in an able note on the subject, gives an interesting quotation from Cyril, of which the following passage is a portion :—

"Just as the Saviour was willing to endure hunger, and thirst, and other sufferings of this kind, so also, as man, He is ignorant of 'that great day.' For He sometimes speaks as God, and sometimes as man, in order that He may show Himself to be both very

There is deep wisdom and mercy in this intentional silence. We have reason to thank God that the thing has been hidden from us. Uncertainty about the date of the Lord's return is calculated to keep believers in an attitude of constant expectation, and to preserve them from despondency. What a dreary prospect the early Church would have had before it, if it had known for certain that Christ would not return to earth for at least fifteen hundred years! The hearts of men like Athanasius, Chrysostom, and Augustine, might well have sunk within them, if they had been aware of the centuries of darkness through which the world would pass, before their Master came back to take the kingdom.—What a quickening motive, on the other hand, true Christians have perpetually had for a close walk with God! They have never known, in any age, that their Master might not come suddenly to take account of His servants. This very uncertainty has supplied them with a reason for living always ready to meet Him.

There is one caution connected with the subject, which

God and very man. As God He said to His disciples, 'Our friend Lazarus sleepeth,' when no one had told Him. As man He asked the sister of Lazarus, when He came to them at the end of His journey, 'Where have ye laid him?' He who, when far off, knew that Lazarus was dead, how could He be ignorant, when present, of the place where the body of Lazarus was? It is utterly improbable that He should have known the one thing, and been ignorant of the other. But the truth is, that He knew both as God, while He was ignorant of both as man. Therefore, in the same way, He both knew not and yet knew 'that day and that hour.' As man He knew not. As God He knew."

It is a sensible remark of Gualter, that pressing an excessively literal interpetation of texts like this, is the sure way to revive old heresies, and to bring into doubt, sometimes the Divine, and sometimes the human nature of Christ.

must not be overlooked. We must not allow the uncertainty of the time of our Lord's second advent to prevent our giving attention to the unfulfilled prophecies of Scripture. This is a great delusion, but one into which, unhappily, many Christians fall. There is a wide distinction to be drawn between dogmatical and positive assertions about dates, and a humble, prayerful searching into the good things yet to come. Against dogmatism about times and seasons, our Lord's words in this place are a standing caution. But as to the general profitableness of studying prophecy, we can have no plainer authority than the Apostle Peter's words: "Ye do well that ye take heed to prophecy;" and the Apostle John's words in Revelation: "Blessed is he that readeth." (2 Peter i. 19; Rev. i. 3.)

We learn, in the second place, from these verses, *what are the practical duties of all true believers in the prospect of the second coming of Jesus Christ.* Our Lord mentions three things, to which His people should attend. He tells them plainly that He is coming again one day, in power and great glory. He tells them at the same time, that the precise hour and date of that coming are not known. What then are His people to do? In what position of mind are they to live? They are to watch. They are to pray. They are to work.

We are to *watch.* We are to live always on our guard. We are to keep our souls in a wakeful, lively state, prepared at any time to meet our Master. We are to beware of anything like spiritual lethargy, dulness, deadness, and torpor. The company, the employment of time, the society which induces us to forget Christ and

His second advent, should be marked, noted, and avoided. "Let us not sleep as do others," says the Apostle, "but let us watch and be sober." (1 Thess. v. 6.)

We are to *pray*. We are to keep up habits of regular communion and intercourse with God. We are to allow no strangeness to come in between us and our Father in heaven, but to speak with Him daily; that so we may be ready at any moment to see Him face to face. Moreover, we are to make special prayer about the Lord's coming, that we may be "found in peace, without spot and blameless," and that our hearts may at no time be "overcharged" with the cares of this life, and so the day come upon us unawares. (2 Peter iii. 14; Luke xxi. 34.)

Finally, we are to *work*. We are to realize that we are all servants of a great Master, who has given to every man his work, and expects that work to be done. We are to labour to glorify God, each in our particular sphere and relation. There is always something for every one to do. We are to strive each of us to shine as a light,—to be the salt of our own times,—to be faithful witnesses for our Master, and to honour Him by conscientiousness and consistency in our daily conversation. Our great desire must be to be found not idle and sleeping, but working and doing.*

Such are the simple injunctions to which our Lord would have us attend. They ought to stir up in the hearts of all professing Christians great self-examination.

---

* "Be doing something," says Jerome, "that the devil may always find you engaged."—It was a common saying of Calvin, towards the end of his life, when his friends would have had him do less work, for his health's sake, "Would you have my Master find me idle?"

Are we looking for our Saviour's return? Do we long for His appearing? Can we say with sincerity, Come Lord Jesus? Do we live as if we expected Christ to come again? These are questions which demand serious consideration. May we give them the attention which they deserve!

Does our Lord require us to neglect any of the duties of life, in the expectation of His return? He requires nothing of the kind. He does not bid the farmer neglect his land, or the labourer his work, the merchant his business, or the lawyer his calling. All He asks is that baptized people should live up to the faith into which they were baptized,—should live as penitent people,—live as believing people,—live as people who know that " without holiness no man can see the Lord."—So living, we are ready to meet our Master. Not living in this way, we are neither fit for death, judgment, nor eternity. To live in this way is to be truly happy, because it is to be truly prepared for anything that may come upon the earth. Let us never be content with a lower standard of practical Christianity than this. The last words of the prophecy are peculiarly solemn : " What I say unto you, I say unto all, Watch ! "

MARK XIV. 1—9.

1 After two days was *the feast of* the passover, and of unleavened bread : and the chief priests and the scribes sought how they might take him by craft, and put *him* to death.

2 But they said, Not on the feast *day*, lest there be an uproar of the people.

3 And being in Bethany, in the house of Simon the leper, as he sat at meat, there came a woman having an alabaster box of ointment of spikenard very precious ; and she brake the box, and poured *it* on his head.

4 And there were some that had indignation within themselves, and said, Why was this waste of the ointment made !

5 For it might have been sold for more than three hundred pence, and have been given to the poor. And they murmured against her.

6 And Jesus said, Let her alone; why trouble ye her? she hath.wrought a good work on me.

7 For ye have the poor with you always, and whensoever ye will ye may do them good: but me ye have not always.

8 She hath done what she could: she is come aforehand to anoint my body to the burying.

9 Verily I say unto you, Wheresoever this Gospel shall be preached throughout the whole world, *this* also that she hath done shall be spoken of for a memorial of her.

THIS chapter begins that part of St. Mark's Gospel which describes our Lord's sufferings and death. Hitherto we have chiefly seen our Saviour as our prophet and teacher. We have now to see Him as our High Priest. Hitherto we have had to consider His miracles and sayings. We have now to consider His vicarious sacrifice on the cross.

Let us first observe in these verses, *how God can disappoint the designs of wicked men, and over-rule them to His own glory.*

It is plain, from St. Mark's words and the parallel passage in St. Matthew, that our Lord's enemies did not intend to make His death a public transaction. "They sought to take Him by craft." "They said, Not on the feast day, lest there be an uproar of the people." In short, it would appear that their original plan was to do nothing till the feast of the passover was over, and the passover-worshippers had returned to their own homes.

The over-ruling providence of God completely defeated this politic design. The betrayal of our Lord took place at an earlier time than the chief priests had expected. The death of our Lord took place on the very day when Jerusalem was most full of people, and the passover feast was at its height. In every way the counsel of these wicked men was turned to foolishness. They thought they were going to put an end for ever to Christ's spiritual kingdom ; and in reality they were helping to establish it. They thought to have made Him vile and contemptible by the crucifixion ; and in reality they made Him glorious. They thought to have put Him to death privily and without observation; and instead, they were compelled to crucify Him publicly and before the whole nation of the Jews. They thought to have silenced His disciples, and stopped their teaching ; and instead, they supplied them with a text and a subject for evermore. So easy is it for God to cause the wrath of man to praise Him. (Psalm lxxvi. 10.)

There is comfort in all this for true Christians. They live in a troubled world, and are often tossed to and fro by anxiety about public events. Let them rest themselves in the thought that everything is ordered for good by an all-wise God. Let them not doubt that all things in the world around them are working together for their Father's glory. Let them call to mind the words of the second Psalm: "The kings of the earth set themselves, and the rulers take counsel together against the Lord." And yet it goes on, "He that sitteth in the heavens shall laugh: the Lord shall have them in derision." It has been so in time past. It will be so in time to come.

Let us observe, secondly, in these verses, *how good works are sometimes undervalued and misunderstood.* We are told of the good work of a certain woman, in pouring ointment on our Lord's head, in a house at Bethany.* She did it, no doubt, as a mark of honour and respect,

---

* The question has often been raised, whether there were one, two, or three women who anointed our Lord during His earthly

and in token of her own gratitude and love towards
Him. Yet this act of her's was blamed by some. Their
cold hearts could not understand such costly liberality.
They called it "waste." "They had indignation within
themselves." They "murmured against her."

The spirit of these narrow-minded fault-finders is unhappily only too common. Their followers and successors
are to be found in every part of Christ's visible Church.

ministry. Theophylact is of opinion that there were three. For
this opinion much may be said.

1. The woman spoken of in the seventh chapter of St. Luke
appears first in order. The city in which this anointing took place
does not appear to be Bethany. The woman is spoken of as having
been a "sinner." The house is described as that of a Pharisee.
The anointing was of our Lord's "feet," and not of His "head."
There is strong internal evidence that the whole transaction took
place at a comparatively early period of our Lord's ministry. All
these points should be noticed.

2. The anointing described by St. John appears next in order.
This, we are distinctly told, was "six days" before the passover.
The person who anointed our Lord was Mary, the sister of Lazarus.
The part of him anointed was again His "feet," and not His "head."
These points ought also to be noticed.

3. The anointing described by St. Matthew and St. Mark comes
third in order. This, we are told, was only "two days" before the
feast of the passover. In this case we are not told the name of the
woman who anointed our Lord. But we are told that the ointment
was poured on His "head."

The question of course occurs to our minds: "Is it likely and
probable that this event would take place no less than three times?"
In reply to that it may be fairly said, that to anoint a person as a
mark of honour and respect, was far more common in our Lord's
time than we in England suppose; and that anointing was a far
more frequent practice than we in this climate can imagine. And it
seems perfectly possible that the same thing may have happened
three times.

The main difficulty, of course, is the close similarity of the
language used at the anointing described by John, and at that
described by Matthew and Mark. This can only be explained by
supposing that our Lord twice said the same things.

There is never wanting a generation of people who decry what they call "extremes" in religion, and are incessantly recommending what they term "moderation" in the service of Christ. If a man devotes his time, money, and affections to the pursuit of worldly things, they do not blame him. If he gives himself up to the service of money, pleasure, or politics, they find no fault. But if the same man devotes himself, and all he has, to Christ, they can scarcely find words to express their sense of his folly.—"He is beside himself." "He is out of his mind." "He is fanatic." "He is an enthusiast." "He is righteous over-much." "He is an extreme man."—In short, they regard it as "waste."

Let charges like these not disturb us, if we hear them made against us because we strive to serve Christ. Let us bear them patiently, and remember that they are as old as Christianity itself. Let us pity those who make such charges against believers. They show plainly that they have no sense of obligation to Christ. A cold heart makes a slow hand. If a man once understands the sinfulness of sin, and the mercy of Christ in dying for him, he will never think anything too good or too costly to give to Christ. He will rather feel, "What shall I render to the Lord for all His benefits." (Psalm cxvi. 12.) He will fear wasting time, talents, money, affections on the things of this world. He will not be afraid of wasting them on his Saviour. He will fear going into extremes about business, money, politics, or pleasure; but he will not be afraid of doing too much for Christ.

Let us observe, in the last place, how *highly our Lord*

Jesus Christ esteems any service done to Himself. Nowhere, perhaps, in the Gospels, do we find such strong praises bestowed on any person as this woman here receives. Three points, in particular, stand out prominently in our Lord's words, to which many who now ridicule and blame others for their religion's sake, would do well to take heed.

For one thing, our Lord says, "Why trouble ye her?" A heart-searching question that, and one which all who persecute others because of their religion would find it hard to answer!—What cause can they show? What reason can they assign for their conduct? None: none at all! They trouble others out of envy, malice, ignorance, and dislike of the true Gospel.

For another thing, our Lord says, "She hath done a good work."—How great and marvellous is that praise, from the lips of the King of kings! Money is often given to the Church, or bestowed on charitable institutions, from ostentation, or other false motives. But it is the person who loves and honours Jesus Himself, who really "does good works."

For another thing, our Lord says, "She hath done what she could."—No stronger word of commendation than that could possibly have been used. Thousands live and die without grace and are lost eternally, who are always saying, "I try all I can. I do all I can." and yet in saying so, they tell as great a lie as Ananias and Sapphira. Few, it may be feared, are to be found like this woman, and really deserve to have it said of them that they "do what they can."

Let us leave the passage with practical self-application.

Let us, like this holy woman, whose conduct we have
just heard described, devote ourselves, and all we have,
to Christ's glory.   Our position in the world may be
lowly, and our means of usefulness few.   But let us,
like her, " do what we can."

Finally, let us see in this passage a sweet foretaste
of things yet to come in the day of judgment.   Let us
believe that the same Jesus who here pleaded the cause
of His loving servant when she was blamed, will one
day plead for all who have been His servants in this
world.   Let us work on, remembering that His eye is
upon us, and that all we do is noted in His book.—Let
us not heed what men say or think of us because of
our religion.   The praise of Christ, at the last day, will
more than compensate for all we suffer in this world
from unkind tongues.

MARK XIV. 10—16.

10 And Judas Iscariot, one of the twelve, went unto the chief priests, to betray him unto them.

11 And when they heard it, they were glad, and promised to give him money. And he sought how he might conveniently betray him.

12 And the first day of unleavened bread, when they killed the passover, his disciples said unto him, Where wilt thou that we go and prepare that thou mayest eat the passover?

13 And he sendeth forth two of his disciples, and saith unto them, Go ye into the city, and there shall meet you a man bearing a pitcher of water: follow him.

14 And wheresoever he shall go in, say ye to the goodman of the house, The Master saith, Where is the guest-chamber, where I shall eat the passover with my disciples?

15 And he will shew you a large upper room furnished and prepared: there make ready for us.

16 And his disciples went forth, and came into the city, and found as he had said unto them: and they made ready the passover.

IN these verses, St. Mark tells us how our Lord was
delivered into the hands of His enemies.   It came to
pass through the treachery of one of His own twelve

disciples. The false Apostle, Judas Iscariot, betrayed Him.

We ought to mark, firstly, in this passage, *to what lengths a man may go in a false profession of religion.*

It is impossible to conceive a more striking proof of this painful truth, than the history of Judas Iscariot. If ever there was a man who at one time looked like a true disciple of Christ, and bade fair to reach heaven, that man was Judas. He was chosen by the Lord Jesus Himself to be an Apostle. He was privileged to be a companion of the Messiah, and an eye-witness of His mighty works, throughout His earthly ministry. He was an associate of Peter, James, and John. He was sent forth to preach the kingdom of God, and to work miracles in Christ's name. He was regarded by all the eleven Apostles as one of themselves. He was so like his fellow-disciples, that they did not suspect him of being a traitor. And yet this very man turns out at last a false-hearted child of the devil,—departs entirely from the faith,—assists our Lord's deadliest enemies, and leaves the world with a worse reputation than any one since the days of Cain. Never was there such a fall, such an apostacy, such a miserable end to a fair beginning, such a total eclipse of a soul!

And how can this amazing conduct of Judas be accounted for? There is only one answer to that question. "The love of money" was the cause of this unhappy man's ruin. That same grovelling covetousness, which enslaved the heart of Balaam, and brought on Gehazi a leprosy, was the destruction of Iscariot's soul. No other explanation of his behaviour will satisfy the plain

statements of Scripture. His act was an act of mean
covetousness, without a redeeming feature about it.
The Holy Ghost declares plainly " He was a thief."
(John xii. 6.)   And his case stands before the world as
an eternal comment on the solemn words, " The love
of money is the root of all evil."   (1 Tim. vi. 10.)

Let us learn from this melancholy history of Judas,
to be " clothed with humility," and to be content with
nothing short of the grace of the Holy Ghost in our
hearts.   Knowledge, gifts, profession, privileges, church-
membership, power of preaching, praying, and talking
about religion are all useless things, if our hearts are not
converted.   They are all no better than sounding brass
and a tinkling cymbal, if we have not put off the old
man and put on the new.   They will not deliver us from
hell.—Above all, let us remember our Lord's caution,
to " beware of covetousness."   (Luke xii. 15.)   It is a
sin that eats like a canker, and once admitted into our
hearts, may lead us finally into every wickedness.   Let
us pray to be " content with such things as we have."
(Heb. xiii. 6.)   The possession of money is not the one
thing needful.   Riches entail great peril on the souls of
those who have them.   The true Christian ought to be
far more afraid of being rich than of being poor.

We ought to mark, secondly, in this passage, the
intentional connection between the time of the Jewish pass-
over and the time of Christ's death.   We cannot doubt
for a moment that it was not by chance, but by God's
providential appointment, that our Lord was crucified in
the passover week, and on the very day that the passover
lamb was slain.   It was meant to draw the attention of

the Jewish nation to Him as the true Lamb of God. It was meant to bring to their minds the true object and purpose of His death. Every sacrifice, no doubt, was intended to point the Jew onward to the one great sacrifice for sin which Christ offered. But none, certainly, was so striking a figure and type of our Lord's sacrifice, as the slaying of the passover lamb. It was preeminently an ordinance which was a "schoolmaster unto Christ." (Gal. iii. 24.) Never was there a type so full of meaning in the whole circle of Jewish ceremonies, as the passover was at its original institution.

Did the passover remind the Jew of the marvellous deliverance of his forefathers out of the land of Egypt, when God slew the first-born? No doubt it did. But it was also meant to be a sign to him of the far greater redemption and deliverance from the bondage of sin which was to be brought in by our Lord Jesus Christ.

Did the passover remind the Jew that by the death of an innocent lamb the families of his forefathers were once exempted from the death of their first-born? No doubt it did. But it was also meant to teach him the far higher truth that the death of Christ on the cross was to be the life of the world.

Did the passover remind the Jew that the sprinkling of blood on the door-posts of his forefathers' houses preserved them from the sword of the destroying angel? No doubt it did. But it was also meant to show him the far more important doctrine that Christ's blood sprinkled on man's conscience cleanses it from all stain of guilt, and makes him safe from the wrath to come.

Did the passover remind the Jew that none of his forefathers were safe from the destroying angel, in the night when he slew the first born, unless he actually ate of the slain lamb No doubt it did.   But it was meant to guide his mind to the far higher lesson,—that all who would receive benefit from Christ's atonement, must actually feed upon Him by faith, and receive Him into their hearts.

Let us call these things to mind, and weigh them well. We shall then see a peculiar fitness and beauty in the time appointed by God for our Lord Jesus Christ's death on the cross.   It happened at the very season when the mind of all Israel was being directed to the deliverance from Egypt, and to the events of that wondrous night, when it took place.   The lamb slain and eaten by every member of the family,—the destroying angel,—the safety within the blood-sprinkled door, would have been talked over and considered in every Jewish household, the very week that our blessed Lord was slain.   It would be strange indeed if such a remarkable death as His, at such a time, did not set many minds thinking, and open many eyes.   To what extent we shall never know till the last day.

Let it be a rule with us, in the reading of our Bibles, to study the types and ordinances of the Mosaic law with prayerful attention.   They are all full of Christ. The altar,—the scape-goat,—the daily burnt offering,— the day of atonement, are all so many finger-posts pointing to the great sacrifice offered by our Lord on Calvary. Those who neglect to study the Jewish ordinances, as dark, dull, and uninteresting parts of the Bible, only show their own ignorance, and miss great advantages.

w

Those who examine them with Christ as the key to their meaning, will find them full of Gospel light and comfortable truth.*

MARK XIV. 17—25.

17 And in the evening he cometh with the twelve.

18 And as they sat and did eat, Jesus said, Verily I say unto you, One of you which eateth with me shall betray me.

19 And they began to be sorrowful, and to say unto him one by one, *Is* it I? and another *said, Is* it I?

20 And he answered and said unto them, *It is* one of the twelve, that dippeth with me in the dish.

21 The Son of man indeed goeth, as it is written of him: but woe to that man by whom the Son of man is betrayed! good were it for that man if he had never been born.

22 And as they did eat, Jesus took bread, and blessed, and brake *it,* and gave to them, and said, Take, eat: this is my body.

23 And he took the cup, and when he had given thanks, he gave *it* to them: and they all drank of it.

24 And he said unto them, This is my blood of the new testament, which is shed for many.

25 Verily I say unto you, I will drink no more of the fruit of the vine, until that day that I drink it new in the kingdom of God.

---

* It may be well to observe in this connection, that it admits of much question whether the common view of the word "passover" is the correct one. At any rate, the following passage from Bishop Lowth on Isaiah xxxi. 5, deserves careful consideration. He says :—

"The common notion of God's passing over the houses of the Israelites is, that in going through the land of Egypt to smite the first-born, seeing the blood on the door of the houses of the Israelites, He passed over, or skipped those houses, and forbore to smite them. But that this is not the true notion of the thing, will be plain from considering the words of the sacred historian, where he describes very explicitly the action : 'For Jehovah will pass through to smite the Egyptians ; and when He seeth the blood on the lintels and on the two side-posts, Jehovah *will spring forward over or before the door,* and will not suffer the destroyer to come into your houses to smite you.' (Exodus xii. 23.) Here are manifestly two distinct agents, with which the notion of passing over is not consistent,—for that supposes but one agent. The two agents are the destroying angel passing through to smite every house, and Jehovah the protector keeping pace with him, who seeing the door of the Israelites marked with blood, leaps forward, throws Himself with a sudden motion in the way, opposes the destroying angel, and protects and saves that house against him, nor suffers him to smite it." The words of Isaiah xxxi. 5, ought to be studied attentively, in order to understand the fitness and propriety of this interpretation.

THESE verses contain St. Mark's account of the institution of the Lord's Supper. The simplicity of the
description deserves special observation. Well would it
have been for the Church, if men had not departed from
the simple statements of Scripture about this blessed
sacrament! It is a mournful fact that it has been
corrupted by false explanations and superstitious additions, until its real meaning, in many parts of Christendom, is utterly unknown. Let us however, at present,
dismiss from our minds all matters of controversy, and
study the words of St. Mark with a view to our own
personal edification.

Let us learn from the passage before us, that *self-
examination should precede the reception of the Lord's
Supper*. We cannot doubt that this was one object of
our Lord's solemn warning, "One of you which eateth
with Me shall betray Me." He meant to stir up in the
minds of His disciples those very searchings of heart
which are here so touchingly recorded: "They began to
be sorrowful, and to say unto Him one by one, Is it I?
and another said, Is it I?" He meant to teach His
whole Church throughout the world, that the time of
drawing near to the Lord's table should be a time for
diligent self-inquiry.

The benefit of the Lord's Supper depends entirely on
the spirit and frame of mind in which we receive it. The
bread which we there eat, and the wine which we there
drink, have no power to do good to our souls, as medicine does good to our bodies, without the co-operation of
our hearts and wills. They will not convey any blessing
to us by virtue of the minister's consecration, if we do

not receive them, rightly, worthily, and with faith. To assert, as some do, that the Lord's Supper must do good to all communicants, whatever be the state of mind in which they receive it, is a monstrous and unscriptural figment, and has given rise to gross and wicked superstition.

The state of mind which we should look for in ourselves, before going to the Lord's table, is well described in the Catechism of the Church of England. We ought to "examine ourselves whether we repent truly of our former sins,—whether we steadfastly purpose to lead a new life,—whether we have a lively faith in God's mercy through Christ,—and a thankful remembrance of His death,—and whether we are in charity with all men." If our conscience can answer these questions satisfactorily, we may receive the Lord's Supper without fear. More than this God does not require of any communicant. Less than this ought never to content us.

Let us take heed to ourselves in the matter of the Lord's Supper. It is easy to err about it on either side.—On the one hand, we are not to be content with staying away from the Lord's table under the vague plea of unfitness. As long as we so stay away, we are disobeying a plain command of Christ, and are living in sin.—But, on the other hand, we are not to go to the Lord's table as a mere form, and without thought. As long as we receive the sacrament in that state of mind, we derive no good from it, and are guilty of a great transgression.—It is an awful thing to be unfit for the sacrament, for this is to be unfit to die. It is a no less awful thing to receive it unworthily, for this is most provoking to God. The only safe course is to be a decided servant of Christ, and to live the life of faith in Him.—Then we may draw near with boldness, and take the sacrament to our comfort.

Let us learn, in the second place, from these verses, that *the principal object of the Lord's Supper, is to remind us of Christ's sacrifice for us on the cross.* The bread is intended to bring to our recollection the "body" of Christ, which was wounded for our transgressions. The wine is intended to bring to our recollection the "blood" of Christ, which was shed to cleanse us from all sin. The atonement and propitiation which our Lord effected by His death as our Surety and Substitute, stand out prominently in the whole ordinance. The false doctrine which some teach, that His death was nothing more than the death of a very holy man, who left us an example how to die, turns the Lord's Supper into an unmeaning ordinance, and cannot possibly be reconciled with our Lord's words at its institution.

A clear understanding of this point is of great importance. It will place us in the right position of mind, and teach us how we ought to feel in drawing near to the Lord's table. It will produce in us true *humilty* of spirit. The bread and wine will remind us how sinful sin must be, when nothing but Christ's death could atone for it. It will produce in us *hopefulness* about our souls. The bread and wine will remind us that though our sins are great, a great price has been paid for our redemption. —Not least, it will produce in us *gratitude*. The bread and wine will remind us how great is our debt to Christ, and how deeply bound we are to glorify Him in our lives. May these be the feelings that we experience, whenever we receive the Lord's Supper!

Finally, we learn from these verses, *the nature of the spiritual benefits, which the Lord's Supper is intended to convey, and the persons who have a right to expect them.* We may gather this lesson from the significant actions which are used in receiving this sacrament. Our Lord commands us to " eat " bread and to " drink " wine. Now eating and drinking are the acts of a living person. The object of eating and drinking is to be strengthened and refreshed. The conclusion we are meant to draw, is manifestly this, that the Lord's Supper is appointed for " the strengthening and refreshing of our souls," and that those who ought to partake of it are those who are lively, real Christians. All such will find this sacrament a means of grace. It will assist them to rest in Christ more simply, and to trust in Him more entirely. The visible symbols of bread and wine will aid, quicken, and confirm their faith.

A right view of this point is of the utmost moment in these latter days. We must always beware of thinking that there is any way of eating Christ's body, and drinking Christ's blood, but by faith,—or that receiving the Lord's Supper will give any man a different interest in Christ's sacrifice on the cross from that which faith gives. Faith is the one grand means of communication between the soul and Christ. The Lord's Supper can aid, quicken, and confirm faith, but can never supersede it, or supply its absence. Let this never be forgotten. Error on this point is a most fatal delusion, and leads to many superstitions.

Let it be a settled principle in our Christianity, that no unbeliever ought to go to the Lord's table, and that the sacrament will not do our souls the slightest good, if we do not receive it with repentance and faith. The Lord's Supper is not a converting or justifying ordinance, and those who come to it unconverted and unjustified, will go away no better than they came, but rather worse. It is an ordinance for believers, and not for unbelievers,—for the living, and not for the dead. It is meant to sustain life, but not to impart it,—to strengthen and increase grace, but not to give it,—to help faith to grow, but not to sow or plant it. Let these things sink down into our hearts, and never be forgotten.

Are we alive unto God? This is the great question. If we are, let us go to the Lord's Supper, and receive it thankfully, and never turn our backs on the Lord's table. If we do not go we commit a great sin.

Are we yet dead in sin and worldliness? If we are, we have no business at the communion. We are on the broad way that leadeth to destruction. We must repent. We must be born again. We must be joined to Christ by faith. Then and not till then, we are fit to be communicants.*

* There are two expressions in the passage now expounded, which deserve a special notice. One is, the "fruit of the vine." The other is, "the kingdom of God."

1. The words, "fruit of the vine," applied by our Lord to the cup of wine which He had just been giving to His disciples, in the institution of the Lord's Supper, appear entirely to overthrow the Romish doctrine of transubstantiation. The wine, it appears, did not really and literally become Christ's blood, as the Roman Catholics say. Our Lord Himself speaks of it as the juice of grapes, "the fruit of the vine." It is clear therefore, that when He said of that cup of wine before, "this is my blood," He meant nothing more than this, "this represents—is an emblem of—my blood."

2. The words, "kingdom of God," applied by our Lord to a time

MARK XIV. 26—31.

26 And when they had sung an hymn, they went out into the mount of Olives.

27 And Jesus saith unto them, All ye shall be offended because of me this night: for it is written, I will smite the shepherd, and the sheep shall be scattered.

28 But after that I am risen, I will go before you into Galilee.

29 But Peter said unto him, Although all shall be offended, yet *will* not I.

30 And Jesus saith unto him, Verily I say unto thee, That this day, *even* in this night, before the cock crow twice, thou shalt deny me thrice.

31 But he spake the more vehemently, If I should die with thee, I will not deny thee in any wise. Likewise also said they all.

WE see in these verses, *how well our Lord foreknew the weakness and infirmity of His disciples.* He tells them plainly what they were going to do. " All ye shall be offended because of Me this night." He tells Peter in particular of the astounding sin which he was about to commit : " This night, before the cock crow, thou shall deny Me thrice."

Yet our Lord's fore-knowledge did not prevent His chosing these twelve disciples to be His Apostles. He allowed them to be His intimate friends and companions, knowing perfectly well what they would one day do. He granted them the mighty privilege of being continually with Him, and hearing His voice, with a clear foresight of the melancholy weakness and want of faith which they would exhibit at the end of His ministry. This is a remarkable fact, and deserves to be had in continual remembrance.

and state of things yet future, appear to show plainly that He did not consider God's kingdom to have come, when He spoke. Moreover the words have not yet received a fulfilment, as it is not known that our Lord administered the Lord's Supper to His disciples after His resurrection. The words therefore are meant to turn our minds towards the time of our Lord's second advent. Then, and not till then, " the kingdom of God" will be fully set up. Then, and not till then, we shall sit down at the marriage supper of the Lamb, and drink the new wine in the kingdom.

Let us take comfort in the thought that the Lord Jesus does not cast off His believing people because of failures and imperfections. He knows what they are. He takes them, as the husband takes the wife, with all their blemishes and defects, and once joined to Him by faith, will never put them away. He is a merciful and compassionate High-priest. It is His glory to pass over the transgressions of His people, and to cover their many sins. He knew what they were before conversion,—wicked, guilty, and defiled; yet He loved them. He knows what they will be after conversion,—weak, erring, and frail; yet He loves them. He has undertaken to save them, notwithstanding all their shortcomings, and what He has undertaken He will perform.

Let us learn to pass a charitable judgment on the conduct of professing believers. Let us not set them down in a low place, and say they have no grace, because we see in them much weakness and corruption. Let us remember that our Master in heaven bears with their infirmities, and let us try to bear with them too. The Church of Christ is little better than a great hospital. We ourselves are all, more or less, weak, and all daily need the skilful treatment of the heavenly Physician. There will be no complete cures till the resurrection day.

We see, in the second place, in these verses, *how much comfort professing Christians may miss by carelessness and inattention*. Our Lord spoke plainly of His resurrection: "After that I am risen, I will go before you into Galilee." Yet His words appear to have been thrown away, and spoken in vain. Not one of His disciples seem to have noticed them, or treasured them up in his heart. When

He was betrayed, they forsook Him. When He was crucified, they were almost in despair. And when He rose again on the third day, they would not believe that it was true. They had heard of it frequently with the hearing of the ear, but it had never made any impression on their hearts.

What an exact picture we have here of human nature! How often we see the very same thing among professing Christians in the present day! How many truths we read yearly in the Bible, and yet remember them no more than if we had never read them at all! How many words of wisdom we hear in sermons heedlessly and thoughtlessly, and live on as if we had never heard them! The days of darkness and affliction come upon us by and by, and then we prove unarmed and unprepared. On sick beds, and in mourning, we see a meaning in texts and passages which we at one time heard listlessly and unconcerned. Things flash across our minds at such seasons, and make us feel ashamed that we had not noticed them before. We then remember to have read them, and heard them, and seen them, but they made no impression upon us. Like Hagar's well in the wilderness, they were close at hand, but, like Hagar, we never saw them. (Gen. xxi. 19.)

Let us pray for a quick understanding in hearing and reading God's Word. Let us search into every part of it, and not lose any precious truth in it for want of care. So doing, we shall lay up a good foundation against the time to come, and in sorrow and sickness be found armed.

Let us mark how little reason ministers have to be surprised, if the words that they preach in sermons are often unnoticed and unheeded. They only drink of the same cup with their Master. Even He said many things which were not noticed when first spoken. And yet we know that "never man spake like this man." "The disciple is not greater than his Master, nor the servant than his Lord." We have need of patience. Truths that seem neglected at first, often bear fruit after many days.

We see, in the last place, in these verses, *how much ignorant self-confidence may sometimes be found in the hearts of professing Christians.* The Apostle Peter could not think it possible that he could ever deny his Lord. "If I should die with Thee," he says, "I will not deny Thee in any wise." And he did not stand alone in his confidence. The other disciples were of the same opinion. "Likewise also said they all."

Yet what did all this confident boasting come to ? Twelve hours did not pass away before all the disciples forsook our Lord and fled. Their loud professions were all forgotten. The present danger swept all their promises of fidelity clean away. So little do we know how we shall act in any particular position until we are placed in it ! So much do present circumstances alter our feelings !

Let us learn to pray for humility. "Pride goeth before destruction, and a haughty spirit before a fall." (Prov. xvi. 18.) There is far more wickedness in all our hearts than we know. We never can tell how far we might fall, if once placed in temptation. There is no degree of sin into which the greatest saint may not run, if he is not held up by the grace of God, and if he does not watch and pray. The seeds of every wickedness lie hidden in our hearts. They only need the convenient season to spring forth into a mischievous vitality. "Let him that thinketh he standeth take heed lest he fall." "He that trusteth his own heart is a fool." (1 Cor. x. 12; Prov. xxviii. 26.) Let our daily prayer be, "Hold Thou me up and I shall be safe."

MARK XIV. 32—42.

32 And they came to a place which was named Gethsemane: and he saith to his disciples, Sit ye here, while I shall pray.

33 And he taketh with him Peter and James and John, and began to be sore amazed, and to be very heavy;

34 And saith unto them, My soul is exceeding sorrowful unto death: tarry ye here, and watch.

35 And he went forward a little, and fell on the ground, and prayed that, if it were possible, the hour might pass from him.

36 And he said, Abba, Father, all things *are* possible unto thee; take away this cup from me: nevertheless not what I will, but what though wilt.

37 And he cometh, and findeth them sleeping, and saith unto Peter, Simon, sleepest thou? couldest not thou watch one hour?

38 Watch ye and pray, lest ye enter into temptation. The spirit truly *is* ready, but the flesh *is* weak.

39 And again he went away, and prayed, and spake the same words.

40 And when he returned, he found them asleep again, (for their eyes were heavy,) neither wist they what to answer him.

41 And he cometh the third time, and saith unto them, Sleep on now, and take *your* rest: it is enough, the hour is come; behold, the Son of man is betrayed into the hands of sinners.

42 Rise up, let us go; lo, he that betrayeth me is at hand.

THE history of our Lord's agony in the garden of Gethsemane is a deep and mysterious passage of Scripture. It contains things which the wisest divines cannot fully explain. Yet it has upon its surface plain truths of most momentous importance.

Let us mark, in the first place, *how keenly our Lord felt the burden of a world's sin.* It is written that He "began to be sore amazed, and to be very heavy; and saith unto them, My soul is exceeding sorrowful unto death,"—and that "He fell on the ground, and prayed that, if it were possible, the hour might pass from Him."

There is only one reasonable explanation of these expressions. It was no mere fear of the physical suffering of death, which drew them from our Lord's lips. It was a sense of the enormous load of human guilt, which began at that time to press upon Him in a peculiar way. It was a sense of the unutterable weight of our sins and transgressions which were then specially laid upon Him. He was being "made a curse for us." He was bearing our griefs and carrying our sorrows, according to the covenant He came on earth to fulfil. He was being "made sin for us who Himself knew no sin." His holy nature felt acutely the hideous burden laid upon Him. These were the reasons of His extraordinary sorrow.

We ought to see in our Lord's agony in Gethsemane the exceeding sinfulness of sin. It is a subject on which the thoughts of professing Christians are far below what they should be. The careless, light way in which such sins as swearing, sabbath-breaking, lying, and the like, are often spoken of, is a painful evidence of the low condition of men's moral feelings. Let the recollection of Gethsemane have a sanctifying effect upon us. Whatever others do, let us never " make a mock at sin."

Let us mark, in the second place, *what an example our Lord gives us of the importance of prayer in time of trouble.* In the hour of His distress we find Him employing this great remedy. Twice we are told that when His soul was exceeding sorrowful, " He prayed."

We shall never find a better receipt than this for the patient bearing of affliction. The first person to whom we should turn in our trouble is God. The first complaint we should make should be in the form of a prayer.

The reply may not be given immediately. The relief we want may not be granted at once. The thing that tries us may never be removed and taken away. But the mere act of pouring out our hearts, and unbosoming ourselves at a throne of grace will do us good. The advice of St. James is wise and weighty: "Is any afflicted? Let him pray." (James v. 13.)

Let us mark, in the third place, *what a striking example our Lord gives us of submission of will to the will of God.* Deeply as His human nature felt the pressure of a world's guilt, He still prays that, "if it were possible," the hour might pass from Him. "Take away this cup from Me: nevertheless not what I will, but what Thou wilt."*

* Men are so apt to run into error on the subject of the divine and human natures in Christ, that the following quotation may be worth reading.

"There are two distinct wills in Christ. But although they be truly distinct and different one from the other, yet they are not contrary one to the other, but they are subordinate each to other; the human will of Christ being always subject to His divine will, and most ready to be ordered and ruled by it. Therefore here we see that He doth submit His will, as He was man, to the divine will of God the Father, which divine will of the Father was also Christ's own will. This truth we are to hold and maintain against those old heretics, which were called Monothelites, because they held there was but one kind of will in Christ, namely His divine will.—This heresy sprung up in the Eastern church about 600 years after Christ; and it did very much molest and trouble the Church for many years. —It was a branch of the gross heresy of Eutyches, which sprung up 200 years before. This Eutyches confounded the two natures in Christ, holding that as there was but one Person after the personal union, so there was but one nature in Christ,—viz. the divine nature, the human nature being swallowed up. To maintain this the better, his followers maintained that Christ had but one kind of will. This heresy was condemned by the 6th General Council at Constantinople, as well as by other ancient councils. And the Fathers of the Church in those times did confute it by these very words of our Saviour which we have now in hand."—*Petter on Mark.*

We can imagine no higher degree of perfection than that which is here set before us. To take patiently whatever God sends,—to like nothing but what God likes,—to wish nothing but what God approves,—to prefer pain, if it please God to send it, to ease, if God does not think fit to bestow it,—to lie passive under God's hand, and know no will but His : this is the highest standard at which we can aim, and of this our Lord's conduct in Gethsemane is a perfect pattern.

Let us strive and labour to have " the mind that was in Christ " in this matter. Let us daily pray, and endeavour to be enabled to mortify our self-will.—It is for our happiness to do so. Nothing brings us so much misery on earth as having our own way.—It is the best proof of real grace to do so. Knowledge, and gifts, and convictions, and feelings, and wishes, are all very un-certain evidences. They are often to be found in uncon-verted persons. But a continually increasing disposition to submit our own wills to the will of God, is a far more healthy symptom. It is a sign that we are really " grow-ing in grace, and in the knowledge of Jesus Christ."

Let us mark, lastly, in these verses, *how much infirmity may be found even in the best Christians.* We have a painful illustration of this truth in the conduct of Peter, James, and John. They slept when they ought to have watched and prayed. Though invited by our Lord to watch with Him, they slept. Though warned a short time before that danger was at hand, and their faith likely to fail, they slept. Though fresh from the Lord's table, with all its touching solemnities, they slept. Never was there a more striking proof that the best of men are but men, and that, so long as saints are in the body, they are compassed with infirmity.

These things are written for our learning. Let us take heed that they are not written in vain. Let us ever be on our guard against the slothful, indolent, lazy spirit in religion, which is natural to us all, and specially in the matter of our private prayers. When we feel that spirit creeping over us, let us remember Peter, James, and John in the garden, and take care.

The solemn counsel which our Lord addresses to His disciples should often ring in our ears : "Watch and pray lest ye enter into temptation. The spirit truly is ready, but the flesh is weak." It should be the Christian's daily motto from the time of his conversion to the hour of his death.

Are we true Christians ? and would we keep our souls awake ? Let us not forget that we have within us a double nature,—ready "spirit" and weak "flesh ;" a carnal nature inclined to evil, and a spiritual nature inclined to good. These two are contrary one to the other. (Gal. v. 17.) Sin and the devil will always find helpers in our hearts. If we do not crucify and rule over the flesh, it will often rule over us and bring us to shame.

Are we true Christians ? and would we keep our souls awake ? Then let us never forget to "watch and pray." We must watch like soldiers,—we are upon enemy's ground. We must always be on our guard. We must fight a daily fight and war a daily warfare. The Christian's rest is yet to come.—We must pray without ceasing, regularly, habitually, carefully, and at stated times. We must pray as well as watch, and watch as well as pray.

Watching without praying is self-confidence and self-conceit. Praying without watching is enthusiasm and fanaticism. The man who knows his own weakness, and knowing it both watches and prays, is the man that will be held up and not allowed to fall.

MARK XIV. 43—52.

43 And immediately, while he yet spake, cometh Judas, one of the twelve, and with him a great multitude with swords and staves, from the chief priests and the scribes and the elders.

44 And he that betrayed him had given them a token, saying, Whomsoever I shall kiss, that same is he; take him, and lead *him* away safely.

45 And as soon as he was come, he goeth straightway to him, and saith, Master, master; and kissed him.

46 And they laid their hands on him, and took him.

47 And one of them that stood by drew a sword, and smote a servant of the high priest, and cut off his ear.

48 And Jesus answered and said unto them, Are ye come out, as against a thief, with swords and *with* staves to take me?

49 I was daily with you in the temple teaching, and ye took me not: but the Scriptures must be fulfilled.

50 And they all forsook him, and fled.

51 And there followed him a certain young man, having a linen cloth cast about *his* naked *body;* and the young men laid hold on him:

52 And he left the linen cloth, and fled from them naked.

LET us notice in these verses, *how little our Lord's enemies understood the nature of His kingdom.* We read that Judas came to take Him "with a great multitude, with swords and staves." It was evidently expected that our Lord would be vigorously defended by His disciples, and that He would not be taken prisoner without fighting. The chief priests and scribes clung obstinately to the idea, that our Lord's kingdom was a worldly kingdom, and therefore supposed that it would be upheld by worldly means. They had yet to learn the solemn lesson contained in our Lord's words to Pilate, "My kingdom is not of this world :—now is my kingdom not from hence." (John xviii. 36.)

We shall do well to remember this in all our endea-

X

vours to extend the kingdom of true religion. It is not
to be propagated by violence, or by an arm of flesh.
"The weapons of our warfare are not carnal." "Not by
might, nor by power, but by my Spirit, saith the Lord of
hosts." (2 Cor. x. 4; Zech. iv. 6.) The cause of truth
does not need force to maintain it. False religions, like
Mahometanism, have often been spread by the sword.
False Christianity, like that of the Roman Church, has
often been enforced on men by bloody persecutions. But
the real Gospel of Christ requires no such aids as these.
It stands by the power of the Holy Ghost. It grows by
the hidden influence of the Holy Ghost on men's hearts
and consciences. There is no clearer sign of a bad cause
in religion than a readiness to appeal to the sword.

Let us notice, secondly, in these verses, *how all
things in our Lord's passion happened according to God's
word.* His own address to those who took Him exhibits
this in a striking manner: "the Scriptures must be fulfilled."

There was no accident or chance in any part of the close
of our Lord's earthly ministry. The steps in which He
walked from Gethsemane to Calvary were all marked
out hundreds of years before. The twenty-second Psalm,
and the fifty-third chapter of Isaiah were literally fulfilled. The wrath of His enemies, His rejection by His
own people, His being dealt with as a malefactor, His
being condemned by the assembly of the wicked,—all had
been foreknown, and all foretold. All that took place
was only the working out of God's great design to provide an atonement for a world's sin. The armed men
whom Judas brought to lay hands on Jesus, were, like

Nebuchadnezzar and Sennacherib, unconscious instruments in carrying God's purposes into effect.

Let us rest our souls on the thought, that all around us is ordered and overruled by God's almighty wisdom. The course of this world may often be contrary to our wishes. The position of the Church may often be very unlike what we desire. The wickedness of worldly men, and the inconsistencies of believers, may often afflict our souls. But there is a hand above us, moving the vast machine of this universe, and making all things work together for His glory. The Scriptures are being yearly fulfilled. Not one jot or title in them shall ever fail to be accomplished. The kings of the earth may take counsel together, and the rulers of the nations may set themselves against Christ (Psalm ii. 2) ; but the resurrection morning shall prove that, even at the darkest time, all things were being done according to the will of God.

Let us notice, lastly, in these verses, *how much the faith of true believers may give way.* We are told that when Judas and his company laid hands on our Lord, and He quietly submitted to be taken prisoner, the eleven disciples "all forsook Him and fled." Perhaps up to that moment they were buoyed up by the hope that our Lord would work a miracle, and set Himself free. But when they saw no miracle worked, their courage failed them entirely. Their former protestations were all forgotten. Their promises to die with their Master, rather than deny Him, were all cast to the winds. The fear of present danger got the better of faith. The sense of immediate peril drove every other feeling out of their minds. They "all forsook Him and fled."

There is something deeply instructive in this incident. It deserves the attentive study of all professing Christians. Happy is he who marks the conduct of our Lord's disciples, and gathers from it wisdom!

Let us learn from the flight of these eleven disciples, not to be over confident in our own strength. The fear of man does indeed bring a snare. We never know what we may do, if we are tempted, or to what extent our faith may give way. Let us be clothed with humility.

Let us learn to be charitable in our judgment of other Christians. Let us not expect too much from them, or set them down as having no grace at all, if we see them overtaken in a fault. Let us not forget that even our Lord's chosen Apostles forsook Him in His time of need; yet they rose again by repentance, and became pillars of the Church of Christ.

Finally, let us leave the passage with a deep sense of our Lord's ability to sympathize with His believing people. If there is one trial greater than another, it is the trial of being disappointed in those we love. It is a bitter cup, which all true Christians have frequently to drink. Ministers fail them. Relations fail them. Friends fail them. One cistern after another proves to be broken, and to hold no water. But let them take comfort in the thought, that there is one unfailing Friend, even Jesus, who can be touched with the feeling of their infirmities, and has tasted of all their sorrows. Jesus knows what it is to see friends and disciples failing Him in the hour of need. Yet He bore it patiently, and loved them notwithstanding all. He is never weary of forgiving. Let us strive to do likewise.   Jesus, at any rate, will never fail us.   It is written, " His compassions fail not." (Lam. iii. 22.) *

* The question has often been asked, "Who was the 'certain young man,' mentioned at the end of this passage, on whom the young men laid hold, and who fled away naked ?" St. Mark is the only Evangelist who relates this circumstance : and he has given us no clue to further knowledge as to who it was, or why the event is mentioned.

No satisfactory answer to these questions has yet been given. The utmost that can be said of any of the explanations attempted is, that they are conjectures and speculations.

"Some," says Petter, in his commentary on Mark, "have thought that it was one of the twelve disciples : viz., James the son of Alpheus, the Lord's brother, or kinsman of our Saviour (whose appearance was perhaps like our Lord's.)"   This is the view of Epiphanius and Jerome.   Others have thought that it was John, the beloved disciple. This is the view of Ambrose, Chrysostom, and Gregory. But it could be neither of them, nor any of the twelve, because it is said immediately before, that they "all fled" upon the taking of our Saviour, whereas this young man followed our Saviour at this time. It is more likely that it was some good young man, who dwelt near the garden of Gethsemane, who, hearing the noise and stir that was made about the taking and binding of our Saviour, did arise suddenly out of his bed to see what was the matter, and perceiving that they had cruelly taken and bound our Saviour, and were leading Him away, did follow after Him to see what would be done with Him, whereby it appears that he was a well-wisher to our Saviour."

Theophylact and Euthymius think it probable that it was some young man who followed our Lord from the house where He ate the passover with His disciples.   Some think that it was the Evangelist Mark himself.

Some have thought that St. Mark's purpose in relating the event, is to show the cruelty, rage, and ferocity of those who took our Lord. They were ready to lay hands on any one who was anywhere near Him, and to make prisoners indiscriminately of all who even appeared to be connected with Him.

Some have thought that the whole transaction exhibits the utter desertion of our Lord.   "This young man," says Clarius, "would rather escape naked than be taken as one of the followers of Christ."

Some have thought that it is related to show the real peril in

MARK XIV. 53—65.

53 And they led Jesus away to the high priest: and with him were assembled all the chief priests and the elders and the scribes.

54 And Peter followed him afar off, even into the palace of the high priest: and he sat with the servants, and warmed himself at the fire.

55 And the chief priests and all the council sought for witness against Jesus to put him to death; and found none.

56 For many bare false witness against him, but their witness agreed not together.

57 And there arose certain, and bare false witness against him, saying,

58 We heard him say, I will destroy this temple that is made with hands, and within three days I will build another made without hands.

59 But neither so did their witness agree together.

60 And the high priest stood up in the midst, and asked Jesus, saying, Answerest thou nothing? what *is it* *which* these witness against thee?

61 But he held his peace, and answered nothing. Again the high priest asked him, and said unto him, Art thou the Christ, the Son of the Blessed?

62 And Jesus said, I am: and ye shall see the Son of man sitting on the right hand of power, and coming in the clouds of heaven.

63 Then the high priest rent his clothes, and saith, What need we any further witnesses?

64 Ye have heard the blasphemy: what think ye? And they all condemned him to be guilty of death.

65 And some began to spit on him, and to cover his face, and to buffet him, and to say unto him, Prophesy: and the servants did strike him with the palms of their hands.

SOLOMON tells us in the book of Ecclesiastes, that one evil he has seen under the sun, is when "folly is set in great dignity, and the rich sit in low place." (Eccles. x. 6.) We can imagine no more complete illustration of his words than the state of thing we have recorded in the passage before us. We see the Son of God, "in whom are

which the disciples were, and to make it plain that they saved their lives only by their flight.

One eminent divine regards the whole event as strongly figurative. He sees in it an antitype of what took place on the day of atonement, and at the cleansing of a leper. He considers the young man escaping to represent the goat let go free, and the bird let loose ; while our Lord represents the goat offered up, and the bird slain. (See Lev. xiv. 7, and xvi. 22.)

I offer no opinion on any of the above explanations, excepting that I look on the last as eminently fanciful and unsatisfactory. Bullinger remarks sensibly, "It does not interest us much to know who this young man was, and it would not bring any very great fruit to us if we did know. If it had been useful and wholesome for us to know, the Spirit of God would not have been silent, seeing that He is often marvellously diligent in relating very minute things."

hid all the treasures of wisdom and knowledge," arraigned as a malefactor before "the chief priests, and elders, and scribes." We see the heads of the Jewish nation combining together to kill their own Messiah, and judging Him who will one day come in glory to judge them and all mankind. These things sound marvellous, but they are true.

Let us observe in these verses, *how foolishly Christians sometimes thrust themselves into temptation.* We are told that when our Lord was led away prisoner, "Peter followed Him afar off, even into the palace of the high priest: and he sat with the servants, and warmed himself at the fire."* There was no wisdom in this act. Having once forsaken his Master and fled, he ought to have remembered his own weakness, and not to have ventured into danger again. It was an act of rashness and presumption. It brought on him fresh trials of faith, for which he was utterly unprepared. It threw him into bad company, where he was not likely to get good but harm. It paved the way for his last and greatest transgression,—his thrice-repeated denial of his Master.

But it is an experimental truth that ought never to be overlooked, that when a believer has once begun to back-

---

* In the expression "warmed himself at the fire," it is worthy of remark, that the Greek word which we translate "fire," is not the same as that translated "fire of coals," in John xviii. 18. It would rather bear the meaning of "light," or a fire so blazing as to give light.

The remark is not without interest, as it explains how easily Peter was recognized and discovered by those who sat around him, as one of Christ's disciples. The bright light of the fire shining upon him made concealment impossible.

slide and leave his first faith, he seldom stops short at his first mistake. He seldom makes only one stumble. He seldom commits only one fault. A blindness seems to come over the eyes of his understanding. He appears to cast overboard his common sense and discretion. Like a stone rolling downhill, the further he goes on in sinning, the faster and more decided is his course. Like David, he may begin with idleness, and end with committing every possible crime. Like Peter, he may begin with cowardice, go on to foolish trifling with temptation, and then end with denying Christ.

If we know anything of true saving religion, let us ever beware of the beginnings of backsliding. It is like the letting out of water,—first a drop and then a torrent. Once out of the way of holiness, there is no saying to what we may come. Once giving way to petty inconsistencies, we may find ourselves one day committing every sort of wickedness. Let us keep far from the brink of evil. Let us not play with fire. Let us never fear being too particular, too strict, and too precise. No petition in the Lord's Prayer is more important than the last but one : " Lead us not into temptation."

Let us observe, in the second place, in these verses, *how much our Lord Jesus Christ had to endure from lying lips, when tried before the chief priests.* We are told that " many bare false witness against Him ; but their witness agreed not together."

We can easily conceive that this was not the least heavy part of our blessed Saviour's passion. To be seized unjustly as a malefactor, and put on trial as a criminal when innocent, is a severe affliction. But to hear men

inventing false charges against us and coining slanders,—
to listen to all the malignant virulence of unscrupulous
tongues let loose against our character, and know that it
is all untrue,—this is a cross indeed! " The words of a
talebearer," says Solomon, " are as wounds." (Prov.
xviii. 8.) " Deliver my soul," says David, " from lying lips
and a deceitful tongue." (Psalm cxx. 2.) All this was a
part of the cup which Jesus drank for our sakes. Great
indeed was the price at which our souls were redeemed!

Let it never surprise true Christians if they are
slandered and misrepresented in this world. They must
not expect to fare better than their Lord. Let them
rather look forward to it, as a matter of course, and see
in it a part of the cross which all must bear after conversion. Lies and false reports are among Satan's choicest
weapons. When he cannot deter men from serving Christ,
he labours to harass them, and make Christ's service uncomfortable. Let us bear it patiently, and not count it
a strange thing. The words of the Lord Jesus should
often come to our minds : " Woe unto you, when all men
shall speak well of you." " Blessed are ye, when men
shall revile you and persecute you, and say all manner
of evil against you falsely, for my sake." (Luke vi. 26 ;
Matt. v. 11.)

Let us observe, lastly, in these verses, *what distinct
testimony our Lord bore to His own Messiahship and second
advent in glory.* The high priest asks Him the solemn
question, " Art thou the Christ, the Son of the Blessed ? "
He receives at once the emphatic reply, " I am : and ye
shall see the Son of man sitting on the right hand of
power, and coming in the clouds of heaven."

These words of our Lord ought always to be had in remembrance. The Jews could never say after these words, that they were not clearly told that Jesus of Nazareth was the Christ of God. Before the great council of their priests and elders, He declared, "I am the Christ." The Jews could never say after these words, that He was so lowly and poor a person, that He was not worthy to be believed. He warned them plainly that His glory and greatness was all yet to come. They were only deferred and postponed till His second advent. They would yet see Him in royal power and majesty, "sitting on the right hand of power," coming in the clouds of heaven, a Judge, a Conqueror, and a King. If Israel was unbelieving, it was not because Israel was not told what to believe.

Let us leave the passage with a deep sense of the reality and certainty of our Lord Jesus Christ's second coming. Once more at the very end of His ministry, and in the face of His deadly enemies, we find Him asserting the mighty truth that He will come again to judge the world. Let it be one of the leading truths in our own personal Christianity. Let us live in the daily recollection that our Saviour is one day coming back to this world. Let the Christ in whom we believe, be not only the Christ who died for us and rose again,—the Christ who lives for us and intercedes,—but the Christ who will one day return in glory, to gather together and reward His people, and to punish fearfully all His enemies.

MARK XIV. 66—72.

66 And as Peter was beneath in the palace, there cometh one of the maids of the high priest:

67 And when she saw Peter warming himself, she looked upon him, and said, And thou also wast with Jesus of Nazareth.

68 But he denied, saying, I know not, neither understand I what thou sayest. And he went out into the porch: and the cock crew.

69 And a maid saw him again, and began to say to them that stood by, This is *one* of them.

70 And he denied it again. And a little after, they that stood by said again to Peter, Surely thou art *one* of them: for thou art a Galilæan, and thy speech agreeth *thereto*.

71 But he began to curse and to swear, *saying*, I know not this man of whom ye speak

72 And the second time the cock crew. And Peter called to mind the word that Jesus said unto him, Before the cock crow twice, thou shalt deny me thrice. And when he thought thereon, he wept.

A SHIPWRECK is a melancholy sight, even when no lives are lost. It is sad to think of the destruction of property, and disappointment of hopes which generally attend it. It is painful to see the suffering and hardship, which the ship's crew often have to undergo in their struggle to escape from drowning. Yet no shipwreck is half so melancholy a sight as the backsliding and fall of a true Christian. Though raised again by God's mercy, and finally saved from hell, he loses much by his fall. Such a sight we have brought before our minds in the verses we have now read. We are there told that most painful and instructive story, how Peter denied his Lord.

Let us learn, in the first place, from these verses, *how far and how shamefully a great saint may fall.* We know that Simon Peter was an eminent Apostle of Jesus Christ. He was one who had received special commendation from our Lord's lips, after a noble confession of His Messiahship: "Blessed art thou Simon Barjona:" —"I will give unto thee the keys of the kingdom of heaven." He was one who had enjoyed special privileges, and had special mercies shown to him. Yet here we see this same Simon Peter so entirely overcome by fear that he actually denies his Lord. He declares that he knows not Him whom he had accompanied and lived with for three years! He declares that he knows not Him who had healed his own wife's mother, taken him up into the mount of transfiguration, and saved him from drowning in the sea of Galilee! And he not only denies his Master once, but does it three times! And he not only denies Him simply, but does it "cursing and swearing!" And, above all, he does all this in the face of the plainest warnings, and in spite of his own loud protestations that he would do nothing of the kind, but rather die!

These things are written to show the Church of Christ what human nature is, even in the best of men. They are intended to teach us that, even after conversion and renewal of the Holy Ghost, believers are compassed with infirmity and liable to fall. They are meant to impress upon us the immense importance of daily watchfulness, prayerfulness, and humility, so long as we are in the body. "Let him that thinketh he standeth, take heed lest he fall."

Let us carefully remember that Simon Peter's case does not stand alone. The Word of God contains many other examples of the infirmity of true believers, which we shall do well to observe. The histories of Noah, Abraham, David, Hezekiah, will supply us with mournful proof that " the infection of sin remains even in the regenerate," and that no man is so strong as to be beyond the danger of falling. Let us not forget this. Let us walk humbly with our God. "Happy is the man that feareth alway." (Prov. xxviii. 14.)

Let us learn, in the second place, from these verses,

how small a temptation may cause a saint to have a great fall. The beginning of Peter's trial was nothing more than the simple remark of "a maid of the high priest:" "Thou also wert with Jesus of Nazareth." There is nothing to show that these words were spoken with any hostile purpose. For anything we can see, they might fairly mean that this maid remembered that Peter used to be a companion of our Lord. But this simple remark was enough to overthrow the faith of an eminent Apostle, and to make him begin to deny his Master. The chiefest and foremost of our Lord's chosen disciples is cast down, not by the threats of armed men, but by the saying of one weak woman!

There is something deeply instructive in this fact. It ought to teach us that no temptation is too small and trifling to overcome us, except we watch and pray to be held up. If God be for us we may remove mountains and get the victory over a host of foes. "I can do all things," says Paul, "through Christ that strengtheneth me." (Phil. iv. 22.) If God withdraw His grace, and leave us to ourselves, we are like a city without gates and walls, a prey to the first enemy, however weak and contemptible.

Let us beware of making light of temptations because they seem little and insignificant. There is nothing little that concerns our souls. A little leaven leaveneth the whole lump. A little spark may kindle a great fire. A little leak may sink a great ship. A little provocation may bring out from our hearts great corruption, and end in bringing our souls into great trouble.

Finally, let us learn from these verses *that backsliding*

brings saints into great sorrow. The conclusion of the passage is very affecting. " Peter called to mind the words that Jesus said unto him, Before the cock crow twice, thou shalt deny me thrice." Who can pretend to describe the feelings that must have flashed across the Apostle's mind? Who can conceive the shame and confusion, and self-reproach, and bitter remorse which must have overwhelmed his soul? To have fallen so foully! To have fallen so repeatedly! To have fallen in the face of such plain warnings! All these must have been cutting thoughts. The iron must indeed have entered into his soul. There is deep and solemn meaning in the one single expression used about him : " when he thought thereon, he wept."

The experience of Peter is only the experience of all God's servants who have yielded to temptation. Lot and Samson and David and Jehosaphat, in Bible history,—Cranmer and Jewell, in the records of our own English Church,—have all left evidence, like Peter, that " the backslider in heart shall be filled with his own ways." (Prov. xiv. 14.) Like Peter, they erred grievously. Like Peter, they repented truly ; but, like Peter, they found that they reaped a bitter harvest in this world. Like Peter, they were freely pardoned and forgiven ; but, like Peter, they shed many tears.

Let us leave the passage with the settled conviction that sin is sure to lead to sorrow, and that the way of most holiness is always the way of most happiness. The Lord Jesus has mercifully provided that it shall never profit His servants to walk carelessly and to give way to temptation. If we will turn our backs on Him we shall be sure to smart for it.   Though He forgives us, He will make us feel the folly of our own ways.   Those that follow the Lord most fully, shall always follow Him most comfortably.   "Their sorrows shall be multiplied who hasten after other gods." (Psalm xvi. 4.)

MARK XV. 1—15.

1 And straightway in the morning the chief priests held a consultation with the elders and scribes and the whole council, and bound Jesus, and carried *him* away, and delivered *him* to Pilate.

2 And Pilate asked him, Art thou the King of the Jews? and he answering said unto him, Thou sayest *it*.

3 And the chief priests accused him of many things: but he answered nothing.

4 And Pilate asked him again, saying, Answerest thou nothing? behold how many things they witness against thee.

5 But Jesus yet answered nothing; so that Pilate marvelled.

6 Now at *that* feast he released unto them one prisoner, whomsover they desired.

7 And there was *one* named Barabbas, *which lay* bound with them that had made insurrection with him, who had committed murder in the insurrection.

8 And the multitude crying aloud began to desire *him to do* as he had ever done unto them.

9 But Pilate answered them, saying, Will ye that I release unto you the King of the Jews?

10 For he knew that the chief priests had delivered him for envy.

11 But the chief priests moved the people, that he should rather release Barabbas unto them.

12 And Pilate answered and said again unto them, What will ye then that I shall do *unto him* whom ye call the King of the Jews?

13 And they cried out again, Crucify him.

14 Then Pilate said unto them, Why, what evil hath he done? And they cried out the more exceedingly, Crucify him.

15 And *so* Pilate, willing to content the people, released Barabbas unto them, and delivered Jesus, when he had scourged *him*, to be crucified.

THESE verses begin the chapter in which St. Mark describes the slaying "of the Lamb of God, which taketh away the sin of the world."   It is a part of the Gospel history which should always be read with peculiar reverence.   We should call to mind, that Christ was cut off, not for Himself, but for us. (Dan. ix. 26.)   We should remember that His death is the life of our souls, and that unless His blood had been shed, we must have perished miserably in our sins.

Let us mark in these verses, *what a striking proof the*

Jewish rulers gave to their own nation that the times of Messiah had come.

The chapter opens with the fact, that the chief priests bound Jesus and "delivered Him to Pilate," the Roman Governor. Why did they do so? Because they had no longer the power of putting any one to death, and were under the dominion of the Romans. By this one act and deed they declared that the prophecy of Jacob was fulfilled. "The sceptre had departed from Judah, and the lawgiver from between his feet," and Shiloh the Messiah, whom God had promised to send, must have come. (Gen. xlix. 10.) Yet there is nothing whatever to show that they remembered this prophecy. Their eyes were blinded. They either could not, or would not, see what they were doing.

Let us never forget that wicked men are often fulfilling God's predictions to their own ruin, and yet know it not. In the very height of their madness, folly, and unbelief, they are often unconsciously supplying fresh evidence that the Bible is true. The unhappy scoffers who make a jest of all serious religion, and can scarcely talk of Christianity without ridicule and scorn, would do well to remember that their conduct was long ago foreseen and foretold. "There shall come in the last days scoffers, walking after their own lusts." (2 Peter iii.)

Let us mark, secondly, in these verses, *the meekness and lowliness of our Lord Jesus Christ.* When He stood before Pilate's bar, and was "accused of many things," He answered nothing. Though the charges against Him were false, and He knew no sin, He was content to endure the contradiction of sinners against Himself, not answering again. (Heb. xii. 3.) Though he was innocent of any transgression, He submitted to hear groundless accusations made against Him without a murmur. Great is the contrast between the second Adam and the first! Our first father Adam was guilty, and yet tried to excuse himself. The second Adam was guiltless, and yet made no defence at all. "As a sheep before her shearers is dumb, so openeth He not His mouth." (Isa. liii. 7.)

Let us learn a practical lesson from our Saviour's example. Let us learn to suffer patiently, and not to complain, whatever God may think fit to lay upon us. Let us take heed to our ways, that we offend not in our tongues, in the hour of temptation. (Psalm xxxix. 1.) Let us beware of giving way to irritation and ill-temper, however provoking and undeserved our trials may seem to be. Nothing in the Christian character glorifies God so much as patient suffering. "If when ye do well and suffer for it, ye take it patiently, this is acceptable with God. For even hereunto were ye called, because Christ also suffered for us, leaving us an example that ye should follow His steps." (1 Peter ii. 20, 21.)

Let us mark, thirdly, in these verses, *the wavering and undecided conduct of Pilate.*

It is clear from the passage before us that Pilate was convinced of our Lord's innocence. "He knew that the chief priests had delivered Him for envy." We see him feebly struggling for a time to obtain our Lord's acquittal, and so to satisfy his own conscience. At last he yields to the importunity of the Jews, and "willing to content the people," delivers Jesus to be crucified,—to the eternal disgrace and ruin of his own soul.

A man in high places without religious principles, is one of the most pitiable sights in the world. He is like a large ship tossed to and fro on the sea without compass or rudder. His very greatness surrounds him with temptations and snares. It gives him power for good or evil, which, if he knows not how to use it aright, is sure to bring him into difficulties, and to make him unhappy. Let us pray much for great men. They need great grace to keep them from the devil. High places are slippery places. No wonder that St. Paul recommends intercession " for kings and for all that are in authority." (1 Tim. ii. 1.) Let us not envy great men. They have many and peculiar temptations. How hardly shall a rich man enter the kingdom of God. "Seekest thou great things for thyself? seek them not." (Jerem. xl. 5.)

Let us mark, fourthly, in these verses, *the exceeding guilt of the Jews in the matter of the death of Christ*. At the eleventh hour the chief priests had an opportunity of repenting, if they would have taken it. They had the choice given them whether Jesus or Barabbas should be let go free. Coolly and deliberately they persevered in their bloody work. They chose to have a murderer let go free. They chose to have the Prince of Life put to death. The *power* of putting our Lord to death was no longer theirs. The *responsibility* of His death they publicly took upon themselves.—"What will ye that I shall do unto Him ?" was Pilate's question. "Crucify Him, crucify Him," was the awful answer.—The agents in our Lord's death were undoubtedly Gentiles. But the guilt of our Lord's death must always rest chiefly upon the Jews.

We marvel at the wickedness of the Jews at this part

of our Lord's history,—and no wonder. To reject Christ and choose Barabbas was indeed an astounding act! It seems as if blindness, madness, and folly could go no further. But let us take heed that we do not unwittingly follow their example. Let us beware that we are not found at last to have chosen Barabbas and rejected Christ. The service of sin and the service of God are continually before us. The friendship of the world and the friendship of Christ are continually pressed upon our notice. Are we making the right choice? Are we cleaving to the right Friend? These are solemn questions. Happy is he who can give them a satisfactory answer.

Let us mark, finally, in these verses, *what a striking type the release of Barabbas affords of the Gospel plan of salvation.* The guilty is set free and the innocent is put to death. The great sinner is delivered, and the sinless one remains bound. Barabbas is spared, and Christ is crucified.

We have in this striking fact a vivid emblem of the manner in which God pardons and justifies the ungodly. He does it, because Christ hath suffered in their stead, the just for the unjust. They deserve punishment, but a mighty Substitute has suffered for them. They deserve eternal death, but a glorious Surety has died for them. We are all by nature in the position of Barabbas. We are guilty, wicked, and worthy of condemnation. But "when we were without hope," Christ the innocent died for the ungodly. And now God for Christ's sake can be just, and yet "the justifier of him which believeth in Jesus."

Let us bless God that we have such a glorious salvation set before us. Our plea must ever be, not that we are deserving of acquittal, but that Christ has died for us. Let us take heed, that having so great a salvation we really make use of it for our own souls. May we never rest till we can say by faith, " Christ is mine. I deserve hell : but Christ has died for me, and believing in Him I have a hope of heaven."

MARK XV. 16—32.

16 And the soldiers led him away into the hall, called Prætorium; and they call together the whole band.

17 And they clothed him with purple, and platted a crown of thorns, and put it about his *head*,

18 And began to salute him, Hail, King of the Jews!

19 And they smote him on the head with a reed, and did spit upon him, and bowing *their* knees worshipped him.

20 And when they had mocked him, they took off the purple from him, and put his own clothes on him, and led him out to crucify him.

21 And they compel one Simon a Cyrenian, who passed by, coming out of the country, the father of Alexander and Rufus, to bear his cross.

22 And they bring him unto the place Golgotha, which is, being interpreted, The place of a skull.

23 And they gave him to drink wine mingled with myrrh : but he received *it* not.

24 And when they had crucified him, they parted his garments, casting lots upon them, what every man should take.

25 And it was the third hour, and they crucified him.

26 And the superscription of his accusation was written over, THE KING OF THE JEWS.

27 And with him they crucify two thieves; the one on his right hand, and the other on his left.

28 And the Scripture was fulfilled, which saith, And he was numbered with the transgressors.

29 And they that passed by railed on him, wagging their heads, and saying, Ah, thou that destroyest the temple, and buildest *it* in three days,

30 Save thyself, and come down from the cross.

31 Likewise also the chief priests mocking said among themselves with the scribes, He saved others; himself he cannot save.

32 Let Christ the King of Israel descend now from the cross, that we may see and believe. And they that were crucified with him reviled him.

THE passage we have now read, is one of those which show us the infinite love of Christ towards sinners. The sufferings described in it would fill our minds with mingled horror and compassion, if they had been inflicted on one who was only a man like ourselves. But when we reflect that the sufferer was the eternal Son of God, we are lost in wonder and amazement. And when we reflect further that these sufferings were voluntarily endured to deliver sinful men and women like ourselves from hell, we may see something of St. Paul's meaning when he says, " The love of Christ passeth knowledge." " God commendeth His love toward us in that while we were yet sinners, Christ died for us." (Ephes. iii. 19 ; Rom. v. 8.)

We shall find it useful to examine separately the several parts of our Lord's passion. Let us follow Him step by step from the moment of His condemnation by Pilate to His last hour upon the cross. There is a deep meaning in every jot and tittle of His sorrows. All were striking emblems of spiritual truths. And let us not forget as we dwell on the wondrous story, that we and our sins were the cause of all these sufferings. " Christ suffered for sins, the just for the unjust, that He might bring us to God." (1 Peter iii. 18.) It is the death of our own Surety and Substitute that we are reading.

First of all we see Jesus delivered into the hands of the Roman soldiers, as a criminal condemned to death. He, before whom the whole world will one day stand and be judged, allowed Himself to be sentenced unjustly, and given over into the hands of wicked men.

And why was this ? It was that we, the poor sinful children of men, believing on Him, might be delivered from the pit of destruction, and the torment of the prison of hell. It was that we might be set free from every charge in the day of judgment, and be presented faultless before God the Father, with exceeding joy.

Secondly, we see Jesus insulted and made a laughingstock by the Roman soldiers. They "clothed Him with purple" in derision, and put "a crown of thorns" on His head, in mockery of His kingdom. "They smote Him on the head with a reed, and did spit upon Him," as one utterly contemptible, and no better than "the filth of the world." (1 Cor. iv. 13.)

And why was this? It was that we, vile as we are, might have glory, honour, and eternal life through faith in Christ's atonement. It was done that we might be received into God's kingdom with triumph at the last day, and receive the crown of glory that fadeth not away.

Thirdly, we see Jesus stripped of His garments and crucified naked before his enemies. The soldiers who led Him away "parted His garments, casting lots upon them."

And why was this? It was that we, who have no righteousness of our own, might be clothed in the perfect righteousness that Christ has wrought out for us, and not stand naked before God at the last day. It was done that we, who are all defiled with sin, might have a wedding-garment, wherein we may sit down by the side of angels, and not be ashamed.

Fourthly, we see Jesus suffering the most ignominious and humiliating of all deaths, even the death of the cross. It was the punishment reserved for the worst of male-factors. The man on whom it was inflicted was counted accursed. It is written, " Cursed is every one that hangeth on a tree." (Gal. iii. 13.)

And why was this? It was that we, who are born in sin and children of wrath, might be counted blessed for Christ's sake. It was done to remove the curse which we all deserve because of sin, by laying it on Christ. "Christ hath redeemed us from the curse of the law being made a curse for us." (Gal. iii. 13.)

Fifthly, we see Jesus reckoned a transgressor and a sinner. "With Him they crucify two thieves." He who had done no sin, and in whom there was no guile, "was numbered with the transgressors."

And why was this? It was that we, who are miserable transgressors, both by nature and practice, may be reckoned innocent for Christ's sake. It was done that we, who are worthy of nothing but condemnation, may be counted worthy to escape God's judgment, and be pronounced not guilty before the assembled world.

Lastly, we see Jesus mocked when dying, as one who was an impostor, and unable to save Himself.

And why was this? It was that we, in our last hours, through faith in Christ may have strong consolation. It all came to pass that we may enjoy strong assurance, —may know whom we have believed, and may go down the valley of the shadow of death fearing no evil.

Let us leave the passage with a deep sense of the enormous debt which all believers owe to Christ. All that they have, and are, and hope for, may be traced up to the doing and dying of the Son of God. Through His condemnation, they have acquittal,—through His sufferings, peace,—through His shame, glory,—through His death, life. Their sins were imputed to Him. His righteousness is imputed to them. No wonder that St. Paul says "Thanks be unto God for His unspeakable gift." (2 Cor. ix. 15.)

Finally, let us leave the passage with the deepest sense

of Christ's unutterable love to our souls. Let us remember what we are,—corrupt, evil, and miserable sinners. Let us remember who the Lord Jesus is,—the eternal Son of God, the maker of all things. And then let us remember, that for our sakes Jesus voluntarily endured the most painful, horrible and disgraceful death. Surely the thought of this love should constrain us daily to live not unto ourselves but unto Christ. It should make us ready and willing to present our bodies a living sacrifice to Him who lived and died for us. (2 Cor. v. 4; Rom. xii. 1.) Let the cross of Christ be often before our minds. Rightly understood, no object in all Christianity is so likely to have a sanctifying as well as a comforting effect on our souls.

MARK XV. 33—38.

33 And when the sixth hour was come, there was darkness over the whole land until the ninth hour.

34 And at the ninth hour Jesus cried with a loud voice, saying, Eloi, Eloi, lama sabacthani? which is, being interpreted, My God, my God, why hast thou forsaken me?

35 And some of them that stood by, when they heard it, said, Behold he calleth Elias.

36 And one ran and filled a spunge full of vinegar, and put it on a reed, and gave him to drink, saying, Let alone; let us see whether Elias will come to take him down.

37 And Jesus cried with a loud voice, and gave up the ghost.

38 And the veil of the temple was rent in twain from the top to the bottom.

WE have in these verses the death of our Lord Jesus Christ. All deaths are solemn events. Nothing in the whole history of a man is so important as his end. But never was there a death of such solemn moment as that which is now before us. In the instant that our Lord drew His last breath, the work of atonement for a world's sin was accomplished. The ransom for sinners was at length paid. The kingdom of heaven was thrown fully open to all believers.—All the solid hope that mortal men enjoy about their souls, may be traced to the giving up the ghost on the cross.

Let us observe, in these verses, *the visible signs and wonders which accompanied our Lord's death.* St. Mark mentions two in particular, which demand our attention. One is the darkening of the sun for the space of three hours. The other is the rending of the veil which divided the holy of holies from the holy place in the temple. Both were miraculous events. Both had, no doubt, a deep meaning about them. Both were calculated to arrest the attention of the whole multitude assembled at Jerusalem. The darkness would strike even thoughtless Gentiles, like Pilate and the Roman soldiers. The rent veil would strike even Annas and Caiaphas and their unbelieving companions. There were probably few houses in Jerusalem that evening in which men would not say, " We have heard and seen strange things to-day."

What did the miraculous darkness teach ? It taught the exceeding wickedness of the Jewish nation. They were actually crucifying their own Messiah, and slaying their own King. The sun himself hid his face at the sight.—It taught the exceeding sinfulness of sin in the eyes of God. The Son of God Himself must needs be left without the cheering light of day, when He became sin for us and carried our transgressions.*

* It is almost unnecessary to remark, that the darkness which covered the heaven on the day of the crucifixion, could not possibly have been occasioned by an eclipse of the sun, because the passover was always held at full moon. It is evident that the darkness was miraculous, and caused by some special interference with the course of nature.

What did the miraculous rending of the veil mean?
It taught the abolition and termination of the whole
Jewish law of ceremonies. It taught that the way into
the holiest of all was now thrown open to all mankind
by Christ's death. (Heb. ix. 8.) It taught that Gentiles
as well as Jews might now draw nigh to God with boldness, through Jesus the one High Priest, and that all
barriers between man and God were for ever cast down.

May we never forget the practical lesson of the rent
veil! To attempt to revive the Jewish ceremonial in the
Church of Christ, by returning to altars, sacrifices, and a
priesthood, is nothing better than closing up again the
rent veil and lighting a candle at noon day.

May we never forget the practical lesson of the miraculous darkness! It should lead our minds on to that
blackness of darkness which is reserved for all obstinate
unbelievers. (Jude 13.) The darkness endured by our
blessed Surety on the cross was only for three hours. The
chains of darkness which shall bind all who reject His
atonement and die in sin, shall be for evermore.

Let us observe, secondly, in these verses, *how truly and
really our Lord Jesus Christ was made a curse for us, and
bore our sins.* We see it strikingly brought out in those
marvellous words which He used at the ninth hour:
"My God, my God, why hast Thou forsaken Me."

It would be useless to pretend to fathom all the depth
of meaning which these words contain. They imply an
amount of mental suffering, such as we are unable to
conceive. The agony of some of God's holiest servants
has been occasionally very great, under an impression of
God's favour being withdrawn from them. What then

may we suppose was the agony of the holy Son of God,— when all the sin of all the world was laid upon His head —when He felt Himself reckoned guilty, though without sin,—when He felt His Father's countenance turned away from Him? The agony of that season must have been something past understanding. It is a high thing. We cannot attain to a comprehension of it. We may believe it, but we cannot explain and find it out to perfection.

One thing, however, is very plain, and that is the impossibility of explaining these words at all, except we receive the doctrine of Christ's atonement and substitution for sinners. To suppose, as some dare to do, that Jesus was nothing more than a man, or that His death was only a great example of self-sacrifice, makes this dying cry of His utterly unintelligible. It makes Him appear less patient and calm in a dying hour than many a martyr, or even than some heathen philosophers. One explanation alone is satisfactory. That explanation is the mighty scriptural doctrine of Christ's vicarious sacrifice and substitution for us on the cross. He uttered His dying cry under the heavy pressure of a world's sin laid upon Him and imputed to Him.

Let us observe, lastly, in these verses, *that it is possible to be forsaken of God for a time, and yet to be loved by Him.* We need not doubt this, when we read our Lord's dying words on the cross. We hear Him saying to His Father, "Why hast Thou forsaken Me?" and yet addressing Him as "My God." We know too that our Lord was only forsaken for a season, and that even when forsaken He was the beloved Son in whom, both in His suffering and doing, the Father was "well pleased."

There is deep experimental instruction in this, which deserves the notice of all true Christians. No doubt there is a sense in which our Lord's feeling of being "forsaken" was peculiar to Himself, since He was suffering for our sins and not for His own. But still after making this allowance there remains the great fact that Jesus was for a time " forsaken of the Father," and yet for all that was the Father's " beloved Son." As it was with the Great Head of the Church, so it may be in a modified sense with His members. They too, though chosen and beloved of the Father, may sometimes feel God's face turned away from them. They too, sometimes from illness of body, sometimes from peculiar affliction, sometimes from carelessness of walk, sometimes from God's sovereign will to draw them nearer to Himself, may be constrained to cry, "My God, my God, why hast Thou forsaken me?"

It becomes believers who feel "forsaken," to learn from our Lord's experience not to give way to despair. No doubt they ought not to be content with their position. They ought to search their own hearts, and see whether there is not some secret thing there which causes their consolations to be small. (Job xv. 11.) But let them not write bitter things against themselves, and hastily conclude that they are cast off for ever, or are self-deceivers, and have no grace at all. Let them still wait on the Lord, and say with Job, "Though He slay me yet will I trust in Him." (Job xiii. 15.) Let them remember the words of Isaiah and David: "Who is among you that feareth the Lord,—that walketh in darkness, and hath no light? let him trust in the name

of the Lord, and stay upon his God." " Why art thou
cast down, O my soul, and why art thou disquieted
within me ? Hope thou in God, for I shall yet praise
Him." (Isaiah l. 10 ; Psalm xlii. 11.)

MARK XV. 39—47.

39 And when the centurion, which
stood over against him, saw that he so
cried out, and gave up the ghost, he
said, Truly this man was the son of God.

40 There were also women looking on
afar off : among whom was Mary Magdalene, and Mary the mother of James
the less and of Joses, and Salome ;

41 (Who also, when he was in Galilee,
followed him, and ministered unto him,)
and many other women which came up
with him unto Jerusalem.

42 And now when the even was come,
because it was the preparation, that is,
the day before the sabbath,

43 Joseph of Arimathæa, an honourable counsellor, which also waited for
the kingdom of God, came, and went in
boldly unto Pilate, and craved the body
of Jesus.

44 And Pilate marvelled if he were
already dead : and calling *unto him* the
centurion, he asked him whether he had
been any while dead.

45 And when he knew *it* of the centurion, he gave the body to Joseph.

46 And he bought fine linen, and took
him down, and wrapped him in the
linen, and laid him in a sepulchre which
was hewn out of a rock, and rolled a
stone unto the door of the sepulchre.

47 And Mary Magdalene and **Mary**
the mother of Joses beheld where he was
laid.

THE death of our Lord Jesus Christ is the most important fact in Christianity. On it depend the hopes of
all saved sinners both for time and eternity. We need
not therefore be surprised to find the reality of His
death carefully placed beyond dispute. Three kinds of
witnesses to the fact are brought before us in the verses
we have now read. The Roman centurion, who stood
near the cross,—the women who followed our Lord from
Galilee to Jerusalem,—the disciples, who buried Him,
were all witnesses that Jesus really died. Their united
evidence is above suspicion. They could not be deceived.
What they saw was no swoon, or trance, or temporary
insensibility. They saw that same Jesus, who was
crucified, lay down His life, and become obedient even

unto death. Let this be established in our minds. Our Saviour really and truly died.

Let us notice, for one thing, in this passage, *what honourable mention is here made of women.* We are specially told that, when our Lord gave up the ghost, " there were women looking on afar off." The names of some of them are recorded. We are also told that they were the same who had followed our Lord in Galilee and ministered unto Him, and that there were " many other women which came up with Him to Jerusalem."

We should hardly have expected to have read such things. We might well have supposed that, when all the disciples but one had forsaken our Lord and fled, the weaker and more timid sex would not have dared to show themselves His friends. It only shows us what grace can do. God sometimes chooses the weak things of the world to confound the things that are mighty. The last are sometimes first, and the first last. The faith of women sometimes stands upright, when the faith of men fails and gives way.

But it is interesting to remark throughout the New Testament how often we find the grace of God glorified in women, and how much benefit God has been pleased to confer through them on the Church, and on the world. In the Old Testament, we see sin and death brought in by the woman's transgression. In the New, we see Jesus born of a woman, and life and immortality brought to light by that miraculous birth. In the Old Testament, we often see woman proving a hindrance and a snare to man. The women before the flood, the histories of Sarah, Rebecca, Rachel, Delilah, Bath-sheba, Jezebel, are all painful examples. In the New Testament, we generally see women mentioned as a help and assistance to the cause of true religion. Elizabeth, Mary, Martha, Dorcas, Lydia, and the women named by St. Paul to the Romans, are all cases in point. The contrast is striking, and we need not doubt intentional. It is one of the many proofs that grace is more abundant under the gospel than under the law. It seems meant to teach us that women have an important place in the Church of Christ, one that ought to be assigned to them, and one that they ought to fill. There is a great work that women can do for God's glory, without being public teachers. Happy is that congregation in which women know this, and act upon it!

Let us notice, for another thing, in this passage, *that Jesus has friends of whom little is known.* We cannot conceive a more remarkable proof of this than the person who is here mentioned for the first time,—Joseph of Arimathæa. We know nothing of this man's former history. We know not how he had learned to love Christ, and to desire to do Him honour. We know nothing of his subsequent history after our Lord left the world. All we know is the touching collection of facts before us. We are told that "he waited for the kingdom of God," and that at a time when our Lord's disciples had all forsaken Him, he "went in boldly unto Pilate, and craved the body of Jesus," and buried it honourably in his own tomb. Others had honoured and confessed our Lord when they saw Him working miracles, but Joseph honoured Him, and confessed himself a disciple when he saw Him a cold, blood-sprinkled corpse. Others had shown love to Jesus while He was speaking and living, but Joseph showed love when He was silent and dead.

Let us take comfort in the thoughts that there are true Christians on earth, of whom we know nothing, and in places where we should not expect to find them. No doubt the faithful are always few. But we must not hastily conclude that there is no grace in a family or in a parish, because our eyes may not see it. We know in part and see only in part outside the circle in which our own lot is cast. The Lord has many " hidden ones" in the Church, who, unless brought forward by special circumstances, will never be known till the last day. The words of God to Elijah should not be forgotten : "Yet I have left me seven thousand in Israel." (1 Kings xix. 18.)

Let us notice, lastly, in this passage, *what honour our Lord Jesus Christ has placed on the grave, by allowing Himself to be laid in it.* We read that He was "laid in a sepulchre hewn out of a rock," and a "stone rolled unto the door."

This is a fact that in a dying world we should always remember. It is appointed unto men once to die. We are all going to one place, and we naturally shrink from it. The coffin and the funeral, the worm and corruption, are all painful subjects. They chill us, sadden us, and fill our minds with heaviness. It is not in flesh and blood to regard them without solemn feelings. One thing, however, ought to comfort believers, and that is the thought, that the grave is "the place where the Lord once lay." As surely as He rose again victorious from the tomb, so surely shall all who believe in Him rise gloriously in the day of His appearing. Remembering this, they may look down with calmness into the "house appointed for all living." They may recollect that Jesus Himself was once there on their behalf, and has robbed death of his sting. They may say to themselves, "the sting of death is sin, and the strength of sin is the law: but thanks be to God who giveth us the victory through our Lord Jesus Christ." (1 Cor. xv. 56, 57.)

The great matter that concerns us all, is to make sure that we are spiritually buried with Christ, while we are yet alive. We must be joined to Him by faith, and conformed to His image. With Him we must die to sin, and be buried by baptism into His death. (Rom. vi. 4.) With Him we must rise again, and be quickened by His Spirit. Except we know these things, Christ's death and burial will profit us nothing at all.

MARK XVI. 1—8.

1 And when the Sabbath was past, Mary Magdalene, and Mary the *mother* of James, and Salome, had bought sweet spices, that they might come and anoint him.

2 And very early in the morning the first *day* of the week, they came unto the sepulchre at the rising of the sun.

3 And they said among themselves, Who shall roll us away the stone from the door of the sepulchre?

4 And when they looked, they saw that the stone was rolled away: for it was very great.

5 And entering into the sepulchre, they saw a young man sitting on the right side, clothed in a long white garment; and they were affrighted.

6 And he saith unto them, Be not affrighted: Ye seek Jesus of Nazareth, which was crucified: he is risen; he is not here: behold the place where they laid him.

7 But go your way, tell his disciples and Peter that he goeth before you into Galilee: there shall ye see him, as he said unto you.

8 And they went out quickly, and fled from the sepulchre; for they trembled and were amazed: neither said they any thing to any *man;* for they were afraid.

LET us observe, in this passage, *the power of strong love*

to Christ. We have a forcible illustration of this in the conduct of Mary Magdalene, and the other Mary, which St. Mark here records. He tells us that they had "bought sweet spices" to anoint our Lord, and that "very early in the morning, the first day of the week, they came unto the sepulchre, at the rising of the sun."

We may well believe that it required no small courage to do this. To visit a grave in the dim twilight of an eastern day-break, would try most women, under any circumstances. But to visit the grave of one who had been put to death as a common malefactor, and to rise early to show honour to One whom their nation had despised,—this was a mighty boldness indeed. Yet these are the kind of acts which show the difference between weak faith and strong faith,—between weak feeling and strong feeling towards Christ. These holy women had tasted of our Lord's pardoning mercies. Their hearts were full of gratitude to Him for light, and hope, and comfort, and peace. They were willing to risk all consequences in testifying their affection to their Saviour. So true are the words of Canticles: "Love is strong as death,—many waters cannot quench love, neither can the floods drown it." (Cant. viii. 6, 7.)

Why is it that we see so little of this strong love to Jesus among Christians of the present day? How is it that we so seldom meet with saints who will face any danger, and go through fire and water for Christ's sake? There is only one answer. It is the weak faith, and the low sense of obligation to Christ, which so widely prevail. A low and feeble sense of sin will always produce a low and feeble sense of the value of salvation. A slight sense of our debt to God will always be attended by a slight sense of what we owe for our redemption. It is the man who feels much forgiven who loves much. " To whom little is forgiven, the same loveth little." (Luke vii. 47.)

Let us observe, secondly, in this passage, how *the difficulties which Christians fear, will sometimes disappear as they approach them.* These holy women, as they walked to our Lord's grave, were full of fears about the stone at the door. " They said among themselves, Who shall roll us away the stone from the door of the sepulchre?" But their fears were needless. Their expected trouble was found not to exist. " When they looked they saw that the stone was rolled away."

What a striking emblem we have in this simple narrative, of the experience of many Christians! How often believers are oppressed and cast down by anticipation of evils, and yet, in the time of need, find the thing they feared removed, and the "stone rolled away." A large proportion of a saint's anxieties arise from things which never really happen. We look forward to all the possibilities of the journey towards heaven. We conjure up in our imagination all kinds of crosses and obstacles. We carry mentally to-morrow's troubles, as well as to-day's. And often, very often, we find at the end, that our doubts and alarms were groundless, and that the thing we dreaded most has never come to pass at all Let us pray for more practical faith. Let us believe that in the path of duty, we shall never be entirely forsaken. Let us go forward boldly, and we shall often find that the lion in the way is chained, and the seeming hedge of thorns is only a shadow.

Let us observe, thirdly, in this passage, *that the friends of Christ have no cause to be afraid of angels.* We are told, that when Mary Magdalene and her companion saw an angel sitting in the sepulchre, " they were affrighted." But they were at once reassured by his words : " Be not affrighted : ye seek Jesus of Nazareth, which was crucified."

The lesson, at first sight, may seem of little importance. We see no visions of angels in the present day. We do not expect to see them. But the lesson is one which we may find useful at some future time. The day is drawing near when the Lord Jesus shall come again to judge the world, with all the angels round Him. The angels in that day shall gather together His elect from the four winds. The angels shall gather the tares into bundles to burn them. The angels shall gather the wheat of God into His barn. Those whom the angels take they shall carry to glory, honour, and immortality. Those whom they leave behind shall be left to shame and everlasting contempt.

Let us strive so to live, that when we die we may be carried by angels into Abraham's bosom. Let us endeavour to be known of angels as those who seek Jesus, and love Him in this world, and so are heirs of salvation. Let us give diligence to make our repentance sure, and so to cause joy in the presence of the angels of God. Then, whether we wake or sleep, when the archangel's voice is heard, we shall have no cause to be afraid. We shall rise from our grave, and see in the angels our friends and fellow-servants, in whose company we shall spend a blessed eternity.

Let us observe, lastly, in this passage, the *exceeding kindness of God towards His backsliding servants.* The message which the angel conveys is a striking illustration of this truth. Mary Magdalene and the other Mary were bid to tell the disciples that "Jesus goeth before them into Galilee," and that "there they shall see Him." But the message is not directed generally to the eleven Apostles. This alone, after their late desertion of their master, would have been a most gracious action. Yet Simon Peter, who had denied his Lord three times, is specially mentioned by name. Peter, who had sinned particularly, is singled out and noticed particularly. There were to be no exceptions in the deed of grace. All were to be pardoned. All were to be restored to favour,—and Simon Peter as well as the rest.

We may well say when we read words like these, "this is not the manner of man." On no point perhaps are our views of religion so narrow, low, and contracted, as on the point of God's exceeding willingness to pardon penitent sinners. We think of Him as such an one as ourselves. We forget that "He delighteth in mercy." (Micah vii. 18.)

Let us leave the passage with a determination to open the door of mercy very wide to sinners, in all our speaking and teaching about religion. Not least, let us leave it with a resolution never to be unforgiving towards our fellow-men. If Christ is so ready to forgive us, we ought to be very ready to forgive others.

MARK XVI. 9—14.

9 Now when *Jesus* was risen early the first *day* of the week, he appeared first to Mary Magdalene, out of whom he had cast seven devils.

10 *And* she went and told them that had been with him, as they mourned and wept.

11 And they, when they had heard that he was alive, and had been seen of her, believed not.

12 After that he appeared in another form unto two of them, as they walked, and went into the country.

13 And they went and told *it* unto the residue : neither believed they them.

14 Afterward he appeared unto the eleven as they sat at meat, and upbraided them with their unbelief and hardness of heart, because they believed not them which had seen him after he was risen.

LET us mark, in these verses, *what abundant proof we have that our Lord Jesus Christ really rose again from the dead.* In this one passage St. Mark records no less than three distinct occasions on which He was seen after His resurrection. First, he tells us, our Lord appeared to one witness,—Mary Magdalene ; then to two witnesses, —two disciples walking into the country; and, lastly, to eleven witnesses,—the eleven Apostles all assembled together. Let us remember, in addition to this, that other appearances of our Lord are described by other writers in the New Testament, beside those mentioned by St. Mark. And then let us not hesitate to believe, that of all the facts of our Lord's history, there is none more thoroughly established than the fact that He rose from the dead.

There is great mercy in this. The resurrection of Christ is one of the foundation-stones of Christianity. It was the seal of the great work that He came on earth to do. It was the crowning proof that the ransom He paid for sinners was accepted, the atonement for sin accomplished, the head of him who had the power of death bruised, and the victory won. It is well to remark how often the resurrection of Christ is referred to by the Apostles. "He was delivered for our offences," says Paul, "and was raised again for our justification." (Rom. iv. 25.) "He hath begotten us again to a lively hope," says Peter, "by the resurrection of Jesus Christ from the dead." (1 Peter i. 3.)

We ought to thank God that the fact of the resurrection is so clearly established. The Jew, the Gentile, the priests, the Roman guard, the women who went to the tomb, the disciples who were so backward to believe, are all witnesses whose testimony cannot be gainsaid. Christ has not only died for us, but has also risen again. To deny it shows far greater credulity than to believe it. To deny it a man must put credit in monstrous and ridiculous improbabilities. To believe it a man has only to appeal to simple undeniable facts.

Let us mark, secondly, in these verses, *our Lord Jesus Christ's singular kindness to Mary Magdalene.* We are told that "when He was risen early the first day of the week, He appeared first to Mary Magdalene, out of whom He had cast seven devils." To her before all others of Adam's children, was granted the privilege of being first to behold a risen Saviour. Mary, the mother of our Lord, was yet alive. John, the beloved disciple, was yet upon earth. Yet both were passed over on this occasion in favour of Mary Magdalene. A woman who at one time had probably been chief of sinners, a woman who at one time had been possessed by seven devils, was the first to whom Jesus showed Himself alive, when He rose victorious from the tomb. The fact is remarkable, and full of instruction.*

* There is nothing in the New Testament to justify the common

We need not doubt, for one thing, that, by appearing " first to Mary Magdalene," our Lord meant to show us how much He values love and faithfulness. Last at the cross and first at the grave,—last to confess her Master while living, and first to honour Him when dead, this warm-hearted disciple was allowed to be the first to see Him when the victory was won. It was intended to be a perpetual memorial to the Church that those who honour Christ He will honour, and that those who do much for Him upon earth shall find Him, even upon earth, doing much for them. May we never forget this. May we ever remember that for those who forsake all for Christ's sake there is " an hundred-fold now in this present time."

We need not doubt, for another thing, that our Lord's appearing "first to Mary Magdalene" was intended to comfort all who have become penitent believers, after having run into great excesses of sin. It was meant to show us that, however far we may have fallen, we are raised to entire peace with God, if we repent and believe the Gospel. Though before far off, we are made nigh. Though before enemies, we are made dear children. Old things are passed away, and all things are become new. (1 Cor. v. 17.)

notion that Mary Magdalene had been a sinner against the seventh commandment more than other commandments. There is no scriptural warrant for calling hospitals and asylums intended for fallen women, "Magdalene Hospitals." No better authority can be discovered for the common idea on the subject than tradition.

At the same time it is only fair to say, that there seems strong probability for supposing that the sins of Mary Magdalene had been very great. There was probably some grave cause for her being possessed by seven devils, though the nature of it has not been revealed to us.

The blood of Christ makes us completely clean in God's sight. We may have begun, like Augustine and John Newton, and been ringleaders in every kind of iniquity. But once brought to Christ, we need not doubt that all is forgiven. We may draw nigh with boldness, and have access with confidence. Our sins and iniquities, like those of Mary Magdalene, are remembered no more.

Let us mark, lastly, in these verses, *how much weakness there is sometimes in the faith of the best Christians.* Three times in this very passage we find St. Mark describing the unbelief of the eleven Apostles. Once, when Mary Magdalene told them that our Lord had risen, " they believed not."—Again, when our Lord had appeared to two of them as they walked, we read of the residue, " neither believed they them."—Finally, when our Lord Himself appeared to them as they sat at meat, we are told that " He upbraided them for their unbelief and hardness of heart." Never perhaps was there so striking an example of man's unwillingness to believe that which runs counter to his early prejudices. Never was there so remarkable a proof of man's forgetfulness of plain teaching. These eleven men had been told repeatedly by our Lord that He would rise again. And yet, when the time came, all was forgotten, and they were found unbelieving.

Let us however see in the doubts of these good men the over-ruling hand of an all-wise God. If they were convinced at last, who were so unbelieving at first, how strong is the proof supplied us that Christ rose indeed! It is the glory of God to bring good out of evil. The very doubts of the eleven Apostles are the confirmation of our faith in these latter days.

Let us learn from the unbelief of the Apostles, a useful practical lesson for ourselves. Let us cease to feel surprise when we find doubts arising in our own heart. Let us cease to expect perfection of faith in other believers. We are yet in the body. We are men of like passions with the Apostles. We must count it no strange thing if our experience is sometimes like their's, and if our faith, like their's, sometimes gives way. Let us resist unbelief manfully. Let us watch, and pray, and strive to be delivered from its power. But let us not conclude that we have no grace, because we are sometimes harassed with doubts, nor suppose that we have no part or lot with the Apostles, because at seasons we feel unbelieving.

Let us not fail to ask ourselves as we leave this passage, whether we have risen with Christ, and been made partakers spiritually of His resurrection. This, after all, is the one thing needful. To know the facts of Christianity with the head, and to be able to argue for them with the tongue, will not save our souls. We must yield ourselves to God, as those alive from the dead. (Rom. vi. 13.) We must be raised from the death of sin, and walk in newness of life. This and this only is saving Christianity.

MARK XVI. 15—18.

15 And he said unto them, Go ye into all the world, and preach the Gospel to every creature.

16 He that believeth and is baptized shall be saved; but he that believeth not shall be damned.

17 And these signs shall follow them that believe; In my name shall they cast out devils; they shall speak with new tongues;

18 They shall take up serpents; and if they drink any deadly thing, it shall not hurt them; they shall lay hands on the sick, and they shall recover.

WE ought to notice, firstly, in these verses, *the parting commission which our Lord gives to His Apostles.* He is addressing them for the last time. He marks out their work till He comes again, in words of wide and deep significance, " Go ye into all the world, and preach the Gospel to every creature."

The Lord Jesus would have us know that all the world needs the Gospel. In every quarter of the globe man is the same,—sinful, corrupt, and alienated from God. Civilized or uncivilized, in China, or in Africa, he is by nature everywhere the same,—without knowledge, without holiness, without faith, and without love. Wherever we see a child of Adam, whatever be his colour, we see one whose heart is wicked, and who needs the blood of Christ, the renewing of the Holy Ghost, and reconciliation with God.

The Lord Jesus would have us know that the salvation of the Gospel is to be offered freely to all mankind. The glad tidings that " God so loved the world that He gave His only begotten Son," and that "Christ has died for the ungodly," is to be proclaimed freely " to every creature." We are not justified in making any exception in the proclamation. We have no warrant for limiting the offer to the elect. We come short of the fulness of Christ's words, and take away from the breadth of His sayings, if we shrink from telling any one, " God is full of love to you, Christ is willing to save you." " Whosoever will, let him take the water of life freely." (Rev. xx. 17.)

Let us see in these words of Christ, the strongest argument in favour of missionary work, both at home and abroad. Remembering these words, let us be un-

wearied in trying to do good to the souls of all mankind.
If we cannot go to the heathen in China and Hindostan
let us seek to enlighten the darkness which we shall
easily find within reach of our own door. Let us labour
on, unmoved by the sneers and taunts of those who disapprove missionary operations and hold them up to
scorn. We may well pity such people. They only
show their ignorance, both of Scripture and of Christ's
will. They understand neither what they say, nor
whereof they affirm.

We ought to notice, secondly, in these verses, *the
terms which our Lord tells us should be offered to all who
hear the Gospel.* "He that believeth and is baptized
shall be saved; but he that believeth not shall be damned."
Every word in that sentence is of deep importance. Every
expression in it deserves to be carefully weighed.

We are taught here the importance of baptism. It is
an ordinance generally necessary to salvation, where it
can be had. Not "he that believeth" simply, but
"he that believeth and is baptized shall be saved."
Thousands no doubt receive not the slightest benefit from
their baptism. Thousands are washed in sacramental
water, who are never washed in the blood of Christ. But
it does not follow therefore that baptism is to be despised
and neglected. It is an ordinance appointed by Christ
Himself, and when used reverently, intelligently, and
prayerfully, is doubtless accompanied by a special blessing.
The baptismal water itself conveys no grace. We must
look far beyond the mere outward element, to Him who
commanded it to be used. But the public confession
of Christ, which is implied in the use of that water, is a

sacramental act, which our Master Himself has commanded ; and when the ordinance is rightly used, we may confidently believe that He seals it by His blessing.

We are taught here, furthermore, the absolute necessity of faith in Christ to salvation. This is the one thing needful. " He that believeth not" is the man that shall be lost for evermore. He may have been baptized, and made a member of the visible Church. He may be a regular communicant at the Lord's Table. He may even believe intellectually all the leading articles of the creed. But all shall profit him nothing if he lacks saving faith in Christ. Have we this faith ? This is the great question that concerns us all. Except we feel our sins, and feeling them flee to Christ by faith, and lay hold on Him, we shall find at length we had better never have been born.

We are taught here, furthermore, the certainty of God's judgments on those who die unbelieving. " He that believeth not shall be damned." How awful the words sound ! How fearful the thought that they came from the lips of Him who said, " My words shall not pass away." Let no man deceive us with vain words. There is an eternal hell for all who will persist in their wickedness and depart out of this world without faith in Christ. The greater the mercy offered to us in the Gospel, the greater will be the guilt of those who obstinately refuse to believe. " Oh, that men were wise ! Oh, that they would consider their latter end." (Deut. xxxii. 29.) He that died upon the cross has given us plain warning that there is a hell, and that unbelievers shall be damned. Let us take heed that His warning is not given to us in vain !

We ought to notice, lastly, in these verses, *the gracious promises of special help which our Lord holds out in His parting words to His Apostles.* He knew well the enormous difficulties of the work which He had just commissioned them to do. He knew the mighty battle they would have to fight with heathenism, the world, and the devil. He therefore cheers them by telling them that miracles shall help forward their work. " Signs shall follow them that believe. In my name they shall cast out devils ; they shall speak with new tongues ; they shall take up serpents; and if they shall drink any deadly thing it shall not hurt them ; they shall lay hands on the sick, and they shall recover." The fulfilment of most of these promises is to be found in the Acts of the Apostles.

The age of miracles no doubt is long passed. They were never meant to continue beyond the first establishment of the Church. It is only when plants are first planted, that they need daily watering and support. The whole analogy of God's dealings with His Church forbids us to expect that miracles would always continue. In fact, miracles would cease to be miracles, if they happened regularly without cessation or intermission. It is well to remember this. The remembrance may save us much perplexity.

But though the age of physical miracles is past, we may take comfort in the thought that the Church of Christ shall never want Christ's special aid in its seasons of special need. The great Head in heaven will never forsake His believing members. His eye is continually upon them. He will always time His help wisely, and come to their succour in the day that He is wanted.

"When the enemy shall come in like a flood, the Spirit of the Lord shall lift up a standard against him." (Isai. lix. 19.)

Finally, let us never forget that Christ's believing Church in the world is of itself a standing miracle. The conversion and perseverance in grace of every member of that Church is a sign and wonder, as great as the raising of Lazarus from the dead. The renewal of every saint is as great a marvel as the casting out of a devil, or the healing of a sick man, or the speaking with a new tongue. Let us thank God for this, and take courage. The age of spiritual miracles is not yet passed. Happy are they who have learned this by experience, and can say, "I was dead, but am alive again: I was blind, but I see."

MARK XVI. 19—20.

19 So then after the Lord had spoken unto them, he was received up into heaven, and sat on the right hand of God.

20 And they went forth, and preached every where, the Lord working with *them*, and confirming the word with signs following. Amen.

THESE words form the conclusion of St. Mark's Gospel. Short as the passage is, it is a singularly suitable conclusion to the history of our Lord Jesus Christ's earthly ministry. It tells us where our Lord went, when He left this world and ascended up on high. It tells us what His disciples experienced after their Master left them, and what all true Christians may expect until He appears again.

Let us mark, in these verses, *the place to which our Lord went when He had finished His work on earth, and*

the place where He is at this present time.　We are told
that "He was received up into heaven, and sat on the
right hand of God."　He returned to that glory which
He had with the Father before He came into the world.
He received, as our victorious Mediator and Redeemer,
the highest position of dignity and power in heaven
which our minds can conceive.　There He sits, not idle,
but carrying on the same blessed work for which He died
on the cross.　There He lives, ever making intercession
for all who come unto God by Him, and so able to save
them to the uttermost.　(Heb. vii. 25.)

There is strong consolation here for all true Christians.
They live in an evil world.　They are often careful and
troubled about many things, and are sorely cast down by
their own weakness and infirmities.—They live in a dying
world.　They feel their bodies gradually failing and
giving way.　They have before them the awful prospect
of soon launching forth into a world unknown.—What
then shall comfort them?　They must lean back on the
thought of their Saviour in heaven, never slumbering,
and never sleeping, and always ready to help.　They
must remember that though they sleep, Jesus wakes,—
though they faint, Jesus is never weary,—though they
are weak, Jesus is Almighty,—and though they die,
Jesus lives for evermore.　Blessed indeed is this thought!
Our Saviour, though unseen, is an actually living person.
We travel on towards a dwelling where our best Friend
is gone before to prepare a place for us.　(John xiv. 2.)
The Forerunner has entered in and made all things ready.
No wonder that St. Paul exclaims, "Who is He that
condemneth?　It is Christ that died; yea, rather that is

risen again, who is even at the right hand of God, who also maketh intercession for us." (Rom. viii. 34.)

Let us mark, for another thing, in these verses, *the blessing which our Lord Jesus Christ bestows on all who work faithfully for Him.* We are told that, when the disciples went forth and preached, the Lord "worked with them," and "confirmed the word with signs following."

We know well, from the Acts of the Apostles and from the pages of Church history, the manner in which these words have been proved true. We know that bonds and afflictions, persecution and opposition, were the first fruits that were reaped by the labourers in Christ's harvest. But we know also that, in spite of every effort of Satan, the word of truth was not preached in vain. Believers from time to time were gathered out of the world. Churches of saints were founded in city after city, and country after country. The little seed of Christianity grew gradually into a great tree. Christ Himself wrought with His own workmen, and, in spite of every obstacle, His work went on. The good seed was never entirely thrown away. Sooner or later there were "signs following."

Let us not doubt that these things were written for our encouragement, on whom the latter ends of the world are come. Let us believe that no one shall ever work faithfully for Christ, and find at last that His work has been altogether without profit. Let us labour on patiently, each in our own position. Let us preach and teach and speak and write and warn and testify, and rest assured that our labour is not in vain. We

AA

may die ourselves, and see no result from our work. But the last day will assuredly prove that the Lord Jesus always works with those who work for Him, and that there were "signs following," though it was not given to the workmen to see them. Let us then be "steadfast, immovable, always abounding in the work of the Lord." We may go on our way heavily, and sow with many tears; but if we sow Christ's precious seed, we shall "come again with joy and bring our sheaves with us." (1 Cor. xv. 58; Psal. cxxvi. 6.)

And now let us close the pages of St. Mark's Gospel with self-inquiry and self-examination. Let it not content us to have seen with our eyes, and heard with our ears, the things here written for our learning about Jesus Christ. Let us ask ourselves whether we know anything of Christ "dwelling in our hearts by faith"? Does the Spirit "witness with our spirit" that Christ is our's and we are His? Can we really say that we are "living the life of faith in the Son of God," and that we have found by experience that Christ is "precious" to our own souls? These are solemn questions. They demand serious consideration. May we never rest till we can give them satisfactory answers! "He that hath the Son hath life, and he that hath not the Son of God hath not life." (1 John v. 12.)

Printed in U. S. A.